MW00606304

AFRICAN AMERICAN HERITAGE IN MASSACHUSETTS

EXPLORING THE LEGACY

PEOPLE AND PLACES OF SIGNIFICANCE

Rosalyn Delores Elder

Photographs by Delores Elder-Jones
and Rosalyn Delores Elder

Boston, MA

African American Heritage in Massachusetts: Exploring the Legacy

Published by African American Heritage Massachusetts,
2016, Boston, MA

Copyright by Rosalyn D. Elder. All rights reserved.
This book or any portion thereof may not be reproduced or used
in any manner whatsoever without the express written permission of
the publisher except for the use of brief quotations in a book review.

African American Heritage in Massachusetts Publishers

www.africanamericanheritagemassachusetts.com

ISBN: 978-0-9975972-0-2

Printed in the USA

Cover and Interior Design by Carla Green, Clarity Designworks
Cover Photograph by Rosalyn Delores Elder
Illustrations by Karen Connolly-Zitt
Maps by Jitan Dahal

I dedicate this book to the memory of my parents:

Mary Odessa Johns Elder

December 10, 1912 – October 17, 1992

"Do your best and the rest will follow."

+ 1931 +

Otis Augustus Elder, II

April 10, 1910 – April 29, 1995

*"No one can ever take away from you
a job well done."*

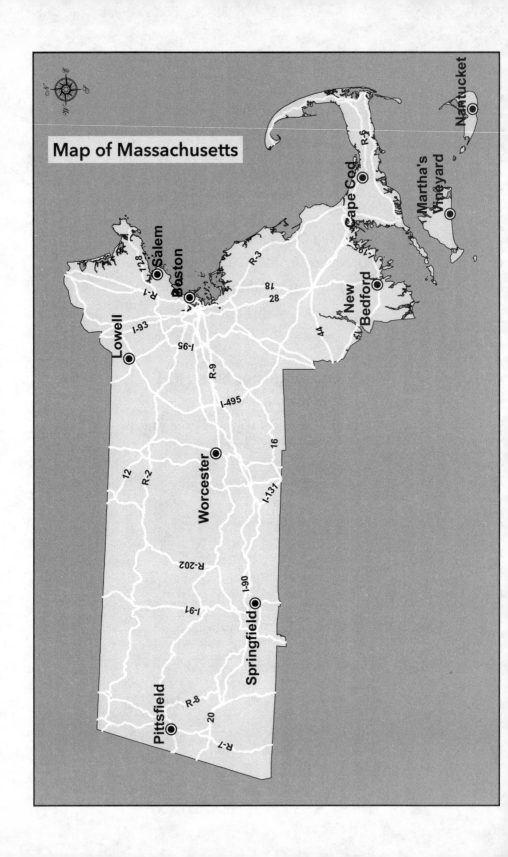

Map of Massachusetts

Table of Contents

Cape Cod and the Islands

The Berkshires

Central MAssachusetts

Other Resources

Western Massachusetts

PREFACE

Knowledge of one's ancestors and their contributions to civilization are prerequisites to appreciate one's heritage and to understand one's potential to make similar contributions. Unfortunately, most historians did not weave African American history into the fabric of early American history except for the inclusion of slavery where African Americans were usually represented as victims rather than instigators of change. A broader knowledge of this history will benefit everyone.

In Massachusetts, African Americans have contributed to every aspect of the legacy of this state including its political, literary, artistic, and scientific realms. This guidebook explores those people and places which are significant to understand and appreciate this rich and inspiring, though often overlooked, history. A list of resources and a bibliography are included to assist those who want to explore this rich heritage further.

One of my inspirations to continue the work of others who documented African American history in Massachusetts was a quote by Sargent Claude Johnson (1888 – 1967), a famous, Boston born, African American artist who flourished during the period of the

Harlem Renaissance. Johnson once explained his main goal to create beautiful sculptures with clearly articulated African American features:

> *"It is the pure American Negro I am concerned with, aiming to show the natural beauty and dignity in that characteristic lip and that characteristic hair, bearing and manner; and I wish to show that beauty not so much to the white man as to the Negro himself."*
> - SARGENT JOHNSON

A similar goal led me to open an African American cultural boutique in Boston, *Treasured Legacy*, which I operated from 1992 to 1998. The store was located at the Dartmouth Street Shops of Copley Place, an up-scale retail mall which included stores such as Neiman Marcus, Gucci, and Tiffany.

At Treasured Legacy, we sold fine art reproductions by African American artists represented in museums across the country, as well as original art by local artists. We felt that more people could become familiar with this important aspect of our American heritage if they viewed the art on a daily basis.

Treasured Legacy was located outside the mall along the Southwest Corridor Park. This location encouraged a lot of casual foot traffic from neighborhood residents. Early one morning in January of 1993, about a month after our grand opening, an elderly African American woman stood outside in the cold as she stared at the displays in the windows. I went to the door to welcome her in but she hesitated. Perhaps because, after all, this was Copley Place with its traditionally expensive stores. She eventually entered at my invitation.

A stroll around the store allowed her time to view all the framed art and sculptures. After she completed her tour of the shop, she placed on the sales counter a single notecard to purchase. It had a reproduction of *The Sharecropper,* an etching by the artist, Elizabeth Catlett, on the front. The customer then placed next to the notecard a handkerchief that she gently opened, and began to deliberately count out coins to pay for her purchase. After I put her notecard in a bag, I ended the sale with a customary but heartfelt, *"Thank you, and have a nice day."* Her response will always stay with me: *"I have had a nice day, now that I see you are here."*

Just as that individual needed affirmation that she was important and that people who looked like her had made important contributions to our society, we all need similar affirmation. When you open this book to explore these sites, please take a moment to think about the daily lives of the individuals described here. Their *vision, faith, and determination* should forever be inspiration to us all.

I will close this preface with another personal story that made me appreciate how critical it is that people have a sense of their history and the contributions of their ancestors, especially young people. In 1998, my daughter, Anghara, was a high school senior at Buckingham, Browne and Nichols, a private, predominantly white school in Cambridge. Throughout her childhood, I tried to instill in Anghara a true sense of her importance as a member of a race who had accomplished much in the world.

When Anghara experienced a blatant example of racism at her school, she was able to react appropriately. Rather than ignore it and pretend that it did not happen, she confronted the issue. To the school's credit, they used the incident as an opportunity to teach their students about racism. Anghara's courage resulted in a request to speak at the school's annual Martin Luther King, Jr. Breakfast. Her speech below, is followed by a letter she received from another student who visited the school the day of the breakfast. The frustration of the two students that existed in 1998 still exists today. It highlights the important need to integrate all of American history into our classrooms.

Hello, my name is Anhgara Abouzied Elder.

I am a senior and have been a BB&N student for six years. I stand before you today, as a frustrated BB&N student to ask the question that has been burning in my mind since Mr. Bryant asked me to speak at this assembly. Can BB&N honestly say that there has been real progress to diversify its community? How far have we really come in the past five years, or even ten years? My class is the only one that I know of that has more than ten black students. What about the Latino students? What about the Asian students?

How long will it be before you are unable to count the minorities in a class on both of your hands. We need more than just students of different backgrounds to label ourselves as diverse, there needs to be a diverse curriculum and a diverse faculty and staff.

Who are students supposed to seek refuge with, if there is no one around they can relate to? You wondered why there seemed to be a black table, because there were twenty-nine other white tables.

The BB&N experience for me has been a long, hard lesson. I'm not saying that I don't appreciate the education that I have received here. On the contrary, everything that I have learned at Buckingham, Browne and Nicols has helped make me the person I am today, socially and academically.

But just when I think that we are past the point of ignorance, I pick up the school newspaper and see a cartoon with a monkey driving a bus to a country in Africa. With all of the negative historical connotations that surround the stereotype of black people looking like monkeys, I was painfully brought back to reality at the sight of this cartoon.

What some might see as harmless comedy, I saw as a derogatory statement about people from Africa. As unintentional as it may have been, it was still printed. The fact that this cartoon was able to slip by the editors and the faculty supervisor, makes me seriously question the so-called cultural sensitivity that BB&N is supposed to possess.

How far have we really come? If Martin Luther King, Jr. were to see us now, more than thirty years after the civil rights movement, would he really be pleased with our progress or ask the question why have you stopped trying?

BB&N prides itself on how multi-cultural it is or attempts to be, but can we really boast this title? This past summer, there were close to fifteen openings for new faculty and staff members. Only two of these positions were filled by people of color. The level of progress that now exists is unsatisfactory.

Why did I have to wait three years to learn about my history, African American history, in school? Why was I never given the opportunity to learn about Asian American history or Latino and Native American history? Aren't we all part of the same country? I shouldn't have to go to a special class to find out about different American cultures, it should all be taught as American history. Otherwise, is it really American history, or just a small part of it?

To combat the ignorance that produces insensitive comics, we must push ourselves to learn the truth of American history, not just the polite Anglo interpretation. We, the American people, and the community of BB&N will never be able to understand each other, unless we know about everyone's culture, not just a select group.

I challenge Buckingham, Browne and Nicols to take that extra step forward and educate themselves, about American history and American culture, not just white or black, but American.

I challenge Buckingham, Browne and Nicols to make sure that all of the ignorance that I have experience is wiped out of our community and the hard lessons that I have learned at this institution will not have to be learned by future students. I know this may sound a bit idealistic, but anything is possible if you really want it.

Thank you.

January 14, 1998

Dear Anghara,

Hi, my name is Hannah Baker-Siroty. I am a senior at Newton North High School. You don't know me, I'm close friends with ------- -------. I came on Monday to hear her speak and I wanted you to know that I heard you too. What you said was so true. You know-it sucks. The world sucks, and it hurts too. It's all about fear. All these people are afraid of what's different from them (not on the surface…obviously). They're afraid for all these stupid reasons.

The courage that you have inside you is amazing. It is not easy to confront an issue such as race, in fact it is rather scary. People are sensitive and close-minded. ------ ------ was telling me how your school was reacting to your speech, and it makes me so mad. You're right. The world needs to be fixed.

In one of my classes I'm reading a book called Common Ground *by J. Anthony Lukas. It takes place in Boston during the time of Dr. Martin Luther King's death. I'm understanding all this stuff about opportunities. Opportunities that white people got and black people didn't. I'm not saying that because I'm reading this book that I understand what it's like to be black, because I'm not black and I can't be something that I'm not. But I do know what it's like to have people make assumptions about me, based on my appearance.*

It took an incredible amount of strength to do what you did on Monday. I believe in fighting for everyone's rights, no matter what. If people are getting you down, don't let them. What you have done is wonderful. People like you – who aren't afraid – are the leaders in this world.

I know that it doesn't really matter much because you don't know me, but at my school, no one would have the courage to do what you did. You had an impact on me. I thought you were very eloquent, poised, and determined. While I continue my fight for equality, it's nice to know that there are people like you who are also getting their feet wet. Thank you for opening another door in my life. The door which holds strength, love, and respect for myself and every other person in this world.

Sincerely,
Hannah

Anghara and Hannah, thank you for the reminder of how important it is for citizens to understand all aspects of their history. Readers, thank you for your time to read this book. New information is discovered daily so I apologize for any omissions and mistakes for which I am solely responsible. I only hope that those omissions will serve as a catalyst for others to discover and document more of this important history.

Rosalyn Delores Elder
August, 2016

Acknowledgments

It takes a village is true for so many things. I want to acknowledge my incredible village of family and friends who lifted me so this book could be realized. Brian, your patience, support, and encouragement gave me the emotional space I needed to take on and complete this incredible journey. Anghara, everyone should have such a cheerleader (Edmund, Ava, and Elly are clueless as to how lucky they are). Delores, your unflappable spirit, determination, and enthusiasm are constant sources of inspiration, I look forward to our next road trip. Cookie, Fred, Beth, Stephanie, Penelope, Linda, Anaezi, Sherril, Selena, John and Diane, thank you for keeping the tunnel lit. Ian and Beatrix, you survived your teen years and your mom wrote a book, sounds like a win-win.

Marie Madison, thank you for taking time out of your busy schedule to review and fact-check the section on Concord. When I visited Deerfield, I appreciated the staff at the Deerfield Memorial Hall Museum, Timothy Car-ter Neumann, Kay Wilby, and Bruce Mahoney, who allowed me to tour the museum when it was time to close. The gift of books on Lucy Terry after my tour was quite an unexpected pleasure. Sven Beckert, thank you for the copies of your booklet, *Harvard and Slavery: Seeking a Forgotten History,* that you mailed me after your lecture. That information certainly enriched my research. Haywood Fennell, thank you for bringing my attention to the contributions of Judge Edward Gourdin. You saved this book from what would have been a glaring omission. Also, thanks to everyone who offered advice, encouragement, and assistance, especially the stranger who escorted Delores and me to the DuBois Homestead site in Great Barrington even though it was twenty minutes out of his way.

A final thank you to the professionals who helped me pull this together, Carla Green, Karen Connolly-Zitt, Jitan Dahal, Delores Elder-Jones, Linda Tate, and Brian Sandiford, it would not have happened without you.

INTRODUCTION

African Americans have been a part of the history of Massachusetts from its establishment in the colonial period to the present. *Desire*, the first ship to leave the colonies specifically to import individuals for the purpose of enslavement, made its maiden voyage from Salem, Massachusetts in 1638. In the colonial period, a dichotomy about slavery developed in the psyche of the citizens of Massachusetts. That dichotomy ranged from those who embraced slavery because of the economic opportunity it provided, to those who opposed it on moral grounds. That dichotomy was so extreme that it often split families. When Wendell Phillips (NAA), a member of a socially prominent, white family in Boston, announced to his family that he intended to become a speaker for the abolitionist movement, they attempted to have him admitted to an insane asylum.

That early history of the importation of individuals for the purpose of enslavement was the basis of many New England fortunes. Those fortunes endowed many of the foremost institutions that still exist today such as Harvard University, Brown University, Yale, Princeton, and other Ivy League universities. The New England textile industry was dominated by the production of cotton from Southern plantations. The economical price of cotton was dependent on a steady supply of cheap labor, hence, the motivation to enslave a large portion of the population sat on an economical stool.

Although most enslaved individuals ended up on plantations in the Caribbean or the southern United States, many Northerners also enslaved individuals. The number of individuals enslaved by a single family in the North was usually limited to those needed as personal servants or farm hands. This difference in the scale of slavery was strictly a function of the difference in the Southern agrarian economy and the Northern mercantile economy.

Those enslaved individuals in Massachusetts interacted closely with the families for whom they labored yet their life was highly constricted by regulations put into place in order to control their movements and actions. An innate desire for fairness compelled enslaved individuals to sue for their freedom in Massachusetts as early as 1701. Those early *Freedom Lawsuits* were individual acts of courage that protested acts of violence or other mistreatment.

By the period of the American Revolution, the enslaved population in Massachusetts was aware of the fight by the colonists to be free of unfair domination by England. Two pivotal freedom lawsuits in the early 1780s, the cases of Quock Walker and Elizabeth *"Mum Bett"* Freeman, used different legal arguments to justify freedom of enslaved plaintiffs than had been used in previous cases. Those two lawsuits leaned heavily on the declaration of individual rights contained in the new Massachusetts state constitution. The state found it impossible to align slavery with that new constitution and Massachusetts effectively ended slavery in 1783. Although slavery ended in the state, limitations continued to restrict the daily life of most African Americans.

Despite those constraints, African Americans made significant contributions to the heritage of this state. In the early 1700s, Onesimus, enslaved by Cotton Mather (NAA) of Boston, shared with Mather how the human body accepted a small amount of the smallpox virus into the bloodstream to protect itself from the deadly virus. This was how the concept of inoculation made its way into western medical practice.

Maria Stewart, an African American abolitionist, was the first female of any race engaged as a public speaker in the United States. She gave lectures on racial pride in the early 1830s in Boston. Lewis Temple's invention of the *"toggle"* harpoon in New Bedford rev-

olutionized the whaling industry. Later in the 19th century, Jan Matzeliger invented the shoe lasting machine and shoe ownership became more affordable to the general public.

Prior to the Civil War, Massachusetts was a beacon of hope for some of the most prominent protestors against slavery in the United States, both black and white. In 1829, David Walker's radical pamphlet, *Appeal to the Colored Citizens of the World*, led the charge for the absolute end to slavery throughout this country, without restrictions, and without compensation to those who held property rights to those enslaved. Abolitionists fought against slavery until the Emancipation Proclamation by President Abraham Lincoln (NAA) took effect on January 1st, 1863. That proclamation ended slavery in the Confederate states. On Dec. 6th, 1865, the United States Congress passed the Thirteenth Amendment which ended slavery in all the states that were not part of the Confederacy.

After the Civil War, one of the foremost intellectuals of the twentieth century, W.E.B. DuBois, was born in Great Barrington in 1868. DuBois was the first African American to receive a Ph.D. from Harvard University. DuBois led the charge for the complete intellectual development of African Americans. He viewed the achievement of that goal to be critically important in order for the entire United States, not just its African American citizens, to fully realize its potential.

Although this book primarily explores sites critical to understand the contributions of African Americans to the history of Massachusetts, many citizens of European ancestry are also included because they participated and contributed to this history as well. For clarity, the notation, (NAA), follows their name to designate that they are not African American if the text did not previously indicate this. Individuals of Native American heritage are also included and identified in this history.

The use of the terms, slave and master, perpetuated the hierarchy of implied superiority of some individuals over others. Instead, the term, enslaved, has been used to indicate the status of African Americans who were bound as property to others. Also, rather than refer to someone as a master, they are referred to as someone who enslaved other individuals.

This book is organized into eight geographical regions of the state to facilitate touring those sites. Those regions are: Boston City Sites; Metro Boston Sites; Northeast Sites; Southeast Sites; Cape Cod and the Islands; Central Massachusetts Sites; Western Massachusetts Sites; and the Berkshires.

The Underground Railroad was an important component of the effort to assist individuals in their escape from enslavement. The ultimate goal was Canada because to stop anywhere short of that destination meant potential re-enslavement. The following lines from a popular song of the era described Canada as that ultimate goal. Henry Bibb, the publication's editor, was a fugitive from enslavement himself.

> *"I've served my master*
> *all my days*
> *Without a dime's reward,*
> *And now I'm forced*
> *to run away*
> *To flee the lash abhorred.*
> *The hounds are baying*
> *on my track –*
> *The master's just behind,*
> *Resolved that he will*
> *bring me back*
> *Before I cross the line.*
> *Farewell old master,*
> *Don't come after me,*
> *I'm on my way to Canada*
> *Where colored men are free."*
> *– THE VOICE OF THE FUGITIVE,*
> *ED. BY HENRY BIBB*

Complete networks of safe houses were organized along the East Coast to assist fugitives in their journey north. Those stations aligned with established transportation corridors that followed rivers or Native American trails. Included in this guide are several sites that have been documented as stations on that Underground Railroad network. They are designated by the listing, *UGRR Station*.

I encourage you to visit many of the sites in this guide to learn more about this rich and important legacy.

TIMELINE

1619 First Africans arrived in Jamestown, VA as indentured servants.

1638 On Dec. 12th, enslaved Africans arrived in Boston onboard the ship, *"Desire"*.

1641 Massachusetts was the first colony to give legal sanction to the practice of enslavement with Section 91 of the Massachusetts Body of Liberties. The other colonies soon followed Massachusetts's lead:

"There can never be any bond, slaverie, villinage or Captivitie among us unless it be lawfull Captives taken in just warres, and such strangers as willingly selle themselves or are sold to us." (sic)

1650 **Massachusetts Census:**
Total Population: 14,037
African American Population: 295

1660 **Massachusetts Census:**
Total Population: 20,082
African American Population: 422

1670 **Massachusetts Census:**
Total Population: 30,000
African American Population: 160

This decrease in the African American population can possibly be attributed to the spread of smallpox that also decimated the indigenous population.

1680 **Massachusetts Census:**
Total Population: 39,752
African American Population: 170

1690 **Massachusetts Census:**
Total Population: 49,504
African American Population: 400

1692 Villagers in Salem accused enslaved resident, Tituba, of the practice of witchcraft. That accusation sparked the Salem Witch Trials. The trials condemned 23 people to death, another 17 died in prison. Tituba avoided execution because of her *"confession."*

1700 **Massachusetts Census:**
Total Population: 55,941
African American Population: 800

1701 **Freedom Lawsuit:** Adam of Boston v. John Saffin (NAA). Adam, an indentured servant, brought this freedom lawsuit before Judge Sewell (NAA). Sewell ruled in favor of Adam on a charge of a broken promise of freedom after seven years work.

1705 Massachusetts imposed a tax of L4 (four pounds/ the British currency, approximately $360 in 2010 dollars) per imported African to discourage the transport of individuals into the country for the purpose of enslavement.

Massachusetts Miscegenation Law prohibited marriage between whites and individuals of African descent.

1710 **Massachusetts Census:**
Total Population: 62,390
African American Population: 1,310

1712 **Revolt:** 21 individuals executed after their revolt against enslavement failed in New York City.

1720 **Massachusetts Census:**
Total Population: 91,008
African American Population: 2,150

1721 Onesimus, an African, enslaved by Cotton Mather (NAA) of Boston, described to Mather how Africans inoculated themselves against smallpox. Mather shared that information with Dr. Zabdiel Boylston who on May 21st, administered the first smallpox inoculations to his son and two enslaved Africans.

1730 **Massachusetts Census:**
Total Population: 114,116
African American Population: 2,780

1740 **Massachusetts Census:**
Total Population: 151,613
African American Population: 3,035

1741 **Revolt:** 34 individuals executed after their revolt against enslavement failed in New York City. 21 were burned at the stake (17 African American men, 2 white men, and 2 white women).

1746 Massacre of Deerfield, MA villagers by Native Americans. Lucy Terry Prince, an enslaved Deerfield resident, commemorated this event in the poem, *"Bars Flight"*. This was the first recorded poem written by an African American.

1750 **Massachusetts Census:**
Total Population: 188,000
African American Population: 4,075

1760 **Publication:** Briton Hammon of Marshfield published in Boston the first autobiography of an enslaved individual, *A Narrative of the Uncommon Sufferings and Surprising Deliverance of Briton Hammon*.

Massachusetts Census:
Total Population: 202,600
African American Population: 4,566

1762 **Freedom Lawsuit:** Jenny Slew of Ipswich v. John Whipple Jr. (NAA). Slew won her lawsuit on a charge of abuse and was awarded her freedom.

1766 **Freedom Lawsuit:** Amos Newport of Hatfield v. Joseph Billing (NAA). Newport's lawsuit was not successful because he did not claim abuse or a broken promise of freedom as in past successful *"Freedom Lawsuits,"* but that he had a natural right to be free.

1768 **Freedom Lawsuit:** Margaret of Lexington v. William Muzzy (NAA). Margaret won her lawsuit and her freedom on a charge of abuse.

1770 **Boston Massacre:** On March 5th, fugitive from enslavement, Crispus Attucks, led a confrontation against British troops. He was the first colonist to die in this first confrontation with British troops in the American Revolution. Five colonists died in that confrontation.

Wage Lawsuit: An enslaved individual, Prince Boston of Nantucket, successfully sued John Swain (NAA) for wages he earned on a vessel, *"The Friendship"*. The wages of enslaved individuals traditionally went to their enslavers.

Massachusetts Census:
Total Population: 235,308
African American Population: 4,754

1772 **Freedom Lawsuit:** Prince Boston v. John Swain (NAA). Boston's successful lawsuit effectively ended the practice of enslavement on Nantucket.

1773 **Boston Tea Party:** On December 16th, colonists openly defied Britain and dumped tea valued at $2 million (in today's dollars) into the Boston harbor.

Publication: Phillis Wheatley's book of poetry, *Poems of Phillis Wheatley, A Native African and a Slave*, was published in England. This was the first book of poetry published by an African American.

Group Freedom Petitions: On Jan. 6th, in April, and again in June, African Americans presented three petitions to Massachusetts Governor Thomas Hutchinson (NAA), His Majesty's Council, and the House of Representatives for freedom on, *"behalf of all thous (sic) who by divine Permission are held in a state of slavery,…"*.

1774 **Freedom Lawsuit:** Juno Larcom-Thistle of Beverly v. David Larcom (NAA). David died prior to the court's decision and Juno simply *"took"* her freedom.

Group Freedom Petitions: In May and again in June, African Americans presented two petitions to the state government. Both petitions requested freedom for those enslaved in the Commonwealth.

1775 American Revolution officially began at the Battle of Lexington and Concord on April 19th. An African American, Prince Esterbrooks, was the first patriot wounded in that historic battle.

On March 6th, Prince Hall received a charter from the Grand Lodge of Ireland to open the first African Lodge.

1776 Prince Hall and fourteen other African Americans united to form African Lodge No. 1.

1777 **Group Freedom Petition:** On January 13th, a group of African Americans presented a petition to the state government that requested freedom for those held in slavery.

Vermont was the first state to officially abolish slavery on July 8th.

1780 **No Taxation without Representation Petition:** A group of African Americans led by Paul Cuffe of Westport filed this petition in the Massachusetts Legislature on March 14th. Cuffe felt it unfair that the state taxed his business but he could not vote because of his race. This unsuccessful petition influenced Massachusetts to grant African American men the right to vote in 1783.

Massachusetts Census:

Total Population:	268,627
African American Population:	4,822

Prior to 1780, most of the African American population in Massachusetts was enslaved. The 1790 census recorded no enslaved residents in the state.

1781 **Freedom Lawsuit:** Quock Walker of Barre vs. Nathaniel Jennison (NAA). On June 12th, 1781, Quock Walker won his lawsuit and his freedom on a charge of '*injury without right.*' He received an award of 50 pounds in damages. A previous owner, James Caldwell (NAA), had already granted Walker his freedom, therefore, Levi Lincoln (NAA), Walker's attorney, argued that Jennison had no right to the property of Walker's free labor. Levi Lincoln went on to serve as U.S. Attorney General under President Jefferson (NAA). Nathaniel Jennison then won a second trial in which he charged two of Caldwell's brothers (NAA) with

interference with his property when they assisted Walker in his escape.

Freedom Lawsuit: Brom and Bett of Ashley Falls v. Col. Ashley (NAA). In August of 1781, Elizabeth "Mum Bett" Freeman and a co-plaintiff, Brom, brought this joint lawsuit against Col. Ashley and won their freedom. Although physical abuse was a factor in the lawsuit, the plaintiffs' attorney, Theodore Sedgwick (NAA), charged that the Massachusetts constitution, passed the year before, had outlawed enslavement. Ashley filed an appeal but later dropped it.

1783 **Freedom Lawsuit:** This was the third and last of the Walker v. Jennison trials. The Massachusetts Attorney General had previously charged Jennison in 1781 with criminal assault and battery on Walker. That trial did not come before the Massachusetts Supreme Court until April, 1783. In his decision, the Supreme Judicial Court Chief Justice William Cushing (NAA) ruled against Jennison. He further stated that involuntary servitude was incompatible with the new state constitution. Massachusetts ceased to enforce the practice of enslavement from that moment forward.

Voting Rights: Massachusetts granted African American men the right to vote.

Reparations Petition: Belinda Royall of Medford v. the Royall Estate. Belinda presented a petition to the Massachusetts Legislature for "*reparations*" against the Royall (NAA) estate for fifty years of unpaid labor. She was awarded reparations for her past service.

American Revolution ended.

1784 On September 29th, African Lodge No. 1 received a charter from the Grand Lodge of England to join as African Lodge No. 459.

1786 **Massachusetts Miscegenation Law** of 1705 expanded to prohibit marriage between a white person to a person of African, Indian, or Mulatto descent.

1787 **Equal Education Petition:** Prince Hall petitioned the Massachusetts State Legislature for equal education facilities for African American children. That same year, Hall received his Masonic Lodge charter from the Grand Lodge of England.

1789 George Washington (NAA) inaugurated as the first President of the United States. He served until 1797. Washington owned legal rights to enslaved individuals as early as age eleven. By the end of his life, the enslaved population on his Mt. Vernon estate in Virginia consisted of 318 individuals. Half of those were enslaved by Washington, and the estate of his wife, Martha Custis Washington (NAA), enslaved the other half. Washington manumitted his enslaved population in his 1799 will.

1790 **Massachusetts Census:**
Total Population: 378,787
African American Population: 5,369

1791 African American astronomer and surveyor, Benjamin Banneker, received an appointment by President Thomas Jefferson to join the team to survey the site for the nation's capital. Banneker later wrote a letter to President Jefferson (NAA) to protest enslavement in the United States.

Revolt: On August 22nd, the Haitian Revolution began in the French colony of Saint Dominique. This was the only successful mass revolt of enslaved people in the Western Hemisphere. That revolt inspired many Americans in their fight to end enslavement in the United States. Toussaint L'Ouverture (1743 – 1803) was embraced as a hero for his role in that victory.

1793 **Fugitive Slave Act:** This U.S. law made it easier to capture fugitives from bondage who fled from one state to another.

1794 Eli Whitney (NAA) patented his Cotton Gin. This invention revolutionized the cotton industry and increased the need for abundant and cheap (a.k.a. enslaved) labor in the South.

1796 **Boston African Society** formed by forty-four African Americans as a mutual benefit organization.

1797 John Adams (NAA) of Quincy, Massachusetts, served as the second President of the United States.

A group of African Americans established the African School in the basement of Primus Hall's house on Beacon Hill in Boston, MA. This was the first school organized to educate African American children in Boston.

1800 **Massachusetts Census:**
Total Population: 422,845
African American Population: 6,452

Revolt: Enslaved African, Gabriel, organized an unsuccessful revolt of several thousand enslaved individuals in Virginia.

1801 Thomas Jefferson (NAA), the primary author of the Declaration of Independence *("...all men are created equal...")* was the third President of the United States. Jefferson enslaved over 600 individuals at his Monticello estate in Virginia. He also maintained a relationship with Sally Hemmings, an enslaved female on his estate. That relationship spanned several decades and produced many children.

In the 1790s, Jefferson viewed enslavement as a cornerstone of American wealth and he did not manumit his enslaved laborers in his will. Jefferson also refused to honor the wishes of a friend, Tadeuz Kosciuszko (NAA), who wanted to free enslaved individuals. Kosciuszko was a Polish national who was a hero of the American Revolution. Kosciuszko desired to have his estate purchase the freedom of enslaved individuals and Jefferson, as executor of his estate, refused to honor that request.

1803 President Jefferson (NAA) authorized the purchase of French territories in North America for $15 million. Known as the Louisiana Purchase, that transaction doubled the geographical size of the U.S. by the addition of 530,000,000 acres. It further embroiled the United States in the issues of whether enslavement could expand into the new territory.

1804 United States Congress prohibited the importation of Africans for the purpose of enslavement. This prohibition led Southern plantation owners to breed and trade enslaved individuals as a method to maintain a steady supply of enslaved labor. This inhumane practice brought with it an increase in violence the enslaved community had to endure.

1806 African Meeting House built on Beacon Hill in Boston.

1807 England passed the **Abolition of the Slave Trade Act**. That Act abolished slavery in the British colonies.

1809 James Madison (NAA) began service as the fourth President of the United States. Madison was the primary author of the United States Constitution. Madison was another example of the conflict of the early leaders of this country about enslavement. Madison recognized the intellectual potential of people of African heritage but he refused to give up the economic benefits that ownership of enslaved individuals provided. His Montpelier estate in Virginia maintained a population of over 100 enslaved individuals and Madison did not manumit any of them.

1810 **Massachusetts Census:**
Total Population: 472,040
African American Population: 6,737

1817 James Monroe (NAA) of Virginia began service as the fifth President of the United States. Monroe actively engaged in the purchase and trade of enslaved individuals.

1820 **Massachusetts Census:**
Total Population: 523,287
African American Population: 6,740

Missouri Compromise passed by the U.S. Congress prohibited the practice of enslavement in certain areas of the newly acquired Louisiana Purchase.

1822 **Revolt:** Enslaved individual, Denmark Vesey organized an unsuccessful revolt in Charleston, SC.

1825 John Quincy Adams (NAA) of Massachusetts served as the sixth President of the United States. Throughout his career, Adams was an ardent advocate of the rights of African Americans and a vocal opponent of the practice of enslavement.

1826 **Massachusetts General Colored Association** formed in Boston, *"to promote the welfare of the race by combatting slavery."(sic)*

1827 **Publication:** Samuel Cornish and John Russworm edited and published *"Freedom's Journal"* in New York City, the first African American newspaper in the country. Russworm was one of the first instructors at the African School in Boston.

1829 **Publication:** David Walker of Massachusetts wrote and published *Walker's Appeal*. It called for the immediate end to slavery throughout the United States without compensation.

1830 **Massachusetts Census:**
Total Population: 610,408
African American Population: 7,048

1831 **Revolt:** Freed African American, Nat Turner, led an unsuccessful revolt in Southampton County, VA. The three day revolt terrorized white citizens throughout the state.

1832 **New England Anti-slavery Society** formed in Massachusetts.

African American, Maria W. Stewart of Boston became the first woman in the United States to give public speeches.

1836 **Freedom Lawsuit :** Commonwealth v. Thomas Aves (NAA). The state of Massachusetts brought this lawsuit against Thomas Aves on behalf of an enslaved individual, 6 year old Med. Aves's daughter, a resident of a state that allowed slavery, brought Med to Massachusetts during a visit. The Court ruled that Med was free since she was not a fugitive from enslavement.

1837 **Publication:** Hosea Easton of Boston wrote and published, *A Treatise on the Intellectual Character and Civil and Political Condition of the Colored People of the U. States; and the Prejudice Exercised Toward Them; With a Sermon on the Duty of the Church to Them.*

1838 Charles Lenox Remond of Salem, MA became the first African American lecturer employed by an anti-slavery society.

Frederick Douglass escaped slavery in Maryland and settled in New Bedford.

1839 **Revolt:** Cinque from West Africa led a revolt of enslaved individuals aboard the ship, the Amistad. During the struggle, the Africans fatally wounded several of their captors. Former President, John Quincy Adams (NAA) of Massachusetts successfully defended the rebels against the murder charges. Justice Joseph Story (NAA) of Salem wrote the U.S. Supreme Court's majority decision to acquit the defendants.

1840 **Massachusetts Census:**
Total Population: 737,699
African American Population: 8,669

1841 **Boston Vigilance Committee** formed on June 4th. An inter-racial group from multiple religious affiliations formed this organization to protect those who sought their freedom from slavery.

1842 Federal marshals captured fugitive, George Latimer, in Boston. Local abolitionists raised funds to purchase his freedom. The public outcry of his capture led the state to pass anti-fugitive capture laws.

1843 **Personal Liberty Law of 1843:** In response to the capture of fugitive, George Latimer, Massachusetts passed this law. It forbade state officials to detain fugitives or to use state facilities to detain fugitives.

School Desegregation Lawsuit: Absalom Boston of Nantucket filed this unsuccessful lawsuit on behalf of his daughter, Phoebe Ann Boston, and Eunice Ross, to attend Nantucket High School.

Repeal of the 1786 Miscegenation Law in Massachusetts. Individuals of different races could now marry legally.

Sojourner Truth, a fugitive from New York State, began her mission to lecture against slavery and for the rights of women. Truth lived for a while in Florence, MA where she was a member of the Northampton Association of Education and Industry (NAEI), an anti-slavery economic cooperative.

1845 **Public School Access Legislation:** Massachusetts State Legislature passed House Bill No 45. That Bill guaranteed all children in the state a right to a public education. This Bill was a direct the result of the Absalom Boston lawsuit in Nantucket. Nantucket and several other school districts integrated their schools because they did not have the resources for a segregated system. Boston public schools remained segregated until 1855.

Macon Allen was the first African American licensed as an attorney in Massachusetts.

1847 **Publication:** Fugitive from slavery, Frederick Douglass published the first issue of "*The North Star*" newspaper in Rochester, NY.

Robert Morris was the second African American licensed to practice law in Massachusetts. Morris stayed at the forefront of legal battles to defend the rights of African Americans.

Whites in the United States who wanted freed African Americans to leave this country founded the country of Liberia in West Africa as the solution.

The first two African American physicians in the United States graduated from medical school the same year. David Peck graduated from Rush Medical School in Chicago, IL, and Henry Jenkins Roberts graduated from the Berkshire Medical Institute in Pittsfield, MA.

1849 **School Desegregation Lawsuit:** Five-year-old African American student, Sarah Roberts, was the lead plaintiff in the unsuccessful case to challenge school segregation in Boston.

Harriet Tubman escaped slavery in Maryland. Tubman made several subsequent trips to the South to liberate enslaved individuals. Southerners put a $10,000 bounty on her head.

William and Ellen Craft escaped slavery in Georgia and eventually settled in Boston. In their escape, Ellen Craft, who possessed a near white complexion, disguised herself as a white male, and William Craft pretended to be her enslaved, but loyal, manservant.

1850 **Massachusetts Census:**
Total Population: 994,514
African American Population: 9,064

Compromise of 1850: This Act put the enforcement of the Fugitive Slave Law under Federal jurisdiction.

1851 In Boston, abolitionists led by African American, Lewis Hayden, stormed a courtroom and successfully rescued fugitive, Shadrach Minkins, from jail.

Publication: William Nell, civil rights activist and historian, published, *Services of Colored Americans in the Wars of 1776 and 1812*.

Publication: Harriet Beecher Stowe (NAA) published the influential book, *Uncle Tom's Cabin*. It galvanized support for abolition.

1853 **Publication:** Fugitive and abolitionist, William Wells Brown, was the first African American to publish a novel, *Clotel*. He published his novel in England.

Publication: Nancy Prince of Newburyport published her memoirs, *A Narrative of the Life and Travels of Mrs. Nancy Prince*.

On Aug. 1th, African Americans in Massachusetts petitioned the state legislature for permission to join the state militia.

1854 Federal marshals captured fugitive, Anthony Burns, in Boston. His return to slavery cost the Federal Government $40,000 (approximately $1.2 million in today's dollars).

Massasoit Guards, an African American militia, was organized in Boston to protect the African American community.

1855 **Public School Access Legislation:** Massachusetts State Legislature ended segregation in all public schools in the state. The victory was due to efforts of several involved in the Sarah Robert's lawsuit in Boston.

Publication: William Nell, civil rights activist and historian, published, *Colored Patriots of the American Revolution* which documented African American participation in that war.

1857 **Dred Scott Decision:** This United States Supreme Court decision declared that African Americans, enslaved or free, could never be U.S. citizens and could not sue in court. Justice Benjamin Robbins Curtis (NAA) of Boston resigned from the court in protest.

1859 **Revolt:** On October 16th, John Brown (NAA) led an unsuccessful raid on Harper's Ferry in Virginia in a revolt against the institution of slavery. That attempted revolt hastened the onset of the Civil War.

Publication: Harriet Wilson's book, *Our Nig, or Sketches from the Life of a Free Black,* was the first novel published by an African American in the United States.

1860 William Nell was the first African American civilian Federal employee with his appointment as a Boston postal clerk.

Massachusetts Census:
Total Population: 1,231,066
African American Population: 9,602

1861 **Civil War Began:** On April 12th, the Confederate Army fired on Fort Sumter in South Carolina.

Publication: Harriet Jacobs published *Incidents in the Life of a Slave Girl.* The book described the seven years Jacobs hid in an attic in NC to be near her enslaved children.

1862 **Emancipation Proclamation** ended slavery in the Confederate States. President Abraham Lincoln (NAA) signed the Proclamation on September 22nd. It took effect on Jan. 1st, 1863:

"That on the first day of January, in the year of our Lord one thousand eight hundred and sixty-three, all persons held as slaves within any State or designated part of a State, the people whereof shall then be in rebellion against the United States, shall be then, thenceforward, and forever free."

1864 Rebecca Lee Crumpler of Boston was the first African American female doctor in the United States.

1865 **Civil War Ended:** On April 9th, Palm Sunday, General Robert E. Lee (NAA) surrendered the Confederate Army to General Ulysses S. Grant (NAA) of the Union Army at Appomattox Courthouse in Virginia. Over 180,000 African Americans served in the war and over 40,000 of them died.

President Abraham Lincoln (NAA) was assassinated on April 14th by John Wilkes Booth (NAA).

The U.S. Congress **passed** the Thirteenth Amendment on January 31st, 1865, a Bill to abolish slavery throughout all the United States except as punishment for a crime. The United States Congress also **ratified and adopted it as law** on December 6th, 1865.

1866 On November 6th, Edward G. Walker and Charles L. Mitchell both won election as the first African Americans to serve in the Massachusetts legislature. Walker's father was David Walker, the author of the radical abolitionist pamphlet, *Walker's Appeal.* The Charlestown polls where Walker stood for election closed before the Boston polls where Mitchell ran and Walker became technically, the first to win.

On June 13th, 1866, the United States Congress **passed** the Fourteenth Amendment, a Bill to give citizenship rights to African Americans.

1868 The U.S. Congress **ratified and adopted as law** the Fourteenth Amendment on July 9th, 1868.

1869 George Ruffin was the first African American graduate of Harvard Law.

The Act to Enfranchise the Indians of Massachusetts, 1869: Legislators allegedly developed this Act to give full citizenship rights to Native Americans who resided on tribal lands. As a condition to receive those rights, they had to divide their communal property. Many lost their land through that process.

On February 26th, 1869, the United States Congress **passed** the Fifteenth Amendment, a Bill to give the right to vote to African American men.

1870 Massachusetts Census:
Total Population: 1,457,351
African American Population: 3,496

The United States Congress **ratified and adopted as law** the Fifteenth Amendment on February 3rd, 1870. Women in the United States did not receive the right to vote until the Nineteenth Amendment in 1920.

1879 Mary Eliza Mahoney of Boston, was the first African American licensed as a nurse in the United States.

1880 Massachusetts Census:
Total Population: 1,783,085
African American Population 5,873

1881 Booker T. Washington founded Tuskegee Institute in Alabama.

1882 Lewis Howard Latimer of Boston, joined Thomas Edison's (NAA) team of engineers. Latimer's 1882 design of the carbon filament improved the light bulb.

1883 Jan Matzelinger of Lynn, MA, invented a shoe lasting machine that produced up to 500 pairs of shoes a day compared to 50 pairs a day produced manually.

George Ruffin of Boston, was the first African American judge in the state with his appointment to the Charlestown Municipal Court.

1890 Massachusetts Census:
Total Population: 2,238,947
African American Population: 8,125

1895 W.E.B. DuBois was the first African American awarded a Ph.D. degree from Harvard University. DuBois co-founded the NAACP in 1910.

1896 Plessy v. Ferguson Decision:
This U.S. Supreme Court decision institutionalized the doctrine of, *"separate but equal,"* the legal precedent used to uphold a plethora of *"Jim Crow"* laws that were enacted throughout the South after the war. Justice Henry Billings Brown (NAA) of Lee, MA wrote the majority opinion to uphold that doctrine. Justice Stephen J. Field (NAA) of Stockbridge also voted in the majority.

1898 Marshall *"Major"* Taylor of Worcester, MA, set a world record for the 1-mile bicycle race on August 27th (1 minute: 41.4 seconds).

1901 Publication: William Monroe Trotter and George Washington Forbes founded the radical civil rights newspaper, *"The Guardian,"* in Boston.

BOSTON SITES

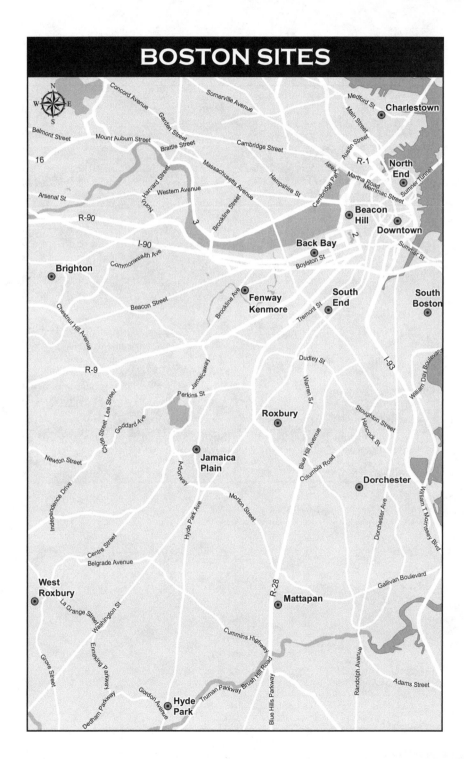

Boston Map, 1770

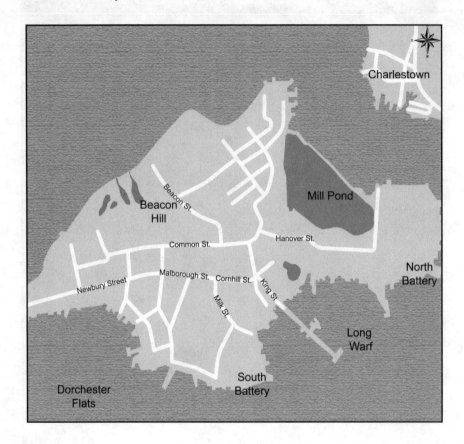

Beacon Hill Map, 2010

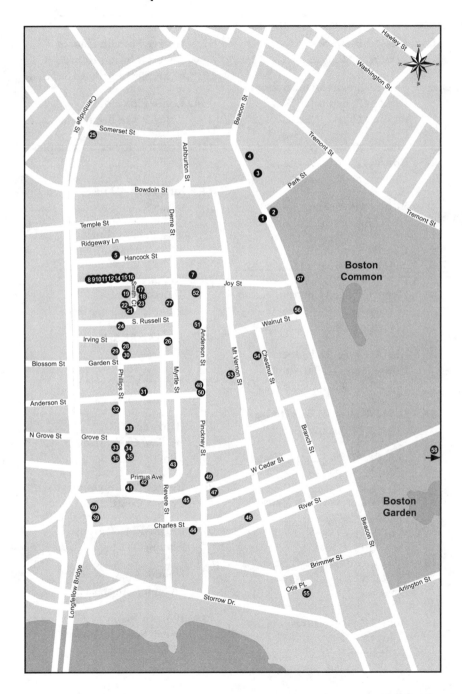

BEACON HILL

BEACON HILL was the location of a prosperous community of African Americans from the late-1700s to the late-1800s. They developed a strong and vibrant social network that sustained the community throughout difficult times. Many of those residents were property owners because property ownership was often the minimum threshold required to assert citizenship rights. They frequently purchased property from each other.

Some of those who purchased property on Belknap (Joy St. today) were: Tobias Locker in 1763; Scipio Fayerweather in 1765; Caesay Wendall in 1771; Prince Watts in 1785; Boston Smith in 1787; Cromwell Barnes in 1787; Brittain Balch in 1787; Samuel Bean in 1789; Peter Smith in 1810; and Hamlet Earle in 1793. Smith Court was another popular location for African American property owners. Some who owned property on Smith Court in the late 18th and early 19th century were: Peter Guss; Hannibal Allen; Peter Fortune Bailey; Scipio Dalton; George Holmes; Peter Branch; Timothy Phillips; Peter Mitchell; Richard Johnson; David Barlett; Peter Jessamine; Cromwell Barnes; Lewis Sylvester; Cato Hancock; Joel Holden; Cuff Buffum; Hamlet Earl; Boston Faddy; Peter Virginia; Oliver Nash; Abel Barbadoes; John Boyce; Thomas Jarvis; and Mrs. Bostille. Several individuals owned multiple properties. Joseph Sprague owned eight properties that he rented out.

The hub of this community was on the north slope of Beacon Hill but many African Americans lived on the South Slope as well. This African American community possessed a strong identity of self and intense racial pride. The label Africa or African often prefaced the names of important community institutions such as the African Meeting House, the African Methodist Episcopal Church and the African Lodge No. 1. The African Meeting House, built in 1806, was the center of civic activity in this community.

Important Institutions in the African American Community on Beacon Hill
- African Meeting House
- African Methodist Episcopal Church
- African Lodge No. 1
- The African School

Howard Thurman, Dean of Theology at Boston University, established the Museum of Negro History during the late-1950s with his wife, Sue Bailey Thurman. The goal of the museum was to document the African American heritage of Boston. Marcus Mitchell was the first curator of that museum. In 1963, Mitchell developed a Black Heritage Trail to document the many historic structures on Beacon Hill significant to African American heritage in Massachusetts.

In 1964, the museum was renamed the Museum of Afro-American History. Byron Rushing became the Director, a position he held for 15 years. Rushing's research documented several additional structures in this area important to African American history, and the Black Heritage Trail was formed. Rushing went on to serve the residents of the South End in the Massachusetts State Legislature with his election in 1982 as a State Representative.

The National Park Service offers guided walking tours of the Black Heritage Trail Monday through Saturday, at 10 a.m., noon and 2 p.m. The tours are free, but reservations are required. Most of the sites on the Black Heritage Trail are private residences and their interiors are not available for tours. This guide includes not only the official sites on the Black Heritage Trail but also sites in the *2002 Historic Resource Study Boston African American National Historic Site* by Kathryn Grover and Janine V. da Silva.

The following list from the 1848–49 Boston City Directory indicated that two hundred and forty residents of Beacon Hill and its adjacent neighborhoods were people of color at the time of that census. The street addresses and the occupation of the residents were included in the original list. Some of the streets were renamed or no longer exist. www.primaryresearch.org/peopleof color.

Andover St.
3: Benjamin F. Roberts, printer; Peter Smith, laborer.

Belknap
2: Sarah Burr, widow.
5: Lewis Smith, cook; Albert Williams, boot maker.
7: Amos Jackson, laborer.
9: Abraham Gaul, laborer.
11: Robert Walker, shoe maker.
12: Isaac Caldwell, boarding; Anthony F. Clark, hair dresser.
14: Peter L. Freeman, porter; Juda George, washing.
15: Cloe C. Jackson, washing.
16: Peter Avory, hair dresser.
17: Isaac Woodland, laborer; John L. Brown, mariner; Catharine Henson, widow; John Leonard, waiter; Theresa M. Turner, seamstress.
18: Maria Bell, widow; Coffin Potts, clothing; Benjamin P. Basset, hair dresser.
20: John Henry, laborer.
22: John Marshall, laborer.
23: James Fisk, laborer; John D. Fowler, cook; George F. Wilson; Uriah Mero, mariner.
24: Robert Baskvell, waiter; Joseph Russell, laborer.
25: Nancy Alexander, washing; Mary Elsbury, washing.
26: Susan Garrison, dress maker; James Johnson, tender.
27: Gilbert F. Gray, laborer; John Griffin; Robert Johnson, waiter; Edward Ruhler, laborer; Phebe A. Smith; Daniel Smith, mariner; William Stith, steward; John Thompson.
28: Catherine L. Barbadoes, dress maker; Augustus Howard, waiter; Jesse Huse, boot polisher.

Belknap Court
5: Odcardo Minot, boot black.

Belknap Place
Caesar Gardner, waiter; John Jenkins, cook; Daniel Smith, tender.

Brattle
12: C. Freeman, boot polisher; Reuben Simpson, clothing.
38: Thomas P. Smith, clothing.
40: Joseph Scarlett, chimney sweeper.

Bridge
33: William Lawson, clothing;
48: Edward B. Lawton, tender; Enoch L. Stallad, barber.

Brighton
27: George H. Boardmen, barber; Robert Bruce, laborer; Jos. W. Butler, waiter; Henry A. Gaskin, laborer; Russell Gaul, laborer; Edward Gray; Charles Mahoney, laborer; Mary Ann Mahoney, widow; John Sampson, mariner; Thomas G. Williams, waiter.

Butolph
1: Eli Caesar, hair dresser.
2: Mrs. William Wright, boarding.
10: Henry Tyler, clothing.
11: William S. Johnson, laborer; Joshua Owen, laborer; George Williams, laborer.
20: John F. Smith, hair dresser.

Cambridge
20: John N. Brown, barber.
110.5: Mrs. D.L. Carteaux, millinery goods.

Cambridge Court
3: Wesley Wilson, mariner.

Derne
10: Juleon B. McCrea, hair dresser.

Garden
2: Andrew T. Bell; John R. Lowry.
21: Phebe Bradshaw, widow.
31.5: Alexander R. Kell, trunk maker; Samuel Scott, waiter.
87: William Mitchell, laborer;

Grove
4: Stephen Boiser; George H. Bordwine; John Hogan, laborer; Lydia Potter, washing; Letecia Scott, washing.
34: William H. Logan, waiter.
35: Thomas Smith, laborer.

Hanover
2: James Collins, mariner.
4: Benjamin Wilson, laborer.

Lindall
2: Henry Smith, tender.

3: William W. Rich, tailor.
19: Harrison Mingo, barber.

Livingston
7: John Williams, laborer; John H. Simpson, waiter.

May
6: Eliza Burrows, washing; George Burton, mariner; Jones Clark, clothing; Mrs. A. Skeen, washing.
10: Hannah Cosey, washing; Thomas Jones, mariner; Mrs. James Jordan; John Miller, jobber; Enoch Saunders, laborer; Sarah Williams, washing; James J. Saunders, laborer.
11: Thomas Cummings, tender; John Debois, laborer; Henry H. Emery; John Johnson, tender; Jacob Sampson, laborer.
17: Charles Rozier, mariner; John Smith, laborer.
19: John Thompson, cigar maker.
24: William H. Gray, waiter; James H. Jackson, waiter; Augustus Murray, waiter; Isaiah Roby, job wagon.

Myrtle
11: Theodore Wells, waiter.
59: Leonard A. Grimes, Reverend; Peter Johnson, laborer.

Nashua
2: Mrs. Geo. H. Brown, washing.

Nashua Court
3: William Kendall, laborer.
5: Henry Johnson, laborer.

North Brighton
2: John Lockley, barber.

Poplar
17: Joseph H. Turpin, boards; Alfred G. Howard, hair cutter and musician; Edwin F. Howard, hair dresser; Mrs. Margaret A. Nahar.
26: Hannah M. Benson, widow.
29: Mrs. Mary Potter, washing; E.F.B. Mundrucu, clothing.

Poplar Court
2: Simpson H. Lewis, clothing.
3: Elias Furbush, laborer; John Rogers.

Portland
34: Peter Byus, tailor.

Second
3: James H. Helt, cook; John T. Hilton, hair dresser.
9: Robert Roberts, stevedore.
12: G.F. Rogers, clothing; John Aikens.
16. Francis Standin, mariner; Joseph Revaleon, hair dresser.

Smith Court
3: George Washington, laborer.
4: Isaac Barbadoes, musician; Samuel Barscom, laborer; Charles Brady, laborer; William Rumsley, laborer; John Smith, whitewasher.

Southac
1: James Butcher, tender.
2: Joseph J. Fatal, laborer; Richard Freeman, mariner; William Delancy, hair dresser; James Elisha; T. Campbell, waiter.
3: Henry L.W. Thacker, waiter; Lemuel Burr, barber.
4: William Riley, clothing; Lewis A. Martin; George S. Sprywood, Reverend.
5: Samuel Snowden, Reverend; George Mandulf, mariner.
6: Franklin Cuttee, caterer; Lewis Gaul, tender; Lewis Robbins, laborer; William Junior, oysters; J.L. Giles; William Robinson, tender.
7: Charles H. Taylor, restorator; William Davis, tender.
8: John St. Pierre, clothing; James A.C. Tilgham, whitner.
9: E. Jackson, boarding; William H. Alley, hair dresser.
11: Henry Cook, laborer; Isaac Watkins, laborer.
12: John Hatten, shoe maker.
13: Peter Randall, laborer; William Johnson, grocer; Grafter Johnson, waiter.
30: Joseph Gibson, laborer.
34: Marcus Huntley, cook; George H. Washington, porter.
35: Thomas Freeman, laborer.
36: Charles, Messick, and Isaac Roberts, furniture; Andress Lewis, barber; George Smith, boarding; John Henderson, laborer.
38: Robert James, laborer; Pompey Thurston.

Southac Court
2: Charles Rose, barber.
6: John Wright, clothing.
39: Isaac Hoye, baker; William Preston, tender; Henry Carter, laborer; George W. Clark.
40: John R. Taylor, temperance.

Southac Place
Richard H. Savoy, waiter; Henry Thomas, laborer.

South May
11: William H. Castell, barber; Joseph Scarlett, printer; Margaret Scarlett, widow.
13: Timothy Paine, laborer.

South Russell
21: Ira S. Gray.
29: Thomas Dalton.
31: Alice Bush, washing; Henry Davis, waiter.

Spring
33: George L. Clark, laborer.
37: James S. Smith, barber.
53: E.R. Davis, tailoress.

Suffolk
2: William E. Gray, laborer.
3: Isaac Henderson, laborer.

Vine
2: John Andrus, mariner; Betsey Gray; Thomas Hosker, laborer.

West Cedar
9: Henry Nichols, laborer; Richmond Tuttle, barber.
10: Mrs. Benjamin Shepherd.
57: Joseph H. Gover, laborer.

West Centre
6: Samuel Wilson, clothing; George Simms, laborer; Edward Williams.
7: Thomas T.M. Duffee, washing.
8: Peter Hawkins, laborer.
9: Mary A. Henson, washing.
12: William Brown, laborer; Nancy Gambo, widow; Lucy Hemenway, widow; Isaac Hill; Catharine Lindsey, widow.
15: Henry J. Johnson, Reverend; William H. Shiloh, hair dresser; Mary A. Eastman, washing.

MASSACHUSETTS STATE HOUSE

24 Beacon St.
Open Daily, 9 to 5

The State House, designed by self-taught architect Charles Bulfinch (NAA) in 1795, is the official seat of government for the state of Massachusetts. This is where the Executive and Legislative branches conduct their business. Throughout its history, African Americans continuously interacted with the state government to assert their civil rights.

In the mid 1700s, African Americans presented several petitions to the Legislature to end slavery in the state. Later, African American participation in the Civil War inspired them to a higher level of political engagement than had been possible earlier. Twelve African Americans in Massachusetts won election to state-wide office after the Civil War.

African Americans Elected to Massachusetts State Legislature in 19th Century
- Edwin G. Walker and Charles L. Mitchell (1866)
- John J. Smith (1868, 1869, and 1872);
- George L. Ruffin (1870, 1871);
- Joshua B. Smith (1873, 1874);
- George W. Lowther (1878, 1879);
- Julius C. Chappelle (1883, 1886);
- William O. Armstrong (1887, 1888);
- Andrew B. Leattimore (1889, 1890);
- William L. Reed (1896, 1897);
- Charles E. Harris (1892);
- Robert T. Teamoh (1894)

A gallery located outside of Doric Hall on the second floor of the State House contains an exhibit to commemorate six women who were influential in our state's history. That exhibit includes two African Americans, Sarah Parker Remond (1814–1894), an aboli-

Massachusetts State House

tionist, and Josephine St. Pierre Ruffin (1842–1924), a noted feminist and the wife of Judge George Ruffin.

April 22, 1965
Martin Luther King, Jr. addressed a joint session of the Massachusetts Legislature

In 1965, Dr. Martin Luther King, Jr. participated in a march in Boston to protest segregation in the city. While here, the Massachusetts State Legislature invited him to address a joint session on April 22nd. In that speech, Dr. King made a direct connection between the colonial struggle of the American Revolution to the civil rights struggle of the 1960s. Dr. King invoked the memory of the Pilgrim Fathers, the *"Declaration of Independence,"* and the *"Star Spangled Banner"* in his speech. He put those patriotic icons under the same umbrella of hope and faith in a just cause that also covered the civil rights movement. Dr. King ended his speech with quotes by two native sons of Massachusetts:

> *"Truth crushed to earth will rise again;"*
> -- William Cullen Bryant (NAA)

> *"Truth forever on the scaffold, wrong forever on the throne; yet that scaffold sways the future, and behind the dim unknown standeth God within the shadows keeping watch above his own..."*
> -- James Russell Lowell (NAA)

On January 4th, 2007, the State House was the location of an event of historic proportions, the inauguration of Deval Patrick as the first African American governor of Massachusetts. Patrick's election was only the second time in United States history that an African American had won a gubernatorial election in this country. Douglass Wilder's election as governor of Virginia in 1990 was the first.

January 4, 2007
Deval Patrick inaugurated as 1st African American Governor of Massachusetts.

Patrick swore his oath on a Bible given to John Quincy Adams (NAA) in the 1840s by members of the Amistad rebellion. Adams successfully defended the Amistad rebels, who were kidnapped from Africa, against charges of murder after they captured the slave ship, the Amistad, on which they were imprisoned in transit to the Caribbean. Members of the rebellion belonged to the Mendi Tribe of West Africa, and the Bible became known as the Mendi Bible. Patrick invoked the memory of the rebels in his inaugural speech to connect his history with theirs.

Governor Patrick (b. July 31st, 1956) and his sister, Rhonda, were raised by their mother, Emily Mae Patrick, and their grandmother, Sally Embers, in the Taylor Homes public housing development on Chicago's South Side. Patrick's father, Laudine Patrick, was a jazz musician. In high school, Deval Patrick won a scholarship to Milton Academy, a prestigious boarding school in Milton, MA.

Deval Patrick

Patrick went on to graduate from Harvard College and Harvard Law School. President Bill Clinton (NAA) appointed Patrick Assistant Attorney General for Civil Rights in 1994. Patrick's election as governor in 2006 was his first attempt at public office. Patrick achieved another historic first when he was re-elected to a second term as governor in 2010.

2 54TH REGIMENT MEMORIAL

Beacon St., opposite the State House

The Massachusetts 54th Regiment Memorial, also known as the Shaw Memorial, is a testament to the bravery and integrity of the first African American

Civil War Regiment organized in the North. In 1863, African American volunteers from all of New England filled the new Boston based regiment. In Massachusetts alone, there were 3,838 African American volunteers.

Joshua B. Smith, a prominent citizen of the African American community, a successful caterer, an active abolitionist, and a future State legislator, was also a former staff member of the Shaw household. In 1865, Smith began to raise funds to build a memorial to recognize the bravery of Shaw and the members of the 54th Regiment. The memorial was finally completed and dedicated in 1897.

May 28, 1863
54th Regiment march down Beacon St. on their way to war.

The bronze bas-relief took sculptor, Augustus Saint-Gaudens (NAA), thirteen years to complete. Saint-Gaudens was a United States citizen of French and Irish ancestry. The 54th Regiment Memorial represents one of the finest examples of his art anywhere. It portrayed the soldiers of the 54th as they marched down Beacon St. on May 28th, 1863, on their way to war. Saint-Gaudens depicted each soldier as unique individuals. That depiction reinforced their individual humanity. It was one of the earliest efforts in American portraiture that depicted African Americans in a realistic and respectful manner.

Located opposite the State House, this memorial honors all the African

54th Regiment Memorial

American volunteers from the North who served in the Civil War. Col. Shaw and ninety-six members of the Massachusetts 54th Regiment died from the assault on Fort Wagner. Another two hundred were injured or captured.

President Abraham Lincoln's (NAA) decision to finally admit African Americans into the armed forces in 1863 was based on two factors, the constant pressure from abolitionists, and the high death rate of the white Union soldiers.

Frederick Douglass and other notable abolitionists recruited for the regiment, and two of Frederick Douglass's sons, Lewis and Charles, volunteered to serve in the regiment. The African

Meeting House on Beacon Hill was the center of this recruitment activity.

> "...Once let the black man get upon his person the brass letter, U.S., let him get an eagle on his button, a musket on his shoulder, and bullets in his pocket, (then) there is no power on earth that can deny that he has earned the right to citizenship."
> -- FREDERICK DOUGLASS

African American leaders in Boston did not universally support the war effort. Robert Morris, an attorney,

54th Regiment Casualties, Battle of Fort Wagner

Colonel Robert Gould Shaw,
Commander

Company A:
Sergeant Andrew Burton
Corporal Ralph Gardner
Private Henry Abbot
Private Henry F. Burghardt
Private George W. Duncan
Private James M. Allen
Private George E. Ellis
Private Joseph Ford
Private Edward Hines
Private Marshall Lamb
Private Harrison Pierce
Private John Smith
Private George F. Waterman
Private Cornelius Watson

Company B:
Sergeant Robert J. Simons
Corporal Charles Hardy
Private S.E. Anderson
Private George Allison
Private Jesse H. Brenn
Private David Baily
Private Morris Brunn
Private John H. Brooks
Private James Elets
Private George Grant
Private Luiden Glascow
Private Alfred Green
Private William Rigby
Private John A. Suellen
Private Daniel Slate
Private Charles Williams
Private Samuel R. Wilson
Private Lemuel Blake

Company C:
Corporal Joseph Campbell
Corporal Abram P. Turner
Private Joseph L. Hall
Private Cornelius Hudson
Private Ira Halsey

Private Samuel Johnson
Private John Lott
Private Treadwell Turner
Private George Rice

Company D:
Private Andrew Clark
Private George E. Cogswell
Private William Edgerly
Private Albert Evans
Private Bay Hogans
Private Thomas Lloyd
Private William Lloyd
Private Stephen Newton
Private Thomas T. Riggs

Company E:
Private Joseph J. Proctor
Private Morris Butler
Private William Grover
Private Nathaniel Hourly
Private Charles W. Lopeman
Private John Weeks
Private William Anderson

Company F:
Private Jefferson Ellis
Private John P. Gray
Private Daniel Kelley
Private Francis Lowe
Private George W. Mashwe
Private David Ropes
Private Sheldon Thomas
Private George K. Thomas
Private Edward Williams

Company G:
Private Charles Body
Private William Meyers
Private Harrison Nichols
Private Charles Straubon
Private John Stereut

Private William Tyler
Private William Underwood

Company H:
Sergeant Walter A. Jeffers
Corporal Amstell Williams
Private James Caldwell
Private James A. Williams
Private J.W. Dickinson
Private Henry Kirk
Private Enos Smith
Private Frederick Wallace
Private H.W. Worthington

Company J:
Sergeant Alfred Whiting
Corporal Charles Augustas
Corporal Robert Lyons
Corporal Randolph Brady
Private J.M. Freeman
Private Noah Gains
Private William Pillow
Private Thomas Stow
Private B.H. Williams
Private Ezekiel Williams
Private J Williamson
Private B. Smith
Private S.W. Woods
Private H.C. Charleton

Company K:
Sergeant Jesse Mahan
Corporal John H. Wilson
Private Colove Morgan
Private Samuel Ford
Private Henry Craig
Private William Brady
Private Joseph Bryant
Private Thomas R. Ampey
Private Allen W. Stevenson

www.archives.gov/exhibits/american_originals/54thmass

180,000
The number of African American troops who served in the Union military

40,000
The number of African American troops who died during the war. Those fatalities represented 22% of those troops who served.

abolitionist, and civil rights activist, refused to participate in recruitment until full equality for the recruits was the law. That included the right for the recruits to become officers. William Wells Brown, a fugitive from slavery, an ardent abolitionist and author, held a similar position:

> *"... equality first, guns afterward..."*
> WILLIAM WELLS BROWN

Despite less than unanimous support, recruitment continued and the Massachusetts 54th Regiment was soon filled to capacity with 1,369 enlisted men and 78 white officers. The commander of the unit was a twenty-six year old volunteer from a prominent white Boston family, Robert Gould Shaw (NAA). After a very short training period at Camp Meigs, in present day Hyde Park, the 54th Regiment went to assist in the capture of the city of Charleston, South Carolina.

In order to capture Charleston, the Union Army had to first capture Morris Island. That victory would allow them to eliminate Fort Wagner which the Confederates used to guard the harbor in which Charleston was located. The Union Army's first assault on the island on July 10th, 1863, resulted in the capture of the southern half of the island but not the more strategic northern half where Fort Wagner was located. Another Union attempt on July 11th was also not successful. Major General Quincy A. Gillmore (NAA) of the Union Army decided to plan a massive attack on July 18th after troop reinforcements arrived. The Confederates had 1,800 troops at the Fort. The Union Army planned to send 5,000 troops in the attack which would be supported by a bombardment from the Atlantic Ocean.

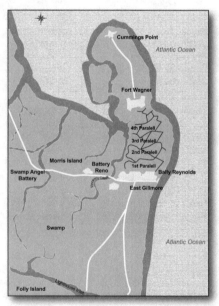

Map of Morris Island and Fort Wagner

Fort Wagner was truly a fort to be reckoned with. It was strategically located to obstruct a ¼ mile wide stretch of beach on the approach to the tip of Morris Island, Cummings Point. Along the eastern side of the beach was the Atlantic Ocean and along the western side lay a swamp. Fort Wagner's parapets were 30 feet tall and the fort contained fourteen cannons, one of which could fire 128-pound shells. On the southern side of the fort, the side where any land assault would have to come, was a 10 foot wide by 5 foot deep moat. Palmetto stakes that had been carved into deadly sharp spears were buried into the ground. Land mines provided an additional protective barrier.

The assault began at 8:15 a.m. on the morning of July 18th with a bombardment from eleven Union ships in the harbor. That attack continued throughout the day in preparation for the land assault. At 7:45 p.m., Col. Shaw of the 54th Regiment organized 624 of his men in formation to lead the first land assault. Behind the 54th were the following regiments in the order of their placement in the assault: the 10th Connecticut, the 48th New York, the 3rd New Hampshire, the 76th Pennsylvania, and the 9th Maine. The symbolic significance to allow the 54th , the only African American regiment in the group, to lead the assault was not lost on any of those present.

When the 54th was within 150 yards of the Fort, the Confederates began to fire. The subsequent battle was horrific. By 8:30 p.m., the 54th had already suffered substantial casualties. The total casualties from the 624 troops of the 54th regiment that charged Fort Wagner that day consisted of 272 troops who were either killed, wounded, or captured. The second assault, which included the 7th New Hampshire, the 63rd Ohio and 67th Ohio, and the 100th New York Regiments, fared no better. The battle finally ended by 10:30 p.m. The 54th fought gallantly in the Battle of Fort Wagner along with all the Union troops, but the Confederate soldiers enjoyed a strategic advantage at Fort Wagner that enabled them to prevail in that battle.

Two hundred and seventy-six troops died that day and ninety-six of those were from the Massachusetts 54th Regiment. Col. Shaw and the other members of the 54th Regiment who died on the battlefield that day were dumped into a mass grave by the Confederate soldiers. That action was intended as an insult to Col. Shaw as a white officer. When his family was informed, they indicated that it was an appropriate memorial to their son to be interred with those with whom he fought so gallantly.

Sgt. William H. Carney of the 54th Regiment became the first African American to receive a United States

July 18th, 1863 – Battle of Fort Wagner		
	Union Army	Confederate Army
Troops	5,000	1,800
Killed	276	36
Wounded	880	133
Captured	389	5

Congressional Medal of Honor for his bravery during the battle of Fort Wagner. See more on Carney under New Bedford sites. Ultimately, the Union Army could not capture Fort Wagner so they laid siege on the Fort until the Confederates abandoned it on Sept. 6th, 1863.

Corporal James Henry Gooding of the 54th Regiment wrote weekly dispatches from the frontlines that gave an up-close and personal view of the war effort. The *New Bedford Mercury* newspaper published his letters on a regular basis.

Morris Island, July 20, 1863

Messrs. Editors: -- At last we have something stirring to record. The 54th, the past week, has proved itself twice in battle. The first was on James Island on the morning of the 16th.

… The men of the 54th behaved gallantly on the occasion – so the Generals say. It is not for us to blow our horn; but when a regiment of white men gave us three cheers as we were passing them, it shows that we did our duty as men should.

I shall pass over the incidents of that day, as regards individuals, to speak of a greater and more terrible ordeal the 54th regiment has passed through. Gen. Strong asked us if we would follow him into Fort Wagner. Every man said, yes – we were ready to follow wherever we were led. You may all know Fort Wagner is the Sebastopol of the rebels; but we went at it, over the ditch and on to the parapet through a deadly fire, but we could not get into the fort. We met the foe on the parapet of Wagner with the bayonet -- we were exposed to a murderous fire from the batteries of the fort, from our Monitors and our land batteries, as they did not cease firing soon enough. Mortal men could not stand such a fire, and the assault on Wagner was failure. The 9th Me., 10th Conn., 63rd Ohio, 48th and 100th N.Y. were to support us in the assault; but after we made the first charge, everything was in such confusion that we could hardly tell where the reserve was. At the first charge the 54th rushed to within twenty yards of the ditches, and, as might be expected of raw recruits, wavered – but at the second advance they gained the parapet. The color bearer of the State colors was killed on the parapet. Col. Shaw seized the staff when the standard bearer fell, and in less than a minute after, the Colonel fell himself. When the men saw their gallant leader fall, they made a desperate effort to get him out, but they were either shot down, or reeled in the ditch below. One man succeeded in getting hold of the State color staff, but the color was completely torn to pieces….

— *James Henry Gooding*

Battle of Fort Wagner
Illustration by Laurence Pierce, AKA Larry Azim

After the battle, the bravery of the Massachusetts 54th Regiment became a rallying cry for the recruitment of African American soldiers throughout the country. The 54th matched their bravery with their integrity. For 18 months, these soldiers refused their pay because it was lower than that for white soldiers of comparable rank.

January 1, 1865
United States Congress Passed a Law mandating equal pay for all soldiers.

Monthly Pay		
	Black Recruits	White Recruits
Pay	$10.00	$13.00
Clothing	$3.00	Free
Net Pay	$7.00	$13.00

 JOHN SWETT ROCK & BOSTON LAW ASSOCIATION
16 Beacon St.

The Boston Law Association hung a commemorative plaque in its lobby to honor John Swett Rock. Rock was the first African American attorney presented to the United States Supreme Court on February 1st, 1865. See more on John Swett Rock in this section and in Downtown Boston.

February 1, 1861
John Swett Rock was the 1st African American attorney presented to the U.S. Supreme Court.

BOSTON ATHENAEUM
10-1/2 Beacon St.
10 a.m. to 5 p.m. daily /
Limited access

This private library contains original documents about the history of African Americans in Massachusetts. Also in their collection are several paintings by Harlem Renaissance artist, Allan Rohan Crite (1910–2006) of Boston. Crite donated his paintings to the Athenaeum. The Athenaeum allows visitors to view the paintings and other documents by special request. Architect Edward Clarke Cabott (NAA) won a competition in 1846 for his neoclassical design for the building.

Boston Athenaeum

 CHARLES SUMNER HOUSE
20 Hancock Street.

Throughout his career, Charles Sumner (1811-1874) (NAA) actively engaged in the movement to end slavery and to

Charles Sumner

ensure equal rights and opportunities for African Americans. After graduation from Harvard College and Harvard Law School, Sumner spent several years abroad. In Paris, Sumner met individuals of African heritage who were also students in that cosmopolitan city. That exposure changed his opinion about the alleged inferiority of people of African descent. Sumner devoted the rest of his life to the fight to end slavery and to promote the equality of the races.

Charles Sumner was the lead attorney in the appeal of the Sarah Roberts vs. City of Boston school desegregation case of 1849. Chief Justice Lemuel Shaw (NAA) was the Chief Justice of the Massachusetts Supreme Court in that case. Sumner lost the case, as did Robert Morris before him, but by 1855, their efforts influenced the state legislature to end segregated public schools throughout Massachusetts. See more on the lawsuit under the Abiel Smith School in Beacon Hill sites.

Charles Sumner House

Charles Sumner became a U.S. Senator in 1851. Sumner nearly died and spent three years in recovery from an assault in 1856 after he delivered an anti-slavery speech on the Senate floor. In that speech, he referred to Senator Andrew Butler (NAA) of South Carolina as a *"pimp for slavery."* Butler was one of the authors of the Kansas-Nebraska Act of 1854. That bill created the new territories of Kansas and Nebraska. It also allowed the new settlers to vote if they would become a pro-slavery state or anti-slavery state.

The Kansas-Nebraska Act nullified a previous congressional bill, the Missouri Compromise of 1850. That bill prohibited slavery in the areas of the Louisiana Purchase that were north of the 36° 30' parallel except for the proposed state of Missouri where slavery would be allowed. Many Northerners were incensed over the Kansas-Nebraska Act because it opened the door to expand slavery into the new territiories.

Excerpt from Sumner's speech that so enraged Brooks:

"The senator from South Carolina has read many books of chivalry, and believes himself a chivalrous knight with sentiments of honor and courage. Of course he has chosen a mistress to whom he has made his vows, and who, though ugly to others, is always lovely to him; though polluted in the sight of the world, is chaste in his sight -- I mean the harlot, slavery. For her, his tongue is always profuse in words. Let her be impeached in character, or any proposition made to shut her out from the extension of her wantonness, and no extravagance of manner or hardihood of assertion is then too great for this senator."

— *Charles Sumner*

A few days after Sumner's speech, Butler's cousin, South Carolina Representative Preston Brooks (NAA), entered the Senate chambers when Sumner was at his desk and began to beat him severely on the head and upper body with a walking cane. The severe blows to Sumner's head caused him to temporarily lose his sight from the blood that flowed from his wounds. Brooks continued to beat Sumner even after his cane snapped in half. His blows to Sumner were so vigorous that he, Brooks, injured himself when one of his backswings struck his own eye.

Several in attendance attempted to assist Sumner but they were blocked by others who approved of the episode. Brooks was finally able to be restrained but only after he had nearly bludgeoned Sumner to death. Sumner received several stitches from that incident and he suffered symptoms of brain trauma for the remainder of his life. Brooks was arrested and convicted for assault and he paid a $300 fine but served no jail time. Although the House could not muster the votes to censor him, Brooks resigned to allow his constituents to judge his actions. He easily won his re-election. Southerners praised Brooks's actions and Northerners condemned it.

The cane that Brooks beat Sumners with is on display in the Old State House, see downtown Boston sites. William Cullen Bryant (NAA), a native of Massachusetts and at that time, editor of the New York Evening Post, said this about the incident:

> "...Has it come to this that we must speak with bated breath in the presence of our southern masters?... Are we to be chastised as they chastise their slaves? Are we too, slaves, slaves for life, a target for their brutal blows, when we do not comport ourselves to please them?"
> – WILLIAM CULLEN BRYANT.

 ## 6 HOME FOR AGED COLORED WOMEN #3
22 Hancock St

This was the final location for this home for elderly African American women. It was originally opened in 1860 at 65 Phillips St. It was located at 27 Myrtle St. from 1863 until 1900 at which time it moved into this house. See more under Beacon Hill site #33.

 ## 7 ABEL & CHLOE BARBADOES HOUSE JAMES G. BARBADOES
19 Joy St., (formerly 19 Belknap St.)

Abel (1756–1817) and Chloe (1759–1843) Barbadoes were the parents of James George Barbadoes (1796–1841), a prominent African American civil rights activist of the nineteenth century. Abel was born in Lexington to Quawk Abel and Kate Barbadoes. His brother, Isaac, died in battle in the American Revolution. Abel petitioned the Legislature for Isaac's pension and he did not receive it until 1816, a year before his death.

After Abel relocated to Boston, he married Chloe Holloway of Maine on September 27th, 1782, at the First Baptist Church in Boston. In Boston, Abel and Chloe had nine children and James was the middle child. Abel was a skilled mason who participated in the construction of the African Meeting House on Beacon Hill.

James George Barbadoes lived at this address during his early years. He married three times, Almira Long, Mary Ann Willis, and Rebecca Brint. James George Barbadoes had eleven children from his three marriages.

Barbadoes was at the forefront of all civil rights activity throughout his life. He was a member of the African Lodge #459 when it broke away from the Grand Lodge of England and became the Prince Hall Freemasonry Lodge. He was one of the founders and Secretary of the Massachusetts General Colored Association in 1826. In 1831, the First National Convention of Free People of Color was held in Philadelphia and James G. Barbadoes attended as one of the delegates from Massachusetts. He was appointed vice-president of the convention.

Barbadoes was one of many African Americans who protested the intent of the American Colonization Society to force free people of color to relocate to Liberia.

Barbadoes continued in his struggle to achieve civil rights for African Americans until his death in Jamaica in 1841 from a fever. He had gone there to establish a silkworm company. The silkworm industry was viewed as a viable option to the cotton industry which depended on enslaved labor.

8A DAVID & ELIZA WALKER HOUSE

81 Joy St.
(formerly 8 Belknap St.)
www.davidwalker
memorial.org

Davis Walker (1785-1830) was one of the most famous and radical of the many anti-slavery activists. His pamphlet, *Walker's Appeal,* stirred up anti-slavery sentiment among both blacks and whites. Walker was born to an enslaved father and a free mother in Wilmington, NC. He lived as a free Black because of his mother's free status.

Walker settled in Boston around 1820 where he was active in the abolitionist community. David Walker lived at this residence with his family from

David Walker House

1827 to 1829. Walker was one of the founders of the Massachusetts General Colored Association, the first all-black abolitionist organization in the United States. He was also a frequent contributor to *Freedom's Journal* of New York City, the nation's first African American newspaper.

His used clothing shop on Brattle St. near Faneuil Hall provided a system for Walker to distribute his radical anti-slavery pamphlet, the *Appeal to the Colored Citizens of the World,* popularly known as *Walker's Appeal.* He hid the pamphlets in clothes purchased by seamen from the South who visited Boston.

Walker argued in his pamphlet that the institution of slavery was a sin before God and that the only solution to it was its total elimination. Walker's pamphlet increased hostilities over slavery in people on both sides of the issue. Southern lawmakers put an award on Walker's head after the publication of the pamphlet.

David Walker died in 1830 after he published the third edition of his pamphlet. The circumstances of Walker's sudden death are not clear. His daughter died of influenza a few months earlier and he may have died from the same illness. Walker's widow, Eliza Butler Walker, remained in Boston to raise their young son, Edwin Garrison Walker. Edwin Walker was the first African American to win election to the Massachusetts Legislature in 1865. Edwin's middle name was in honor of William Lloyd Garrison, the white abolitionist. A group in Boston was recently formed to raise awareness about the importance of David Walker in the history of our country with, "*The David Walker Memorial Project.*"

September 25, 1829
David Walker published *Walker's Appeal.* Southerners put out an award for his capture:
$3,000 Dead
$10,000 Alive

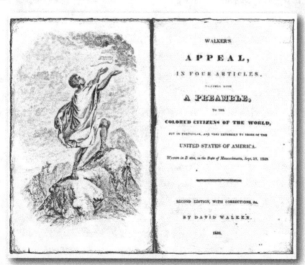

Walker's Appeal Cover

This excerpt is from the introduction of *Walker's Appeal*:

"My dearly beloved Brethren and Fellow Citizens.

Having traveled over a considerable portion of these United States,...--the result of my observations has warranted the full and unshaken conviction, that we, (coloured people of these United States,) are the most degraded, wretched, and abject set of beings that ever lived since the world began; and I pray God that none like us ever may live again until time shall be no more.

They tell us of the Israelites in Egypt, the Helots in Sparta, and of the Roman slaves, which last were made up from almost every nation under heaven, whose sufferings under those ancient and heathen nations, were in comparison with ours, under this enlightened and Christian nation, no more than a cipher—or, in other words, those heathen nations of antiquity, had but little more among them than the name and form of slavery; while wretchedness and endless miseries were reserved, apparently in a phial, to be poured out upon our fathers, ourselves and our children, by Christian Americans!

These positions I shall endeavour, by the help of the Lord, to demonstrate in the course of this Appeal, to the satisfaction of the most incredulous mind—...

The causes, my brethren, which produce our wretchedness and miseries, are so very numerous and aggravating, that I believe the pen only of a Josephus or a Plutarch, can well enumerate and explain them.

...I am fully aware, in making this appeal to my much afflicted and suffering brethren, that I shall not only be assailed by those whose greatest earthly desires are, to keep us in abject ignorance and wretchedness, and who are of the firm conviction that Heaven has designed us and our children to be slaves and BEASTS OF BURDEN to them and their children.

I say, I do not only expect to be held up to the public as an ignorant, impudent and restless disturber of the public peace,... —and perhaps put in prison or to death, for giving a superficial exposition of our miseries, and exposing tyrants. But I am persuaded, that many of my brethren, particularly those who are ignorantly in league with slave-holders or tyrants, who acquire their daily bread by the blood and sweat of their more ignorant brethren—and not a few of those too, who are too ignorant to see an inch beyond their noses, will rise up and call me cursed—Yea, the jealous ones among us will perhaps use more abject subtlety, by affirming that this work is not worth perusing, that we are well situated, and there is no use in trying to better our condition....

...can our condition be any worse?—Can it be more mean and abject? If there are any changes, will they not be for the better, though they may appear for

the worst at first? Can they get us any lower? Where can they get us? They are afraid to treat us worse, for they know well, the day they do it they are gone.... I appeal to heaven for my motive in writing—who knows that my object is, if possible, to awaken in the breast of my afflicted, degraded and slumbering brethren, a spirit of inquiry and investigation respecting our miseries and wretchedness in this REPUBLICAN LAND OF LIBERTY!!! "

– David Walker.

8B JAMES & MARIA STEWART HOUSE

81 Joy St., (formerly 8 Belknap St.)

James and Maria Stwart also resided at 8 Belknap St. In 1832, Maria Stewart (1803-1879) was the first documented female of any race to deliver public speeches in the United States. Stewart was an early anti-slavery activist who suggested that African Americans should not wait for deliverers but must deliver themselves from oppression, and that freedom began with the cultivation of the mind.

> *"...It is of no use for us to sit with our hands folded, hanging our heads like bulrush, lamenting our wretched condition; but let us make a mighty effort, and arise; and if no one will promote or respect us, let us promote and respect ourselves."*
> — MARIA STEWART

> *"...It is not the color of the skin that makes the man, but...the principles formed within the soul."*
> - MARIA STEWART

Born in Connecticut, Stewart became an orphan at the age of five. A clergyman and his family raised Stewart until she was fifteen. That family instilled in her a deep sense of religion and a thirst for knowledge.

Maria Stewart

In 1826, Maria married James W. Stewart, a successful independent shipping agent, in Boston. His death in 1829, and the court's refusal to recognize Maria's rights to his estate, forced her to begin a career as a public speaker to support herself. Stewart's husband had been an associate of David Walker, the radical abolitionist. That association influenced Stewart's politics and her proud demeanor.

This excerpt is from Stewart's speech, "Knowledge is Power":

"...African rights and liberty is a subject that ought to fire the breast of every free man of color in these United States, and excite in his bosom a lively, deep, decided and heart-felt interest. When I cast my eyes on the long list of illustrious names that are enrolled on the bright annals of fame among the whites, I turn my eyes within, and ask my thoughts, "Where are the names of our illustrious ones?" ...

We have made ourselves appear altogether unqualified to speak in our own defense, and are therefore looked upon as objects of pity and commiseration. We have been imposed upon, insulted and derided on every side; and now, if we complain, it is considered as the height of impertinence. We have suffered ourselves to be considered as dastards, cowards, mean, faint-hearted wretches; and on this account (not because of our complexion) many despise us, and would gladly spurn us from their presence.

These things have fired my soul with a holy indignation, and compelled me thus to come forward, and endeavor to turn their attention to knowledge and improvement; for knowledge is power. I would ask, is it blindness of mind, or stupidity of soul, or the want of education that has caused our men who are 60 or 70 years of age, never to let their voices be heard, nor their hands be raised in behalf of their color? Or has it been for the fear of offending the whites? If it has, O ye fearful ones, throw off your fearfulness, and come forth in the name of the Lord, and in the strength of the God of Justice, and make yourselves useful and active members in society; ...

While our minds are vacant and starve for want of knowledge, theirs are filled to overflowing. Most of our color have been taught to stand in fear of the white man from their earliest infancy, to work as soon as they could walk, and to call "master" before they could scarce lisp the name of mother. Continual fear and laborious servitude have in some degree lessened in us that natural force and energy which belong to man; or else, in defiance of opposition, our men, before this, would have nobly and boldly contended for their rights. But there is no such opportunity for the sons of Africa, and I fear that our powerful ones are fully determined that there never shall be.

...Is it possible,..., that for the want of knowledge we have labored for hundreds of years to support others, and been content to receive what they chose to give us in return? Cast your eyes about, look as far as you can see; all, all is owned by the lordly white, except here and there a lowly dwelling which the man of color, midst deprivations, fraud, and opposition has been scarce able to procure. Like King Solomon, who put neither nail nor hammer to the temple, yet received the praise; so also have the white Americans gained themselves a name, like the names of the great men that arte in the earth, while in reality we have been their principal foundation and support. We have pursued the shadow, they have obtained the substance; we have performed the labor, they have received the profits, we have planted the vines, they have eaten the fruits of them.

...The unfriendly whites first drove the native American from his much loved home. Then they stole our fathers from their peaceful and quiet dwellings, and brought them hither, and made bondmen and bond-women of them and their little ones. They have obliged our brethren to labor; kept them in utter ignorance; nourished them in vice, and raised them in degradation; and now that we have enriched their soil, and filled their coffers, they say that we are not capable of becoming like white men, and that we can never rise to respectability in this country. They would drive us to a strange land (Liberia). But before I go, the bayonet shall pierce me through. African (American) rights and liberty is a subject that ought to fire the breast of every free man of color in these United States, and excite in his bosom a lively, deep, decided, and heartfelt interest."

–Maria Stewart

Stewart believed in the potential of all individuals to achieve. She was not sympathetic to those who limited the scope and range of anyone's accomplishments because of their sex or race. Stewart's speeches were met with coldness, even from those of her own race. That

September 21, 1833
During Stewart's last public speech at the African Masonic Hall, she exhorted African American women to help save the race.

chilly reception forced her to reconsider that vocation.

Maria Stewart eventually relocated to Washington, DC, to become a public school teacher to support herself. In 1878, one year before her death and forty-nine years after she became a widow, Stewart finally received the pension that she was entitled to in 1829 for her late husband's service in the War of 1812.

REV. SAMUEL SNOWDEN HOUSE #1
UGRR Station
79 Joy St (formerly 5 or 9 Belknap St.)

Rev. Samuel Snowden (d. 1850) was an abolitionist and the first pastor of May St. Church. May St. Church was the predecessor of today's Union United Methodist Church in the South End. Snowden was born enslaved in Maryland. By 1800, he was a preacher in Maine with a reputation that extended throughout the New England states.

In 1818, Snowden was recruited to pastor May St. Church in Boston and he accepted. Snowden must have been a person of persuasion because the congregation built a new church by 1823. Snowden immediately became active in Boston's anti-slavery efforts. He was a member of the New England Anti-Slavery Society and a delegate to the first convention for freed African Americans that was held in Philadelphia. Rev. Snowden had widely established the fact that his doors were always open for those who sought shelter. Snowden lived with his family at this address from 1818 until 1843. See more on Snowden under Beacon Hill site #36.

 ### JOHN T. HILTON HOUSE
73-75 Joy St.
(formerly 12 Belknap St.)

The John T. Hilton House was owned or occupied by African Americans from the time of its original construction in 1825 until 1921. John Telemachus Hilton (1801–1864), a famous abolitionist, anti-colonialist, and entreprenuer, lived at 73–75 Joy St. for a short time in the early 1830s and he was the most well known resident of that dwelling. Hilton was born in Pennsylvania and when he relocated to Boston in 1820, he entered fully into the African American activism of that community. Some of Hilton's civic affiliations were: Grand Master of the Prince Hall Masonic Lodge; one of the founders of the Massachusetts General Colored Association; member of the Boston Vigilance Committee; and member of the Anti-Slavery Society.

John T. Hilton married Lavinia Ames in 1825. Their family included three sons and two daughters. One of Lavinia Ames ancestors was Prince Ames, a veteran of the American Revolution. The couple also belonged to the African Baptist Church on Beacon Hill and they both were active in the temperance movement. Hilton's various entrepreneurial enterprises included at various times: hairdresser; ownership of an employment agency; ownership of a retail shop; ownership of a furniture shop; and manager of ticket sales for various events. The Hilton's eventually moved to Cambridge to protest Boston's segregated public schools.

The original owner and builder of 73–75 Joy St. was George B. Holmes, a hairdresser and musician. Holmes built this house in 1825 but he only occupied it for a short time because he died within four years. Holmes' father, George Holmes, a laborer, built a home in the vicinity on what was renamed Holmes Alley after him.

 11 ROBERT ROBERTS HOUSE
71 Joy St
(formerly 14 Belknap St.)

Robert Roberts (1780–1860) wrote, *The House Servant's Directory, or a Monitor for Private Families, 1827,* a very popular manual on how to run a gentleman's household. Roberts wrote this book while he ran the household of Gore Place, the estate of diplomat and politician, Christopher Gore (NAA) in Waltham. Robert Roberts published his book after Christopher Gore's death in 1827. Robert Roberts accrued substantial personal wealth from the success of this book.

Roberts was born in Charleston, SC, and he relocated to Boston sometime after 1805. In Boston, Roberts joined a close-knit African American community. That strong community bond protected many free African Americans who were constantly exposed to the dangers of kidnappers who sold them into bondage, even from states as far north as Massachusetts. Roberts had intimate knowledge of those dangers because kidnappers sold three of his first wife's brothers into bondage in 1810. Roberts was unable to locate them despite his extensive efforts.

Roberts' first wife, Dorothy Hall, was the daughter of Jude Hall, a veteran of the American Revolution. After the death of Dorothy Hall in 1813, Roberts married Sarah Easton, the daughter of another veteran of the Revolution, James Easton (1754–1830) of Bridgewater, MA. Easton was a prominent business leader and civil rights activist. James Easton's son and Roberts's brother-in-law, Hosea Easton (1798–1837), was a prominent minister, abolitionist, and author.

Roberts lobbied against the American Society for Colonization's efforts to relocate freed African Americans to Liberia in an effort to minimize their presence in the United States. Roberts was the father of Benjamin Roberts, the printer, and the grandfather of Sarah Roberts, the plaintiff in the Roberts vs. Boston school desegregation case of 1849.

Robert Roberts was buried at Woodlawn Cemetery in Everett, MA. When he died, Roberts left an estate valued at nearly $8,000, a substantial sum at that time.

GEORGE PUTNAM HOUSE / ROBERT JOHNSON HOUSE

69 Joy St.
(formerly 16 Belknap St.)

African American hairdresser and abolitionist, George Putnam purchased this lot in 1826 for $439 and he built the house on it within two years. Putnam frequently hosted meetings in his home to discuss anti-slavery efforts and how to combat the colonization movement. Another of his key proposals was the development of a high school for African American students. Both George and his wife, Jane, were active in the temperance movement. The locations of George's hair salons were, in sequential order, 211 Washington St., 14 School St., and 150 Court St. the Putnams relocated to Salem in the late 1840s.

In 1853, Putnam sold this house to another African American, Robert Johnson (d. 1880). Johnson was a fugitive from Richmond, Virginia who escaped slavery around 1834. In Boston, Johnson was a clothes merchant and a waiter. He and his wife, Clarissa, and their family, lived across the street from 69 Joy St. from 1834 until they purchased 69 Joy St in 1853. One of Johnson's sons, Robert Johnson, Jr., recruited for the 54th Regiment before he enlisted. He died as a prisoner of war in South Carolina in 1865. Three other sons, Henry, Frederick, and William, were also veterans of the Civil War. This house stayed in the Johnson family for five decades.

 ## COFFIN PITTS HOUSE

UGGR Station
67 Joy St. (18 Belknap St.)

The first known African American resident of 67 Joy St. was William Vassall who began to pay taxes on the property in 1821. Vassall was at various times, a clothes dealer and and waiter. From 1823 to 1835, African American waiter, Lewis York, occupied 67 Joy St. In 1835, the property was purchased by African American abolitionist and clothes merchant, Coffin Pitts for $1,400. The property remained in his family until 1900.

Pitts, an abolitionist, was active in the Massachusetts General Colored Association, and in the fight against colonialization. When Pitts was a member of Twelfth Baptist Church, he met Anthony Burns who visited the church shortly after he arrived in Boston. Pitts agreed to lodge Burns at his residence and he gave Burns employment at his clothes shop at 24 Brattle St. When Burns was arrested, members of Twelfth Baptist raised $1,200 to free him but the judge refused. After Burns was sent back to slavery, the church raised $1,300 to free him and that sum was accepted. The trial and deportation of Anthony Burns left Boston in an uproar for years.

13B ARTHUR & REBECCA CRUMPLER
67 Joy St.

Rebecca Lee Crumpler boarded with the Pitts family at 67 Joy St. in 1869. Crumpler was the first African American female to become a physician. Rebecca Lee Crumpler (1831–1895) spent her formative years in Delaware where she was born. She moved to Charlestown, MA in 1852, where she worked as a nurse for the next eight years. Crumpler graduated from the New England Female Medical College in 1864 as the first African American female doctor in the United States.

After she and her husband, Arthur Crumpler, worked for several years

Pitts / Crumpler House

with freed, indigent ex-slaves in Richmond, VA, Dr. Rebecca Crumpler set up her medical practice in Boston in the early 1870s. Crumpler eventually wrote, *A Book of Medical Discourses,* a popular book which described various medical ailments and the household remedies to cure them. Crumpler intended the book to be a self-help guide for individuals who were not trained physicians. Dr. Crumpler moved to Hyde Park during the 1880s. At the time of her death, she resided in Fairview, MA.

14 JOHN HENRY HOUSE
65 Joy St.
(formerly 20 Belknap St.)

65 Joy St. was occupied by African American residents as early as 1818 when the family of civil rights activist, William Nell, lived there. They moved in 1824 and the house was occupied for brief periods by other African American tenants such as Coffin Pitts and James G. Barbadoes until 1837 when it was purchased by mariner, John Henry. Henry owned the property until 1865.

15 JOHN B. PERO HOUSE
59–61 Joy St
(formerly Belknap St.)

On this site stood a double house whose address was at various times, 28–30 Belknap, and 22–24 Belknap St.

John B. Pero, a hairdresser with a shop at 2 Dock Sq., occupied this house from 1825 through the 1850s with his wife, Martha. Pero was a Prince Hall Mason. Pero let rooms to other African Americans, a common practice, during the time they lived here. The house was demolished and replaced by a new structure in 1854.

 ## 16 POMPEY AND MARTHA THURSTON HOUSE
55 Joy St.
(formerly Belknap St.)

This was another house whose address changed even before the street name changed to Joy St. It was originally identified as 32-34 Belknap St. until 1833 to 1854, when it was identified as 26-28 Belknap St. Pompey and Martha Thurston moved into the house as early as 1822, and they remained there until approximately 1850. Thurston's occupation ranged from shoeblack, laborer, coachman, and waiter. After 1850, the couple boarded with Rev. Leonard Grimes and his family on Grove St. Through her connection with Grimes, Martha Thurston became the first matron of the Home for Aged Colored Women in 1860.

 ## 17 ABIEL SMITH SCHOOL
46 Joy St.

The Abiel Smith School was built in 1835 on a site adjacent to the African Meeting House. It was the first school built specifically for the education of African American children. After the Abiel Smith School was completed, all African American students in Boston attended this school for their education. The school's benefactor was Abiel Smith (NAA), a wealthy, white Bostonian. Architect, Richard Upjohn (NAA), designed the structure with large windows that bathed the interior in bright sunlight to enhance the educational experience of the students.

Abiel Smith School

Prior to the construction of the Abiel Smith School, African American children in Boston attended school in the basement of Primus Hall's house on Beacon Hill. After the African Meeting House was constructed in 1806, the children attended the African School in the basement of the Meeting House. In the early part of its history, the African School was organized, funded, and maintained by the African American community in Boston. One of its original teachers was John Russworm. He later published *"Freedom's Journal,"* the first African American newspaper in New York City.

Around 1812, the City of Boston began to partially fund the African school. Each subsequent year, those allocation of funds increased and with that increase, the City exercised its power to make operational decisions for the school that had previously been made by the African American community. Those decisions led to a decrease in the quality of the education of the students to the extent that by 1835, African American parents were in full protest mode. One of the concessions of those protests was the construction of the new Abiel Smith School.

That construction project did not end the protests because the quality of education in the newly built school continued to decline. Many prominent African Americans opposed the Abiel Smith School due to its inferior resources compared to those in all-white schools. The students received an inferior education because of those inequities. Their parents felt that segregation of the students implied that the students were secondary citizens.

In 1849, Benjamin Roberts engaged attorney Robert Morris to file a lawsuit on behalf of his daughter, Sarah Roberts. Sarah, who was five, had to by-pass five schools to go to the Abiel Smith School on Beacon Hill. Morris cited the 1845 Massachusetts State Statute that guaranteed every child a right to a public school education. Interestingly, that 1845 victory was possible only after another African American challenged the status quo. In 1840, Absalom Boston sued the Town of Nantucket to allow two teenagers, his daughter and Eunice Ross, to attend the local high school. See Nantucket Sites.

William Nell, a strong advocate for equal education opportunities for African Americans, worked with Morris on the Sarah Roberts case. Morris lost the case but the trio, Roberts, Morris, and Nell, decided to appeal to the Supreme Judicial

December 4, 1849
Sarah Roberts vs.
City of Boston School
Desegregation
case began.

Court of Massachusetts. They engaged a white attorney, Charles Sumner, to argue the appeal. Sumner's appeal, *"Argument Against the Constitutionality of Separate Colored Schools,"* was published by Benjamin Roberts's printing company. Sumner lost the appeal as well. Judge Lemuel Shaw (NAA), the chief judge on the case, stated that the existence of a public school, the Abiel

Smith School for African American students, satisfied the state's obligation to provide an education to African American students.

> **Separate but Equal Doctrine**
>
> Born: 1849
> Sarah Roberts vs. City of Boston
> School Desegregation Case
>
> Died: 1954
> Brown vs. Kansas Board of Education
> School Desegregation Case

Judge Shaw's 1849 decision established the legal precedent of *"separate but equal."* That precedent was referenced in the United States Supreme Court case of Plessy vs. Ferguson in 1896. The decision from the Plessy case sanctioned legalized segregation of public facilities in the United States in the first half of the twentieth century until the 1954 U.S. Supreme Court case of Brown vs. the Kansas Board of Education, another school desegregation case. Thurgood Marshall, the lead attorney for the plaintiff in the Brown case, successfully convinced the court to overturn Plessy vs. Ferguson. In 1967, Marshall became the first African American United States Supreme Court Justice. See more on the Plessy case under Lee, MA sites.

"Argument Against the Constitutionality of Separate Colored Schools," by Charles Sumner, excerpt:

"May it please your Honors:

Can any discrimination, on account of color or race, be made, under the constitution and Laws of Massachusetts, among the children entitled to the benefit of our public schools? This is the question which the Court is now to hear, to consider, and to decide.

...are the committee, having the superintendence of the public schools of Boston, entrusted with the power, under the constitution and laws of Massachusetts, to exclude colored children from these schools, and to compel them to resort for their education to separate schools, set apart for colored children only, at distances from their homes less convenient than those open to white children?

This important question arises in an action by a colored child, only five years old, who, ... sues the city of Boston for damages, on account of a refusal to receive her into one of the public schools...

I. I begin with the principle, that, according to the spirit of American institutions, and especially of the constitution of Massachusetts, all men, without distinction of color or race, are equal before the law...

The equality which was declared by our fathers in 1776, and which was made the fundamental law of Massachusetts in 1780, was equality before the law. Its object was to efface all political or civil distinctions, and to abolish all institutions founded upon birth. "All men are created equal," says the Declaration of Independence. "All men are born free and equal," says the Massachusetts Bill of Rights. These are not vain words. …no person can be created, no person can be born, with civil or political privileges, not enjoyed equally by all his fellow-citizens, nor can any institution be established recognizing any distinctions of birth. This is the Great Charter of every person who draws his vital breath upon this soil, whatever may be his condition, and whoever may be his parents. He may be poor, weak, humble, black—he may be of Caucasian, of Jewish, of Indian, or of Ethiopian race—he may be of French, of German, of English, of Irish extraction—but before the constitution of Massachusetts all these distinctions disappear. He is not poor, or weak, or humble, or black—nor French, nor German, nor English, nor Irish; he is a man,--the equal of all his fellow-men. He is one of the children of the State, which, like an impartial parent, regards all its offspring with an equal care…

…Their rights are equality before the law; nor can they be called upon to renounce one jot of this. They have an equal right with white children to the general public schools. A separate school, though well endowed, would not secure to them that precise equality, which they would enjoy in the general public schools. The Jews in Rome are confined to … the ghetto. In Frankfort they are condemned to …the Jewish quarter. It is possible that the accommodations allotted to them are as good as they would be able to occupy, if left free to choose throughout Rome and Frankfort; but this compulsory segregation from the mass of citizens is of itself an inequality which we condemn with our whole souls. It is a vestige of ancient intolerance directed against a despised people. It is of the same … with separate schools in Boston.…

…The law contemplates not only that they shall all be taught, but that they shall be taught all together. They are not only to receive equal quantities of knowledge, but all are to receive it in the same way. All are to approach together the same common fountain; nor can there be any exclusive source for any individual or any class. The school is the little world in which the child is trained for the larger world of life. It must, therefore, cherish and develop the virtues and the sympathies which are employed in the larger world. And since, according to our institutions, all classes meet, without distinction of color, in the performance of civil duties, so should they all meet, without distinction of color, in the school, beginning there those relations of equality which our Constitution and laws promise to all…"

-- Charles Sumner.

18 AFRICAN MEETING HOUSE

8 Smith Court
Mon. - Sat. 10 am - 4 pm
617-725-0022
www.afroammuseum.org

Completed in 1806, the African Meeting House is the oldest continuously used structure in the country built specifically for African American worship. Prior to the construction of the African Meeting House, many African Americans worshipped with white congregations in segregated pews. As African American worshippers increased in population, a need for separate African American congregations became apparent.

Rev. Thomas Paul (1780–1831), an itinerant minister from New Hampshire, led some of those early African American worship services at Faneuil Hall. Those services formed the basis of the African Baptist Church, the congregation that built the African Meeting House.

August 8, 1805
African Baptist Church formed with 22 members: 7 male and 16 female.

Rev. Paul and two other male members of the congregation, Scripio Dalton and Cato Gardner, raised funds for a permanent structure. Gardner personally raised over $1,500. The African Meeting House was finished in 1806. The final cost of $7,700 consisted primarily of African American funds and labor.

Rev. Thomas Paul

Under Paul's leadership, the African Meeting House was a beacon of African American social and civic life in Boston for nearly one hundred years. The construction of the new Meeting House included a one-room school on the first floor. The African School was relocated from Primus Hall's house to here after construction was complete. The African School remained here until the Abiel Smith School was constructed in 1835.

December 6, 1806
First service of African Meeting House

One civic group, the Massachusetts General Colored Association, was organized at the African Meeting House in 1826. The first officers were: Thomas Dalton, President; William G. Nell, Vice-president; and James Barbados, Secretary. David Walker was an active

During the Civil War, the African Meeting House served as the recruitment center for the all-Black regiment, the Massachusetts 54th. In 1972, the African Meeting House and the adjacent Abiel Smith School jointly became the Museum of Afro American History. Boston activists, Henry Hampton and Ruth Batson, led the redevelopment effort of the museum.

African Meeting House

member of the group as well. The mission of that group was:

> *"...to promote the welfare of the race by combatting slavery." (sic)*

Many African American orators, including Frederick Douglass, spoke at the African Meeting House. It was often referred to as the Abolition Church as well as the Black Faneuil Hall. William Lloyd Garrison (NAA), founded the New England Anti-slavery Society here in 1832. Garrison was one of the many white abolitionists who spoke here.

January 6, 1832
William Lloyd Garrison founded the New England Anti-Slavery Society at the African Meeting House.

19 HENRY SCOTT / WILLIAM C. NELL HOUSE
UGRR Station
3 Smith Court

The residences at 3, 5, 7, 7A, and 10 Smith Court housed several African American families in the 1800s as both renters and homeowners. African American tenants began to rent at 3 Smith Court as early as 1830. Some of those tenants were George Washington, a waiter, barber Andrew and Rachel Telford, and long-time tenant, Henry Scott and his family. Scott rented from 1839 until 1865 at which time he purchased the house. Scott achieved notoriety for his role in the jail escape of Shadrach Minkins in 1851 (see downtown Boston sites #8, and #15). Scott was arrested and tried for his participation in the event but he was found innocent because of lack of evidence. Between 1856 and 1860, Scott and his family gave refuge to several fugitives from slavery.

William C. Nell

The most prominent resident of Smith Court was William C. Nell (1816-1874), the African American historian and civil rights activist. Nell lived with his family at Number 3 Smith Court from 1851 to 1865.

William Nell was instrumental in the efforts to eliminate school segregation in Boston. In 1829, while a student at the African School in the basement of the African Meeting House, Nell, and two others, won the prestigious Franklin Medal, a medal given annually to a select group of students in Boston for outstand-

ing scholarship. The committee refused to allow Nell to attend the banquet to which the foremost white citizens of the city were invited, because of his race.

Determined to be present at the event where he was to be honored, Nell disguised himself as a waiter. The irony and injustice of the occasion sparked a life of activism against educational inequality and for civil rights that lasted throughout his life. Nell led a persistent crusade against segregated schools and he was actively involved in the 1849 lawsuit brought by Benjamin Roberts on behalf of his five-year-old daughter, Sarah. The efforts of William Nell and others culminated in the integration of Boston public schools in 1855. At a ceremony to honor him for his participation to end the segregation of Boston public schools, Nell stated:

Henry Scott / William Nell House

"...In the year 1829, while a pupil in the basement story of the Belknap Street Church (aka, the African Meeting House), the Honorable Harrison Gray Otis, then mayor of the city, accompanied the Honorable Samuel T. Armstrong to an examination of the colored school. It chanced that Charles A. Battiste, Nancy Woodson and myself were pronounced entitled to the highest regard of merit. In lieu of Franklin Medals, legitimately our due, Mr. Armstrong gave each an order on Deacon James Loring's bookstore...

The white medal scholars were invited guests to the Faneuil Hall dinner. Having a boy's curiosity to be spectator at the "feast of reason and the flow of soul, " I made good my court with one of the waiters, who, allowed me to seem to serve others as the fee for serving myself, the physical being then with me subordinate. Mr. Armstrong improved a prudent moment in whispering to me., "You ought to be here with the other boys." Of course, the same idea had more than once been mine, but his remarks, while witnessing the honors awarded to white scholars only augmented my sensitiveness all the more, by the intuitive inquiry which I eagerly desired to express: "If you think so, why have you not taken steps to bring it about?"

The impression made on my mind, by this day's experience, deepened into a solemn vow that, God helping me, I would do my best to hasten the day when the color of the skin would be no barrier to equal school rights... While I would not in the smallest degree detract from the credit justly due the men for their conspicuous exertions in this reform, truth enjoins upon me the pleasing duty of acknowledging that to the women, and the children also, is the cause especially indebted for success...."

– *William Nell*

William Nell wrote for *"The Liberator"* newspaper and he authored several histories on African American participation in the American Revolution and the War of 1812. Nell's appointment as a Boston postal clerk in 1860 made him the first African American civilian employed by the Federal government.

 20 GEORGE WASHINGTON HOUSE
5 Smith Court

In 1802, African American laborer, Peter Wilcox, purchased this site for $150. By 1813, Wilcox had built a house on the site and lived there with his wife, Chloe, and their three children, Eliza, Sarah, and Caroline. Wilcox sold the property to African American, Samuel

D. Parker in 1815 because Wilcox had made plans to migrate with his family to Sierre Leone with a group sponsored by Paul Cuffe. See more on Cuffe under Westport sites.

Samuel Parker owned the property until he sold it in 1849 to waiter, George Washington. George Washington (d. 1871), his wife, Rachel, and their ten children kept the house in the family until 1924. The children ran various businesses in Boston which included a tailor shop, a hair salon, music instruction, and employment agency.

 ### JOSEPH SCARLETT HOUSE
7 Smith Court

African American renters occupied 7 Smith Court as early as 1822. In 1857, Joseph Scarlett purchased the house for $800. Scarlett's father, John Scarlett, a chimney sweeper, a grocer, and a used clothing merchant, purchased properties with his hard earned savings, and his son, Joseph, continued in that business. Joseph Scarlett never resided at 7 Smith Court but he rented it out along with the fourteen other properties that he owned at the time of his death in 1898.

 ### HOLMES ALLEY HOUSE
7A Smith Court

7A Smith Court was once Holmes Alley. This property was primarily a rental property with white owners and African American tenants. In 1858, Joseph Scarlett purchased the property and kept it in his portfolio of properties throughout his life.

 ### WILLIAM HENRY / JOSEPH SCARLETT HOUSE
2 Smith Court

African American tailor, William Henry, purchased this property in 1803 and built a house on it by 1804. Henry died in 1834 and his wife and children continued to live in the house until they sold it to Joseph Scarlett in 1852. This was the first of the three properties that Scarlett purchased on Smith Court.

 ### THOMAS & LUCY DALTON HOUSE
29 South Russell St.

Thomas (1794–1883) and Lucy Lew Dalton (1790–1865) married in 1834. They were prominent African American civil rights advocates active in the effort to improve access to education for African American youth. Thomas Dalton was born in Gloucester, MA. Lucy Lew was born in Dracut, MA into the family of a veteran of the American Revolution, Brazillai Lew.

Thomas Dalton moved to Boston where he owned several businesses including a successful clothing store on Brattle St. Dalton was also active in

Thomas and Lucy Dalton House

In 1836, the Daltons helped found the Infant School Association which prepared African Americans for secondary education. Dalton, William Nell, and Robert Morris knew that it was critical for African Americans to obtain a quality education if they were to assert their full rights as citizens. In the early 1840s, the group petitioned the Legislature to integrate Boston Public Schools. Their goal was finally achieved in 1855.

> "...People are apt to become what they see is expected of them... It is very hard to retain self-respect if we see ourselves set apart and avoided as a degraded race by others...Do not say to our children that however well-behaved, their very presence in a public school is contamination to your children."
>
> -- INFANT SCHOOL ASSOCIATION PETITION

the African Methodist Episcopal Zion Church and the Prince Hall Freemasonry Lodge. In 1826, he was one of the founders of the Massachusetts General Colored Association, an abolitionist group. In 1833, Dalton and his wife, Lucy Lew, helped co-found the Boston Mutual Lyceum which promoted educational lectures for citizens of color.

**Thomas and Lucy Lew Dalton
Civic Activities:**
- African Methodist Episcopal Zion Church
- Prince Hall Freemasonry Lodge
- Massachusetts General Colored Association
- Boston Mutual Lyceum
- Infant School Association

 25 # PETER HOWARD'S BARBERSHOP
UGRR Station
Somewhere on Cambridge St.

REV. LEONARD GRIMES HOUSE #1
59 Mrytle St.

Leonard Grimes (1815–1874) was born free in Virginia. He relocated to the District of Columbia after he decided as a young man to dedicate his life to help others obtain their freedom. Grimes's occupation as a hack driver allowed him the flexibility to assist other enslaved individuals.

In 1839, law enforcement officials discovered his Underground Railroad activities and convicted him to two years of hard labor. After Grimes served his time in the Richmond Penitentiary, he relocated his family to New Bedford. In 1848, Leonard Grimes moved to Boston where he took over the ministry of Twelfth Baptist Church. Grimes's leadership of Twelfth Baptist

Rev. Leonard Grimes

turned it into one of the prominent abolitionist institutions in Boston. He remained as minister until his death. Grimes also assisted in the escape of Shadrach Minkins in 1851.

 ## HOME FOR AGED COLORED WOMEN #2
27 Myrtle St.

This facility was created specifically to care for elderly African American women. It existed from 1860 to 1944. It was located at this site from 1863 until 1900. See more under Beacon Hill site #33.

 ## JOHN COBURN HOUSE
2 Phillips St.

In 1843, John Coburn (1811–1872), a successful entrepreneur built this house for his wife, Emmeline, and his adopted son, Wendell. The house was designed by Boston architect Asher Benjamin (NAA). Coburn's entrepreneurial instincts led him to establish Coburn's Gaming House at this location as a private facility where African Americans could gamble.

Coburn's membership in the Boston Vigilance Committee put him at the forefront of abolitionist activity in Boston. He was arrested and acquitted for his role in Shadrach Minkins' escape from jail. In 1854, Coburn along with other members of Boston's African American community decided that the boldness of fugitive slave bounty hunters and violence against African Americans were on the rise because no deterrent existed to discourage such activity. They formed an African American militia, the Massasoit Guards, in an attempt to curb this violence. The unit was named after a local Native American tribe, the Massasoits, who had defied the colonists two hundred years earlier.

1854
Massasoit Guards – an African American Militia formed to protect the African American community against violence.

30 JOHN SWETT ROCK HOUSE #1
34 Garden St.

John Coburn House

29 SITE: HENRY THACKER HOUSE
UGRR Station
5 Phillips St.

A house on this site was purchased by Henry L.W. Thacker in 1833. Henry Thacker's son, also Henry Thacker, participated in Underground Railroad activities and in 1847, he sheltered fugitives at this site. The property stayed in the family until 1874.

Thacker House

30 JOHN SWETT ROCK HOUSE #1
34 Garden St.

John Swett Rock (1825-1866), an ardent abolitionist, was a talented professional who succeeded in several professions. His personal achievements served to contradict those who suggested that African Americans were intellectually inferior to whites. Rock was born in New Jersey where he became a dentist after a brief apprenticeship. He later relocated to Philadelphia and there he attended medical school and practiced medicine and dentistry. In 1853, Rock with his bride, Catherine Bowers, moved to Boston because of its reputation as a focal point for abolitionist activity.

American attorney, Robert Morris, and in 1861, the Massachusetts' bar admitted him to practice law. On Feb. 1st, 1865, John Swett Rock became the first African American attorney to be presented before the United States Supreme Court.

John Swett Rock House

John Swett Rock

In Boston, Rock quickly became a well-known public figure who frequently spoke against slavery and for African American pride. Rock decided to add law to his professional resume. He apprenticed under the African

Rock suffered from poor health throughout his life and his death from tuberculosis at the young age of forty-one made his achievements that much more impressive. Rock was buried in Woodlawn Cemetery in Everett, MA.

Excerpt from Rock's speech, "I Will Sink or Swim with My Race":

"...I would have you understand, that I not only love my race, but am pleased with my color; and while many colored persons may feel degraded by being called Negroes, and wish to be classed among other races more favored, I shall feel it my duty, my pleasure and my pride, to concentrate my feeble efforts in elevating to a fair position a race to which I am especially identified by feeling and by blood.

My friends, we can never become elevated until we are true to ourselves. We can come here and make brilliant speeches, but .... Let us go to work—each man in his place, determined to do what he can for himself and his race. Let us try to carry out some of the resolutions which we have made, ... If we do this, friends will spring up in every quarter,

...But we must not rely on them. They cannot elevate us. Whenever the colored man is elevated, it will be by his own exertions. ...The colored man who, by dint of perseverance and industry, educates and elevates himself, prepares the way for others, gives character to the race, and hastens the day of general emancipation.

While the Negro who hangs around the corners of the streets, or lives in the grogshops or by gambling, or who has no higher ambition than to serve, is by his vocation forging fetters for the slave, and is, to all intents and purposes, a curse to his race. "

-- John Swett Rock

31 REV. HOSEA EASTON WEST CENTER ST. CHURCH

Somewhere on Anderson St., formerly West Center St.

Hosea Easton (1799–1837) was the son of James Easton, Sr., a veteran of the American Revolution and civil rights activist from North Bridgewater. Hosea Easton became a Methodist minister and moved to Boston in 1828 after he married. He pastored the West Center Street Church (which no longer exists) on Beacon Hill. Easton was heavily involved in abolitionist activities in Boston and he became one of the members of the Massachusetts General Colored Association.

In 1837, Easton published a book that suggested that the basis for slavery was purely economic and that the American clergy was hypocritical to encourage its perpetuation. The lengthy title was, *A Treatise on the In-*

tellectual Character and Civil and Political Condition of the Colored People
of the U. States; and the Prejudice Exercised Toward Them; With a Sermon on
the Duty of the Church to Them.

"...Excuses have been employed in vain to cover up the hypocrisy of this nation. The most corrupt policy which ever disgraced its barbarous ancestry, has been adopted by both church and state, for the avowed purpose of withholding the inalienable rights of one part of the subject of the government.

The injury sustained by the colored people, is both national and personal; indeed, it is national in a twofold sense. In the first place, they are literally stolen from their native country, and detained for centuries, in a strange land, as hewers of wood and drawers of water. In this situation, their blood, habits, minds, and bodies, have undergone such a change, as to cause them to lose all legal or natural relations to their mother country. They are no longer her children; therefore, they sustain the great injury of losing their country, their birthright, and are made aliens and illegitimates. Again, they sustain a national injury by being adopted subjects and citizens, and then be denied their citizenship, and the benefits derivable therefrom—accounted as aliens and outcasts, hence, are identified as belonging to no country—denied birthright in one, and had it stolen from them in another...they belong to no people, race, or nation; subjects of no government—citizens of no country—scattered surplus remnants of two races, and of different nations—severed into individuality—rendered a mass of broken fragments, thrown to and fro, by the boisterous passions of this and other ungodly nations.

...There could be nothing more natural, than for a slaveholding nation to indulge in a train of thoughts and conclusions that favored their idol, slavery. ... What could accord better with the objects of this nation in reference to blacks, than to teach their little ones that a Negro is part monkey?

...The effect of this instruction is most disastrous upon the mind of the community; having been instructed from youth to look upon a black man in no other light than a slave, and having associated with that idea the low calling of a slave, they cannot look upon him in any other light. If he should chance to be found in any other sphere of action than that of a slave, he magnifies to a monster of wonderful dimensions, so large that they cannot be made to believe that he is a man and a brother....

—Hosea Easton

SITE: TWELFTH BAPTIST CHURCH
43-47 Phillips St.

Twelfth Baptist Church originated in 1840 after a portion of the congregation of the African Meeting House decided to split. In 1848, Leonard Grimes (1815–1874) took over the ministry of Twelfth Baptist. Grimes' turned Twelfth Baptist Church, also known as the, *"Fugitive Slave's Church,"* into one of the dominant abolitionist institutions in Boston. Grimes remained the minister for the rest of his life. Between 1850 and 1855, Twelfth Baptist built a church home at this location.

February 22, 1855 Grimes galvanized Twelfth Baptist Church to raise $1,500 to purchase Anthony Burns's freedom from slavery.

Some of the most prominent fugitives from slavery in Boston belonged to this church such as Shadrach Minkins, Thomas Sims, and Anthony Burns. The abolitionists, Lewis and Harriet Hayden, and John Swett Rock were also members.

George Washington Williams (1849–1891) served as minister for a brief time between 1875 and 1880. Williams, a Civil War veteran, was the first African American graduate of Newton Theological Seminary. Williams eventually relocated to Ohio where he became the first African American elected to the Ohio State Legislature. Williams also was a diplomat and an historian. Williams wrote a famous open letter to King Leopold II (NAA) of Belgium in 1890. In that letter, he exposed the abuses of the Belgium authorities on people of the Congo. His adventures in Africa were incorporated into a recent movie in which the actor Samuel Jackson portrayed the character of George Washington Williams.

Twelfth Baptist Church remained at this location until 1906 when they relocated to Shawmut Avenue in the South End. Although the Twelfth Baptist Church building was demolished, some of the pews from the church were purchased by the Vilna Shul congregation that installed them in their synagogue on nearby Garden St.

 ## HOME FOR AGED COLORED WOMEN #1
65 Phillips St.
(65 Southac St.)

Many elderly women outlived their spouses and for those women who did not have children, their situation in old age was very precarious. Old age homes for women had been created previously but none of them accepted African American women. In 1859, Rebecca Parker Clarke (NAA) recognized a need for a home specifically for African American women. She organized a committee that included Rev. Leonard Grimes of Twelfth Baptist Church, and attorney John Albion Andrew, who would soon become governor. By 1860, the group rented out this house and the first clients moved in. In 1863, the home had outgrown this house and they relocated to 27 Myrtle St. The home remained at the Myrtle site until 1900 when it relocated to its final site at 22 Hancock St. where it remained until 1944.

34 LEWIS & HARRIET HAYDEN HOUSE

UGRR Station
66 Phillips St.

Lewis Hayden (1811-1889), one of the most influential African Americans in Massachusetts in the mid to late 1800s, lived here with his second wife, Harriet, and their child. Hayden escaped slavery from Kentucky with his family in the late 1830s. His first wife and child were lost to him forever after they were purchased in Kentucky. After

they escaped slavery, Lewis and Harriet Hayden settled in Boston, where Lewis opened a used clothing shop in 1849, first at 101 Cambridge St. and then at 121 Cambridge St. His personal experience led Hayden to become a vocal abolitionist and civil rights activist.

Lewis Hayden

This excerpt was from Lewis Hayden's personal narrative as contained in *A Key to Uncle Tom's Cabin, Presenting the Original Facts and Documents Upon Which the Story is Founded* by Harriet Beecher Stowe, 1853.

"...I never saw anything in Kentucky which made me suppose that ministers or professors of religion considered it any more wrong to separate the families of slaves by sale than to separate... animals.

There may be ministers and professors of religion who think it is wrong, but I never met with them. My master was a minister, and yet he sold my mother, as I have related.

When he was going to leave Kentucky for Pennsylvania, he sold all my brothers and sisters at auction. I stood by and saw them sold. When I was just going up on to the block, he swapped me off for a pair of carriage-horses. I looked at those horses with strange feelings. I had indulged hopes that master would take me into Pennsylvania with him, and I should get free. How I looked at those horses, and walked round them, and thought for them I was sold!

...my master had said in the pulpit that there was no more harm in separating a family of slaves than a litter of pigs....

It may seem strange, but it is a fact,--I had more sympathy and kind advice, in my efforts to get my freedom, from gamblers and such sort of men, than Christians. Some of the gamblers were very kind to me.

I never knew a slave-trader that did not seem to think, in his heart, that the trade was a bad one.... They were like Haley, --they meant to repent when they got through....

Intelligent colored people in my circle of acquaintance,..., felt no security whatever for their family ties. Some, it is true, who belonged to rich families, felt some security, but those of us who looked deeper, and knew how many were not rich that seemed so, and saw how fast money slipped away, were always miserable. The trader was all around, the slave-pens at hand, and we did not know what time any of us might be in it. Then there were the rice-swamps, and the sugar and cotton plantations; we had had them held before us as terrors, by our masters and mistresses, all our lives. We knew about them all; and when a friend was carried off, why, it was the same as death, for we could not write or hear, and never expected to see them again.

I have one child who is buried in Kentucky, and that grave is pleasant to think of. I've got another that is sold nobody knows where, and that I never can bear to think of."

—*Lewis Hayden*

Hayden, one of the founders of the Boston Vigilance Committee, thrusted himself at the forefront of all anti-slavery activity in the city. In 1851, he spearheaded one of the most celebrated of their ventures, the jailbreak of fugitive, Shadrach Minkins, after his capture in Boston. After the group broke Minkins out of jail, they smuggled him safely into Canada.

Mission of the Vigilance Committee: *"...to take all measures which we shall deem expedient to protect the colored people of this city in the enjoyment of their lives and liberties."*

Hayden's defiance to the institution of slavery was legendary and the couple sheltered many fugitives who made their way to Boston. In one instance when bounty hunters approached Hayden's home to capture some fugitives from slavery, Hayden stood on his front porch with a loaded shotgun and threatened to ignite a keg of gunpowder he kept under the porch if they took another step. The bounty hunters decided not to take the chance. When they left to get reinforcements, the fugitives escaped.

Hayden headed the effort to persuade Gov. Andrews to form the Massachusetts 54th Regiment, the African American volunteer regiment and he became an effective recruiter for the Regiment. After the war, Hayden continued his leadership role in the African American community as a legislative liaison in the Massachusetts State House. That role allowed him to advocate regularly to powerful legisla-

tors on behalf of the African American community.

> **Lewis Hayden's Civic Activities**
> - Abolitionist
> - Ran a station on the Underground Railroad
> - Co-founder of the Boston Vigilance Comm.
> - Orchestrated excape of Shadrach Minkins
> - Persuaded Gov. Andrews to form the 54th
> - Spearheaded Memorial to Crispus Attucks
> - Legislative Liaison in the State House

Hayden led a group to establish a memorial to acknowledge Crispus Attuck's role in the American Revolution. That effort resulted in the Boston Massacre Memorial on Boston Common. After Hayden's death, his widow established a scholarship in his honor at Harvard University. Lewis Hayden was buried at Woodlawn Cemetery in Everett.

Lewis & Harriet Hayden House

 ## WILLIAM RILEY HOUSE
UGRR Station
68 Phillips St. (68 – 70 Southac St.)

African American clothes merchant, William Riley (d. 1849), purchased 68 Phillips St. in 1835. The following year he purchased the property next door, 70 Phillips St. He lived at these houses with his wife, Elizabeth, and their children. Riley was a member of the Massachusetts General Colored Association and he was outspoken against the efforts to repatriate African American citizens to Africa.

The barber, Thomas Cole who ran an Underground Railroad Station out of his barbershop on Atkinson St. boarded with the Rileys from 1836 until 1843.

Elizabeth Riley (d. 1867) was also an activist and a member of the Boston Female Anti-Slavery Society. Elizabeth hid Shadrach Minkins from authorities after he was broken out of jail. The property stayed in the family through 1874.

REV. SAMUEL SNOWDEN HOUSE #2
UGRR Station
71 Phillips St.
(73 Southac St.)

Rev. Snowden came to Boston to pastor May St. Church in 1818. Rev. Snowden lived with his family at 5 Phillips St. from the time they arrived in Boston until 1842 when they moved to this residence. The Snowdens were known to be fervent abolitionists. Their reputation was so established that on the day of Snowden's death on Oct. 8th, 1850, thirteen fugitives arrived to be sheltered.

Snowden's two sons, Isaac and Charles, and his daughter, Isabella, all participated in their father's legacy. The sons were members of the Boston Vigilance Committee and in 1851, they were arrested for apparently being on guard at one a.m. in front of the Court House. The Fugitive Slave Law of 1850 had been recently passed and tensions were high because of rumors that free African Americans were being kidnapped. When the fugitives were brought to court in the middle of the night and there was no one to vouch for their free status, they would be summarily sent to slavery. When the two were searched that night, loaded weapons were found in their possession. Isabella and her husband, barber, Henry Holmes, lived on Holmes Alley where they also gave shelter to fugitives.

JOHN R. TAYLOR BOARDINGHOUSE/ WM. T. MANIX BOARDINGHOUSE/ JOHN SWETT ROCK HOUSE #2
UGRR Station
81-83 Phillips St.

Mariner, John Taylor and his wife, provided shelter to fugitives from slavery at their house between 1849 to 1850. When William T. Manix moved into the house in 1855, he provided shelter for fugitives as well.

John Swett Rock lived in two residences on Beacon Hill. He lived at 83 Phillips during 1860. His other residence was 34 Garden St. on Beacon Hill.

38 REV. GRIMES HOUSE #2

28 Grove St.

Rev. Grimes, the pastor of Twelfth Baptist Church, also lived at this address during part of the time that he lived on Beacon Hill.

Grimes House #2

39 SITE: AFRICAN MASONIC HALL

28 Cambridge St.

This facility was a popular venue for anti-slavery lecturers and speakers on race pride. Maria Stewart was one of many to speak here.

40 SITE: WILLIAM & ELLEN CRAFT HOUSE

51 Cambridge St.

In December of 1848, William (1824-1900) and Ellen (1826-1897) Craft devised a bold scheme to escape slavery in Georgia. They eventually settled in Boston at this address. In their escape, they disguised Ellen as a white male because of her near-white complexion. William, who possessed a darker complexion, acted the role of the devoted servant who accompanied his *"master."* The Crafts wrapped bandages around Ellen's face and pretended that she had a severe mouth infection that prevented speech. That disguise masked her lack of facial hair and her female voice. To deflect notice of the fact that Ellen could not write, they wrapped her hand in bandages and pretended that she had acute arthritis. Their ploy worked and the couple successfully escaped from Georgia.

In Boston, William worked as a cabinet-maker and Ellen worked as a tailor. Fugitive bounty hunters found them after two years and attempted to return them to Georgia. The struggle between the Crafts and the bounty hunters caused quite a stir in Boston. The couple refused to allow well-intentioned abolitionists to purchase their freedom.

William Craft sent Ellen to a safe-house away from Beacon Hill. He then armed himself with every conceivable weapon and carried on his daily rou-

Ellen Craft

William Craft

tine, as if to taunt the bounty hunters to try to take him. His neighbors also armed themselves and the immediate neighborhood soon became as heavily armed as any fortress. Concerned that the situation would escalate into uncontrollable violence, friends persuaded the couple to relocate to England.

The Crafts lived abroad for nineteen years until after the Civil War. When the couple returned to the United States, they settled in Georgia where they raised their five children and opened a school for newly emancipated African Americans.

An excerpt from the Craft's personal narrative entitled,
Running a Thousand Miles for Freedom:

"*...My wife and myself were born in different towns in the state of Georgia, which is one of the principal slave States. It is true, our condition as slaves was not by any means the worst; but the mere idea that we were held as chattels, and deprived of all legal rights—the thought that we had to give up our hard earnings to a tyrant, to enable him to live in idleness and luxury—the thought that we could not call the bones and sinews that God gave us our own: but above all, the fact that another man had the power to tear from our cradle the new-born babe and sell it in the shambles like a brute, and then scourge us if we dared to lift a finger to save it from such a fate, haunted us for years.*

My wife's first master was her father, and her mother his slave, and the latter is still the slave of his widow. Notwithstanding my wife being of African extraction on her mother's side, she is almost white—in fact, she is so nearly so that the tyrannical old lady to whom she first belonged became so annoyed, at finding her frequently mistaken for a child of the family, that she gave her when eleven years of age to a daughter, as a wedding present. ...This separated my wife from her mother, and also from several other dear friends. But the incessant cruelty of her old mistress made the change of owners ... so desirable, that she did not grumble much at this cruel separation.

...My old master had the reputation of being a very humane and Christian man, but he thought nothing of selling my poor old father, and dear aged mother, at separate times, to different persons, to be dragged off never to behold each other again, till summoned to appear before the great tribunal of heaven.

My old master also sold a dear brother and a sister, in the same manner as he did my father and mother. The reason he assigned for disposing of my parents, as well as of several other aged slaves, was, that "they were getting old, and would soon become valueless in the market, and therefore he intended to sell off all the old stock, and buy in a young lot." A most disgraceful conclusion for a man to come to, who made such great professions of religion!

My old master, then, wishing to make the most of his slaves, apprenticed a brother and myself out to learn trades... before our time expired, my old master wanted money; so he sold my brother, and then mortgaged my sister, a dear girl about fourteen years of age, and myself, then about sixteen, to one of the banks, to get money to speculate in cotton. ...the money became due, my master was unable to meet his payments; so the bank had us placed upon the auction stand and sold to the highest bidder.

My wife was torn from her mother's embrace in childhood, and taken to a distant part of the country. She had seen so many other children separated from their parents in this cruel manner, that the mere thought of her ever becoming the mother of a child, ...appeared to fill her very soul with horror....

...We therefore resolved to get the consent of our owners, be married, settle down in slavery, and endeavor to make ourselves as comfortable as possible under that system. We were married, and prayed and toiled on till December, 1848, at which time a plan suggested itself that proved quite successful, and in eight days after it was first thought of we were free from the horrible trammels of slavery."

...Our old masters sent agents to Boston after us. They took out warrants, and placed them in the hands of the United States Marshal to execute. But the following letter from our highly esteemed and faithful friend, the Rev. Samuel May, of Boston, to our equally dear and much lamented friend, Dr. Estlin of Bristol (England), will show why we were not taken into custody.

– William and Ellen Craft

21 Cornhill, Boston
November 6th, 1850
My dear Mr. Estlin,

I trust that in God's good providence this letter will be handed to you in safety by our good friends, William and Ellen Craft. They have lived amongst us about two years, and have proved themselves worthy, in all respects, of our confidence and regard. The laws of this republican and Christian land...regard them only as slaves—chattels—personal property. But they nobly vindicated their title and right to freedom two years since, by winning their way to it; at least, so they thought. But now, the slave power, with the aid of Daniel Webster and a band of lesser traitors, has enacted a law, which puts their dearly-bought liberties in the most imminent peril; holds out a strong temptation to every mercenary and unprincipled ruffian to become their kidnapper; and has stimulated the slave-holders generally to such desperate acts for the recovery of their fugitive property, as have never before been enacted in the history of this government.

Within a fortnight, two fellows from Macon, Georgia, have been in Boston for the purpose of arresting our friends William and Ellen. A writ was served against them from the United States District Court; but it was not served by the United States Marshal; why not, is not certainly known: perhaps through fear, for a general feeling of indignation, and a cool determination not to allow this young couple to be taken from Boston into slavery, was aroused, and pervaded the city. It is understood that one of the judges told the Marshal that he would not be authorized in breaking the door of Craft's house.

Craft kept himself close within the house, armed himself, and awaited with remarkable composure the event. Ellen, in the meantime, had been taken to a retired place out of the city. The vigilance committee (appointed at a late meeting in Faneuil Hall) enlarged their numbers, held an almost permanent session, and appointed various subcommittees to act in different ways. One of these committees called repeatedly on Messers. Hughes and Knight, the slave-catchers, and requested and advised them to leave the city. At first they peremptorily refused to do so, 'till they got hold of the niggers.'

On complaint of different persons, these two fellows were several times arrested, carried before one of our county courts, and held to bail on charges of 'conspiracy to kidnap,' and of 'defamation,' in calling William and Ellen 'slaves.' At length, they (the slave-catchers) became so alarmed, that they left the city by an indirect route, evading the vigilance of many persons who were on the look-out for them. Hughes, at one time, was near losing his life at the hands of an infuriated coloured man. While these men remained in the city, a prominent

Whig gentleman sent word to William Craft, that if he would submit peaceably to an arrest, he and his wife should be bought from their owners, cost what it might.

Craft replied, in effect, that he was in a measure the representative of all the other fugitives in Boston, some 200 or 300 in number; that, if he gave up, they would all be at the mercy of the slave-catchers, and must fly from the city at any sacrifice; and that, if his freedom could be bought for two cents, he would not consent to compromise the matter in such a way. This event has stirred up the slave spirit of the country, south and north; the United States government is determined to try its hand in enforcing the fugitive Slave law; and William and Ellen Craft would be prominent objects of the slaveholder's vengeance.

Under these circumstances, it is the almost unanimous opinion of their best friends, that they should quit America as speedily as possible, and seek an asylum in England! Oh! Shame, shame upon us, that Americans whose fathers fought against Great Britain, in order to be FREE, should have to acknowledge this disgraceful fact! God gave us a fair and goodly heritage in this land, but man has cursed it with his devices and crimes against human souls and human rights. Is America the 'land of the free, and the home of the brave?' God knows it is not; and we know it too. A brave young man and a virtuous young woman must fly the American shores, and seek, under the shadow of the British throne, the enjoyment of 'life, liberty, and the pursuit of happiness.".…

I am, very respectfully yours,
Samuel May,
Jun.

Ellen Craft in Disguise

41 PRIMUS HALL HOUSE & THE AFRICAN SCHOOL
SE Corner of W. Cedar & Phillips St.

On October 17th, 1787, Prince Hall, a prominent civil rights advocate, unsuccessfully petitioned the Massachusetts State Legislature to provide funds for a public school for African American children. African Americans persisted in their determination to provide their children with an education, and in 1798, Primus Hall, Prince Hall's son, opened up a privately funded school for African American students in his home at this location.

The African School was the first privately funded school for Black children in the state of Massachusetts. The school relocated to the basement of the African Meeting House after that structure was completed in 1806.

October 17, 1787
Prince Hall petitioned Massachusetts Legislature for funds for public schools for African American Children

1798
Primus Hall opened The African School in his home.

Excerpt from Prince Hall's petition for schools for African American children:

October 17, 1787

"To the Honorable Senate and House of Representatives of the Commonwealth of Massachusetts Bay, in General Court assembled.

The petition of a great number of blacks, freemen of this Commonwealth, humbly sheweth (sic), that your petitioners are held in common with other freemen of this town and Commonwealth and have never been backward in paying our proportionate part of the burdens under which they have, or may labor under; and as we are willing to pay our equal part of these burdens, we are of the humble opinion that we have the right to enjoy the privileges of free men. But that we do not will appear in many instances, and we beg leave to mention one out of many, and that is of the education of our children which now receive no benefit from the free schools in the town of Boston, which we think is a great grievance, as by woeful experience we now feel the want of a common education. We, therefore, must fear for our rising offspring to see them in ignorance in a land of gospel light when there is provision made for them as well as others and yet can't enjoy them, and for no other reason can be given this that they are black...

We therefore pray your Honors that you would in your wisdom... some provision may be made for the education of our dear children. And in duty bound shall ever pray."

Prince Hall was not yet a freed man when Primus Hall (1756–1842) was born to him and Sarah Ritchie, his first wife. Ezra Trask (NAA) claimed ownership rights over Primus at birth. Although Ezra Trask named the child, Primus Trask, at birth, Primus always acknowledged Prince Hall as his father and he changed his last name as soon as he was legally able. Ezra Trask manumitted Primus at an early age, probably in his late teens, and he was free to pursue his life within his abilities. Primus followed in his father's footsteps as a soldier in the American Revolution. Many African American men felt that participation in the war was necessary in order for African Americans to assert their rights to full citizenship.

During the American Revolution, Primus obtained work with Timothy Pickering (NAA) of Salem. Pickering eventually served as Secretary of State in the administrations of both George Washington (NAA) and John Adams (NAA). Through that early relationship, Primus met Washington on several occasions and Washington was the officer to sign Hall's honorable discharge from service.

Primus Hall relocated to Boston after the war where he entered the soap-boiling trade. Hall was an active participant in the African American community of Boston and a member of the Prince Hall Freemasonry lodge.

Despite his honorable discharge, Hall had to sue the Federal Pension Commission before he received his pension as a veteran of the American Revolution.

June 28, 1828 Primus Hall won his lawsuit against the Federal Pension Commission and was awarded a pension of $60 per year.

42 PRIMUS HALL SOAPWORKS
Primus Avenue (formerly Wilberforce Place)

Primus Hall owned property that spanned from Cedar St. to the other side of Wilberforce Place. His soapworks business was located here. Wilberforce Place received its name from a Canadian colony of freed Africans. The street was renamed Primus Avenue in the 1860s to honor Primus Hall.

43 SITE: REVERE ST. METHODIST EPISCOPAL CHURCH
Somewhere on Revere St.

Rev. Samuel Snowden (d. 1850) was an abolitionist and the first pastor of May St. Church, the predecessor of today's Union United Methodist Church in the South End. May St. originated when African American worshippers outgrew Bromfield St. Methodist Church. They petitioned church leadership for a separate church which they named, May St. Church. They requested Rev. Samuel Snowden as pastor.

Membership in May St. Church quickly outgrew the facility and the congregation relocated to the larger Revere St. Church facility in 1818. Under Rev. Snowden's leadership, Revere St. Church became an abolitionist center and a stop on the Underground Railroad. David Walker, the fervent abolitionist and writer, was one of its more radical members.

The congregation of Revere St. Church had to find a new home when their building was sold in 1903. In 1949, after several moves, they settled into their current location at 485 Columbus Ave. in the South End and renamed themselves, Union United Methodist Church.

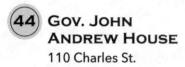 44 GOV. JOHN ANDREW HOUSE
110 Charles St.

Gov. Andrew (1818–1866) (NAA) was sworn in as Governor of Massachusetts in January, 1861. Gov. Andrew led the state throughout the Civil War years. He was instrumental in the formation of the first African American Regiment in the North, the 54th Massachusetts Regiment.

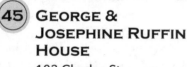 45 GEORGE & JOSEPHINE RUFFIN HOUSE
103 Charles St.

In 1869, George Ruffin (1834-1886) was the first African American awarded a law degree from Harvard University. In 1870 and 1871, he served for two terms in the Massachusetts State legislature. Ruffin's political career continued with his election in 1875 to the Boston City Council. In 1883, Ruffin became the first African American

judge in the state with his appointment to the Charlestown Municipal Court.

George Ruffin

George Ruffin's Achievements:
- 1869 - First African American awarded a law degree from Harvard
- 1870 & 1871 - State Legislature
- 1875 - Served in Boston City Council
- 1883 - 1st African American Judge

Ruffin House

Mrs. Josephine St. Pierre Ruffin's (1842-1924), portrait is in a gallery of notable women at the State House because of her achievements as one of the primary African American feminists at the turn of the 20th century. She financed and edited *"Woman's Era,"* the first magazine written for and by African American women. She also founded the *National Federation of Afro-American Women* in 1895. In 1910, she was a charter member of the *National Association for the Advancement of Colored People* (NAACP).

Josephine Ruffin

Josephine Ruffin's Life of Service:
- Leading African American feminist
- Editor of *Women's Era* magazine
- Founder of National Federation of Afro-American Women
- Charter member of NAACP

Excerpt of a speech delivered by Mrs. Ruffin in 1895:

"...Now for the sake of the thousands of self-sacrificing young women teaching and preaching in lonely southern backwoods or the noble army of mothers who have given birth to these girls, mothers whose intelligence is only limited by their opportunity to get at books, for the sake of the fine cultured women who have carried off the honors in school here and often abroad, for the sake of our own dignity, the dignity of our race, and the future good name of our children, it is "mete, right and our bounden duty" to stand forth and declare ourselves and principles, to teach an ignorant and suspicious world that our aims and interests are identical with those of all good aspiring women. Too long have we been silent under unjust and unholy charges; we cannot expect to have them removed until we disprove them through ourselves.

... Year after year southern women have protested against the admission of colored women into any national organization on the ground of the immorality of these women, and because all refutation has only been tried by individual work, the charge has never been crushed, as it could and should have been at

the first. Now with an army of organized women standing for purity and mental worth, we in ourselves deny the charge and open the eyes of the world to a state of affairs to which they have been blind, often willfully so, and the very fact that the charges, audaciously and flippantly made, as they often are, are of so humiliating and delicate a nature, serves to protect the accuser by driving the helpless accused into mortified silence."

– Josephine St. Pierre Ruffin

46 CHARLES ST. MEETING HOUSE
70 Charles St.

The Third Baptist Church of Boston, a white congregation, originally built this structure in 1807. In 1836, Timothy Gilbert (NAA), a member

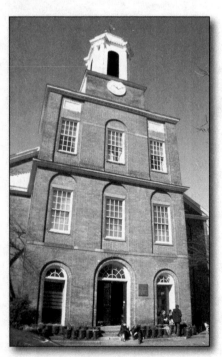
Charles St. Meeting House

of Third Baptist, decided to challenge the church's segregationist policy by direct confrontation, he invited some African American friends to sit with him during service. After that encounter, the congregation expelled Gilbert. Gilbert organized Tremont Temple in downtown Boston as the nation's first integrated church in protest. See downtown Boston Sites.

In 1876, the African Methodist Episcopal Church bought the Third Baptist Church building and renamed it Charles St. A.M.E. Church. By 1939, Charles St. A.M.E. Church was the last African American institution to remain on Beacon Hill. That year they moved to Roxbury at 551 Warren St.

47 REV. THOMAS PAUL & SUSAN PAUL HOUSE
36 West Cedar St.

Rev. Thomas Paul (1780–1831), founder of the African Meeting House, was an itinerant minister from New Hampshire. He eventually settled in Boston where he founded the congregation that organized the construction of the African Meeting House in 1806.

Paul House

Susan Paul

Susan Paul (1809–1841), the daughter of Thomas Paul, gained distinction as one of the first African American members of the Boston Female Anti-Slavery Society. Susan was one of the first female teachers at the Abiel Smith School. She also wrote the first biography by an African American, *The Memoir of James Jackson, the Attentive and Obedient Scholar, Who Died in Boston, October 31, 1833.* Jackson was seven years of age at the time of his death.

 ## GEORGE STILLMAN HILLARD HOUSE

UGRR Station
62 Pinckney St.

The Hillard (NAA) household was an example of how the issue of slavery split families. Mrs. Hillard operated a safe house for fugitives despite the fact that Mr. Hillard was a U.S. Commissioner whose job it was to issue warrants to Federal Marshals for the capture of fugitives.

49 JOHN J. SMITH HOUSE
86 Pinckney St.

John J. Smith (1820-1893) lived in this house from 1878 until his death. Smith, born free in Richmond, Virginia, moved to Boston in the late 1840s after he failed to make his fortune in the California Gold Rush. That effort left him poorer than when he started. In Boston, John J. Smith was a barber whose shop at the corner of Howard and Bulfinch St. served as a community center for abolitionist activity.

In 1851, Smith, a member of the Boston Vigilance Committee, participated in the jail escape of fugitive from slavery, Shadrach Minkins. Smith also recruited volunteers for the all-black 5th Calvary during the Civil War. After the war, Smith was active in politics. He won election to the state legislature for three terms, 1868, 1869, and 1872.

John J. Smith House

Elizabeth Smith, John's daughter, was an educator. Her appointment to the faculty of the Phillips School made her the first African American in Massachusetts to teach in an integrated school.

50 PHILLIPS SCHOOL
Anderson and Pinckney St.

In 1855, the Phillips School became the first integrated public school in Boston. The school was built in 1824 as the Boston English High School. In 1844 it was renamed Phillips Grammar School af-

John J. Smith

ter John Phillips (1770 – 1823) (NAA), Boston's first mayor (1822–1823) and the father of Wendell Phillips, the famous abolitionist.

Prior to 1855, African American children who lived in Boston had two options for an education. They either were privately tutored, or they attended the segregated Abiel Smith School on Beacon Hill. Many African Americans, led by civil rights activists such as Robert Morris and William Nell, were not satisfied with this arrangement, especially given the poor quality of the resources available at the Abiel Smith School. They advocated for equality in education for African American children.

1855
Phillips School was the first integrated Public School in Boston

In 1849, Benjamin Roberts, a local printer, filed a lawsuit on behalf of his five-year old daughter, Sarah Roberts, to protest school segregation in Boston. He engaged Robert Morris as attorney. Charles Sumner, a white attorney, abolitionist, and later a United States Senator, led the appeal process. The initial lawsuit and the appeal were both unsuccessful but they influenced the eventual integration of Boston public schools in 1855. Elizabeth Smith, the daughter of abolitionist John J. Smith, was appointed to teach at the school in the 1870s. Robert Morris spoke in New Bedford in 1855 to celebrate the integration of Boston public schools:

Phillips School

"...When we wanted our children to go the Public Schools in Boston, they offered them schools, and white teachers; but no, we wouldn't have them. Then they offered to give us colored teachers; no, we wouldn't stand that neither. Then the School Committee said—"Well, if you won't be satisfied either way, you shall have them as we choose." So we decided on a desperate step, but it turned out to be a successful one. We went round to every parent in the city, and had all the children removed from the "Cast" Schools; we made all our people take their children away. And in six months we had it all our own way—and that's the way we always should act.

Let us be bold, and they'll have to yield to us. Let us be bold, if any man flies from slavery, and comes among us. When he's reached us, we'll say, he's gone far enough. If any man comes here to New Bedford, and they try to take him away, you telegraph to us in Boston, and we'll come down three hundred strong, and stay with you; and we won't go until he's safe. If he goes back to the South, we'll go with him. And if any man runs away, and comes to Boston, we'll send for you, if necessary, and you may come up to us three hundred strong, if you can—come men, and women too."

– Robert Morris

(51) MED'S "FREEDOM LAWSUIT" COMMONWEALTH V. AVES AVES HOUSE
21 Pinkney St.

On Aug. 16th, 1836, the Commonwealth of Massachusetts brought this lawsuit on behalf of a 6-year-old enslaved child, Med. Med was brought to Massachusetts by her enslaver, Mary Slater (NAA) of New Orleans, when Slater came to Boston to visit her father, Thomas Aves. During the visit, Slater became ill. While she recuperated in Roxbury, she asked her father to take care of Med in her absence.

When the Boston Female Anti-Slavery Society learned of Med's plight, they lobbied the state and a Petition for a Writ of Habeas Corpus was filed on Med's behalf for her freedom. Attorneys for the state were Ellis Gray Loring (NAA), Rufus Choate (NAA), and Samuel Sewall (NAA). Attorneys for Aves were Benjamin Robbins Curtis (NAA), and C.P. Curtis (NAA). The case was heard in the Massachusetts Supreme Judicial Court by Justice Lemuel Shaw.

The defendants argued that Federal law required fugitives from slavery to be returned to the individuals with ownership rights over them. The Commonwealth argued that Slater could not exercise any property rights over Med because she (Slater) brought Med into a free state voluntarily. They further argued that since Med was not a fugitive, the state of Massachusetts, as a free state, was not obligated to respect the property rights of a person from a slave state when that person entered the Commonwealth freely. On Aug. 27th, 1836, Justice Shaw ruled in Med's favor and she was allowed to remain in the state. A guardian for her was appointed by the state. Judge Shaw's decision stated:

> "...all persons coming within the limits of a state, become subject to all its municipal laws, civil and criminal, and entitled to the privileges which those laws confer;... this rule applies as well to blacks as white."
> - JUSTICE LEMUEL SHAW

That decision added fuel to the fire of Southern indignation of what they perceived to be Northern violation of the Southerner's rights as property owners. One of the attorneys for the defense, Benjamin Robbins Curtis, was eventually appointed to the United States Supreme Court where he served as an associate justice in the Dred Scott trial. See more on Curtis under Watertown sites.

(52) GEORGE MIDDLETON / LOUIS GLAPION HOUSE
5-7 Pinckney St.

George Middleton (1735–1815) led an all-black unit, the Bucks of America, in the American Revolution. After the war, Governor John Hancock (NAA), presented a flag to the unit as testament to their bravery during the war. The embroidered flag depicted a pine tree, a deer, and the name, the Bucks of America. African American historian, William Nell donated the flag to the Massachusetts Historical Society in the 1850s. The unit also adopted as an emblem, a silver medallion embossed with the same symbols.

George Middleton /
Louis Glapion House

After the American Revolution, Middleton worked as a liveryman on Beacon Hill. Middleton and Louis Glapion, a hair-dresser and fellow member

*Bucks of
America
Medallion*

*Bucks of
America
Flag*

of the African Lodge of Masons, built this home in 1787 for their families. Glapion operated his hair salon out of his residence at 5 Pinckney St. This Federalist style townhouse was one of the few structures built on Beacon Hill with an exterior of wood siding. It is also the oldest known home still in existence in the United States built by and for African Americans.

Middleton's bravery was legendary. Abolitionist Lydia Maria Child (NAA) remembered an occurrence that illustrated Middleton's boldness under pressure:

> "...Our negroes, for many years, were allowed peaceably to celebrate the abolition of the slave trade; but it became a frolic with the white boys to deride them on this day, and finally, they determined to drive them, on these occasions, from the Common. The colored people became greatly incensed by this mockery of their festival, and this infringement of their liberty, and a rumor reached us, on one of these anniversaries, that they were determined to resist the whites, and were going armed, with this intention. About three o'clock in the afternoon a shout of a beginning fray reached us. Soon, terrified children and women ran down Belknap street, pursued by white boys, who enjoyed their fright. The sounds of battle approached; clubs and brickbats were flying in all directions. At this crisis, Col. Middleton opened his door, armed with a loaded musket, and, in a loud voice shrieked death to the first white who should approach. Hundreds of human beings, white and black, were pouring down the street, the blacks making but a feeble resistance, the odds in numbers and spirit being against them. Col. Middleton's voice could be heard above every other, urging his party to turn and resist to the last. His appearance was terrific, his musket was levelled, ready to sacrifice the first white man that came within its range. The colored party, shamed by his reproaches, and fired by his example, rallied, and made a ... show of resistance...."
>
> – *Lydia Maria Child*
> *(The Colored Patriots of the American Revolution by William Nell).*
> *(See Beacon Hill Sites)*

Middleton was one of the founders of the African Society, a members only, mutual aid organization formed in 1796. Through dues collected, this society assisted its members during periods of financial, medical, or legal difficulties.

The Rules of the African Society:

1st. WE, the AFRICAN MEMBERS, form ourselves into a Society, under the above name, for the mutual benefit of each other, which may fro time to time offer; behaving ourselves at the same time as true and faithful Citizens of the Commonwealth in which we live; and that we take no one into the Society, who shall commit any injustice or outrage against the laws of their county.

2nd. That before any person can become a Member of the Society he must be presented by three of the Members of the same; and the person, or persons, wishing to become Members, must make application one month at least beforehand, and that at one of the monthly, or three monthly meetings, Person, or persons if approved of shall be received in the Society. And, that before the admittance of any person into the Society, he shall be obliged to read the rules, or cause the same to be read to him; and not be admitted as a member unless he approves them.

3rd. That each Member on admittance, shall pay one quarter of a Dollar to the Treasurer; ...and his name added to the list of the Members.

4th. That each Member shall pay one quarter of a Dollar per month to the Treasurer, ...but no benefit can be tendered to any Member, until he has belonged to the Society one year.

5th. That any Member...not able to attend the regular meetings...may pay their part by appointing one of their brother to pay the same for him: so that any traveling...shall still be considered as brothers and belonging to the Society.

6th. That no money shall be returned to any one, that shall leave the Society; but if the Society should see fit to dismiss any one from their community it shall then be put to a vote, whether the one, thus dismissed shall have his money again,...

7th. That any Member, absenting himself from the Society, for the space of one year, shall be considered as separating himself from the same; but, if he should return at the end of that time, and pay up his subscription, he shall in six months be re-established in all the benefits of a Societain...

8th. That a committee, ...shall be chosen by the members...; and that their chief care shall be, to attend to the sick, and see that they want nothing that the Society can give...and inform the Society, at their next meeting of those who stand in need of the assistance of the Society,... The committee shall likewise be empowered to call the Society together as often as may be necessary.

9th. That all monies paid into the Society, shall be credited to the payers; and all going out, shall be debted to whom, or what for; and a regular account kept by one, chosen by the Society for that purpose.

10th. When any Member, or Members of the Society is sick, and not able to supply themselves with necessaries, suitable to their situations, the committee shall then tender to them and their family whatever the Society have, or may think fit for them. And should any Member die, and not leave wherewith to pay the expenses of his funeral, the Society shall then see that any, so situated, be decently buried. But it must be remembered, that any Member, bringing on himself any sickness, or disorder by intemperance, shall not be considered, as entitled to any benefits, or assistance from the Society.

11th. Should any Member die, and leave a lawful widow and children, the Society shall consider themselves bound to relieve her necessities, so long as she behaves herself decently, and remains a widow; and that the Society do the best in their power to place the children so that they may in time be capable of getting an honest living.

12th. Should the Society, with the blessing of Heaven, acquire a sum, suitable to bear interest, they will then take into consideration the best method they can, of making it useful.

13. The Members will watch over each other in their Spiritual concerns;...

14th. That each Member traveling for any length of time...shall leave a Will with the Society, or being married, with his wife, all other Members to leave a Will with the Society, for to enable them to recover their effects, if they should not return, but on their return, this Will is to be returned to the one that gave it, but if he should not return, and leave a lawful heir, the property is to be delivered to him; otherwise deemed to the Society.

A List of Members names.

PLATOAlderson*	Scipio Dalton	Juber Howland	Cato Morey
Hannible Allen*	Aurther Davis	Richar Holsted	Richard Marshal
Thomas Burdine	John Decruse	Thomas Jackson	Joseph Ocraman
Peter Bailey	Hamlet Earl*	George Jackson	John Phillips*
Joseph Ball*	Ceazer Fayerwather	Lewis Jones*	Cato Rawson
Peter Branch*	Mingo Freeman	Isaac Johnson	Richard Standley*
Prince Brown	Cato Gardner	John Johnson	Cyrus Vassall
Boston Ballard	Jeramiah Green	Sears Kimball	Derby Vassall*
Anthoney Battis	James Hawkins*	Thomas Lewis*	(SIC)
Serio Collens	John Harrison	Joseph Low	
Rufus Callehorn	Glosaster Haskins*	George Middleton	
John Clark	Prince M. Harris*	Derby Miller	

REV. WILLIAM E. CHANNING HOUSE
83 Mt. Vernon St.

Rev. William Ellery Channing (1780–1842) (NAA) was the pastor of Federal Street Church in downtown Boston. He was also the primary spokesperson for the new liberal theology of Unitarianism. Channing's influence was widespread. His theology influenced the liberal views of many Transcendentalists.

In 1840, Channing, a dedicated abolitionist, published *Emancipation*, a pamphlet that argued that the success of the British abolition of slavery was a practical model which the United States should adopt. Channing was honored with a statue in the Boston Public Garden. He was buried in Mt. Auburn Cemetery.

> *"He who cannot see a brother, a child of God, a man possessing all the rights of humanity, under a skin darker than his own, wants the vision of a Christian...to look unmoved on the degradation and wrongs of a fellow-creature, because burned by a fiercer sun, proves us strangers to justice and love."*
> -- CHANNING

> *"The deliberate, solemn conviction of good men through the world, that slavery is a grievous wrong to human nature, will make itself felt. To increase this moral power is every man's duty. To embody and express this great truth is in every man's power; and thus every man can do something to break the chain of the slave."*
> – CHANNING

 ## DR. SAMUEL GRIDLEY HOWE & JULIA WARD HOWE HOUSE
13 Chestnut St.

Dr. Samuel Gridley Howe (1801–1876) (NAA), a medical reformer, participated in most abolitionist activities in Boston prior to the Civil War. Howe received an undergraduate degree from Brown University and his medical degree from Harvard University in 1824. Youthful idealism led Howe to join the Greek War of Independence and the July Revolution in France during the 1820s.

Howe returned to Boston in 1831 where he began his medical career. His innovative treatment of those with physical and mental disabilities led to the development of the Perkins School for the Blind in his father's home in

Howe House

1832 and to the formation of the Fernald School in Waltham for the mentally disabled in 1848.

Dr. Gridley Howe's efforts to destroy slavery were legendary. In 1854, he participated with the group that stormed the Federal courthouse in Boston in the unsuccessful attempt to rescue Anthony Burns prior to his return to bondage. During John Brown's (NAA) trial, Howe, as a member of the *"Secret Committee of Six,"* briefly went into exile in Canada to escape persecution for his solicitation of funds to support the Harper's Ferry event. Howe served as a member of the Sanitary Commission during the Civil War to improve health conditions in the Union camps. After the war, he served with the Freedmen's Bureau. Howe was buried at Mt. Auburn Cemetery in Cambridge.

Dr. Samuel Gridley Howe

> "...so long as the labors and drudgery of the world is thrown actively upon one class, while another class is entirely exempt from it. There is radical injustice in it. And injustice in society is like a rotten timber in the foundation of a house."
> -- Dr. Samuel Howe

In 1843, Dr. Howe married Julia Ward (1819–1910) of New York City. Julia, an ardent abolitionist and feminist, wrote *"The Battle Hymn of the Republic"* on Nov. 18th, 1861, during a visit with her husband to President Abraham Lincoln (NAA) in Washington, D.C.

Julia Ward Howe

On that occasion, she heard a parade of soldiers sing, *"John Brown's Body,"* for the first time. It inspired her to write that same evening, *"The Battle Hymn of the Republic."*

"Battle Hymn of the Republic"
By Julia Ward Howe

*My eyes have seen the glory of the
coming of the Lord;
He is trampling out the vintage where
the grapes of wrath are stored;
He hath loosed the fateful lightning of
His terrible swift sword:
His truth is marching on.*

*Chorus: Glory, glory, hallelujah!
Glory, glory, hallelujah!
Glory, glory, hallelujah!
His truth is marching on.*

*I have seen Him in the watch-fires of a
hundred circling camps,
They have builded Him an altar in the
evening dews and damps;
I can read His righteous sentence by the
dim and flaring lamps:
His day is marching on.*

Chorus: Glory, glory, hallelujah!

*I have read a fiery gospel writ in
burnished rows of steel:
"As ye deal with my condemners, so
with you my grace shall deal;
Let the Hero, born of woman, crush the
serpent with his heel,
Since God is marching on.*

Chorus: Glory, glory, hallelujah!

*He has sounded forth the trumpet that
shall never call retreat;
He is sifting out the hearts of men
before His judgment-seat:
Oh, be swift, my soul, to answer Him!
Be jubilant, my feet!
Our God is marching on.*

Chorus: Glory, glory, hallelujah!

*In the beauty of the lilies Christ was
born across the sea,
With a glory in His bosom that
transfigures you and me.
As he died to make men holy,
let us die to make men free,
While God is marching on.*

Chorus: Glory, glory, hallelujah!

He is coming like the glory of the morning on the wave,
He is Wisdom to the mighty, He is Succour to the brave,
So the world shall be His footstool, and the soul of Time His slave,
Our God is marching on.

Chorus: Glory, glory, hallelujah!

That song helped to rally soldiers of the Union Army in the Civil War. In the years since, it became a favorite patriotic song and a staple of the Civil Rights Movement of the 1960s.

 ## DR. HENRY I. BOWDITCH HOUSE
UGRR Station
8 Otis Place

Dr. Bowditch (NAA) was very active in the Boston Vigilance Committee and in all aspects of the anti-slavery struggle. Frederick Douglas stated that Bowditch, *"was the first in Boston to treat me as a man."*

 ## SITE: WENDELL PHILLIPS CHILDHOOD HOME
Beacon St. & Walnut St.

This was the location of the childhood home of the famous abolitionist and orator, Wendell Phillips (1811–1884) (NAA). Phillips was the son of John Phillips (NAA), the first mayor of Boston. See more on Wendell Phillips under downtown Boston sites.

 ## BOSTON COMMON RIOTS
Beacon St. at Joy St.

The Boston Common consists of 44 acres of land in the middle of downtown Boston. From Boston's earliest settlement in 1622, the area originated as a communal space for cows to graze. The land eventually evolved into public recreation space. African Americans frequently gathered here for public celebrations on the anniversary of the end of slavery in the state in 1783. On those days, they became the frequent target of white hecklers who harassed and physically brutalized them.

Prince Hall delivered this speech on June 24th, 1797, to a group at the Masonic Lodge, in response to the violence that African Americans experienced regularly in the hands of white rioters, especially on the Boston Common during those anniversary celebrations held to mark the end of slavery in the state.

Prince Hall Speech, excerpt:

> "... *Patience I say; for were we not possessed of a great measure of it, you could not bear up under the daily insults you meet with in the streets of Boston; much more on public days of recreation, how are you shamefully abus'd (sic), and that at such a degree that (we) may truly be said to carry our lives in our hands, and the arrows of death are flying about your heads; helpless old women have their clothes torn off their backs, even to the point of exposing their nakedness; and by whom are these disgraceful and abusive actions committed, not by the men born and bred in Boston, for they are better bred; but by a mob or horde of shameless, low-lived, envious, spiteful persons, some of them not long since, servants in gentlemen's kitchens, scouring knives, tending horses, and driving chaise. 'Twas said by a gentleman who saw that filthy behaviour (sic) in the common (Boston Common), that in all the places he had been in, he never saw so cruel behavior in all his life." -*

> *- Prince Hall, excerpt from speech*

BOSTON GARDEN
Along Boylston St.

The city of Boston erected several monuments in Boston Garden to honor the memory of some of the heroes of Massachusetts. Four of those honored, Charles Sumner (NAA), Wendell Phillips (NAA), Col. Thomas Cass (NAA), and Edward Everett Hale (NAA) were active in the abolitionist movement or in the effort to win the Civil War. Another of the heroes honored, Tadeuz Kosciuszko (1746–1817) (NAA), was an engineer of high rank in the American Revolution. Kosciuszko came from Poland specifically to assist the colonies in their fight for freedom.

Agrippa Hull of Stockbridge, was assigned as Kosciuszko's personal assistant during the war. Hull so impressed Kosciuszko that Kosciuszko requested that his estate be used to buy the freedom of as many African Americans as possible and bestow upon them an amount sufficient to purchase farmland so that they could maintain they independence. Unfortunately, the executer of his estate, Thomas Jefferson (NAA), did not follow his friend's wishes.

59 JOSEPH & THANKFUL SOUTHWICK HOUSE

UGRR Station
Site not known

The Southwick's were early supporters of the anti-slavery movement. Joseph was one of the founders of the American Anti-Slavery Association when he lived in Maine. When the couple relocated to Boston, they joined the movement here as well. Thankful was a founder of the Boston Female Anti-Slavery Association and Joseph was a founder of the Boston Vigilance Committee. He was also an early subscriber to Garrison's newspaper, *"The Liberator."* The couple used their home as a station on the Underground Railroad.

60 LOCAL RESOURCES

Black Heritage Trail
www.nps. gov

Museum of African American History
46 Joy St. / 617-725-0022
www.maah.org

African American Patriots in American Revolution by Municipality

The National Liberty Mall Fund compiled this list. This lists contradicts some of the other information contained in this volume, particularly the number of Patriots of color from Mashpee. I attribute that to the possibility that the Mashpee Patriots of color were listed as Native American rather than African American. What is clear is that African Americans from practically every municipality in the Commonwealth served in the American Revolution and the total number of those participants range from 1,150 up to 1,500.

Abington	5	Cohasset	2	Hingham	7	Newburyport	9	Stoughton	5
Acton	3	Colrain	4	Holden	2	Newton	2	Stow	2
Adams	3	Concord	15	Holliston	6	Northampton	10	Sturbridge	2
Amesbury	8	Conway	3	Ipswich	9	Northborough	1	Sudbury	4
Amherst	3	Cummington	1	Kingston	4	Northfield	1	Sunderland	1
Andover	23	Danvers	13	Lancaster	23	Norton	4	Sutton	3
Arlington	1	Dartmouth	25	Lanesborough	4	Oakham	1	Swansea	10
Ashby	1	Dedham	5	Lee	1	Oxford	2	Taunton	17
Ashfield	2	Deerfield	4	Leicester	13	Palmer	3	Templeton	1
Attleborough	3	Dighton	16	Lenox	1	Paxton	3	Tewksbury	4
Auburn	1	Dorchester	7	Leominster	1	Pelham	5	Topsfield	2
Barnstable	9	Douglas	1	Lexington	9	Pembroke	5	Tyringham	2
Barre	4	Dracut	6	Lincoln	5	Pepperell	2	Upton	3
Becket	1	Dunstable	5	Littleton	5	Petersham	2	Uxbridge	1
Bedford	6	E. Bridgewater	1	Ludlow	1	Pittsfield	12	Waltham	5
Belchertown	3	Eastham	4	Lunenburg	4	Plymouth	26	Ware	2
Bellingham	5	Easton	3	Lynn	5	Plympton	5	Wareham	3
Berkley	4	Edgartown	2	Malden	7	Raynham	2	Warren	3
Berkshire	8	Essex	1	Manchester	2	Reading	10	Warwick	1
Beverly	11	Falmouth	12	Mansfield	4	Rehoboth	15	Watertown	6
Billerica	4	Fitchburg	1	Marblehead	15	Richmond	4	Wellfleet	1
Bolton	3	Framingham	14	Marlborough	5	Rochester	6	Wenham	4
Boston	93	Franklin	3	Marshfield	4	Rowley	3	West Springfield	7
Boxford	3	Freetown	17	Martha's Vineyard	5	Roxbury	5	West Stockbridge	2
Braintree	9	Georgetown	1	Mashpee	2	Salem	25	Westborough	1
Bridgewater	40	Gloucester	3	Medfield	6	Salisbury	3	Westfield	6
Brookfield	4	Grafton	9	Medford	15	Sandisfield	3	Westford	2
Brookline	4	Granville	5	Medway	5	Sandwich	17	Weston	1
Cambridge	13	Great Barrington	6	Mendon	2	Scituate	10	Westport	1
Cape Ann	1	Groton	4	Methuen	1	Sharon	3	Weymouth	1
Carlisle	1	Hadley	4	Middleborough	10	Sheffield	6	Whately	1
Charlestown	10	Halifax	1	Middleton	5	Shelburne	7	Wilbraham	3
Charlton	5	Hampshire	6	Monson	1	Shrewsbury	2	Williamstown	1
Chatham	3	Hanover	8	Montague	1	South Hadley	3	Wilmington	1
Chelmsford	3	Hardwick	4	Nantucket	5	Southampton	5	Woburn	16
Chelsea	2	Harvard	3	Natick	11	Spencer	2	Worcester	21
Cheshire	3	Harwich	6	Needham	3	Springfield	10	Wrentham	5
Chester	1	Hatfield	4	New Braintree	1	Stockbridge	9	Yarmouth	2
Chesterfield	3	Haverhill	2	Newbury	18	Stoneham	11		

www.partingways.org

Boston Harbor Map, 1775

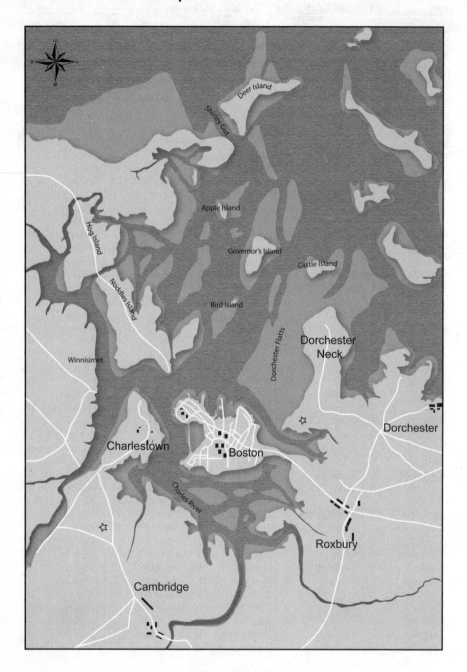

CHARLESTOWN

Settlers founded Charlestown in 1629 as an independent town, one year earlier than the settlement of Boston. By the early 1700s, Boston's growth outpaced that of Charlestown. After the American Revolution, Charlestown thrived because of the maritime industries located there and the large influx of Irish immigrants who worked in those industries. In 1800, the U.S. Government built the Navy Yard on the Charlestown harbor and Boston annexed the successful town in 1874.

1 MALCOLM X SITE: SITE OF CHARLESTOWN STATE PRISON

Bunker Hill Community College
250 New Rutherford Ave.

Malcolm Little (1925–1965), also known as Malcolm X, served time in 1946 at the Charlestown State Prison for a burglary conviction. He stayed there for one year before he was transferred to the Concord Reformatory. The state demolished the jail in the mid-1970s and redeveloped the site as Bunker Hill Community College. It is ironic and appropriate that an educational institution replaced the building where Malcolm X was incarcerated because he absolutely believed in the transformative power of education.

2 SITES: EDWIN G. WALKER HOUSES

28 Belmont St. /
36 Belmont St.

In 1866, Edwin Walker (1830–1901), the son of abolitionist, David Walker, won election as the first African American to serve in the state legislature. David Walker's fiery anti-slavery pamphlet, *Walker's Appeal*, called for the violent overthrow of slavery in 1829. David Walker died suddenly in 1830, a few months before Edwin Walker's birth, and after the publication of the third edition of his pamphlet. His widow, Eliza Butler Walker, remained in

Boston, where she raised their son, Edwin Garrison Walker. Edwin's middle name honored William Lloyd Garrison (NAA), the abolitionist and publisher of "*The Liberator*" newspaper.

Edwin Garrison Walker

Edwin lived at residences at these addresses after he married Hannah Jane Van Vronker of Lowell in 1858. Walker, who owned a successful leather-goods business, studied law in his spare time. In 1861, he passed the bar and became a licensed attorney. Walker continued the activist tradition of his family with participation in anti-slavery efforts. In 1845, his mother, Eliza Walker, also an activist, cofounded the United Daughters of Zion, a benevolent organization for African American women. Eliza lived with Edwin and Hannah at the Charlestown residences. Both structures were demolished.

In 1866, Walker won election to the Massachusetts Legislature to represent Charlestown's Third Ward. Walker shared the honor of election as the first African American legislator with Charles Lewis Mitchell of Boston because they both won election on the same day. Since Charlestown's polls closed earlier than the Boston polls, Walker officially became the first.

1866
Edwin Walker and Charles Mitchell won election as 1st African American legislators in the state.

 3 **BUNKER HILL MONUMENT**
Bunker Hill Square
Daily 9 to 5; Closed
New Year's, Thanksgiving, and Christmas Day
Free Admission /
617- 242-5641

The colonists engaged the British in battle on June 17th, 1775, in Charlestown at the misnamed Battle of Bunker Hill. That battle, which actually occurred on Breed's Hill, changed the course of the war. Two of the heroes of that battle were African Americans, Peter Salem and Salem Poor. It was the first major battle of the American Revolution. The British with their well-trained, well-equipped soldiers, felt confident they would win the battle because they outnumbered the colonists,

June 17, 1775
Battle of Bunker Hill

who were mostly untrained farmers and merchants.

Fortunately, what the colonists lacked in training and equipment, they made up for in determination and a strong belief that their cause was just. The British ultimately won the battle, but suffered greater casualties. That outcome rallied the spirits of the colonists and reaffirmed their determination to continue their fight for freedom.

Battle of Bunker Hill Casualties		
	British	American
Killed	226	139
Wounded	928	278

Bunker Hill Monument

Some of the African American and Native American Patriots who fought at the Battle of Bunker Hill were: Peter Salem; Salem Poor; Cato Howe; Barzillai Lew; Phillip Abbot (died at Bunker Hill); Alexander Ames; Isaiah Bayoman; Cuff (Chambers) Blanchard; Titus Coburn; Grant Cooper; Caesar (Dickenson) Bailey; Charlestown Eaads; Alexander Eames; Asaba Grosvenor; Blaney Grusha; Jude Hall of New Hampshire; Cuff Haynes; Caesar Jahar; Pompy of Braintree; Caesar Post; Job Potaa; Robin of Sandowne, New Hampshire; Seasor of York County; Sapson Talbot; Cato Tufts; Cuff Whittemore; John Ashbow (Native American) of CT; Pompey (Blackman) Freeman; Sampson Coburn; Jonathan Occum (Native American) of CT; and Joseph Paugenit (Native American).

The design for the 220-foot tall Bunker Hill Monument resulted from a competition won by Solomon Willard (NAA). The builders laid the cornerstone on June 17th, 1825, fifty years after the battle. The monument was finally completed in 1843.

Peter Salem (1750-1816) of Framingham enlisted in the Patriot army, as did many other enslaved individuals, because freedom was promised as reward for their enlistment. Salem achieved one of the main victories at the Battle of Bunker Hill when he killed Major Pitcairn, the first English officer killed in that battle. Pitcairn's death rallied the colonists and encouraged them to continue to fight despite their limited military resources. The gun Peter Salem used that day is exhibited at the monument. Aaron White of Connecticut made this eyewitness report:

> "The British Major Pitcairn had passed the storm of our fire and had mounted the redoubt, when waving his sword, he commanded in a loud voice, the rebels to surrender. His sudden appearance and his commanding air at first startled the men immediately below him. They neither answered nor fired, probably not being exactly certain what was to be done. At this critical moment, a Negro soldier (Peter Salem) stepped forward and aiming his musket at the major's bosom, blew him through."
>
> *-- Aaron White*

Salem Poor's (circa 1750–1780) service in that battle and in the entire war was also exceptional. Freedom was not the goal of Salem Poor. Born in Andover, MA, Poor worked and saved the sum of 27 pounds (approximately $1900.00 in 2014 dollars) to purchase his freedom in 1769 from John Poor. Salem Poor enlisted in May of 1775, and served until March of 1780. He so impressed his superior officers that fourteen of them petitioned the Massachusetts legislature for compensation for him. In 1975, the United States Postal Service issued a stamp to honor Salem Poor's service.

> "The Reward due to so great and distinguished a Character. The Subscribers beg leave to Report to your Honorable House (Which We do in justice to the Character of so Brave a man) that under Our Own observation, we declare a A Negro Man Called Salem Poor of Col. Fryes Regiment, Capt. Ames. Company in the late Battle of Charleston, behaved like an Experienced Officer, as Well as an Excellent Soldier, to Set forth Particulars of his Conduct would be Tedious, We Would Only beg leave to say in the Person of this Negro Centers a Brave & gallant Soldier."
>
> *– Excerpt from the Legislative Petition to reward Salem Poor*

4 AFRICAN AMERICAN VETERANS OF THE AMERICAN REVOLUTION IN MASSACHUSETTS

Enslaved Africans participated in the Americn Revolution as both Loyalists and as Patriots. Both sides used the incentive of potential freedom to entice enslaved individuals to serve. The British realized that the enslaved population had the potential to influence the outcome of the war because of their high numbers. They could fight on the front lines, they could disrupt crop production, and they could encourage unrest in the enslaved population.

Lord Dunmore (NAA), the Governor of Virginia for Britain, issued a proclamation in 1775, that offered freedom to any enslaved individual who joined the British Loyalist Army. Three hundred Africans immediately formed an Ethiopian unit under the English banner.

> "Nov. 7, 1775
>
> ...And I do hereby further declare all indentured servants, Negroes, or others, (appertaining to rebels,) free that are able and willing to bear Arms, they joining His MAJESTY'S Troops as soon as may be, for the more speedily reducing this Colony to a proper Sense of their Duty..."
> – Lord Dunmore, Governor of Virginia.

The Patriots eventually realized the logic of this strategy. By 1778, General George Washington (NAA) approved the formation of a Regiment of free African soldiers in Rhode Island. Later, enslaved Africans were also allowed to serve and they received their freedom as reward for their service. By the end of the war, Africans had served in large numbers on both sides of the war effort. An estimate of the number of African Americans who served in Massachusetts was as high as 1,500, or over 25% of the African American population at the time.

A large volume of the enslaved population also used the confusion of the war to escape bondage. In South Carolina, that figure was approximately one-quarter of the enslaved population. In Georgia, that number rose to one-third of the enslaved population.

Approximate Number of African American Troops who served in the American Revolution	
American Continental Army	5,000
English Loyalist Army	10,000
African Amer. Troops in Mass.	1,150 to 1,500

 SITE: EDWIN WALKER'S LAW OFFICE
25 City Square

Edwin Garrison Walker practiced law at this location after he became a licensed attorney. He eventually relocated his offices to Pemberton Sq. in Boston.

 CHARLESTOWN DISTRICT COURT
3 City Square

George Ruffin, the first African American awarded a law degree from Harvard University in 1869, became the first African American judge in the state with his appointment to the Charlestown District Court bench in 1883. He served at the Charlestown District Court from the time of his appointment until his death in 1886. Ruffin also served for two terms in the Massachusetts State Legislature, in 1870 and in 1871. Charlestown District Court commissioned a portrait of Judge Ruffin in 1990. That portrait hung in the courtroom where Ruffin presided.

Charlestown District Court

 7 **MARK AND PHILLIS**
Charlestown Neck
Today: Sullivan Sq.,
1 Cambridge St.

In colonial Charlestown, as in the rest of New England, enslaved individuals were deeply embedded into colonial life but not necessarily to the mutual satisfaction of both parties. Enslaved individuals were aware of other Africans who obtained their freedom so it was natural that they desired those same freedoms for themselves.

Mark and Phillis were two of many who desired their freedom. They were enslaved by Captain John Codman (NAA), a resident of Charlestown. On September 18th, 1755, the two were executed for the murder of Codman with arsenic. Apparently, Codman was a particularly cruel individual. Mark and Phillis burned one of his buildings in an earlier effort to be released but Codman continued to enslave them. Their final effort to gain their freedom from Codman was successful but they were found guilty of his murder and executed at the Cambridge Gallows. See Cambridge Sites.

Phillis was burned alive at the Gallows. Mark was garroted and his body returned to Charlestown where it hung on display for several decades at the main road into Charlestown, at a place known as the, *"Charlestown Neck."* In 1755, Charlestown was located on a peninsula that was connected to Somerville by a narrow isthmus that was known as the *"Charlestown Neck."* Over the years, that narrow strip of land was filled in by land and the neck disappeared.

Mark's body was displayed there to warn other enslaved individuals against similar attempts. The place where Mark's body hung became a local landmark that was referenced by many who passed that spot. Paul Revere (NAA) referred to that infamous landmark in an undated letter he wrote around 1798 to Jeremy Belknap (NAA) which described his famous midnight ride of 1775, nearly twenty years after Mark was hung.

"... I set off upon a very good Horse; it was then about 11 o'Clock, & very pleasant. After I had passed Charlestown Neck, nearly opposite where <u>Mark was hung in chains</u>, I saw two men on horse back, under a Tree. When I got near them, I discovered they were British officer. One tried to git a head of Me, & the other to take me...." (sic)

-- Paul Revere in undated letter to Jeremy Belknap

The underlined portion was added by me. That reference to the place where Mark was hung was also included in Henry Wadsworth Longfellow's (NAA) famous poem, *"The Midnight Ride of Paul Revere."*

Massachusetts regularly gathered data on the number of enslaved individuals in the population. The census from 1754, the year before Mark and Phillis were executed, quantified the number of enslaved individuals by municipality. It was not 100% accurate because every municipality did not respond. Some towns not included in this census were Framingham where the first Patriot to die in the American Revolution, Crispus Attucks, was a fugitive from slavery around the time of this census, as well as Deerfield, and Plymouth. The town of Medford was also under-represented in the census. Based on recent information, we know that the Royall estate in Medford enslaved over sixty-three individuals from 1737 until the period of the American Revolution. What this census does accomplish, is to give a relative indication of how the enslaved population was spread across the state during this period.

1754 Mass. Census of Enslaved People

Abington	7	Danvers	25	Leominster	50	Pembroke	82	Sudbury	69
Acton	105	Dartmouth	42	Lexington	31	Plympton	13	Sutton	66
Amesbury	20	Dedham	76	Lincoln	35	Reading	24	Taunton	41
Andover	99	Dighton	87	Littleton	4	Rowley	27	Tewksbury	15
Attleborough	19	Dorchester	91	Lunenburg	55	Roxbury	48	Topsfield	23
Barnstable	105	Dudley	65	Malden	11	Rutland	22	Townsend	103
Bedford	92	Easton	4	Manchester	95	Rutland Dist.	26	Uxbridge	56
Bellingham	21	Eastham	89	Marlboro	60	Salem	74	Walpole	46
Berkley	18	Falmouth	43	Marshfield	2	Salisbury	94	Waltham	5
Beverly	21	Freetown	39	Medfield	44	Sandwich	88	Watertown	62
Billerica	29	Hadley	114	Medford	6	Scarborough	111	Wenham	96
Bolton	57	Halifax	17	Medway	58	Scituate	17	Westboro	53
Boston	33	Hanover	3	Middleboro	38	Sherborn	15	Western	48
Boxford	73	Harwich	85	Middleton	36	Shirley	59	Westfield	10
Bradford	90	Hatfield	37	Milton	79	Shrewsbury	54	Westford	63
Braintree	93	Haverhill	71	Montague	84	Southampton	49	Weston	7
Brookfield	25	Holden	67	Natick	64	Southborough	51	Weymouth	47
Brookline	45	Hopkinson	104	Needham	98	SouthHadley	63	Wilmington	75
Cambridge	83	Hull	80	Newbury	100	Spencer	52	Woburn	70
Chelmsford	86	Ipswich	101	Newton	34	Springfield	9	Worcester	8
Chelsea	102	Kingston	12	N. Yarmouth	109	Stoneham	72	Wrentham	13
Chilmark	40	Lancaster	16	Oxford	30	Stoughton	97		
Concord	60	Leicester	32	Palmer	78	Sturbridge	94		

NORTH END

> "Here lies the Body of Margaret Colley
> a Free Negro
> Died May 4, 1761 aged 75 years."

The North End developed in 1630 as part of Boston and it soon became the center of a prosperous merchant community. That community included a large group of Africans. Some of them were freed, and others were still enslaved. Those Africans settled in a section of the North End neighborhood known as New Guinea. Many African communities in New England were called New Guinea as a reference to the African origins of the residents and the mistaken belief that many came from the West African country of Guinea. The Italian immigration for which the North End is famous today did not begin until the late 1890s.

Margaret Colley was another individual buried at Copp's Hill. Colley's (1686–1761) epitaph was the only history of her life that was recorded. We know from that epitaph that she was free at the time of her death. Colley was obviously proud of that status which was why it was indicated on her grave marker. We don't know if her free status was self-attained, i.e., did she save and purchase her freedom, or was she manumitted. We do know that Colley had achieved some stature in life because either she could afford a stone marker, or someone thought highly enough of her that they installed one to honor her life. Colley also lived to the age of

 ## COPP'S HILL
BURYING GROUND

21 Hull St.
April through Oct. 31:
9:00 am to 5:00 pm;
Nov. 1 to March 30:
9:00 am to 3:00 pm.

Copp's Hill Burying Ground contains the gravesites of many early African residents of Boston including some of its more prominent members. Prince Hall, a community activist and founder of the African Lodge of Masons, and Rev. Thomas Paul, organizer of the construction of the African Meeting House, were two of the notable citizens buried here.

Copp's Hill Entrance

75 years, a significant achievement at a time when the average life expectancy was only 50 or 60 years of age.

Another person interred at Copp's Hill, Mary Hammond Augustus (1734–1759) died at the young age of 25. Her marker also describes her as a, *"free negro."* She and her husband, Ceasor Augustus, a freedman, married on November 28th, 1757. They had achieved a level of financial stability because Ceasor could afford a stone grave marker for Mary. Abel Barbados (d. 1817), another African American buried here, belonged to the congregation of Rev. Thomas Paul at the African Meeting House. Barbados, a skilled mason, assisted in the construction of the Meeting House (see Beacon Hill sites). Zipporah Potter, the first known African American to purchase property in Boston in 1670, was also buried on Copp's Hill.

Over 1,000 people of African descent were buried in the Copp's Hill Burying Ground, and based on what we know, many of those were probably people who had achieved stature in the community. Unfortunately, many of their graves had wood markers which disintegrated over time or the stone markers were removed.

② PRINCE HALL BURIAL SITE
Copp's Hill Burying Ground

Copp's Hill Burying Ground contains the grave of Prince Hall (1735-1807), one of the most influential African American leaders in the United States during the eighteenth century. Hall's grave was sited next to the grave of his first wife, Sarah Ritchie (d. 1769). Prince Hall lived his early years enslaved in the British West Indies. In 1749, he ended up in Massachusetts enslaved by William Hall (NAA) of Medford. William Hall taught Prince Hall the leather dressing trade which enabled him to earn an independent living as an adult.

Prince Hall Monument

In 1770, Hall obtained his manumission papers and began a life of commerce and civic leadership. In 1775, after service in the American Revolution, Hall, and fourteen other free African men, petitioned the Grand Lodge of Ireland for membership and they were accepted. Hall and his fellow African American Masons united to form African Lodge No. 1 in 1776. That lodge petitioned the Grand Lodge of England for a charter for an African American chapter in 1784 and they received the charter on Sept. 29th, 1784 as African Lodge No. 459.

Hall frequently sought redress through the legislature for injustices to African Americans. In 1777, he petitioned the legislature to abolish slavery:

The petition of a great number of negroes, who are detained in a state of slavery in the very bowels of a free and Christian country, humbly showing,--

That your petitioners apprehend that they have, in common with all other men, a natural and inalienable right to that freedom, which the great Parent of the universe hath bestowed equally on all mankind, and which they have never forfeited by any compact or agreement whatever. But they were unjustly dragged by the cruel hand of power from their dearest friends, and some of them even torn from the embraces of their tender parents,--from a populous, pleasant and plentiful country, and in violation of the laws of nature and of nations, and in defiance of all the tender feelings of humanity, brought hither to be sold like beasts of burden, and, like them, condemned to slavery for life—...

Your honors need not to be informed that a life of slavery like that of your petitioners, deprived of every social privilege, of everything requisite to render life even tolerable, is far worse than nonexistence.

...They humbly beseech Your Honors to give their petition its due weight and consideration and cause an act of the legislature to be passed, whereby they may be restored to the enjoyment of that freedom, which is the natural right of all men, ..."

Lancaster Hill
Peter Bess
Brister Slenfen
Prince Hall

Jack Pierpont, (his X mark)
Nero Funelo, (his X mark)
Newport Sumner, (his X mark)

In 1787, Hall unsuccessfully petitioned the Massachusetts legislature to support repatriation of African Americans back to Africa:

> *"...where we shall live among our equals, and be more comfortable and happy, than we can be in our present situation."*
>
> *– Prince Hall*

Also in 1787, Hall petitioned for public school access for African American children but again, to no success. In 1798, Prince Hall's son, Primus Hall, opened a privately funded school in his home on Beacon Hill for African American students. Prince Hall consistently acted to uplift the African American community. He gave frequent speeches to encourage and motivate his community to continue to work to improve their daily existence. The next excerpt is from a speech Prince Hall delivered on June 24th, 1747. It illustrated how Prince Hall connected world events with the African struggle in the colonies. In this speech, Hall used the Haitian Revolution of 1791 to 1804, an as example of how people of African descent overthrew their oppressors.

> *"...My brethren, let us not be cast down under these and many other abuses we at present labour under: for the darkest is before the break of day. My brethren, let us remember what a dark day it was with our African brethren six years ago, in the French West Indies. Nothing but the snap of the whip was heard from morning to evening; hanging, broken on the wheel, burning, and all manner of tortures inflicted on those unhappy people for nothing else but to gratify their masters pride, wantonness, and cruelty: but blessed be God, the scene is changed; they now confess that God hath no respect of persons, and therefore receive them as their friends, and threat them as brothers. Thus doth Ethiopia began to stretch forth her hand, from a sink of slavery to freedom and equality."*
>
> *– Prince Hall*

The African Lodge No. 459 broke away from the Grand Lodge of England in 1827 and renamed itself the African Grand Lodge No. 1. Today, this fraternal organization consists of over 4,500 lodges worldwide with over 300,000 members. The African Lodge No. 1 erected this monument to Hall's memory in 1895. It was designed as a broken column, the Masonic symbol of a life interrupted.

Prince Hall's Life of Service	
1770	Obtained Manumission Papers
1775	Accepted as Masons with 14 other African Americans into Lodge #441 of the Grand Lodge of Ireland.
1776	Hall and his colleagues formed the African Lodge #1.
1777	Petitioned to abolish slavery
1784	Grand Lodge of England issued a Warrant for African Lodge #1 to join as African Lodge #459 on Sept. 29th.
1787	Petitioned For repatriation to Africa
1787	Petitioned for public school access for African American children
1788	Petitioned to protest slave trade
1788	Petitioned to Protest kidnapping of freed African Americans
1791	Grand Lodge of England made Prince Hall a Provincial Grand Master

3   ONESIMUS SITE: SECOND CHURCH
24 Clark St.

In the colonial era, the smallpox pestilence often had deadly consequences for anyone who contracted it. Around 1720, Onesimus, an African enslaved by Cotton Mather (1663-1728) (NAA), the prominent Puritan minister, shared with Mather how Africans protected the body against the disease through inoculation. A healthy person would receive the contaminated pus from a smallpox victim into their bloodstream. That process allowed the recipient's body to develop immunity to the disease.

Mather shared this concept with a prominent colonial physician, Dr. Zabdiel Boylston (NAA). Boylston tested the procedure on May 21st, 1721 on his son and two enslaved Africans during a smallpox outbreak. The success of the tests led to the wide-spread use of inoculation as protection against the disease.

Cotton Mather also achieved notoriety for his earlier involvement with the Salem Witch Trials.

Enslaved individuals frequently attended church services with their enslavers. Second Church, also known as Old North Church, was where Onesimus likely attended services with Cotton Mather and his family. By 1727, as many as twenty-three enslaved Africans worshipped at Old North Church. Despite a relationship that sounds almost familial, Mather was quite clear in his opinion of the place of African Americans. His pamphlet, *"The Negro Christianized"* recommended Christianity as a tool to make enslaved individuals more likely to accept their status in life.

The Second Church was originally erected in 1714. It was also known as The New North Meeting House. The Church was rebuilt in 1802 based on a design by the prominent architect, Charles Bulfinch (NAA). By 1862, the demographics of the North End had changed and the neighborhood became the destination of immigrants from Ireland and then, Italy. Both those groups had strong Catholic religious affiliations and in 1862, the Second Church became St. Stephen Roman Catholic Church.

4 ZIPPORAH POTTER ATKINS MARKER

Rose Kennedy Greenway
Hanover St. and Surface
Road

In 1670, Zipporah Potter Atkins (c. 1645–1705) purchased a property at this site for 46 pounds, approximately $3,200 in today's dollars. Potter-Atkins, a free woman, purchased the property with funds left her by her enslaved father. That purchase, made over one hundred years before slavery ended in Massachusetts, made her the first known African American female property owner in Massachusetts. Potter-Atkins sold a portion of the property in 1693 for 100 pounds. She sold the remainder of the property in 1699 for 25 pounds. Her total profit from her initial investment was nearly three times what she originally paid for the property. Potter-Atkins was buried at Copp's Hill Burying Ground. This remarkable discovery was made by Dr. Vivian Johnson, a retired professor from Boston University.

Zipporah Potter Marker

Boston Peninsula Map, 1815

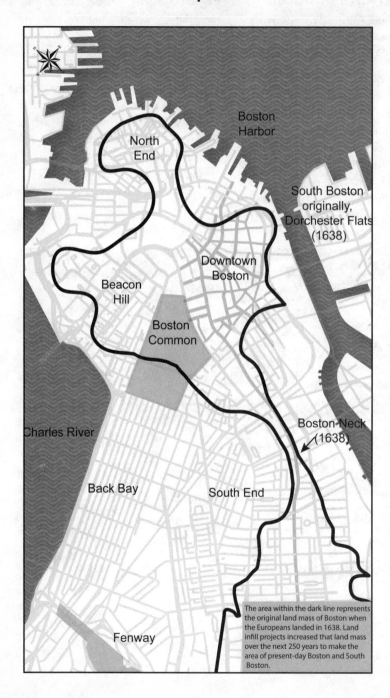

The area within the dark line represents the original land mass of Boston when the Europeans landed in 1638. Land infill projects increased that land mass over the next 250 years to make the area of present-day Boston and South Boston.

Downtown Boston Map, 2010

DOWNTOWN BOSTON

250 YEARS AGO, downtown Boston had a much different physical layout from Boston of today. The city developed on a peninsula known as the Shawmut Peninsula. The area of that peninsula consisted of most of present-day downtown Boston and part of Beacon Hill.

Significant water coves and ponds existed around its perimeter. A narrow neck of land, known as the 'Boston Neck" that aligned roughly with present-day Tremont St., connected that peninsula to the colonial town of Roxbury.

On the outer harbor side of Boston, the area of present-day South Boston, two large coves of water existed where parts of downtown Boston is today. South Boston did not exist north of West Broadway during the colonial era and most of today's South End laid under a body of water that was known as the South Bay. Knowledge of the difference in geography between Boston of 1750 and Boston today helps one understand the close community relationships at that time.

Two institutions central to the cultural and economic activity in colonial Boston were Faneuil Hall and Quincy Market. Boston's original harbor line extended up to those buildings, and the hub of wharf activity flowed over into the markets. Eventually, the harbor moved further out to the ocean as the water coves and bays were filled to expand the city's land mass.

 SITE: BENJAMIN ROBERTS HOUSE
Site of 3 Andover St., now North Station

Benjamin Roberts (1818-1881), a printer by trade, resided in a house at this site with his wife, Adeline Allen and their five children. Daughter Sarah, five-years-old and the second born, was the plaintiff in an historic school desegregation case in 1849, Sarah Roberts vs. the City of Boston. That case influenced the desegregation of Boston public schools in 1855. See Beacon Hill sites.

 BROOKE COURTHOUSE
24 New Chardon St.

The Brooke Courthouse, built in 1999, was named to honor Senator Edward Brooke (1919 – 2015), the first African American senator from Massachusetts. See more on Edward Brooke under Oak Bluffs sites.

 SARAH PARKER REMOND & SITE: HOWARD ATHENAEUM
Near Somerset St. & Cambridge St.

In 1853, Sarah Parker Remond (1826–1894), a prominent speaker and abolitionist, was one of the first African Americans to file an anti-discrimination lawsuit in the Commonwealth. She sued the Howard Athenaeum, one of the premier performance theaters in Boston during the mid-1800s. The management did not allow Remond and her guests to sit in the premium seats she had purchased by mail. Instead, they attempted to force the group into a segregated balcony area. Athenaeum staff also injured Remond in a scuffle related to the incident. She won the lawsuit and $500.00 in damages, a significant sum at that time.

May 4, 1853
Howard Athenaeum refused to honor tickets that Sarah Parker Remond purchased through the mail. she filed one of the 1st antidiscrimination lawsuits and won.

Sarah Parker Remond

The Howard Athenaeum remained in operation at 42 Howard St. until a fire in 1953 caused it to close. By 1960, this neighborhood, known as Scollay Square, had become seedy and run-down. The City consolidated parcels and demolished the buildings in the area through eminent domain to clear land for the new Government Center complex. Howard St. no longer exists.

William Nell's account of the incident was published in *"The Liberator"* newspaper on December 17th, 1853:

"On May 4, 1853, Sarah Parker Remond, her sister Caroline Remond Putnam, and William C. Nell presented their one dollar tickets to the doorkeeper at the Howard Athenaeum in Boston having purchased tickets through an expressman for seats in the Family Circle to hear Madame Henriette Sontag in the opera Don Pasquale. Sarah and her friends were given the customary checks. While quietly proceeding to their seats, they were stopped by Mr. A. Palmer, the manager of the house, who refused to let them take their seats.

C. P. Philbrick, a police officer at the theater, was called and ordered the party out. They were told they could get their money back or take seats in the gallery. They refused. Philbrick attempted to push Sarah down the stairs, tearing her dress and injuring her shoulder.

Sarah made a legal protest against this treatment, and Palmer and Philbrick were brought before the police court. The case was tried before Judge Russell. The lawyer Charles G. Davis appeared for Miss Remond. Shortly afterwards, Sarah Remond brought a civil suit to recover damages against Palmer and Philbrick in the First District Court of Essex County. She agreed to accept a small sum on the condition that she and her friends should have tickets to the opera, for seats as good as those originally purchased on the night they were rejected...."

-- William Nell

"Why Slavery is Still Rampant":

"...The free colored people of the northern states are, for no crime but merely the fact of complexion, deprived of all political and social rights. Whatever wealth or eminence in intellect and refinement they may attain to, they are treated as outcasts; and white men and women who identify themselves with them are sure to be insulted in the grossest manner.

...I shall only add that in Maryland there is at present a gentleman in prison, condemned for ten years, because a copy of Uncle Tom's Cabin was found in his possession. The laws are equally severe against teaching a slave to read— against teaching even the name of the good God."

— *Sarah Parker Remond.*

4 JUDGE HARRY ELAM, SR. JUDGE EDWARD GOURDIN

Suffolk County Courthouse
3 Pemberton Sq.

In 1978, the Massachusetts Supreme Judicial Court appointed Judge Harry Elam, Sr. to the position of Chief Justice of the Boston Municipal Court. Elam was the first African American to hold that position. Today, the main offices for the Boston Municipal Court are located in the Brooke Courthouse but when Elam served, they were located in the Suffolk County Courthouse.

Judge Harry Elam, Jr.

Judge Elam (1922–2012) was born in Cambridge and educated in Boston. He graduated from the Boston Latin School in 1940. A veteran of World War II, Elam attended Boston University where he received his undergraduate and law degrees. In 1971, Gov. Sargent (NAA) appointed Elam to the Boston Municipal Court. Judge Elam acknowledged the influence of African American activists, Melnea Cass, Edith Williams, and Edith Brothers, in his appointment.

In 1958, Edward Orval Gourdin (1897-1966) was the first African American appointed to the Mass. Superior Court. Gourdin, an Olympic track star and a 1924 graduate of Harvard Law School, also served twice in the National Guard from which he retired in 1951 with the rank of Brigadier General. That year he was appointed to the bench at Roxbury District Court.

Chief Justice Roderick Ireland

can Justice at the Mass. Supreme Judicial Court in the over 300 years of the court's history. A graduate of Lincoln Univ., Ireland received law degrees from Columbia and Harvard, and a Ph.D. from Northeastern Univ.

In 2010, Gov. Patrick nominated Ireland to be Chief Justice of the Supreme Judicial Court, another first for Ireland. Ireland retired from the bench in 2014.

 CHIEF JUSTICE RODERICK IRELAND MASS. SUPREME JUDICIAL COURT
John Adam's Courthouse
3 Pemberton Sq.

Judge Roderick Ireland (b. 1944) was first appointed to the bench in 1977 by Gov. Michael Dukakis (NAA). In 1997, Judge Ireland was appointed to the Mass. Supreme Judicial Court by Gov. William Weld (NAA), as the first African American Justice in the 300 years of the court's history. That appointment made Ireland the first African Ameri-

 BOSTON CITY HALL
City Hall Plaza
Cambridge St.

The current Boston City Hall was built in the 1960s as part of the Government Center redevelopment complex. City officials assembled and cleared a fifty-six acre site in the Scollay Square neighborhood of downtown Boston through the process of, *"urban renewal."* The master plan for the complex combined city, state, and federal government offices with private commercial office and retail space. The design firm of Kallmann, McKinnell and

Boston City Hall

Knowles (NAA) won the competition for the design for Boston City Hall. Their scheme featured massive concrete forms designed in an archtectural style known as *"brutalism"*. City Hall became a symbol of controversy with Boston citizens, they either loved it or hated it.

On April 5th, 1976, Boston City Hall plaza was the stage for an incident that represented for many African Americans, the symbol of Boston as a bastion of Northern racism. In the mid-1970s, Boston was torn asunder by a federal order to desegregate the Boston Public Schools through busing. Boston City Hall Plaza was a popular stage for public protests against the busing order. On that day, a delegation of white students from Charlestown

High School and South Boston attended a meeting at City Hall to discuss the issue of busing with city officials.

After that meeting, an African American attorney, Theodore Landsmark, was intercepted by the students on the plaza as he made his way to a different meeting, also scheduled at City Hall. One of the students attempted to stab Landsmark with the United States flag and the image was captured by Stanley Forman (NAA), a photographer for the Boston Herald. That Pulitzer Prize photo was widely distributed both nationally and internationally. It came to represent the extent that deep roots of racist attitudes existed in Boston. The busing turmoil in Boston spanned over three years. The damage that resulted included substantial destruction of property at key locations throughout the city, physical violence, and at least one fatality.

The politics of City Hall also angered many Bostonians. A citizen activist, Chuck Turner, formed the Third World Jobs Clearing House in 1975 to pressure the unions to hire minority workers. That effort led to a mandate for local residents to receive local construction jobs. Turner served for ten years on the Boston City Council after he won election in 1999.

In the early 1980s, citizens were frustrated that the Boston Redevelopment Authority made too many decisions in favor or downtown development at the expense of the neighborhoods. A fee to link downtown development to neighborhood development was conceived. After a coalition of tenant groups and Mass. Fair Share, a state-wide grassroots organization, put the concept on the ballot and it won by 70%, Mayor Kevin White (NAA) formed an Advisory Group to study how the measure could be implemented.

June 3, 1983
Mayor White (NAA) formed an Advisory Group to look at Linkage between Downtown Development and Neighborhood Housing. City Councilor Bruce Bolling was Co-Chair.

White appointed two Co-Chairs, City Councilor Bruce C. Bolling, and Edward J. McCormack (NAA). In October of 1983, the advisory group's report shared recommendations to implement the linkage concept in Boston. State legislation was finally passed in 1986 to legalize the linkage fee.

Bruce Bolling

In the early 1980s, citizens were frustrated that the Boston Redevelopment Authority made too many decisions in favor or downtown development at the expense of the neighborhoods. A fee to link downtown development to neighborhood development was conceived. After a coalition of tenant groups and Mass. Fair Share, a state-wide grassroots organization, put the concept on the ballot and it won by 70%, Mayor Kevin White (NAA) formed an Advisory Group to study how the measure could be implemented.

Bruce Bolling (1945–2012) first won election to the Boston City Council in 1981. His father, Royal Bolling, Sr., was a state senator and his brother, Royal Bolling, Jr. was a state representative. Bruce Bolling's leadership of the linkage advisory group helped the group achieve realistic goals that could actually be implemented. The success of the linkage fee concept stimulated development in many Boston neighborhoods. Several municipalities across the country followed Boston's lead and enacted similar linkage requirements for developers. In 1986, Bruce Bolling became the first African American to serve as President of the Boston City Council.

Another Boston City Councilor, Charles Yancey, took a leadership position on a different issue, one that polarized the country during the 1980s, the anti-apartheid struggle in South Africa. Some United States citizens wanted to ignore the issue because they felt that we should not interfere in the domestic policies of other countries. Other citizens felt that since South Africa was a very prosperous country, we should continue to engage in an economic relationship with them and enjoy the residual profits from that relationship. A third

July 11, 1984
Boston City Council passed 10 to 3 the South Africa Divestment Ordinance Drafted by City Councilor, Charles Yancey.

group of citizens felt that the apartheid policies of South Africa were just as morally reprehensible as slavery was in the mid-1800s, and that the U.S. should take a moral stand against them.

Yancey, a new Boston City Councilor at the time, drafted the 1984 South Africa Divestment Bill. That bill led to the withdrawal of $12.5 million of Boston City investments from South Africa. The first of its kind, that strategy encouraged other cities across the country to do the same. Soon, divestment from South Africa became a popular protest strategy that was adopted not only by other cities but universities, corporations, and other institutions that wanted to contribute to pressure on South Africa.

That consolidated pressure was one of many factors that persuaded South Africa to release Nelson Mandela from prison in 1990, and to finally dismantle apartheid in 1994. Mandela made Boston one of the first stops on his world tour after he was released from prison. Yancey, one of the longest serving members of the city council, lost his bid for re-election in 2015.

Charles Yancey

7 BILL RUSSELL STATUE
City Hall Plaza

William "Bill" Russell's (b. Feb. 12th, 1934) achievements in basketball were so spectacular that in 2009, the NBA (National Basketball Association) renamed their Most Valuable Player awards, the Bill Russell NBA Finals Most Valuable Player Award.

Russell joined the Boston Celtics in 1959 as a Center. He served the team for thirteen seasons, ten of them as a player and the last three as a player/coach. His role as coach made Russell the first African American coach in NBA history. The Boston Celtics won eleven NBA championships during Russell's tenure.

Bill Russell experienced extensive racism during his career with the Celtics but through it all, he remained focused on the development of a championship team. On November 1st, 2013, a statue of Russell, by sculptor, Ann Hirsch (NAA), was unveiled on City Hall Plaza to celebrate his achievements both on and off the court.

> *"All of us have prejudices that grow out of our egos... The struggle is to keep the prejudice from turning into bigotry and hatred. Bigotry takes possession of people, and is mankind's biggest enemy."*
> – BILL RUSSELL, *SECOND WIND*

Bill Russell Statue

 8 ## SHADRACH MINKINS SITE: TAFT'S CORNHILL COFFEEHOUSE

Cornhill St., on Boston City Hall Plaza

Shadrach Minkins (1814–1879) escaped slavery in Norfolk, Virginia in 1850. He relocated to Boston where he settled on the north slope of Beacon Hill, an area that was heavily populated with an enlightened African American community. On February 15th, 1851, fugitive bounty hunters led U.S. marshals to this coffeehouse where Minkins worked. The officers arrested Minkins while he served breakfast.

The marshals took Minkins to the nearby Federal Courthouse and jail on Court St. Members of the Boston Vigilance Committee staged a bold escape for Minkins from that facility. That successful effort emboldened abolitionists in their fight against the Fugitive Slave Laws.

Cornhill St. Shops

As part of the Government Center redevelopment complex of the 1960s, Cornhill St. was eliminated, but some of the shops on the south side of Cornhill Street were not demolished. They provide a reasonable representation of the appearance of the remainder of the street during that period. Their scale, and brick construction provide an interesting juxtaposition to the massive poured concrete structure of the new Boston City Hall and the all glass exterior of the recently remodeled Government Center subway station.

⑨ Site: Liberator Newspaper Offices #2
UGRR Station
21 Cornhill St., on Boston City Hall Plaza

William Lloyd Garrison moved his newspaper offices to a building on this site in the early 1830s. When the Bos-

ton Vigilance Committee was active in the 1840s, Garrison used these offices as a safe haven for fugitives. He also stored clothing donations at this office to distribute to the newcomers.

Rev. Samuel May (NAA) of the Boston Vigilance Committee wrote a letter from this address on behalf of William and Ellen Craft to introduce the couple to the English community when they fled fugitive bounty hunters in the United States.

⑩ Site: Benjamin Roberts Print Shop
9 Washington St.

In 1849, Benjamin Franklin Roberts (1814–1881) filed a crucial school desegregation lawsuit on behalf of his five-year-old daughter, Sarah. Despite its defeat, the lawsuit, Sarah Roberts v. City of Boston, paved the way for the Massachusetts State Legislature to end segregated public schools in 1855. Benjamin Roberts's genealogy influenced his early sense of self-assurance and assertiveness. His father, Robert Roberts, was an activist and established member of the African American community of Boston. His mother, Sarah Easton Roberts, was the daughter of a veteran of the American Revolution.

Roberts initially opened a printing office in Boston in 1838 where he published New England's first African American newspaper, "*The Anti-Slavery Herald.*" That paper could not compete with Garrison's newspaper, "*The Liberator,*" and it went out of business after a very short run. Roberts relocated to Lynn where he published Lynn's first city directory.

He continued his publishing business after he returned to Boston in the mid-1840s. Roberts' company published handbills and pamphlets for the abolitionist movement. It also published Charles Sumner's appeal in the Sarah Roberts vs. City of Boston case. A key purpose to publish this document was to educate the general public about the legal process as it related to the civil rights of African Americans. In 1853, Roberts tried again to publish

a newspaper, "*The Self-Elevator,*" but it was also short-lived.

 ## 11 FANEUIL HALL AND MARKET
Congress St. opposite Boston City Hall

The successful merchant, Peter Faneuil (1700–1743) (NAA), donated Faneuil Hall to the City of Boston. Designed by John Smibert (NAA), the market opened for business in 1742. In addition to a market on the ground floor, Faneuil Hall contained a large meeting hall on the second floor. Charles Bulfinch's (NAA) enlargement of the building in 1806 added a floor, doubled its width, and added balconies to the second-floor meeting hall.

Faneuil Hall

In May of 1764, Faneuil Hall, also known as the *"Cradle of Liberty,"* was the location of one of many gatherings that protested British dominance over the colonies.

March 8, 1770
Funeral Service for
Boston Massacre
Martyrs

The funeral service for the Boston massacre martyrs also took place here. Crispus Attucks, an African American, was the first to die in that massacre. After the funeral service, attendees marched the caskets through the streets to their final burial place in a single grave at the Granary Burying Ground on Tremont Street.

As early as 1791, Rev. Thomas Paul led worship services at Faneuil Hall for African American congregations prior to the construction of the African Meeting House on Beacon Hill in 1806.

Meetings to discuss the plight of fugitives from slavery took place regularly at Faneuil Hall between 1845 and 1856. The passing of the second Fugitive Slave Act of 1850 by the U.S. Congress led to another important meeting at Faneuil Hall in October of that year. Over 6,000 attendees

September 24, 1846
A Meeting at Faneuil Hall convened to sever ties with the U. S. Constitution because it condoned slavery.

listened as speakers encouraged militant disobedience to the new law. Frederick Douglass warned that bloody violence would result if the government passed the law. Ironically, Peter Faneuil who funded the construction

of Faneuil Hall, built his fortune on the slave trade.

12 SAMUEL COPELAND BUSINESS WILLIAM LAWSON BUSINESS BLACKSTONE BLOCK
95 & 166 Blackstone St.

Barbers, wig-makers and hair dressers, caterers, and dealers in used clothes were a few of the limited business opportunities available to African Americans in the nineteenth century. Those who were able to accrue wealth usually began that process through one of those businesses. Samuel Copeland and William Lawson, two successful dealers in used clothes, had their shops in the Blackstone Block, a block of buildings that housed small businesses. Their economic success was symbolized by family portraits they commissioned by the artist, William Matthew Prior (NAA). Only the most economically secure families could afford to commission family portraits. Read more about Copeland under Chelsea sites.

William Lawson (1807–1854), a resident of 33 Bridge St. on Beacon Hill, commissioned two portraits, one of himself and one of his wife, Nancy (b. 1810) by Prior in 1843. The portraits are in the collection of the Shelburne Museum in Shelburne, Vermont. Both portraits revealed the social status of the sitters.

Nancy Lawson
Replication of a painting by
Matthew Prior

William Lawson
Replication of a painting by
Matthew Prior

Nancy was very fashionably dressed as only a woman of means could afford. The book she held indicated her literacy. The backdrop of lush drapery in front of a pastoral landscape were further indications of Nancy's high social status. William was also stylishly dressed as befitted a successful businessman. The cigar he held was another indicator of his economic success. Both individuals gazed directly at the viewer, evidence that they were confident and not easily intimidated. William Matthew Prior's abolitionist views influenced his respectful depiction of his African American sitters.

 ## SITE: THOMAS COLE'S BARBERSHOP
UGRR Station
Somewhere on Atkinson St.

Thomas Cole (d. 1847) was a member of the Massachusetts General Colored Association and an out-spoken critic of colonization efforts. Cole also regularly participated in any and all activities that encouraged the elevation of the African American community. He attended the first convention for free African Americans in Philadelphia and he was part of a group on Beacon Hill that wanted to create a college for African American men. Cole lived at 68 Phillips St. in Beacon Hill. He spread the word that his barbershop was always available as a shelter for fugitives.

SITE: JOHN SWETT ROCK'S LAW OFFICE
6 Tremont St.

John Swett Rock (1825–1866) maintained a law office at this location. On February 1st, 1861, the multi-talented Rock became the first African American attorney presented to the United States Supreme Court. See more on Rock under Beacon Hill Sites.

 ### SITE: FEDERAL COURT TRIALS OF FUGITIVES FROM SLAVERY:
• THOMAS SIMS
• SHADRACH MINKINS
• ANTHONY BURNS
26 Court St.

The Federal Courthouse and Jail where trials for fugitives from slavery took place stood on this site in the 19th century. Many citizens in Northern states, Massachusetts in particular, did not readily comply with the Fugitive Slave Acts and the Federal government found it difficult to enforce those laws. Eventually, the concern that the Federal government could not / did not do

> **Fugitive Slave Act of 1793**
> Facilitated capture of fugitives from slavery even in Free States.
>
> **Fugitive Slave Act of 1850**
> Required private citizens to assist in the capture of fugitives from slavery. It became a violation of the law not to assist.

enough to protect what they considered their property influenced the decision of Southern states to secede from the Union in 1861.

In 1842, Massachusetts boldly defied the Fugitive Slave Act of 1793 with the case of George Latimer, a fugitive from slavery who sought refuge in Boston. See more on Latimer under Lynn sites. The result of that case led Massachusetts to pass the Personal Liberty Law of 1843. The Federal government strengthened the Federal Fugitive Slave Act of 1793 with the passage of the Fugitive Slave Act of 1850. They also built a Federal courthouse and jail in Boston where they detained and tried fugitives.

> **Massachusetts Personal Liberty Act of 1843:**
> Forbade state officials to detain fugitives or to use state facilities for their detention.

Boston citizens formed the Boston Vigilance Committee to resist those Fugitive Slave Acts. They diligently helped fugitives avoid the return to bondage. That assistance put both fugitives and those who helped them in danger, both ran the risk of arrest. Also, bounty hunters frequently kidnapped free people and the burden of proof fell on the captured person to prove their free status. These conditions created a heightened level of tenseness in Boston.

The most audacious and successful effort of the Boston Vigilance Committee occurred in 1851. Shadrach Minkins escaped slavery in 1850 and settled on Beacon Hill in Boston. On Feb. 15th,

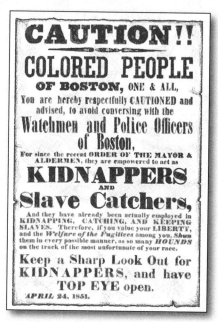

Poster Warning of Kidnappers

Robert Morris, the successful attorney and civil rights advocate, defended Shadrach Minkins against the charges. During the trial which occurred within days of Minkins arrest, Lewis Hayden and other members of the Boston Vigilance Committee, rushed the courtroom and ferreted Minkins outside to a *"get-away"* carriage. The entire episode took less than thirty minutes. The group escorted Minkins safely out of town and he eventually settled in Canada. The Federal government, outraged at this blatant challenge to their authority, attempted to convict several individuals for their involvement in the escape including Robert Morris and Lewis Hayden. The contradictory testimony of witnesses made conviction impossible and all the defendants were acquitted.

1851, U.S. marshals arrested Minkins and took him to the Federal jail at this location. They charged Minkins with violation of the Fugitive Slave Act.

United States Senator, Daniel Webster (NAA) (1782-1852) advocated for strong enforcement of the Fugitive Slave Act of 1850. Webster aspired to become President and he felt the need to pander to Southern politicians in the belief that they would support his bid for president.

Boston's Famous Fugitives from Enslavement

Fugitive	Date Captured
George Latimer	October 18th, 1842
Shadrach Minkins	February 15th, 1851
Thomas Sims	April 4th, 1851
Anthony Burns	May 24th, 1854

26 Court St. today

Thomas Sims, another fugitive from slavery, had a less fortunate experience. Sims stowed away on a vessel to escape slavery from Georgia in February of 1851 but his freedom was short-lived. Soon after he arrived in Boston, agents intercepted a telegraph he sent to his wife for funds, and they arrested him on April 4th, 1851. This time, the authorities took extra precautions. Federal officials declared Sims the human property of a citizen of Georgia on April 11th, 1851 and the very next day 300 armed militia escorted him to the wharves. Sim's return to bondage left Boston in an uproar. For several years after that event, an anti-slavery rally was held in Boston on the anniversary of Sim's capture.

 16 ANTHONY BURNS RETURN TO BONDAGE
State St. to Long Wharf

On May 24th, 1854, bounty hunters in Boston captured Virginia native, Anthony Burns (1834-1862) as a fugitive. Richard Henry Dana, Jr. (NAA) and Robert Morris were his defense attorneys. Dana, an active abolitionist, also wrote the well-known memoir, *Two Years Before the Mast*. See more on Dana under Cambridge sites.

Two days after Burns was captured, an ominous tenseness spread throughout the community. The abolitionists did not want a repeat of the Sims's experience and the pro-slavery coalition did not want a repeat of the Minkins's experience. Two separate anti-slavery

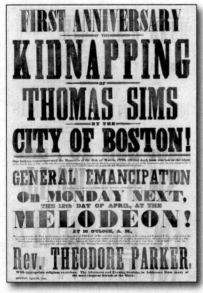

Poster of Anniversary of Sim's Capture

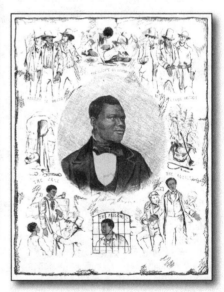

Poster to Protest Burn's Trial

meetings convened that night, one at Tremont Temple, and another at Faneuil Hall. Both groups demanded the release of Burns.

Many citizens not previously engaged by the debate, took a stand. Anti-slavery citizens who were not active abolitionists developed a radical zeal about the situation. Wendell Phillips (NAA) delivered this speech to the crowd at Faneuil Hall:

"...A poor ignorant man, arrested by a lie - overawed by his master - surrounded with jailors - dragged into court at the earliest hour - about to be hurried into slavery, without friends, a moment of deliberation, or the aid of counsel - this is Boston!

Well gentleman, we sued out a writ. The State of Massachusetts has a statute, made to meet this very case, by which the man shall be taken from the hands of the Marshal, on proper security, - and we offered him five thousand dollars bonds, - and then it should be placed before a jury, to say how much, if anything, a kidnapper is entitled to. Mr. Freeman puts his foot against the door of that slave pen, and defies the State of Massachusetts. I say again, when law ceases in the city of Boston, it is time for the sovereignty of the people to begin. (Repeated cheers.) The city government stands neutral; let us govern the city. (Cries of "good," "good" and loud cheers.)

The question, to-morrow, is, fellow-citizens, whether Virginia conquers Massachusetts. - ("No." "Never.") If that man leaves the city of Boston, Massachusetts is a conquered State. There is not a State in the Union - not one, even the basest, - that would submit to have that fugitive slave leave it. ...

Now, fellow citizens, in the celebrated case of Boston and the slave Shadrach, which you will recollect took place in the Court House, and Mr. Shadrach took up his residence in Canada on that occasion - in that celebrated case, we settled the slave law one way - that slaves were not to go back. Well, the next year, they settled the slave law the other way, and sent Thomas Sims back to bondage. To-morrow the question is, which way will you stick? Will you adhere to the precedent of Thomas Sims? ("No! No!") carried down State St. betwixt two or three hundred men, between moon-setting and sun-rising? Or will you adhere to some other precedent, of the year before, when we exhibited such love for the increase of our population, that we preferred to keep these strangers about us? (Cries of "That's it," and cheers.) If you have any feeling about it, let me say to you that I have been engaged for seventeen years in talking about the slave. I have talked often in these halls. I do not know that I have talked to any purpose; but it seems to me that if two fugitives are taken out of the city of Boston within three years, I have talked to no purpose. ...

...For God's sake, let us make Boston worth living in. (Cheers.) My friend, the Chairman, says he hopes to live and die in a land of liberty. If he lives over to-morrow, and a slave warrant is executed in State Street, I advise him to change his domicile, for he will be no longer in a land of liberty....

– Wendell Phillips

Unitarian minister Rev. Theodore Parker (NAA) also delivered a speech that night:

"...I say, there are two great laws in this country. One is the slave law. That is the law of the President of the United States; it is Senator Douglas's law; it is the law of the Supreme Court of the United States; it is the law of the Commissioner; it is the law of every Marshal, and of every meanest ruffian whom the Marshal hires to execute his behests. —There is another law, which my friend, Mr. Phillips, has described, in language such as I cannot equal, and therefore shall not try; I only state it in its plainest terms. It is the law of the people, when they are sure they are right, and determined to go ahead. [Cheers.] Now, gentlemen, there was a Boston once, and you and I had fathers —brave fathers; and mothers who stirred up those fathers to manly deeds. Well, gentlemen, once it came to pass that the British parliament enacted a "law" — they called it a law — issuing stamps here. What did your fathers do on that occasion? They said, in the language of Algernon Sydney, quoted in your resolutions, "that which is not just is not law, and that which is not law ought not to be obeyed." —was an instance of the people going behind a wicked law to enact absolute justice into their justice, and making it common law. You know what they did with the tea. Well, gentlemen, I say there is one law —slave law; it is everywhere. There is another law, which also is a finality; and that law, it is in your hands and your arms, and you can put that in execution just when you see fit. Gentlemen, I am a clergyman and a man of peace; I love peace. But there is a means, and there is an end; Liberty is the end, and sometimes peace is not the means towards it.

– Theodore Parker

Rather than meet the next day, the two groups converged into a mob at the federal jail. Led by a coalition of African American and white abolitionists, including Lewis Hayden, Thomas Wentworth Higginson (NAA), and Wendell Phillips (NAA), the mob successfully rammed through the door only to find themselves blocked by armed Federal Marshals.

In the fight that developed, someone fatally stabbed a United States Marshal and several individuals were injured. After a short while, reinforcements arrived and the mob fell back. Thirteen people received arrest warrants after the confrontation including Wendell Phillips and Lewis Hayden. In their trials, the court dismissed Phillips's case for lack of evidence. The witness in Hayden's case changed his testimony and the Judge had to dismiss that case as well. Rev. Thomas Higginson received a saber cut on the chin that night that he bore proudly for the rest of his life. Both Rev. Theodore Parker and Rev. Thomas Higginson later became members of the *"Secret Committee of Six,"* the group that funded John Brown's raid on Harper's Ferry in 1859.

June 2, 1854
Burns Returned to Bondage. Cost to the U.S.: 2,000 armed militia at $40,000 ($1.2 million in today's dollars). 50,000 abolitionists turned out to protest.

In their defense of Burns, Dana and Morris declared the Fugitive Slave Law unconstitutional. Judge Edward G. Loring (NAA), refused to accept that defense. He ordered Burns returned to slavery. That decision overwhelmingly angered abolitionists in the region. Over 50,000 protesters flocked into Boston to witness the horrendous act of Burns forced return. On June 2nd, 1854, Burns was marched to Long Wharf to be returned to slavery. The U.S. had to deploy 2,000 armed militia to escort Burns to the wharf because of the high volume of protests.

A Southern newspaper, the *"Richmond Enquirer"*, made this sarcastic comment about the high cost to return Burns to bondage:

> *"...a few more such victories and the South will be undone."*

The portrayal of that day from the journal of Attorney Richard Henry Dana, Jr. (NAA) described the level of alarm felt by the abolitionists.

"Mr. Grimes & I walked to & fro in front of the C't. Hs. for an hour or so, the entire Square being cleared of people, & filled with troops. Every window was filled, & beyond the lines drawn up by the police, was an immense crowd.

Whenever a body of troops passed to or fro, they were hissed & hooted by the people, with some attempts at applause from their favorers. Nearly all the shops in C't & State streets were closed & hung in black, & a huge coffin was suspended across State St., and Union flags hanging down. A brass field piece, belonging to the 4th Artillery was ostentatiously loaded in sight of all the people and carried by the men of that corps in rear of the hollow Square in which Burns was placed. Some 1500 or 1800 men of the Vol. Militia were under arms, all with their guns loaded & capped, & the officers with revolvers. These men were stationed at different posts in all the streets & lanes that lead into Court or State streets, from the C't. Hs. to Long Wharf...

...Gen Edmands gave orders to each commander of a post to fire on the people whenever they passed the line marked by the police in a manner he should consider turbulent & disorderly. So, from 9 o'clk, in the morning until towards night, the city was really under Martial law. The entire proceeding was illegal.

Mr. Grimes & I remained in the C't. Hs. until the vile procession moved. Notwithstanding their numbers & the enormous military protection, the Marshal's company were very much disturbed & excited. They were exceedingly apprehensive of some unknown & unforeseen violence. The "guard" at length filed out & formed a hollow square. Each man was armed with a short Roman sword & one revolver hanging in his belt. In this square marched Burns with the Marshal. The S.S. troops & the squadron of Boston light house preceded & followed the square, with the field piece. As the procession moved down it was met with a perfect howl of Shame! Shame! & hisses." (sic)

- Richard Henry Dana – document
(www.nps.gov/boaf/burns)

Abolitionist Henry David Thoreau (NAA) of Concord, saw abolition as a moral imperative and the Fugitive Slave Act of 1850 as an abomination. He recalled the forced return of Burns to slavery in this speech on July 4th, 1854, in Framingham, Massachusetts:

"... Massachusetts sat waiting Mr. Loring's decision, as if it could in any way affect her own criminality. Her crime, the most conspicuous and fatal crime of all, was permitting him to be the umpire in such a case. It was really the trial of Massachusetts. Every moment that she hesitated to set this man free—every moment that she now hesitates to atone for her crime, she is convicted.

...I wish my countrymen to consider, that whatever the human law may be, neither an individual nor a nation can ever commit the least act of injustice against the obscurest individual without having to pay the penalty for it. A government which deliberately enacts injustice, and persists in it, will at length even become the laughing-stock of the world.

Much has been said about American slavery, but I think that we do not even yet realize what slavery is. If I were seriously to propose to Congress to make mankind into sausages, I have no doubt that most of the members would smile at my propositions, and if any believed me to be in earnest, they would think that I proposed something much worse than Congress had ever done. But if any of them will tell me that to make a man into a sausage would be much worse - worse—than to make him into a slave—than it was to enact the Fugitive Slave Law,....

... It is to some extent fatal to the courts, when the people are compelled to go behind them. I do not wish to believe that the courts were made for fair weather, and for very civil cases merely; but think of leaving it to any court in the land to decide whether more than three millions of people, in this case a sixth part of a nation, have a right to be freemen or not! But it has been left to the courts of justice, so called—to the Supreme Court of the land—and, as you all know, recognizing no authority but the Constitution, it has decided that the three millions are and shall continue to be slaves. Such judges as these are merely the inspectors of a pick-lock and murderer's tools, to tell him whether they are in working order or not, and there they think that their responsibility ends. ...

The law will never make men free; it is men who have got to make the law free. They are the lovers of law and order who observe the law when the government breaks it....

I have lived for the last month—and I think that every man in Massachusetts capable of the sentiment of patriotism must have had a similar experience—with the sense of having suffered a vast and indefinite loss. I did not know at first what ailed me. At last it occurred to me that what I had lost was a country. ...I feel that my investment in life here is worth many per cent less since Massachusetts last deliberately sent back an innocent man, Anthony Burns, to slavery. I dwelt before, perhaps, in the illusion that my life passed somewhere only between heaven and hell, but now I cannot persuade myself that I do not dwell wholly within hell....

Slavery and servility have produced no sweet-scented flower annually, to charm the senses of men, for they have no real life: they are merely a decaying and a death, offensive to all healthy nostrils. We do not complain that they live, but that they do not get buried. Let the living bury them: even they are good for manure."

– Henry David Thoreau

The Massachusetts State Legislature passed the Personal Liberty Act of 1855 as a result of the forced return of Anthony Burns to slavery. This bill built upon the Personal Liberty Act of 1843 that the Legislature passed in response to the case of fugitive George Latimer in 1842.

Massachusetts Personal Liberty Act of 1855
- Any Judge can bring a Fugitive Slave case into a State Court to determine if the Prisoner was being rightfully detained.
- In State Court, the burden to prove innocence was removed from the Defendant and the burden to prove guilt was placed on the Plaintiff.
- Neither the statement of the defendant nor the Plaintiff could be allowed as evidence but "Two Credible Witnesses," were necessary.
- Violation of this Act was Punishable by a $5,000 fine and 5 years in jail.

Several states issued similar Personal Liberty Laws until the Federal Government decided to fight back. In the case of *Ableman v. Booth* of 1859 (62 U.S. 506) the U.S. Supreme Court overturned a decision by the Supreme Court of Wisconsin which gave local officials power to interfere with U.S. marshals who enforced the Fugitive Slave Act. The Supreme Court cited the Supremacy Clause of the U.S. Constitution in their decision.

Supremacy Clause of the U.S. Constitution
The U.S. Constitution, federal statutes, and U.S. treaties are, *"the supreme law of the land."* This is also referred to as the Preemption Doctrine, i.e., in the case of a conflict, federal law preempts state law.

Burns was the last fugitive returned to bondage from Massachusetts. His church, The Church of Jesus Christ, in Fauquier County, Virginia, excommunicated him because he ran away. Burns wrote this letter on July 13th, 1854, in response to that action.

"...*you have excommunicated me, on the charge of "disobeying both the laws of God and men," in absconding from the service of my master, and refusing to return voluntarily.*"

I admit that I left my master (so called), and refused to return; but I deny that in this I disobeyed either the law of God, or any real law of men.

Look at my case. I was stolen and made a slave as soon as I was born. No man had any right to steal me. That man-stealer who stole me trampled on my dearest rights. He committed an outrage on the law of God; therefore his man-stealing gave him no right in me, and laid me under no obligation to be his slave. God made me a man—not a slave; and gave me the same right to myself that he gave the man who stole me to himself. The great wrongs he has done me, in stealing me and making me a slave, in compelling me to work for him many years without wages, and in holding me as merchandize,--these wrongs could never put me under obligation to stay with him or to return voluntarily, when once escaped.

You charge me that, in escaping, I disobeyed God's law. No, indeed! That law which God wrote on the table of my heart, inspiring the love of freedom and impelling me to seek it at every hazard, I obeyed, and, by the good hand of my God upon me, I walked out of the house of bondage.

I disobeyed no law of God revealed in the Bible. I read in Paul (Cor. 7:21), "But, if thou mayest be made free, use it rather." I read in Moses (Deut. 23:15-16), "Thou shalt not deliver unto his master the servant which is escaped from his master unto thee. He shall dwell with thee, even among you in that place which he shall choose in one of thy gates, where it liketh him best; thou shalt not oppress him." This implies my right to flee if I feel myself oppressed, and debars any man from delivering me again to my professed master.

I said I was stolen. God's Word declares, "He that stealeth a man and selleth him, or if he be found in his hand he shall surely be put to death." (Ex. 21:16) Why did you not execute God's law on the man who stole me from my mother's arms? How is it that you trample down God's law against the oppressor, and wrest it to condemn me, the innocent and oppressed? Have you forgotten that the New Testament classes "mansteelers" with "murderers of fathers" and "murderers of mothers" with "manslavers and whoremongers?" (1 Tim. 1:9-10)

The advice you volunteered to send me, along with this sentence of excommunication, exhorts me, when I shall come to preach like Paul, to send every runaway home to his master, as he did Onesimus to Philemon. Yes, indeed I would, if you would let me. I should love to send them back as he did, "NOT AS A SERVANT, but above a servant: -- A BROTHER—a brother beloved—both in the flesh and in the Lord;"...

You charge me with disobeying the laws of men. I utterly deny that those things which outrage all right are laws. To be real laws, they must be founded in equity.

You have thrust me out of your church fellowship. So be it. You can do no more. You cannot exclude me from heaven; you cannot hinder my daily fellowship with God..."

– Anthony Burns

Rev. Leonard A. Grimes of the Twelfth Street Baptist Church, *"the fugitive slave's church,"* raised the $1,500 to purchase the freedom of Burns. Anthony Burns went on to study theology at Oberlin College. He eventually moved to Canada where he became a minister. In 1858, the Boston Vigilance Committee organized a petition that removed Judge Loring from office.

17 OLD STATE HOUSE
• BOSTON MASSACRE
• EARLY FREEDOM PETITIONS

206 Washington St. Marker Behind Old State House

The Old State House was originally the seat of British colonial government. It was appropriated by the colonists in the American Revolution.

On March 5th, 1770, a confrontation between British soldiers and colonists occurred at this spot. A crowd harassed a lone British soldier until he loaded his gun and called for assistance. Eight soldiers from the British 29th regiment responded. The crowd grew rowdier and the soldiers became more tense. Crispus Attucks (1723-1770), a tall, stout African American, struck the first blow and was the first to die that evening.

Attucks escaped slavery from Framingham around 1750 and he ended up in Boston where he worked various jobs around the wharves.

March 5, 1770
Boston Massacre

He most likely felt agitated because of his own fugitive status and he may have become emboldened by the revolutionary fervor in Boston.

Regardless, Crispus Attucks found himself at the head of an angry mob on the night of March 5th, 1770. He apparently struck one of the soldiers with a stick and that action instigated the riot. Attucks displayed incredible fearlessness when he boldly challenged the authority of the British military. He also had to possess a high level of confidence and charisma to successfully persuade strangers to follow him into that very dangerous, and what proved to be deadly, situation.

Site of Boston Massacre

130

The soldiers panicked and fired into the crowd. Five civilians were killed. Their deaths rallied the colonists and directly led to the American Revolution. The courts charged the British soldiers with murder but John Adams (NAA) successfully defended them against that charge.

Boston Massacre Marker

Boston Massacre
Illustrated by Laurence Pierce, AKA Larry Azim

An account of the actions of that evening was recalled in William Nell's book, *Colored Patriots of the American Revolution*:

"*The people were greatly exasperated. The multitude ran towards King Street, crying, 'Let us drive out these ribald; they have no business here!' the rioters rushed furiously towards the Custom House; they approached the sentinel, crying, 'Kill him kill him!' They assaulted him with snowballs, pieces of ice, and whatever they could lay their hands upon. The guard were then called, and, in marching to the Custom House, they encountered," continues Botta, "a band of the populace, led by a mulatto named ATTUCKS, who brandished their clubs, and pelted them with snowballs. The maledictions, the imprecations, the execra-*

tions of the multitude, were horrible. In the midst of a torrent of invective from every quarter, the military were challenged to fire. The populace advanced to the points of their bayonets. The soldiers appeared like statues; the cries, the howlings, the menaces, the violent din of bells still sounding the alarm, increased the confusion and the horrors of these moments; at length, the mulatto and twelve of his companions, pressing forward, environed the soldiers, and striking their muskets with their club, cried to the multitude: 'Be not afraid; they dare not fire: why do you hesitate, why do you not kill them, why not crush them at once?' the mulatto lifted his arm against Capt. Preston, and having turned one of the muskets, he seized the bayonet with his left hand, as if he intended to execute his threat. At this moment, confused cries were hears: 'The wretches dare not fire!' Firing succeeds. ATTUCKS is slain."

Early Freedom Petitions: Individual African Americans had sued for their freedom as early as 1700, but the spirit of the revolution, inspired them to act as a unit. By the 1770s, groups of African Americans petitioned government officials who met in this building half a dozen times to unilaterally end perpetual bondage throughout the state. The following petition was typical of those group *"Freedom Petitions"*:

"Boston, April 20th, 1773

Sir,

The efforts made by the legislative of this province in their last sessions to free themselves from slavery, gave us, who are in that deplorable state, a high degree of satisfaction. We expect great things from men who have made such a noble stand against the designs of their fellow-men to enslave them. We cannot but wish and hope Sir, that you will have the same grand object, we mean civil and religious liberty, in view in your next session. The divine spirit of freedom, seems to fire every humane breast on this continent, except such as are bribed to assist in executing the execrable plan.

We are very sensible that it would be highly detrimental to our present masters, if we were allowed to demand all that of right belongs to us for past services; this we disclaim. Even the Spaniards, who have not those sublime ideas of freedom that English men have, are conscious that they have no right to all the services of their fellow-men, we mean the Africans, whom they have purchased with their money; therefore they allow them one day in a week to work for themselves, to enable them to earn money to purchase the residue of their time which they have a right to demand in such portions as they are able to pay for (a due appraisement of their services being first made, which always stands at the purchase money.) We do not pretend to dictate to you Sir, or to the Honorable Assembly, of which you are a member. We acknowledge our obligations to you for what you have already done, but as the people of this province seem to be actuated by the principles of equity and justice, we cannot but expect your house will again take our deplorable case into serious consideration, and give us that ample relief which, as men, we have a natural right to.

But since the wise and righteous governor of the universe, has permitted our fellow men to make us slaves, we bow in submission to him, and determine to behave in such a manner as that we may have reason to expect the divine approbation of, and assistance in, our peaceable and lawful attempts to gain our freedom.

We are willing to submit to such regulations and laws, as may be made relative to us, until we leave the province, which we determine to do as soon as we can, from our joint labours procure money to transport ourselves to some part of the Coast of Africa, where we propose a settlement. We are very desirous that you should have instructions relative to us, from your town, therefore we pray you to communicate this letter to them, and ask this favor for us.

In behalf of our fellow slaves in this province, and by order of their Committee,

Peter Bestes, Sambo Freeman, Felix Holbrook, Chester Joie"

Massachusetts informally ceased to enforce slavery in the state in 1783 after two African Americans, Quock Walker of Barre, MA and Elizabeth *"Mum Bett"* Freeman of Ashley Falls, MA, successfully challenged the legality of the institution in 1781 in two unrelated *"Freedom Lawsuits."* Their challenges were based on the 1781 Massachusetts state constitution that declared:

> *"...all men are born free and equal, and have...the right of enjoying and defending their lives and liberties."*

Their legal victories built on the cumulative victories of over thirty previous *"Freedom Lawsuits"* by enslaved

1783
Slavery ceased to be enforced in Massachusetts

individuals in this state that dated from as early as 1700 and the half dozen group *"Freedom Petitions"* that African Americans submitted to the state government. Supreme Court Justice William Cushing ruled in 1783 in a third trial from the Quock Walker vs. Nathaniel Jennison lawsuit that a system of perpetual bondage was inconsistent with the state's new constitution.

Old State House

Citizens of the Commonwealth first heard the Declaration of Independence read from the east balcony of this building on July 18th, 1776. The building was used as the seat of government for the state until 1798. It served as the City Hall for Boston from 1830 to 1848.

Today, the Old State House contains exhibits that relate to the Boston Massacre and other aspects of Massachusetts history. One of the exhibits is the cane that U.S. Representative, Preston Brooks (NAA) of SC, used to violently beat Senator Charles Sumner with on the floor of the Senate Chambers in Washington, D.C. after Sumner presented an anti-slavery speech in 1856.

 SITE: PHILLIS WHEATLEY'S RESIDENCES

Wheatley Residence: Somewhere on State Street (then known as King St.)

Peters Residence: Somewhere on Court Street (then known as Queen St.)

In 1761, kidnappers abducted a frail female child from western Africa and brought her to this country. On the Boston wharves, Thomas Wheatley (NAA) enslaved the child whom he named Phillis, as a personal servant for his wife, Mrs. Susanna Wheatley (NAA). Phillis (d. 1784), approximately seven years old at the time, possessed a superior mind that captivated Mrs. Wheatley. Impressed by Phillis' quick intelligence, Mrs. Wheatley decided to teach Phillis to read and write. She soon began to treat her as a companion instead of as someone enslaved. Phillis quickly developed a talent as a poet.

The Wheatleys were very prosperous due to John Wheatley's lucrative retail business. The family maintained a residence on King Street which was named in honor of King George of England. After the American Revolution, the street was renamed State Street. Although the Wheatley's retained several enslaved individuals as servants, Phillis was not allowed to mingle with them.

*Engraving of Phillis Wheatley
Book Cover*

While Phillis was a teenager, Mrs. Wheatley attempted to have her poetry published but to no avail. The British publisher she eventually found did not believe that a young native-born African could compose poetry of the high caliber that Phillis produced. The publisher wanted a guarantee that the poems originated with Phillis. Some of the foremost citizens of Boston subjected Phillis to an oral exam to prove her intelligence. After that exam, they signed an attestation that verified Phillis as the author of her first book of poems. That attestation was included in her volume of poetry.

Dignitaries who signed the attestation
- Governor Thomas Hutchison (NAA)
- Lieutenant Gov. Andrew Oliver (NAA)
- The Honorable Harrison Gray (NAA)
- The Honorable James Bowdoin (NAA)
- John Hancock, Esq. (NAA)
- Rev. Samuel Mather (NAA)
- Rev. John Moorhead (NAA)

In 1773, Phillis traveled to England to have her volume of poetry published. While there, the English persuaded the Wheatleys to manumit Phillis. An engraving of Phillis, seated at her desk with pen in hand and deep in thought, graced the cover of the slim volume. The unsigned engraving was the work of an African American artist, Scipio Moorhead. Scipio was enslaved by Rev. John Moorhead (NAA), the pastor of the Church of the Presbyterian Strangers, now known as Arlington Street Church. Rev. Moorhead was also one of the signers of the attestation for Phillis's volume of poetry.

Upon publication of her first volume of poetry, *Poems of Phillis Wheatley: A Native African and a Slave*, Phillis became the first person of African birth in the United States to publish a volume of poetry. The next year, Mrs. Wheatley became ill, and Phillis returned home immediately. Mrs. Wheatley died shortly after Phillis returned to Boston. Mr. Wheatley died soon after his wife passed.

Phillis Wheatley wanted her readers to understand that the colonists were not the only people to suffer from oppression. Africans such as herself were in this country because they had been kidnapped from their families and whole groups of people were enslaved. Phillis Wheatley expressed that anguish in many of her poems.

"To the Right Honorable William, Earl of Dartmouth"

…"No more, America,
in mournful strain,
Of wrongs and grievance
unredressed complain;
No longer shall thou dread
the iron chain
Which wanton Tyranny,
with lawless hand,
Has made, and with it meant
t'enslave the land.
Should you, my lord,
while you peruse my song,
Wonder from whence my love
of Freedom sprung,
Whence flow these wishes for
the common good,
By feeling hearts alone best understood,
I, young in life, by seeming cruel fate
Was snatched from Afric's
fancied happy seat:
What pangs excruciating must molest,
What sorrows labor in
my parent's breast!
Steeled was that soul,
and by no misery moved,
That from a father seized
his babe beloved:
Such, such my case.
And can I then but pray
Others may never feel tyrannic sway!"

Milestones of Phillis Wheatley's Life	
1754	Approximate year of birth
1761	Kidnapped from Africa & Enslaved
1773	Book of Poetry published
1773	Manumitted
1778	Married John Peters in April
1784	Died on December 5th

Wheatley used her literary influence whenever she could to advocate for the liberty of all Africans. On March 11th, 1774, the Connecticut Gazette published a letter Wheatley wrote to Reverend Samson Occom (1723-1792) (NAA). In it, Phillis criticized the hypocrisy of New England ministers and other whites who advocated freedom from the British for themselves while they persisted to enslave others. Occom, a Mohegan Indian who converted to Christianity, became a minister and missionary for the Native American tribes of Southern New England. He co-founded Dartmouth College. His brother, Jonathan, was a veteran of the American Revolution.

"Rev'd and honor'd Sir,

I have this Day received your obliging kind Epistle, and am greatly satisfied with your Reasons respecting the Negroes, and think highly reasonable what you offer in Vindication of their natural rights: Those that invade them cannot be insensible that the divine Light is chasing away the thick Darkness which broods over the Land of Africa; and the chaos which has reign'd so long, is converting into beautiful Order, and reveals more and more clearly, the glorious Dispensation of civil and religious Liberty, which are so inseparably united, that there is little or no Enjoyment of one without the other: Otherwise, perhaps, the Israelites had been less solicitous for their Freedom from Egyptian Slavery; I do not say they would have been contented without it, by no means, for in every human Breast, god has implanted a Principle, which we call Love of Freedom; it is impatient of Oppression, and pants for Deliverance; and by the Leave of our Modern Egyptians I will assert, that the same Principle lives in us. God grant Deliverance in his own Way and time, and get him honor upon all those whose Avarice impels them to countenance and help forward the calamites of their fellow Creatures. This I desire not for their Hurt, but to convince them of the strange Absurdity of their conduct whose Words and Actions are so diametrically opposite. How well the Cry for Liberty, and the reverse Disposition for the Exercise of oppressive Power over others agree, -- I humbly think it does not require the Penetration of a Philosopher to determine."

– Phillis Wheatley

Phillis married John Peters in April of 1778. They resided at his residence somewhere on Queen St., which was renamed Court St. after the Revolution. Peters, an educated and free African American, earned his income in the grocery trade. The economic hardships of the American Revolution took its toll on the Peters family and John Peters lost his Queen St. grocery. All of his other business interests went into decline as well.

For the first time in her life, Phillis experienced extreme poverty. She delivered three children in her short marriage but her poor health and the family's dire circumstances took their toll. All the children died in infancy and Phillis, at approximately thirty years of age, died on Dec. 5th, 1784. Phillis Wheatley Peters was buried in an unmarked grave in the Boston area with her third child. Wheatley's resolve to compose verses that criticized the status quo demonstrated her strength of character despite her physical frailty.

> **"On Being Brought From Africa to America"**
> *– Phillis Wheatley*
>
> *T' was mercy brought me from my pagan land,*
> *Taught my benighted soul to understand*
> *That there's a God—that there's a Saviour too;*
> *Once I redemption neither sought nor knew.*
> *Some view our sable race with scornful eye—*
> *"Their color is a diabolic dye."*
> *Remember, Christians,*
> *Negroes black as Cain*
> *May be refined, and join the angelic train."*

(19) ROBERT MORRIS LAW OFFICE
27 State Street

Robert Morris (1823-1882) maintained his lucrative law practice at this location. Ellis Gray Loring (NAA) brought Morris from Salem to Boston to help at Loring's Washington St. home. Morris's quick intelligence and ambition influenced Loring to promote him to a position of office assistant that had recently become available at Loring's downtown Boston law office. Morris received the promotion, but he had to maintain his household duties as well. That promotion served as a law apprenticeship for Morris.

Morris used his position of influence to fight many legal battles for African Americans. He served as original counsel in the Sarah Roberts vs. City of Boston school desegregation case. He also defended Shadrach Minkins against fugitive slave charges.

Robert Morris

Morris helped organize the para-military group, the Massasoit Guards. His group formed this short-lived entity in 1855 to protect African Americans from daily assaults in Boston. Morris believed that African Americans should bear arms to protect themselves but once the Civil War began, he refused to recruit soldiers for the 54th Regiment until full equality for the recruits, including equal pay and the right to be officers, was the law.

1845
Macon Allen was the first African American licensed attorney in Massachusetts

1847
Robert Morris was the second African American licensed attorney in Massachusetts

138

27 State St.

Some Pro-bono Legal Activities of Morris
- Attorney for Sarah Roberts vs. Boston
- Defense Council for Shadrach Minkins
- Assist. Attorney For Anthony Burns
- Co-organizer of Massasoit Guards
- Advocate of Equality in the Military

 SITE: DAVID WALKER'S SHOP

Brattle St. near Faneuil Hall (street no longer exists)

Radical abolitionist David Walker (1785–1830), opened a used clothing shop on Brattle St. near Faneuil Hall. The shop provided a venue for Walker to distribute his anti-slavery book, *Walker's Appeal*, to sailors in Boston harbor. See more on Walker under Beacon Hill sites.

 SITE: PRINCE HALL'S SHOP AND AFRICAN LODGE NO. 1

Somewhere on Water St.

Prince Hall, (1735–1807), a veteran of the American Revolution, was one of the most prolific civil rights activists of his time. Hall also organized the first Masonic Lodge in this country specifically for African Americans. Hall operated his leather dressing business at a site on this street in a building known as, the Golden Fleece.

When Hall's original petition for a lodge was turned down by the Grand Lodge of Massachusetts, he and fourteen other free men of color were accepted as Masons in Lodge #441 of the Grand Lodge of Ireland on March 6th, 1775. On July 3rd, 1776, Hall and his fourteen colleagues formed the African Lodge #1.

The Original members of African Lodge #1	
Prince Hall	Peter Best
John Canton	Peter Freeman
Forten Horward	Cyrus Johnston
Prince Rayden	Prince Rees
Duff Ruform	Thomas Santerson
Bueston Slinger	Boston Smith
Cato Speain	Benjamin Tiler
Richard Tiley	

On March 2nd, 1784, Hall wrote a letter to the Grand Lodge of England to request that the African Lodge #1 be allowed to receive a charter for membership. The Grand Lodge issued that charter on Sept. 29th, 1784, and was renamed, African Lodge #459. The African Lodge originally met at Prince

Hall's place of business at this site.

The early Grand Masters of the African Lodge and its initial members were at the forefront of the struggle for African American civil rights and the fight to end slavery. Members of the Barbadoes family and David Walker were other prominent associates of the African Lodge.

Building across Street from the Site of 83 Broad St.

Original African Lodge Grand Masters	
Prince Hall	1791 – 1807 Boston
Nero Prince	1808 Boston
George Middleton	1809 – 1810 Boston
Peter Lew	1811 – 1816 Dracut
Sampson Moody	1817 – 1825
John T. Hilton	1826 – 1827
Walker Lewis	1829 – 1830 Lowell
Thomas Dalton	1831 – 1832 Boston

 ## SITE: JAMES STEWART'S SHOP
83 Broad St.

James Stewart (d. 1829), a veteran of the War of 1812, and Maria Stewart (Beacon Hill Sites) married during the mid-1820s. James Stewart maintained a successful business as a shipping agent in a building at this location. The building which contained his business has been demolished but this photograph is of a building across the street from the site. This structure was constructed

during the colonial period and is very likely, similar in scale and appearance to 83 Broad St.

 ## SITE: "THE LIBERATOR" OFFICE #1
12 Post Office Sq.

William Lloyd Garrison (NAA) began publication of his influential abolitionist newspaper, *"The Liberator,"* at this location on Jan 1st, 1831. The office stayed at this site until 1834 when Garrison relocated to Cornhill St. The building was destroyed in the Great Boston Fire of 1872.

24 SCIPIO MOORHEAD & THE CHURCH OF THE PRESBYTERIAN STRANGERS

REV. WILLIAM ELLERY CHANNING FEDERAL STREET CHURCH

Site: Somewhere on Federal St.

The Church of the Presbyterian Strangers was established in 1727. It was originally located somewhere on Federal St. in what is now Boston's Financial District. By the 1760s, the pastor of the Church of the Presbyterian strangers was Rev. John Moorhead (NAA). Rev. Moorhead also enslaved Scipio Moorhead, an African with artistic talents. Scipio most likely attended church services with the Moorhead family at the Federal St. location.

Scipio Moorhead engraved the portrait of Phillis Wheatley on the cover of her volume of poetry. Scipio's talents so impressed Phillis that she dedicated a poem to the artist in her book. That poem and Moorhead's engraving of Wheatley are the most tangible evidence of the existence of the artist that remain. Those verses document Phillis Wheatley's pride in those of African heritage whose talents served as a reminder that high intelligence and cultural achievement were not limited to those of European ancestry.

"To S.M., A Young African Painter,..."
– Phillis Wheatley

To show the lab'ring bosom's deep intent,
And thought in living characters to paint,
When first thy pencil did those beauties give,
And breathing figures learnt from thee to live,
How did those prospects give my soul delight,
A new creation rushing on my sight!
...
Still may the painter's and the poet's fire,
To aid thy pencil and thy verse conspire!
And may the charms of each seraphic theme
Conduct thy footsteps to immortal fame!
High to the blissful wonders of the skies
Elate thy soul,
and raise thy wishful eyes....

Rev. Moorhead was one of the signers of the attestation in Phillis Wheatley's volume of poetry which verified her authenticity. The Church of the Presbyterian Strangers evolved from Presbyterianism to Congregationalism in 1786. It eventually settled on Unitarian Christianity and renamed itself, Federal Street Church. The colonists gathered at the church in 1788 to debate the new constitution of the United States.

Rev. William Ellery Channing (1780–1842) (NAA) was pastor of the Federal Street Church from 1803 until his death. Channing was the primary spokesperson of his day for the liberal theology of Unitarianism. In 1740, Channing, a dedicated abolitionist, published *Emancipation*, a pamphlet that argued that the success of the British abolition of slavery was a practical model which the United States should adopt. The congregation of Federal Street Church relocated their building to 351 Boylston St. in Back Bay in 1861 and renamed it Arlington St. Church.

George Middleton & Site: Old Trinity Church
Summer St. and Hawley St.

A group of worshippers formed Trinity Church at this location in 1733. Prior to the construction of the African Meeting House on Beacon Hill in 1806, African American Christians worshipped with white congregations but they were seated in segregated pews or in the balcony. George Middleton, a veteran of the American Revolution, worshipped at Trinity Church when it was at this location. It was only after a sizable increase in their population that African Americans formed their own congregations.

The Great Boston Fire of 1872 destroyed the Trinity Church building at this location and the church relocated to the more spacious Copley Square area. The reknown architect, Henry Hobson Richardson's (NAA) Romanesque design for the new structure has become a Boston landmark.

Boston Vigilance Committee Site: Marlboro Chapel, Hall No. 3
229 Washington St. between Bromfield & Winter

On June 4th, 1841, an inter-racial group decided to form the Boston Vigilance Committee, a new organization, to protect, clothe, and feed fugitives from slavery. The group's mission statement was:

> "...to secure to persons of color the enjoyment of their constitutional and legal rights."

Initially, the Committee was dedicated to peaceful and legal strategies to achieve their goals. Unfortunately, the harshness of the Fugitive slave laws forced them to revised their strategy and to embrace violence as an additional crucial component. Some of the leaders of the group were: William C. Nell, Lewis Hayden, Rev. Theodore

Parker (NAA), Deacon Timothy Gilbert (NAA), Frances Jackson (NAA), Charles T. Torrey (NAA), Joseph Southwick (NAA), and others.

Francis Jackson, Treasurer of the group, kept detailed logs of payments made to individuals who regularly assisted the Vigilance Committee. The cost of the rescues were quite expensive. The total outlay for the rescue of Shadrach Minkins alone amounted to $1,820.32, a considerable sum in that day.

Some of the African Americans who assisted in that rescue work were: Cornelia Atkins; Eli Baney; David Brown; Susan Brown; Susan Burroughs; Lewis E. Caswell; Milton Crew; Mr. Dale; E.D. Eddy; Samuel Flint; Elizabeth Fullerton; Henry Garnet; Elizabeth Gilmore; Catherine Greeland; C.H. Greeland; Benjamin Giger; Rev. Leonard Grimes; Dr. M.P. Hanson; Lewis Hayden; Lewis Howard; Isabella S. Holmes; Margaret Irwin; William Mannix; John Oliver; Elizabeth Peters; Peter Randolph; Henry Richardson; John Robertson; Phillip Russell; James Scott; Mrs. Scott; Adeline Skeene; Burrill Smith; Rev. Samuel Snowden; John M. Spears; R.C. Taft; John B. Taylor; Sarah A. Taylor; Calvin Terry; Henry Tyler; Clara Vaught; James Watson; Mrs. Charles Williams; C.D. Williams; Henry Williams; Jane Woodfolk; and Maria Young.

 SITE: CARTEAUX'S HAIR SALON #1
284 Washington St.

Christiana Carteaux (1820-1902), the wife of African American artist, Edward Bannister (1828-1901), owned hair salons in several cities over the course of her career. This was the site of one of her Boston salons.

 OLD SOUTH MEETING HOUSE
310 Washington St.
617- 482-6439
Daily: 10 am to 4 pm

This historic church, originally built in 1729, was the church home of Phillis Wheatley. In 1773, Wheatley became the first African American to publish a book of poetry, *Poems on Various Subjects, Religious and Moral*. The church and its minister, Rev. Sewell, had a great moral influence on Wheatley,

Old South Meeting House

and in 1769, she wrote, *"On the Death of the Rev. Sewell"* to commemorate his passing.

> ### On the Death of the Rev. Dr. Sewell
> – Phillis Wheatley
>
> *Ere yet the morn its lovely*
> *blushes spread,*
> *See Sewell number'd with*
> *the happy dead.*
> *Hail, holy man, arriv'd*
> *the immortal shore,*
> *Though we shall hear*
> *thy warning voice no more.*
> *Come, let us all behold*
> *with wishful eyes*
> *The saint ascending to*
> *his native skies;*
> *From hence the prophet wing'd*
> *his rapt'tous way*
> *To the blest mansions*
> *in eternal day.*
> *Then begging for the spirit*
> *of our God,*
> *And panting eager the same abode,*
> *Come, let us all with the*
> *same vigour rise*
> *And take a prospect of*
> *the blissful skies;*
> *While on our minds*
> *Christ's image is imprest,*
> *And the dear Saviour glows*
> *in ev'ry breast.*
> *Thrice happy saint!*
> *To find thy heav'n at last,*
> *What compensation for*
> *the evil past!...*
> *"Sewell is dead." Swift-pinion'd*
> *fame thus cry'd.*

> *"Is Sewell dead," my trembling*
> *tongue reply'd.*
> *O what a blessing in*
> *his flight deny'd!*
> *How oft for us*
> *the holy prophet pray'd!*
> *How oft to us*
> *the word of Life convey'd!*
> *By duty urg'd my mournful*
> *verse to close,*
> *I for his tomb*
> *this epitaph compose...*

Prior to the American Revolution, the Old South Meeting House served as a place where the Patriots assembled to organize protests against the British. On the cold night of December 16th, 1773, over 5,000 colonists came here to attend what became known as the Boston Tea Party to protest a tea tax imposed by Great Britain. They dumped a shipment of tea, valued in today's dollars at approximately $2 million, into Boston Harbor. During the American Revolution, the British used Old South Meeting House as a horse stable while they occupied Boston.

29 SITE: CARTEAUX'S HAIR SALON #2
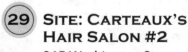
365 Washington St.

This was the site of another of Christiana Carteaux's hair salons. Carteaux was the wife of landscape painter, Edward Bannister. Her financial success enabled him to devote all of his time to his art career.

Carteaux's Hair Salon

 SITE: LAW FIRM OF WALKER, WOLFF, AND BROWN
46 School St.

In 1866, Edwin Walker (1830–1901) became the first African American to win election to the Massachusetts Legislature. See Charleston sites. Walker, James H. Wolff, and Edward Everett Brown formed a partnership in 1888 and opened a law firm in a building on this site. Their firm was the first law firm in Massachusetts with all African American partners. The location directly across the street from Boston

City Hall allowed the attorneys to have quick access to the city's politicians.

 OLD BOSTON CITY HALL
45 School Street

The second half of the nineteenth century was a dynamic time for African American politicians. In Boston, ten African Americans won election to the Boston City Council which operated in this building. African Americans did not serve on the Boston City Council again until the 1960s.

African Americans felt tremendous pride in the successful outcome of the Civil War and their participation in it. That sense of success gave them the will to flex their political muscles in the post-war years of the late 1800s. Twelve African Americans also won election as state legislators in Massachusetts (see Beacon Hill sites).

> **African Americans who served on the Boston City Council during the late 1800s**
> - George L. Ruffin, 1876-1877
> - James W. Pope, 1881
> - William O. Armstrong, 1885-1886
> - Andrew B. Leattimore, 1887-1888
> - Charles E. Harris, 1889-1890
> - Nelson Gaskins, 1891
> - Walden Banks, 1892-1893
> - Stanley Ruffin, 1894-1895
> - J. Henderson Allston, 1894-1895
> - Charles H. Hall, 1895

Gridley Bryant (NAA) and Arthur Gilman (NAA) designed this building in the Neoclassical style. It opened in

Old Boston City Hall

on the railroads. The fact that Malcolm X held such a wide variety of positions as a teenager indicated his industrious nature. The fact that he did not last long in any of those positions indicated the frustration he felt on jobs that stymied his intellectual growth. It was only after he was imprisoned in 1946 that Malcolm X dedicated the time to develop his intellectual capabilities.

1865 and it remained as the seat of Boston government until 1965.

 32 MALCOLM X SITE: PARKER HOUSE HOTEL
60 School St.

Malcolm X (1925–1965) worked as a bus boy at this famous hotel during his teen years. Other positions he held were at the Sears and Roebuck warehouse in the Fenway, and various service jobs

The Parker House Hotel, constructed in 1856, originated as one of Boston's premier luxury hotels. It has hosted numerous dignitaries such as President Ulysses S. Grant (NAA) and President John F. Kennedy (NAA). Two Boston culinary specials, the Parker House Roll and the Boston Cream Pie, were both created here.

Parker House Hotel

 33 TREMONT TEMPLE
88 Tremont St.
www.tremonttemple.com

In the early 1800s, churches charged parishioners rent for the use of their pews during worship. Those who could not afford to pay could not participate in the services. African American parishioners who paid those fees were seated in inferior and separate pews because of the segregation policies of the churches.

Tremont Temple

In 1838, one of the members of Charles St. Meeting House, Thomas Gilbert (NAA), also an original member of the Boston Vigilance Committee, decided to test those policies. When he invited some African American friends to worship with him in his pew, the congregation expelled him from the church. Outraged by this non-Christian attitude, Gilbert founded First Baptist Free Church. First Baptist Free Church began to meet at this building in the early 1840s. In 1841, they adopted the name, Tremont Temple Baptist Church. They purchased the building in 1843. The church rented out its ground floor space to retail stores. The revenue generated allowed the church to keep its doors open to all. The congregation's vision was:

> "...a church with free seats, where every(one), rich or poor, white or black, should be on the same religious level, and the Sabbath home for the stranger and the traveler."
> -- THOMAS GILBERT

Just after midnight on January 1st, 1863, a group of abolitionists gathered here to await the news via telegraph, that the Emancipation Proclamation, signed by President Lincoln, was now the law of the land.

 SITE: EDMONIA LEWIS STUDIO
SE corner Bromfield and Tremont St., now Suffolk Law School

Edmonia Lewis (1845–1901) was one of the few female artists of any race to make a career with her art during the nineteenth century. Her father was African American and her mother a Native American from the Chippewa Tribe. After Edmonia became an orphan at the age of five, she and her brother lived with their mother's tribe until she was twelve. Edmonia's brother was a gold miner in California. That income allowed him to finance her education to Oberlin College.

Edmonia Lewis

In 1863, Edmonia Lewis's brother advised her to move to Boston after several racial incidents at Oberlin made it difficult for her to continue her education there. In Boston, she studied sculpture under the direction of a local sculptor. Lewis produced sculptures of famous anti-slavery leaders to earn income. Her most famous sculpture, *"Free at Last,"* depicted individuals at the point of their awareness of their newly freed status.

Free at Last Sculpture

35 GRANARY BURYING GROUND
- ### BOSTON MASSACRE VICTIMS
- ### JUDGE SAMUEL SEWELL

Tremont St. near
Bromfield St.

Boston citizens buried the five victims of the Boston Massacre in a joint grave here on March 8th, 1770. They held the funeral at Faneuil Hall, and carried the coffin through the streets to the Granary Burying Ground. The massacre and funeral agitated the colonists to such an extent that it directly precipitated the American Revolution.

Granary Burying Ground Gates

Gravesite of Boston Massacre Victims

Other prominent residents buried here:
- Samuel Adams (NAA),
- John Hancock (NAA),
- Paul Revere (NAA),
- Benjamin Franklin's (NAA) parents,
- Judge Samuel Sewell (NAA).

John Hancock, one of the signers of the Declaration of Independence, was also buried here. Hancock was one of the many founding fathers who enslaved several individuals during his lifetime. The grave of one of those enslaved individuals, Frank, was placed in close proximity to Hancock's memorial on the grounds of the cemetery.

Judge Samuel Sewell (1652–1730) (NAA), an influential personality during the colonial period, was also buried here. Sewell achieved permanent notoriety because of his involvement in the Salem Witch Trials. Those trials led to the death of forty citizens. Sewell later apologized for his participation in those events.

Sewell did not believe in slavery on moral grounds. In 1700, he wrote an essay, *"The Selling of Joseph,"* which made the case for the abolition of slavery. That essay used the Biblical story of Joseph, son of Jacob, who had been sold into slavery by his brothers as an example of the injustice of the practice.

"…Forasmuch as liberty is in real value next to life, none ought to part with it themselves, or deprive others of it,….

The numerousness of slaves at this day in the province, and the uneasiness of them in their slavery has put many upon thinking whether the foundation of it be firmly and well laid, so as to sustain the vast weight that is built upon it. It is most certain that all men, as they are the sons of Adam, are co-heirs and have equal right to liberty, and all other outward comforts of life. "God hath given the Earth (with all its commodities) onto the Sons of Adam" (Psal. 115:16), "And hath made of one blood all nations of men, for to dwell on all the face of the earth,…Yet through the indulgence of God to our first parents after the fall, the outward estate of all and each of their children remains the same as to one another. So that originally and naturally, there is no such thing as slavery. Joseph was rightfully no more a slave to his brethren than they were to him; and they had no more authority to sell him than they had to slay him...

And seeing that God has said, "He that stealeth a man, and selleth him, or if he be found in his hand, he shall surely be put to death." (Exod, 21:16) This law being of everlasting equity, wherein man-stealing is ranked among the most atrocious of capital crimes; What louder cry can there be made of that celebrated warning, Caveat emptor!"(sic)

- Sewell

Judge Sewell was also involved in one of the earliest freedom suits in the Commonwealth, the 1701 case of Adam of Boston against his enslaver, John Saffin (NAA). Saffin hired Adam out to Thomas Shepard (NAA) in 1694 for a seven year term. In return, Adam was to receive his freedom at the end of that period but he did not. The case was heard by Judge Sewell, who sat on the Superior Court. Sewell ruled in Adam's favor in 1703. This decision was more unusual because of the extent to which Saffin attempted to portray Adam as an unruly and recalcitrant individual who, presumably, did not deserve his freedom.

Park Street Church

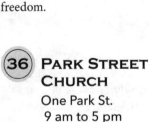

36 PARK STREET CHURCH

One Park St.
9 am to 5 pm

1829	William Lloyd Garrison delivered his first anti-slavery speech here
1831	Patriotic hymn, *America*, performed here for the first time
1910	Boston NAACP formed

This Boston landmark, with its 217-foot spire, was founded in 1809 on the former site of the town granary. On July 4th, 1829, William Lloyd Garrison delivered his first anti-slavery speech here. Garrison rallied abolitionists throughout the country with his newspaper, *"The Liberator."* Garrison's *July 4th* speech sparked an abolitionist spirit in all who heard it, a spirit that did not slow down until the United States ended slavery in the Confederate States in 1863:

"...Every Fourth of July, our Declaration of Independence is produced, with a sublime indignation, to set forth the tyranny of the mother country, and to challenge the admiration of the world. But what a pitiful detail of grievances does this document present, in comparison with the wrongs which our slaves endure! In the one case, it is hardly the plucking of a hair from the head; in the other, it is the crushing of a live body on the wheel; the stings of the wasp contrasted with the tortures of the inquisition. Before God, I must say, that such a glaring contradiction, as exists between our creed and practice, the annals of six thousand years cannot parallel.

In view of it, I am ashamed of my country. I am sick of our unmeaning declamation in praise of liberty and equality; of our hypocritical cant about the unalienable rights of man. I could not, for my right hand, stand up before a European assembly, and exult that I am an American citizen, and denounce the usurpations of a kingly government as wicked and unjust; or, should I make the attempt, the recollection of my country's barbarity and despotism would blister my lips, and cover my cheeks with burning blushes of shame."

– Excerpt from William L. Garrison's July 4th, 1829 speech.

In 1831, singers performed here for the first time the patriotic hymn, *"America,"* composed by Samuel Francis Smith (NAA):

"My country, 'tis of Thee,
Sweet Land of Liberty
Of thee I sing;
Land where my fathers died,
Land of the pilgrims' pride,
From every mountain side
Let Freedom ring."

Those stirring words inspired a famous African American, Martin Luther King, Jr. (1929-1968), in his historic *"I Have A Dream"* speech during the Civil Rights Movement's *"March on Washington"* in August of 1963. Frederick Douglass also delivered abolitionist speeches from the pulpit of this church. Park Street Church's leadership as a center for civil rights activity influenced the Boston chapter of the NAACP (National Association for the Advancement of Colored People) to form here in 1910.

(37) CARTEAUX & BANNISTER HOUSE
31 Winter St.

In 1857, Christiana Carteaux (1828-1901), married barber and landscape artist, Edward Bannister (1828-1901). Carteaux and Bannister lived at this address during the late 1800s. Christiana Carteaux was a very successful entrepreneur who owned several hair salons in downtown Boston. Two of her salons were located on Washington St. Their marriage gave Bannister the economic security required to concentrate on his art full-time.

Bannister was born in Nova Scotia, Canada to an African American father and a white mother. Bannister's father

died when he was two. His mother's death when he was sixteen, forced Bannister and his brother to relocate in 1848. In Boston, Bannister worked as a barber by day and attended the Lowell Institute Art School at night.

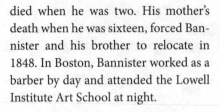

Christiana Carteaux

Carteaux / Bannister House Site

Edward Bannister

In 1876, Bannister entered his landscape painting, *"Under the Oaks,"* in the

Philadelphia Centennial Exposition. It won the first prize bronze medal in that exhibit. The officials of the exposition were unaware that the artist of the award winning painting was an African American:

> "Upon learning that No. 54 had received a first prize medal, I hurried to the Committee room where I gained the attention of an official who demanded in a most exasperating tone of voice, 'Well, what do you want here anyway, speak lively.'
>
> "I want to inquire concerning No. 54, is it a prize winner?' I replied.
>
> 'What's that to you', he said. In an instant my blood was up. Controlling myself I said with deliberation, 'I am interested in the report that "Under the Oaks" has received a prize, I painted that picture."
>
> The explosion of a bomb could not have created more of a sensation in that room. Without hesitation, the official apologized to me and soon all were bowing and scraping to me."
>
> – Bannister

Eventually, Bannister and his wife moved to Providence, RI. In Providence, Carteaux operated more hair salons and Edward Bannister became one of the sixteen founders of the Providence Art Club. That art club eventually evolved into the Rhode Island School of Design. Bannister's painting, "Workers in the Field," is in the collection of the Museum of Fine Art, Boston.

 38 NEW ENGLAND EMIGRANT AID SOCIETY

Somewhere on Winter St.

Eli Thayer (1819–1899) (NAA), originally from Worcester, founded the New England Emigrant Aid Society in 1854. The goal of that company was to send settlers, both African American and whites, to the new territory of Kansas in order to increase its potential to become a free state. This action was in response to the Kansas-Nebraska Act of 1854 which stated that the residents of the new Territory would determine whether it would become a free state or a slave state.

Although the company was a for-profit enterprise, the altruistic motives of the founders and investors minimized any concern for an immediate return on their investment. The company subsidized the travel of the settlers and it assisted with their transition to the new community. The fact that many of the settlers were urban dwellers and ill-suited to farm-life resulted in a high rate of return to the east. The settlers who remained founded the Kansas towns of Topeka, Manhattan, and Osawatomie.

The New England Emigrant Aid Society maintained offices in a building somewhere on Winter St. The charter of the Emigrant Aid Society remained in effect until 1907. Thayer later served as a Representative in the United States Congress.

 ## 39 BOSTON MASSACRE MEMORIAL
Boston Common, Tremont & Avery

On March 5th, 1851, the anniversary date of the Boston Massacre which occurred on March 5th, 1770, a group of African Americans petitioned the Massachusetts legislature for a memorial for Crispus Attucks. Attucks, an African American, was the first to die in that massacre. Since that initial petition was unsuccessful, they submitted a second petition for a monument to memorialize all five Patriots who died

African Americans who signed the Petition for a Memorial to Crispus Attucks
- William C. Nell
- Charles Lenox Remond
- Henry Weeden
- Lewis Hayden
- Frederick G. Barbadoes
- Joshua B. Smith
- Lemuel Burr

that evening; Attucks, Samuel Maverick, James Caldwell, Samuel Gray, and Patrick Carr.

Sculptor Robert Kraus (NAA), designed the monument. Two quotes etched on the monument represented the importance of that historic night to the formation of the United States:

> *"From that moment we may date the severance of the British Empire"*
> DANIEL WEBSTER (NAA)

> *"On that night the foundation of American independence was laid."*
> - JOHN ADAMS (NAA)

At the 1888 dedication ceremony, John Boyle O'Reilly (NAA), read a poem he wrote in honor of the slain men.

> *"...And honor to Crispus Attucks*
> *Who was the leader and voice*
> *that day*
> *The first to defy*
> *And the first to die,*
> *With Maverick, Carr and Gray.*
> *Call it riot or revolution,*
> *Or mob or crowd as you may...*
> *Such deaths have been*
> *seeds of nations,*
> *Such lives shall be honored for aye."*
>
> *– John Boyle O'Reilly*

Boston Massacre Memorial

of men saved Garrison when they took him to the Leverett St. jail in the West End for protection until the mob dispersed. Outraged that such violence could occur in Boston, Phillips decided to dedicate his life to end slavery.

Attitudes on slavery polarized the community to such an extent that Phillips's family attempted to have him admitted to an insane asylum when he joined the American Anti-slavery Society. He eventually became a popular speaker for that group. Phillips also participated in the *"free produce"* movement.

> **Free Produce Movement**
> Boycotts of products that were dependent on slave labor in their production such as cane sugar and clothing made of cotton.

The engraving on the base of the memorial features a depiction of the famous Paul Revere (NAA) etching of that historical event. Crispus Attucks lies slain in the foreground.

 ## 40 WENDELL PHILLIPS HOUSE
50 Exeter St.

Wendell Phillips (1811–1884) (NAA), a graduate of Harvard College and Harvard Law School, had embarked on a traditional legal career when he viewed an event that changed the direction of his life. On Oct. 21st, 1835, Phillips witnessed an angry pro-slavery mob's attempt to lynch abolitionist, William Lloyd Garrison (NAA). A small group

Wendell Phillips

Phillips's participation in the failed attempt to break Anthony Burns out of jail resulted in a court indictment but he did not serve any time. He spoke with pride about that indictment his entire life.

> "What is defeat? Nothing but education; nothing but the first step to something better."
> – WENDELL PHILLIPS

The City of Boston erected a statue in Boston Garden to honor Phillips. His house received designation on the National Register of Historic Places. Phillips was buried in the Milton Cemetery in Milton, MA.

> "Eternal vigilance is the price of liberty."
> – WENDELL PHILLIPS

41 SITE: THEODORE PARKER HOUSE
UGRR Station
**1 Exeter Place
now, Harrison Ave. Ext.**

Rev. Theodore Parker (1810–1860) (NAA), a prominent activist in the abolitionist movement, performed the official wedding ceremony of William and Ellen Craft in his home at this location on Nov. 7th, 1850. The couple had previously married informally in Georgia.

42 SITE: HARRIET E. WILSON HOUSE
46 Carver St., Street no longer exists, now Charles Street South in Bay Village

Harriet E. Wilson (1825–1900) was the first African American to publish a novel in the continental United States with the publication of *Our Nig, or Sketches from the Life of a Free Black* in 1859. Wilson lived at this address from 1870 to 1877 with her second husband, John Gallatin Robinson (NAA). Wilson's novel was discovered in 1981 by Harvard scholar, Henry Louis Gates, Jr. See more on Wilson under South End Sites.

43 SITE: AVERY WHARF
Near Beach & Tyler St.

The first African American to publish a book of poetry, Phillis Wheatley, received her name from the ship of her captivity, Phillis, which docked at Avery Wharf. Wheatley arrived in America in 1761 onboard the Phillis. During the 1700s, Avery Wharf was located near the site of today's Chinatown Gate. Several land infill projects over the next 100 years eliminated the wharf and extended the harbor further out to sea.

Site of Avery Wharf / Now: Chinatown Gate

44 LINCOLN TOWER
1 Lincoln St.

Through a mechanism known as, *"Linkage,"* a consortium of minority developers, the Columbia Plaza Associates, developed this new office tower in a joint venture with the developers, Gale International. Linkage was an urban real estate development concept that required minority business participation in real estate development of downtown parcels as an incentive for development of the parcels on the 143 acres of vacant land of the Southwest Corridor. The linkage concept was one

Lincoln Tower

of the concessions local citizens demanded from the development of the Southwest Corridor in the 1980s. See South End sites.

The construction of Lincoln Tower was initially approved in 1990, but delayed because of a downturn in the economy. Developers resumed the project in the year 2000. The final cost of the project was over $350 million.

 FORT WARREN
Georges Island,
Boston Harbor
Open: mid-May to
early October

Soldiers created the folksong, *"John Brown's Body,"* at Fort Warren in memory of the martyr, John Brown (NAA). Brown failed in his attempt to take the Federal Arsenal in Harper's Ferry, VA, on Oct. 16th, 1859, but his valiant effort hastened the start of the Civil War.

May 12, 1861
*John Brown's Body
sung for the first
time during a flag-
raising ceremony.*

Sung for the first time on May 12th, 1861, at a flag-raising ceremony, the song quickly became a favorite of Union troops. The composition was a group effort of the troops of the 2nd Infantry Battalion of the Massachusetts militia. George Kimball (NAA) of the 2nd Infantry wrote this account of the song's origin:

> *"…We had a jovial Scotchman in the battalion, named John Brown…and as he happened to bear the identical name of the old hero of Harper's Ferry, he became at once the butt of his comrades. If he made his appearance a few minutes late among the working squad, or was a little tardy in falling into the company line, he was sure to be greeted with such expressions as "Come, old fellow, you ought to be at it if you are going to help us free the slaves"; or, "This can't be John Brown—why John Brown is dead." And then some wag would add, in a solemn, drawling tone, as if it were his purpose to give particular emphasis to the fact that John Brown was really, actually dead: "Yes, yes, poor old John Brown is dead; his body lies mouldering in the grave."*
>
> *– George Kimball*

The teasing became so popular that additional lines were added. It was sung to the tune of a well-known Methodist camp-song composed by William Steffe (NAA) in 1856, *"Brothers, Will You Meet Me at Canaan's Hap-*

py Shore." "John Brown's Body" was the inspiration for *"The Battle Hymn of the Republic"* by Julia Ward Howe.

John Brown's Body

John Brown's body lies a-moldering in the grave (3 times)
His soul goes marching on

Chorus:
Glory, Glory, Hallelujah (3 times)
His soul goes marching on.
He captured Harper's Ferry with his nineteen men so true (3 times)
His soul goes marching on

Chorus:
Glory, Glory, Hallelujah...

He frightened old Virginia till she trembled through and through (3 times)
His soul goes marching on

Chorus:
Glory, Glory, Hallelujah...

They hung him for a traitor, themselves the traitor crew (3 times)
His soul goes marching on

Chorus:
Glory, Glory, Hallelujah...

John Brown died
that the slave might be free (3 times)
His soul goes marching on

Chorus:
Glory, Glory, Hallelujah...

The stars above in Heaven are looking kindly down (3 times)
On the grave of old John Brown

Last Chorus:
Glory, Glory, Hallelujah...

Fort Warren was built on a 28-acre island strategically located at the entrance to Boston Harbor. Its role was to protect the harbor from attack. After 28 years, the fort was completed in 1861 at the start of the Civil War. During that war, the government imprisoned captured Confederate soldiers there. The Fort served until 1947 when it was decommissioned. Today, it is a National Historic Landmark. It is accessible by ferry from downtown Boston.

46 Local Resources

Boston Freedom Trail
Tours: April 15 - Nov. 28

Black Heritage Trail Tour:
Daily, www.nps.gov

African American Patriots Tour: February,
Sat. & Sun. at 12:45
www.nps.gov/bost

Emancipation Trail:
www.unityfirst.com/2013/emancipationtrail

Institute of Contemporary Art:
100 Northern Ave.
617-478-3100
www.icaboston.org

Map of Back Bay, 2010

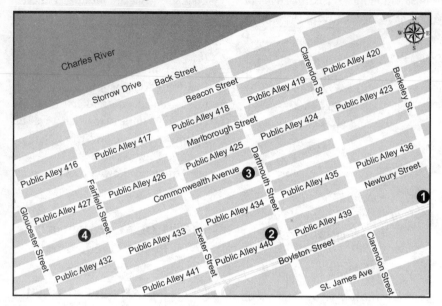

BACK BAY

Boston's Back Bay neighborhood was originally the area of a tidal bay before it was a neighborhood. That bay extended almost to where today's Tremont Street is located. The City of Boston began a land-infill project in this area in 1857 and it was substantially completed by 1882. Streets and other infrastructure were put in place to create a very exclusive residential neighborhood. Building lots were purchased by developers and construction commenced on what would become one of the most expensive and intact Victorian residential neighborhoods in the United States.

① ROBERT TAYLOR & MIT SCHOOL OF ARCHITECTURE

Site: Boylston between Berkeley & Claredon

In 1892, Robert Taylor (1868–1942) became the first African American to graduate from a professional school of architecture when he graduated from MIT. He was also the first African American to graduate from MIT. Robert Taylor was born in Wilmington, NC, where his father owned a construction company. Taylor stood to inherit the family construction business, but instead, he chose to enroll in MIT when he was twenty. Robert Taylor excelled in his studies and received the highest marks of any of his classmates.

Robert Taylor

a more spacious campus in Cambridge, but the architecture program remained in this building until 1937 at which time that program joined the rest of the school. The building was demolished shortly after the architecture program relocated to Cambridge.

 ## MURIEL SNOWDEN INTERNATIONAL SCHOOL
150 Newbury St.

Muriel Snowden (1916-1988) was a prominent community activist in Roxbury for most of her adult life. Snowden founded Freedom House (see Roxbury sites) in 1949 with her husband, Otto Snowden (1911-1990). The couple organized many other civic initiatives to benefit Boston residents.

After his graduation in 1892, Booker T. Washington recruited Taylor to teach at Washington's new school, Tuskegee Institute, in Alabama. Taylor designed and supervised the construction of many of the buildings at the school until his death in 1942. Tuskegee represents one of the largest collections of structures in the United States in a contiguous setting designed by a single architect. In 2015, the United States Post Office issued a stamp to honor Taylor.

In 1866, MIT was located in a five-story building at this location. In 1916, most of the school relocated to

Muriel Snowden International School

③ WILLIAM LLOYD GARRISON STATUE
Commonwealth Ave. between Dartmouth St. & Exeter St.

William Lloyd Garrison (1805–1879) (NAA) was an influential abolitionist and the founder of *"The Liberator"* newspaper. In his newspaper, Garrison published speeches, information about anti-slavery rallies, and narratives of fugitives from slavery. He viewed slavery as a moral issue on which one should never compromise.

That abhorrence of slavery was not universal in the North. Once, a pro-slavery mob interrupted a speech Garrison was about to deliver and attempted to lynch him. He was rescued by a local police officer. That event inspired Wendell Phillips, who viewed it from his downtown office, to join the abolition movement. Garrison also encouraged Frederick Douglass to join the movement as a speaker in 1841.

④ BOSTON WOMEN'S MEMORIAL
Commonwealth Ave. between Fairfield St. and Gloucester St.

This bronze monument honors three Massachusetts women who made significant contributions to the heritage of this state: Phillis Wheatley, Abigail Adams (NAA), and Lucy Stone (NAA). In 1773, Phillis Wheatley became the first African American to publish a book of poetry. Wheatley corresponded with many prominent dignitaries of the time such as General George Washington (NAA). Wheatley's correspondence revealed a calm yet determined individual

Boston Women's Memorial

Phillis Wheatley Sculpture

5 MASS. HISTORICAL SOCIETY

1154 Boylston St.
M - Sat.: 9 to 4
617-646-0560
www.masshist.org

The Massachusetts Historical Society has a wealth of documents on African American history in Massachusetts. The Society is home to the pen President Lincoln used to sign the Emancipation Proclamation. The pen was given to Senator Charles Sumner, who witnessed that historic event, as a gift to George Livermore (NAA), a Cambridge abolitionist.

who refused to accept the condition of slavery as the status quo.

Abigail Adams (1744–1818) was a prolific writer and social commentator in the mid to late 1700s. She wrote extensive letters to her husband, John Adams (NAA), who was the second President of the United States. John Adams spent a great deal of time away from home because of various political and diplomatic assignments. Through those letters, Abigail Adams acted as his confidant and unofficial advisor. Abigail Adams had a personal distain for the institution of slavery and she was a role model for her children with her active participation in the fight against slavery.

Lucy Stone (1818–1893) was the mother of the women's suffrage movement in the United States and an active proponent of the abolition of slavery. Meredith Bergmann (NAA) completed this memorial in the mid-1990s.

Another exhibit is a copy of a famous photo, *"The Branded Hand."* This photo depicted the hand of abolitionist, Captain Jonathan Walker (NAA), of Harwich. Captain Walker's hand was branded with the initials, S.S. for Slave Stealer after he was convicted for his role in the attempted escape of fugitives from slavery in Florida. The photo was exhibited widely at the time to bolster support for the abolitionist cause. See Harwich sites. Lectures and seminars are presented annually at the Society.

6 LOCAL RESOURCES

Boston Public Library
700 Boylston St.,
Copley Sq.
www.bpl.org

Fenway / Kenmore Map

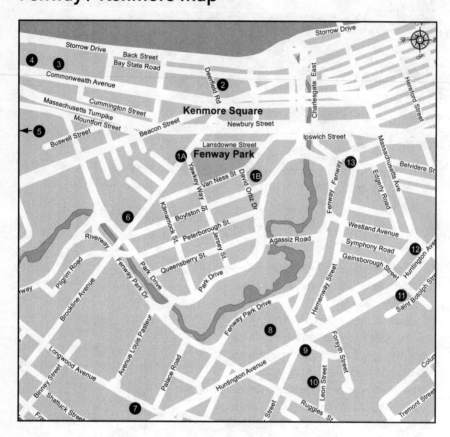

FENWAY / KENMORE

**DAVID ORTIZ
BRIDGE**
Formerly Brookline Ave.
Bridge

two transportation corridors near Fenway Park, Boston's home field, to honor Ortiz, a bridge over the Massachusetts Turnpike and a street near the Park.

 DAVID ORTIZ DRIVE
Formerly Yawkey Way
Extension St. between
Van Ness and Boylston St.

David Ortiz (b. 1975), affectionately known as "Big Papi," became one of the most popular players in Red Sox history. Ortiz, a native of the Dominican Republic, joined the team in 2003 as a pinch hitter and he ended the season with 31 homeruns. In his next season, the Red Sox won their first World Series in 86 years and Ortiz was instrumental in that victory.

Over the course of his 13-year career with the Red Sox, Ortiz became one of the top hitters in baseball history. In October of 2016, the state of Massachusetts and the city of Boston renamed

2 **HOWARD THURMAN
CENTER**
19 Deerfield Street
Boston University
617- 353-4745

Howard Thurman (1899–1981) served as the first African American spiritual leader of a predominantly white school when he was Dean of the Chapel at Boston University, from 1953 to 1965. Thurman preached a philosophy of non-violence that was inspired by the writings of Mohandas Gandhi (NAA), the leader for India's independence.

Thurman's lectures inspired Martin Luther King, Jr. while King studied theology at Boston University and influenced his powerful philosophy of non-violence.

"Don't ask what the world needs. Ask what makes you come alive, and go do it. Because what the world needs ... people who have come alive."
-- HOWARD THURMAN

"There is something in every one of you that waits and listens for the sound of the genuine in yourself. It is the only true guide you will ever have, and if you cannot hear it, you will all of your life spend your days on the ends of strings that somebody else pulls."
-- HOWARD THURMAN

Howard Thurman married Sue Bailey Thurman (1903–1996) in 1932. Mrs. Thurman worked extensively throughout her life in the areas of international peace and intercultural relationships. In the 1930s, she participated in a peace delegation to visit India, Burma, and Ceylon with her husband. There, she and Rev. Thurman became the first African Americans to visit Mohandas Gandhi after Gandhi attained his position of spiritual leader of India. The Rev. and Mrs. Thurman founded the Museum of Afro- American History on Beacon Hill in 1964. Mrs. Thurman went on to establish museums of African American history in several other cities across the United States.

Howard Thurman

Sue Bailey Thurman

3 MLK Site: "Free at Last" Memorial

Boston University,
Marsh Plaza
735 Commonwealth
Avenue

Chilean artist, Sergio Castillo (1925–2010) (NAA) designed this sculpture in 1975 to memorialize the legacy of Rev. Martin Luther King, Jr. The name for the memorial was based on the last words of King's famous, *"I Have a Dream,"* speech that he delivered at the March on Washington on April 28th, 1963: *"Free at last, free at last; thank God Almighty, we're free at last."* The sculpture represented fifty doves in

Free at Last Memorial

flight to symbolize the fifty states that should be united in a common struggle for human rights. Martin Luther King, Jr. received a Doctor of Theology Degree from Boston University in 1954.

4 MLK Site: King Reading Room

Boston University,
Mugar Library,
771 Commonwealth Ave.
617-353-3696

Martin Luther King, Jr. bequeathed his papers to his Alma Mater, Boston University. Some of those papers are on display in this exhibition room on the third floor of the Mugar Library at Boston University.

Mugar Memorial Library also contains papers on the life of Edward Gourdin. In 1958, Gourdin, a track star and veteran, was the first African American appointed to the Mass. Superior Court.

5 Frances Jackson House

UGRR Station
31 Hollis Place

Frances Jackson (NAA) was one of the founders of the Boston Vigilance Committee. He also served as treasurer. Jackson kept a detailed record book from 1850 to 1861 that listed all funds expended by the committee to assist fugitives in their escapes.

⑥ MALCOLM X SITE: SEARS & ROEBUCK BUILDING
401 Park Drive

Malcolm X worked at this Sears and Roebuck warehouse in the 1940s when the company approached the height of its success. The facility was built in 1929 specifically for Sears. At its peak during the 1950s and 1960s, Sears at this location employed over 1,200 people. A new post office had to be created on-site and extra street cars had to be added to the local service to handle the increased customer traffic. The warehouse closed during the 1980s and it was eventually redeveloped into a popular urban retail complex, the Landmark Center.

⑦ DR. GEORGE FRANKLIN GRANT HARVARD DENTAL SCHOOL
188 Longwood Ave.

Dr. George Franklin Grant (1846-1910) began his fascination with dentistry at the age of fifteen when he worked as an apprentice to a dentist in his hometown of Oswego, NY. At the age of twenty-one, Grant applied to and was accepted at Harvard Dental School. After graduation, Grant accepted an offer by Harvard to join their dental faculty. That appointment made him the first African American faculty member at the Harvard Dental School.

Grant specialized in the non-surgical treatment of cleft palates, especially those in children. His research led him to invent the oblate palate, a device that

Sears & Roebuck Building

helped realign his client's palates. Dr. Grant's inventive curiosity and love of golf also led him to invent the wooden golf tee in 1899.

 MUSEUM OF FINE ART

465 Huntington Avenue
617-267-9300
www.mfa.org
Free admission on
Wednesdays at 4 pm

Dr. George Franklin Grant

The Museum of Fine Art, one of the largest museums in the world, has over 450,000 items in its collection. The popular museum receives over one million visitors each year. Founded in 1870, the MFA was originally located in Copley Square. The trustees decided to relocate it to the current site in 1909.

Under the leadership of Malcolm Rogers (NAA), Museum Director, 1994-2014, the MFA developed several initiatives to improve its outreach to and representation of communities of color. One of those efforts was

Museum of Fine Art

a self-guided audio tour of a selection of African American art from its permanent collection. Edmund Barry Gaither, Executive Director of the Museum of the National Center of African American Artists, curated the tour and narrated the audio recording.

Another initiative occurred in 2005 when the Museum established the Heritage Fund to make acquisitions that better represented the diverse cultural heritage of the United States. That was followed in 2011 by the creation of the Heritage Remixed Friends Group. That group was created to give members a deeper exposure to the diverse art in the Museum's collections.

The museum regularly presents exhibits that celebrate African American culture, and in 2015, it commissioned a book to document the work by African American artists in its collection, *Commonwealth: Art by African Americans in the Museum of Fine Arts, Boston* by Lowery Stokes Sims, editor. That book accommpanied an exhibit of that same name. The MFA also has galleries dedicated to its extensive collection of African art.

Significant works that pertain to African American history and culture by white artists and at least one piece of art by an anonymous designer have been acquired by the museum. Some of those notable works of art are:

African American Artists in the Permanent Collection of the MFA (circa 2014)

Benny Andrews	William H. Johnson
Edward Bannister	Lois Mailou Jones
Richmond Barthe	Wifredo Lam
Romare Bearden	Jacob Lawrence
John Biggers	Norman Lewis
Grafton T. Brown	Glenn Ligon
Magdalena Campos-Pons	Alvin Loving
Elizabeth Catlett	Kerry James Marshall
Nick Cave	David McGee
Willie Cole	Archibald Motley
Eldzier Cortor	Horace Pippin
Allan Crite	Harriet Powers
Frank Cummings	Walter Simon
Beauford Delany	Art Smith
Aaron Douglass	Hughie Lee Smith
Dave Drake	Henry Ossawa Tanner
Robert Duncanson	Kara Walker
William Edmundson	Fred Wilson
Robert Freeman	John Wilson
Ellen Gallagher	Hale Woodruff
Sedrick Huckaby	Richard Yarde
Sargent Johnson	

John Ahearn	"Raymond and Freddy"
John Singleton Copley	"Watson and the Shark"
Robert Gwathmey	"Sharecropper & Blackberry Pickers"
William Sidney Mount	"The Bone Player"
William Matthew Prior	"Three Sisters of the Copeland Family"
John Singer Sargent	"Nude Study of Thomas E. McKeller"
Thomas Sully	"The Passage of the Delaware"
John Turnbull	"The Death of General Warren at Battle of Bunker's Hill 17 June 1775"
J.M.W. Turner	"The Slave Ship"
Anonymous	"Portrait Pitcher of Toussaint L'Ouverture"

EKUA HOLMES MURAL: "CROSSWALKS & BUS STOPS"
Northeastern Campus
Huntington Ave. &
Parker St.

In 2016, Northeastern University installed a major public art mural by Boston artist, Ekua Holmes, a graduate of Massachusetts College of Art. *"Crosswalks and Bus Stops"* celebrated Holmes's memory of the close-knit Roxbury community in which she was raised.

> *"Those relationships left impressions that are now infused in the layers of my collages and elicit both fond recollections and universal life lessons..."*
> - EKUA HOLMES.

The mural is prominently sited on the exterior of the Computer Technology Building, at the gateway from Northeastern's institutional campus to the residential neighborhoods of Roxbury and Mission Hill.

In 2015, Google commissioned Holmes to create a work of art for their home page to honor Martin Luther King, Jr. on the MLK holiday. That work of art received extensive rcognition. Holmes also won the Caldecott

Honor in 2016 for her illustrations for the children's book, *Voice of Freedom, Fannie Lou Hamer.*

 CEDRIC DOUGLAS MURAL: "A WORLD OF INNOCENT DISCOVERY"
Northeastern University,
Behrakis Health Sciences
Center
30 Leon St.

Cedric Douglas, a public artist, completed this mural at the end of a 2015–2016 artist-in-residence position at Northeastern's Center for the Arts. Douglas's first art creation occurred in 1994. Sixteen at the time, he painted a cartoon on a basketball court in his hometown of Quincy. Although that effort led to an encounter with the police, Douglas has created art ever since.

Douglas has a firm belief in the power of public art to influence community outcomes. Two of the initiatives that he developed were "Up the Walls" to encourage the installation of more street art in Boston; and the UpTruck, a mobile arts lab to engage as many residents of Upman's Corner, a Boston neighbhood, as possible to collaborate on ideas for a public art installation for that community.

11 CORETTA SCOTT KING NEW ENGLAND CONSERVATORY

290 Huntington Ave.
617-585-4018
www.necmusic.edu

Founded in 1867, the New England Conservatory of Music is the oldest music school in the United States and one of the foremost schools in the world for the study of classical music. Coretta Scott King (1927–2006) was one of its famous graduates. She studied voice here in the early 1950s. During her studies in Boston, Coretta Scott married Martin Luther King, Jr.

The New England Conservatory is the only music school listed on the National Register of Historic Places because of its world-wide influence. Jor-

dan Hall, its main concert hall, is one of the premier performance halls for its size, 600 seats, in the world. The New England Conservatory has spread an appreciation and love of music in the region because of the free concerts it offers most evenings throughout the year.

12 ROLAND HAYES SYMPHONY HALL

301 Massachusetts Ave.
617-266-1492
www.bso.org
Three annual discounted family concerts. Free tours of the building.

On November 15th, 1917, the African American tenor, Roland Hayes (1887–1977), rented Symphony Hall

New England Conservatory of Music Jordan Hall

for a self-sponsored concert. He advertised the concert through the mail with over 3,000 announcements. That sold-out performance launched his phenomenally successful music career.

Born in Georgia on a tenant farm, Hayes received his first music lessons from his father and an appreciation of African American spiri-

Symphony Hall

tuals from his childhood church. After his father's death when he was eleven, Hayes's mother moved the family to Chattanooga, Tennessee. His first formal music lessons were at Fisk University in Nashville. There he toured with the Fisk Jubilee Singers.

Hayes eventually relocated to Boston to continue his music training. After his successful performance at Symphony Hall, Hayes went on a concert tour around the world which included a command performance for the King and Queen of England. Symphony Hall eventually engaged Roland Hayes to give concerts on a regular basis. His love of African American spirituals led him to include them in his concerts at every opportunity.

Roland Hayes experienced high levels of discrimination throughout his career yet he never allowed that to discourage him. Hayes shared his love of music through individual music lessons to private students from his home in Brookline.

Roland Hayes

BERKLEE COLLEGE OF MUSIC
1140 Boylston St.

Berklee College of Music

Some of the great African American names in jazz graduated from Berklee College of Music. Those famous alumni included: Quincy Jones, Branford Marsalis, Keith Jarrett, and Cyrus Chesnutt. The school's founder, Lawrence Berk (NAA), opened the school in 1945 as Schillinger House. He envisioned the school as a place to train musicians specifically for positions in the emergent radio and TV industries. By 1954, the school had grown to over 500 students. That year, Berk changed the school's name to Berklee College of Music, to reflect its larger enrollment and to focus on contemporary music.

Berklee presented its first honorary doctorate in 1971 to jazz composer, Duke Ellington (1899-1974). Ellington's selection was an acknowledgment of the importance to Berklee of its jazz roots. The John Coltrane Memorial Jazz Concert has become an annual Spring event, and the annual Berklee Beantown Jazz Festival in the Fall has grown into one of the premier jazz festivals in New England. Today's annual enrollment of over 4,000 students has made Berklee one of the largest independent music schools in the country.

Duke Ellington

BRIGHTON

 ## HORATIO JULIUS HOMER AND EVERGREEN CEMETERY
2060 Commonwealth Ave.

Horatio Julius Homer (1848–1923) was Boston's first African American police officer after his appointment in 1878. Homer was interred at Evergreen Cemetery.

South End Map, 2010

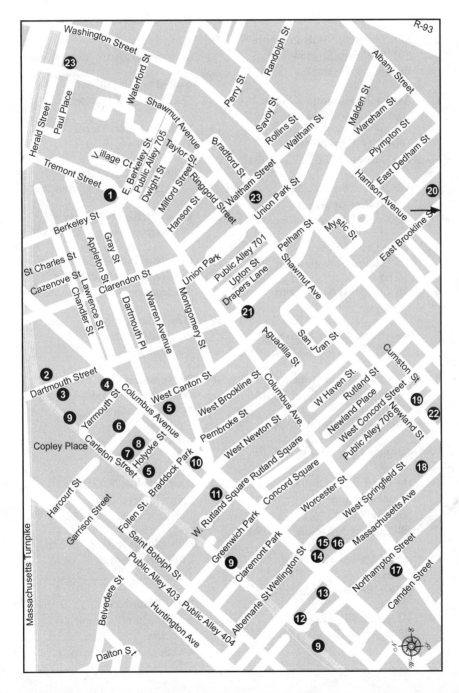

SOUTH END

THE GEOGRAPHICAL area of the South End, as we know it today, did not exist when Boston was founded in the mid-1600s. Instead, colonial Boston was connected to Roxbury by a narrow strip of land called the *"Boston Neck."* This strip of land, little more than one block wide in some areas, stretched along Washington St. from Essex St. in Chinatown, to roughly where Union Park St. is today in the South End. During the colonial era, a fortified gate existed at Washington and E. Berkeley St., the narrowest point of the *"Boston Neck."*

On the southeast side of that narrow neck of land was the marshland of South Boston Bay. In the early 1800s, real estate developers filled in South Boston Bay, laid out a grid of streets, and named the area the South End to acknowledge its position as Boston's southern anchor.

Developers intended for this newly created land to become a gracious neighborhood and they began to build a community of elegant townhomes by 1848. Before the new neighborhood had an opportunity to become established, waves of immigrants poured into Boston and quickly filled the area. The South End soon became a neighborhood of boarding houses. In the late 1800s and early 1900s, African American institutions that previously called Beacon Hill home relocated to the South End to follow their constituents.

 SITE: HARRIET E. WILSON HOUSE

Site: 15 Village St.,
now East Berkeley &
Tremont St.

Harriet E. Wilson (1825–1900) was the first African American to publish a novel in the continental United States with the publication of *Our Nig, or Sketches from the Life of a Free Black* in 1859. Wilson's novel was discovered in 1981 by African American studies scholar, Henry Louis Gates, Jr. Wilson lived at this address from 1879 until 1897. She served as general housekeeper and manager of this two-story boardinghouse.

Wilson was born free as Hattie Adams in Milford, NH. At a young age, Hattie's father died and her mother abandoned her. Those circumstances forced Hattie to become an indentured servant to the Hayward family (NAA) until she was eighteen. The cruelty of that existence was the basis of *Our Nig*. It exposed the oppressive treatment that African Americans frequently were forced to endure at the hands of some white Northerners.

Wilson became a single parent after her first husband, Thomas Wilson, abandoned her. She wrote the novel as a way to support her infant but her candid observations of Northern racism hindered the novel's success. Wilson placed her son in an orphanage because she could not support him. Her economic struggles took a toll on her family and her son died at the age of seven.

After her son's death, Wilson moved to Boston for better opportunities. In Boston, she married her second husband, John Gallatin Robinson (NAA). They lived from 1870 until 1877 at 46 Carver St. in the area of downtown Boston known today as Bay Village. The couple separated but never divorced. Wilson relocated to the South End shortly after. She worked as a spiritualist and a housekeeper for the remainder of her life. Harriet Wilson died in Quincy Hospital and was buried at Mount Wollaston Cemetery in Quincy. The town of Milford, NH has erected a statue in her honor.

Preface to *Our Nig*:

"In offering to the public the following pages, the writer confesses her inability to minister to the refined and cultivated, the pleasure supplied by abler pens. It is not for such these crude narrations appear. Deserted by kindred, disabled by failing health, I am forced to some experiment which shall aid me in maintaining myself and child without extinguishing this feeble life. I would not from these motives even palliate slavery at the South, by disclosures of its appurtenances North. My mistress was wholly imbued with southern principles. I do not pretend to divulge every transaction in my own life, which the unprejudiced would declare unfavorable in comparison with treatment of legal bondmen; I have purposely omitted what would most provoke shame in our good anti-slavery friends at home.

My humble position and frank confession of errors will, I hope shield me from severe criticism. Indeed, defects are so apparent it requires no skilful hand to expose them.

I sincerely appeal to my colored brethren universally for patronage, hoping they will not condemn this attempt of their sister to be erudite, but rally around me a faithful band of supporters and defenders.

H.E.W." (sic)

2 ASA PHILLIP RANDOLPH STATUE
Back Bay Station
Dartmouth and Stuart St.

In 1986, the Massachusetts Department of Transportation honored Asa Phillip Randolph (1889–1979), a civil rights activist and union organizer, with a statue, designed by African American sculptor, Tina Allen, at this transportation hub because he organized the Brotherhood of Sleeping Car Porters in 1925. This 10,000 member organization was the first labor union organized specifically for African Americans.

A. Phillip Randolph

hour, led Ashley Totten, a Sleeping Car Porter, to attempt to organize the workers in 1924. When the Pullman Company fired Totten, he asked Randolph to take over. The Brotherhood was officially founded on August 25th, 1925.

After the organized workers were unable to negotiate with the Pullman Company, they began a bitter strike in 1925. A panel exhibit on the history of the Sleeping Car Porters and the struggle they undertook to organize their union is located in the lobby of Back Bay Station. The strike lasted twelve years until 1937 when the union won a contract with the Pullman Company.

A job as a sleeping car porter was one of the few secure jobs available to African American men from the 1920s through the 1950s. The stability of those positions allowed the men who held them to give their families financial security. That security allowed those families to take the first steps toward economic mobility.

Despite that security, the life of a sleeping car porter was anything but easy. Strenuous work conditions, (they worked an average of 400 hours a month, nearly three times today's average of 160 hours of work a month), and the low pay, $0.26 an

Asa Phillip Randolph Statue

Brotherhood of Sleeping Car Porters		
	Pre-strike	Post-strike
Hours per month	400	240
Pay	$0.26 / hour	$0.50 / hour
Name	George	Birth name

the Presidential Medal of Freedom in 1964 for his contributions to social justice. The United States Postal Service issued a stamp to honor Randolph in 1989.

Before the strike, all the men had to answer to the name of George, which was the first name of the founder of the company. It was derisive and undignified, a throwback to the ante-bellum era when African American men were frequently called, *"Uncle."* One of the concessions of the strike was that the men were to be called by their birth name and not the generic name of *"George."*

Randolph spearheaded several other civil rights victories in the first half of the 20th century. In 1941, his threat of a protest march on Washington, D.C. led President Franklin Delano Roosevelt (NAA) to issue Executive Order 8802 which ended discrimination in the industries that supported the war efforts. In 1948, he used similar tactics to persuade President Harry S. Truman (NAA) to issue Executive Order 9981 that ended discrimination in the armed forces.

Randolph also co-organized the famous, *"March on Washington"* protest in 1963 with Bayard Rustin. That march was attended by over 250,000 people, one of the largest marches to date on the nation's capital. The climax was Martin Luther King, Jr., when he delivered his *"I Have A Dream"* speech.

President Lyndon Baines Johnson (NAA) awarded A. Phillip Randolph

A. Phillip Randolph's Civic Achievements	
1925	Organized the Brotherhood of Sleeping Car Porters
1941	Persuaded President Roosevelt to issue Executive Order 8802 that ended discrimination in war industries
1948	Persuaded President Truman to issue Executive Order 9981 that ended discrimination in the Armed Forces
1963	Organized the March on Washington with Bayard Rustin
1964	Awarded the Presidential Medal of Freedom by President Johnson

"...Justice is never given; it is exacted, and the struggle must be continuous for freedom is never a final fact, but a continuing, evolving process to higher and higher levels of human, social, economic, political, and religious relationships".
- A. PHILLIP RANDOLPH

"...A community is democratic only when the humblest and weakest person can enjoy the highest civil, economic, and social rights that the biggest and most powerful possess".
- A. PHILLIP RANDOLPH

Back Bay Station is one of the largest stations on the Orange Line. It is the hub for several modes of mass transportation including the Orange Line subway, Amtrak train service, the commuter rail, and local bus service.

 ### 3 TENT CITY APARTMENTS
130 Dartmouth St.

Tent City, a 269-unit, mixed-income apartment complex, owes its existence to the persistence and dedication of many housing activists in the Boston community. Those activists felt that the interests and needs of the poor residents of the city were ignored when city officials in the late 1960s planned Copley Place, a $500 million, high-end office, retail, and hotel complex.

Inspired by the Poor People's March of the civil rights era, African American community activist, Mel King, and several others, organized protests against the massive construction project after developers demolished a three-acre block of townhouses to clear land for a parking garage for the development.

These protests morphed into demonstrations by individuals on the site on April 25th, 1968. On that day, police arrested twenty-three protesters, including Mel King. Released on bond, they immediately returned to the site. Within three days, between 100 and 300 protesters lived and slept in tents on the grounds of the construction site. Thousands of others came to support their cause. The media named the protest site, Tent City, because so many citizens joined the struggle.

April 25th, 1968
Tent City Protests led to the arrest of 23 Protesters

April 30th, 1988
Tent City Housing Development finally opened

The city and the developers negotiated with the protesters, and one of the concessions led to the construction of a mixed-income housing complex on the site, Tent City. The architecture firm of Goody Clancy Associates (NAA) designed the housing complex to relate to the residential design features of the ur-

Tent City Apartment Complex

ban neighborhood. Tent City Housing Development finally opened in 1988, twenty years after the initial protests. An exhibit that documented the history of the protest effort was installed in the lobby of the Tent City development.

In addition to the housing development, the community won another concession, the developers had to reserve a portion of retail space at the mall for locally owned, small businesses. Those retail shops were called, The Dartmouth Street Shops.

4 MEL KING & SOUTH END TECHNOLOGY CENTER
359 Columbus Ave.

Community activist, Mel King (b. 1928), spearheaded the Tent City protests during the 1960s and 1970s. He also founded the South End Technology Center to provide computer training to teenagers. King grew up in the South End. After he graduated from Claflin College in South Carolina in the late 1960s, he returned to the South End to help his community.

Mel King decided to do something about the problem faced by many of his South End neighbors who lost their homes due to gentrification. His protests of the Boston Redevelopment Authority's attempts to centralize planning for South End communities led him to organize the group CAUSE, Community Assembly for a United

South End. CAUSE forced the city to include citizen input in their planning for the South End. The development of Tent City was a direct outcome of CAUSE's efforts. Mel King also participated in the protests over the Southwest Corridor Project.

Mel King

In 1972, King won election to the Massachusetts State Legislature. In his role as a legislator, King sponsored a study to replace federal programs with state programs for the development of vacant parcels along the Southwest Corridor. This led to the formation of the Massachusetts Community Development Finance Corporation (MCDFC). Funds from this agency allowed community development corporations to organize in order to address development for their respective neighborhoods along the corridor. This agency still exists and continues to provide funds for community development.

These community development groups dedicated their resources to the development of low-income housing for residents displaced by the Southwest Corridor project. They also created opportunities for minority businesses. Several of the groups still operate today, including Madison Park Development Corp., Urban Edge, and the Jamaica Plain Neighborhood Development Corp. They have been able to build hundreds of low and middle-income housing units throughout Southwest Corridor parcels, as well as on parcels in their communities.

Mel King's Civic Activities
- Led Tent City Protests
- Organized CAUSE, Community Assembly for a United South End
- Won election as a State Legislator in 1972
- Was a Professor in MIT's Urban Studies Dept.
- Spearheaded the formation of MCDFC, Mass. Comm. Develop Finance Corp.
- Was the first African American to mount a serious campaign for Mayor of Boston in 1983
- Founded the South End Technology Center

"...I grew up at a time when the images shown of people like me were negative. Then I got a chance to go to college in South Carolina. There was a movie theater there, the State. It was owned by and run by black folks. They showed films with people who looked like me, who were doing everyday things. I learned then the big issue was who controlled the content."
- MEL KING

"...for all they've talked about improving the city schools, we've had a system of low expectations. We've had algebra as a ceiling when calculus should be the floor."
- MEL KING

"...I was in the legislature ten years. The day it felt good that somebody opened the door for me and said, "Hello, Mr. Representative"—I knew that it was the time to go."
- MEL KING

"...A statement I picked up way back was, "We complain about the dirt, and we have the broom in our hands."
- MEL KING

In 1983, King was the first African American to mount a serious campaign to become mayor of Boston. Although that effort was unsuccessful, it raised the political participation of African Americans in Boston. They cast 90% of their votes for King.

5 ALLAN CRITE HOUSE
410 Columbus Avenue

Allan Crite's (1910–2006) family relocated to Boston from New Jersey before he was ten years old. They settled in this house on Tremont St. where Crite lived for the remainder of his life. Allan Crite received his early art education at the Museum School, the education arm of the Museum of Fine Arts.

Allan Crite House

Allan Crite

In the 1930s, he participated in the Harmon Foundation exhibits. Those exhibits highlighted the work of African American artists in exhibition tours across the country. Crite recorded many of the social activities in his community during the 1930s in his paintings. The architecture of the South End served as a prominent backdrop to those scenes. Those paintings documented the history of the changes in the South End that occurred in his lifetime.

Crite's paintings reside in many prominent museum collections in the United States such as the Boston Museum of Fine Art, the Athenaeum on Beacon Hill, and the Smithsonian in Washington, D.C. Allan Crite was an inspiration and mentor to many Boston artists due to his longevity, talent, and generousity of time and resources.

6 DR. CORNELIUS N. GARLAND
225 West Canton St.

In 1908, Dr. Cornelius N. Garland (d. 1952) founded the first hospital in Boston, Plymouth Hospital, to specifically cater to African American clients. Dr. Garland also maintained a private practice at this location.

Dr. Garland was born in Alabama and he received his medicsl degree from Shaw University in 1901. He moved to Boston after he completed post-graduate studies in England. Dr. Garland opened Plymouth Hospital when he could not obtain an medical affiliation with any of the local hospitals. See more under South End site #22. Dr. Garland was buried at Forest Hills Cemetery in Jamaica Plain.

 7 SUSIE KING TAYLOR HOUSE
23 Holyoke St.

Born enslaved on a Georgia plantation, Susie King Taylor (1848–1912) went to live in Savannah, GA with her grandmother, Mrs. Dolly Reed, at the age of seven. Mrs. Reed had acquired a degree of financial and personal autonomy and this enabled her to pay a white tutor to secretly teach Susie how to read and write. It was against the law to teach an African American to read or write in the South in that period. At the outbreak of the Civil War, Susie joined the Union Army at Fort Pulaski. From 1862 through 1865, she served in the Union Army as a teacher, laundress, and nurse.

After the war, Susie, by then, a young widow, settled in Boston where she served as President of the Women's Relief Corps, a volunteer organization that provided aid and assistance to soldiers and veterans. In 1902, Susie Taylor

Susie King Taylor House (23 Holyoke) and Harriet Tubman House (25 Holyoke)

published a memoir of her life and life at the Union Camp, *Reminiscences of My Life in Camp with the 33D United States Colored Troops.*

"...*My mother was born in 1834. She married Raymond Baker in 1847. Nine children were born to them, three dying in infancy. I was the first born. I was born on the Grest Farm (which was on an island known as Isle of Wight), Liberty County, about thirty-five miles from Savannah, Ga., on August 6, 1848, my mother being waitress for the Grest family. I have often been told by mother of the care Mrs. Grest took of me. She was very fond of me, and I remember when my brother and I were small children, and Mr. Grest would go away on business, Mrs. Grest would place us at the foot of her bed to sleep and keep her company. Sometimes he would return home earlier than he had expected to; then she would put us on the floor.*

...When I was about seven years old, Mr. Grest allowed my grandmother to take my brother and me to live with her in Savannah. ...

...My grandmother went every three months to see my mother. She would hire a wagon to carry bacon, tobacco, flour, molasses, and sugar. These she would trade with people in the neighboring places, for eggs, chickens, or cash, if they had it. These, in turn, she carried back to the city market, where she had a customer who sold them for her. The profit from these, together with laundry work and care of some bachelors' rooms, made a good living for her.

...The hardest blow to her was the failure of the Freedmen's Savings Bank in Savannah, for in that bank she had placed her savings, about three thousand dollars, the result of her hard labor and self-denial before the war, and which, by dint of shrewdness and care, she kept together all through the war. She felt it more keenly, coming as it did in her old age, when her life was too far spent to begin anew; but she took a practical view of the matter, for she said, "I will leave it all in God's hand. If the Yankees did take all our money, they freed my race; God will take care of us."

...He said Captain Whitmore had spoken to him of me, and that he was pleased to hear of my being so capable, etc., and wished me to take charge of a school for the children on the island. I told him I would gladly do so, if I could have some books. He said I should have them, and in a week or two I received two large boxes of books and testaments from the North. I had about forty children to teach, beside a number of adults who came to me nights, all of them so eager to learn to read, to read above anything else. ...There were about six hundred men, women, and children on St. Simon's, the women and children being in the majority, ...;"

– Susie King Taylor

Susie King Taylor

Taylor was buried in an unmarked grave at the Mount Hope Cemetery in Roslindale.

⑧ HARRIET TUBMAN HOUSE
25 Holyoke St.

In 1904, six African American women opened a settlement house in this building to assist African American girls recently relocated from the South. This structure was originally the home of Julia Henson (NAA), a good friend of Harriet Tubman. Tubman often stayed here on her frequent trips to Boston. Henson donated her home to the new group and they appointed Harriet Tubman as honorary president in 1913. The group renamed itself, the *Harriet Tubman House,* shortly thereafter to honor Ms. Tubman whose steely determination and bravery freed thousands.

> *"Every great dream begins with a dreamer. Always remember, you have within you the strength, the patience and the passion to reach for the stars to change the world."*
> —HARRIET TUBMAN

Harriet Tubman

⑨ SOUTHWEST CORRIDOR PROJECT
Orange Line Subway and Southwest Corridor Park

The state developed the Orange Line Subway along a tract of land known as the Southwest Corridor in the mid-1980s. This subway line and the development that occurred adjacent to it,

187

owed their existence to a group of determined and concerned citizens. The genesis of the project dated from 1948. That year, the Federal Government developed a Master Highway Plan for Metropolitan Boston. They wanted to provide easy access from downtown Boston to nearby suburban communities which contained newly built residences for the veterans of WWII.

That trend to develop new residential communities on the outskirts of cities occurred all across the country. Those developments required massive highways to bring commuters quickly into the city for jobs and quickly out at the end of the day, without the need to drive through what was commonly perceived as, unacceptable urban neighborhoods.

The highways and the new suburban communities they serviced were subsidized by the Federal Government. Although the GI bill was available to any recent veteran, the new communities incorporated covenant restrictions to keep certain ethnic groups out, primarily African American families. Those new suburban communities, and the highways that serviced them, represented two blatant examples of the physical and financial manifestation of institutionalized racism in this country.

Land acquisition for the Southwest Corridor highway began in the late 1950s through a process of eminent domain. Demolition cleared a swath of land through Boston in the 1960s. It destroyed neighborhoods, it uprooted families, and it demolished over 120 acres of urban neighborhoods.

Southwest Corridor Map

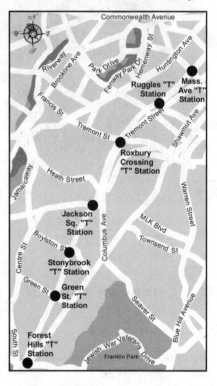

Timeline of Southwest Corridor Project	
1948	Federal government developed a Master Highway Plan to extend an 8- to 12- lane highway through Boston
1950s	Land acquired by eminent domain
1960s	Design finalized and demolition begun
1960s	Hundreds of demonstrations to stop the I-95 Connector through Boston led Gov. Sargent to cancel the highway
1973	Gov. Sargent persuaded Congress to transfer the Fedederal Highway funds to the state for local Mass Transit
1976	Consultants selected
1977	Design and engineering began
1979	Construction began
1987	Orange Line opened

Meanwhile, the old diesel trains, which the highway was supposed to displace, continued to roll on the tracks. Environmentally contaminated exhaust continued to be spewed into the air of the adjacent communities. The strong history of environmentally compromised transportation and manufacturing systems located in those neighborhoods led to a direct correlation between those facilities and the high incident of people, especially children, in urban Boston neighborhoods, who suffered from respiratory illnesses, notably asthma.

The federal government intended for the highway to cut a swath through Boston and continue through Cambridge, but by the 1960s, Boston and Cambridge citizens had enough. They mobilized to limit any further destruction of their communities with protests that declared: *"Stop I-95: People before Highways"*.

Their protests forced an end to the highway project. It was replaced with the Orange Line Subway. The African American architecture firm of Stull and Lee won the award for urban design and architectural coordination for the entire project. Stull and Lee also won the award as architect for one of the largest stations in the project, the Ruggles St. "T" Station. At its completion, the Southwest Corridor Subway Project was the largest and most expensive infrastructure project in the state.

> **Orange Line Subway**
> - Completed 1988
> - $800 million Total Cost
> - 30 different consultants
> - 47 separate contracts
> - Eight subway stations
> - 50 - acre park adjacent to corridor
> - 4.7 miles in length

The citizens also demanded that the development of the parcels adjacent to the subway, known as the SW Corridor, should primarily benefit the communities displaced by the massive construction project. That demand led to the development of 143 adjacent acres into a new community college, two new high schools, a regional track and gym, nearly 1,000 units of affordable housing, a neighborhood health center, and many community gardens. Public art was integrated throughout the new subway stations and along the corridor.

This process also required that the privilege for developers to develop any of those 143 acres of parcels was linked to the opportunity for minority developers to participate in the development of downtown properties (see Lincoln Tower in downtown sites). This urban development concept was known as *"Linkage."*

A residual accomplishment of the Southwest Corridor project was that it was able to successfully nurture minority businesses. Many minority firms, especially those in the construction industries, gained valuable business experience through their participation on Southwest Corridor contracts.

10 HARRIET TUBMAN SQUARE "EMANCIPATION" "GET ON BOARD"

450 Columbus Avenue

In 1999, Boston dedicated this square to honor Harriet Tubman (1820–1913). Tubman often visited Boston before the Civil War to speak to abolitionists in the area. Tubman was famous for her legendary escape from bondage in Maryland in 1849. The tenacity and courage she exhibited during many subsequent trips to the South to lead others to freedom, despite personal danger, elevated her life to a level of heroic statue in the African American community.

Harriet Tubman, born Araminta Ross, refused to be defined by others, and she did not allow others to determine her destiny. She experienced much cruelty in her early life. In her youth, she was beaten so severely that she suffered blackouts for the remainder of her life. During her adolescent and teen years, her parents taught her how to navigate through the woods and how to use nature to survive. That knowledge served her well on her later journeys. After her marriage to John Tubman in 1844, Harriet, desperate to be free, decided to escape bondage. She tried to get her husband to accompany her but he refused. Undeterred, Harriet made a successful solo journey. She adopted her mother's first name after her escape.

Encouraged by her success, Harriet Tubman made several subsequent trips to the South to assist many more individuals in their escape from bondage. She led her parents to freedom when they were both over seventy. Tubman worked as a scout for the Union Army in the Civil War. She also spearheaded raids during the war that led to the freedom of over 1,000 enslaved individuals. Those raids led to the destruction of many plantations. Tubman helped so many to escape bondage that she became known as, *"Moses."*

Meta Vaux Warrick Fuller designed this sculpture, *"Eman-*

"Emancipation" by Meta Vaux Warrick Fuller

cipation," in 1913. It was commissioned to honor the fiftieth anniversary of the *Emancipation Proclamation.* Fuller described her sculpture as:

> "Humanity weeping over her suddenly freed children, who, beneath the gnarled fingers of Fate step forth into the world, unafraid."
> - META VAUX WARRICK FULLER

> "I had reasoned this out in my mind, there was one of two things I had a right to, liberty or death; if I could not have one, I would have the other, for no man should take me alive. I should fight for my liberty as long as my strength lasted."
> -- HARRIET TUBMAN

"Get on Board" by Fern Cunningham

twenty dollar bill. She will be the first female portrayed on United States currency.

Fern Cunningham designed the sculpture, *"Get on Board,"* in the late 1990s. It depicted Tubman at the forefront of a group of men, women, and children as she led them to freedom. Tubman was a naturally assertive leader who always carried a bible and a gun. She threatened death to anyone who started the journey but wanted to quit mid-way.

In April of 2016, the U.S. Treasury announced plans to put a portrait of Harriet Tubman on the back of the

> "On my underground railroad I never ran my train off the track. And I never lost a passenger."
> - HARRIET TUBMAN

> "I freed a thousand slaves. I could have freed a thousand more if only they knew they were slaves."
> - HARRIET TUBMAN

(11) UNION UNITED METHODIST CHURCH
485 Columbus Ave.

Union United Methodist Church's original location during the early nineteenth century was on Beacon Hill. Its membership included activist, David Walker. By the late nineteenth century, the African American community and churches had nearly completely relocated from Beacon Hill. They primarily settled in the South End..

Union United Methodist Church relocated from Beacon Hill after the congregation built this new structure in 1872. The architect, Alexander Estey (NAA), designed this Gothic Revival style building which featured Roxbury puddingstone in its construction. Its tall stone spire has served as a landmark on Columbus Avenue since it opened.

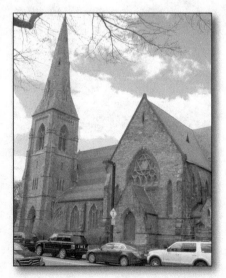
Union United Methodist Church

(12) MLK SITE: KING RESIDENCE
397 Massachusetts Ave.

The most famous African American in United States history, Martin Luther King, Jr. (1929–1968), lived here when he was a theology student at Boston University in the 1950s. King studied philosophical theology and was influenced by such spiritual leaders as Howard Thurman, St. Thomas Aquinas (NAA) and Mohandas Gandhi (NAA).

Martin Luther King, Jr.

After graduation, King returned to the South where he became the most influential figure of the Civil Rights movement through his leadership of the Southern Christian Leadership Council (SCLC). Martin Luther King, Jr. practiced a philosophy of nonviolent civil disobedience. He won a Nobel

Peace Prize in 1964 because of his widespread influence. In 1983, the United States Congress established a national holiday, the third Monday in January, to honor him.

Martin Luther King, Jr. House

 WALLY'S JAZZ CLUB
427 Massachusetts Avenue
2 pm to 2 am daily
617-424-1408

Wally's Jazz Club is Boston's only jazz club still in operation out of several clubs that were popular in the 1930s, 40s, and 50s. Some of those clubs were the High Hat, the Savoy Ballroom, and the Wig Wam. Several famous musicians, such as Charlie Parker, Billie Holiday, and Art Blakely, performed at Wally's during the big-band era.

Joseph Walcott (1905-1998), the founder, immigrated from Barbados in 1910. In 1947, he opened his first venture, Wally's Paradise, across the street at 428 Mass. Ave. Walcott was the first African American to own a nightclub in New England with Wally's. In 1979, Walcott changed the name to Wally's Jazz Club and moved the club to its current location. Today, it features live music 365 days a year.

When the Big Band era ended, Wally's remained relevant through its connections to younger musicians. It provided a venue for young jazz musicians from local music schools, such as Berklee College of Music, the Boston Conservatory and the New England Conservatory of Music, to jam with professionals on tour in order to improve the students' technique. Today, Walcott's children operate Wally's Jazz Club.

Wally's Jazz Club Sign

United South End Settlements

14 UNITED SOUTH END SETTLEMENTS

566 Columbus Avenue
617- 536-8610

The United South End Settlements was constructed in 1988 as the new home of the Harriet Tubman Center. The Center was formed to provide a wide range of social services for local residents. A gallery is located in the lobby with displays on contemporary art and exhibits on the life of Harriet Tubman.

Pullman Porter House

15 PULLMAN PORTER HOUSE

218 West Springfield St.

The Pullman Company used this traditional South End style 1860s boarding house as a dependable residence for its porters. Asa Phillip Randolph held the early meetings of the Brotherhood of Sleeping Car Porters on the first floor. The Brotherhood was the first union organized specifically for African Americans.

16 WOMEN'S SERVICE CLUB

464 Massachusetts Avenue

The Women's Service Club of Boston originated at the start the 20th century as a social service organization to assist African American women in need. Mary Evans Wilson (1865-1928) founded the organization with a group of African American women who originally met to knit for soldiers during WWI. The Women's Service Club purchased 464 Mass. Ave. in 1919. Melnea Cass (1896–1978), the Roxbury activist, served as president for nearly two decades.

Mary Evans Wilson

Mary Evans Wilson, born in Oberlin, Ohio, came from a long line of activists. Her uncle fought with John Brown at Harper's Ferry, and her father was jailed after he assisted a fugitive from slavery. After graduation from Oberlin College, Wilson taught for ten years in the Washington, D.C. schools. She and her husband, Butler Roland Wilson, a civil rights attorney, moved to Boston in 1894.

Wilson led the charge in many civil rights protests in Boston. She also transformed the leadership of the Boston NAACP from a predominantly white led organization to that run by African Americans.

 ## 17 PIANO FACTORY & GALLERY
791 Tremont Street

This was the largest piano factory in the nation when the Chickering Piano Company opened this building in 1854. At its peak, the factory employed over 600 workers and it produced 60 pianos a week. During the Civil War, a portion of the factory was used to produce the Spencer Repeating rifle.

In the late 1980s, developers converted this building into affordable housing for artists. Notable contemporary artists such as Paul Goodnight and Milton Derr have their studios here. A gallery that features the work of local contemporary African American artists such as Ekua Holmes is located on the lower level of the building.

Piano Factory

18 LEAGUE OF WOMEN FOR COMM. SERVICE / FARWELL MANSION
UGRR Station
558 Massachusetts Avenue

John Farwell (NAA), a wealthy sea captain and abolitionist, built this house in 1860 with a hidden staircase and tunnel to accommodate fugitives from slavery. The League of Women for Community Service has owned the house since 1920.

This African American women's service organization began in the early 1900s to assist women who sought employment. The organization also provided a safe place for African American women to board after they relocated to Boston. Maria Baldwin (1856-1922), the first African American to serve as a public school principal in the state, was the first president. See Cambridge sites for more on Baldwin. Coretta Scott King (1927-2006), Martin Luther King, Jr.'s wife, lived here in the 1950s when she was a student at the New England Conservatory of Music.

Coretta Scott King was instrumental in the establishment of Martin Luther King, Jr.'s birthday as a national holiday. She continued to advocate for the civil rights of others all her life.

Coretta Scott King

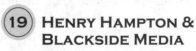

"...Hate is too great a burden to bear. It injures the hater more than it injures the hated..."
– CORETTA SCOTT KING

19 HENRY HAMPTON & BLACKSIDE MEDIA
486 Shawmut Ave.

Filmmaker, Henry Hampton (1940-1998) conceived and produced the award winning documentary, *"Eyes on the Prize,"* in the 1980s. This series about the civil rights movement forever changed America's perception of the people who made that pivotal movement happen. It also brought the history of the movement alive for a younger generation. Hampton formed Blackside Media in 1968 as an independent film production company. In the 1970s, he focused on films that raised awareness about African American history.

> *"...If you're black in America, race is a factor in your life. Start with that assumption."*
> – HENRY HAMPTON

> *"...Food might be more important than history but if you don't understand what's been done to you - by your own people and the so-called 'they' - you can never get around it."*
> – HENRY HAMPTON

Henry Hampton

Hampton contributed to many aspects of social activism and cultural enlightenment in Boston. One volunteer position was Chair of the Board of the Museum of Afro-American History. In that role, he and Ruth Batson spearheaded efforts to raise funds to renovate the museum in the late 1980s. Hampton received several honorary degrees for his accomplishments. He died from complications from lung cancer at Brigham and Women's Hospital in 1988.

Blackside Media Productions

20 DR. SOLOMON CARTER FULLER DMH COMM. HEALTH CENTER
85 East Newton St.

Solomon Carter Fuller (1872–1953), the first African American licensed to practice psychiatry in the United States, dedicated his career to research to understand how Alzheimer's disease affects the brain. The Massachusetts Department of Mental Health dedicated this mental health research facility to honor Dr. Fuller in 1974.

Dr. Solomon Carter Fuller Plaque

Dr. Fuller was born in Liberia where his father emigrated to from America. Solomon Carter Fuller relocated to the United States where he pursued medical studies at Boston University Medical School. After he graduated in 1897, he practiced medicine in Boston and Framingham. Dr. Fuller married the sculptor, Meta Vaux Warrick and they settled in Framingham. See Framingham and South End sites.

21 VILLA VICTORIA HOUSING
640 Tremont

In the early 1960s, cities cleared inner city neighborhoods around the country in the name of urban renewal. Behind the concept of urban renewal was the theory that urban neighborhoods were incubators of crime and decay. Many politicians believed that the only way to solve that problem was to wipe the slate clean and began anew, hence the term, *"urban renewal."*

Dr. Solomon Carter Fuller Building

In preparation for its urban renewal plan for Boston, the government cleared parts of the South End for the planned I-95 highway project and for other new residential and commercial construction. The community brought the I-95 project to a halt

Villa Victoria

recreation, and social service uses interwoven throughout the development. John Sharratt (NAA) Associates designed the complex in 1972 to successfully incorporate many ideas about public and private space fundamental to Latino communities.

but not before many residents had been displaced as a result of the demolition.

The Villa Victoria housing site, a block bound by West Dedham, Tremont, Shawmut, and Brookline, was known as Parcel 19. Many of the displaced Puerto Rican residents of Parcel 19 organized into the group, Inquilinos Boricuas en Accion (IBA). Their rallying cry was, *"We shall not be moved from Parcel 19."* They demanded to be part of any process to plan for the site. Villa Victoria was the outcome. Villa Victoria included a multi-generational residential community with retail,

 ## DR. CORNELIUS N. GARLAND & PLYMOUTH HOSPITAL
12 East Springfield St.

Dr. Cornelius N. Garland (d.1952) founded Plymouth Hospital in 1908 at this location. This was the first hospital founded specifically for African American patients. Dr. Garland operated the facility as both a hospital and a facility to train nurses. He originally opened the hospital because none of the local hospitals would grant him affiliation status. Dr. Garland was pressured to close Plymouth in 1928 because many in the local African American community felt that the existence of that facility took the obligation away from the white hospitals to integrate their facilities.

Villa Victoria Sign

23 HUBIE JONES & BOSTON CHILDREN'S CHORUS
112 Shawmut St.

Hubie Jones (B. 1933), a social activist and retired Dean of Boston University's School of Social Work, founded the Boston Children's Chorus (BCC) in 2003. Inspired by Kenneth Clark, his professor at the City College of New York, Jones dedicated his life to use the social sciences to create social change, particularly for children.

Jones formed numerous organizations that improved the quality of life for Boston youth. When he was Director of the Roxbury Multi-Service Center from 1967 to 1971, Jones orchestrated the enactment of two state laws to improve education access, the Special Education Law, and the Bilingual Education Law.

Boston Children's Chorus began with twenty students in its first year. Today, over 450 students a year participate in its various programs. The Chorus combines a rigorous immersion in choral music with social activism. In 2010, Jones received the $50,000 Purpose Prize for seniors who are catalysts for social change.

> "We do not merely have a social responsibility to assure that our children and youth have decent life chances and prosper. We have a sacred obligation to do so."
> – JONES

Hubie Jones

24 LOCAL RESOURCES
Massachusetts Historical Society
1154 Boylston St.
617-536-16098
www.masshist.org
Free admission

O'Bryant African American Institute
Northeastern University
40 Leon St.
617-373-3143
www.northeastern.edu/aai

SOUTH BOSTON

ARTISTS FOR HUMANITY
100 West Second St.
www.afh.com

Three African American teenagers, Damon Butler, Rob Gibbs, and Jason Talbot founded Artists for Humanity (AFH) in 1990 with artist, Susan Rodgerson (NAA) as an entrepreneurial incubator for teen artists. Their mission:

> *"...to bridge economic, racial and social divisions by providing underserved youth with the keys to self-sufficiency through paid employment in the arts".*
> - AFH MISSION STATEMENT.

AFH has become well known for the high caliber of artistic products produced by its members. They have successfully provided alternative paths to teens who risked juvenile delinquency. Many other art groups across the country now replicate AFH's successful model for artistic mentorship.

In 2004, AFH moved into its headquarters at 100 West Second St. in South Boston, the EpiCenter. This new facility was the city's first LEED Platinum building. LEED was developed as a metric to measure the sustainability of buildings and a Platinum rating was the highest that could be achieved.

SOUTH BOSTON HIGH SCHOOL, NOW EXCEL HIGH SCHOOL
95 G. Street

In the early 1970s, South Boston High School was the site of much of the violence that occurred from Boston's mandate to bus students to achieve an integrated school population. In 1974, the inequities that resulted from Boston's historically segregated communities had escalated to an explosive level. Employment discrimination was rampant, especially in government jobs, and the

Artists for Humanity Building

banks redlined those residents into crowded neighborhoods such as Roxbury, Mattapan, and North Dorchester where the public schools were extremely deteriorated with few resources.

On June 21st, 1974, Federal Judge Arthur Garrity (NAA) determined that the inequitites of those schools were due to a deliberate decision by the Boston School Committee to maintain two separate systems. He ordered the city to immediately end the inequities through a city-wide busing desegregation program. The buses began to roll on Sept. 12th, 1974. That date became emblazoned in Boston's collective memory because of the violence that ensued. The violence lasted the entire school year.

The next school year, 1974–1975, the violence and protests by the white community against busing escalated.

Some of the most violent incidents occurred at South Boston High where on some days, 75% of the expected 1,500 students stayed home. At one point, 400 police were present to protect 500 students. The violence in the schools was matched by violence in the streets.

3 HAWES BURYING GROUND
East 5th Street

David Walker, the author of the radical abolitionist book, *Walker's Appeal*, was buried here in an unmarked grave. Hawes Burying Ground is the oldest cemetery in South Boston.

Roxbury Map

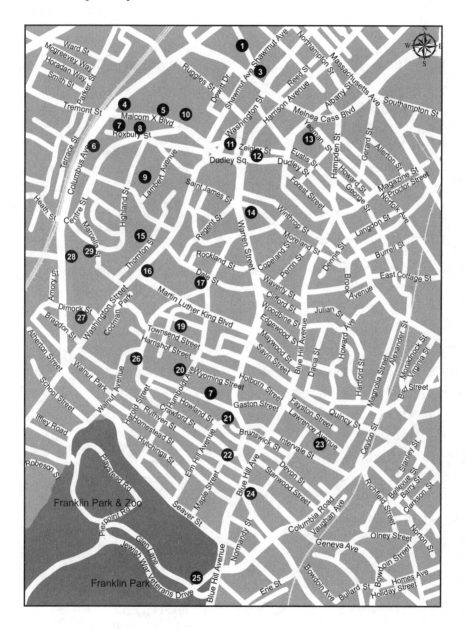

ROXBURY

EARLY COLONISTS settled Roxbury in 1630 as a farming community. It was the closest town on the key road of Washington St. which led to and from the important destination of Boston. That critical location made it an important stop for travelers. Its proximity to Boston and its high geographical elevation made it a strategic site in the American Revolution.

Roxbury eventually evolved into a suburb of the City of Boston. In Roxbury, Boston's wealthy families built spacious mansions as weekend and summer getaways in the mid-1800s to escape the crowded, urban environment of the city. Roxbury's name derived from the abundance of Puddingstone, a natural stone used in construction, found in the area.

Annexed by the City of Boston in 1867, Roxbury was home to many different immigrant groups over the years. A strong Irish presence existed in the late 1800s to the early 1900s. Several former synagogues were located in Roxbury because many in the Jewish community called it home at a time that overlapped with the Irish presence. Many of those structures remain. By the mid-1930s, African Americans began to move to Roxbury in large numbers. Today, Roxbury serves as the cultural center of the African American community of Boston.

 SITE: MARY ELIZA MAHONEY HOUSE
31 Westminister St.

This was the site of the childhood home of Mary Eliza Mahoney (1846-1926). Mahoney was the first African American registered nurse after she graduated from the nursing program at New England Hospital. Despite this exceptional accomplishment, only three others in Mahoney's class of forty finished the program, she still was not able to obtain work in her chosen profession.

Mary Eliza Mahoney

Mahoney took any nursing related job she could find because of her love for her occupation. That passion led her to co-found the National Association of Colored Graduate Nurses, NACGN, in order to encourage other African Americans to pursue that career.

August 1st, 1879
Mahoney became first African American registered nurse in the U.S.

Mahoney advocated for equal opportunity for women and supported the movement to give women the right to vote. In 1920 after women in the United States won the right to vote, Mahoney, at the age of 76, was among the first women in Boston to register to vote. The NACGN established an annual award in her honor in 1936 that continues to this day. Mahoney was buried at Woodlawn Cemetery in Everett.

2 COLUMBUS AVE.
Between Jackson Sq. "T" Station and the Ruggles "T" Station

Several important institutions in the Boston community were sited in this area of Columbus Ave.; Boston's Main Police Station, Madison Park Community Health Center, Roxbury Community College, and the Reggie Lewis Track and Athletic Facility. The African American architecture firm, Stull & Lee, designed three of those facilities, Ruggles "T" Station, the Main Police Station, and Roxbury Community College.

3 MELNEA CASS BOULEVARD

Melnea Cass (1896–1978) actively participated in Boston's African American civic community her entire adult life. In fact, she received the nickname, *"First Lady of Roxbury,"* because of her efforts to improve conditions for Boston's communities of color.

Despite her graduation as valedictorian of her high school class, few employment opportunities existed at the time for African American women with Cass's potential. She married Marshall Cass in 1917, and became a housewife and community organizer.

Melnea Cass

Melnea Cass's Civic Initiatives
- initiated policy to provide social security benefits to domestic workers
- co-founded Action for Boston Community Development (ABCD), a leading anti-poverty agency in the city
- demanded employment for African Americans in downtown department stores and hospitals

Northeastern University, Simmons College, and Boston College all bestowed honorary doctorates on Cass to thank her for her service to the community. The Melnea Cass Boulevard and the Melnea Cass MDC Swimming Pool and Skating Rink were named to honor her.

4 REGGIE LEWIS TRACK FACILITY
1350 Tremont St.

The Reggie Lewis Track and Athletic Center was named for the Boston Celtics basketball star, Reggie Lewis. Lewis served as a positive role model for young boys in the community when he prematurely died of a heart attack in 1993. Lewis was 27 at the time of his

death. The Reggie Lewis Athletic Center is the site of regional track meets and community functions.

Reggie Lewis

Reggie Lewis Athletic Center

5 MALCOLM X BOULEVARD

This important boulevard was renamed in the mid-1980s to honor Malcolm X, one of the most famous residents of Roxbury. Malcolm X Boulevard has served as a vital connection between the neighborhoods of Mission Hill and Dudley Square in Roxbury.

6 ROXBURY COMMUNITY COLLEGE
1234 Columbus Ave.

The State of Massachusetts established Roxbury Community College in 1968. Construction was completed on the campus in the late 1980s. Roxbury Community College was one of the projects developed on the Southwest Corridor parcels as a community benefit. The African American architecture firm of Stull and Lee designed this major project.

A significant sculpture, *"Father Reading to Son,"* by African American artist, John Wilson (1922–2015), was

Father Reading to Son by John Wilson

installed on the campus grounds after construction of the college was completed. A Roxbury native, Wilson graduated from the School of the Museum of Fine Arts in 1945 and from Tufts University in 1947. While a student, he discovered the Mexican muralists, Jose Clemente Orozco (NAA) and Diego Rivera (NAA). Those two artists focused on art as an agent for social change as did other Mexican artists in that period. Orozco and Rivera also used art to raise public awareness about important political and social issues. In 1950, John Wilson moved to Mexico to study firsthand the work of those art activists.

Wilson relocated to the United States in 1956. Back in Boston, he joined the art faculty at Boston Univer-

Roxbury Community College

sity in 1964. Although Wilson began his career with a focus on drawing and print-making, he is best known for his larger than life sculptures. See more on Wilson under Roxbury site, MN-CAAA.

7 ISLAMIC SOCIETY OF BOSTON MOSQUE
100 Malcolm X Blvd.

This mosque serves as the center of worship for over 70,000 Muslims throughout the metropolitan Boston area. In addition to worship space, the design included an elementary school for 300 students, a social hall, and funeral facilities. The 2005 building with its towering dome and minaret has served as a new landmark for the community. Its location on Malcolm X Blvd. is appropriate since Malcolm X was one of the most famous contemporary converts to the Muslim faith.

Islamic Society of Boston Cultural Center & Mosque

8 DILLAWAY THOMAS HOUSE
UGRR Station
183 Roxbury St.
10 to 4 Mon.-Fri.
617-445-3399

This parsonage was built in 1750 across the street from the First Church in Roxbury. The British used it in the American Revolution as headquarters for General John Thomas (NAA). Over 5,000 British troops were stationed here during that war. In the 1840s to the 1860s, the house was believed to be a station on the Underground Railroad. That history was discovered in the 1990s when renovation of the house revealed secret passageways.

Dillaway Thomas House

The Headmaster of Boston Latin School, Charles K. Dillaway (NAA), lived here during the early 1920s. After the house fell into disrepair, the Roxbury Historical Society saved it from demolition in 1927. It became their headquarters until the mid-1980s when the National Park Service took over its operation. The restored house is now the home of Roxbury Heritage

State Park. The restoration included a detailed layering of the architectural components of the construction to document and exhibit how the house was constructed and has changed over the years.

9 EDWARD EVERETT HALE HOUSE
12 Morely St.

Unitarian minister and author, Edward Everett Hale (1822–1909) (NAA) rallied those sympathetic to the Union cause with his famous short story, "*The Man Without a Country.*" The story was published in 1863, just at the start of the Civil War. Hale came from a distinguished family that included the orator, Edward Everett, and the American Revolutionary war hero, Nathan Hale (NAA). Nathan Hale was executed by the British as a spy. A statue of Edward Everett Hale was erected in the Boston Gardens.

> "...I am only one, but I am one. I cannot do everything, but I can do something. And I will not let what I cannot do interfere with what I can do...."
> -EDWARD EVERETT HALE

Since 1979, African American artist, Napoleon Jones-Henderson has resided in the historic Hale house.

Jones-Henderson was one of the founders of the art collective, Afri-Cobra. Afri-Cobra gave artistic expression to the principles of Black Nationalism in the 1960s and the 1970s. Henderson-Jones is a public artist whose medium is kilm-fired ceramics.

10 JOHN D. O'BRYANT SCHOOL & MADISON PARK TECHNICAL H.S.
75 Malcolm X Blvd.

The John D. O'Bryant School of Math and Science originated in 1893 as the Mechanics Arts High School. In 1944, it became the Boston Technical High School as one of only three public exam schools for Boston students. In 1992, the Boston School Committee renamed it to honor the first African American member of the Boston School Committee, John D. O'Bryant. O'Bryant won election to the Boston School Board in 1977.

The Madison Park Technical Vocational High School has served as Boston's premier technical vocational high school with an annual enrollment of over 1,600 students. Both of these institutions were relocated in the 1980s to newly constructed buildings on land that became available from the development of the Southwest Corridor.

On June 25th, 1990, Nelson Mandela visited the school during his worldwide tour after he was released from prison in

O'Bryant High School

South Africa. Mandela encouraged the students to use the force of education to make changes in the world. Twenty-five years after that visit, the gym where Mandela spoke was renamed the Nelson Mandela Gymnasium.

 11 DUDLEY SQUARE & DUDLEY STATION
Washington St. and
Dudley St.

Dudley Square has always been the commercial and cultural heart of Roxbury. This vibrant neighborhood center has constantly evolved to reflect the demographics of the residents of the immediate community. The earlier Irish and German immigrants established such institutions as Ferdinand's Blue Store, a popular New England department store, and Hiberian Hall, a social center for Irish Americans.

The period between 1910 to about 1935, saw the community change with an influx of Jewish residents.

Roxbury became the African American center of Boston as a result of the Northern migration of a great wave of African Americans from the South between World War I and II. Many African American churches relocated from Beacon Hill to Roxbury and the South End during this time to be near their new constituents.

Concurrent with this mass migration, discrimination in retail establishments became more entrenched. Retailers refused credit to African Americans and refused to allow them to try on clothes in downtown Boston department stores. Stores in Dudley Square were not as stringent as those downtown stores and they accommodated all customers. The result was that their business with African Americans increased.

Dudley Station

Although those stores catered to a predominantly African American clientele, they were still white-owned. It was not until the early 1960s that the store, *A Nubian Notion,* opened to respond to the lack of African American-owned retail businesses in the Dudley area. *A Nubian Notion* was founded by Sayid Malik A. Abdal-Khallaq. The family closed the business in 2016.

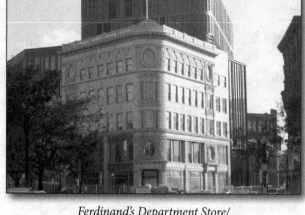

Ferdinand's Department Store/ Bruce C. Bolling Municipal Building

Dudley Square evolved into a transportation hub because of this bustling commercial development. As early as 1901, the Boston Elevated Railway ran a line from Dudley Sq. to Sullivan Sq. in Charlestown. After the elevated line was taken down in 1989, Dudley Station became a major hub for most of the city's bus routes. In the mid-1990s, the rapid transit Silver Line began operation with direct service to the airport.

Recently, Dudley Sq. has undergone a major city-led revitalization. The hallmark of that effort was the renovation and expansion of Ferdinand's Department Store into a new municipal building with headquarters for the Boston Public Schools. In 2015, that newly renovated building was dedicated as the Bruce C. Bolling Municipal Building. Bolling was the first African American president of the Boston City Council.

The city commissioned a public art mural, *"Roxbury Rhapsody,"* for the lobby. Roxbury artist, Napoleon Jones-Henderson, designed the mural. A group of art students from Massachusetts College of Art assisted with the production and installation of the kiln-fired ceramics of the mural.

> *"Roxbury Rhapsody: as an expression of community + visual music; weaves Roxbury's many strands of life, culture and people into a single tapestry of glass, metal and color."*
> -Napoleon Jones-Henderson

12 HIBERIAN HALL
184 Dudley St.
617-541-3900
www.madison-park.org

Between the 1870s and the 1920s, the Dudley area of Roxbury was predominantly populated with Irish immigrants. The community dance halls that were a hallmark of Irish social life all but disappeared when the Irish residents moved out of the neighborhood. Hiberian Hall was one of the last buildings to remain that was used for that entertainment. It stood vacant for several decades until the Madison Park Development Corporation revitalized it into the Roxbury Center for the Arts in the late 1990s.

Hiberian Hall

That effort, spearheaded by Candelaria Silva of ACT (Arts, Culture & Trade) Roxbury, transformed the vacant building into a cultural resource for the community. Silva, a cultural activist, also participated in the organization of the Roxbury Film Festival and Roxbury Open Studios, two of the most popular cultural activities that occur in Roxbury today.

 13 ORCHARD GARDENS
25 Ambrose St.

One of the primary efforts that contributed to the resuscitation of Dudley Square in the mid-1990s was the redevelopment of the Orchard Park Housing complex. Orchard Park was one of Boston Housing Authority's largest and most problematic developments. BHA resident Edna Bynoe and the Orchard Park Tenant Task Force spearheaded this revitalization effort.

Orchard Gardens Housing

The redevelopment included a new public school that received high accolades from the architectural community. The African American architecture firm, Stull & Lee, designed the new school in collaboration with TLCR Architects.

Orchard Gardens Public School

213

(14) MLK SITE: TWELFTH BAPTIST CHURCH
150 Warren Street

Twelfth Baptist Church, established in 1840, and Boston's oldest Black church still in continuous operation, developed from a split between the African Baptist Church and the African Meeting House on Beacon Hill. This church was a prominent center of abolitionist activity. Rev. Leonard Grimes (1815-1874) led the church in its early years. Grimes suffered imprisonment for two years in the 1840s for his assistance in the escape of a family of eight from Virginia. See more on Twelfth Baptist and Rev. Grimes under Beacon Hill sites.

Twelfth Baptist Church

Rev. Martin Luther King, Jr. and Rev. Michael Haynes served this con-gregation as youth ministers, while King studied theology at Boston University in the 1950s. Haynes eventually became pastor of Twelfth Baptist. King and Haynes remained good friends throughout King's life and Rev. Haynes invited King to Boston in 1965 for a march to protest segregation in this city. During that visit, King spoke before both houses of the Massachusetts legislature. Rev. Haynes is the brother of jazz musician, Roy Haynes.

(15) WILLIAM LLOYD GARRISON HOUSE
125 Highland St., private residence

William Lloyd Garrison (1805–1879) (NAA) influenced a generation of anti-slavery activists as one of the most prominent abolitionists in the United States. His newspaper, *The Liberator*, founded in 1830, shared the narratives of many who managed to escape slavery and it related the stories of those who contined to suffer because they remained enslaved. In the first issue of *The Liberator* on January 1st, 1831, Gar-

William Lloyd Garrison House

rison declared his intentions to never compromise his views on slavery:

> "...I am aware that many object to the severity of my language; but is there not cause for severity? I will be as harsh as truth, and as uncompromising as justice. On this subject, I do not wish to think, or to speak, or write, with moderation. No! No! Tell a man whose house is on fire to give a moderate alarm; tell him to moderately rescue his wife from the hands of the ravisher; tell the mother to gradually extricate her babe from the fire into which it has fallen; -- but urge me not to use moderation in a cause like the present. I am in earnest–I will not equivocate–I will not excuse–I will not retreat a single inch–AND I WILL BE HEARD. The apathy of the people is enough to make every statue leap from its pedestal, and to hasten the resurrection of the dead."
> –William Lloyd Garrison, in the first issue of The Liberator

William Lloyd Garrison

noose had actually been placed around his neck when the police rescued him. Wendell Phillips (NAA) witnessed the entire episode from his office window and decided at that moment to dedicate himself to the abolition movement. Garrison also encouraged Frederick Douglass to share his story when Douglass first arrived in the Boston area. That encouragement influenced Douglass to become a speaker on the anti-slavery lecture circuit in the early 1840s.

October 21st, 1835
Garrison nearly lynched by an angry mob in downtown Boston

Garrison who co-founded the New England Anti-Slavery Society in 1832, constantly put his life at risk with his radical views. On October 21th, 1835, he substituted for another speaker at an anti-slavery lecture in Boston. When word spread about Garrison's presence, a lynch mob formed outside the hall. The mob captured him and the

Liberator Newspaper
January 1st, 1831   First Issue
December 29th, 1865   Last Issue

The final issue of Garrison's newspaper was released on December 29th,

1865, at the end of the Civil War. His house has been listed as a National Historic Landmark. Garrison was buried at Forest Hills Cemetery in Jamaica Plain.

> "...Enslave the liberty of but one human being and the liberties of the world are put in peril."
> —WILLIAM LLOYD GARRISON

16 MELNEA CASS RECREATION COMPLEX
120 Martin Luther King, Jr. Blvd.

The Melnea Cass Recreation Complex originally opened in the mid-1980s. It was named to honor the, *"First Lady of Roxbury,"* Melnea Cass. This popular community facility with its indoor tennis courts, basketball courts, roller skating rink, track, showers, function rooms, classrooms, and outdoor pool,

Melnea Cass Recreation Complex

recently reopened after a complete renovation.

17 MALCOLM X SITE: COLLINS HOUSE
72 Dale Street

Malcolm X (1925–1965) was born Malcolm Little in Omaha, Nebraska. Local whites assassinated his father, Earl Little (1890–1931), when Malcolm was seven years old. Many whites in the community feared that he would encourage the local African American community to challenge the status quo when Earl Little preached Marcus Garvey's philosophy of self-empowerment to the locals. A few years after his father's death, Malcolm's mother, Louise Little, suffered a nervous breakdown. Malcolm and his siblings were separated and sent to live with relatives around the country.

Malcolm arrived in Boston in the early 1940s to live with his half-sister, Ella Mae Little Collins (1914–1996), and her family in this house. Here, Malcolm spent his formative teen and early adult years. He eventually became a local thug and ended up in jail. A detailed account of his life can be found in, *The Autobiography of Malcolm X*, written with Alex Haley.

Malcolm X converted to the Muslim faith while in jail. After his released, he became active in the Black Muslim brotherhood. As a leader, Malcolm X gave voice to the thoughts of

Malcolm X

disenfranchised African Americans. Many were impatient with the lack of progress in this country on behalf of African Americans and a movement emerged which challenged the complacency of the majority of white citizens in the United States.

This movement put America on notice that violence would now be considered a viable option to obtain rights that many white Americans took for granted. While some African Americans saw integration as a goal to be achieved, Malcolm X articulated the sentiment of this militant segment who wanted to distance themselves from white Americans.

The energy of this militant core greatly expanded the envelope of how African Americans saw themselves and what they would now accept. In fact, the use of the term, *"black,"* as a descriptive label was used at this time as a very, *"in your face,"* response to the more non-confrontational labels of, *"colored"* or *"Negro."* Many African Americans viewed Malcolm X as a hero for his bravery to speak up for those not empowered to do so.

Malcolm X also became a hero of anti-establishment activists of other races. By the time of his assassination, Malcolm X's opinion of how the races could work together had evolved into one of more collaboration. Unfortunately, he did not have time to share those ideas fully with the world before his murder.

Malcolm X House

This house was designated a Boston Landmark in 1998. After many years of neglect, Historic Boston, Inc. and the National Trust for Historic Preservation initiated a joint effort in 2012 to raise funds to renovate this historic structure into a resource for college students whose studies focused on African American history, social justice, and human rights.

18 MLK SITE: MARTIN LUTHER KING, JR. BLVD.

This street was renamed to honor Martin Luther King, Jr. after his assassination on April 4th, 1968, in Memphis, TN.

19 MALCOLM X SITE: TOWNSEND ST.

Two of the community institutions that Malcolm X frequented during his teen years were located on Townsend St. He sang briefly in the Townsend St. Baptist Church choir when he first arrived in Boston in the early 1940s and the Townsend Drug Store and Soda Fountain was one of the first businesses that employed Malcolm X in his teen years. Neither institution exists today.

20 WILLIAM M. TROTTER SCHOOL
135 Humboldt Ave.

The Boston Public School Dept. named this school to honor William Monroe Trotter (1872–1934), a fervent civil rights activist in Boston. It opened in 1969 as the city's first Magnet school. See Trotter in Dorchester sites.

21 CHARLES ST. AME CHURCH
551 Warren Street

Charles St. AME, Boston's oldest African American congregation still in existence, was established in 1833 on what is now Joy St. on Beacon Hill. The original 35 members received a charter for a church from the state legislature in 1839. The church grew steadily until the end of the Civil War, when various forces and the dynamic leadership of a new minister, Rev. John T. Jennifer, resulted in a church membership that exceeded 500 members.

Charles St. AME Church

Trotter School Mural

A decision by the city of Boston to widen Charles Street on Beacon Hill and the general migration of African Americans from Beacon Hill to Roxbury influenced the church's decision to relocate to its current location in 1939. The church was listed on the National Historic Register in 1983.

Freedom House

 ## MURIEL & OTTO SNOWDEN FREEDOM HOUSE
14 Crawford Street

Community activists, Otto (1914–1995) and Muriel (1916–1988) Snowden, founded this non-profit in 1949, to stimulate civic empowerment and community participation. It sponsors education programs, and programs for the elderly. The organization announced plans to relocate to Grove Hall in 2017. The Muriel Snowden International High School in Back Bay was dedicated in the early 1990s to honor Mrs. Snowden, see Back Bay sites.

 ## MARTIN LUTHER KING, JR. SCHOOL
77 Lawrence Ave.

This Boston Public School was renamed to honor Martin Luther King, Jr. after his assassination in 1968.

 ## MALCOLM X SITE: MOHAMMED'S MOSQUE #11
10 Washington Street

Malcolm X was Minister of Temple #11 in 1953 shortly after it was founded as the first mosque in Boston. Mohammed's Mosque #11 serves as the center of the Black Muslim community in Boston.

Otto and Muriel Snowden

Mohammed's Mosque #11

25 FRANKLIN PARK & ZOO
1 Franklin Park Road

World renowned landscape architect, Frederick Law Olmsted (1822–1903) (NAA) planned Franklin Park in the 1870s as the terminus of the, *"Emerald Necklace,"* a seven mile long system of nine inter-connected parks woven throughout Boston neighborhoods.

Franklin Park Entrance Gates

The 500-acre park was designed as a scenic escape from the congestion of the city. This was at a time when Roxbury, as a suburb of Boston, contained mansions built by the wealthy of Boston as weekend retreats. In the demographic changes that occurred in Boston in 1900 to the 1930s, as African Americans gradually relocated from other parts of the city and the South, Roxbury became the social and civic center of that community. Today, it is the location of numerous celebrations and festivals popular in the African American and Latino communities.

Franklin Park is reknown for its world-class golf course, the William

J. Devine Golf Course, and its 72-acre zoo. A frequent golfer on the greens was Dr. George Franklin Grant (1846–1910). Dr. Grant's love of the game as an amateur golfer led him to invent the first wooden golf tee in 1899. Dr. Grant also was the first African American faculty member at Harvard University's Dental School. See more on Grant in Kenmore sites. In 1992, the William Devine Golf Course was the site of a golf clinic held by world champion golfer, Tiger Woods for junior golfers.

26 ELMA LEWIS & MNCAAA
300 Walnut Ave.
www.ncaaa.org
617-442-8614
Tues.-Sun., 1 p.m. to 5 p.m.

Elma Lewis (1921-2004) established the Museum of the National Center of African American Artists (MNCAAA) in 1970 to celebrate the achievements of African American artists. Barry Gaither has served as the Executive Director and curator since it was found-

MNCAAA

ed. In 1976, the MNCAAA relocated to this historic 1872 Victorian Gothic villa, named Abbotsford, that was constructed entirely of Roxbury puddingstone by local industrialist, Aaron Davis Williams, Jr. (1821–1899) (NAA).

Boston benefited from several cultural traditions that Lewis initiated. Every holiday season she staged a production of, *"Black Nativity,"* a Christmas musical based on a play by Langston Hughes. Local composer, John Andrew Ross (1940–2006) wrote the music and each year he served as director of the production. The play is performed annually during the holiday season at various performance venues in Boston. The annual summer concert series in Franklin Park, Playhouse in the Park, was also initiated by Lewis. In the 1980s, Elma Lewis won the prestigious MacArthur Fellowship for her many contributions to the arts in Boston.

Elma Lewis

> **Major Cultural Initiatives of Elma Lewis**
> - Elma Lewis School of Fine Art
> - Museum of the National Center of African American Artists
> - Annual Production of Black Nativity
> - Playhouse in the Park at Franklin Park

Her parents were diligent and cultured individuals who immigrated from Barbados. They met through the United Negro Improvement Association founded by Marcus Garvey. The sense of pride and determination to uplift their community that all Garvey disciples held dear was instilled in the Lewis children. Elma had two brothers, one became a physician and the other trained as a classical musician. Ms. Lewis received a B.A from Emerson College in 1943 and a M. ED from Boston University in 1944. In this excerpt from a 1997 interview, Lewis shared some of her deeply held convictions:

"...My earliest memory is three years old, standing on the stage reciting a poem about the beauty of black women. I played with dolls that looked like me. ...I had a very strong cultural identity from the beginning. And it was not very possible for me to be denigrated by white people because I always had a strong sense of self, always. And I have been encouraged in my teaching and in my directing of people to give them that same sense. That liberates. That does not want to do

any damage to anybody else but it strengthens one's self. I don't know, that seems to have been hard for non-blacks to accept. I don't know why, because everybody wants that for himself. Every man wants it.

...He (her father) had gone to school with Melvin King's father. In fact, he was the best man at their wedding. But that is not surprising because in immigrant communities, immigrants all live together when they come over. And they've known each other from the old country at that age. And when they come that's what they do. Now, those men were serious men. There was no frivolity in them. They couldn't afford to be. Had they been, you would not know the names of their children because the children, black children in America, particularly male, who have not had really serious raising are soon demolished by society. And if you see any black man over 40 standing up then you know he has had very serious raising....

...Yes. I don't remember them seeing it as making a mark. I remember seeing it as salvation, self-salvation and the advancement of the race. You were taught to advance the race, to do everything for first your family and then others like you, because that was their only opportunity out of destruction. The society was made to destroy them and if they were not going to be destroyed that was your responsibility. It was not so that somebody would know my name, it was so that I may do good. We were raised to do good, to be good people, advance the cause of other people. ...

...Yes, we were determined people. We were determined people. And I look at people my age. I look at the black population that's 60 or 70 years old and I think that people should look at them with tremendous respect instead of abuse. How they went through what they went through to arrive at this, how there comes to be a John Wilson or any of those people is remarkable. They had to come from very determined people, very determined people. That's not just true in my case, that's true all along. ... these children (today) say, "I'm going to be a movie star." We didn't say those things. We said, "I'm going to do magnificent things," whatever they were, different in each case. And they were all for the edification of someone else. It was never, "I'm going to buy a big Cadillac," or any of that.

...When people talk about affirmative action, there had to be affirmative action. ...It angers me, because we had to have affirmative action to keep from being robbed. That's what affirmative action's about. It's not about for giving the undeserving. And everybody knows that but nobody articulates it. That's what it was about and is about. And if it's being wrongly used, use it rightly, but don't say it isn't needed. Big difference. ...

(Her brother was admitted to Harvard and eventually graduated from medical school)...and when he didn't have a hospital - he went around to every hospital and asked them one by one by one by one until he met a just man ... Harry Derow, who was a Jewish doctor at Beth Israel. And Dr. Derow took him ...and they went to the board of Beth Israel....And he (her brother) was the first black doctor in Boston with hospital affiliation, and that was Beth Israel.

...I never developed a life of leisure. A life of pleasant work, yes, but work. You must be a contributor. And that's what we do with children in our family until today. You have to be productive. There's no entertaining you. You don't come in the world to be entertained, you come into the world to make it a better place. And that's automatic. You come into the world with that. That's what you're here for, to make the world a better place....

...I never, ever heard of anyone who couldn't read and write when I was a child growing up. I never, ever heard of anybody who couldn't get some kind of menial job. The menial jobs are gone. So a large segment of your colored - I say colored in the sense of many colors - population is out of work. There's nothing for them. I never heard of a black man in prison when I was a child. Now they're there wholesale.......

...it's not the arts that are my concern. It is the culture. It is what the arts are telling you. The arts are how man speaks about his life. The arts are not something of beauty. ... The arts teach the virtues. And the arts explain the culture so that you can correct the culture, preserve it, discuss it, think on it. It's what tells you who man is and where he's been and where he's apt to go. That's what the arts do for you. It gives you the culture..... The arts interpret the culture. When you see Henry Tanner paint a picture of an old man praying with a little boy over a measly meal, that addresses itself a lot to what those black old men had to do in the South getting those children up and over..."

— *Excerpt from an oral history interview with Elma Lewis, July 25th, 1997 and Sept. 19th, 1997, conducted by Robert Brown for the Archives of American Art, Smithsonian Institution.*

> *"Our role is to support anything positive in black life and destroy anything negative that touches it."*
> – ELMA LEWIS

A monumental sculpture, *"Eternal Presence,"* by internationally famous African American artist, John Wilson (1922–2015) was installed on the museum grounds in 1987. This eight-foot bronze head of an African American

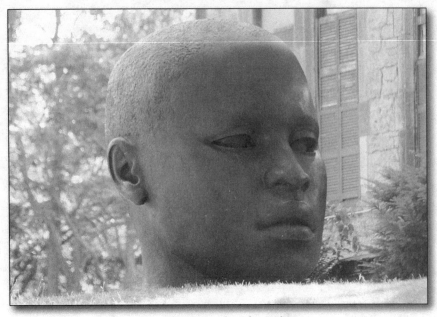

Eternal Presence by John Wilson

youth was described by Wilson to represent:

> "...a symbolic Black presence infused with a sense of universal humanity."
> -- JOHN WILSON

Wilson received a commission in 1983 to complete a sculpture of Martin Luther King, Jr. in Buffalo, NY. That design resulted in an eight -foot tall bronze head of the leader. In 1985, Wilson won a national competition to complete a sculpture of Martin L. King, Jr. for the United States Capital. Edmund Barry Gaither, Executive Director of the MNCAAA, headed the panel of judges. That sculpture, an eight - foot tall bronze bust on top of a five - foot tall marble base, was placed in the Rotunda of the U.S. Capital. Some of the most prestigious museums in the country have collected John Wilson's art such as the DeCordova Museum in Lincoln, MA, the Museum of Modern Art in New York City, and the MFA in Boston.

ELMA LEWIS SCHOOL OF FINE ART
7 Waumbeck St.

Elma Lewis (1921–2004) founded the Elma Lewis School of Fine Art in Boston in 1950 at this location. That institution trained over 6,000 students and influenced many Roxbury youth to pursue a career in the arts.

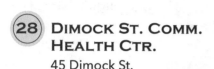

28 DIMOCK ST. COMM. HEALTH CTR.
45 Dimock St.

Dr. Marie Zakrewska (1829–1902) (NAA) opened the New England Hospital for Women and Children at this site in 1862. It was the first New England Hospital founded by women for women, and only the second such facility in the entire country. Mary Eliza Mahoney, the first African American licensed nurse in the country, received her training here in 1879. It became Dimock Community Health Center in 1969. Today, over 70,000 patients a year receive affordable health care from the facility. In 1991, the National Historic Commission designated the nine-acre site as a National Historic Landmark.

Dimock Community Health Center

Jackie Jenkins Scott led and transformed the organization from 1983 at a time when it faced bankruptcy, until 2004 when she resigned to become the 13th President of Wheelock College in Boston. Under Scott's tenure, Dimock CHC sponsored a yearly fund-raiser, *"Steppin' Out,"* in the fall of each year. The theme of the fund-raiser was to be a replication of music clubs of the big band era. *"Steppin' Out"* has become a major cultural event in New England.

29 RUTH BATSON & METCO
40 Dimock St.

Ruth Batson (1921–2003) was born in Roxbury at a time when the focus of educated people was to serve, build, and uplift the community. In addition to her job as a tenured psychiatry professor at Boston University School of Medicine, Batson actively participated in the Boston chapter of the NAACP. There she focused on the educational

Ruth Batson

METCO Building

disparities of low-performing schools in Boston.

In 1963, Ruth Batson and Ellen Jackson initiated, *"Operation Exodus,"* popularly known today as METCO, the Metropolitan Council for Educational Opportunity Program. That program voluntarily bused elementary, middle, and high school students from under-performing schools in Boston neighborhoods such as Mattapan, Hyde Park, Roxbury, and Dorchester, to high-performing schools in towns such as Brookline, Newton, Milton, and Weston.

METCO received its initial funds from the Carnegie Foundation in 1966. Batson served as administrator of METCO until 1969. In 1973, Jean McGuire became the Executive Director of METCO. In 1981, McGuire was the first African American female to win a seat on the Boston School Committee in what was a very contested election. She has guided the program to its current participation of over 3,300 students annually including 150 who participate from Springfield. METCO is so popular that many parents put their children on the waitlist as soon as they are born.

In 1969, Batson endowed the Ruth M. Batson Educational Foundation. By 2003, that foundation had awarded over $1.2 million in grants to African American students for tuition and emergency assistance. In 1997, the Boston University School of Medicine established the Ruth Batson Scholarship. That scholarship had distributed over $500,000 to deserving students by 2003. Batson also spearheaded the revitalization of the Museum of African American History on Beacon Hill with Henry Hampton.

 LOCAL RESOURCES

Discover Roxbury
Tours; Roxbury Open Studios & Film Festival;
www.discoverroxbury.org

Hamill Gallery of Tribal Art
2164 Washington St.
617-442-8204
www.hamillgallery.com

DORCHESTER

1 WILLIAM MONROE TROTTER HOUSE

97 Sawyer Ave., private residence

William Monroe Trotter (1872–1934) came from a family of civil rights activists. His father, James Trotter, served in the 55th Regiment during the Civil War. William Trotter excelled in his studies and became both valedictorian and class president in high school.

In 1895, he graduated *magna cum laude* from Harvard University and was the first African American inducted into the honors organization, Phi Beta Kappa. Trotter moved into this house with his new bride, Geraldine Louise

William Monroe Trotter

Pindell, in 1899. The house was designated a National Historic Landmark in 1976.

William Trotter founded the radical newspaper, *"The Guardian,"* in 1901. He also founded the *"Boston Literary and Historical Association,"* a literary venue to promote a progressive agenda for African American development. Trotter used his paper to criticize unjust policies against African Americans. He also led protests against Booker T. Washington's policy of accommodation.

Trotter, through his speeches and his newspaper, fought tirelessly for full equality for all African Americans. His remarks to President Wilson during a delegation of African Americans to the White House in November, 1914, protested Wilson's decision to reinstate segregation of Federal employees,--this

William Monroe Trotter House

after Wilson promised in his campaign to deal fairly with African Americans if elected. That initial promise led many African American leaders such as W.E.B. Du Bois and Trotter, to support Wilson. Their support changed to disgust as the reality of Wilson's administration practices became obvious.

The William Monroe Trotter Elementary School in Roxbury, Trotter Park at 135 Humboldt Avenue in Dorchester, and the William Monroe Trotter Institute for the Study of Black Culture at the University of Massachusetts, Boston, were all named to honor his legacy.

> "Persistent manly agitation is the way to liberty. We refuse to allow the impression to remain that the Negro American assents to inferiority."
> –WILLIAM MONROE TROTTER

Trotter's comments to President Wilson:

"...Only two years ago you were heralded as perhaps the second Lincoln, and now the Afro-American leaders who supported you are hounded as false leaders and traitors to their race. What a change segregation has wrought!

You said that your "colored fellow citizens could depend upon you for everything which would assist in advancing the interests of their race in the United States." Consider that pledge in the face of the continued color segregation! Fellow citizenship means congregation. Segregation destroys fellowship and citizenship. ....

As equal citizens and by virtue of your public promises we are entitled at your hands to freedom from discrimination, restriction, imputation and insult in government employ. Have you a "new freedom" for white Americans and a new slavery for your "Afro-American fellow citizens'? God forbid!...

Segregation is in itself an injury and denial of the equality of citizenship. It is unfair to separate the Afro-American when there is no similar segregation of the Semitic, Teutonic, Latin, Celtic or Slavic government employees...."

–William Monroe Trotter

SITE: LUCY STONE HOUSE
45 Boutwell St.

In 1847, women's rights activist and abolitionist, Lucy Stone (1818–1893) (NAA), was the first woman in Massachusetts to earn a college degree when she graduated from Oberlin College. Shortly after graduation, Stone accepted a position as a speaker for the American Anti-Slavery Society.

> *"I expect to plead not for the slave only, but for suffering humanity everywhere. Especially do I mean to labor for the elevation of my sex."*
> –LUCY STONE

At her marriage to Henry Blackwell, Lucy Stone announced that she would keep her own name because marriage laws:

> *"...refuse to recognize the wife as an independent, rational being, while they confer on the husband an injurious and unnatural superiority, investing him with legal powers which no honorable man would exercise, and which no man should possess."*
> -LUCY STONE

Stone was one of the few white women's rights activists to join Frederick Douglass in support of the Fifteenth Amendment which gave the right to vote to African American men. She saw that initial, though limited, progress as a step in the right direction. Stone later joined with Julia Ward Howe to focus on the adoption of women's suffrage at the state level while a fraction led by Susan B. Anthony (NAA) held out for federal laws to ensure women's rights.

 JAMES GEORGE BARBADOES SECOND CONGREGATIONAL
600 Washington St.

James George Barbadoes (1796–1841) was a key African American activist in the early to mid-1800s. Barbadoes married his second wife, Mary Ann Willis, at this church on Oct. 14th, 1821.

 LOCAL RESOURCES
William Monroe Trotter Institute
UMass Boston, Healy Library, 10th floor
www.umb.edu/trotter

Massachusetts Archives
220 Morrissey Blvd.
617-727-9268
www.sec.state.ma..us/sec/mus/museum

Strand Theater
543 Columbia Rd.
617-635-1403
www.strandboston.com

JAMAICA PLAIN

AFRICAN AMERICAN MASTER ARTISTS IN RESIDENCE (AAMARP)
76 Atherton St.

Northeastern University's Department of African American Studies has sponsored the African American Master Artist in Residence Program, known as AAMARP, since 1977. African American artist, Dana Chandler, a professor at Northeastern University at the time, founded the program to provide a link between African American artists, the local community, and the Northeastern community. It has provided studio space to artists since its inception. Public access to the galleries and studios has occurred through a series of regularly scheduled exhibits and lectures. Some of the artists affiliated with AAMARP are:

Ellen Banks	Gloretta Baynes
Jeff Chandler (Dana Chandler's brother)	
Walter Clark	Milton Derr
Marlon Forester	L'Merchie Frazier
Tyrone Geter	Ricardo Gomez
Reginald Jackson	Shea Justice
Kofi Kayiga	Khalid Kodi
Bryan McFarlane	Hakim Raquib
Susan Thompson	Don West

HYDE SQUARE TASK FORCE
375 Centre St.
www.hydesquare.org

Hyde Square and Jackson Square define an area of Jamaica Plain known for its predominantly Latino residential and business community. The Hyde Square Task Force was created in the late 1980s to reverse the trend of youth violence that overtook that community. It has empowered local youth to initiate positive change in their community through art and political involvement.

The organization under the leadership of Claudio Martinez (NAA) received national recognition and numerous awards for its youth leadership development programs. Public art installations at the Jackson Sq. "T" Station and the Roxbury Crossing "T" Station

AAMARP Building

were painted by youth of the Hyde Sq. Task Force in 2004 under the direction of Roberto Chao (NAA). Roxbury native, Melnea Cass was featured on the public art installation at Roxbury Crossing.

Hyde Sq. Task Force

Jackson Sq. "T" Station

 ### THE LUCY PARSONS CENTER

358A Centre St.
617-522-6098
www.lucyparsons.org

A community collective founded *"The Lucy Parsons Center"* in Boston in 1970 as a bookstore and resource for those interested in socialist and communist ideologies. The bookstore has relocated several times during its existence. The store was named to honor Lucy Eldine Gonzalez Parsons (1853–1942), a Chicago-based, labor organizer and radical orator, once described by the Chicago Police Department as, *"more dangerous than a thousand rioters."*

Parsons was of mixed African American, Native American, and Mexican heritage. Her 1871 marriage in Texas to Albert Parsons (1848–1887) (NAA), a white, former Confederate soldier, was very controversial. Albert Parsons was interesting in his own right. His family hailed from Maine and Massachusetts but members relocated to the South before Albert Parsons was born. Parsons volunteered for the Confederate Army at the age of thirteen. After the war, as a newspaper publisher, he advocated for

Lucy Parsons

the rights of the formerly enslaved. That position and his marriage to Lucy ostracized him from most of his community and the couple eventually relocated to Chicago.

In Chicago, as a cornerstone of the radical left, Parsons advocated for worker's rights. In 1887, a strike to support the eight-hour day ended in a riot in which seven people died, including one police officer. Parsons, along with six of his radical colleagues were directly implicated in the crime. This trial was oddly prescient of the *"Chicago Seven"* trials nearly 80 years later that also resulted from protests during the 1968 Democratic convention in Chicago. Members of the 1887 group were tried, found guilty, and received the death penalty, despite evidence that none of them were near the crime scene.

Lucy Parsons' participation in the socialist movement increased after the execution of her husband. In addition to frequent articles published in two socialist periodicals, *"The Socialist,"* and *"The Alarm,"* Parsons also published, *"Freedom: A Revolutionary Anarchist-Communist Monthly."* She was also one of the founders of the *"Industrial Workers of the World"* (IWW) and she edited the *"Liberator,"* the newspaper affiliated with the IWW. Parsons's focused her efforts to alleviate unemployment and poverty. That focus often put her in conflict with contemporary feminist anarchists who focused on gender concerns and sexual politics.

Throughout all this activity, Parsons maintained a strenuous schedule as a public speaker, both in the United States, Europe, and South America. Lucy Parsons died on March 7th, 1942, at the age of 89 in a fire in her home. Her personal library of over 1,500 books and her personal papers were immediately seized by the Chicago police and handed over to the FBI.

"Never be deceived that the rich will permit you to vote away their wealth."
–LUCY PARSONS

"Oh misery, I have drunk thy cup of sorrow to its dregs, but I am still a rebel."
–LUCY PARSONS

"My conception of the strike of the future is not to strike and go out and starve, but to strike and remain in and take possession of the necessary property of production."
–LUCY PARSONS

"Anarchism has but one infallible, unchangeable motto, 'Freedom.' Freedom to discover any truth, freedom to develop, to live naturally and fully."
–LUCY PARSONS

SITE: MARY TYLER PEABODY MANN HOUSE
8 Gordon St.

Abolitionist and educator Mary Tyler Peabody Mann (1806–1887) (NAA) organized a petition in 1864 that was signed by 195 school children in Concord to protest continued enslavement in the United States. Known as the, *"Little People's Petition,"* it was delivered to President Abraham Lincoln (NAA) by Senator Charles Sumner (NAA) of Massachusetts. Mann was the widow of the education reformer, Horace Mann (NAA). She lived in Jamaica Plain with her sister Elizabeth Peabody (NAA). Peabody originated the system of kindergartens in the United States. See more on Mary Mann in Concord sites.

5 CIVIL WAR MEMORIAL: WEST ROXBURY SOLDIER'S MONUMENT
Center St. & South St

This monument was originally known as the West Roxbury Soldier's Monument because Jamaica Plain was a part of the town of West Roxbury when it was dedicated on September 14th, 1871. Forty-three troops from that community of 6,310 lost their lives in the Great Rebellion, as the Civil War was commonly known. One of the casualties from West Roxbury was Col. Robert Gould Shaw. Shaw was the Commander of the Massachusetts 54th Regiment, the first African American regiment raised in the North.

 6 MONUMENT TO TRAYVON MARTIN *"STILL, 2014"*
Center & Eliot St.

On February 26th, 2012, Trayvon Martin, an unarmed African American teenager, was gunned down in Florida by a local citizen. The Florida police had licensed that citizen to carry a firearm as a neighborhood watch volunteer. The murderer stated that Martin, who wore a hoodie at the time, presented a hostile image. Hoodies are popular jackets worn by many urban youth. The unprovoked murder of Martin and the acquittal of the perpetrator highlighted the vulnerability of African Americans, particularly young males, who are in-

Still, 2014

nocently killed under the auspices of law enforcement.

In June of 2014, artist, Matthew Hincman (NAA) installed this art installation in close proximity to the Civil War Monument to remind the public that the freedom that this country fought for in 1865 still was not a reality 150 years later for many African Americans who are murdered without consequences for the murderers.

 7 FOREST HILLS CEMETERY

96 Forest Hills Ave.
617-524-3150
www.foresthillstrust.org

Forest Hills Cemetery was established in 1848 as a picturesque Victorian buri-

al garden on 250 acres. It was designed with lavishly landscaped grounds and sculptures as the final resting place for many important literary, historical, political, and cultural figures. Some of the notable individuals discussed in this book who were buried there include: Dr. Cornelius N. Garland, William Lloyd Garrison (NAA), Elma Lewis, William Cooper Nell, John J. Smith, Lucy Stone (NAA), Joseph "Wally" Walcott, and Mary Evans Wilson. In 2009, a local African American historian, Sylvia McDowell, began a project, *"Finding Voices in the Silence,"* to identify people of African ancestry who are buried at Forest Hills Cemetery.

The sculpture, *The Sentinel,* completed by African American artist, Fern Cunningham in 2001, was one of the many sculptures placed on the paths

"The Sentinel" by Fern Cunningham

Forest Hills Entrance Gates

that encircle the cemetery. Cunningham, stated the sculpture was inspired by a photo of an unknown market woman to represent, *"the memory of black ancestral endurance."*

veterans. That section is marked by a Civil War Monument.

Susie King Taylor, who served as a nurse and teacher during the Civil War at Fort Puslaki in Georgia, was buried here in 1912 in an unmarked grave. See her listing under South End sites.

MATTAPAN

 ### CIVIL WAR MEMORIAL: MOUNT HOPE CEMETERY
355 Walk Hill Street

Mount Hope Cemetery has dedicated an entire section of its grounds to hold the remains of Civil War casualties and

 ### RISE / GATEWAY SCULPTURES
Blue Hill Ave. and River St.

In the mid-1990s, the City of Boston commissioned these sculptures to mark the entrance into Boston from Milton. The sculptures were created by cousins, Fern Cunningham and Karen Eutemey in 2005. Both artists formerly resided in Mattapan. The sculptures were designed to be symbolic of the diversity of Mattapan's population and its hope for the future.

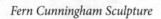

Fern Cunningham Sculpture

Karen Eutemey Sculpture

HYDE PARK

1 CIVIL WAR MEMORIAL: CAMP MEIGS CAMPGROUND
19 Stanbro Street

Camp Meigs was one of the locations where troops from Massachusetts trained for the Civil War. The first African American, all-volunteer regiment from the North, the 54th Regiment, trained there as did the 55th Regiment, and the 5th Calvary. A monument was constructed on the grounds to honor those African American regiments.

Camp Meigs Monument I

The Civil War was second only to the American Revolution as one of the most defining conflicts in United States history. The reasons given for that cataclysmic event were numerous, but the single, most dominant cause was the South's insistence to maintain a large portion of its population in a state of slavery.

The war began on April 12th, 1861, when the Confederates fired on Fort Sumter in South Carolina. It lasted until April 9th, 1865, when the Confederates surrendered to the Union Army at Appomattox Courthouse in Virginia. The Union Army was victorious but the lost in casualties suffered by both sides has had no parallel in United States history.

The population of the United States in 1860 was 31,500,000. The approximate number of troops, Union and Confederate, that fought in the war was 3,800,500. The 2,672,341 Union troops included 178,975 African Americans and 3,530 Native Americans. The combined casualties suffered by both sides were 1,200,000. That figure included 40,000 African American troops. Those casualties were nearly doubled the total casualties suffered by the United States in all the other wars it engaged in from the American Revolution up to the current conflicts in the Middle East.

The individual battles of the Civil War were also some of the deadliest ever experienced in U.S. history. Nine of those battles claimed over 20,000 casualties each, and that figure topped 30,000 casualties for three of those battles, yet the average duration of a Civil War battle was approximately one to three days. The Battle of Gettysburg which lasted from July 1st to July 3rd, 1863, claimed 51,116 lives in that single battle. To compare the order of magnitude of that casualty figure, the ten bloodiest years of the Vietnam War

Camp Meigs Monument II

instruction camp. It was named after one of the Generals of the Union Army. Over 26,000 soldiers trained at Camp Meigs. Today, the site is a Boston City playground.

Governor Andrew (NAA) of Massachusetts received authorization to recruit for an African American regiment in the North on January 26th, 1863. Prior to that authorization, five other African American Regiments had already been created in the South:

1st Kansas Colored Regiment	Aug. 4th, 1862
1st South Carolina Volunteers	Aug. 25th, 1862
1st Louisiana Colored	Aug. 25th, 1862
2nd Louisiana Colored	Aug. 25th, 1862
3rd Louisiana Colored	Aug. 25th, 1862

claimed 58,200 U.S. troops. This was at a time when the population of this country was 179 million (compared to our 1860 population of 31,500,000) and our country still has not completely healed from the trauma of the Viet Nam War nearly fifty years later. By the end of the Civil War, 159,165 troops from Massachusetts, 13% of the state's population, had participated in the war effort. Massachusetts suffered 12,976 casualties from that conflict.

The grounds of Camp Meigs were originally part of a family farm. The state confiscated 125 acres of that farmland in 1861 for a military

Readville Recruitment Poster

So many from all over the North answered the first recruitment call that the 54th Regiment was quickly filled. The overflow formed the nucleus of the 55th Regiment which moved into the vacated barracks when the 54th Regiment was mobilized on May 28th, 1863. The 55th Regiment began to train immediately. The pattern for the organization of those African American regiments was that the regiment of African American enlisted men would be led by white officers. Gov. Andrew's initial request to commission African American officers was denied by the War Department.

African American Military Units trained at Camp Meigs			
	54th Reg.	55th Reg.	5th Calvary
Officers	78	82	61
Enlisted	1,369	1,144	1,325
Enlisted Men commissioned in the Regiments			
	5	8	0
Killed or died of Wounds			
Officers	5	3	0
Enlisted	88	59	5
Missing	43	0	0
Died of accidents or disease			
Officers	1	2	0
Enlisted	107	118	121
Died as prisoners			
Officers	0	0	0
Enlisted	34	1	128

(Massachusetts in the Army and Navy during the War of 1861-65 by Thomas Wentworth Higginson)

This data documented the results of the harsh conditions that African American recruits endured in the Civil War. The statistics of those who died of disease or accidents in hospitals or as prisoners indicated that to survive a battle was no guarantee that one would survive the war.

Timeline for 54th Regiment	
Jan. 16th, 1863	Gov. Andrews issued call for African American volunteers
May 28th, 1863	54th Left Boston for War
July 18th, 1863	Battle of Fort Wagner
July 21st, 1863	55th sent into active service
Aug. 22nd, 1864	U.S. ended pay discrimination after 18 month protest
Nov. 30th, 1864	54th and the 55th joined forces at battle of Honey Hill in SC
Sept. 2nd, 1865	54th disbanded by Gov. Andrew

The 54th saw action immediately, but none so momentous as what they experienced on July 18th, 1863. That day they were ordered to capture Fort Wagner on Morris Island in South Carolina. That failed attack led to the death of nearly 100 troops from the 54th Regiment. Many more died later from wounds received in battle that day. Though defeated in that battle, the soldiers were victorious in spirit. Their bravery proved, unequivocally, that African American soldiers were just as courageous as their white comrades. Their valor encouraged other African Americans to enlist.

The 55th Regiment was sent to the front on July 21st, 1863, to Folly Island near Charleston, S.C. On November 30th, 1864, the 55th Regiment and the 54th Regiment joined forces at the Battle of Honey Hill in South Carolina.

Map of Camp Meigs

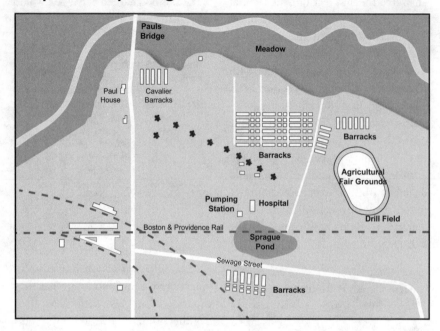

The 54th and the 55th Regiments joined ranks again in their fight against the U.S. Government, for discrimination in pay. For 18 months, the soldiers continued to fight, but they refused their pay until the United States Congress intervened and corrected the injustice. This action personified the willingness of these volunteers to endure personal hardship and sacrifice in the spirit of group advancement. It exemplified the high level of integrity and moral courage they possessed.

African American recruits knew that they faced immediate execution if caught by the enemy. White soldiers were normally taken as prisoner if caught. The massacre of over 300 African American troops at Fort Pillow in Tennessee by Confederates on April 12th, 1864, was one of the more egregious examples of the treatment African American troops could expect if they were captured.

All of the troops had to subsist on meager food rations that often left them hungry. Those food rations included a pound of *"Hard Tack Bread."* Hard Tack was dense bread that each soldier received with their food rations along with their pound of beans and bacon. Hard Tack received its descriptive name because it was so hard that troops claimed that it could only be broken on a rock or with a rifle butt. The advantages were that it traveled well, and the high levels of protein and Vitamin B in the whole-wheat flour could be depended upon to fill the hungry soldier's stomach.

With this knowledge of the harsh conditions, the 54th and the 55th persisted in their service and their protest. The basis of the protest was that African American recruits were promised the same pay as white recruits, $13.00 a month, as well as the same rations and the same clothing allowance. Despite that promise, the government attempted to pay the African American recruits the sum of only $10.00 a month and to charge them $3.00 a month for clothing.

Governor Andrew passed a bill through the Massachusetts State Legislature on Nov. 16th, 1863, to make up the difference in pay between what the Federal Government promised the African American recruits and what they actually tried to pay them. The 54th and the 55th Regiments jointly refused

Soldier of the 54th Regiment

the Governor's offer. They felt that the Federal Government delivered the insult, and that only the Federal Government could correct the injustice.

The "*New Bedford Mercury*" published the following letter of protest from James Henry Gooding of New Bedford which Gooding sent to President Abraham Lincoln:

Camp of the 54th Mass. colored regt., Morris Island.
Dept. of the South. Sept. 28th, 1863.
Your Excellency, Abraham Lincoln:

Your Excellency will pardon the presumption of an humble individual like myself, in addressing you, but the earnest Solicitation of my comrades in Arms beside the genuine interest felt by myself in the matter is my excuse, for placing before the Executive head of the Nation our Common Grievance.

On the 6th day of the last Month, the Paymaster of the department informed us, that if we would decide to receive the sum of $10 per month, he would come and pay us that sum, but that, on the sitting of Congress, the Regt., would, in his opinion, be allowed the other three. He did not give us any guarantee that this would be, as he hoped; certainly he had no authority for making any such guarantee, and we cannot suppose him acting in any way interested.

Now the main question is, Are we Soldiers, or are we Labourers? We are fully armed and equipped, have done all the various Duties pertaining to a Soldiers life, have conducted ourselves to the complete satisfaction of General Officers, who were, if anything, prejudiced against us, but who now accord us all the encouragement and honour due us; have shared the perils and labour of Reducing the first stronghold that flaunted a Traitor Flag; and more, Mr. President. Today the Anglo-Saxon Mother, Wife, or Sister are not alone in tears for departed Sons, Husbands and Brothers. The patient, trusting Descendents of Africa's Clime have dyed the ground with blood, in defense of the Union, and Democracy. Men, too, your Excellency, who know in a measure the cruelties of the Iron heel of oppression, which in years gone by, the very Power their blood is now being spilled to maintain, ever ground them to the dust.

But When the war trumpet sounded o'er the land, when men knew not the Friend from the Traitor, the Black man laid his life at the altar of the Nation– and he was refused. When the arms of the Union were beaten, in the first year of the War, and the Executive called for more food for its ravaging men, again the black man begged the privilege of aiding his country in her need to be and again refused.

And now he is in the War, and how has he conducted himself? Let their dusky forms rise up, out of the mires of James Island, and give the answer. Let the rich mould around Wagner's parapets be upturned, and there will be found an Eloquent answer. Obedient and patient and Solid as a wall as are they. All we lack is a paler hue and a better acquaintance with the Alphabet.

Now your Excellency, we have done a Soldier's Duty. Why Can't we have a Soldier's pay? You caution the Rebel Chieftain, that the United States knows no distinction in her Soldiers. She insists on having all her soldiers of whatever creed or Color, to be treated according to the usages of War. Now if the United States exacts uniformity of treatment of her soldiers from the Insurgents, would it not be well and consistent to set the example herself by paying all her soldiers alike?

We of this Regt. were not enlisted under any "contraband" act but we do not wish to be understood as rating our Service of more Value to the government than the service of the ex-slave. Their Service is undoubtedly worth much to the Nation, but Congress made express provision touching their case, as slaves freed by military necessity, and assuming the Government to be their temporary Guardian. Not so with us. Freemen by birth and consequently having the advantage of thinking and acting for ourselves so far as the laws would allow us, we do not consider ourselves fit subjects for the Contraband act.

We appeal to you, Sir, as the Executive of the Nation, to have us justly Dealt with. The Regt. Do pray that they be assured their service will be fairly appreciated by paying them as American Soldiers, not as menial hirelings. Black men, you may well know, are poor; three dollars per month for a year will (barely) supply their needy Wives and little ones with fuel. If you, as Chief magistrate of the Nation, will assure us of our whole pay, we are content. Our Patriotism, our enthusiasm will have a new impetus, to exert our energy more and more to aid our Country. Not that our hearts ever flagged in Devotion, spite the evident apathy displayed in our behalf, but We feel as though our Country spurned us, now that we are sworn to serve her. Please give this a moment's attention."

-- James Henry Gooding

This protest against pay discrimination continued until August 22nd, 1864, after African American troops had suffered for 18 months. On that date, the federal government decided that equal pay for all soldiers would be the law, effective January 1st, 1865. The sacrifice of the 54th and the 55th Regiments benefited all African American troops who joined after the protest ended. Unfortunately, Gooding, as did many others of the 54th and 55th Regiment, did not survive the war to enjoy that victory. Gooding was captured on Feb. 20th, 1864, at the Battle of Olustee in Florida. He died in Andersonville Prison in Georgia.

Recipe for Hard Tack Bread

4 cups whole wheat flour
4 teaspoons salt
2 cups water or less

1. *Mix flour and salt together. Add enough water so that the mixture sticks together but not on hands or pan.*
2. *Roll the dough into a rectangle, ½" thick and cut into 3" x 3" squares.*
3. *Using a nail, press four rows of four holes into each square but do not punch through the dough. Turn the squares over and do the same.*
4. *Place on an ungreased cookie sheet and bake at 350 degrees for 30 minutes. Turn each square over and bake for another 30 minutes.*
5. *The squares dry as they cool and as they dry they take on the consistency of fired brick. This durability made them very suitable to the rigors of a soldier's life in a battle campaign.*

2 JAMES MONROE TROTTER HOUSE
68 Neponset Ave.

James Monroe Trotter (1842–1892), was born enslaved in Mississippi. Trotter's white father manumitted Trotter's mother, their two daughters, and James, and sent them to Cincinnati to live. In Cincinnati, Trotter's family was able to live freely and the children obtained an education. After graduation, Trotter taught school in several Ohio towns. He also met his wife, Virginia Isaacs, in Ohio.

James Monroe Trotter

When the request went out for African American volunteers for the war effort, Trotter immediately attempted to enlist in the Massachusetts 54th Regiment. Since it had already reached its capacity, he enlisted in the Massachusetts 55th.

Trotter was active in the wage discrimination protest against the Federal government which resulted in equal pay for all soldiers. He quickly rose through the ranks, first as a Private, then Sergeant, and finally he became the first African American to achieve the rank of 2nd Lieutenant.

James Monroe Trotter House

After the war, Trotter joined the U.S. Postal Service in Boston but after several years, he resigned that position in protest of their unfair promotion policies. In 1887, Trotter was appointed Recorder of Deeds for Washington, D.C. by President Grover Cleveland (NAA). That appointment made Trotter the highest ranking African American in the Federal government. James Monroe Trotter died of tuberculosis shortly after he returned to Boston. Trotter was the father of civil rights activist, William Monroe Trotter.

3 SITE: ANGELINA GRIMKE WELD HOUSE

212 Fairmount Ave.

Prominent abolitionists and feminists, Angelina Grimke Weld (1805–1879) (NAA) and her older sister, Sarah, had first-hand knowledge of the brutality of slavery. Their prominent Charleston, SC family, one of the wealthiest families in the area, enslaved many on their sizeable plantation. Sarah left home when she became an adult to protest her family's participation in the enslavement of individuals. She joined the Quaker Sect in Philadelphia. Angelina followed her sister after a few years.

Neither sister could reconcile their Christian beliefs with the harsh reality of human bondage that surrounded them in their youth. After *"The Liberator"* newspaper published Angelina Grimke's abolitionist tract, *"Appeal to Christian Women of the South,"* in the early 1830s, the sisters were warned under threat of physical violence to never visit their family in Charlestown again. They became speakers on the Anti-Slavery lecture circuit in the North.

Angelina Grimke Weld

> "...The doctrine of blind obedience and unqualified submission to any human power, whether civil or ecclesiastical, is the doctrine of despotism, and ought to have no place among Republicans and Christians."
>
> —ANGELINA GRIMKE

Angelina Grimke Weld delivered this speech in 1838 at the second Anti-Slavery Convention of American Women in Philadelphia:

"...As a Southerner, I feel that it is my duty to stand up here tonight and bear testimony against slavery. I have seen it-- I have seen it. I know it has horrors that can never be described. I was brought up under its wing: I witnessed for many years its demoralizing influences and its destructiveness to human happiness. It is admitted by some that the slave is not happy under the worst forms of slavery. But I have never seen a happy slave. I have seen him dance in his chains, it is true; but he was not happy. There is a wide difference between happiness and mirth. Man cannot enjoy the former while his manhood is destroyed, and

that part of the being which is necessary to the making and to the enjoyment of happiness, is completely blotted out. The slaves, however, may be, and sometimes are, mirthful. When hope is extinguished, they say, "let us eat and drink, for tomorrow we die." ...

Many persons go to the South for a season, and are hospitably entertained in the parlor and at the table of the slave-holder. They never enter the huts of the slaves; they know nothing of the dark side of the picture, and they return home with praised on their lips of the generous character of those with whom they had tarried....

...I wonder when I reflect under what influence I was brought up that my heart is not harder than the nether millstone. But in the midst of temptation I was preserved, and my sympathy grew warmer, and my hatred of slavery more inveterate, until at last I have exiled myself from my native land because I could no longer endure to hear the wailing of the slave. I fled to the land of Penn.; for here, thought I, sympathy for the slave will surely be found. But I found it not. The people were kind and hospitable, but the slave had no place in their thoughts. Whenever questions were put to me as to his condition, I felt that they were dictated by an idle curiosity, rather than by that deep feeling which would lead to effort for his rescue....

...We may talk of occupying neutral ground, but on this subject, in its present attitude, there is no such thing as neutral ground. He that is not for us is against us, and he that gathereth not with us, scattereth abroad. If you are on what you suppose to be neutral ground, the South look upon you as on the side of the oppressor. ...

...Women of Philadelphia! Allow me as a Southern woman, with much attachment to the land of my birth, to entreat you to come up to this work. Especially let me urge you to petition. Men may settle this and other questions at the ballot-box, but you have no such right; it is only through petitions that you can reach the Legislature. It is therefore peculiarly your duty to petition. Do you say, "It does no good? The South already turns pale at the number sent. They have read the reports of the proceedings of Congress, and there have seen that among other petitions were very many from the women of the North on the subject of slavery.... Men who hold the rod over slaves, rule in the councils of the nation: and they deny our right to petition and to remonstrate against abuses of our sex and of our kind. We have these rights, however, from our God. Only let us exercise them: ..."

—Angelina Grimke Weld

Back home in Charleston, Henry Grimke (NAA), a brother of the two sisters, maintained a second family outside of town with an enslaved woman, Nancy Weston. The couple had three sons, Archibald, Francis, and John. After their father died, the mother and three sons felled on extremely hard times and their white step-brother continued to enslave them. Despite their poverty, Archibald and Francis obtained a scholarship to Lincoln University.

After Sarah and Angelina learned about their nephews, Archibald and Francis, the sisters decided to contribute to the cost of their education. Read more on Francis under Salem sites and more on Archibald under Cambridge sites. Angelina, her husband, Theodore Weld, and her sister, Sarah who never married, moved to Hyde Park, MA, after the Civil War and lived in a house at this site.

Brown's raid on Harper's Ferry on Oct. 16th, 1859. Parker possessed an adamant belief that slavery had to be overturned by any means. He wrote this of John Brown's attack on Harper's Ferry:

> *"...One held against his will as a slave has a natural right to kill everyone who seeks to prevent his enjoyment of liberty."*
> -THEODORE PARKER

Theodore Parker

WEST ROXBURY

1 THEODORE PARKER (NAA) UNITARIAN UNIVERSALIST CHURCH
1859 Center Street

Theodore Parker (1810-1860) (NAA) joined the *"Secret Committee of Six,"* a group that provided funds for John

Parker received degrees from Harvard College and Harvard Divinity School. He became a Unitarian minister and a strong proponent of Transcendentalism. Early in his career, Parker took a moral stance against slavery, and he maintained that posi-

Theodore Parker Unitarian Universalist Church

tion throughout his life. Parker also held strong convictions against other social injustices of his time such as the inequality of women, the inhumane conditions of prisons, and the inequities between the rich and the poor.

Theodore Parker served as minister of the Unitarian Universalist Church of West Roxbury from 1837 until 1846. His congregation remained faithful to him despite the fact that Parker was ostracized by other members of the Unitarian community because of his radical beliefs. The West Roxbury Church renamed itself to honor Theodore Parker in 1962. Seven Tiffany stained glass windows were installed in the church to further commemorate Parker.

Many slaveholders used the authority of the Bible to justify slavery, but Parker, in his famous 1848, *"Letter To a Southern Slaveholder,"* pointed out that hypocrisy.

Letter to a Southern Slaveholder,

"...You need not suppose that I have any spite against the slaveholders; I wish them well not less than their slaves. ... I think slave holding is a wrong in itself, and therefore, a sin; but I cannot say that this or that particular slave-holder is a sinner because he holds slaves. I know what sin is—God only knows who is a sinner. ...

So as a Christian, you appeal to the Old Testament for your authority to hold slaves. Now, look ..., and see the difference between the Old Testament and New Testament. The Old Testament demands circumcisions, a peculiar priesthood, sacrifice of certain animals, and observance of certain fast days,... It demands them all in the name of a Lord. Yet you do not observe any of them.

...No, I do not think God changes; therefore, I don't believe he uttered those dreadful commands in the Old Testament. I believe that God has the attributes of universal justice and universal love. Doubtless, you will call me an "Infidel", but that makes no odds; I try to be a Christian, but do not begin by discarding conscience, reason, and common sense....

Dear sir, Christianity does not consist in believing stories in the Old Testament, about Noah's curse and all that, but in loving your brother as yourself, and God with your whole heart. Do not think that I covet your slaves. No consideration would induce me to become a slaveholder. ... Let me ask you, while you take from a man his liberty, his person, do (you) not violate that command, "Thou shalt not covet anything that is thy neighbor's"? ...

Do not think that I assume any airs of superiority over you because I am not a slave holder. ...I am working for the truth and right. I have nothing to gain personally by the abolition of slavery, and have by opposing that institution got nothing but a bad name. I shall not count you my enemy, but am truly your friend."

–Theodore Parker

Theodore Parker's sermons and essays influenced a widely diverse group of people such as Abraham Lincoln (NAA), Martin Luther King, Jr., and Betty Friedan (NAA), a modern feminist:

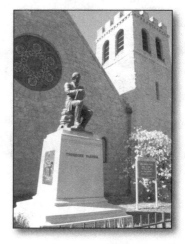

Theodore Parker
Unitarian Universalist Church II

"...There is what I call the American idea... The idea that all men have unalienable rights; that in respect thereof, all men are created equal; and that government is to be established and sustained for the purpose of giving every man an opportunity for the enjoyment and development of all these unalienable rights. This idea demands, ...a democracy, that is, a government of all the people, by all the people, for all the people; ..."
–THEODORE PARKER,
EXCERPT FROM A SPEECH THAT
INFLUENCED ABRAHAM LINCOLN

"...I do not pretend to understand the moral universe; the arc is a long one, my eye reaches but little ways; I cannot calculate the curve and complete the figure by the experience of sight, I can divine it by conscience. And from what I see I am sure it bends towards justice."
–THEODORE PARKER,
EXCERPT FROM A SPEECH THAT
INFLUENCED MARTIN LUTHER KING, JR.

"...The domestic function of the woman does not exhaust her powers...To make one half of the human race consume its energies in the functions of housekeeper, wife, and mother is a monstrous waste of the most precious material God ever made."
–THEODORE PARKER,
EXCERPT FROM A SPEECH THAT
INFLUENCED BETTY FRIEDEN

2 MYRTLE HART MACKINLEY & WILLIAM MACKINLEY
Site Unknown

Myrtle Hart MacKinley (1877–1966) was born in Indiana into a family of musicians. Her father, Henry Hart, was a violinist, and her mother, Sarah, was a concert pianist. The family traveled and performed throughout the mid-West. Myrtle gravitated to the harp early in life. Her mastery of that instrument provided her with an opportunity to perform at the Chicago World's Fair in 1893. She married William MacKinley, also a musician in 1926. William was music director at the Colonial Theater in Boston for over 40 years and Myrtle frequently performed there as well. The couple was buried at Mt. Auburn Cemetery in Cambridge.

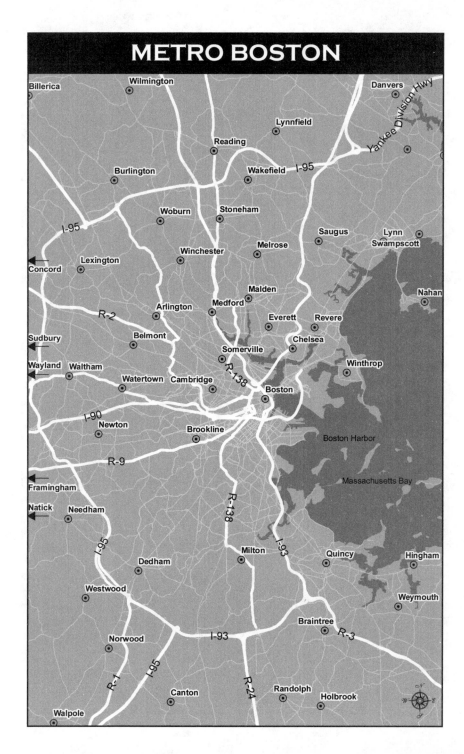

METRO BOSTON

Cambridge Map

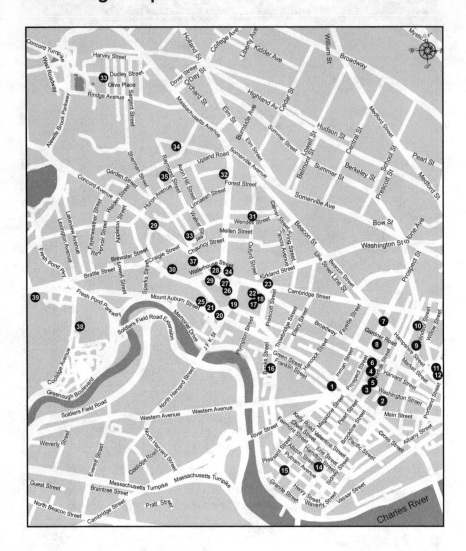

CAMBRIDGE

TODAY, Cambridge, Massachusetts enjoys an international reputation as a strong bastion of liberal and progressive views. One of the primary reasons for that reputation is the location of prominent universities in the town such as Harvard, which was founded in 1636, MIT, and others. Once African Americans were able to attend college, Harvard stood as the pinnacle to be reached in that goal, but Harvard has not always been a beacon of hope for African Americans. Harvard's legacy on the subject of slavery encompassed a duality. It educated and employed individuals who perpetuated that bondage, and it also educated those who dedicated their lives to abolish it.

That heritage has been documented in a publication, *"Harvard and Slavery: Seeking a Forgotten History,"* written by Harvard professor, Sven Beckert (NAA) and Katherine Stevens (NAA) and the students of their Harvard and Slavery Research seminars. That research documented the extent to which Harvard and the Cambridge community benefited from the system of slavery. In April of 2016, Harvard acknowledged the contributions of four of those enslaved individuals with a plaque mounted on Wadsworth House. Titus and Venus were two of those individuals. They worked for Harvard President, Benjamin Wadsworth (1725–1739) (NAA). Juba and Bilah were enslaved by Harvard President Edward Holyoke (1737–1769) (NAA).

In the 1700s, many retired Caribbean planters and other businessmen who had prospered financially from the trade and labor of those enslaved, relocated to Cambridge and other nearby towns. They brought with them a cadre of enslaved African household servants whose role it was to maintain the lifestyle of those relocated planters. Those newcomers used their money as their entre into respectable society. One favorite practice was to donate large sums of money to established institutions such as Harvard. Those newly rich families were neighbors to Harvard Presidents, faculty, and students who also maintained enslaved individuals both on and off campus.

Harvard's reputation as the pillar of education and refinement in the "new world" made it the destination of choice for wealthy, southern plantation heirs. That unique demographic made up a large sector of Harvard's student population and the resident population of Cambridge in the mid-1700s to the mid-1800s.

After slavery ended in Massachusetts around 1783, many Africans in Cambridge relocated to the port cities of Boston, Salem, and New Bedford, because of the economic opportunities those bustling ports provided. By the mid-1840s, Cambridge experienced a spurt in its African American population because many relocated back to Cambridge to take advantage of the integrated Cambridge public school system unlike the school system in Boston which remained segregated until 1855.

1 PATRICK H. RAYMOND HOUSE
10 Pleasant Street

Patrick H. Raymond (1831–1892) was the first African American Chief of the Fire Department for the City of Cambridge, and the first African American Fire Chief in the country with his appointment by Mayor Hamlin Harding (NAA) in 1871. Raymond stayed in that position for eight years, despite fierce criticism.

The late 1800s was a very controversial period for fire departments across the United States. The Great Chicago Fire occurred in 1871. It claimed 300 lives and caused a proportionate level of property damage. The next year, the Great Boston Fire occurred on November 9th, 1872. That blaze demolished 65 acres and destroyed over 770 buildings in the current Financial District of downtown Boston.

Patrick Raymond House

Raymond spearheaded reforms in Cambridge during his tenure as Fire Chief to ensure that the densely built city did not experience a fate similar to that of Boston. He created two new fire companies and built new firehouses in several Cambridge neighborhoods. Raymond lived in this house while he was Fire Chief for the city.

2 ST. PAUL'S AME CHURCH
37 Bishop Allen Drive

The two most influential African American leaders at the turn of the 20th century, W.E.B. DuBois and Booker T. Washington, both spoke at St. Paul's

Patrick Raymond

St. Paul's AME Church

African Methodist Episcopal Church, the oldest African American church in Cambridge. St. Paul's AME, established in 1873, has served as a prominent resource for many African American students from out of town who attended Harvard and MIT. The church and its related Christian Life Center continue to be active fixtures in the community.

 ## ROBERT MOSES AND THE ALGEBRA PROJECT

99 Bishop Allen Drive
617-491-0200
www.algebra.org

Robert Moses (b. 1935) was born in New York City and he received a PhD in mathematics from Harvard University. Moses spearheaded the *Mississippi Freedom Summer Project* of 1964, a project that brought national attention to the Civil Rights Movement in the South. The goal of that project was to end African American disfranchisement during southern elections. The organizers decided to focus their attention on Mississippi where in some areas of the state, the ratio of eligible African American voters to actually registered African American voters was as wide as 5,000 to 1. Before Moses developed the idea of the *Freedom Summer Project*, the Civil Rights struggle had been a regional one that primarily involved African Americans who orchestrated demonstrations and protests against southern institutions.

White involvement on the side of the Civil Rights struggle was minimal until Moses developed the idea to recruit northern white college students to participate in a voter registration project in the summer of 1964. The project had barely begun when on June 21st, three young male college students, a local African American, James Chaney, and two New Yorkers, Andrew Goodman (NAA), and Michael Schwerner (NAA), were reported missing. The murders outraged the American public, primarily because of the race of the two New Yorkers.

Robert Moses

The continued efforts of the Southern white establishment to intimidate the volunteers to leave failed, largely due to Moses who kept them focused on their goal. Moses himself was beaten and jailed several times but he stayed and continued to organize local communities to enable them to influence their destinies.

In 1982, Moses won the prestigious MacArthur *"Genius"* Fellowship. He used his $100,000 fellowship award to start the Algebra Project, a project to teach advanced math to students of color. Moses felt that a lack of math and science literacy effectively limited the potential of students of color to achieve economic access and parity in our technology based world. The program began with after-school tutors in one school in Cambridge. It has grown to serve over 10,000 students annually across the country. It also trains educators in how to use the techniques that Moses developed.

Moses understood that change must be internalized before it can be achieved and that peer to peer encounters have proven to be very effective in that process. To that end, he developed the Young People's Project to train teenagers to run math camps for other teens.

> "The absence of math literacy in urban and rural communities throughout this country is an issue as urgent as the lack of registered Black voters in Mississippi was in 1961."
> -- ROBERT MOSES

④ SITE: CHARLOTTE HAWKINS BROWN HOUSE
55 Essex St.

Charlotte Hawkins Brown (1883–1961) founded Palmer Memorial Institute in Greensboro, NC, in 1902. Brown's large family of nineteen moved to Cambridge from Henderson, NC, when she was seven. At Cambridge English High School, Brown excelled in her studies and there she met her future mentor and benefactor, Alice Freeman Palmer (NAA), the former president of Wellesley College. After graduation from high school, Brown enrolled in Salem Normal School, now Salem State College. In her second year at Salem Normal, Brown accepted an offer to operate the Bethany Institute, a school in Sedalia, NC, for the American Missionary Association.

Charlotte H. Brown

Although the school closed after only five months, Brown was encouraged by the success she achieved in that short time. Brown returned north to raise funds to open another school in the same location. In October of 1902, Brown opened Palmer Memorial Institute, named after her benefactor, with four hundred dollars and a donation of fifteen acres of land.

Palmer Memorial Institute eventually grew to encompass over three hundred acres. It evolved from classes in basic education and manual training, into a college preparatory institution. The school closed in 1971. Over the course of its existence, it prepared hundreds of African Americans for higher education.

5 JOSHUA BOWEN SMITH HOUSE
79 Norfolk St.

Joshua Bowen Smith (1813–1879) relocated to Boston from Pennsylvania while in his early twenties. A series of fortunate positions as a caterer enabled

Joshua Bowen Smith House

Smith to associate with some of the prominent abolitionists of the day, such as the families of Robert Gould Shaw (NAA), the leader of the Mass. 54th Regiment, and Charles Sumner (NAA), the future United States Senator. Smith moved to 79 Norfolk Street in 1852.

Joshua Bowen Smith

His economic success allowed him to actively participate in the abolitionist movement. Those activities included membership on the Boston Vigilance Committee. Smith also was the original fund-raiser for the 54th Regiment Memorial opposite the State House because of his close relationship with the Shaw household. Smith maintained a close relationship to Senator Sumner throughout the senator's career, and became a trusted advisor to the senator on matters related to slavery. Smith won election to the Massachusetts State Legislature for two terms, in 1873 and 1874.

6 BISHOP GEORGE A. McGUIRE — ST. BARTHOLOMEW'S CHURCH

239 Harvard St.

St. Bartholomew Church & Sign

Bishop George McGuire (1866–1934) founded the African Orthodox Church in Cambridge in 1921. Born and educated in Antigua, British West Indies, McGuire was ordained into the Episcopalian ministry in 1896. He pastored a congregation in Arkansas in 1905. In 1909, he relocated to Cambridge where he took over the predominantly African American congregation of St. Bartholomew's Episcopal Church.

The racism of the Episcopal Church frustrated McGuire. He left St. Bartholomew's to take other positions, including some in his native Antigua. In 1919, for a few years before he founded the African Orthodox Church, McGuire was Chaplain of the UNIA (Universal Negro Improvement Association). The UNIA was Marcus Garvey's movement to facilitate repatriation back to Africa for African Americans.

7 SITE: CLEMENT G. MORGAN HOUSE

265 Prospect St.

Clement G. Morgan (1859–1929), born to enslaved parents in Virginia, was the first African American to graduate from both Harvard College and Harvard Law School. After the Civil War, his family relocated to Washington, D.C. where Morgan graduated from high school. He entered Harvard College at the age of twenty-six in 1885, and he graduated from Harvard Law in 1893.

Clement Morgan, W.E.B. DuBois, and William Trotter, all Harvard graduates, were some of the original founders of the Niagara Movement, the

Bishop George A. McGuire

predecessor of the NAACP. Morgan achieved another first with his election to the Cambridge Board of Aldermen in 1895. He remained active in politics and maintained a successful law practice in Boston for the remainder of his life. Clement G. Morgan was buried in Mt. Auburn Cemetery.

Maria Baldwin

Clement Morgan

 ## 8 MARIA BALDWIN HOUSE
196 Prospect St.

Maria Baldwin (1856–1922) was the first African American principal of a public school in Cambridge with her appointment as head of the Agassiz School in 1889. Born in Cambridge, Baldwin graduated from Cambridge High School in 1874. After her studies at the Teacher's Training School, Baldwin taught for a few years in Maryland.

The African American community of Cambridge protested Baldwin's inability to obtain a position in her hometown despite her excellent qualifications. Those protests influenced the Cambridge School Board to offer Baldwin a position to teach at the Agassiz School. After seven years, she was promoted to the position of Principal of the Agassiz School. Baldwin remained at the school until her death in 1922. In addition to her role as a prominent

Maria Baldwin House

educator in Cambridge, Baldwin was well known for her public lectures on women's suffrage and African American historical figures. The Agassiz was renamed the Maria Baldwin School in 2002.

9 ALBERTA V. SCOTT HOUSE
28 Union St.

In 1898, Alberta V. Scott (1875–1902) became the first African American to graduate from Radcliffe College. Scott's blue-collar family lived at this address for a time. She devoted herself to her studies at an early age, and her diligence was rewarded when she graduated from Radcliffe.

Shortly after she graduated, Booker T. Washington recruited Scott to teach

at Tuskegee Institute in Alabama. A sudden illness after one year brought Scott's career to an end. She returned to Cambridge and died in her family's new home at 37 Hubbard Ave.

Alberta Scott House & Sign

Alberta Scott

10 JOHN FATAL HOUSE
49 Lincoln St.

Abolitionist and civil rights advocate, John Fatal (1816–1904) was born in Newburyport. He moved to Boston as an adult where he was active in the abolitionist movement as a member of the Boston Vigilance Committee. Fatal was also active in the fight to desegregate Boston Public Schools. The failure of that effort led Fatal to relocate his family to Cambridge to take advantage of Cambridge's integrated school system.

John Fatal Sign

John Fatal achieved success as a business owner prior to his election for one term to the Cambridge Common Council. Fatal eventually took a position at the United States Sub-treasury in Boston, where he worked for 25 years.

John Fatal House

11 LUNSFORD LANE HOUSE
44 Webster Ave.

Born enslaved in Raleigh, NC, Lunsford Lane (1810-1879) learned to read and write at an early age. He eventually purchased his freedom with money earned through odd jobs. Lane opened a shop and purchased a house in the Raleigh area with his earnings, and he began to save the $2,500 needed to purchase the freedom of his wife and children.

Lunsford Lane

The ability of Lane and other formerly enslaved African Americans to contribute economically to the community should have been seen as positive. Instead, local whites felt Lane's success, and the success of those in similar circumstances, would inspire the local, enslaved community to try to purchase their freedom as well. That trend would destabilize the local economy which depended on a bountiful supply of enslaved labor.

Lunsford Lane House & Sign

After Lane had already paid $620 toward his family's freedom, local whites ran him out of town. Lane escaped with one of his daughters but the rest of his family remained enslaved. He traveled as an abolitionist lecturer for a year in the Boston area in an effort to raise funds to complete the purchase of his family.

When Lane returned to the South, to purchase the freedom of the remainder of his family, he was tarred and feathered and driven out of town again. This time he was able to escape with everyone. Lane returned to Massachusetts and settled in Cambridge. There he wrote the well-received autobiography, *The Narrative Life of Lunsford Lane*. Lane lived here from 1848 to 1860.

SITE: WILLIAM WELLS BROWN HOUSE

1 Lilac Court, previously 15 Webster Street - demolished

In 1853, William Wells Brown (1814–1884), a fugitive from slavery and later an abolitionist, was the first African American author to publish a novel, *Clotel,* which was published in England. Brown was born in Lexington, KY, and he managed to escape bondage at the age of twenty. He moved first to Buffalo, NY, and then to Boston, where he educated himself and became a lecturer for the American Anti-Slavery Society. Brown lectured his entire life against slavery and for the civil rights of African Americans.

William Wells Brown

This excerpt from Brown's speech, *"I Have No Constitution, and No Country,"* was delivered at the Paris Peace Congress in August of 1849. *"The Liberator"* newspaper reprinted it a few months later:

"I Have No Constitution, and No Country"

"...Before resuming my seat, I would say to our friend from Boston, as I said to another gentleman a short time before I left America, who talked in a similar manner about the slave States, and the good treatment the slaves received, and so forth. At the close of a meeting, that gentleman rose, and requested permission to ask me some simple questions, which were as follows: Had I not enough to eat when I was in slavery? Was I not well clothed while in the southern States? Was I ever whipped? And so forth. I saw that he only wanted a peg on which to hang a pro-slavery speech, but I answered his questions in the affirmative. He immediately rose and made a speech, in which he endeavored to make his audience believe that I had run away from a very good place indeed. (Laughter.) He asked them if they did not know hundreds and thousands of poor people in America and England, who would be willing to go into the state of Missouri and there fill the situation I had run away from. (Cries of Oh, Oh!)

A portion of the assembly for a moment really thought his plea for slavery was a good one. ...in consequence of the lateness of the hour, and therefore that it would not do for me to reply at any length, I accordingly rose and made a single remark in answer to this pro-slavery speech. I said, the gentleman has praised up the situation I left, and made it appear quite another thing to what it ever appeared to me when I was there; but however that may be, I have to inform him that that situation is still vacant, and as far as I have anything voluntary to do with it, it shall remain so; but, nevertheless, if that gentleman likes to go into Missouri and fill it, I will give him a recommendation to my old master, and I doubt not that he would receive him with open arms, and give him enough to eat, enough to wear, and flog him whenever he thought he required it."

-- William Wells Brown

William Wells Brown House Sign

13 MAYOR KENNETH REEVES AND MAYOR E. DENISE SIMMONS
Cambridge City Hall
795 Mass. Ave.

St. Augustine's Orthodox Church

Two African Americans were elected to the position of mayor in Cambridge, the only municipality in the Commonwealth with such a distinction. Kenneth Reeves served from 1992 to 1995, and again from 2006 to 2007. E. Denise Simmons served from 2008 to 2009, and she was re-elected in 2016. Both initial elections marked the first time that an openly gay African American, Reeves, and an openly lesbian African American, Simmons, were elected mayor of a major U.S. city.

14 BISHOP GEORGE A. MCGUIRE
ST. AUGUSTINE'S AFRICAN ORTHODOX CHURCH
137 Allston St.

Bishop George McGuire (1866–1934) founded the African Orthodox Church in Cambridge in 1921. St. Augustine's is the only church of this denomination that remains in Cambridge. See Cambridge Site #6. Bishop McGuire began his ministry as an Episcopalian priest but the racism of the Church frustrated him. He moved to his native Antigua to take other positions in the ministry.

McGuire moved back to the States in 1919 and became chaplain-general of the Universal Negro Improvement Association (UNIA), the African American empowerment organization founded by Marcus Garvey. McGuire's efforts to establish the official church of the UNIA failed. The level of ritual of the Episcopal service that McGuire instituted proved to be uncomfortable to the UNIA membership.

McGuire founded the African Orthodox Church in 1921. Membership reached 12,000 by the mid-1920s with

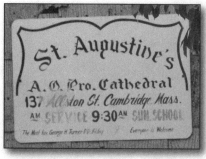

St. Augustine's Orthodox Church Sign

congregations spread throughout the Northeastern United States, Nova Scotia, and the Caribbean.

15 SITE: J. MILTON CLARKE & LEWIS CLARKE HOUSE
2 Florence Place

The brothers, J. Milton Clarke (1820–1902) and Lewis Clarke (1818–1897), escaped slavery in Kentucky together in their early twenties. After they arrived in Cambridge, they wrote a successful book in 1846, *Narrative of the Sufferings of Lewis and Milton Clarke*. Harriet Beecher Stowe (NAA) based one of the characters in *Uncle Tom's Cabin* on Lewis Clarke.

Lewis Clarke

Lewis eventually left Cambridge, but Milton stayed and became the first African American elected to public office in Cambridge, with his election to the Cambridge Common Council in 1870. Milton Clarke also worked at the United States Sub-treasury in downtown Boston for thirty-three years.

J. Milton Clarke

16 W.E.B. DuBois HOUSE
20 Flagg Street

William Edward Burghardt Dubois (1868–1963), the foremost African American intellectual in the first half of the 20th century, lived here while he was a student at Harvard University. After graduation, DuBois relocated to the South where his research on African American cul-

1895
W.E.B. DuBois was the first African American to earn an academic doctorate from Harvard.

W. E. B. DuBois

July 13, 1905
"Niagara Movement" meeting in Buffalo, NY led to the creation of the NAACP in 1910.

ture resulted in the classic book, *The Souls of Black Folk.*

DuBois was the leader and spokesman for the anti-Booker T. Washington forces. Booker T. Washington rejected higher education for African Americans. He felt their focus should be to learn a trade in order to develop a strong economic base. In contrast, DuBois firmly believed that intellectual development of African Americans was equally critical to improve their conditions in life.

DuBois brought civil rights activists together in the famous *"Niagara Movement"* at Buffalo, NY, in 1905. This movement joined with white reformers to found the NAACP in 1910. DuBois personified a new manner for African Americans, a spirit of militant protest and self-assertion.

DuBois in his essay, *"The Immediate Program of the American Negro,"* outlined his controversial idea to cultivate a class of Negro leaders, a class he termed, *"The Talented Tenth"*:

W. E. B. DuBois House

"...The immediate program of the American Negro means nothing unless it is mediate to his great ideal and the ultimate ends of his development. We need not waste time by seeking to deceive our enemies into thinking that we are going to be content with half a loaf, or by being willing to lull our friends into a false sense of our indifference and present satisfaction.

The American Negro demands equality—political equality, industrial equality and social equality; and he is never going to rest satisfied with anything less. He demands this in no spirit of braggadocio and with no obsequious envy of others, but as an absolute measure of self-defense and the only one that will assure to the darker races their ultimate survival on earth...."

—W.E.B. DuBois

17 HARVARD CAMPUS (HC): JULIAN ABELE & WIDENER LIBRARY

Harvard Univ. Main Quad off Mass. Ave.

African American architect, Julian Abele (1881–1950) was the primary designer for Widener Library during his employment with the Philadelphia architecture firm of Horace Trumbauer (NAA). Born in Philadelphia, Abele was the first African American to graduate with an architecture degree from the University of Pennsylvania. After

Julian Abele

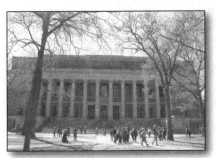

Widener Library

graduation, Abele traveled throughout Europe to expand his architectural education.

Upon his return to the states, Abele joined the firm of Horace Trumbauer in Philadelphia, as an assistant designer. He rose to the position of chief designer in 1909, a position he held until the death of the firm's owner in 1938. In addition to Widener Library, Abele was primarily responsible for the design of the Philadelphia Museum of Art, many mansions in Newport, RI, and multiple buildings at Duke University in North Carolina.

 ## HC: ALLAN CRITE AT GROSSMAN LIBRARY
311 Sever Hall-3rd floor

Several drawings by the Harlem Renaissance artist, Allan Crite, are on display in Grossman Library.

 ## HC: RICHARD T. GREENER
Harvard College House, 1430 Mass. Ave.

The path Richard Theodore Greener (1844–1922) took to become the first African American to graduate from the country's most prestigious university was not the typical one. He was not nurtured in a family of privilege and he did not receive his education from a prestigious school. His family's poor circumstances forced him to leave middle school to work to help support them.

1870
Richard Theodore Greener was the first African American graduate of Harvard College.

After six years of work, Greener managed to resume his studies. He be-

gan with a college preparatory program at Oberlin College and he finished his secondary studies at Phillips Andover Academy. Greener entered Harvard in 1865. Despite the fact that he had to repeat his first year, Greener perservered and graduated in 1870. After graduation, Greener eventually served as a diplomat for several U.S. Presidents.

Richard T. Greener

 ## HC: DuBois INSTITUTE/ HUGGINS CTR FOR AFRICAN & AFRICAN AMERICAN RESEARCH
104 Mount Auburn St., 3R
www.dubois.fas.harvard.edu

The Dubois Institute, which in 2013 was renamed the Huggins Center for African and African American Research, is one of the foremost centers in the world for the research and study of the history and culture of people of the African diaspora. Created in 1975, the DuBois Institute annually awards up to twenty fellowships to scholars from around the world. It also sponsors research projects, conferences, and lectures that are opened to the general public.

In 1991, Harvard appointed Henry Louis Gates, Jr., as Head of the Department of Afro-American Studies. That same year, Gates became director of the W.E.B. DuBois Institute. Under the leadership of Gates, the influence of the Institute has extended throughout the world.

DuBois Institute / Huggins Center

The Neil and Angelica Zander Rudenstine (NAA) Gallery at the Institute features art by and about people of the African diaspora. Some of the artists represented by past exhibits include: Romare Bearden, Elizabeth Catlett, Jacob Lawrence, and contemporary artists, Carrie Mae Weems, and Maria Magdalena Campos-Pons.

The international architect, David Adjaye (b. 1966), designed a new home for the Ethelbert Cooper Gallery of African and African American Art of the Center. This is the only building in Massachusetts designed by this internationally known African architect. He is principal of the London based international firm of Adjaye Associates.

Adjaye's firm was lead designer for the new National Museum for African American History and Culture of the Smithsonian. Located on the national mall in Washington, D.C., that museum opened in September of 2016. The design team that won the competition in April of 2009, was the Freelon Adjaye Bond / Smith Group. Two of the other member firms also had Cambridge connections. Phillip Freelon was educated at MIT and later was a Loeb Fellow at Harvard's Graduate School of Design (GSD). He is now on the faculty of MIT's School of Architecture. In 2016, a fellowship was established in Freelon's name at the GSD. J. Max Bond was educated at Harvard's School of Design. Unfortunately, J. Max Bond died shortly before the team won the award.

There are two major research areas at the DuBois Institute, the Hip-Hop Archive, dedicated to understand and promote Hip-Hop culture, and the Image of the Black in Western Art Research Project and Photo Archive. This project is an outgrowth of a four volume series, *The Image of the Black in Western Art,* first published in the early 1990s by Harvard University Press.

The Image of the Black in Western Art series was based on research sponsored by art patrons, Jean and Dominique de Menil (NAA) in the early 1960s to protest segregation in the U.S. The archive of over 30,000 works of art studied how Western art represented people of African descent over the past 5,000 years. The DuBois Institute partnered with Harvard University Press to continue the series.

(21) HC: CHARLES HAMILTON HOUSTON INSTITUTE FOR RACE & JUSTICE
125 Mount Auburn St., 3rd Floor
www.charleshamilton houston.org

Charles J. Ogletree, Jr. founded the Charles Hamilton Houston Institute for Race and Justice at Harvard Law School in 2005. Ogletree, a tenured professor at Harvard Law School, mentored both President Barack Obama and Governor Deval Patrick while both were students at Harvard Law. The Charles Hamilton Houston Institute was formed to continue the legacy of Charles Hamilton Houston (1895-1950) who dedicated his life to the reversal of racial discrimination by the implementation of changes in the law. Houston graduated from Harvard Law in 1923.

Houston attended Amherst College as an undergraduate prior to his enrollment in Harvard Law, see more under Amherst sites. Soon after graduation from the law school, Houston took the position of Vice-Dean of Howard Law School in Washington, D.C. He wanted to train as many African American lawyers as possible to send South to fight segregation. In some Southern states in this era, the ratio of African American citizens to African American attorneys was as high as 200,000 to 1. Houston also served on the Legal Defense Team of the NAACP.

Charles Hamilton Houston

Houston very methodically laid the groundwork for contemporary legal challenges against institutional segregation; in fact, he became known as the man who began to dismantle *Jim Crow* in America. Houston's legacy as a legal strategist equaled his reputation as a teacher of the law.

> *"...a lawyer's either a social engineer or ... a parasite on society."*
> – CHARLES HAMILTON HOUSTON

Charles Hamilton Houston used his limited resources to dismantle segregation in education. He felt that the inequities from a deficient education limited an individual's ability to compete in society. The results of that disparity plagued many African Americans throughout their life. Houston also realized that a poor education was, in many instances, no accidental, *"luck of the draw,"* in life but a calculated effort to indoctrinate African Americans to accept an inferior status in life without a struggle. As Houston stated:

> *"Discrimination in education is symbolic of all the more drastic discrimination which Negroes suffer in American life."*
> –CHARLES HAMILTON HOUSTON

Thurgood Marshall, Houston's most famous student at Howard Law School, successfully argued the Brown vs. Kansas Board of Education case of 1954 in the United States Supreme Court. Marshall won a unanimous (9–0) victory in that seminal school desegregation case. President Lyndon Baines Johnson (NAA) appointed Thurgood Marshall as the first African American Supreme Court Justice in 1967.

The Charles Hamilton Houston Institute hosts film presentations, lectures, conferences, and symposiums related to its mission. Most of their events are open to the general public. Harvard Law School established the Charles Hamilton Houston Professorship of Law, a tenured faculty position, to honor Houston.

Charles Hamilton Houston Institute:
- The Citizenship Project: explores the ambivalence of the United States toward immigrants.
- The O'Connor Project: named after Supreme Court Justice, Sandra Day O'Connor (NAA), investigates the relationship of the diversity admissions policies of schools to social and educational inequities.
- One Nation Indivisible: investigates how people sustain diverse communities.
- Pathways Home: explores the ways in which formerly incarcerated people rebuild their lives.
- Race and the Death Penalty: investigates the connection between racial profiling and the death penalty.
- Redirecting the School to Prison Pipeline: investigates the correlation between substandard schools and youth who land in detention facilities and prison.

(22) HC: PETER GOMES & MEMORIAL CHURCH
One Harvard Yard
617-495-5508

After World War I, Harvard University President, Abbott Lawrence Lowell (NAA), decided to combine a new chapel with a war memorial. The architects Coolidge, Shepley, Bulfinch & Abbott (NAA) designed Memorial Church as a nondenominational church. The Harvard community dedicated the structure on Armistice Day in 1932, in memory of University alumni and students who died during WWI.

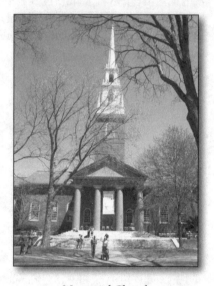

Memorial Church

lican, Gomes delivered the inaugural sermons for both President Ronald Reagan (NAA) and the first President George W. Bush (NAA).

Peter Gomes

In 1970, Reverend Peter Gomes (1942–2011) became the first African American minister of Memorial Church. Harvard Divinity School appointed Gomes as Plummer Professor of Christian Morals in 1974. A Repub-

In 1991, Gomes announced that he was gay, to protest widespread homophobia. He dedicated the rest of his career to eradicate the many levels of intolerance that exist in our society. Gomes's longevity at Memorial Church combined with his bravery to publicly declare his sexual orientation were two of the factors for the widespread respect that he received. In 2006, Gomes, a registered Republican, switched his party affiliation to support his friend, Deval Patrick, in Patrick's campaign to become the first African American Governor of Massachusetts. Gomes served at Harvard for four decades until his death.

23 HC: MEMORIAL HALL
45 Quincy St.

In 1870, construction began on Memorial Hall, a building dedicated to honor the memory of the sons of Harvard who served in the Civil War. The memorial, dedicated in 1878, consisted of three components, Annenberg Hall, Memorial Transept, and Sanders Theater. The building, a superior example of Victorian Gothic architecture, was designated as a National Historic Landmark in 1970.

Twenty-eight marble tablets that list 136 Harvard alumni who died in the Civil War were installed in Memorial Transept. Robert Gould Shaw (NAA), Class of 1860, was one of the names listed. Shaw was the Colonel of the Massachusetts 54th Regiment, the first African American regiment raised in the North. There was no reference to slavery as the primary cause of that

war. That omission was typical of most Civil War memorials and monuments. Also, no fallen Confederate alumni were listed on the tablets. The Harvard community has recently engaged in a lively discussion about whether it would be appropriate to include Confederate alumni in the memorial. There has been no resolution on that debate.

Sanders Theater, renowned for its superior acoustics, has hosted some of the most distinguished speakers in contemporary history such as Martin Luther King, Jr., Winston Churchill (NAA), and Mikhail Gorbachev (NAA).

24 HC: HARVARD LAW SCHOOL
1563 Massachusetts Ave.

Harvard Law School, established in 1817, has long nurtured African Americans into positions of leadership. The first African American to graduate from Harvard Law was George Ruffin in 1862. Ruffin went on to be appointed the first African American judge in the state. See Beacon Hill and Charlestown sites.

The second African American to graduate from Harvard Law School was Archibald Grimke (1849–1930).

Memorial Hall at Harvard

Harvard Law School

He graduated in the mid-1870s. Grimke was the nephew of Sarah (NAA) and Angelina Grimke (NAA), the white abolitionists from Charleston, SC. Sarah and Angelina left Charleston in the early 1830s because they could not live with the hypocrisy of fellow Southerners, including their own family, who enslaved individuals but called themselves Christians.

Archibald Grimke's father, Henry (NAA), left his white wife and maintained a second family with an enslaved woman, Nancy Weston, on the outskirts of Charleston. Henry and Nancy had three sons, Archibald, Francis, and John. Henry kept the entire family enslaved yet he lived with them as a family. After their father's death in 1852, their white half-brother maintained the boys in a semi-enslaved status.

The boys eventually enrolled in Lincoln University in Pennsylvania on scholarship. Lincoln University was the nation's first historically Black college. Supreme Court Justice, Thurgood Marshall, poet, Langston Hughes, and Kwame Nkrumah, the first President of Ghana, all graduated from Lincoln.

While at Lincoln University, their aunts, Sarah and Angelina Grimke (NAA), discovered them and began to assist in their support. Francis went on to study at Princeton Theology Seminary and Archibald matriculated to Harvard Law. Archibald became an activist attorney after graduation. He helped found and wrote for "*The Guardian*" newspaper with William M. Trotter. In 1894, President Grover Cleveland (NAA) appointed Grimke as Consul to Santo Domingo. Grimke's involvement with the NAACP led him to become national Vice-President in 1899.

Archibald Grimke married Sarah Stanley (NAA) and they had one child, Angelina Weld Grimke (1880–1958), named after Archibald's aunt. Sarah's family did not approve of the marriage and Sarah abandoned Archibald and Angelina while Angelina was still a toddler.

Angelina Weld Grimke became an accomplished poet. Many of her poems were not published in her lifetime because they described her romantic preferences for females, a reality that was very controversial in the early twentieth century.

Archibald Grimke was a very outspoken advocate for the civil rights of African Americans his entire life. In 1920, his speech, *"The Shame of Amer-*

Archibald Grimke

ica, or the Negro's Case Against the Republic," lambasted the United States for the hypocritical way it treated African Americans.

**"The Shame of America, or the Negro's Case Against the Republic,"
excerpt:**

"... Thus it happened that black men fought in that war shoulder to shoulder with white men for American Independence. In every colony from Massachusetts to Georgia, they were found faithful among the faithless, and brave as the bravest during those long and bitter years, fighting and dying with incomparable devotion and valor,... Such was the priceless contribution which the poor, oppressed Negro made to American Independence.

What was his guerdon? In the hour of their triumph did the patriot fathers call to mind such supreme service to reward it? In the freedom which they had won by the aid of their enslaved countrymen, did they bethink then of lightening the yoke of those miserable men? History answers, no! Truth answers, no! the descendants of those black heroes answer, no! what then? They founded the Republic on slavery, rested one end of its stately arch on the prostrate neck of the Negro. They constructed a national Constitution which safeguarded the property of man in man, introducing into it for that purpose its three fifths slave representation provision, its fugitive slave clause, and an agreement by which the African slave trade was legalized for nineteen years after the adoption of that instrument. That was the reward which the founders of the Republic meted out with one accord to a race which had shed freely its blood to make that Republic a reality among the nations of the earth. Instead of loosening and lifting his heavy yoke of oppression they strengthened and tightened it afresh on the loyal and long suffering neck of the Negro....

...You may ransack the libraries of the world, and turn over all the documents of recorded time to match that Preamble of the Constitution as a piece of consummate political dissimulation and mental reservation, as an example of how men juggle deliberately and successfully with their moral sense, how they raise above themselves (a) huge fabric of falsehood, and go willingly to live and die in a make believe world of lies. The muse of history, dipping her iron pen in the generous blood of the Negro, has written large across the page of the Preamble, and the face of the Declaration of Independence, the words, "sham, hypocrisy." ..."

–Archibald Grimke, excerpt from speech

The first African American elected Governor of Massachusetts, Deval Patrick, also graduated from Harvard Law School. See more on Patrick under Beacon Hill sites. Barack Obama, the first African American elected President of the United States in 2008, graduated from Harvard Law as did his wife, Michelle Obama. Obama entered Harvard Law in 1988 at the age of 27. He made history at the school in 1990 as the first African American President of the Harvard Law Review. Obama won election to a second term in 2012.

Two other African Americans affiliated with Harvard Law whose professional legacies have greatly impaced all our lives were Charles Hamilton Houston and Derrick Bell. See more on Houston under Cambridge site

#21 and Amherst sites. Derrick Bell (1930–2011), a Harvard Law professor, achieved a significant impact on our society through his development of a new area of legal scholarship known

> **Famous African American Alumni of Harvard Law**
> - Judge George Ruffin, first African American Judge in the State in 1883
> - Archibald Grimke, civil rights advocate
> - Charles Hamilton Houston, paved the way to legally dismantle segregation laws
> - Reginald Lewis (1942-1993) graduated in 1968. Lewis was the first African American to own a billion dollar company, Beatrice Foods.
> - Edward Gourdin, first African American appointed to Mass. Superior Court, 1958.
> - Massachusetts Governor Deval Patrick
> - U.S. President Barack Obama
> - First Lady Michelle Obama, 1988.
> - Chief Justice Roderick Ireland, Mass. Supreme Court, 2010

President Barack Obama

First Lady Michelle Obama

as *"Critical Race Theory."* Critical Race Theory was developed to analyze institutional racism to better understand how those in power can manipulate the law to perpetuate their control of that power.

The ultimate goal of Critical Race Theory was to transform the disparity between the races in order to achieve real and meaningful racial equality. Critical Race Theory has become an established theory of law now taught in law schools across the United States.

In 1991, Bell was the first African American to achieve tenure at Harvard Law School. Despite this accomplishment, he refused to rest on his laurels. Instead, Bell utilized his position as a platform to protest the disparity between the number of tenured faculty of color at Harvard Law School and their white counterparts. The lack of any Af-

rican American female tenured faculty at Harvard Law led Bell to take an unpaid leave of absence in 1991.

> *"It appears my worst fears have been realized: we have made progress in everything yet nothing has changed."*
> —DERRICK BELL

> *"Courage means putting at risk your immediate self-interest for what you believe is right."*
> —DERRICK BELL

Derrick Bell ended his affiliation with Harvard four years later, because they still had not appointed an African

American female to a tenured faculty position. His decision to take that leave of absence was a testament to his belief that each individual has the potential to transform their world by personal acts of courage.

Derrick Bell

In 1998, Harvard Law School appointed its first African American female, Lani Guinier, to a tenured faculty position. Her appointment ended the disparity that led to Bell's resignation. After he left Harvard, Bell taught at New York University until his death.

25 MARY WALKER HOUSE

54 Brattle St., now the Cambridge Center for Adult Education

Mary Walker (1818–1872) was enslaved by the Cameron (NAA) family in North Carolina. A talented seam-stress, she often accompanied the family on trips to the North. On one such trip to Philadelphia in 1848, she escaped but the family she left back in NC, remained enslaved. Mary eventually made her way to Boston and settled in Cambridge where she continued to work. She received much praise as a seamstress.

Mary, with the help of several abolitionists, attempted numerous times to be reunited with her three children but all the attempts failed. One son finally escaped in 1852 but Mary had to wait until after the Civil War to be reunited with her other children. A benefactor purchased this house for Mary and she lived there with her extended family until her death. The home was in her family until 1912.

26 HARRIET A. JACOBS HOUSE

17 Story St.

Harriet Jacobs (1813-1897), wrote one of the most powerful narratives to come out of slavery, *Incidents in the*

Harriet Jacobs House

Life of a Slave Girl. Abolitionist and author, Lydia Maria Child (NAA) edited the book and was instrumental in its publication in 1861. Jacobs lived in this house after she settled in Cambridge.

The Norcom family (NAA) of Edenton, NC, enslaved Jacobs and her brother when they were still young. In Harriet's teenage years, she attracted the attention of a wealthy, white landowner and future government official, Samuel Tredwell Sawyer (NAA). Harriet entered into a relationship with Sawyer and bore him two children, Louisa and Joseph, in the mistaken belief that he would free them all.

After the birth of her children, the father purchased the children but not Harriet, and he freed none of them. In anger, Harriet ran away from the Norcom's; but she could not bear to be away from her children, so she devised a way to hide in their attic so that she could watch over them. Harriet stayed in that attic for seven years.

Harriet Jacobs

Harriet Jacobs's second escape took her to New York, and then to Boston. In Boston, she met abolitionists who purchased her freedom and helped her to obtain the freedom of her children. Her narrative is a brutal reminder of the harsh existence of those forced to depend on the whims of others.

An excerpt from the first chapter:

The New Master and Mistress:

"...Mrs. Flint, like many southern women, ...her nerves were so strong, that she could sit in her easy chair and see a woman whipped, till the blood trickled from every stroke of the lash. She was a member of the church; but partaking of the Lord's Supper did not seem to put her in a Christian frame of mind. If dinner was not served at the exact time on that particular Sunday, she would station herself in the kitchen, and wait till it was dished, and then spit in all the kettles and pans that had been used for cooking. She did this to prevent the cook and her children from eking out their meager fare with the remains of the gravy and other scrapings. The slaves could get nothing to eat except what she chose to give them. Provisions were weighed out by the pound and ounce, three times a day.

... she gave them no chance to eat wheat bread from her flour barrel. She knew how many biscuits a quart of flour would make, and exactly what size they ought to be.

Dr. Flint was an epicure. The cook never sent a dinner to his table without fear and trembling; for if there happened to be a dish not to his liking he would either order her to be whipped, or compel her to eat every mouthful of it in his presence. The poor, hungry creature might not have objected to eating it; but she did object to having her master cram it down her throat till she choked.

...When I had been in the family a few weeks, one of the plantation slaves was brought to town, ... Dr. Flint ordered him to be taken to the work house, and tied up to the joist, so that his feet would just escape the ground. In that situation he was to wait till the doctor had taken his tea. I shall never forget that night. Never before, in my life, had I heard hundreds of blows fall, in succession, on a human being. His piteous groans, and his "O, pray don't massa," rang in my ear for months afterwards. There were many conjectures as to the cause of this terrible punishment. Some said master accused him of stealing corn; others said the slave had quarreled with his wife, in the presence of the overseer, and had accused his master of being the father of her child. They were both black, and the child was very fair.

I went into the work house next morning, and saw the cowhide still wet with blood, and the boards all covered with gore. The poor man lived, and continued to quarrel with his wife. A few months afterwards Dr. Flint handed them both over to a slave-trader. ... When the mother was delivered into the trader's hands, she said, "You promised to treat me well." To which he replied, "You have let your tongue run too far; damn you!" She had forgotten that it was a crime for a slave to tell who was the father of her child."

-- Harriet Jacobs, Incidents in the Life of a Slave Girl

 27 ## OLD BURYING GROUND

Harvard Square, Corner of
Mass Ave. & Garden St.

Two African American Revolutionary War Heroes were buried here, Cato Steadman and Neptune Frost. Steadman fought at the historic Battle of Lexington and Concord on April 19th,

Old Burying Ground Cemetery Plaque

1775. Though not buried here, Cuff Whittemore of Cambridge also served in the American Revolution. Several enslaved individuals who lived in Cambridge were also buried here.

 ## PRINCE HALL MONUMENT
Cambridge Common, Garden St.

Prince Hall (1735–1807) was a veteran of the American Revolution, an activist for African American rights, and the founder of the African Order of Masons. On Sept. 12th, 2006, Cambridge City Councilor and the first African American female mayor of Cambridge, Denise Simmons, proposed a resolution for a memorial to honor Hall. The memorial was unveiled on May 15th, 2010. See more on Hall under North End Sites and downtown Boston Sites.

 ## MEMORIAL TO GEN. WASHINGTON
Cambridge Common at Garden St.

General George Washington (NAA) took control of the Continental Army near this site. Washington was stationed at this camp when he received correspondence that included a poem from Phillis Wheatley in 1775 that praised his accomplishments. Washington thanked Wheatley by letter on February 28th, 1776. In that letter, he also invited Wheatley to visit him at the Cambridge camp. That correspondence represents the only known written communication between General Washington and an African American civilian.

Prince Hall Monument

To His Excellency General Washington
By Phillis Wheatley, excerpt

"Celestial choir! enthron'd in realms of light,
Columbia's scenes of glorious toils I write.
While freedom's cause her anxious breast alarms,
She flashes dreadful in refulgent arms.
See mother earth her offspring's fate bemoan,
And nations gaze at scenes before unknown!
See the bright beams of heaven's revolving light
Involv'd in sorrows and the veil of night!
...
Shall I to Washington their praise recite?
Enough thou know'st them in the fields of fight.
Thee first in place and honours, -- we demand
The grace and glory of thy martial band.
Fam'd for thy valour, for thy virtues more,
Hear every tongue thy guardian aid implore!
...
Proceed, great chief, with virtue on thy side,
Thy every action let the goddess guide.
A crown, a mansion, and a throne that shine,
With gold unfading, WASHINGTON! Be thine."

Cambridge, Feb. 28, 1776
Miss Phillis –

Your favor of the 26th of October did not reach my hands till the middle of December. Time enough, you will say, to have given an answerere this. Granted. But a variety of important occurrences, continually interposing to distract the mind and withdraw the attention, I hope will apologize for the delay, and plead my excuse for the seeming but not real neglect. I thank you most sincerely for your polite notice of me in the elegant lines you enclosed: and however undeserving I may be of such encomium and panegyric, the style and manner exhibit a striking proof of your poetical talents; in honor of which, and as a tribute justly due to you, I would have published the poem had I not been apprehensive that, *while I only meant to give the world this new instance of your genius, I might have incurred the imputation of vanity. This, and nothing else, determined me not to give it place in the public prints.*

If you should ever come to Cambridge, or near headquarters, I shall be happy to see a person so favored by the Muses, and to whom nature has been so liberal and beneficent in her dispensations. I am, with great respect, you obedient, humble servant,

Geo. Washington"

Cambridge Memorial to Gen. Washington

30 BLACK WOMEN ORAL HISTORY RUTH EDMONDS HILL & DR. HUGH MORGAN HILL, AKA BROTHER BLUE
Radcliffe College
Schlesinger Library /
Ten Garden Street.

Between 1976 and 1985, under the sponsorship of the Schlesinger Library, 71 interviews were conducted with vari-

ous African American women who had made significant contributions to society. Ruth Edmonds Hill was co-editor of those interviews. Those documents are stored in Schlesinger Library at Radcliffe College. They are available for research on-line. The following Massachusetts women were included in that collection; Melnea Cass, May Chinn, Clara Dickson, Florence Edmonds, Beulah Hester, Ellen Jackson, Lois Mailou Jones, Muriel Snowden, Ann Tanneyhill, Mary Thompson, Ozeline Wise, and Dorothy West.

Ruth Hill, a scholar, storyteller, and historian, was married to Dr. Hugh Morgan Hill (1921-2009), a recipient of several graduate and post-graduate degrees. Dr. Hill, AKA, Brother Blue,

Schlesinger Library

was a fixture at Cambridge festivals and events, where he mesmerized people with his unique ability to tell stories. He utilized storytelling as a way to build peace in his community.

Ruth Edmonds Hill and Brother Blue

Ruth Hill's grandfather was Rev. Samuel Harrison of Pittsfield, MA. Rev. Harrison was a Chaplain for the Massachusetts 54th Regiment. He was involved in the fight with the federal government against wage discrimination. Hill successfully petitioned to have Harrison's house in Pittsfield designated a national landmark.

(31) LONGFELLOW HOUSE / GEN. WASHINGTON'S HEADQUARTERS NATIONAL HISTORIC SITE
105 Brattle St.

While General George Washington's Continental Headquarters was based in Cambridge, he resided at this Georgian style house from July, 1775, until April, 1776. The next historical figure to live here was Henry Wadsworth Longfellow (1807–1882) (NAA), the noted poet and abolitionist. Longfellow lived in this house from 1837 until his death. His family was the last to live in the house. In 1913, they established a trust to preserve the residence.

Longfellow wrote many of his beloved works here. Those included, "The Midnight Ride of Paul Revere," "The Song of Hiawatha," and, "The Courtship of Miles Standish." Longfellow counted many prominent abolitionists in his circle of friends such as Charles Sumner (NAA), Ralph Waldo Emerson (NAA), and Nathaniel Hawthorne (NAA). Initially, Longfellow preferred to keep his distance from the politics of slavery and his primary contributions to the abolitionist cause were financial ones. That changed in 1842 when Longfellow compiled and published

Henry Wadsworth Longfellow

the collection, *Poems on Slavery, 1842.* "The Witnesses" was one of the poems from that collection.

"The Witnesses"
By Henry Wadsworth Longfellow

"In Ocean's wide domains,
Half buried in the sands,
Lie skeletons in chains,
With shackled feet and hands.
Beyond the fall of dews,
Deeper than plummet lies,
Float ships, with all their crews,
No more to sink nor rise.
There the black Slave-ship swims,
Freighted with human forms,
Whose fettered, fleshless limbs
Are not the sport of storms.
These are the bones of Slaves;
They gleam from the abyss;
They cry, from yawning waves,
"We are the Witnesses!"
Within Earth's wide domains
Are markets for men's lives;
Their necks are galled with chains,
Their wrists are cramped with gyves.
Dead bodies, that the kite
In deserts makes its prey;
Murders, that with affright
Scare school-boys from their play!
All evil thoughts and deeds;
Anger, and lust, and pride;
The foulest, rankest weeds,
That choke Life's groaning tide!
These are the woes of slaves,
They glare from the abyss;
They cry, from unknown graves,
"We are the Witnesses!"'

By the time the Fugitive Slave Law of 1850 was passed, many who were moderates in politics, such as Longfellow, had become more radical. Longfellow wrote the poem, "The Midnight Ride of Paul Revere," as a call to arms to those who continued to be complacent about the harms of slavery. It appeared on newsstands on Dec. 20th, 1860, when the first Confederate state seceded from the Union.

 ## 32 LEWISVILLE SETTLEMENT
Garden St. near Shepard St.

The family of Mark Lewis, a tenant farmer in Cambridge in 1799, established an African American settlement in Cambridge complete with its own burying ground at this location. Mark Lewis owned and farmed 29 acres of land near Observatory Hill. His son, Adam Lewis and Adam's wife, Catherine Vassall, built a large house at Concord and Garden St. in 1820. In 1821, Adam Lewis's brother, Peter Lewis, and Peter's family from Barre, MA, joined the family compoound.

In 1830, Peter Lewis purchased an acre of land at this location and Lewisville began. The self-sufficient settlement thrived until a group of the family relocated to Liberia in 1859. Another group of the family remained in Cambridge. The last direct descendant of the family in Cambridge, Jerome Lewis, died in 1976.

(33) MARIA L. BALDWIN SCHOOL
28 Sacramento St.

In 1889, Maria Baldwin (1856-1922) became the first African American principal of a public school in Cambridge when she took over the helm of the Agassiz School, a predominantly white school. Baldwin had previously taught at the Agassiz for seven years. African Americans who worked in a professional capacity were rare at this time, and Ms. Baldwin's leadership position over a white staff was doubly remarkable.

Baldwin led the school until her death from a heart attack. During her tenure at the Agassiz, she developed many educational practices that are the norm today but were innovative for their time. One was the appointment of a school nurse to be on the staff. Baldwin's reputation for excellence persuaded many Harvard and MIT faculty to enroll their children. One of her students, the poet, e. e. cummings (NAA), labelled her a, *"gentle dictator"* whose *"delicious voice,"* and *"charming manner,"* made being in her presence, *"an honour and a glory..."*

In 2002, the Cambridge School Committee renamed the Agassiz School to honor Maria Baldwin. The Agassiz was originally named after Harvard faculty member and scientist, Louis Agassiz (1807–1873) (NAA), and his wife, scientist and co-founder of Radcliffe College, Elizabeth Cabot Agassiz (NAA). Louis Agassiz also had a connection to African American history, although, not a positive one. Agassiz's article, *"The Diversity of Origin of the Human Races,"* which was published in 1850, expressed his theory that people of African origin and people of European origin were two distinctly different species just as different animal species existed. He further hypothesized that the species of African origin was inferior to the species of European origin. This theory of *"polygenesis,"* as it was known, was embraced by those who sought to maintain inequality between the races.

Baldwin School

EXECUTION OF MARK AND PHILLIS: CAMBRIDGE GALLOWS

End of Stone Court, at Mass. Ave. between Arlington & Lancaster

On September 18th, 1755, an event occurred in Cambridge that illustrated the inevitable outcome when a sector of the population was maintained in a state of pertetual bondage. Two enslaved individuals, Mark and Phillis, were found guilty of murder when their enslaver, Captain John Codman (NAA) of Charlestown, died after he was poisoned with arsenic. Their public execution took place at the Cambridge Gallows at this location. Mark was gibbetted (hung) and Phillis was burned to death.

The gruesome nature of their execution stayed in the public memory for many years. After their execution, Mark's body was taken to Charlestown where it was hung on display for several decades until it rotted. See more under Charlestown sites.

 PAULINE HOPKINS HOUSE

53 Clifton St.

Pauline Hopkins (1856–1930) created an independent literary career for herself at a time when women's professional options were limited, especially options for African American women. The two primary options available were the role of housewife or work in some menial capacity such as a maid or cook. Hopkins wrote a musical drama while still in her early twenties that was performed locally.

Pauline Hopkins

Eventually, she became editor of the new *"Colored American Magazine."* Hopkins' very political agenda as editor of this magazine was to make African Americans throughout the country aware of their impressive achievements despite the barriers placed in their path. Hopkins also wrote several novels which she distributed in a serial format in the magazine. When Booker T. Washington purchased the magazine, he fired Hopkins who was a Dubois sympathizer. She subsequently started her own company as a publisher.

"...The recent attacks made by many prominent persons upon our race, and the efforts which have been made in some states in the South to deprive our people, by legislation, of the political and other rights guaranteed us by the constitution, make it imperative for us everywhere to appeal to the conscience and heart of the American people.

This can only be accomplished by making our white brothers and sisters realize the work we are doing, and that, in a single generation after the abolition of slavery, we have produced not only farmers and mechanics but singers, artists, writers, poets, lawyers, doctors, successful business men and even some statesmen...."

-- Pauline Hopkins, Colored American Magazine, March 1904.

Hopkins House

 ## WILLIAM H. LEWIS HOUSE
226 Upland Road

Harvard Law School graduate, William H. Lewis (1868–1949), achieved several firsts in both college sports and law. He was the first African American college football player (Amherst College–1888); he was the first African American to be named an All American player (Harvard Law–1900); and in 1895, he was the first African American college football coach (Harvard 1895–1906).

Most of these accomplishments occurred while he attended Harvard Law School. It was his job as Harvard football coach that led to his appointment by President Theodore Roosevelt (NAA) to be Assistant Attorney General for Massachusetts. Roosevelt, another Harvard alumni, wanted to keep Lewis in Cambridge to continue to coach the Harvard team.

 ## ALBERTA V. SCOTT HOUSE
37 Hubbard Ave.

In 1898, Alberta V. Scott (1875–1902) was the first African American to graduate from Radcliffe College. See information on Scott in Cambridge Site #9.

After a prolonged illness, Scott died in her family's home at this address.

the highest ranked African American in federal government. Lewis held that position until Woodrow Wilson's (NAA) election in 1912. Lewis lived at this house with his wife, Elizabeth B. Baker, who attended Wellesley College, and their three children.

William H. Lewis

In addition to his talents as an athletic, Lewis was equally talented as an attorney. He used his skills as an orator to successfully defend his clients or to get them reduced sentences. He also filed several anti-discrimination lawsuits. In 1910, President William Taft (NAA) appointed Lewis as the Assistant Attorney General of the United States, an appointment that made him

 ## THOMAS W. HIGGINSON HOUSE
29 Buckingham St.

A Unitarian minister, Thomas Wentworth Higginson's (1823–1911) (NAA) vigorous contribution to abolitionist activities culminated in his role as one of the, *"Secret Committee of Six,"* the group that provided funds for John Brown's (NAA) raid on Harper's Ferry on October 16th, 1859. Higginson who came from a family of privilege, received degrees from both Harvard College and Harvard Divinity School.

William H. Lewis House

Thomas Wentworth Higginson

Higginson's first congregation in Newburyport turned against him because of what they considered to be radical ideas against enslavement. From 1852 to 1862, he served as pastor of the Free Church in Worcester. He was a member of the Boston Vigilance Committee and in the failed attempt to break Anthony Burns out of jail in 1854, Higginson received a saber cut on the chin which he flaunted for the rest of his life. After John Brown's capture, Higginson endeavored to raise funds for Brown's defense and he made plans to break Brown out of jail.

Higginson House

Higginson enlisted in the army as soon as the Civil War began. From 1862 to 1864, he commanded the first African Americans recruited by the Federal government, the 1st South Carolina Volunteers. After the war, he recorded his experiences in the book, *Army Life of a Black Regiment*. Higginson's house has been listed on the National Register of Historic Places.

> "...Great men are rarely isolated mountain-peaks; they are the summits of ranges."
> —THOMAS WENTWORTH HIGGINSON

39 RICHARD HENRY DANA, JR. HOUSE
4 Berkeley St.

Richard Henry Dana, Jr. (1815 - 1882) (NAA) was one of the many white allies who aided the struggle to abolish slavery. Dana served as lead attorney for Anthony Burns, one of the most famous fugitives from slavery to be tried in Massachusetts. Although Dana lost the case, the cost to the United States to return Burns to bondage amounted to over $40,000 (about $1.2 million in today's currency). That high cost and the

Richard Henry Dana, Jr.

fact that anti-slavery advocates in the north refused to allow fugitives to be returned to slavery without an expensive legal fight were two of the reasons that made secession appear as a viable option to Southerners.

Born into privilege in Cambridge, Dana graduated from both Harvard College and Harvard Law School. Dana dedicated his life to assist those less fortunate than himself. Traditionally, privileged individuals toured Europe after they graduated from College and before they settled down to a career. Dana chose to become a merchant seaman instead. His classic memoir, *Two Years Before the Mast,* described his experiences at sea. The events he witnessed at sea informed his decision to study law to help the less fortunate in life.

Dana House

Dana's abolitionist activities inspired him to become one of the founders of the Free Soil Party in 1848. The Free Soil Party was formed to limit the expansion of slavery in the new territories of the west.

 ## 40 CAMBRIDGE CEMETERY
76 Coolidge Ave.

Some of the African Americans who played important roles in Cambridge's history were buried at Cambridge Cemetery. They included Patrick H. Raymond, Clement G. Morgan, and William Wells Brown. Thomas Wentworth Higginson (NAA), an ardent abolitionist, was also buried here.

Cambridge Cemetery

 ## 41 MT. AUBURN CEMETERY & CIVIL WAR MONUMENT
580 Mt. Auburn St.
Black History Walking Tour

Mt. Auburn's 175 acres of landscaped gardens forever changed the way Americans viewed cemeteries after it was founded in 1831. The beautiful grounds, which were designated a National Historic Landmark in 2003, contain several thousand monuments and receive more than 250,000 visitors each year.

Mt. Auburn Cemetery Gates

The cemetery has compiled an African American Heritage Trail of some of the notable African Americans buried here:

Clethra Path, Lot 4389
Harriet Jacobs, and her brother, John S. Jacobs, also a fugitive from slavery, and Harriet's daughter, Louisa.

Cuphea Path, Lot 3847
Myrtle Hart MacKinley and William MacKinley. Myrtle was an accomplished harp player and her husband, William, was the music director of the Colonial Theatre in Boston.

Cypress Ave., Lot 1562
Joshua Bowen Smith, abolitionist and legislator.

Glen Ave., Lot 6308
William Henry Lewis was the African American Assistant Attorney General of the United States.

Indian Ridge Path Lot 4960
George, Josephine, and Florida Ruffin. George Ruffin was the first African American judge in the state and his wife, Josephine, was a pioneering feminist.

Kalmia Path, Lot 4312
Mary Walker, a fugitive from NC.

Magnolia Ave., Lot 3752
Peter Byus, a fugitive who resided on Beacon Hill and worked as a tailor.

Mound Ave., Lot 7503
Clement Morgan was the first African American to graduate from both Harvard College and Harvard Law School.

St. John, Fir Ave., Lot 1736
Benjamin Franklin Roberts filed the 1849 Boston school desegregation lawsuit for his daughter, Sarah.

Vesper Path, Lot 5000, No. 385
Kittie Knox (1874–1900) was a pioneer cyclist. Born in Cambridge to a white mother and black father, Knox lived on Beacon Hill with her mother and brother for most of her life. Knox created quite a bit of controversy when she appeared at races dressed in knickerbockers (men's pants) with a man's bike. She completed several Century Rides (100 miles) before her early death.

White abolitionists and anti-slavery activists buried at Mt. Auburn include Charles Sumner, Samuel Gridley Howe, and his wife Julia Ward Howe, George Luther Stearns, James Russell Lowell, Henry Wadsworth Longfellow, Rev. William Ellery Channing, and Rev. Charles Torrey (1813–1846). Torrey, a Massachusetts native, was honored with a monument in the cemetery when he died in a Maryland prison while he served a sentence for anti-slavery activity. United States Supreme Court Justice Benjamin Robbins Curtis was also buried here. Curtis was one of only two Justices to dissent in the Dred Scott decision.

Hygeia by Edmonia Lewis

The Edmonia Lewis sculpture, *"Hygeia,"* was sited on Poplar Ave at Lily Path. Edmonia Lewis (1845–1901) was the first African American female sculptor to earn an income with her art. See more on Lewis under downtown Boston sites.

A Civil War Monument, *"American Sphinx,"* was created to honor Col. Robert Gould Shaw. It was sculpted by Martin Milmore (NAA), an Irish immigrant who also sculpted the Civil War Memorial in Boston Garden and in Charlestown. Shaw was the white leader of the Massachusetts 54th Regiment at their original formation. He died with 96 of his troops in the assault on Fort Wagner.

 LOCAL RESOURCES

Harvard University Art Museums
485 Broadway
617-495-9400
www.harvardartmuseums.org

African American Heritage Trail of Cambridge
www.cambridgema.gov/historic/aahtrail.html

African American Heritage Trail of Mt. Auburn Cemetery
www.mountauburn.org/tag/african-american-heritage-trail

Massachusetts Institute of Tech. Public Art Tour
77 Massachusetts Ave.
617-253-4795
www.listart.mit.edu/publicart
Free tours of campus and its public art.

WATERTOWN

① WILLIAM S. WHITE (NAA) HOUSE
UGRR Station
Site Unknown

William White's safe house was one of the places that fugitive, Shadrach Minkins stayed after his 1851 escape from a federal jail in downtown Boston.

② BENJAMIN ROBBINS CURTIS
Site Unknown

Benjamin Robbins Curtis (1809–1874) (NAA) was born in Watertown. Curtis graduated from both Harvard College and Harvard Law School. He participated in two significant court decisions that impacted the rights of African Americans. In 1836, Curtis was one of the attorneys for the defense in the case of the Commonwealth of Masssachusetts vs. Aves. In that case, the state successfully sued Thomas Aves (NAA) for the freedom of an enslaved child, Med, that his daughter, Mary Slater (NAA), had voluntarily brought into the state. See more on this case under Beacon Hill sites. Southerners were incensed by that decision.

Robbins was eventually appointed to the United States Supreme Court under President Andrew Jackson (NAA) where he served as associate justice in the Dred Scott trial. In that trial, the Supreme Court ruled that descendants of African slaves were not citizens and could not, therefore, bring lawsuits in a court. Justice Curtis was one of only two justices who dissented from the majority opinion. He resigned from his position as Justice in protest of that decision. Curtis was buried at Mt. Auburn Cemetery in Cambridge. See more on Dred Scott decision under Springfield sites.

WALTHAM

① NATIONAL ARCHIVES
380 Trapelo Rd.

This repository of the United States contains an extensive amount of documents and records that relate to the enslavement of individuals in the United States. It also has documents on various court cases related to the trials of fugitives from slavery, and documents on the Freedmen's Bureau. The Freedmen's Bureau was established to aid those newly emancipated after the Civil War.

② ROBERT ROBERTS & GORE PLACE
52 Gore St.

Robert Roberts (1780–1860) of Beacon Hill ran the household of Gore Place, the estate of diplomat and politician, Christopher Gore (NAA). Roberts wrote a successful book on how to run a gentleman's household based on his experience at Gore Place. See more on Roberts under Beacon Hill sites.

Gore Place

Successful Boston attorney, Christopher Gore (1758–1827) (NAA), became Governor of Massachusetts in 1809 and a United States Senator in 1813. Christopher and Rebecca (NAA) Gore purchased 400 acres of land in Waltham shortly after their marriage in 1785. They built Gore Place in 1805 as a summer home after the original house burned to the ground in 1799. Gore constructed the mansion at a cost of over $24,000, at a time when the average income for a male was $500 a year.

In 1825, African American, Robert Roberts, joined the staff at Gore Place as head butler. The Gores entertained lavishly at their estate where they lived all year by the time Roberts joined the household. Some of their visitors included such notables as President James Monroe (NAA).

ARLINGTON

PRINCE HALL MASONIC CEMETERY
48 Gardner Street

William Kendall purchased this land in 1856 for a burial ground for members of the African Order of Masons. He deeded the land to the Prince Hall Grand Lodge in 1864. It was the first cemetery owned and exclusively used by African Americans. This cemetery was the burial place of several Civil War veterans.

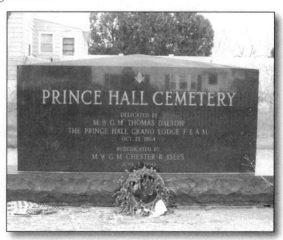

Prince Hall Masonic Cemetery

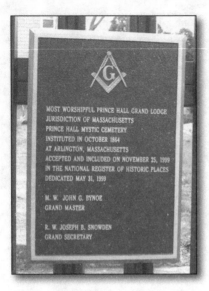

Prince Hall Masonic Cemetery Sign

MEDFORD

 DUGGER PARK & RHONE TENNIS COURTS
Harvard St. & Mystic Valley Pkwy

Edward Dugger, Sr. of the 367th Infantry, 92nd Division, received a commission as a Lt. Col. in World War I at a time when few African American were commissioned officers. The town of Medford renamed this park to honor Dugger's accomplishments in 1939, the year of his death.

Medford renamed these tennis courts in 1972 to honor Clarence Rhone's (1893–1970) lifelong dedication to share his love of tennis to the youth of Medford.

 BELINDA (ROYALL) SUTTON *"REPARATIONS LAWSUIT"*
15 George St.
781-396-9032
www.royallhouse.org
Saturdays and Sundays, June–Oct.

In 1783, Belinda Sutton, also known as Belinda Royall, approximately sixty-five years of age, successfully sued for reparations for the uncompensated work that she performed for fifty years for the Royall family household on this estate, Ten Hills Farm. The estate originally included over 600 acres of land. Today, it contains the only extant quarters constructed specifically for enslaved Africans in the northern United States. Belinda was kidnapped from Ghana at the age of twelve and sold into bondage in Antigua to Isaac Royall, Sr.

Royall House Sign

Royall House

In 1732, Isaac Royall, Sr. (NAA), one of the richest men in New England, began construction on this house to reflect the wealth that he had accumulated as a sugar cane planter and slave trader in Antigua, where he lived for forty years. When the Royalls relocated to Medford after the house was finished in 1737, they brought with them twenty-seven enslaved Africans from their estate in Antigua. Throughout the Royall's occupancy of the estate, the family enslaved over sixty-three individuals, including Belinda. Those enslaved individuals maintained the family's lavish lifestyle until the American Revolution forced Royall, Jr. (NAA), a Loyalist, to flee to England. His flight ended his family's dynasty.

Although the Quock Walker and Mum Bett Freeman cases effectively ended the practice of slavery in Massachusetts in 1783, elderly, formerly enslaved individuals did not have today's safety nets such as Social Security to depend on. They usually continued to work for the families that formerly enslaved them but for meager wages. In Belinda's case, the family fled from the country before they resolved the financially precarious position of the unpaid staff.

Royall made accommodations for Belinda in his will for three years but at the end of those three years, by 1781, she had no financial resources. Belinda, who also was responsible for a sickly daughter, chose not to go on the public dole. Instead, she decided to sue for repartions. Prince Hall, a prominent civic leader, assisted her in the process. Belinda's award from her lawsuit was fifteen pounds, twelve shillings annually.

Quarters for Enslaved Workers

Excerpt from her petition to the Massachusetts Legislature:

"...Fifty years her faithful hands have been compelled to ignoble servitude, for the benefit of an ISAAC ROYALL, until, as if nations must be agitated, and the world convulsed, for the preservation of that freedom which the Almighty Father intended for all the human race, the present war commenced. The terrors of men, armed in the cause of freedom, compelled her master to fly, and to breathe away his life in a land, where lawless domination fits enthroned, pouring bloody outrage and cruelty on all who dare to be free.

The face of your petitioner is now marked with the sorrows of time, and her frame feebly bending under the oppression of years, while she, by the laws of the land, is denied the enjoyment of one morsel of that immense wealth, a part whereof hath been accumulated by her own industry, and the whole augmented by her servitude.

Wherefore, casting herself at the feet of your Honors, as to a body of men, formed for the extirpation of vassalage, for the reward of virtue, and the just returns of honest industry—She prays, That such allowance may be made her, out of the estate of Col. Royall as will prevent her, and her more inform daughter from misery in the greatest extreme, and scatter comfort over the shore and downward path of their lives–And she will ever pray.

Belinda"

Extensive archeological research has revealed detailed information about the lives of the enslaved individuals of the Royall Estate. They were treated very similar to their southern counterparts in the harshness of their work conditions and the total disregard that the Royalls showed to their worker's family relationships. Today, the house exists as an archaeological resource and museum.

 ## 3 LYDIA MARIA CHILD HOUSE

114 South Street, Tufts University

Lydia Maria Child (1802–1880) (NAA), a noted abolitionist, author, and feminist, had a profound influence on the abolitionist movement through her involvement in many of the anti-slavery events of her time. Born into a Calvinist family in Medford, Child was a precocious thinker who constantly searched for truth throughout her life.

Although Child was informed that a career as an author was the surest way to ruin her reputation as a lady, she persistently shared her views through the printed media. In 1824, Child wrote, *Hobomok, A Tale of Early Times.* The unconventional plot of this novel, the marriage between a white woman and a Native American man, clearly indicated Child's respect for the Native American cause for equality.

Child House

Lydia Maria Child

By the late 1820s, the hypocrisy of the institution of slavery troubled Child and she aligned herself with the abolitionist cause. She wrote *An Appeal in Favor of that Class of Americans Called Africans* in 1833. This was the second book that called for the immediate emancipation of enslaved individuals without compensation to their enslavers. David Walker's *Appeal* was the first.

Child and her husband joined the Northampton Association for Education and Industry (NAEI) in the early 1840s. They attempted various enterprises to make the association financially viable. In one effort, they purchased agricultural land and tried to grow beet sugar as an affordable substitute for cane sugar. Cane sugar depended on slave labor in its production whereas beet sugar did not. Child also facilitated African American abolitionist, David Ruggles' move to Northampton after he suffered from poor health and financial difficulties in New York.

Lydia Child's assistance enabled Harriet Jacobs to settle in Cambridge and purchase the freedom of her children. In 1861, Child edited Harriet Jacobs' novel, *Incidents in the Life of a Slave Girl,* The novel was based on Jacobs' experiences during the seven years she spent in an attic in order to be near her enslaved children. Child and her husband moved to Wayland in their later years. Child was buried at the North Cemetery in Wayland.

"I do feel as if it required some apology to attempt to convince men of ordinary humanity and common sense that the Fugitive Slave Bill is utterly wicked, and consequently ought never to be obeyed. Yet Massachusetts consents to that law! Some shadow of justice she grants, inasmuch as her Legislature have passed what is called a Personal Liberty Bill, securing trial by jury to those claimed as slaves. Certainly it is something gained, especially for those who may get brown by working in the sunshine, to prevent our Southern masters from taking any of us, at a moment's notice, and dragging us off into perpetual bondage. It is something gained to require legal proof that a man is a slave, before he is given up to arbitrary torture and unrecompensed toil. But is it the measure of justice becoming the character of a free Commonwealth? "Prove that the man is property, according to your laws, and I will drive him into your cattle-pen with sword and bayonet," is what Massachusetts practically says to Southern tyrants. "Show me a Bill of Sale from the Almighty!" is what she ought to say. No other proof should be considered valid in a Christian country."

–Lydia Maria Childs

"While we bestow our earnest disapprobation on the system of slavery, let us not flatter ourselves that we are in reality any better than our brethren of the South. Thanks to our soul and climate, and the early exertions of the Quakers, the form of slavery does not exist among us; but the very spirit of the hateful and mischievous thing is here in all its strength. The manner in which we use what power we have, gives us ample reason to be grateful that the nature of our institutions does not entrust us with more. Our prejudice against colored people is even more inveterate than it is at the south. "

–Lydia Child

"That a majority of women do not wish for any important change in their social and civil condition, merely proves that they are the unreflecting slaves of custom."
-LYDIA MARIA CHILD

"They [the slaves] have stabbed themselves for freedom—jumped into the waves for freedom—starved for freedom—fought like very tigers for freedom! But they have been hung, and burned, and shot—and their tyrants have been their historians!"
-LYDIA CHILD

4 GEORGE LUTHER STEARNS & FIRST PARISH UNITARIAN CHURCH
147 High Street

George Luther Stearns (1809-1867) (NAA), a businessman, and prominent abolitionist, belonged to the *"Secret Committee of Six,"* the group that funded John Brown's raid on Harper's Ferry in 1859. Stearns lived in Medford where he was a member of First Parish Church. Stearns personally supplied the 200 Sharps rifles and pikes that John Brown possessed at Harper's Ferry.

Stearns made his fortune from the pipe fabrication industry, a trade he learned at the age of nine when he entered the work force to help support his family. Stearns wife, Mary Elizabeth Preston (NAA), knew Maria Lydia Childs, the noted abolitionist. Childs most probably introduced Stearns to the abolitionist movement.

In 1854, the Nebraska-Kansas Act opened up new territories for settlement and voters could decide whether those territories would be anti-slavery states or pro-slavery states. Kansas became a battle ground because both sides attempted to populate the territories with settlers loyal to their cause.

So many violent confrontations ensued that the phrase, *"Bleeding Kansas,"* entered popular language to describe it. Stearns personally financed the Emigrant Aid Company that assisted the anti-slavery settlers. John Brown's

George Luther Stearns

Pottowatomie Creek Massacre was just one of the many violent incidents in Kansas during this turbulent time.

First Parish Unitarian Church

During the Civil War, Stearns recruited African American soldiers for the Union Army, in fact, some credited him with recruitment of over 13,000 African American soldiers for the war effort. After the war, Stearns was a major supporter of the Freedman's Bureau. Ralph Waldo Emerson gave the eulogy at Stearns funeral on April 9th, 1867, at this church.

MEDFORD HISTORICAL SOCIETY

10 Governors Ave.
781-391-8739
www.medfordhistorical.org
Open every Sunday,
noon to 4 pm.

The Medford Historical Society maintains many documents on the history of slavery in Massachusetts.

5A MEDFORD SLAVE TRADE LETTERS

Between 1759 and 1765, the merchant, Timothy Fitch (NAA) corresponded with one of his employees, Captain Peter Gwinn (NAA). The correspondence centered on Fitch's various merchant activities and the cargo on his ships which included the transport and sale of enslaved individuals. This correspondence reaffirms the fact that many New England families built their wealth on the slave trade. The letters were placed in the collection of the Medford Historical Society after a group of students from Tufts University transcribed them.

5B WEST MEDFORD AFRO-AMERICAN REMEMBRANCE PROJECT

Under the auspices of the Medford Historical Society, a committee of local residents worked on a project to doc-

ument the contributions of fellow residents: Madeleine Dugger Andrews; Edward "Buddy" Clayton; Alonzo Fields; Walter Isaacs; The Honorable Marie Oliver Jackson; Shirley Kountze; Miriam Faulcon Phillips; and James and Ada Sherwood. The multi-year project is a collaboration with Tufts University and Brandeis University.

EVERETT

1 WOODLAWN CEMETERY

302 Elm St.
617-387-0800

This garden cemetery, founded in 1850, was designed with 130 acres of trees, shrubs, and manicured lawns. Robert Roberts, John Swett Rock, Mary Eliza Mahoney, Lewis and Harriet Hayden, and Tunis G. Campbell were all buried here. Campbell, an abolitionist, wrote, *Hotel Keepers, Head Waiters, and Housekeepers' Guide*. That book, published in the 1830s, was the first to

Woodlawn Cemetery

offer systematic instruction on how to operate a hotel. Campbell later served in the Georgia legislature.

Woodlawn Cemetery published a self-guided pedestrian tour of the gravesites of individuals of historical significance. Except for Campbell, the individuals mentioned above have been included in other sections of this book.

CHELSEA

 ## SITE: LEWIS HOWARD LATIMER
Oswego Street

Lewis Howard Latimer's (1848–1928) innovative design of the carbon filament greatly expanded the life and durability of the incandescent light bulb. That invention so impressed Thomas Edison that he recruited Latimer to join his team of engineers, the Edison Pioneers. Latimer lived for a time on Oswego Street.

George Latimer, Lewis Latimer's father, was captured in Boston as a fugitive from slavery in 1842. His capture created an uproar in the town that led the state to pass the Personal Liberty Act of 1843. Bostonians raised funds to purchase George Latimer's freedom. See Lynn sites.

Lewis Latimer initially worked as a draftsperson in the Boston patent office

of Crosby & Gould (NAA). There, he drafted the patent application of Alexander Graham Bell's (NAA) telephone invention. Latimer was recruited by the U.S Electric Company where he developed his carbon filament invention.

Lewis Howard Latimer

Latimer worked with Edison for the remainder of his career. He became a patent expert and successfully defended Edison's patents in courts against copycat inventors.

 ## ROBERT MORRIS HOUSE
Site Unknown

In 1845, Robert Morris was the second African American licensed to practice law in Massachusetts after Macon Allen. See more on Morris under downtown Boston sites.

③ SAMUEL COPELAND
UGRR Station
Somewhere on
Chestnut St.

Samuel Copeland (1823–1893) was born in Virginia. He relocated to Boston where he married Alice Welch (NAA) who was Irish. Copeland was a successful dealer of used clothes in Boston. Copeland was active in the abolitionist movement, and he and his wife used their home as a station on the Underground Railroad. Whenever a neighbor asked too many questions about their visitors, Copeland stated that the guest was a relative on a visit.

Copeland's economic success enabled him to commission a portrait of his three daughters by the artist, William Matthew Prior (NAA) in 1854. The Museum of Fine Art in Boston obtained that painting for its collection. The daughters, Eliza, six years old, Margaret, four years old, and Nellie, two years old, were all stylishly dressed to reflect their family's economic prosperity.

*Three Sisters of the Copeland Family
Replica of a painting by
Matthew Prior*

MALDEN

---

① SITE: PETER SHILOH HOUSE
Corner of Lowell &
Walnut St.

A local African American barber, Peter Shiloh, received a house at this location as a reward for his bravery when he testified against a bank robber.

② JUDSON HOUSE (NAA)
UGRR Station
145 Main St.

Judson House

③ MOREY HOUSE (NAA)
UGRR Station
34 Hillside Avenue

Morey House

4 LOUISE STOKES– FRASER MEMORIAL
77 Salem St.
Malden High School

Just after she finished high school, Louise Stokes (1913–1978) placed third in a national 100-meter race. That placement won her a place on the women's 400-meter relay team in the 1932 Olympic Games, the first African American to attain that achievement. Stokes qualified for the team along with another African American, Tidye Pickett. Despite the qualifications of the two African American team members, the white coach only allowed white members to participate on the final relay team.

After she returned home, Stokes continued to race. She qualified for the 1936 races, again based on her time in the 100-meter races. History repeated itself, and the coach still did not allow her to compete. Despite these setbacks,

Louise Stokes-Fraser Monument

the Town of Malden welcomed her home with a victory parade and they eventually installed this plaque to honor her. Stokes retired from sports after the cancellation of the 1940 Olympics due to the on-set of World War II.

5 JAMES REDPATH HOUSE
54 Maple St.

James Redpath (1833-1891) (NAA) used his skills as a journalist to advance the agenda of the abolitionist movement. Redpath's family emigrated from Scotland and settled in Michigan while he was still a teenager. His early employment as a printer evolved into a journalism career.

His initial interest in the anti-slavery movement began with a journalism assignment to interview John Brown in the aftermath of the Pottawatomie Creek Massacre in the Kansas Territory. After that interview, Redpath became an ardent believer in Brown's views that slavery was a moral sin that

Louise Stokes-Fraser

could only be ended by violence. Redpath moved to Boston specifically to stir up support for Brown's plans for a slave insurrection.

After John Brown's raid on Harper's Ferry failed, Redpath traveled to Haiti in 1860, to report on that government's efforts to establish international legitimacy nearly seven decades after that country's successful slave revolt of 1790. Within two years, Redpath established diplomatic relations between the United States and Haiti.

Redpath opened a publishing company in Boston in 1863. His company published such books as William Wells Brown's, *The Blackman,* and a biography, *Toussaint L'Ouverture*, by John R. Beard (NAA). In another business venture, he established the Boston Lyceum Bureau, a speaker's bureau.

Redpath House

Represented by the Boston Lyceum Bureau
- Susan B. Anthony (NAA)
- Henry Ward Beecher (NAA)
- Frederick Douglass
- Ralph Waldo Emerson (NAA)
- Julia Ward Howe (NAA)
- Wendell Phillips (NAA)
- Charles Sumner (NAA)
- Mark Twain (NAA), among others.

James Redpath

 6 COX–HAVEN HOUSE (NAA)
UGRR Station
35-37 Clifton St. /
private residence

Cox-Haven House

MELROSE

(1) WESTON WYMAN HOUSE (NAA)
UGRR Station
28 Greenwood Street

Weston Wyman House

SAUGUS

(1) BENJAMIN FRANKLIN & DOROTHY NEWHALL (NAA) HOUSE
UGRR Station
17–19 Ballard St.

Franklin & Newhall House

LYNN

(1) GEORGE WASHINGTON RADDIN (NAA) HOUSE
UGRR Station
768 Boston St.

(2) FREDERICK DOUGLASS MARKER
Bandstand at Lynn Common
Market Sq., N. Common St., and S. Common St.

Frederick Douglass (1818-1895) lived in Lynn with his wife, Anna during 1841 and 1842. Douglass worked for the American Anti-Slavery Society at this time when he delivered one of his most famous speeches from this bandstand in October of 1842, *"I Have Come to Tell You Something About Slavery."*

Frederick Douglass, as young man

Douglass developed into such an eloquent speaker that many doubted his fugitive slave status. In 1845, he wrote his first autobiography, *Narrative of the Life of Frederick Douglass, An American Slave,* in order to put those doubts to rest. After publication of that biography, Douglass fled to England, because he had revealed details of his former life that put his safety from fugitive slave hunters in jeopardy.

Frederick Douglass Plaque

Lynn Bandstand

Excerpt from Lynn speech:

"...My friends, I have come to tell you something about slavery—what I know of it, as I have felt it. When I came North, I was astonished to find that the abolitionists knew so much about it, that they were acquainted with its effects as well as if they had lived in its midst. But, though they can give you its history---though they can depict its horrors, they cannot speak as I can from experience; they cannot refer you to a back red with scars, as I can; for I have felt these wounds; I have suffered under the lash without the power of resisting. Yes, my blood has sprung out as the lash embedded itself in my flesh. And yet my master has the reputation of being a pious man and a good Christian. He was a leader in the Methodist Church. I have seen this pious class leader cross and tie the hands of one of his young female slaves, and lash her bare skin and justify the deed by the quotation from the Bible, 'he who knoweth his master's will and doeth it not, shall be beaten with many stripes'...."

-- Frederick Douglass

3 JAN MATZELIGER MONUMENT
145 Boston St., Pine Grove Cemetery-25 Gentian Path

Jan Matzeliger's (1852-1889) invention of the shoe lasting machine revolutionized the manufacture of shoes. That invention made the purchase of shoes affordable for most citizens.

Born in Dutch Guyana, South America, to an African mother and a Dutch father, Matzeliger became interested in the way machines work at an early age, thanks to his father's work as an engineer. During his late teens, Matzeliger traveled around the world as a sailor. In 1873, he settled in the United States, first in Philadelphia, PA, and then in Lynn, MA.

Jan Matzeliger

Matzeliger's mechanical aptitude enabled him to repair machinery for income. His curiosity led him to experiment with the labor intensive last step in the production of shoes, the attachment of the upper part of the shoe to the sole. The name of that final step was called *"lasting."* Matzeliger's invention of a shoe lasting machine changed the production of shoes from 50 in a ten-hour day to 200 to 300 produced daily by machine.

Matzeliger Monument

The town of Lynn constructed this monument to honor Matzeliger's contributions to the industrial revolution. In 1991, the U.S. Postal Service also issued a stamp to honor the inventor.

4 SITE: GEORGE LATIMER HOUSE
Newhall St., exact address unknown

George Latimer (1819-1896), the father of the famous inventor, Lewis Howard

George Latimer, 1842

Latimer, fled slavery in 1842 with his wife. His dramatic capture galvanized abolitionists in Boston. Latimer was born in Norfolk, VA, and enslaved by his biological uncle while very young. By the time Latimer was in his late teens, he had passed through a series of individuals who had bondage rights over him. The last of those was James B. Gray (NAA). Gray abused Latimer so extensively that Latimer decided to escape to the North with his pregnant wife, Rebecca.

George and Rebecca Latimer arrived in Boston on Oct. 4th, 1842. They had been in Boston only four days when a former employee of Gray recognized Latimer and sent word to Gray of his location. Gray arrived in Boston on Oct. 18th, and proceeded to have Latimer detained by the police on a false charge of larceny in order to hold him in preparation to send him back to Virginia. Word soon spread in the Boston community about Latimer's situation, and a few days later, over 300 free African Americans surrounded the jail to prevent Latimer's removal by the bounty hunters.

On Oct. 30th, abolitionists organized a meeting at Faneuil Hall to protest Latimer's detention. Some of Latimer's supporters organized a newspaper, *"Latimer's Journal and North Star,"* that was published from November 11th, 1842, to May 16th, 1843. The newspaper had over 20,000 subscribers during its short time in print. It related information to the public about George Latimer's case as well as information about the cases of other fugitives from bondage.

Excerpt from Latimer's autobiographical narrative as dictated to John W. Hutchinson in 1894:

"I have known John W. Hutchinson since 1842. That was the year I came North. I started in September from my home in Norfolk, Virginia. With my wife, also a slave, I secreted myself under the fore-peak of the vessel, we lying on stone ballast in the darkness for nine weary hours. As we lay concealed in the darkness we could peek through the cracks of the partition into the bar-room of the

vessel, where men who would have gladly captured us were drinking. When we went aboard the vessel at Frenchtown a man stood in the gangway who was a wholesaler of liquors. He knew me, for my master kept a saloon and was his customer. But I pulled my Quaker hat over my eyes and passed him unrecognized. I had purchased a first-class passage and at once went into the cabin and stayed there. Fortunately he did not enter. From Baltimore to Philadelphia I travelled as a gentleman, with my wife as a servant. After that, it being a presumably free country, we travelled as man and wife. I was twenty-one when married. Eleven days after leaving my home I was arrested as a fugitive slave in Boston. William Lloyd Garrison was living then, and took great interest in my case. I well remember the exciting scenes which finally culminated in the decision of Chief Justice Shaw that my master had a right to reclaim me. I recall with gratitude the generous act of Rev. Dr. Caldwell, of the Tremont Temple Baptists Society, who raised the money with which I was redeemed. My wife belonged to another master, Mr. DeLacy, and he sent a requisition to take her if I was taken. During my incarceration in Leverett Street jail she was secreted at the house of a friendly Abolitionist on High Street. Her whereabouts were never disclosed, and her master made no further trouble after I was released. A short time after this my first child was born, on Newhall Street, in Lynn.

Immediately after my release I began to attend anti-slavery conventions and appeal for signatures to the famous "Latimer" petitions, to be presented to the Legislature and to Congress. These asked the respective bodies to erase from the statute books every enactment making a distinction on account of complexion, and the enactment of law to protect citizens form insult by alleged arrest......"

–George Latimer

Local citizens raised $400 to manumit Latimer from slavery. After Latimer obtained his freedom, abolitionists circulated two petitions throughout the state. Charles Francis Adams (1807–1886) (NAA), scion of the Adams political dynasty, presented one petition to the Massachusetts State Legislature that contained over 60,000 signatures. The State petition resulted in the passage, in 1843, of the Personal Liberty Law. That law forbade state officials to detain fugitives from slavery or to use state facilities for such detention.

A second petition that proposed an amendment to the United States Constitution with a similar intent received over 43,000 signatures. John Quincy Adams (NAA), the sixth President of the United States and the father of Charles Francis Adams presented the second petition to Congress. The petition to Congress did not result in any legislation.

"To the Senate and House of Representatives of the State of Massachusetts

The undersigned citizens of the State of Massachusetts, earnestly desiring to free this Commonwealth and themselves from all connection with domestic slavery and to secure the citizens of this state from the danger of enslavement, respectfully pray your honorable body,

1. *To forbid all persons holding office under any law of this state from in any way officially or under color of office, aiding or abetting the arrest or detention of any person claimed as a fugitive from slavery.*

2. *To forbid the use of our jails or public property of any description whatever within the commonwealth in the detention of any alleged fugitive from slavery.*

3. *To propose such amendments to the Constitution of the United States as shall forever separate the people of Massachusetts from all connection with slavery. "*

5 NATHAN BREED HOUSE (NAA)

UGRR Station
3 Broad St.

Breed House

6 SITE: NEHEMIAH BASSETT HOUSE (NAA)

UGRR Station
Nahant St. Exact address not known.

The locals named Nahant St., *"escape alley,"* because it's direct route to the Lynn harbor facilitated quick escapes. Several houses along Nahant St. were Underground Railroad Stations for this reason. Nehemiah Bassett and Isaac Bassett who resided at the next listing were related. Family members who held similar political beliefs usually banded together to support those beliefs.

(7) ESTES NEWHALL HOUSE (NAA)
UGRR Station
4 Nahant St.

(8) ISAAC BASSETT HOUSE (NAA)
UGRR Station
17 Nahant St.

Bassett House

(9) SITE: HUTCHINSON COURT
UGRR Station
High Rock, address unknown

(10) SITE: SAMUEL SILSBEE (NAA) HSE
UGRR Station
10 Burchstead Court

(11) JONATHAN BUFFUM (NAA) HOUSE
UGRR Station
Site Unknown

Buffum was a Quaker and the owner of the newspaper, *"The Record."*

(12) JAMES BUFFUM (NAA) HOUSE
UGRR Station
Site Unknown

(13) JOHN B. TOLMAN (NAA) HOUSE
UGRR Station
Site Unknown

WAKEFIELD

(1) CHARLES LENOX REMOND FARM
Site Unknown

Charles Lenox Remond (1810–1878), the abolitionist and women's rights activist, settled on a farm in Wakefield with his family toward the end of his life. Remond was the first African American hired as a speaker by a white anti-slavery organization, the American Anti-Slavery Society.

READING

1 JONAS PARKER HOUSE

UGRR Station
Ash and Cross St.

Jonas Parker (NAA) operated a safe house at this location with his wife, Sally Bancroft Parker (NAA). They hid fugitives in the barn. Sally was the Vice-President of the Female Anti-Slavery Society.

STONEHAM

1 SITE: DEACON ABIJAH BRYANT HOUSE

UGRR Station
307 Main St.

Deacon Abijah Bryant (NAA) co-founded the Stoneham branch of the Massachusetts Anti-Slavery Society in 1838. Bryant's home at this location was a stop on the Underground Railroad.

2 VETERANS OF THE AMERICAN REVOLUTION

Three African Americans, who at various times, listed Stoneham as their place of residence, fought at the Battle of Bunker Hill; Isaiah Bayoman, Job Potama, and Garshom Prince.

3 FIRST CONGREGATIONAL CHURCH
1 Church St.

The First Congregational Church of Stoneham was an activist church against slavery. When the Fugitive Slave Act of 1850 was passed, Rev. William C. Whitcomb (NAA) outraged fellow clergy members when he preached a sermon of armed violence to the death against slavery and its oppressors.

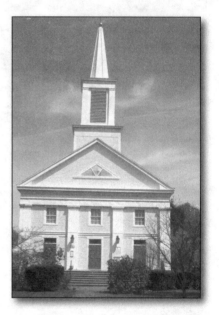

First Congregational Church

4 NEWHALL (NAA) HOUSE
UGRR Station
Somewhere on Green St.

WOBURN

 ## ST. JOHN'S BAPTIST CHURCH
38 Everett St.

Saunders Sims founded St. John's Baptist Church in 1886 with twenty members in his home on Everett St. St. John's remains one of the oldest African American churches in the metropolitan Boston area.

St. John's Baptist Church

The congregation built a permanent church home in 1899. In 1900, the Rev. William Henry Scott (1848–1910), a fugitive from Virginia, became the minister, a position he held until 1906. Rev. Scott fought his entire life for human rights. He was one of the original members of the Niagara Movement, which was later renamed, the NAACP.

 ## LORING (NAA) HOUSE
UGRR Station
Site Unknown

LEXINGTON

 ## PRINCE ESTERBROOKS BATTLE OF LEXINGTON & CONCORD
Lexington Square at Bradburn Tavern

Over 5,000 African Americans served with the Continental Army in the American Revolution. Prince Esterbrooks (1740–1830), one of those many African American men, joined the Lexington Minutemen in 1773 and earned his emancipation through ten years of military service. Lexington dedicated a memorial on Lexington Common to honor Prince Esterbrooks in 2008.

April 19th, 1775 Battle of Lexington and Concord, first Battle of American Revolution, Esterbrooks was one of the first Patriots shot.

Esterbrooks Memorial

Esterbrooks was one of the first Patriots wounded in the Battle of Lexington and Concord. The night before that battle, Paul Revere (NAA) warned the Minutemen that the British were on their way in his famous midnight ride. In 1861, Henry Wadsworth Longfellow (NAA) memorialized that battle in his famous poem, *"The Midnight Ride of Paul Revere."* Longfellow wrote that poem on the eve of the Civil War to rally Northerners against the perils of the institution of slavery.

Lexington Minutemen gathered in Lexington Square to halt that advance of British troops who marched on the town to capture ammunitions stored in Concord. In Lexington on April 19th, 1775, colonial troops fired the famous, *"shot heard 'round the world,"* and the first battle of the American Revolution began. Ralph Waldo Emerson (NAA) honored this event in his poem, *"Concord Hymn"* of 1837.

Concord Hymn (1st stanza)

By Ralph Waldo Emerson

"By the rude bridge that arched the flood.

Their flag to April's breeze unfurled,

Here once the embattled farmers stood

And fired the shot heard round the world."

 2 **POMPEY (BLACKMAN) FREEMAN, VETERAN OF THE AMER. REVOLUTION & FIRST CONGREGATIONAL CHURCH**
7 Harrington Rd.

Pomey (Blackman) Freeman (c. 1755–1790) was a veteran of the American Revolution who fought at the Battles of Lexington and Concord, and the Battle of Bunker Hill. Freeman enlisted in Concord in April, 1775. At the time of his enlistment, his last name was Blackman. He re-enlisted numerous times until his final discharge on November 1st, 1780. During his service, he changed his last name from Blackman to Freeman. After the war, Freeman settled in Lexington where he worked as a tanner and joined the First Congregational Church. He eventually resettled in New Hampshire.

 3 **ISAAC BARBADOES VETERAN OF THE AMER. REVOLUTION**
Site Unknown

Isaac Barbadoes (1755–1777) was born free. His father, Quawk Abel Barbadoes (d. 1757) was enslaved in Lexington but he became free before Isaac was born. Isaacs's parents, Quawk and Kate were married on April 19th, 1754. They had three children, Isaac, Mercy, and Abel. Isaac served in the 15th

Massachusetts Regiment of Col. Timothy Bigelow. Isaac was a casualty of the war. His brother, Abel, was the father of Boston activist, James Barbadoes.

4 LEMUEL HAYNES
Lexington Square

Lemuel Haynes, (1753-1833), the first African American ordained as a minister, joined the military in 1774. He served at the Battle of Lexington and Concord, and during the siege of Boston. Haynes was abandoned at the age of five months by his parents, an African father and a white mother. Deacon David Rose (NAA) in Granville raised Haynes as an indentured servant.

Haynes used his skill an amateur poet to memorialize the action of the first battle of the Revolution in, "*The Battle of Lexington*." This poem, as did the poems of Phillis Wheatley, equated the position of the colonies under British domination as the same as being enslaved.

Lemuel Haynes

> ### The Battle of Lexington, excerpt
> #### By Lemuel Haynes
>
> The nineteenth Day of April last
> We ever shall retain
> As monumental of the past
> Most bloody shocking Scene
> Then Tyrants fill'd with horrid Rage
> A fatal Journey went
> & Unmolested to engage
> And slay the innocent...
> At Lexington they did appear
> Array'd in hostile form
> And tho our Friends were peacefull there
> Yet on them fell the Storm
> Eight most unhappy Victims fell
> Into the Arms of death
> Unpitied by those Tries of Hell
> Who curs'd them with their Breath
> The Savage Band still march along
> For Concord they were bound
> While Oaths & Curses from their Tongue
> Accent with hellish Sound
> To prosecute their felo Desire
> At Concord they unite
> Two Sons of Freedom there expire
> By their tyrannic Spite
> Thus did our Friends endure their Rage
> Without a murm'ring Word
> Till die they must or else engage
> And join with one Accord
>   ...
> For liberty, each Freeman strives
> As it's a Gift of God

And for it willing yield their Lives
And Seal it with their blood
Thrice happy they who thus resign
Into the peaceful Grave
Much better there, in Death Confin'd
Than a Surviving Slave
This Motto may adorn their Tombs,
(Let tyrants come and view)
"We rather seek these silent Rooms
Than live as Slaves to You"

Haynes relocated to Vermont where he enjoyed a long and distinguished career as a minister. He was the first African American ordained as a minister. He was also the first African American minister to lead a white congregation with his leadership of the Hemlock Church of Torrington, CT, and the West Parish Church of Rutland, VT. In 1804, Middlebury College awarded Haynes the first honorary Master of Arts degree received by an African American in the United States.

Haynes spoke out against the hypocrisy of colonial leaders who fought for liberty from England yet continued to condone forced enslavement of Africans. He documented those views in the pamphlet, *"Liberty Further Extended, or Free thoughts on the illegality of Slave-Keeping; Where in those arguments that Are used in its vindication Are plainly confuted."*

"...To affirm, that an Englishman has a right to his Liberty, is a truth which has Been so clearly Evinced Especially of Late, that to spend time in illustrating this, would be But Superfluous tautology. But I query, whether Liberty is so contracted a principle as to be Confined to any nation under Heaven; nay, I think it not hyperbolical to affirm, that Even an African, has Equally as good a right to his Liberty in common with Englishmen. I know that those that are concerned in the Slave-trade, Do pretend to Bring arguments in vindication of their practice; yet if we give them a candid Examination, we shall find them (Even those of the most cogent kind) to be Essentially Deficient.

We live in a day wherein Liberty & freedom is the subject of many millions Concern; and the important Struggle hath already caused great Effusion of Blood; men seem to manifest the most sanguine resolution not to Let their natural rights go without their Lives go with them; a resolution, one would think Every one that has the Least Love to his country, or future posterity, would fully confide in, yet while we are so zealous to maintain, and foster our own invaded rights, it cannot be thought impertinent for us Candidly to reflect on our own conduct, and I doubt not But that we shall find that subsisting in the midst of us, that may with propriety be styled Oppression, nay, much greater oppression, than that which Englishmen seem so much to spurn at.

I mean an oppression which they, themselves, impose upon others....

The main proposition, which I intend for some Brief illustration is this, Namely, That an African, or, in other terms, that a Negro may Justly Challenge, and has an undeniable right to his...Liberty. Consequently, the practice of Slave-keeping, which so much abounds in this Land is illicit....

Consequently, we may suppose that what is precious to one man, is precious to another, and what is irksome, or intolerable to one man, is so to another, ...Therefore we may reasonably conclude, that Liberty is Equally as precious to a Black man, as it is to a white one, and Bondage Equally as intolerable to the one as it is to the other: ....

But, as I observed Before, those privileges that are granted to us By the Divine Being, no one has the least right to take them from us without our consent; and there is Not the Least precept or practice, in the Sacred Scriptures, that constitutes a Black man a Slave, any more than a white one....

It is a Lamentable consequence of the fall, that mankind, have an insatiable thirst after Superiority one over another: .... God has been pleased to distinguish some men from others, as to natural abilities, But not as to natural right, as they came out of his hands....

As there should be Some rule whereby to govern the conduct of men; so it is the Duty, and interest of a community, to form a system of Law, ... But when, instead of contributing to the well Being of the community, it proves baneful to its subjects over whom it Extends, then it is high time to call it in question...."

-- Lemuel Haynes, 1776

(5) MARGARET VS. WILLIAM MUZZY "FREEDOM LAWSUIT"

Lexington was the location of one of the thirty lawsuits that enslaved individuals filed in Massachusetts between 1700 and 1781 in pursuit of freedom. Each of those lawsuits chipped away at the legality of slavery in this state. Margaret filed her case in 1768 in Middlesex County Court for recovery of personal property, herself, from William Muzzy (NAA). John Adams (NAA) represented the defendant. In 1770, the courts ruled in favor of the plaintiff, Margaret. This was one of five freedom lawsuits that Adams was involved in. In all the cases, Adams represented the defendants.

Concord Map

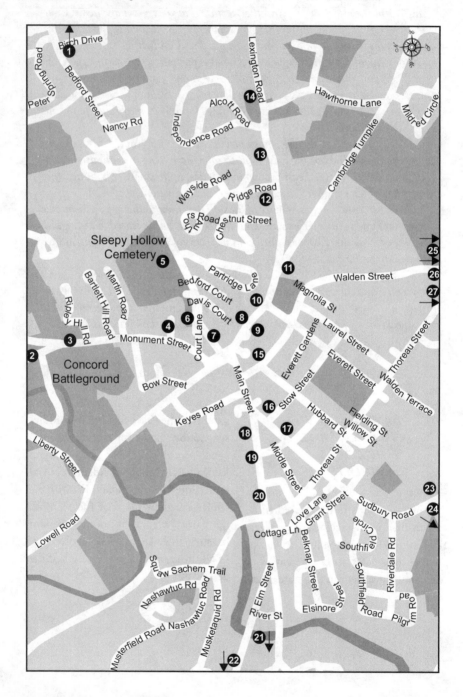

CONCORD

CONCORD'S RICH African American heritage began with the earliest settlers and their colonial struggles for independence. These early African American residents of Concord often lived separate and independent lives, away from the white population. Many of them chose to live alone, or with their immediate families in the woods. Their common characteristics of independence, self-reliance, determination, and a strong bond with nature, impressed some of their more philosophically inclined white neighbors. Those qualities influenced the *Transcendentalist Movement* of Concord.

The Transcendentalist philosophy expressed the supremacy of the spiritual over the material. It believed that man was inherently good, and that being close to nature enabled one to reach a higher spiritual awareness. The foremost proponents of this movement were also some of the most famous advocates of freedom and abolition in the years that preceded the Civil War. This group included Ralph Waldo Emerson (NAA), Henry David Thoreau (NAA), Nathaniel Hawthorne (NAA), the family of Louisa May Alcott (NAA), and many others.

In 2000, a group of Concord citizens, led by resident, Maria Madison, recognized this important period of American history and organized The Drinking Gourd Project. That effort established the African American and Abolitionist Heritage Tours of Concord. The Robbins House Foundation was organized in 2010 to reflect a larger mission as custodian of the The Robbins House, an interpretive museum that was the former residence of one of the original African American families of Concord.

1 GREAT FIELD SITES
Great Field off Monsen Road

Several African Americans in Concord had homesteads in this area of town known as the Great Field.

JOHN JACK HOUSE SITE

John Jack (1713–1773) was one of the earliest African American residents of Concord. The epitaph created for Jack (see Old Hill Burying Ground) made him world famous. Jack purchased his freedom after the age of forty with funds he earned as a shoemaker. Jack also used his earnings to purchase an 8.5-acre plot in the vicinity of this site.

> John Jack was the first African American property owner in Concord.

CAESAR ROBBINS HOUSE SITE

Caesar Robbins (1745–1822), previously enslaved in Chelmsford, was the patriarch of an extended African American family in Concord in the late 1770s. Robbins was a veteran of the French and Indian War, and the American Revolution. He built a one-room cabin in the Great Field, opposite the gate of the Old Manse, the family home of Ralph Waldo Emerson. There Robbins lived with his first wife, Cate Boas, and his second wife, Rose Bay, and their extended family whose members included his son, Peter Robbins, and his daughter, Susan (Robbins) Garrison.

PETER ROBBINS & FATIMA

Peter Robbins (1792–1855), Caesar Robbins's son, built a more substantial home on his family's thirteen-acre home site in the early 1800s where he lived with his wife, Fatima. After Peter entered into a relationship with another resident, Elmira, and had thirteen children by her, Fatima successfully sued for divorce. New owners purchased the house from the family in 1871, and moved it to the current location of 324 Bedford St.

JACK GARRISON & SUSAN ROBBINS

Jack Garrison (1769–1860), a fugitive from slavery in New Jersey, married Susan Robbins (1780–1841) and had eight children. The family lived in an addition on her parents' house. Susan Robbins Garrison was active in the abolitionist movement as one of the founders of the Concord Female Anti-Slavery Society. The town of Concord named Garrison Road to honor Jack and Susan Garrison.

*Jack Garrison
(photo in Concord Museum)*

Ellen Garrison (1823–d. circa 1890), the daughter of Jack and Susan, was a scholar who was embedded in the activism of Concord in her formative years. She moved to Boston at the age of seventeen where she was involved in various anti-slavery and civil rights acivities. One of the many petitions she signed during this time was to desegregate Massachusetts railroads.

She eventually obtained a position as a teacher through the Freedmen's Bureau to teach in Maryland and Virginia. Ellen documented the injustices she experienced in the South in the many letters she wrote of which over 100 remain.

> *"...who will help us if we don't help ourselves"*
> —ELLEN GARRISON

PETER HUTCHINSON & NANCY DAGER

Peter Hutchinson (1799–1882) was the stepson of Peter Robbins and the step-grandson of Caesar Robbins. Peter Hutchinson lived here with his wife, Nancy Dager, and their five daughters. They were the last residents of the family homestead. The town of Concord named Peter Spring Road and Peter's Path both in honor of Hutchinson.

1881
Hutchinson was the first African American to vote in Concord

2 ROBBINS HOUSE INTERPRETIVE CENTER
320 Monument St.
opposite Old Manse
978-254-1745

This is the original home of Peter Robbins. In 2010, The Drinking Gourd Project acquired the house and relocated it closer to its original site. The organization restored this house as the Robbins House Interpretative Center. Historical exhibits about Concord's African American heritage are disiplayed here.

Robbins House

3 OLD MANSE
269 Monument Street

Caesar Robbins married Cate Boas at this historic house in 1769. Rev. William Emerson (NAA), grandfather of Ralph Waldo Emerson (NAA), officiated. Rev. Emerson also built the Old Manse. In 1842, John Garrison, the grandson of Caesar Robbins, developed a garden on the property with the help of Henry David Thoreau (NAA), to celebrate the wedding of Nathaniel

Old Manse

Hawthorne (NAA) to Sophia Peabody (NAA).

In the spring of 1859, John Brown (NAA) spoke before an audience in the parlor. That fall, he led his raid on Harper's Ferry, an event that precipitated the Civil War. Franklin Benjamin Sanborn (NAA) of the *"Secret Committee of Six,"* a group that financed John Brown's raid on Harper's Ferry, also lived briefly at the Old Manse in 1863.

 ### 4 JOHN GARRISON HOUSE
78 Monument Street

John Garrison, son of Jack and Susan Garrison, and grandson of Caesar Robbins, built this cottage in the mid-1800s.

Garrison House

 ### 5 SLEEPY HOLLOW CEMETERY
Bedford St.

Peter Hutchinson (1799–1882), the first African American resident of Concord to vote in town elections, was buried here in an unmarked grave. Hutchison was the stepson of Peter Robbins, who, in turn, was the son of Caesar Robbins, one of the earliest African American residents of Concord.

Numerous famous white authors were buried in Authors' Ridge, a section of Sleepy Hollow Cemetery. Some of them were Ralph Waldo Emerson, Henry David Thoreau, Louisa May Alcott, and other members of her family. Franklin Benjamin Sanborn (NAA) was also buried here. Sanborn was a member of the *"Secret Committee of Six,"* a group that funded John Brown's raid on Harper's Ferry.

6 MARY TYLER PEABODY & HORACE MANN HOUSE
UGRR Station
44 Bedford St.

Mary Tyler Peabody Mann (NAA) (1806–1887) actively participated in abolitionist efforts in Concord. Mary Mann was the widow of the education reformer, Horace Mann (NAA) (1796–1859). Her sister, Elizabeth Peabody (NAA) originated the system of kindergartens in the United States. Anoth-

Mary Tyler Peabody Mann

er sister, Sophia Peabody (NAA), was the spouse of Nathaniel Hawthorne (NAA).

When the students of a school that Mann operated in Concord learned that the Emancipation Proclamation of January 1st, 1863, did not free all enslaved individuals but only those who resided in the Confederate states, they wanted to do something. Mrs. Mann organized a petition for them in the winter of 1864. 195 schoolchildren signed that petition. She gave the petition to Senator Sumner (NAA) of Massachusetts who delivered it to President Lincoln.

1864
Petition of the children of the United States (under 18 years); that the President will free all slave children.

A copy of Lincoln's reply to what he called the, *"Little People's Petition,"* is stored at the Concord Free Public Library.

Executive Mansion
Washington, April 5, 1864
Mrs. Horace Mann

Madam,

The petition of persons under eighteen, praying that I would free all slave children, and the heading of which petition it appears you wrote, was handed me a few days since by Senator Sumner. Please tell these little people I am very glad their young hearts are so full of just and generous sympathy, and that, while I have not the power to grant all they ask, I trust they will remember that God has and that, as it seems, He wills to do it.

Yours truly
A. Lincoln

President Lincoln's reply stated that he did not have the power to grant their request but that, *"God...wills to do it."* That was a possible reference to the fact that the the United States Con-

Thirteenth Amendment
abolished slavery and involuntary servitude throughout all the United States except as punishment for a crime.

April 8th, 1864
Thirteenth Amendment passed by U.S. Senate

January 31st, 1865
Thirteenth Amendment passed by House

December 6th, 1865
Thirteenth Amendment adopted as law

gress had already begun the process to negotiate the 13th Amendment which ended slavery throughout the U.S. Mrs. Mann's reply to Lincoln's letter did not reach the President before his assassination on April 14th:

Mrs. Mann's reply:

"...We look with more hope than ever for the day when perfect justice shall be decreed, which shall make every able bodied colored man spring to the defence (sic) of the nation which it is plain the white man alone cannot save. You who can hasten it must be the happiest of men, for in saving the colored man you will feel that you are doing equal service to the white man."

Mann House

 ## ⑦ JOHN JACK HEADSTONE
Old Hill Burying Ground Monument Square

John Jack (1713–1773), the first African American property owner in Concord was buried here. The epitaph on Jack's headstone memorialized him throughout the centuries because it articulated the hypocrisy of the artificial distinctions between those enslaved and those free. A local attorney, Daniel Bliss (NAA), the executor of Jack's estate, created that epitaph for Jack's headstone.

John Jack Headstone

"God wills us free; man wills us slaves.
I will as God wills; God's will be done.
Here lies the body of
JOHN JACK
a native of Africa who died
March 1773 aged about 60 years
Tho' born in a land of slavery,
He was born free.
Tho' he lived in a land of liberty,
He lived a slave.
Till by his honest, tho' stolen labors,
He acquired the source of slavery,
Which gave him his freedom;
Tho' not long before
Death, the grand tyrant
Gave him his final emancipation,
And set him on a footing with kings.
Tho' a slave to vice,
He practised those virtues
Without which kings are but slaves"

8 JONAS LEE HOUSE CONCORD ART ASSOCIATION
UGRR Station
37 Lexington Rd.

When the Jonas Lee (NAA) family resided here, this residence was a stop on the Underground Railroad. It is now home to the Concord Art Association.

Jonas Lee House

9 FIRST PARISH CHURCH
20 Lexington Road

Concord's national reputation as a beehive of abolitionist activity was reinforced by the large number of anti-slavery speakers who regularly delivered lectures to the local community. The First Parish Church was often the chosen venue for those programs. Harriet Tubman and Frederick Douglass both spoke from its podium and the Middlesex County Anti-Slavery Society regularly held their meeting here.

First Parish Church

10 REUBEN BROWN HOUSE
77 Lexington Road

Reuben Brown (NAA), a good friend of Ralph Waldo Emerson (NAA), was active in a group of white abolitionists in Concord. Brown often allowed out of town abolitionist speakers to stay at his house. John Brown (NAA was one of his most famous visitors.

Reuben Brown House

11 RALPH WALDO EMERSON HOUSE
UGRR Station
28 Cambridge Turnpike

Ralph Waldo Emerson (NAA) (1803-1882) was one of the principal proponents of Transcendentalism, a philosophy that encouraged the inherent goodness of man and the strong connection of man to nature. Emerson and the other Transcendentalists were also fervent abolitionists. That support included the endorsement of John Brown's position that violence was justified to achieve the overthrow of slavery.

Ralph Waldo Emerson

Emerson's influential essay, *"Self-Reliance,"* encouraged independence of thought. He promoted the idea that each individual had the potential to develop true wisdom through a reliance on their personal internal thoughts and should not allow the conventions of society to influence their behavior.

Emerson House

> *"Whoso would be a man, must be a nonconformist. He who would gather immortal palms must not be hindered by the name of goodness, but must explore if it be goodness. Nothing is at last sacred but the integrity of your own mind. Absolve you to yourself, and you shall have the suffrage of the world."*
> –RALPH WALDO EMERSON

> *"A foolish consistency is the hobgoblin of little minds."*
> –RALPH WALDO EMERSON.

> *"Do not go where the path may lead, go instead where there is no path and leave a trail."*
> –RALPH WALDO EMERSON

> *"What lies behind you and what lies in front of you, pales in comparison to what lies inside of you."*
> –RALPH WALDO EMERSON

> *"Without ambition one starts nothing. Without work one finishes nothing. The prize will not be sent to you. You have to win it."*
> –RALPH WALDO EMERSON

(12) JOHN JACK & BENJAMIN BARRON HOUSE
249 Lexington Rd.

John Jack (1713–1773) lived here when he was enslaved by Benjamin Barron (NAA). After Barron's death, Jack purchased his freedom from Barron's widow with money he earned as a shoemaker, a craft he learned from Barron.

John Jack became the first African American landowner in Concord when he purchased eight and one-half acres of land shortly after he purchased his freedom. John Jack is world renown for the epitaph on his headstone at the Old Hill Burial Burying Ground in Concord.

John Jack & Benjamin Barron House

(13) ALCOTT *"ORCHARD"* HOUSE
UGRR Station
399 Lexington Road

The Alcott family members were active abolitionists who also operated an Underground Railroad Station from their home at 399 Lexington Road. Louisa May Alcott (NAA) (1832-1888) authored the classic children's books, *Little Women* and *Little Men*.

> "Let my name stand among those who are willing to bear ridicule and reproach for the truth's sake, and so earn a right to rejoice when the victory is won."
> -LOUISA MAY ALCOTT

Louisa May Alcott House

(14) WAYSIDE INN CASEY FEEN / SAMUEL WHITNEY HOUSE & CASEY'S PLAQUE
UGRR Station
455 Lexington Road

African American, Casey Feen who was enslaved by Samuel Whitney (NAA), gained his freedom when he joined the militia in the American Revolution. A few yards from the Wayside Inn, local citizens erected a plaque to honor Feen. Samuel Whitney (NAA), the original owner of the Wayside Inn, was also a member of the Concord Minutemen.

Wayside Inn

Many white abolitionists and authors, such as Louisa May Alcott (NAA) and Nathaniel Hawthorne (NAA), lived at this historic inn at some point during their residence in Concord. Fugitives from slavery were also welcomed here during their journey to Canada. The importance of the Wayside Inn to the history of our country led the National Register of Historic Places to designate the building as a National Historic Landmark.

(15) TRINITARIAN CONGREGATIONAL
54 Walden Street

Audiences flocked to the Trinitarian Congregational Church to hear many popular abolitionist speakers who lectured from its podium.

Trinitarian Congregational Church

The minister, Rev. John Wilder (NAA), and his wife, Mary Wilder (NAA), were ardent anti-slavery activists. The Concord Female Anti-Slavery Society elected Mrs. Wilder to serve as its first President.

 ## 16 NATHAN AND MARY BROOKS HOUSE
UGRR Station
45 Hubbard St.

The Brooks (NAA) House was originally located at 129 Main St. It was relocated to this site in 1872.

17 SHADRACH MINKINS'S REFUGE BIGELOW HOUSE
UGRR Station
19 Sudbury Rd.

The Fugitive Slave Act of 1850 required United States citizens to assist in the capture of fugitives from slavery; to not assist was a violation of Federal law. The Boston Vigilance Committee actively resisted this unfair law when they helped fugitives avoid capture. The Committee carried out one of the most bold and courageous escapes of a fugitive held in jail during this time, the rescue of Shadrach Minkins.

The group orchestrated Minkins's escape from jail after his capture on February 15th, 1851. He passed through a series of safe houses, including the Bigelow (NAA) house in Concord, before his rescuers took him to Canada. Minkins settled in Canada and became a successful business owner.

Bigelow House

(18) FRANKLIN SANBORN SCHOOL
49 Sudbury Road

Franklin Benjamin Sanborn (NAA) (1831-1917), a journalist, a Transcendentalist, and an abolitionist, lived and ran a school here with Mary Mann (NAA). Sanborn was also a member of the *"Secret Committee of Six,"* a group of wealthy, white individuals who funded John Brown's raid on Harper's Ferry. Shortly after Brown's trial, Sanborn temporarily fled to Canada to avoid prosecution for his involvement in the Harper's Ferry Raid. Sanborn later wrote and published, *The Life and Letters of John Brown.*

Sanborn House

(19) SITE: NATHAN & MARY BROOKS HOUSE NOW: CONCORD FREE PUBLIC LIBRARY
129 Main St.

Nathan and Mary Brooks (NAA) used their house at this location as a station on the Underground Railroad. The house was relocated to 45 Hubbard St. in 1872. Today, many documents that pertain to Concord's anti-slavery history and its early African American residents reside at this library.

Concord Free Public Library

(20) WILLIAM WHITING HOUSE
UGRR Station
169 Main Street

William Whiting's (NAA) participation in the abolition movement included the shelter of fugitives from slavery. Many abolitionists, such as William Lloyd Garrison and John Brown, were guests of Whiting at his home.

Whiting House

(21) HENRY DAVID THOREAU HOUSE
UGRR Station
255 Main St.

Thoreau House

Henry David Thoreau (1817-1862) (NAA), one of the leaders in the Transcendentalist Movement, was also an active abolitionist. He documented in his *Journal* how he helped fugitive, Henry Williams, escape to Canada. Thoreau was also influenced by African American residents of Concord who lived close to nature to do so himself. He documented that effort in his book, *Walden Pond*. His other significant book, *Civil Disobedience*, influenced such historical figures as Mohandas Gandhi (NAA) and Martin Luther King, Jr.

"Talk about slavery! It is not the peculiar institution of the South. It exists wherever men are bought and sold, wherever a man allows himself to be made a mere thing or a tool, and surrenders his inalienable rights of reason and conscience. Indeed, this slavery is more complete than that which enslaves the body alone.... I never yet met with, or heard of, a judge who was not a slave of this kind, and so the finest and most unfailing weapon of injustice. He fetches a slightly higher price than the black men only because he is a more valuable slave."
–Henry David Thoreau

Henry David Thoreau

"Disobedience is the true foundation of liberty. The obedient must be slaves."
-HENRY DAVID THOREAU

> "...a government in which the majority rule in all cases cannot be based on justice, ... Can there not be a government in which majorities do not virtually decide right and wrong, but conscience?... Why has every man a conscience, then? I think that we should be men first, and subjects afterward. It is not desirable to cultivate a respect for the law, so much as for the right."
> –HENRY DAVID THOREAU

22 BRISTER FREEMAN/ JOHN CUMING HOUSE
998 Elm Street

African American, Brister Freeman, lived here while he was enslaved by John Cuming (NAA). Brister earned his freedom after he served in the militia on the side of the Patriots in the American Revolution.

Brister Freeman / John Cuming House

23 MALCOLM X SITE: SITE OF CONCORD REFORMATORY
965 Elm St.

The state transferred Malcolm X to the Concord Reformatory in 1947 from the Charlestown Prison. He spent fifteen months here before he was transferred to the Norfolk MCI prison. In 1972, the name of this medium security prison was changed to the Massachusetts Correctional Institute at Concord.

24 ABIEL WHEELER (NAA) HOUSE
UGRR Station
387 Sudbury Road

25 SITE: THOMAS & JENNIE DUGAN HOMESTEAD
End of Jennie Dugan Road

Thomas Dugan emancipated himself from slavery in Virginia in the early 1800s. He moved to Concord where his frugality and resourceful nature made it possible for him to become the third African American to own land in Concord. Dugan introduced the rye cradle, a farm tool, to the community. He also taught the farmers how to graft apples.

Thomas Dugan had five children by his first wife, Catherine. His second wife, Jennie, was a well-known personality in Concord who had two landmarks named after her, Jennie Dugan

Road and Jennie Dugan Brook. Thomas and Jennie had three children. Their youngest son, George Dugan, enlisted in the Massachusetts 54th Regiment during the Civil War. Another son, Elisha Dugan, lost the family property and had to live in the woods near Old Marlborough Road, near their homestead. Thoreau memorialized him in the poem, "The Old Marlborough Road."

"The Old Marlborough Road"
By Henry David Thoreau

Where they once dug for money,
But never found any;
Where sometimes Martial Miles
Singly files,
And Elijah Wood,
I fear for no good:
No other man,
Save Elisha Dugan,—
O man of wild habits,
Partridges and rabbits,
Who hast no cares
Only to set snares,
Who liv'st all alone,
Close to the bone,
And where life is sweetest
Constantly eatest.
When the spring stirs my blood
With the instinct to travel,
I can get enough gravel
On the Old Marlborough Road.
Nobody repairs it,
For nobody wears it;
It is a living way,
As the Christians say...."

26 SITE: ZILPAH WHITE HOUSE
Route 126 and Route 2

Zilpah White, a single, formerly enslaved woman, lived alone in a one-room cabin near Walden Pond. To survive, she spun flax into linen. Despite the harsh conditions of her daily existence, White lived on her terms. Her independence gained the respect of Thoreau.

27 SITE: CATO & PHYLLIS INGRAHAM HOMESTEAD
Route 2 near Walden Pond

Cato Ingraham was presented with an ultimatum by Duncan Ingraham (NAA), his enslaver, when Cato expressed a desire to marry Phyllis. Duncan, who planned to relocate to Medford, indicated that Cato would lose all support he received as the property of Duncan if he, Cato, married Phyllis. Despite that threat, Cato and Phyllis married and settled in a small house on an acre of sandy land in Walden Woods. The harsh conditions caused both Cato and Phyllis to die of malnutrition. Their courage inspired Thoreau to live on Walden Pond.

**SITE: BRISTER &
FEENA FREEMAN
HOMESTEAD**
Marker off Walden St.
near Route 2
Brister's Hill Road across
the street

Brister Scipio was enslaved by John
Cuming (NAA) for over twenty-five
years before he obtained his freedom
through service in the American Revolution. After the war, Brister renamed
himself Freeman and married Feena.
The couple had three children. Brister
worked as a day laborer and bought an
acre of land near what was renamed
Brister's Hill Road in his honor. Brister's Spring was also named in his
honor. Brister was the second emancipated person to purchase property
in Concord. The couple's perseverance
inspired Thoreau.

*Brister Freeman Marker written by
Henry David Thoreau*

*"Near here lived Brister Freeman
(d. 1820) formerly enslaved in
Concord, Feena Freeman (d. 1811)
and their family.*

*Down the road and on the right
hand, on Brister's Hill, lived Brister
Freeman...there where grow still the
apple trees which Brister planted
and tended..."*

– Thoreau, Walden, 1854

Brister Hill Road Sign

 **EPHRAIM ALLEN
(NAA) HOUSE**
UGRR Station
Site Unknown

 LOCAL RESOURCES
**African American
Heritage Trail of Concord**
www.RobbinsHouse.org

WAYLAND

1 LYDIA MARIA CHILD HOUSE
91 Old Sudbury Road

Lydia Maria Child (1802-1880) (NAA), a famous abolitionist, feminist, and author, lived at this address during the later period of her life. Child was buried in the North Cemetery at 65 Old Sudbury Road in Sudbury. See Medford and Florence sites for more on Child.

Child House

SUDBURY

1 OLD BURYING GROUND AKA: OLD TOWN CEMETERY
Sudbury Centre
Concord Rd. & Old Sudbury Rd.

As early as 1750, African Americans, though small in number, were woven into the fabric of Sudbury. At that time, among the population of 1,745 were twenty-seven African Americans. Many of them were buried in the Old Burying Ground of Sudbury Centre.

MARLBOROUGH

1 CIVIL WAR MEMORIAL: JOHN BROWN LIBERTY BELL
Union Common
Main St. and Bolton

In May of 1861, sixteen members of the Marlborough Company I, 13th Massachusetts Volunteer Militia, many of whom were local firemen, were dispatched to Harper's Ferry, Virginia with orders to seize anything of value so that it would not fall into the hands of the Confederates. Over the Engine House where John Brown had been captured was a bell that weighed approximately seven to eight hundred pounds. The sixteen members of the unit managed to get the bell down from the tower and take it back to where their unit was stationed.

When the Union Army decided they did not want the bell, the volunteer unit from Marlborough petitioned the army to keep the bell, which they named, *"John Brown's Bell."* They intended to install it in their local firehouse in Marlborough which did not have a bell. The army agreed, but the men, who were stationed outside of Williamsport, had no way to ship the bell to Marlborough. In Williamsport, members of the unit met Mrs. Elizabeth Ensminger (NAA), a local shopkeeper, and she agreed to protect the bell until they returned.

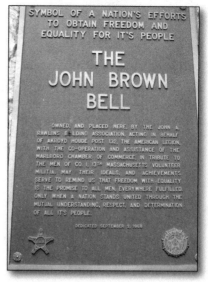

Liberty Bell Tower Sign

John Brown's Bell

Five of the original sixteen members of the rescue unit did not survive the war. The rest returned home to Marlborough. The members of the unit eventually became affiliated with the veteran's organization, the G.A.R. (Grand Army of the Republic) and they managed to build a Veteran's Hall in downtown Marlborough. During a reunion in 1892, some of the members

reminiscenced about the Civil War and a discussion about the bell began. The members decided to raise funds to ship the bell from Williamsport where Mrs. Ensminger, now remarried as Mrs. Snyder, still kept it in safety.

The veterans installed the bell in the front of the newly built Veteran's Hall in 1892. The next year, the town hosted a reception to honor Mrs. Snyder. On the program was a musical solo by Hattie Goins. Goins's father was Luke Goins, a musician who had been enslaved at Harper's Ferry. After the war, he relocated to Marlborough where he and his wife, Annie, raised their eleven children. Goins was able to identify the bell as authentic because of his highly developed ability to recognize musical tone. The Engine House in Harper's Ferry has been rebuilt as a Historic Site. The town of Harper's Ferry has petitioned the town of Marlborough for return of the bell but without success.

This monument also serves as a memorial to all 831 men from Marlborough who served in the Civil War out of a total population of 6,200. The town suffered ninety-one casualties of those enlisted.

Meta Vaux Warrick Fuller

SOUTHBOROUGH

(1) **REV. DANIEL WHITNEY WHITNEY HOUSE**
UGRR Station
Site Unknown

FRAMINGHAM

(1) **DR. SOLOMON CARTER FULLER & META VAUX WARRICK FULLER HOUSE**
31 Warren Road /
Private residence

Dr. Solomon Carter Fuller

The first African American to practice psychiatry in the United States, Dr. Solomon Carter Fuller (1872–1953), was born in Liberia. Dr. Fuller's father was a formerly enslaved African American from the United States who purchased his freedom and immigrated back to Africa. See Dr. Fuller under South End sites. Meta Vaux Warrick Fuller (1877–1968), a leading sculptor during the period of the Harlem Renaissance, married Dr. Solomon Carter Fuller in

Fuller House

1909. The couple settled in Framingham where Dr. Fuller maintained a medical practice and Mrs. Fuller continued her artistic career.

Dr. Fuller graduated in 1897 from Boston University School of Medicine. Throughout his career, he focused on medical research to understand the physical changes to the brain due to Alzheimer's disease. Massachusetts dedicated the Dr. Solomon Carter Fuller Mental Health Center at 85 East Newton St. in the South End in Boston in honor of Dr. Fuller's innovative research in mental health. Dr. and Mrs. Fuller raised their family in this house.

 ### SITE: META WARRICK FULLER STUDIO
135 Warren Road

Meta Vaux Warrick Fuller moved to Framingham with her husband, Dr. Solomon Carter Fuller, in 1910. Fuller was born in Philadelphia she studied with the sculptor, Auguste Rodin in

Paris. After she returned to the states, Fuller lost all her earlier work in a warehouse fire in Philadelphia. Many of her subsequent sculptures explored socially relevant themes.

"Ethiopia Awakening," one of her most famous sculptures, was completed in 1914. It symbolized the cultural awareness that people of the African Diaspora had begun to experience, a need to break free of the mummy shrouds that had bound us to limitations of the past. The phase, the *"New Negro"* was coined to describe those who possessed this newly asserted awareness. Meta Vaux Warrick Fuller was one of the artists who gave visual expression to the philosophy of this, New Negro Movement, which was the momentum behind the period known as the Harlem Renaissance.

Ethiopia Awakening

③ **DANFORTH MUSEUM**
123 Union Avenue
508-620-0050
www.danforthmuseum.org

The Danforth Museum has sculptures by the artist, Meta Vaux Warrick Fuller in its permanent collection. The museum has featured in the past, special exhibits on the artist's work. They have also developed an educational toolkit on the artist for elementary schools.

Danforth Museum

④ **OLIVIA DAVIDSON WASHINGTON FRAMINGHAM STATE UNIVERSITY**
100 State Street

Olivia Davidson (1854–1889) helped establish Tuskegee Institute with her husband, Booker T. Washington. Born in Virginia, Davidson grew up in the state of Ohio. She began her career as a teacher while still a teenager. After she graduated from Hampton Institute in 1879, Davidson enrolled in the State

Normal School in Framingham, MA, now, Framingham State University. Upon her graduation in 1881 as one of six honor students, Booker T. Washington invited her to Tuskegee Institute as a teacher and an administrator.

Olivia Davidson Washington

They married in 1886 after the death of Washington's first wife. Davidson became seriously ill in the late 1880s after she contracted laryngeal tuberculosis. Washington brought her to Massachusetts General Hospital in Boston but the treatment was unsuccessful and she died on May 9th, 1889.

⑤ **CIVIL WAR MEMORIAL: EDGELL MEMORIAL LIBRARY**
3 Oak St. / 508-626-9091

The Edgell Memorial Library was dedicated in 1873 to honor those 530 citizens of Framingham who served in the Civil War when the population of Framingham was only 4,227. Fifty-two of that number never returned. The library has also installed a permanent exhibit on Framingham's involvement in the anti-slavery movement.

SITE: SAXONVILLE MILLS

Concord and Central St.

The Saxonville Mills were the primary manufacturers of the fabric used for Union Army uniforms, the sky-blue Kersey wool.

PETER SALEM MONUMENT

Old Burying Ground
66 Main St.

One of the heroes of the American Revolution, Peter Salem (1750–1816) was born in Framingham. He was enslaved by two individuals, Jeremiah Belknap (NAA) and Lawson Buckminster (NAA), before he enlisted in the militia to obtain his freedom. Salem saw service in several battles but the most important of those was the Battle of Bunker Hill on June 17th, 1775.

In that battle, the Patriots were out-numbered and out-gunned by the British. Salem managed to shoot and kill Major Pitcairn, the first British officer killed during the battle. That victory rallied the Patriots and gave them the courage to continue the fight. His

gravesite is located in a shallow valley at the end of the main entrance path.

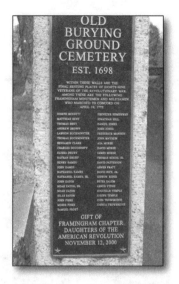

Old Burying Ground Gates

Peter Salem Headstone

8 PLYMOUTH CHURCH
87 Edgell Road
508-875-1364

The Framingham Anti-Slavery Society was founded here in 1837. In 1862, this was the site of the first public performance of, *"The Battle Hymn of the Republic"* by Julia Ward Howe (NAA).

Plymouth Church

9 SITE: HARMONY GROVE
Henry and Franklin St.

Harmony Grove was a cleared area in the woods where Emancipation Day events were held in the 19th century. It was also the site of abolitionist and suffragette rallies.

10 SITE: GENERAL GORDON HOUSE
936 Central St.

The 2nd Massachusetts Volunteer Infantry Regiment in the Civil War was organized by General Gordon (NAA). That Regiment was a model for the entire Union Army. Gordon also trained Col. Robert Gould Shaw, the leader of the Massachusetts 54th Regiment.

11 CRISPUS ATTUCKS
Site Unknown

Crispus Attucks was the first person to be in killed in the Boston Massacre. That attack was one of the primary factors that sparked the American Revolution. Before that eventful day, Attucks escaped from slavery during the mid-1750s from a farm in the vicinity of Framingham.

12 FULLER MIDDLE SCHOOL
31 Flagg Drive

In 1995, the town of Framingham renamed this school to honor Dr. Solomon Carter Fuller, the first African American psychiatrist, and Meta Vaux Warrick Fuller, a sculptor from the Harlem Renaissance.

NATICK

 ## NATICK HISTORICAL SOCIETY MUSEUM
58 Eliot St.
508-647-4841

The Natick Historical Society has permanent exhibits on the involvement of many of its citizens in the Civil War effort. Seven hundred volunteers from Natick enlisted in the war and the town suffered eighty casualties.

 ## SITE: HENRY WILSON'S COBBLER SHOP
Corner West Central (Rt. 135) & Mill St.

Henry Wilson (NAA) began his adult career as a shoe cobbler. Wilson, a staunch abolitionist, became an elected official and Chairman of the Senate Committee on Military Affairs. He later served as Vice-President under Ulysses S. Grant (NAA).

 ## SQUIRE EDWARD WALCOTT (NAA) HOUSE
UGRR Station
89 W. Central St.

 ## ISRAEL HOW BROWN HOUSE
UGRR Station
Lowell Rd.

Israel How Brown (NAA) hid his transient visitors in his produce wagon to transport them to the next station.

NEWTON

 ## JACKSON HOMESTEAD NEWTON HISTORY MUSEUM
UGRR Station
527 Washington St.
Daily 12 to 5 pm
www.newtonhistory museum.org

The participation and financial support of many influential and economically well-off white families in Massachusetts made this state a major route as well as destination for travelers on the Underground Railroad. This assistance was not without personal sacrifice. The Fugitive Slave Act made it a federal crime to aid and assist fugitives in their escape from slavery.

The brothers, William and Francis Jackson (NAA) of Newton were two of many individuals who used whatever resources were at their disposal to fight for the abolitionist cause. Their father,

Timothy Jackson (NAA), a veteran of the American Revolution, built this house.

Jackson Homestead

In 1820, William Jackson returned to the family home to live. He served in the Massachusetts General Court and the U.S. Congress. He also founded the Newton Savings Bank and Eliot Church. William used his political and financial influence to support the abolitionist movement. Francis Jackson was the Treasurer of the Boston Vigilance Committee.

After William's death in 1855, Mary Jackson (NAA), his widow, with his three daughters, continued to aid and abet fugitives from slavery. Mary was one of the founders and the president of the Freedman's Aid Society in Newton. The major beneficiaries of the society were the Southern African American universities, Hampton Institute and Tuskegee Institute. Their home is now the Newton History Museum. It has permanent exhibits on the abolitionist movement and the Underground Railroad.

Ellen Jackson, one of the daughters of William and Mary Jackson, gave this account of one night when another abolitionist, William Bowditch of Brookline, brought a fugitive to her father:

> "...*One night between 12 and one o'clock, I well remember father was awakened by pebbles thrown against his window. He rose and asked what was wanted? Bowditch replied it was he, with a runaway slave whom he wished father to hide till morning, and then help him on his way to Canada, for his master was in Boston looking for him. Father took him in and next morning carried him 15 miles to a Station where he could take a car for Canada. He could not have safely left by any Boston Station.*"
> -- Ellen Jackson

 CORNELIUS LENOX
Site: Unknown

Veteran of the American Revolution, Cornelius Lenox lived in Newton with his family on two acres of land that he owned. Lenox was the father of Nancy Lenox. Nancy was the wife of John Remond of Salem, and the mother of Charles Lenox Remond and Sarah Parker Remond.

CIVIL WAR MONUMENT
Newton Centre
Newton Cemetery,
Walnut St.

The town of Newton erected this monument to honor those who died in the Civil War from Newton in 1864 while the war continued. It was one of the first Civil War monuments erected in New England. The names of forty-three troops were engraved when the monument was completed. Eighteen additional names were added after the war ended. The population of Newton in 1860 was 8,382.

One of the names listed was Lieut. Eben White (NAA) of the 7th U.S. Colored Troops, Company B. White was a white officer assigned to a regiment of African American troops. Confederate soldiers and sympathizers treated harshly the white officers assigned to lead African American troops because those white officers were viewed as traitors to the white race.

White had an unusual history because he was murdered off the battlefield by Confederate sympathizers. Under the Confiscation Act of 1862, Union officers were authorized to seize property of those who sympathized with and gave aid to the Confederate cause. On Oct. 19th, 1863, White approached a Maryland plantation whose owner had openly given solace to Confederate troops.

White planned to recruit those enslaved on the plantation to the Union Army. The Plantation owner and his son challenged White's authority and threatened bodily harm if he did not leave immediately. White refused and the owner and his son shot White point blank in the head and chest. The incident was witnessed by two African American troops from Company B, John Bantam and Benjamin Black. Bantam was also wounded in the encounter. In 1866, after the war ended, the plantation owner was indicted for murder based on Bantam's and Black's testimony. Unfortunately, he was found not guilty.

 ## GEORGE WASHINGTON WILLIAMS & NEWTON THEOLOGICAL SEMINARY
210 Herrick Rd.
Newton Centre

George Washington Williams' (1849–1891) life expanded the boundaries of what could be accomplished with determination and vision. During the course of his short life, Williams was a soldier, a minister, a politician, an historian, and a diplomat. Portions of his remarkable life were captured in a feature movie released in the summer of 2016. That movie related the efforts of Williams, played by actor, Samuel Jackson, to expose the atrocities of the Belgium government during their colonization of the Congo.

Williams was born in Bedford Springs, PA as one of four sons to Thomas and Ellen Rouse Williams. His restless and curious nature, at a time when African American boys were expected to know their place, resulted in his placement in a youth corrections facility where he received a limited education.

At the age of fourteen, Williams enlisted in the Union Army under an assumed name. After stints in the Civil War and the war for Mexican independence, Williams enrolled in college, first at Howard University in Washington, D.C., and then at Newton Theological Seminary where he was the first African American graduate in 1874. During his stay in Boston, Williams pastored at Twelfth Baptist Church on Beacon Hill.

George Washington Williams relocated to Cincinatti where he studied law. He won election as the first African American in the Ohio legislature and served a single term, 1880-1881. At some point, Williams interest in history led him to write two pivotal books: *A History of Negro Troops in the War of Rebellion*; and *The History of the Negro Race in America 1619–1880*.

Williams had connections in Washington which led to several Presidential appointments. One by President Benjamin Harrison (NAA) in 1890 led him to investigate conditions in the Congo. That investigation resulted in a public letter to King Leopold II (NAA) of Belgium which highlighted the atrocities committed in Congo under King Leopold's name. Some of those atrocities included: the native population was constripted for slave labor; native women were sold into forced prostitution; and enslaved people were beheaded and buried alive. Williams hoped that public outrage and exposure of Belgium's flagrant abuse of international law would force a change. He died in England in 1891 from diseases contracted in Africa.

5 MAYOR SETTI WARREN
Newton City Hall
1000 Commonwealth Ave.

Setti Warren (b. 1970) won the mayoral election in Newton in 2009. He was sworn into office on January 1st, 2010. That election victory made him one of the few African Americans to be elected as mayor in Massachusetts. Warren won re-election in 2013.

Setti Warren

MYRTLE BAPTIST CHURCH
21 Curve St.

Myrtle Baptist Church, one of the oldest African American churches still in operation, was added to the National Register of Historic Places in 2008. It was founded in 1874 when African American members of First Baptist Church of Newton desired a separate church independent of that majority white congregation. The 130 African American residents in Newton in 1873 were enough of a critical mass to support an independent congregation. Members of the church who requested the separation were Jane Brewer, Lymus Hicks, Thomas Johnson, Henry Jones, Henrietta Rose, and Sarah Simms.

Reverend Edmund Kelley served as the first minister. Rev. Kelley began his career as a minister in 1843 while he was still enslaved in Tennessee. Rev. Kelley organized many African American churches both, before and after his tenure at Myrtle Baptist. Rev. Martin L. King, Jr. preached from the pulpit of Myrtle Baptist while he was a student at Boston University.

BROOKLINE

 WILLIAM BOWDITCH HOUSE
UGRR Station
9 Toxteth St.,
private residence

William Ingerson Bowditch (1819-1909) (NAA) lived in this house from 1845 until 1867.

During that time he participated in several abolitionist efforts, and his house was a stop on the Underground Railroad. Bowditch also served on the Boston Vigilance Committee.

William Ingersoll Bowditch House

The most famous fugitives to stay at his house were William and Ellen Craft in 1849. See Beacon Hill site. Their stay in Brookline was prior to their move to Boston, where they lived on Beacon Hill. John Brown's son also sought refuge in the Bowditch home, after his father's execution for the raid on Harper's Ferry in 1859.

2 TAPPAN–PHILBRICK HOUSE

UGRR Station
182 Walnut St.,
private residence

When Samuel Philbrick (1789–1859) (NAA) moved with his family to this house in 1829, he was already a dedicated abolitionist. Philbrick was a respected member of the community and he used that position to introduce anti-slavery speakers to his neighbors. His guests included the Grimke sisters, Angelina and Sarah (NAA). They stayed with the Philbricks for two years while they lectured throughout the North on the harsh realities of slavery.

Once, Philbrick insisted that a free African American child who temporarily stayed with them should attend Sunday services and sit in the family pew. Their Unitarian congregation was horrified and demanded that the child sit in the balcony, the designated place reserved for African American worshippers. Philbrick refused and after several Sundays of this disruption, the family withdrew from the congregation.

William and Ellen Craft were also hidden here prior to their escape to England after fugitive bounty hunters arrived in Boston to return them to slavery.

3 POMPEY BLACKMAN, VETERAN OF THE AMERICAN REVOLUTION

Pompey Blackman of Brookline was one of the many African Americans who served in the American Revolution.

DEDHAM

---

1 MALCOLM X SITE: NORFOLK SUPERIOR COURT

650 High Street

Malcolm X and two of his African American male associates were sentenced to eight to ten years for five counts of burglary at this court in the winter of 1946. The sentences of their two white female accomplices were suspended despite the fact they were enthusiastic participants in the crimes.

Tappan–Philbrick House

Norfolk Superior Court

2 WILLIAM GOULD VETERAN OF THE CIVIL WAR
Milton St.

William Gould (1837–1923) and six other individuals rowed a boat 28 nautical miles down the Cape Fear River to escape slavery in Wilmington, NC, on September 21st, 1862. They were eventually picked up by a Navy warship, the USS Cambridge. After his escape, Gould joined the Navy and saw service on that same warship. Gould's diary, which he kept throughout the war, was one of only three diaries written during that time by a formerly enslaved individual.

Gould, a skilled plasterer, and Cornelia Read of Nantucket, married in November, 1865, after he was discharged from the Navy. They settled in Dedham where he became a contractor. The high quality of his professional work and his involvement in the local post of the Grand Army of the

Republic were known throughout the community. Two of the structures his company helped build were St. Mary's Church, and the Episcopal Church of the Good Shepherd.

The family grew to include six sons and two daughters. All of the sons went on to serve in later U.S. wars. Gould was buried at the Brookdale Cemetery. His great grandson, William B. Gould IV, a professor at Stanford University Law School, edited and published his great-grandfather's diary, *Diary of a Contraband: The Civil War Passage of a Black Sailor.*

William Gould with His Six Sons in Uniform

3 ST. MARY'S CHURCH
420 High St.

William Gould participated in the construction of this church.

4 THE EPISCOPAL CHURCH OF THE GOOD SHEPHERD
62 Cedar St.

William Gould participated in the construction of this church.

5 BROOKDALE CEMETERY
86 Brookdale Ave.

William Gould was buried at Brookdale Cemetery.

MILTON

1 WENDELL PHILLIPS GRAVESITE
Milton Cemetery - 211 Centre St.

Prominent abolitionist Wendell Phillips (1811-1884) (NAA), was buried here. See his listing under downtown Boston sites.

2 MILTON ACADEMY
170 Centre St.

Deval Patrick, (B. 1956), the first African American Governor of Massachusetts, graduated from this elite private school.

QUINCY

1 ADAMS NATIONAL HISTORICAL PARK
135 Adams St.
617-770-1175

John Adams (1735-1826) (NAA), the second President of the United States, and his eldest son, John Quincy Adams (1767-1848) (NAA), the sixth President of the United States, both played integral roles in aspects of African American history in Massachusetts. Their home has been preserved by the National Park Service as the Adams National Historical Park.

Early in his career, John Adams was an ambitious attorney. Several of his clients were defendants in five *"Freedom Lawsuits"*: the 1762, Slew v. Whipple lawsuit in Ipswich; the 1766, Newport v. Billing lawsuit in Hatfield; the 1768, Margaret v. Muzzy lawsuit in Lexington; the 1771, Watson v. Caesar lawsuit in Plymouth; and the 1771, Caesar v. Taylor lawsuit in Newburyport. In all but one of those cases, the enslaved plaintiffs won their lawsuits based on their arguments of personal injury. In the single case where Adam's client was victorious, Newport v. Billing, Newport based his case on an argument of his inalienable right to be free as a human rather than on the claim of personal injury.

Adam was also defense attorney for the British soldiers who fired on the

Adams National Historical Park

of the impromptu group of protesters. Adam's defense strategy painted Attucks as a dangerous thug of whom the soldiers were deathly afraid.

That defense strategy succeeded and the British soldiers were spared the gallows for the murders. Unfortunately, that defense strategy is still used today in many situations where police have been accused of the murder of unarmed African American men. Unwittingly, what Adams also achieved was to document for perpetuity, the key role of Attucks as the spark that ignited the American Revolution.

colonists and fatally wounded five of them in the event known as the Boston Massacre on March 5th, 1770. Crispus Attucks, an African American, was the first to die in that encounter. John Adams described Attucks as the organizer

"...Bailey 'saw the Mulatto seven or eight minutes before the firing, at the head of twenty or thirty sailors in Cornhill, and he had a large cordwood stick.' So that this Attucks, by this testimony of Bailey compared with that of Andrew and some others, appears to have undertaken to be the hero of the night; and to lead this army with banners to form them in the first place in Dock square, and march them up to King-street with their clubs; they passed through the main street up to the main guard, in order to make the attack. If this was not an unlawful assembly, there never was one in the world. Attucks with his myrmidons comes round Jackson's corner, and down to the party by the sentry-box; when the soldiers pushed the people off, this man with his party cried, "do not be afraid of them, they dare not fire, kill them! Kill them! Knock them over!"—and he tried to knock their brains out. It is plain the soldiers did not leave their stations but cried to the people, standoff: now to have this reinforcement coming down under the command of a stout Mulatto fellow, whose very looks was enough to terrify any person, what had not the soldiers then to fear? He had hardiness enough to fall in upon them, and with one hand took hold of a bayonet, and with the other knocked the man down: this was the behaviour of Attucks; to whose mad behaviour, in all probability, the dreadful carnage of that night is chiefly to be ascribed."

–excerpt from John Adams' defense during the trial of the British soldiers.

Towards the latter half of his life, Adams did not believe in the institution of slavery and he liked to boast of that fact, but his pragmatism influenced him to omit the issue from the Declaration of Independence out of fear that it would antagonize the Southern colonists.

> "I have, through my whole life, held the practice of slavery in such abhorrence, that I have never owned a negro or any other slave; though I have lived for many years in times when the practice was not disgraceful; when the best men in my vicinity thought it not inconsistent with their character; and when it has cost me thousands of dollars of the labor and subsistence of free men, which I might have saved by the purchase of negroes at a time when they were very cheap."
>
> —John Adams

John Adams

posed her children to become ardent abolitionists.

John Adams wrote the first draft of the Massachusetts Constitution in 1779. In an instance of historical paradox, that document served as inspiration and legal precedent for the court cases of Brom and Bett v. Ashley, and Quock Walker v. Jennison. In both cases, enslaved individuals in Massachu-

On the other hand, John's wife, Abigail Adams (1744–1818) (NAA), was open in her distain of the institution of slavery. While John's political career was on the ascent and he was absent from home for long periods of time, Abigail held primary responsibility for their farm and family of five children whom she home-schooled. Abigail freely employed African Americans on their farm and taught them to read and write when she had the opportunity. It was Abigail's influence that predis-

> "I wish most sincerely there was not a slave in this province. It always appeared a most iniquitous scheme to me-to fight ourselves for what we are daily robbing and plundering from those who have as good a right to freedom as we have."
>
> —ABIGAIL ADAMS

setts sued their enslavers for violations of their rights as outlined under Article 1 of the Massachusetts Constitution. Their victory in those lawsuits effectively ended the practice of slavery in Massachusetts in 1783. Article 1 of that constitution stated:

> "All men are born free and equal, and have certain natural, essential, and unalienable rights; among which may be reckoned the right of enjoying and defending their lives and liberties; that of acquiring, possessing, and protecting property; in fine, that of seeking and obtaining their safety and happiness."
> —*Massachusetts Constitution*

John Quincy Adams

John Quincy Adams, John Adams's son, took an active role to assert the rights of Africans and African Americans. After he served as sixth president of the United States, John Quincy Adams served as an attorney, and as a Representative to Congress for the State of Massachusetts. Adams' most important case was as defense attorney for the Amistad rebels. They were charged with murder in 1840 after they staged a revolt on the slave-ship, the Amistad.

The background of that case was as follows. In the winter of 1839, fifty-three men and women were kidnapped from Africa, as were many of those who ended up enslaved in Amer-

ica. They were forced to board the slave ship, the Amistad. One of their group, Cinque, organized a rebellion on the ship in July of 1839, when the ship was near the Caribbean Islands. The captain and some of the crew were killed in the rebellion.

The rebels ordered the crew who survived to sail the ship back into the direction of the sunrise, the only knowledge they had of the direction of the African continent. The crew sailed the ship along a zigzag route, east by day and north by night. After several weeks, the ship ended up off the coast of Long Island Sound in August. There it was seized by the Coast Guard. The U.S. government imprisoned the rebels in Connecticut and charged them with murder.

> **Amistad Case**
>
> Winter, 1839: Individuals kidnapped from Africa
>
> July, 1839: Cinque organized a successful rebellion
>
> Aug., 1839: Ship seized by Coast Guard off Long Island
>
> Sept., 1839: Africans charged with murder
>
> Fall, 1839: John Quincy Adams led the defense team
>
> March 9, 1841: U.S. Supreme Court found the Africans innocent and freed them

John Quincy Adams stated that the kidnappers violated the liberty of the Africans as free people, and they, the Africans, acted in self-defense to regain that liberty. The trial put the United States in an uproar because of Adams' assertion that the rebels were free people against whom a criminal act had been committed. That assertion took away the comfort many Americans had in which they justified their slave holdings as legitimate. It fed the flames of a emergent abolitionist movement. This excerpt is from Adams' final argument in the case:

"...the case of the Amistad, if, when captured by Lieutenant Gedney, she and her cargo had been in possession of the Spaniards, and the Africans in the condition of slaves, the vessel would have been condemned, and the slaves liberated, by the laws of the United States; because she was engaged in the slave-trade in violation of the laws of Spain. She was in possession of the Africans, self-emancipated, and not in the condition of slaves. ... Thus, the opinion of the Supreme Court, as declared by the Chief Justice, in the case of the Antelope, was a fact, an authority in point, against the surrender of the Amistad, and in favor of the liberation of the Africans taken in her, even if they had been, when taken, in the condition of slaves. How monstrous, then, is the claim upon the Courts of the United States to re-enslave them, as thralls to the Spaniards, Ruiz and Montes! or to transport them beyond the seas, at the demand of the Minister of Spain! I said, when I began this plea, that my final reliance for success in this case was on this Court as a court of JUSTICE;.... I have endeavored to show that they are entitled to their liberty from this Court. .... I have shown that Ruiz and Montes, the only parties in interest here, for whose sole benefit this suit is carried on by the Government, were acting at the time in a way that is forbidden by the laws of Great Britain, of Spain, and of the United States, and that the mere signature of the Governor General of Cuba ought not to prevail over the ample evidence in the case that these Negroes were free and had a right to assert their liberty. ...."

–John Quincy Adams

On March 9th, 1841, the United States Supreme Court issued a verdict of not guilty. Justice Joseph Story (NAA) of Salem, Massachusetts wrote the decision. The Africans returned to Africa. Ka-Le, one of the Amistad rebels, wrote this letter to John Quincy Adams during their trial. It described their anguish and their hope that human fairness would prevail in their case.

"New Haven, Jan. 4, 1841
Dear Friend Mr. Adams,

I want to write a letter to you because you love Mendi people and you talk to the grand court. We want to tell you one thing—Jose Ruiz say we born in Havana, he tell lie. We stay in Havana 10 days and 10 nights, we stay no more. We all born in Mendi—we no understand the Spanish language. Mendi people been in America 17 moons. We talk American language little, not very good; we write every day: we write plenty letters; we read most all time; we read all Matthew and Mark, and Luke, and John, and plenty of little books. We love books very much. We want you to ask the court what we have done wrong. What for Americans keep us in prison. Some people say Mendi people crazy; Mendi people dolt, because we no talk American language. America people no talk Mendi language; America people dolt? They tell bad things about Mendi people, and we not understand. Some men say Mendi people very happy because they laugh and have plenty to eat. Mr. Pendleton (the jailer) come and Mendi people all look sorry because they think about Mendi Land and friends we no see now. Mr. Pendleton say Mendi people angry; white men afraid of Mendi people. Then Mendi people no look sorry again—that why we laugh. But Mendi people feel sorry; …Some people say Mendi people no got souls. Why we feel bad we no got souls: we want to be free very much.

Dear friend Mr. Adams, you have children, you have friends, you love them, you feel very sorry if Mendi people come and carry them all to Africa. We feel bad for our friends, and our friends all feel bad for us. Americans no take us in ship. We on shore and Americans tell us slave ship catch us. They say we make you free. If they make us free, they tell truth, if they no make us free they tell lie. If America people give us free we glad, if they no give us free we sorry— we sorry for God punish liars. We want you to tell court that Mendi people no want to go back to Havana, we no want to be killed. Dear friend, we want you to know how we feel. Mendi people think, think, think. Nobody know what we think; teacher he know, we tell him some. Mendi people have got souls. We think we know God punish us if we tell lie. We never tell lie; we speak truth. What for Mendi people afraid? Because they got souls. Cook say he kill, he eat Mendi people—we afraid—we kill cook. Then captain kill one man with knife, and cut Mendi people plenty. We never kill captain, he no kill us. If court ask who brought Mendi people to America? We bring ourselves. Ceci hold the rudder. all we want is make us free.

Your friend, Ka-Le."

John Quincy Adams was also active in the case of George Latimer, another fugitive from bondage. In the early 1840s, Latimer escaped enslavement in Virginia, only to be caught in Massachusetts with the threat of a return to bondage. Citizens of Massachusetts raised the funds to free Latimer. After he was manumitted, two petitions were circulated throughout the state. One of those petitions proposed an amendment to the United States Constitution to limit the involvement of Federal officials and use of Federal property in the pursuit of fugitives from bondage. It received over 43,000 signatures, and John Quincy Adams presented it to Congress. That petition to Congress did not result in any legislation.

John Quincy Adams's son, Charles Francis Adams (1807–1886) (NAA) presented a similar petition to the Massachusetts State Legislature with over 60,000 signatures. It was passed as the Personal Liberty Law of 1843. John Quincy Adams accurately predicted that slavery would only end through civil war.

2 MOUNT WOLLASTON CEMETERY CIVIL WAR MONUMENT
20 Sea St. Merrymount Neighborhood

This Civil War monument was dedicated in 1868 to the one hundred and five Quincy residents who died in the Civil War. Mount Wollaston Cemetery has been included on the National Register of Historic Places.

One of the notable individuals buried in this cemetery was Harriet Wilson. Wilson was the first African American to publish a novel in the United States with the publication of, *Our Nig* in 1852.

WEYMOUTH

1 MARIA WESTON CHAPMAN AND THE WESTON FAMILY

Sentiments about slavery tended to be shared within individual families. The Weston (NAA) family of Weymouth was no different. Warren and Nancy Bates Weston encouraged their eight children, six girls and two boys, to be independent thinkers with a strong sense of justice.

Maria Weston Chapman (1806–1885) (NAA), the firstborn and a socialite, became the leader of a group of women, which included three of her sisters, to actively support the anti-slavery movement and the efforts of William Lloyd Garrison. The Weston sisters organized the Boston Female Anti-Slavery Society in 1834 along with eight other women. Maria Weston Chapman frequently contributed to "*The Liberator*" newspaper and edited it in Garrison's absence.

The Boston Female Anti-Slavery Society, with Maria at the helm, organized fairs to raise funds for the movement. The death of her husband, Henry Chapman (NAA), in 1842 caused Maria to become even more intensely involved in the anti-slavery efforts. Maria Weston Chapman moved back to Weymouth in 1855 and her sisters joined her there at the outbreak of the Civil War. All the sisters were buried in the family plot in the Weymouth Cemetery.

> "Slavery can only be abolished by raising the character of the people who compose the nation; and that can be done only by showing them a higher one."
> –MARIA WESTON CHAPMAN

Maria Weston Chapman

HINGHAM

1 GOV. ANDREW GRAVESITE OLD SHIP BURYING GROUND
107 Main St.

Gov. John A. Andrew (1818–1867) (NAA) became governor of Massachusetts in 1860. Andrew led the state throughout the tumultuous years of the Civil War. After he was buried here, a statue was erected in his honor.

The Old Ship Church, adjacent to the Burying Grounds, was built in 1681. It is the oldest church structure in the United States still in continuous use for religious purposes. The building was designated a National Historic Landmark.

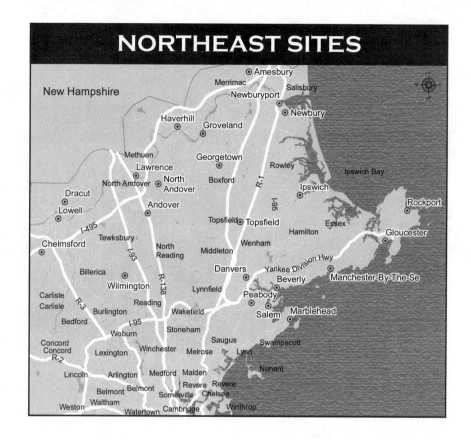

NORTHEAST SITES

New Hampshire

Amesbury
Merrimac
Salisbury
Newburyport
Newbury

Haverhill
Groveland

Methuen
Georgetown
Lawrence
Rowley
North Andover
North
Boxford
Ipswich Bay
Dracut
Andover
Ipswich
Lowell
Andover
Rockport

Topsfield
Topsfield
Essex
Chelmsford
Tewksbury
Hamilton
Gloucester
Billerica
North
Wenham
Reading
Middleton
Danvers
Yankee Division Hwy
Wilmington
Lynnfield
Beverly
Manchester-By-The-Se
Carlisle
Reading
Peabody
Carlisle
Burlington
Wakefield
Salem
Marblehead
Bedford
Stoneham
Woburn
Concord
Saugus
Swampscott
Concord
Winchester
Melrose
Lynn
Lexington
Lincoln
Arlington
Medford
Malden
Nahant
Belmont
Revere
Revere
Belmont
Somerville
Chelsea
Weston
Waltham
Watertown
Cambridge
Winthrop

I-495
I-93
R-138
R-3
I-95
R-2
R-1
I-95

PEABODY

1 DR. ANDREW NICHOLS (NAA) HOUSE
UGRR Station
Main St. near the Square

MARBLEHEAD

1 ORNE HOUSE
UGRR Station
21 State St.

Dr. Samuel L. Young (NAA) hosted anti-slavery meetings and he also allowed fugitives to seek refuge here.

2 AMBROSE ALLEN HOUSE
UGRR Station
9 Merrit St.

Ambrose Allen (NAA) was an active abolitionist and a member of the Liberty Party.

Ambrose Allen House

Orne House

Ambrose Allen Sign

4 SAMUEL GOODWIN (NAA) HOUSE
UGRR Station
Site Unknown

5 JOHN A. PURVIS (NAA) HOUSE
UGRR Station
Site Unknown

6 MERCY THOMAS MORRIS

Mercy Thomas Morris, the mother of Robert Morris, the second African American licensed to practice law in Massachusetts was born in Marblehead. Mercy married Yorkshire Morris in 1813, and they settled in Salem, where they raised eight children.

3 SIMEON & BETSY DODGE HOUSE
UGRR Station
236 Washington St.

Among the fugitives who stayed with the Dodges (NAA) were William and Ellen Craft, and Henry *"Boxcar"* Brown. The Dodges used their house as a stop on the Underground Railroad for over twenty years.

Simeon & Betsy Dodge House

Salem Map

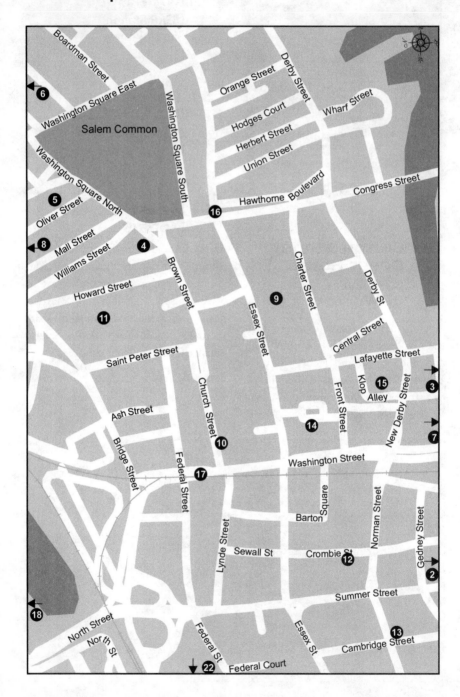

Salem

AFRICAN AMERICANS have always been an integral part of the history of Salem. A ship, *Desire*, owned by a Salem captain, brought the first enslaved Africans to the Massachusetts Bay Colony in 1638. That initial group grew into a substantial community of enslaved, as well as free, Africans. By 1790, so many African American families lived in Salem that the white citizens asked them to leave town because Salem did not want to be responsible for their welfare. Despite this lack of hospitality, African Americans persevered and distinguished themselves in the community.

 ## ROBERT MORRIS BIRTHPLACE
Location unknown

Robert Morris (1823–1882), the second African American licensed as an attorney in Massachusetts, was born in Salem, MA. Morris was the son of Yorkshire Morris and Mercy Thomas Morris. Yorkshire Morris' meager wages as a waiter made it difficult to provide for his family. Despite their poverty, the family actively participated in local politics. Yorkshire Morris regularly organized and campaigned for local political parties.

Salem was very racially polarized. In churches, African Americans sat in segregated balconies which were referred to as, "n_____ heaven," after a pejorative term frequently used to label African Americans. The Salem public schools during the 1830s were for white students only, African American students had no reliable schools in which to obtain an education. Those inequities between the races that Morris experienced during his childhood influenced his life of social activism.

After his father died, Robert Morris, at age eleven, obtained employment in the household of John King (NAA), a prominent Salem attorney, to help support his family. King, a graduate of Harvard University, and at various times, a State Senator and Representative, entertained many prominent guests. Ellis Gray Loring (NAA), a King family friend, met Morris when Loring visited the King family for Thanksgiving in 1836. Loring, impressed with Robert Morris' quick intelligence, offered Morris a position as a house servant in his Boston house, and Morris accepted. After a few years in Boston, Loring offered Morris an apprenticeship in his law firm. That apprenticeship trained Morris to become an attorney. See more on Morris in Beacon Hill sites and downtown Boston sites.

 ## CHARLOTTE FORTEN
Salem Normal School, now Salem State University
One Broad St.

Charlotte Forten (1837-1914), an educator, women's rights advocate, poet, and essayist, was the first African American to attend Salem Normal

School, a training school for teachers, in 1855. Charlotte was the daughter of Robert Forten, a very prominent Philadelphia abolitionist, and the granddaughter of James Forten, a prominent and successful African American businessperson.

Charlotte Forten

Philadelphia's segregated school system forced Charlotte's parents to provide her with a private tutor at home until she reached the age of sixteen. At that time, Robert Forten, Charlotte's father, decided to send her to the integrated school system in Salem, MA, to complete her secondary education. While in Salem, Charlotte lived with the Remond family.

Immediately after graduation, Charlotte became the first African American to receive a position to teach in the integrated Salem school system. In 1862, she left Salem to teach African Americans on the island of St. Helena, South Carolina. Throughout her life, Charlotte Forten maintained a diary that documented her observations about the events of the day. She married Rev. Francis Grimke in 1878, and they settled in Washington, D.C. where Rev. Grimke pastored the 15th Street Presbyterian Church.

Salem Normal School

Rev. Francis Grimke (1850–1937) and his brother, Archibald who was an attorney, were the nephews of Sarah and Angelina Grimke (NAA), the prominent abolitionists from Charleston, SC. The Grimke sisters eventually settled in Boston. See Boston: Hyde Park sites and Cambridge sites. Both Rev. Grimke and his brother, Archibald were at the forefront of civil rights activism during the turn of the century.

Excerpts from the journal of Charlotte Forten:

Tuesday, March 13, 1856.

Went through the examination and entered the Normal School. I have not yet heard from father; but as I had to give no pledge to remain a certain length of time, and this is the only opportunity I should have until another term, I thought it best to enter the school. It was with a very delightful sensation of relief that I received the welcome intelligence of my being admitted; for greatly had I feared it might be otherwise.

Friday, March 16, 1856.

To my great surprise, received a letter from father summoning me to return home as soon as possible. I feel deeply grieved; it seems harder than ever to leave now that I have just entered upon a course of study which I so earnestly hoped would thoroughly qualify me for the duties of a teacher. The few days I have spent at the Normal School have been very pleasant although I have felt a little strange and lonely. But the teachers are kind, and the teaching so thorough and earnest that it increases the love of knowledge and the desire to acquire it. Although it would give me much pleasure to see my kind friends at home, I cannot but regret that I must go now, feeling as I do that a year longer at school would be of great benefit to me. This evening went to Miss Shepard who earnestly declared that I must not go, and who made me a very kind offer, which I do not think can be accepted with the little hope I now possess of being able to repay it.

Saturday, March 17, 1856.

This morning Mr. Edwards came to see me, and told me that he had no doubt of my being able to obtain a situation as teacher here if I went through the Normal School. He wished me to write to father and assure him of this. Miss Shepard urged me to consent to her writing to him about what she proposes. I do indeed feel obliged to her for her very great kindness to me, whether it be as she wishes it or not. I shall continue at school until I hear from home again, as Mr. Edwards said he would like to have me do so.

–Charlotte Forten

3 CEDAR STREET

As long as slavery was legal in any part of the United States, African Americans, free or enslaved, lived with the constant threat of kidnapers. To protect themselves from this threat, they created residential communities where neighbors looked out for each other.

Cedar Street was one such residential community in Salem during the 1800s.

4 TITUBA: SALEM WITCH MUSEUM

19 ½ Washington Square North
508-744-1692

This museum was developed to document the history of the Salem witch hysteria of the late 1690s. An African American, Tituba, began the hysteria with bedtime stories she told to children in her care. See Danvers Sites.

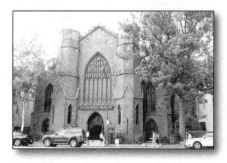

Salem Witch Museum

5 JOSEPH STORY HOUSE

26 Winter Street

Joseph Story (1779-1845) (NAA), wrote one of the most important Supreme Court decisions of the nineteenth century that related to the civil rights of people of the African diaspora, the Amistad decision. At age 32, Story, a local politician and circuit court judge, became the youngest Justice with his appointment to the U.S. Supreme Court. Story graduated 2nd in his class from Harvard College and he co-founded Harvard Law School.

Joseph Story

Story's Supreme Court decision on March 9th, 1841, found the Amistad rebels innocent of the deaths which resulted from their slave rebellion. That decision reverberated throughout the United States and abroad, and it emboldened abolitionists to raise the stakes in their fight against slavery. The case involved a group of Africans who killed some of their kidnappers during

Joseph Story House

a rebellion aboard the Amistad ship in 1839 (see John Quincy Adams under Quincy Site). They attempted to force the rest of the crew to sail the ship back to Africa.

John Quincy Adams of Massachusetts defended the Amistad rebels. He argued that the kidnappers violated the liberty of the Africans and they, the Africans, simply acted in self-defense to regain their freedom. The U.S. Supreme Court issued a verdict of not guilty, and Justice Story wrote the decision. The Africans were finally able to return to Africa.

March 9th, 1841 Justice Joseph Story's Supreme Court Decision found the Amistad Plaintiffs Innocent

"...If then, these negroes are not slaves, but are kidnapped Africans, who, by the laws of Spain itself, are entitled to their freedom, and were kidnapped and illegally carried to Cuba, and illegally detained and restrained on board the Amistad; there is no pretence to say, that they are pirates or robbers. We may lament the dreadful acts, by which they asserted their liberty, and took possession of the Amistad, and endeavored to regain their native country; but they cannot be deemed pirates or robbers in the sense of the law of nations, or the treaty with Spain, or the laws of Spain itself; ...

... supposing these African negroes not to be slaves, but kidnapped, and free negroes, the treaty with Spain cannot be obligatory upon them; and the United States are bound to respect their rights as much as those of Spanish subjects. A fortiori, the doctrine must apply where human life and human liberty are an issue; and constitute the very essence of the controversy. The treaty with Spain never could have intended to take away the equal rights of all foreigners, who should contest their claims before any of our courts, to equal justice; or to deprive such foreigners of the protection given them by other treaties, or by the general law of nations. Upon the merits of the case, then, there does not seem to us to be any ground for doubt, that these negroes ought to be deemed free; ...
--Joseph Story, 1841 U.S. Supreme Court Decision on Amistad Case

6 SALEM WILLOWS PARK
167 Fort Ave.

Each year, on the third Saturday in July, Salem Willows Park is the location of an annual picnic for the African American community from Salem, and nearby towns. This tradition began with a celebration of the cessation of slavery in Massachusetts in the 1780s.

7 POND STREET

Many African Americans in Salem earned a living in the maritime industry in the 1800s. Pond St. was a popular residential street for African Americans in that industry.

8 CHARLES A. BENSON
Somewhere on Rice St.

Charles A. Benson (1830–1881), a sailor in the mid-1800s, lived on both Rice St. and Pond St. Benson documented his experiences at sea in a series of journals. Some of those journals are in the collection of the Peabody Essex Museum and one is in the collection of the Beinecke Library at Yale University. Benson's journals provide a rare glimpse into the personal thoughts and aspirations of an educated African American sailor during those tumultuous times. Though life at sea was dangerous at best, it was still one of the few opportunities available to African American men who desired economic independence.

9 PEABODY / ESSEX MUSEUM
161 Essex Street
www.pem.org

Several artifacts and documents critical to understand the role of African Americans in Salem's history such as the journals of Charles Benson reside in the collection of the Peabody/ Essex Museum. Portraits of John and Nancy

Remond, and two of their children, Sarah Parker Remond and Charles Lenox Remond also hang here.

Peabody Essex Museum

10 SALEM LYCEUM
43 Church Street

The Salem Lyceum was a popular venue for many different types of lectures and concerts in the mid-1800s. It was especially popular for abolitionist speakers. William Lloyd Garrison and Frederick Douglass both spoke from this podium. The Salem Female Anti-Slavery Society also held their meetings here.

Salem Lyceum

11 HOWARD STREET CEMETERY
Howard Street

Howard Street Cemetery dedicated a portion of its plots for members of the African American community in Salem. Prince Farmer, a successful Salem oyster dealer, was one of those residents buried here.

12 PRINCE FARMER HOUSE PIKE HOUSE
UGRR Station
18 Crombie Street

Pike (NAA) was active in the Salem abolition movement. He used his house as a stop on the Underground Railroad and he frequently rented to African American families. One of his tenants, Prince Farmer lived here in the early 1840s. Farmer was an oyster dealer with a successful business on Derby St., a member of the Masonic fraternity, and an abolitionist.

Prince Farmer / Pike House

13 HAMILTON HALL
9 Chestnut Street

Hamilton Hall was the venue for numerous events catered by African American caterer, John Remond. One event was a dinner held in 1826 to celebrate the two hundredth anniversary of the city of Salem. Another of his signature events was a dinner he catered for President Andrew Jackson (NAA), when Jackson visited Salem in 1833.

Hamilton Hall

14 SITE: JOHN AND NANCY REMOND & FAMILY
5 Higginson Sq.

Members of the prosperous Remond family were influential abolitionists as well as strong advocates for full civil rights for African Americans and women. The patriarch, John Remond (1785–1874) came to Salem from Curacao at the age of ten. The matriarch, Nancy Lenox Remond, came from a family of land owners in Newton. Nancy's father, Cornelius Lenox, fought for the Continental Army during the American Revolution.

The businesses of John and Nancy Remond included hair and wig salons, and they were caterers. Those businesses gave the family the economic independence to educate their eight children at the highest levels. Two of their children, Charles Lenox Remond and Sarah Parker Remond, were prominent abolitionists prior to the civil war, and civil rights and women rights activists after. Portraits of John and Nancy, and their children, Charles and Sarah, hang in the Peabody Essex Museum.

Nancy Lenox Remond

John Remond

John Remond was an initial member of the Massachusetts Anti-Slavery Society and the Salem Anti-Slavery Society. He also actively organized African American support for the Federalist political party. The efforts of John and Nancy Remond led to the early desegregation of Salem public schools. Their daughters, Sarah, and her sister, passed the rigorous entrance exams for Salem High School in 1835, but the school denied them admission. John and Nancy challenged that decision in a highly publicized and drawn-out confrontation.

The Remonds temporarily moved their family to Newport, Rhode Island in order for their daughters to continue their secondary education. The Massachusetts Legislature passed a bill in 1844 that mandated access to a public education for every child. That mandate resulted from a challenge by Eunice Ross, an African American teenager on Nantucket Island.

The town of Salem complied with the order, probably because of the pressure the Remonds had brought to the issue, and because the town could not afford a separate system for African American youth. The Remonds moved back to Salem after the mandate.

Their other children also were notable citizens and business owners of Salem. The business accomplishments of their daughters were particularly note-worthy because women were encouraged to stay at home in the 19th century. The oldest daughter, Nancy (b. 1809) married James Sherman in 1834. They operated an Oyster Bar at 14 Derby St. and an ice cream parlor at 5 Higginson Sq.

Two other daughters, Cecelia and Maritcha, operated a shop to manufacture wigs at 175 ½ and 185 Essex St. Cecelia married James Babcock in 1843. Babcock operated a wig shop at 15 Washington St. His book, _How Hair is Wove,_ was published in 1872. The youngest daughter, Caroline (b. 1826), married Joseph Hall Putnam, a schoolteacher. Putnam died at the young age of thirty-three and Caroline went into business for herself as manufacturer of a successful hair tonic, _Mrs. Putnam's Medicated Hair Tonic._ That product gave her financial independence for the rest of her life.

The City of Salem announced plans in January of 2016 to create a park, Remond Park, adjacent to the Salem-Beverly Bridge to honor the legacy of this entrepreneurial African American family.

CHARLES LENOX REMOND

Charles Lenox Remond's popularity as an abolitionist speaker in the 1840s and 1850s stemmed from his dynamic and forceful presentation style. Remond (1810-1878), the first African

American employed as a speaker by the American Anti-Slavery Society, traveled extensively throughout the United States and abroad on behalf of the society.

Charles Lenox Remond

In 1840, Remond was one of the United States delegates to the World Anti-Slavery Convention in London, England. Remond was initially a supporter of William Lloyd Garrison's approach to the abolition of slavery, that of gradual, non-violent civil disobedience. During the early 1840s, Remond aligned himself with a group impatient with the slow pace of change. By 1844, Remond and others, believed that the only solution to end slavery was the dissolution of the Union. They felt that the United States Constitution condoned that despicable practice. Remond delivered this speech at the annual convention of the American Anti-Slavery Society on May 7th, 1844:

376

"I Give My Voice for the Dissolution of the Union", excerpt:

"...With all my knowledge of the origin and the progress, and my experience of the present practical workings of the American constitution, shall I be found here advocating it as a glorious means to a glorious end? No! my fellow countrymen, I am here to register my testimony against it! Not because I do not feel how valuable it might be, were its provisions secured to the few as they are to the many—not because I wish to claim anything more for the few than an equality of privileges—not because I am not ready to "yield everything to the Union but Truth—Honor—Liberty"—but because we have, as a people, yielded even these; and with such a people, I feel that I must not, an individual, be numbered.

...Go the rounds of the Union, and tell me at what tribunal the man of color can have justice? Court, Judge, Jury—all are against him; and to what is it owing? Why, as an honest Buckeye told me in Cincinnati, "it is this everlasting yielding to Slavery," which always must take place, when Freedom yields the first step, by coming into union with it. If the Union had been formed upon the supposition that the colored man was a man, a man he would have been considered, whether in New Hampshire or Kentucky. But under the Union as it was, and as it is, he is kicked, stoned, insulted, enslaved, ...

... I have tried in my own mind to make out a case for those who do not see eye to eye with us in this matter. But the more I have labored at it, the stronger becomes my conviction of duty in calling for a dissolution of the union between Freedom and Slavery. ... I have taken all things into consideration; and in view of each and of all, I say here, as I did in New York, that if I can only sustain the constitution, by sustaining slavery, then— "live or die—sink or swim—survive or perish," I give my voice for the dissolution of the Union."

-- Charles Lenox Remond

SARAH PARKER REMOND

During her teen years, Sarah Parker Remond's (1826–1894) family challenged the Salem school system's refusal to admit Sarah and her sister after the two had passed a rigorous entrance exam. That marked the start of Sarah's life of activism. In 1854, Sarah was the first to win an anti-discrimination lawsuit in Massachusetts. She sued when the manager at the theater refused to seat her and her guests in the premium seats she purchased through the mail.

Sarah Parker Remond maintained an extensive schedule as a public speaker, both in the United States and abroad. After the Civil War, she relocated to Italy where she studied medicine and married a local citizen. Sarah Remond practiced as a physician in Italy until her death. See Beacon Hill sites.

Sarah Parker Remond, older

15 **SITE: NANCY REMOND SHERMAN & JAMES SHERMAN'S OYSTER BAR**
14 Derby St.

In addition to an Oyster Bar at this location, the Shermans operated an Ice Cream parlor at the family homestead at 5 Higginson Sq.

16 **SITE: CECELIA & MARITCHA REMOND'S WIG SHOP**
175 ½ & 184 Essex St.

17 **SITE: JAMES BABCOCK'S WIG SHOP**
15 Washington St.

James Babcock was the spouse of Cecelia Remond.

18 **HARMONY GROVE CEMETERY**
30 Grove Street

Several members of the Remond family were buried here, including husband and wife, John and Nancy Remond and one of their eight children, Charles Lenox Remond.

Luis Fenollosa Emilio (1844–1918) (NAA), a veteran of the Civil War, was also buried here. A large statue was placed at his gravesite. Emilio belonged to a family of fervent abolitionists. He enlisted at the early age of sixteen at the onset of the war. When the Massachusetts 54th Regiment was formed in 1863, Emilio won an assignment as one of the commissioned officers. In 1891, he recounted the bravery of the regiment in his book, *A Brave Black Reg-*

Harmony Grove Cemetery

iment. The History of the Fifty-Fourth Regiment, or Massachusetts Voluntary Infantry, 1863-65.

⑲ PETER SALEM
Site Unknown

Peter Salem (1750–1816), a veteran and hero of the American Revolution, killed Major Pitcairn of the British Army at the Battle of Bunker Hill in Charlestown on June 17th, 1775. Pitcairn was the first English officer to fall in that battle.

Peter Salem lived in Salem for a short while after the war with Katy Benson whom he married in September of 1783. Salem died in Framingham in 1816. Framingham erected a monument at the Old Burying Ground in his honor in 1882.

⑳ WILLIAM CHASE (NAA) HOUSE
UGRR Station
206 Essex St.

㉑ JOSIAH HAYWARD (NAA) HOUSE
UGRR Station
48 Federal St.

㉒ JOHN A. INNIS (NAA) HOUSE
UGRR Station
18 Beckford St.

㉓ LOCAL RESOURCES
African American Heritage Sites of Salem
www.nps.gov/sama/
historyculture/ upload/
SalemafAmsitessm.pdf

BEVERLY

① JUNO LARCOM-THISTLE, FIRST PARISH CHURCH
225 Cabot St.

Thanks to the research of local historian, Terri McFadden (NAA), some of the African American history of Beverly has been revealed. The town of Beverly was the location of one of the early *"Freedom Lawsuits"* that paved the way towards the end of slavery in Massachusetts. That lawsuit was filed by Juno Larcom-Thistle in 1774.

In the 1730s, Juno Larcom (c.1724–1816) was enslaved by the Herrick family of Beverly as a young child. Juno married Jethro Thistle in 1751 at the First Parish Church. Thistle was also enslaved by a Beverly family. All of their children were baptized at the First Parish Church of Beverly.

2 SITE: LARCOM-THISTLE HOUSE "FREEDOM LAWSUIT"
Pride's Crossing & Hale St.

Jethro Thistle, enslaved by Jeffrey This-tle (NAA), and Juno Larcom married in 1751. They settled in a home on the property of the Larcom family at this location. The couple eventually had ten children. When David Larcom sold two of their children into bondage, Juno Je-thro decided to fight back and sued Da-vid Larcom for her freedom in 1774. By this time, several legal precedents had been established for African Ameri-cans to obtain their freedom through lawsuits in Massachusetts. Juno Lar-com's defense was that throughout forty-six years of service, she had been treated badly and her children sold. Juno Larcom-Thistle stated at the end of her defense,

> *"... Judge Ye Weather or noe I hadent ort to Be set at Liberty...." (sic)*

David Larcom died before the court decision and the following year, in an action accepted by David Larcom's family, the Larcom-Thistle family sim-ply asserted their freedom. They were allowed to maintain their home at this site. Jethro Thistle joined the Conti-nental Army in 1777 and served until his death in 1778.

The youngest child of Juno and Je-thro was Cloe Larcom Turner. She lived in the family house until she died in the 1850s at the age of ninety-five. A poem that Cloe wrote in her hymnbook is testament to the difficult existence of African Americans during the colo-nial period, especially those who found themselves in small towns where work was scarce:

> *"Cloe Turner is my name*
> *Nevermyland is my station*
> *Beverly is my dwelling place*
> *And Christ is my salvation.*
> *When I am dead and in my grave*
> *Only my bones are rotten*
> *When this you read*
> *Remember me*
> *So I won't be forgotten."*
> *– Cloe Larcom Turner*
>
> (Courtesty of the
> Beverly Historical Society)

Cloe Turner's hymnbook is in the collection of the Beverly Historical So-ciety.

3 DR. INGALLS KITTREDGE (NAA) HOUSE

UGRR Station
Site Unknown

4 LOCAL RESOURCES:

Beverly Historical Society
117 Cabot St.
978-922-1186
www.beverlyhistorical
society.org

Danvers

1 Site: Tituba & Salem Village Parsonage
67 Centre Street

Today, Salem enjoys a vibrant tourist industry based on an early, unfortunate history, the witch hysteria that resulted in the death of forty people in the community. During the 1690s, Salem Village was located in what is now present day Danvers. In 1692, local villagers accused nearly 200 citizens from the village and the nearby towns of witchcraft. The local juries decided that twenty-three of the accused were guilty and condemned them to death. An additional seventeen of the accused died in prison.

One of those accused and hanged was Rev. George Burroughs (NAA). Rev. Burroughs served as minister of this parsonage from 1681 to 1683. Those horrible events forever tainted the reputation of the entire community. The parsonage, originally built in 1681, was demolished in 1784. This site contains the foundations of the parsonage and three other structures.

Tituba, a young enslaved individual of African and Arawak/ Native ancestry, was at the center of this tragedy. The local pastor, Samuel Parris enslaved Tituba when he lived in the Caribbean. Parris brought her and another enslaved individual, John, with him when he relocated to Salem to be the village pastor. Parris served the parish from 1689 to 1696.

Tituba served as nanny to the three Parris children. She entertained nine-year-old Betty Parris and her cousin, twelve-year-old Abigail Williams, on cold winter evenings, with stories of magic that she remembered from her childhood in the Caribbean. Another neighbor, young Ann Putnam often joined them for the evening tales. The Puritan religion, which Samuel Parris followed, forbade any references to demonology and witchcraft. Unfortunately, those were the very stories that kept the children entertained on the long, cold, New England winter evenings.

The girls began to act out some of Tituba's stories to add to their fun.

Salem Village Parsonage Ruins

Salem Village Parsonage Ruins & Sign

When villagers noticed them, they attributed their strange behavior to magic. The villagers became alarmed that the girls might be possessed, and they accused Tituba of witchcraft. Mr. Parris beat Tituba until she confessed. She was then imprisoned.

During her *"confession,"* Tituba implied that other villagers were involved in a local *"witch community."* This was probably done to divert attention away from herself. The girls also accused other villagers, and the hysteria began.

The villagers never put Tituba on trial, because of her confession but she remained in jail for the duration of the trials. Within four months, the villagers found twenty-three people guilty of the practice of witchcraft and executed them.

This excerpt is from an oral examination of Tituba on March 1st, 1692:

"Q: *Why doe you hurt these poor Children? Whatt harme have they done ont you?*

A: *thay doe noe harme to me I noe hurt them att all.*

Q: *Why have you done itt?*

A: *I have done nothing, I can't tell when the Devill works.*

382

Q: what doe the Devill tell you that he hurts them?

A: noe he tells me nothing.

Q: doe you never see Something appeare in Some shape?

A: noe never See any thing

Q: what familiarity have you w'th the devilo, or w't is itt if you converse q'th all? Tell the truth whoe itt is that hurts them.

A: the Devill for ought I know

Q: w't appearance or how dothe he appeare when he hurts them, w'th w't shape or what is he like that hurts them

A: like a man I think yesterday I being in the Lentoe Chamber I saw a thing like a man, that tould me Searve him & I tould him noe I would nott doe Such thing. (Recorder's note: she chargtes Goody Osborne & Sarah Good as those that hurt the Chilodren, and would have had hir done itt, she sayth she Seen foure two of w'ch she knew nott she saw them last night as she was washing the Roome) thay tould me hurt the Children & would have had me if I woud nott goe & hurt them ....

Q: would they have had you hurt the Children the Last Night

A: yes, butt I was Sorry & I sayd, I would doe Soe noe more, but tould I would feare God.

Q: butt wy did nott you doe Soe before

A: why they tell mee I had done Soe before & therefore I must goe on, these were the 4 woemen & the man (Recorder's note: but she knew none but Osburne & Good only, the others were of Boston)

Q: att first beginning w'th them, w't then appeared to you w't wasw itt like that ot you to doe itt

A: one like a man Jusat as I was goeing to sleep Came to me this was when the Children was first hurt he sayd he would kill the children & she would never be well, and he Sayd if I would nott Serve him he would do soe to mee

Q: is that the Same man that appeared before to you that appeared the last night & tould you this?

A: Yes

Q: w't Other likenesses beside a man hath appeared to you?

A: Sometimes like a hogge Sometimes like a great black dogge, foure tymes

Q: but w't did they Say unto you?

A: they tould me Serve him & that was a good way; that was the black dogge I tould him I was afraid, he tould me he would be worse then to me..."

D. BROOKS BAKER HOUSE
UGRR Station
Elm & Putnam Streets

The Bakers (NAA) engaged their whole family to assist fugitives in their escape. Their seven year old daughter, Sarah, once described how she held a lamp in 1857, while her mother prepared a bed of warm, brown sugar to help heal the raw whip wounds on the back of one fugitive.

 ALFRED FELLOWS HOUSE
UGRR Station
48 Elm Street

The Alfred Fellows (NAA) house was a stop on the Underground Railroad as well as the location of many abolitionist meetings. Some of the guest speakers were Frederick Douglass, Julia Ward Howe, Ralph Waldo Emerson, William Lloyd Garrison, and Harriet Beecher Stowe.

Fellows House

 AFRICAN AMERICAN VETERANS OF THE AMERICAN REVOLUTION

During the American Revolution, enslaved African American men who desired their freedom were encouraged to take up arms in exchange for that freedom. Five individuals from Danvers choose that route to freedom. Primus Jacobs (1750–1817) enlisted for two, three-year tours of duty. The first in 1777 and the second in 1781. After the war, Primus settled in Danvers with his wife, Dinah, and their five children.

Other African Americans from Danvers who served were: Peter Buxton (1736–1797); Scipio Shaw; Fortune Felton (b.1750); and Zachariah Bray (b.1750).

TOPSFIELD

 GOULD (NAA) BARN
UGRR Station
1 Howlett St.

MANCHESTER

1 DELUCENA LATHROP & EMMELINE BINGHAM HOUSE (NAA)

UGRR Station
7 Central Street

Bingham House

2 DANIEL FRIEND HOUSE (NAA)

UGRR Station
8 Friend Street

Friend House

3 LEE FAMILY HOUSE (NAA)

UGRR Station
78 School Sreet

Lee House

GLOUCESTER

1 THOMAS DALTON BIRTHPLACE

Thomas Dalton (1794–1883) was born here on October 17th, 1794. Dalton was an influential abolitionist and civic leader. See Beacon Hill sites for more information.

ROCKPORT

1 SAMPSON COBURN, VETERAN OF THE AMERICAN REVOLUTION
Location Unknown

Sampson Coburn enlisted in the militia on May 20th, 1775. His rank at enlistment was that of Corporal which made him one of the few African Americans to have that position during the war. Coburn participated in many engagements including the Battle of Bunker Hill until his service ended on April 1st, 1776.

2 REV. GEORGE WAUGH (NAA) HOUSE
UGRR Station
Site Unknown

IPSWICH

1 YORKSHIRE MORRIS

Yorkshire Morris (b. 1786) the father of Robert Morris, was born in Ipswich. Robert Morris was the second African American licensed as an attorney in the state after Macon Allen. Robert Morris actively championed the civil rights of African Americans.

2 DR. THOMAS MANNING HOUSE
Old Parsonage

UGRR Station
19 North Main Street

Dr. Manning (NAA) built this house in 1799. It became a parsonage in 1858. Its location adjacent to the river made it an ideal place to hide fugitives until they could be transported to the next safe stop.

Manning House

3 SITE: COLONIAL HOUSE FEATURED IN SMITHSONIAN EXHIBIT: "WITHIN THESE WALLS"
www.americanhistory.si.edu
16 Elm St.

In 2001, the National Museum of American History of the Smithsonian Museums in Washington, D.C. opened a new exhibit, *"Within These Walls."* That exhibit relocated a Georgian style house from this address in Ipswich to illustrate two hundred years of American history through the lives of the occupants of a single house.

That exhibit illustrated the transition of one of the occupants, Chance, from enslavement to freedom. Chance was originally enslaved by one of the families who occupied this house. When slavery ceased to be enforced in Massachusetts in 1783, he became a paid member of the household staff. The house was also the location of meetings of the Ipswich Female Anti-Slavery Society through another occupant. The house is a permanent exhibit of the Smithsonian Museum at 14th St. and Constitution Ave. N.W. in Washington, D.C.

4 JENNY SLEW V. JOHN WHIPPLE *"FREEDOM LAWSUIT"* IPSWICH RIVERWALK MURAL
EBSCO Publishing Company Bldg.
55 South Main St.

On March 5th, 1762, Jenny Slew sued John Whipple, Jr. for "trepass." The term, "trepass," was legalese for enslavement. Slew based her case on the fact although her father was African American, her mother was white. According to an amendment to the Mass. Body of Liberties in 1670, the status of a female's offspring would correspond with her status. An enslaved mother's children would be enslaved, and a freed mother's children would be free. Slew lost her case in the Common Court but a later appeal to the Superior Court in November of 1766 proved victorious. John Adams was the attorney for the defendant, John Whipple.

The court awarded Slew monetary damages and costs. That incident in Ipswich history was recorded on the Ipswich Riverwalk Mural by artist, Alan Pearsall (NAA).

5 SITE: HANGING OF POMP
Pingreys Plain
aka *"Gallow's Lot"*
Mile Lane and High St.

Every region had a *"Hangman's Gallows"* during the colonial period and Pingrey's Plain was the location for this region. The last execution took place on August 6th, 1795. On that date, Pomp was hanged for the murder of his enslaver, Captain Charles Furbush (NAA) of Andover. That execution was witnessed by thousands. Jonathan Plummer (NAA) of the region allegedly witnessed Pomp's last minute confession. Plummer later transcribed and published that, *"confession."*

NATHANIEL WARD (NAA) *"THE BODY OF LIBERTIES"*

Nathaniel Ward (1578–1652) moved to Ipswich in 1634 where he served as minister for two years. While in Ipswich, Ward authored, *"The Body of Liberties,"* for the General Court. That document laid the foundation for the first laws of the Commonwealth. The 91st article of that document legalized enslavement in Massachusetts in an ambivalent manner:

> *"91. There shall never be any bond slaverie, villinage or Captivitie amongst us unles it be lawfull Captives taken in just warres, and such strangers as willingly selle themselves or are sold to us. And these shall have all the liberties and Christian usages which the law of god established in Israell concerning such persons doeth morally require. This exempts none from servitude who shall be Judged thereto by Authoritie." (sic)*

NEWBURY

JOSHUA COFFIN (NAA) HOUSE
UGRR Station
Site Unknown

NEWBURYPORT

WILLIAM LLOYD GARRISON MONUMENT
Brown Square
opposite City Hall
Pleasant and Green St.

Newburyport was the birthplace of William Lloyd Garrison (1805-1879) (NAA). Garrison gave voice to the abolitionist movement through his Boston based newspaper, *"The Liberator"*.

Garrison, impressed by the eloquence and conviction of a young Frederick Douglass at one of Douglass's earliest public appearances, recruited him to become a speaker on the anti-slavery lecture circuit. The town of Newburyport dedicated this statue to honor Garrison on July 4th, 1893, the anniversary of his first abolitionist speech in Boston on July 4th, 1829.

Garrison Statue #1

Three quotes by Garrison were inscribed on three sides of the base of the statue:

"I solicit no man's praise,
I fear no man's censure,
The liberty of a people is
The gift of God and nature."

"Neither God nor the world
Will judge us by our professions
But by our practices."

"I am in earnest –
I will not equivocate –
I will not excuse –
I will not retreat a single inch,
And I will be heard."

Garrison Statue #2

 2 FLORA MARSTON ST. PAUL'S CHURCHYARD
166 High St.

A nineteen year old African American, Flora Marston (1769–1788), was buried in the cemetery of this Anglican church. It is not known how she came to be buried in the cemetery. Neither her mother, Delia Marston, nor her father, Benjamin Marston, were buried there. Flora Marston had to be a member of the congregation in order to be buried there but how she achieved that accomplishment has yet to be discovered. Members in Anglican congregations were followers of the Church of England.

3 RICHARD PLUMER HOUSE (NAA)
UGRR Station
62 Federal St.

Plumer House

4 NANCY GARDNER PRINCE AUTOBIOGRAPHY
Birthplace

Nancy Gardner Prince (1799–c.1856) was born in Newburyport. Her biological father, Thomas Gardner, died when she was an infant. Her mother suffered a nervous breakdown after Nancy's stepfather deserted the family. Nancy and her six siblings were forced to support themselves.

Nancy's eventual marriage to Nero Prince allowed her to live a more stable existence. The Princes traveled abroad to countries as diverse as Russia and Jamaica. After she returned to the United States, Mrs. Prince became active in the Boston Female Anti-Slavery Society. In 1853, Nancy Prince wrote her autobiography, *A Narrative of the Life and Travels of Mrs. Nancy Prince.*

5 MR. JACKMAN (NAA) HOUSE
UGRR Station
Site Unknown

6 CAPT. ALEXANDER GRAVES (NAA) HOUSE
UGRR Station
Site Unknown

7 CAESAR V. TAYLOR "*FREEDOM LAWSUIT*"

In 1771, after Taylor (NAA) reneged on a promise to allow Caesar to purchase his freedom, Taylor enslaved him to another individual. Caesar sued Taylor because of injuries he received after the transaction and on the basis of the broken promise. John Adams was unsuccessful in his defense of Taylor's rights to maintain Caesar as his property. Caesar received his freedom, and the monetary award of 5 pounds, 13 shillings in damages and 24 pounds, 7 shillings in costs.

8 CAESAR V. GREENLEAF "*FREEDOM LAWSUIT*"

Newburyport was the site of another "*Freedom Lawsuit*" in 1773. Caesar brought a charge of "trespass," against Greenleaf (NAA) which he won. The court also awarded Caesar 18 pounds in damages.

WEST NEWBURY

1 ROBERT BROWN (NAA) HOUSE
UGRR Station
Site Unknown

AMESBURY

 ### JOHN GREENLEAF WHITTIER HOUSE
UGRR Station
86 Friend Street

John Greenleaf Whittier (1807-1892) (NAA) used his influence as a popular Quaker poet to assist the abolitionist movement. Whittier, an outspoken critic of slavery, worked for the American Anti-Slavery Association. This house, which he moved to in 1836, was a regular stop on the Underground Railroad. John Greenleaf Whittier wrote 93 poems that either illustrated the cruelty of slavery or celebrated anti-slavery leaders as diverse as Toussaint L'Ouverture and William Lloyd Garrison.

John Greenleaf Whittier

The first stanza from a six stanza poem by Whittier entitled, *"The Farewell of a Virginia Slave Mother to Her Daughters Sold into Southern Bondage,"* was typical of his dramatic style.

> *"I hate slavery in all its forms, degrees and influences and I deem myself bound by the highest moral and political obligations not to let that sentiment of hate lie dormant and smoldering in my own breast, but to give it free vent and let it blaze forth, that it may kindle equal ardor through the whole sphere of my influence."*
> –JOHN GREENLEAF WHITTIER.

The Farewell of a Virginia Slave Mother to Her Daughters Sold into Southern Bondage
By John Greenleaf Whittier

"Gone, gone,---sold and gone,
To the rice-swamp dank and lone.
Where the slave-whip ceaseless swings,
Where the noisome insect stings,
Where the fever demon strews
Poison with the falling dews,
Where the sickly sunbeams glare
Through the hot and misty air;
Gone, gone, --- sold and gone,
To the rice-swamp dank and lone.
From Virginia's hills and waters;
Woe is me, my stolen daughters!..."

John Greenleaf Whittier House

 ### DAVID P. HARMON HOUSE
UGRR Station
Summer Street and Maple Avenue

David Harmon (NAA) was close friends of the Quaker abolitionist, John Greenleaf Whittier (NAA).

Harmon House

 ### MOSES HUNTINGTON (NAA) HOUSE
UGRR Station
Pond Hills

HAVERHILL

 ### JOHN GREENLEAF WHITTIER (NAA) BIRTHPLACE
305 Whittier Road

DANIEL HOYT (NAA) HOUSE
UGRR Station
Savoy Road and Saunders Hill

GROVELAND

LEMUEL MARDEN HOUSE
UGRR Station
239 Main Street

The basement of the Lemuel Marden (NAA) house has a network of tunnels that were used to hide fugitives from slavery.

Marden House

GEORGETOWN

1 CHARLES BEECHER/ CAPT. SAMUEL BROCKLEBANK HOUSE
108 East Main Street

Anti-slavery activist, Charles Beecher (NAA), lived in this house, which was also known as the Brocklebank (NAA) House, with his family from 1859 through 1869. Beecher's sister, Harriet Beecher Stowe (NAA), wrote *Uncle Tom's Cabin.* That novel influenced anti-slavery sentiment in the U.S. in the years directly prior to the Civil War.

Brocklebank House

2 KING DAVIS BUILDING
UGRR Station
2 Central St.

Theodore Elliot (NAA) operated this building as a station on the Underground Railroad.

King Davis Building

3 CUFFEE DOLE, VETERAN OF THE AMERICAN REVOLUTION
Andover St.

Cuffee Dole (c. 1743–1816), a veteran of the American Revolution, was the first African American landowner in Rowley. Rowley was annexed by Georgetown in 1838.

4 UNION CEMETERY
East Main St.

This cemetery contains the grave of Cuffee Dole. This inscription was engraved on his headstone:

> *Cuffee Dole*
> *A Respectable Man of Colour,*
> *Died Rejoicing in the lord*
> *Aug. 17, 1816*
> *Age 73*
> *White Man Turn Not Away in*
> *Disgust, Thou Art My Brother,*
> *Like Me Akin to Earth and Worms*

Dole's epitaph hinted at the many hardships that he endured throughout his life. Dole served in the Continental Army on various occasions between August, 1777, to December, 1780. During that time, he suffered the stigma of what was, most likely, a racially motivated arrest while he was stationed in Cambridge in March, 1776. A white soldier claimed Dole stole eight dollars from him. Dole was never convicted and the charges were ultimately dropped. Dole continued to serve in the militia until his discharge in 1780.

NORTH ANDOVER

 CATO FREEMAN
Pleasant St.

Cato Freeman (1768–1853) was born to Salem and Remas. The family was enslaved by the Phillips (NAA) family of North Andover. The Phillips taught Cato to read, write, and play the violin. When slavery ceased to be enforced in Massachusetts, the family offered Cato a position. Cato married Lydia Bistrow in 1789. After their family grew to include four children, they moved to a house Freeman purchased on Pleasant St. That purchase made Freeman one of the earliest African American property owners in North Andover.

 OLD BURYING GROUND & NORTH PARISH CHURCH CEMETERY
190 Academy Road

The North Parish Church allowed African Americans to join as early as the 1780's but the church maintained a strict segregationist policy. African Americans could not purchase pews and white women who had relationships with African American men had to sit with the African American women.

Some of the African American residents buried here were Cato Freeman (plot 389), Rose Coburn, Pompey Lovejoy, and Primus. The short epitaphs of Rose, Pompey and Primus documented their life for posperity. Cato Freeman's history was documented under North Andover site #1.

> *Rose Coburn:*
> *"Here Lies the Body of*
> *Rose Coburn*
> *Who Died March 19,1859*
> *At Age 92 Years*
> *She was Born a Slave in Andover*
> *And was the Last Survivor of All*
> *Born Here in That condition"*

Pompey: *"Born in Boston a Slave;*
Died in Andover
A Free Man
February 23, 1826
Much Respected as a Sensible,
Amicable And Upright Man"

Primus: *"In Memory of Primus*
Who was a Faithful
Servant of Mr. Benjamin
Stevens, Jr.
Who Died July 25, 1792
Aged 72 Years, 5 months, 16 Days"

③ HAROLD PARKER STATE FOREST
UGRR Station
305 Middleton Road

This 3,000 acre state forest was an established Underground Railroad Station. It was widely used by the local abolitionist network to conceal fugitives from marshals in pursuit.

ANDOVER

---

① SALEM POOR, VETERAN OF THE AMERICAN REVOLUTION
Site unknown

Salem Poor (1747–1802), a veteran of the American Revolution and a hero of the Battle of Bunker Hill on June 17th, 1775, was born in Andover.

② CUFF CHAMBERS, VETERAN OF THE AMERICAN REVOLUTION
Site Unknown

Cuff (Blanchard) Chambers (c. 1738–1818) of Andover was one of the many African Americans who served in the American Revolution on a promise of freedom. Both he and his wife, Bette, were enslaved at the time of their marriage on September 16th, 1762. Chambers joined the militia in the spring of 1775, for a term of eight months. After his service, which included duty at the Battle of Bunker Hill, Chambers relocated with his family to New Hampshire and eventually to Leeds, Maine.

③ WILLIAM JENKINS HOUSE
UGRR Station
8 Douglass Street

From the early 1830s, William Jenkins (NAA) ran this Underground Railroad stop with his wife, Mary Saltmarsh Farnham Jenkins (NAA), for about thirty years. Abolitionist meetings were also hosted here with speakers such as Harriet Beecher Stowe, Frederick Douglass, and William Lloyd Garrison. Jenkins broke away from South Church in 1844 in protest of their position on slavery.

4 HOLT COGSWELL (NAA) HOUSE
UGRR Station
373 South Main Street

Cogswell House

5 REV. RALPH EMERSON / MARK NEWMAN HOUSE
UGRR Station
210 Main Street

Rev. Ralph Emerson (NAA), a relative of Ralph Waldo Emerson, resided here from 1829 to 1853 when he taught at the Theological Seminary. During that time, he provided shelter for fugitives from slavery. This house was also known as the Mark Newman House (NAA).

Newman House

6 HARRIET BEECHER STOWE HOUSE
UGRR Station
80 Bartlett Street

Harriet Beecher Stowe (NAA) lived here from 1852 to 1864 when her husband taught at the Theological Seminary. In addition to fugitives from slavery, other guests included Fredrick Douglass, Sojourner Truth, and William Lloyd Garrison. Stowe wrote, *The Key to Uncle Tom's Cabin* while she resided here.

Stowe House

7 JOSEPH POOR HOUSE, FRYE VILLAGE
UGRR Station
66 Poor Street

Frye Village was a thriving business and residential community dedicated to the abolition movement. In 1846, these residents, who included Elijah Hussey (NAA), a sawmill owner, William C. Donald (NAA), owner of an ink factory, William Poor (NAA), a wagon manufacturer, and Joseph Poor (NAA), owner of a blacksmith shop, united to form the Free Christian Church. Frye Village assisted several hundred fugitives in their escapes. The Joseph Poor house is all that remains of the Village.

Frye Village

(8) FREE CHRISTIAN CHURCH
UGRR Station
31 Elm St.

The Free Christian Church was formed in 1846 when members of the Frye Village separated from the South Church. Abolitionist activity was actively promoted by members.

(9) MOSES PARK HOUSE
UGRR Station
166 Lowell St.

Moses Park (NAA) and his wife were members of the West Parish Anti-Slavery Society. They also harbored fugitives in their home.

(10) SITE: POOR WAGON FACTORY
NOW: CHRISTIAN SCIENCE CHURCH
UGRR Station
278 N. Main St.

William Poor (NAA), one of the founders of Frye Village, manufactured wagons at this location. Many of the wagons contained hidden compartments to conceal fugitives. Fugitives also found refuge at this site.

LAWRENCE

(1) SHAW (NAA) HOUSE
UGRR Station
High St.

(2) SITE: DANIEL SAUNDERS HOUSE
UGRR Station
215 South Broadway

Daniel Saunders (1796–1872) (NAA) lived at this location from 1847 until 1872. During the period prior to the Civil War, he used his house as a station on the Underground Railroad. Saunders established a business and political dynasty in Lawrence. His sons, Daniel, Jr. and Caleb, both served as mayor of Lawrence. A memorial to mark the location of the site was created from the foundation of Daniel, Jr.'s demolished house next door.

WILMINGTON

---

(1) JOSHUA HARNDEN (NAA) TAVERN AKA: WILMINGTON MUSEUM

UGRR Station
Open Tues. & Thurs., 10-2, free
430 Salem Street

Harnden Tavern

Lowell Map

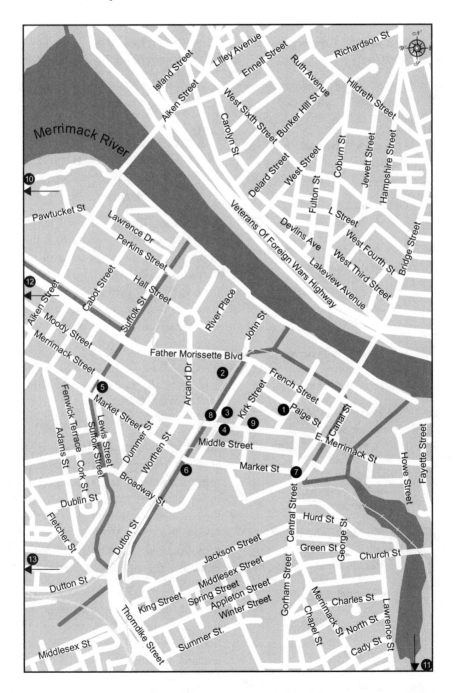

LOWELL

SITE: JOHN ST. CONGREGATIONAL CHURCH
John St. & Paige St.

The John St. Congregational Church, constructed in 1840, was known as the, *"Anti-Slavery Church,"* because of the fiery sermons delivered from the pulpit by Rev. Eden B. Foster (NAA). Foster served as pastor from the early 1850s until the start of the Civil War in 1861.

SITE: LOWELL HIGH SCHOOL
Kirk St. & Anne St.

The City established Lowell High School in 1831 in one of the mill buildings on Middlesex Street. An increase in population led to several moves until the city built a school building on this site in 1840. The 1840 building was demolished in the 1890s and a larger building was constructed on the site.

When other Massachusetts towns debated the issue of school desegregation in the mid-1840s, Lowell boasted that all its school age children were welcome to attend their neighborhood schools. Admission to the high school was by a rigorous examination and many in the African American community in Lowell passed the exam and attended the school.

The first African American documented as a student at Lowell High was Caroline Van Vronker in 1843. Although Lowell boasted of its liberal policy of non-discrimination towards all students, after graduation, those students had to accept an adult world where discrimination was very much the norm. After she obtained a teacher's certificate, Caroline was unable to become a teacher in Lowell because of her color. A relative, Hannah Jane Van Vronker, married Edwin Garrison Walker of Charlestown in 1858. Walker was the first African American elected to the state legislature in 1866.

 3 ## ST. ANNE'S EPISCOPAL CHURCH & PARSONAGE
UGRR Station
8 Kirk St.

St. Anne's Episcopal Church, built in 1825, was led by Rev. Theodore Edson

St. Anne's Episcopal Parsonage

(NAA). Edson was President of the Lowell Anti-Slavery Society. Evidence suggests that he used the parsonage next door to conceal fugitives on their route to freedom.

 4 ## OLD CITY HALL
226 Merrimack St.

Lowell's Old City Hall building, constructed in 1830, was the venue for many abolitionist speakers and meetings. Famous figures such as Frederick Douglass, William Lloyd Garrison, Henry David Thoreau, Ralph Waldo Emerson, and even Abraham Lincoln spoke from its second floor lecture hall.

Old City Hall

 5 ## SITE: WALKER LEWIS BARBERSHOP
Merrimack St.

Walker Lewis (1798–1856) operated a barbershop at a location somewhere on

Merrimack St. Walker Lewis' uncle was Quock Walker of Barre. Quock Walker initiated one of the two *"Freedom Lawsuits"* that ended the enforcement of slavery in Massachusetts in 1783.

Quock Walker's sister, Minor Walker, married Peter P. Lewis in 1792. The couple relocated to Cambridge where they raised eleven children one of whom was Walker Lewis. In 1830, Walker Lewis and his new wife, Elizabeth Lovejoy, relocated to Lowell with six of Walker's siblings and their families.

Walker Lewis participated in most of the activities that pertained to the advancement of African Americans in Lowell during his lifetime. He was a member of the African Lodge and served as Grand Master in 1829 and 1830. Walker was also one of the founders of the Massachusetts General Colored Association. His Lowell home served as a station on the Underground Railroad during the 1840s and 50s.

Lewis became a member of the Church of Jesus Christ of Latter Day Saints in 1842. He was ordained as an Elder in 1843 and was one of only three African Americans to be ordained as an Elder in that denomination. In 1851, Walker relocated to Utah to be closer to other Mormons but the racial prejudice of his fellow Mormons in Utah made that stay last only six months. Lewis died early the next year after he returned to Lowell.

"NEGRO CLOTH" LOWELL MANUFACTURING COMPANY
256 Market St.

The Lowell Manufacturing Company was founded in 1828. In its early years, the company which consisted of a complex of multiple buildings, produced carpets and a textile that was commonly termed, *"Negro Cloth."* *"Negro Cloth"* was a course, durable fabric made of a blend of wool and cotton. It was so named because its primary destinations were the Southern plantations where plantation owners used it to clothe their enslaved workforce.

The coarseness of the fabric made it very uncomfortable to the wearer but that rough quality was encouraged as a way to reinforce a perception of the inferiority of the laborers that the plantation owners wanted the laborers to internalize. In 1835, South Carolina required enslaved individuals to wear *"Negro Cloth"* to identify themselves in public. The Lowell Manufacturing Company eventually ceased the manufacture of that particular cloth.

Many of the buildings of the Lowell Manufacturing Company were demolished by 1960. The buildings that remained were redeveloped into affordable rental units in 1982 and were renamed, Market Mills.

SITE: HORACE B. PROCTOR BARBER SHOP

Central & Market Sts.

Horace Proctor was the first African American in Lowell to be placed on a jury list. This historic event occurred in 1868. Proctor operated a barber shop and bath house at this location for many years.

 SITE: HUNTINGTON HALL

Merrimack St. & Dutton St.

Huntington Hall was constructed in 1852 as Lowell's largest public hall. It was located on the second floor above the Merrimack Depot. The hall was an extremely popular venue for many different events including prominent abolitionist speakers. The hall contained 1,812 fixed seats and it had standing room capacity for 1,200 additional people. A fire on November 4th, 1904, destroyed the building. The only component of the structure that survived was a portion of the first floor arched openings through which the trains passed.

 NATHANIAL BOOTH & MECHANICS HALL

155 Merrimack St.

Mechanics Hall was constructed in 1830 with spaces for educational, social, and cultural activities on the sec-
ond floor and commercial space on the first floor. One of the occupants of the commercial space was Nathanial Booth, a fugitive from Virginia. Booth operated a barber shop at this location from 1845 until 1850. In 1850, Booth fled to Canada when bounty hunters arrived in Lowell for his capture. Booth was assisted in his escape by many Lowell residents. After sympathetic abolitionists purchased his freedom, Booth returned to Massachusetts where he relocated to Boston and resumed his former occupation as a barber.

 ADRASTUS & ELIZABETH LEW HOUSE

UGRR Station
89 Mount Hope St.

In 1844, Adrastus Lew (c.1821–1886) built a house at this location with his wife Elizabeth (1821–1917). The family actively participated in the escape of fugitives from slavery. Adrastus Lew was the grandson of Barzillai Lew, a veteran of the American Revolution.

Lew House

The couple had six children, all of whom became accomplished musicians throughout the region. In 1902, one of their grandchildren, Harry Lew, was the first African American to integrate professional basketball.

⑪ LOWELL CEMETERY
381 Rogers St.

The Lowell Cemetery was incorporated in 1841. The cemetery was designed on thirty acres in the garden style which was very popular during that time. The family of Walker Lewis (1798–1856) located their family plot here. Walker Lewis was a descendent of Quock Walker whose 1783 lawsuit contributed to the end of slavery in Massachusetts. A lone headstone for one of the descendants, Walker Lewis (1839–1901) is all that remains. Walker Lewis served as a

Lewis Burial Plot

Landsman in the U.S. Navy aboard the USS Rhode Island during the Civil War.

Lowell Cemetery Gates

⑫ PAWTUCKET CHURCH
15 Mammoth Road & Riverside St.

Pawtucket Congregational Church originated in 1796 in what was then Dracut. Barzillai and Dinah Lew attended service at this church with their thirteen children. The Lews were a family of talented musicians and many of their children participated in the orchestra which accompanied the church during worship.

The Female Charitable Educational Society with some of the deacons of the Church, organized anti-slavery activity in the church and in Lowell as early as 1834. The church bell tolled in respect for John Brown (NAA) on Dec. 2nd, 1859, the day he was hanged. John Brown organized the unsuccessful raid on the Federal arsenal at Harper's Ferry on October 16th, 1859, in an effort to instigate a slave rebellion. Lowell annexed Pawtucketville from Dracut in 1874. The current church was built in 1899.

Pawtucket Congregational Church

13 CLAY PIT CEMETERY
Between 647 & 705 Pawtucket Blvd.

Barzillai Lew, a veteran of the American Revolution, was buried here. Today, the cemetery has been overgrown with weeds. Many of the gravestones have been destroyed or removed.

CHELMSFORD

1 BARZILLAI LEW, VETERAN OF THE FRENCH & INDIAN WAR AND THE AMERICAN REVOLUTION
Site unknown

Barzillai Lew (1743–1822), who sometimes was referred to as Zeal, moved to Chelmsford after he sold his family farm in Groton. In Chelmsford, Lew made barrels as a copper. That occupation gave him a high level of financial security and in 1766 he was able to purchase the freedom of his future wife, Dinah Bowman (1744–1837) for 400 pounds, today's equivalent of approximately $28,000. A portrait of Barzillai Lew was painted by the famous artist, Gilbert Stuart (NAA). Stuart is best known for his portrait of Gen. George

Recreation of painting by Gilbert Stuart

Washington (NAA). The fact that such a renowned artist painted his portrait indicated that Lew had achieved some distinction in his community.

Lew enlisted in the 27th Regiment of Chelmsford in May of 1775. He served in the war as a fifer, drummer, and soldier during the Battle of Bunker Hill and other battles. The role of the regiment fifer was quite important and required a high level of bravery. The musicians were located at the front of the regiment to rally the troops and keep morale high as the men went into battle. Lew, who was over six feet tall, probably made quite an imposing image, and target, as he marched in front of his regiment.

DRACUT

 DRACUT
UGRR Station

During the nineteenth Century, the town of Dracut went by the moniker of *"Black North"* because of its large African American settlement. The entire town served as a safe haven for those en-route to New Hampshire.

 HARRY LEW
Site Unknown

Harry "Bucky" Lew (1884–1963) was the first African American signed as a professional basketball player. He joined the Lowell Pawtucketville Athletic Club of the New England Professional Basketball League at the age of 18. Although he was recruited for the team, early racism of the coach kept him on the bench more than the court. After a series of lost games, the fans demanded that Lew be placed on the court. Lew played and coached professionally for the next twenty years. Despite the remarkable fact that, at 5'-8", Lew was one of the greatest defensive players in the league, he was never inducted into the Basketball Hall of Fame.

 BARZILLAI LEW
Varnum Ave. and
Totman Road

Barzillai Lew purchased a farmstead at this site after he left the militia. The Lew family grew to include thirteen children. For several generations, the family was known throughout the region as talented musicians.

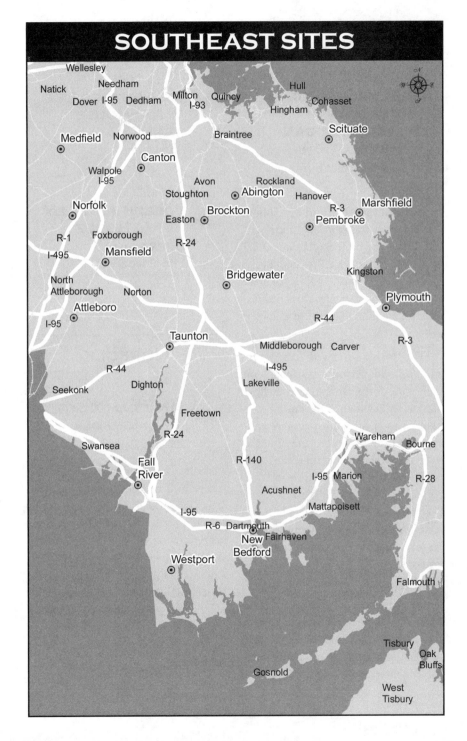

SOUTHEAST SITES

Wellesley
Natick
Needham
Dover I-95 Dedham
Milton Quincy
I-93
Hull
Hingham
Cohasset

Medfield
Norwood
Braintree
Scituate

Canton

Walpole
I-95

Avon
Stoughton
Rockland
Abington
Hanover
Marshfield

Norfolk
Brockton
R-3
Pembroke
Easton

R-1 Foxborough
I-495 Mansfield
R-24

North
Attleborough
Norton
Bridgewater
Kingston

Attleboro
Plymouth

I-95
R-44

Taunton
Middleborough Carver
R-3

R-44
I-495

Seekonk
Dighton
Lakeville

Freetown

R-24
Wareham
Bourne

Swansea
R-140

Fall
River
I-95 Marion
R-28

Acushnet

I-95
Mattapoisett

R-6 Dartmouth
New Fairhaven
Westport
Bedford

Falmouth

Tisbury
Oak
Bluffs

Gosnold

West
Tisbury

CANTON

① SEYMOUR BURR, VETERAN OF THE AMERICAN REVOLUTION
Graveyard at Burr Land

Seymour Burr (b. circa 1754 - d. 1837), a veteran of the American Revolution, was buried at this cemetery. Burr's enslaver was the brother of Aaron Burr (NAA), the third Vice President of the United States whose political career ended after he mortally wounded Alexander Hamilton (NAA) in a duel in 1804.

The British promised freedom to any enslaved person who fought on their side during the American Revolution so Seymour Burr ran away to fight for the British. That attempt ended when he was captured and returned to his enslavers. By that time, the Patriots also promised freedom to enslaved persons who fought for their cause, so Seymour Burr agreed to fight in the American Continental Army instead. He saw service at Fort Catskill and Valley Forge.

In 1805, Burr married Mary Wilbore, a member of the Ponkapoag tribe. They lived on six acres in Canton that Mary Wilbore inherited through her first husband. There they raised two daughters, Polly and Sarah Burr.

MEDFIELD

① REV. LUTHER LEE (NAA) HOUSE
UGRR Station
Site Unknown

② JOSEPH A. ALLEN (NAA) HOUSE
UGRR Station
Site Unknown

NORFOLK

① MALCOLM X SITE: MCI NORFOLK
2 Clark St.

Malcolm X served part of his sentence, 1948 to 1952, at the Massachusetts Correctional Institute at Norfolk. Malcolm's transfer to MCI Norfolk occurred after he spent fifteen months at MCI Concord. His half-sister, Ella Collins, lobbied for that transfer on his behalf. MCI Norfolk was more of a rehabilitation prison than MCI Concord. Norfolk also had an incredible library where Malcolm was able to read in abundance.

MANSFIELD

 1 ## NATIONAL BLACK DOLL MUSEUM
288 N. Main St.
774-284-4729
www.nbdmhc.org

Debra Britt, Felicia Walker, and Laverne Cotton were collectors of African American dolls. After they had amassed an impressive collection, they founded this museum in 2012. The trio envisioned the museum of over 6,000 dolls as a vehicle for African Americans, especially children, to learn about African American culture and history through dolls.

ABINGTON

 1 ## CIVIL WAR MEMORIAL ISLAND GROVE PARK
200 Park Ave.

Island Grove Park was the site of abolitionist meetings prior to the Civil War. One of Abington's two Civil War Memorials was sited in Island Grove Park. Abington, with a population of 8,527 in 1860, suffered 29 casualties during the war and 35 more died from war related diseases shortly after they returned home.

 2 ## CIVIL WAR MEMORIAL DYER MEMORIAL LIBRARY
28 Centre St.

In the Civil War, Abington played an important role in the Union effort. Abington factories manufactured half of all the footwear used by the Union Army troops. This Civil War Memorial documented the role that Abington played during that war.

 3 ## MICOB, HERO OF THE AMERICAN REVOLUTION
Site Unknown

Micob, enslaved by Josiah Torrey (NAA), was a casualty of war in the American Revolution.

SCITUATE

 1 ## REV. CHARLES T. TORREY BIRTHPLACE

Rev. Charles Torrey (1813–1846) (NAA), a Scituate native and one of the more radical abolitionists from Massachusetts, died in a Maryland prison while he served a sentence for anti-slavery activity. After Torrey attended Exeter Academy and Yale University, he enrolled in Andover Theological Seminary where he was exposed to the ab-

Rev. Charles T. Torrey

olitionist movement. His radical views on how to end slavery differed from William Lloyd Garrison's more moderate views. On April 1st, 1840, Torrey joined with like-minded spirits to form the Liberty Party, a political party focused solely on the abolition of slavery.

Impatient with the slow pace of political change, Torrey left his wife and child in Massachusetts and went to Washington, D.C. in 1841 disguised as a reporter. There he and Thomas Smallwood, a freed African American, recruited enslaved African Americans in D.C. to escape via a series of safe houses along a route from Washington to Baltimore, Philadelphia, and Albany. The pair assisted over four hundred enslaved people in their escape. Many of them were enslaved by Congressmen. In the spring of 1843, both Torrey and Smallwood left D.C. because they were under police investigation for their anti-slavery activity. The pair returned in the fall of 1843 but fled again before a police arrest.

Smallwood relocated to Canada but Torrey settled in Baltimore where he continued his assistance of fugitives. The police persisted in their pursuit and Torrey was arrested and sentenced to six years in a Maryland penitentiary. The poor conditions in the prison caused a return of an earlier bout with tuberculosis. Torrey died after sixteen months in prison. His funeral at Tremont Temple was attended by a packed house. A monument was erected at his grave in Mount Auburn Cemetery.

"...Liberty may be taken from me; my good name cannot, until I have done something more to forfeit it, than acts which nine-tenths of the civilized world deem to be the bare performance of the duties imposed on us by common humanity and the Christian faith.

I said, I make no appeal to public sympathy. Let the guilty do that! I shall give the eminent counsellors who plead my cause in the courts, but one instruction; it is, that they make no admission, even by way of argument, that it can be a crime to aid one of God's children, formed in his image, to escape from slavery. The crime is, to make God's child a slave!

If any who read this deem my language that of pride I have only to say that the world will judge. I am a man, and I am right, and therefore speak boldly to those who are my equals and no more."

-- Charles T. Torrey, Letter from a Baltimore Jail, Aug. 29, 1844

PEMBROKE

1 **DR. ANTHONY COLLAMORE (NAA)**
UGRR Station
225 Washington St.

MARSHFIELD

1 **BRITON HAMMON AUTOBIOGRAPHICAL NARRATIVE WINSLOW HOUSE**
634 Careswell St.

In 1760, Briton Hammon (birthdate unknown) returned to Boston from thirteen years of the most remarkable adventures imaginable. Hammon related those adventures in the book, *A Narrative of the Uncommon Sufferings and Surprising Deliverance of Briton Hammon, A Negro Man, -- Servant to General Winslow, of Marshfield, in New-England.* This was the first published narrative by an individual of African descent, free or enslaved.

Hammon traveled to Jamaica to conduct business on behalf of the Winslow (NAA) family. On his return home, he was captured off the coast of Florida. That capture set off a series of escapes and captures that lasted for thirteen years and spread over several countries.

2 **MOSES FOLGER ROGERS (NAA) HOUSE**
UGRR Station
540 Highland St.

NORTH BRIDGEWATER / BROCKTON

1 **JAMES EASTON, SR., VETERAN OF THE AMERICAN REVOLUTION**
Site: Baptist Church, Stoughton Corner

James Easton, Sr. (1754–1830), a veteran of the American Revolution, included many abolitionists and civil rights activists among his family members. Easton married Sarah Dunbar, a Native American, and they had four sons, Caleb, Joshua, Sylvanus, and Hosea Easton. They also had one daughter, Sarah Easton. North Bridgewater, where the Easton's raised their family, was absorbed into Brockton in 1874. From 1816 until 1830, James Easton, Sr. founded and operated a school to teach African American youth to become blacksmiths.

James Easton, Sr. was also a civil rights activist who challenged the segregation of the local churches. When some of the family were dragged from the porch of the Orthodox Church, Easton's family quit that church and bought a pew at the Baptist Church in Stoughton Corner. Once the parishioners discovered that the pew had been purchased by a family of African descent, they attempted to have the purchase cancelled. When that failed, the church tarred the pew. The family attended service anyway with seats they brought in their wagon. Next the church pulled the pew down and the Easton family sat in the aisle. The church continued to harass the family until they quit their membership.

Their daughter, Sarah, was the second wife of Robert Roberts. That union made James Eaton, Sr., the great-grandfather of Sarah Roberts, the plaintiff in the school desegregation case of Roberts v. the City of Boston. The entire family actively engaged in efforts to abolish slavery. One of their sons, Hosea Easton, wrote a controversial book which argued against racial prejudice. It laid some of the blame for racial prejudice on the American clergy because he strongly believed they condoned slavery. See more on the family under Beacon Hill Sites.

TAUNTON

1 ELIJAH & JERUSHSA BIRD (NAA) HOUSE
UGRR Station
Site Unknown

BARROWSVILLE

1 SITE: REV. SOLOMON P. SNOW (NAA) PARISH
UGRR Station
Norton Post Office

NORTH ATTLEBORO

1 REV. SETH CHAPLIN (NAA) HOUSE
UGRR Station
Site Unknown

FALL RIVER

1 ISAAC FISKE HOUSE
UGRR Station
263 Pine St.

Dr. Isaac Fiske (1791–1873) (NAA), an activist in anti-slavery efforts in Fall River, lived in this house with his family from 1845 until his death. According to his daughter, Annie Fiske, fugitives from slavery were often hidden in the attic. One of the guests in the Fiske home was Henry *"Boxcar"* Brown. Brown often retold how he shipped his body as a parcel to escape slavery. That narrative made him a popular speaker on the anti-slavery lecture circuit.

Isaac Fiske House

2 MR. & MRS. SAMUEL BUFFUM CHASE (NAA) HOUSE
UGRR Station
Hunt and Broad St.

WESTPORT

---

1 PAUL CUFFE *"NO TAXATION WITHOUT REPRESENTATION"*
1504 Drift Road

Paul Cuffe (1759-1817), built his fortune as a *"Black Jack,"* a term used to describe African American sea captains in the 19th century. Cuffe settled in Westport where he purchased this 140-acre farm and built the farmhouse on it. He also built an interracial school on the property. Cuffe's African father, Coffe Slocum, purchased his freedom and married a Native American, Ruth Moses, of the Wampanoag tribe from Gay Head on Martha's Vineyard. The couple settled in New Bedford where Paul Cuffe was born. The couple eventually purchased a 100 acre farm in Westport where they raised ten children. Paul Cuffe was the youngest child. Another son, Jonathan Cuffe, moved to Martha's Vineyard where he became a fully integrated member of his mother's tribe.

Paul Cuffe

While he was still a teenager, Paul Cuffe rejected the slave name of his father, Slocum, and instead adopted his father's African name, Cuffe. Cuffe's ap-

Cuffe Farm

for unpaid taxes. He felt it was unfair that he had to pay taxes but was not able to vote. Cuffe, and his brother, along with six other African Americans from Dartmouth, petitioned the Massachusetts Legislature for relief from taxes. The legislature denied their petition, but it led to the successful effort, in 1783, to grant African American men in Massachusetts the right to vote.

prenticeship on a whaling ship taught him the intricacies of navigation and whaling. That knowledge laid the foundation for the business he began in 1779 with one of his brothers in a single boat that they built.

In 1780, Paul Cuffe and his brother, John Cuffe, found themselves in arrears

March 14th, 1780 – Signed Petition Against Taxation Without Representation:

Paul Cuffe	John Cuffe
Adventure Childe	Paul Cuve
Samuel Gray	Pero Howland
Pero Russel	Pero Coggeshall

"To the Honorable Council and House of Representatives in General Court assembled for the State of Massachusetts Bay in New England, March 14, A D 1780.

The petition of several poor Negroes and Mulattos who are Inhabitant of the Town of Dartmouth Humbly Sheweth—That we being chiefly of the African extract and by Reason of Long Bondag and hard Slavery we have been deprived of Injoying the Profits of our Labouer or the advantage of Inheriting Estates from our Parents as our Neighbouers the white peopel do (haveing some of us not long Injoyed our own freedom), & yet of late, Contrary to the invariable Custom & Practice of the country we have been & now are Taxed both in our Polls and that small Pittance of Estate which through much hard Labour & Industry we have got together to Sustain our selves & families withal— We apprehend it therefore to be hard usag and doubtless if Continued will reduce us to a State of Beggary, whereby we shall become a Berthan to others if not timely prevented by the Interposition of your Justice & power...

We apprehend ourselves to be Aggreeved, in that while we are not allowed the Privilege of freemen of the State having no vote or Influence in the Election *of those that Tax us, yet many of our Colour (as is well known) have cheerfully Entered the field of Battle in the defense of the Common Cause, and that (as we conceive) against a similar Exertion of Power (in Regard to taxation) too well Known to need a recital in this place—*

That these the Most honouerable court we Humbley Beseech they would to take this into consideration and Let us aside from Paying tax or taxes or cause us to Be Cleaired for we ever have Been a people that was fair from all these thing ever since the days of our four fathers and therefore we take it as aheard ship that we should be so delt By now in these Difficulty times for there is not to exceed more than five or six that hath a cow in this town and theirfore in our distress we send unto the peaceableness of thee people and the mercy of God that we may be Releaved for we are not allowed in voating in the town meating in nur to chuse an officer neither their was not one ever heard in the active Court of the General Asembly the poor dispised miserable Black people, & we have not an equal chance with white people neither by Sea nur by Land therefore we take it as a heard ship that poor old Negroes should be Rated which have been in Bondage some thirty some forty and some fifty years and now just got their Liberty some by going into the serviese and some by going to Sea and others by good fortan and also poor Distressed mongrels which have no larning and no land and also no (word illegible—ed.) Neither where to put their head but some shelter themselves into an old rooten but which thy dogs would not lay in.

...therefore We most humbley Request therefore that you would take our unhappy case into your serious Consideration and in your wisdom and Power grant us Relief from Taxation ....." (sic)

Cuffe lived in Dartmouth before he settled in Westport with his wife, Alice Pequit, also of the Wampanoag tribe. He and his wife had eight children. Although Cuffe was self-taught, he had higher ambitions for their children. Unfortunately, there was no school in their town. In 1797, Cuffe convened a group of his neighbors to organize the construction of a school. As with many committees, no consensus was reached. Frustrated, but not prepared to give up

his goal, Cuffe built a school on his property with his personal funds. He offered the school to the community for the education of all children.

By 1806, Cuffe owned a fleet of ten ships. His economic success made him one of the wealthiest and most influential African Americans in the colonies. He consistently used that wealth to give back to his community, through jobs and civic improvements in his town. Cuffe strongly believed that a settlement in Africa would allow African Americans an opportunity to achieve without the constraints of discrimination and racism that limited them in the United States. His wealth allowed Cuffe to finance an African American settlement in Sierra Leone.

Friend's Meeting House

CUFFE GRAVE & MONUMENT FRIENDS MEETING HOUSE
930 Main Road

Paul Cuffe joined the Society of Friends (Quakers) in 1808. In 1814, he became a major contributor to rebuild the local Friends Meeting House. Cuffe's grave was placed in the adjacent cemetery. The town erected a monument to honor him on June 15th, 1913. They re-dedicated the monument in 2009.

Cuffe Monument

416

New Bedford Map

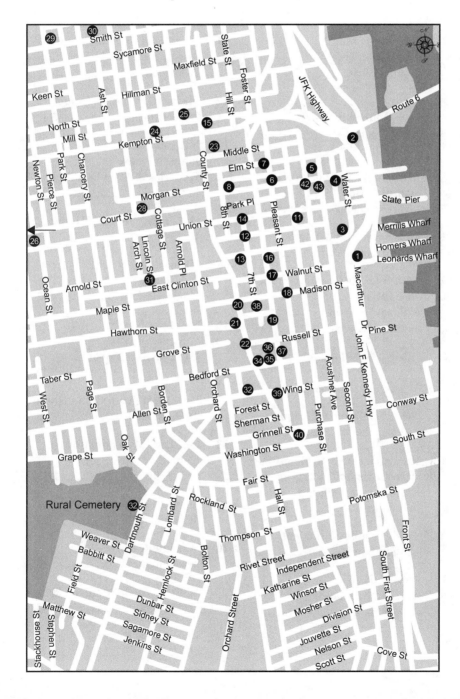

NEW BEDFORD

NEW BEDFORD and other seafaring communities attracted many African Americans during the 18th and 19th centuries. The maritime industries those towns supported provided a level of financial compensation and personal freedom that the more inland communities did not offer. Work on the wharfs and on the ships, especially the whaling ships, made it possible for many African Americans to accumulate the finances to obtain financial independence to open other businesses.

New Bedford contained the largest population of African Americans of any other New England city during the mid-1800s, between six to eight percent of the population. Many in this prosperous community joined the abolitionist movement to support fugitives from slavery. The fugitive population in New Bedford during the mid-1800s fluctuated between 300 to 700 members.

 ## SITE: LEWIS TEMPLE BLACKSMITH SHOP
Coffin's Wharf, foot of Walnut St.

Lewis Temple (1800-1854), a blacksmith, was one of the many who took advantage of the possibilities that were open to industrious and creative individuals during this time. At his blacksmith shop at this site, Temple invented the famous *"toggle"* harpoon, a tool that revolutionized the whaling industry.

Lewis Temple, born in Richmond, VA, made his way to New Bedford, MA, where he settled by 1829. Temple actively participated in the abolitionist movement, as did many prosperous African Americans in New Bedford. During the 1830s, he served as vice-president of an anti-slavery society known as the New Bedford Union Society.

 ## SITE: WILLIAM P. POWELL BOARDING HOUSE
UGRR Station
94 North Water St.

Abolitionist William P. Powell, Sr., (1806–1875) operated a boarding house for sailors at this site. Born in New York State, Powell, Sr. worked in the sea industries early in life. Powell settled in New Bedford around 1833, after he married a member of the Wampanoag Tribe.

William P. Powell, Sr. was one of the founders of the New England Non-Resistance Society, formed in 1838 to condemn violence, in all forms, for any means, including self-defense. Powell, Sr. and his wife relocated their family to England in 1851, in order to escape fugitive slave laws and to allow their children to receive a good education. The family stayed in England until 1861, when they returned to the states.

William P. Powell, Jr.

One of their children, William P. Powell, Jr. (1834–1915), served as one of thirteen African American surgeons, out of 13,000 total surgeons to work for the Union Army during the Civil War. Powell, Jr. was trained at the College of Physicians and Surgeons in London during the family's stay there. After the family returned to the United States, Powell, Jr. received a contract from the Union Army as an assistant surgeon at Contraband Hospital in Washington, DC. That hospital served fugitives from slavery and African American soldiers.

36 Water St.

Powell, Jr. began his work in May of 1863. By October of that same year, he was promoted as head of the hospital. He served in that capacity until October of 1864. After the war, Powell continued to practice medicine until poor health forced him to stop. His petition to the U.S. government for an army pension was denied. They justified the decision on the basis that Powell, Jr. had been a contract surgeon and not a military officer.

 ### 3 WILLIAM BUSH & LUCINDA CLARK BOARDING HOUSES
UGRR Station
Site: 36 & 69½ South Water St.

New Bedford's most active abolitionist, William Bush (1798–1866), operated a series of boarding houses at these two locations with his wife, Lucinda Clark, a relative of Lewis Temple. The couple operated these boarding houses until the start of the Civil War. The boarding houses provided critical housing for African Americans who worked on the wharfs and the ships of New Bedford. The couple also used the boarding houses as stops on the Underground Railroad. Born free in Virginia, Bush and his wife, Lucinda, first lived in Washington, D.C. There Lucinda Clark and Captain Daniel Drayton (NAA) participated in the attempted escape of seventy-seven enslaved individuals in April of 1848, onboard the ship, *the Pearl*.

The authorities arrested and jailed Drayton because of his participation in that rescue effort. Bush and Clark relocated to New Bedford out of concern for Lucinda's safety. Her involvement in the Pearl escape attempt made her a target for arrest, the fate that Captain Drayton experienced. See more on Drayton under other New Bedford sites.

Bush was the uncle of Leonard Grimes, the minister of Twelfth Baptist Church in Boston. While Grimes served a prison sentence in Virginia because he helped fugitives escape slavery, Bush took care of Grimes' family. William Bush was buried in Rural Cemetery in New Bedford.

4　NEW BEDFORD WHALING MUSEUM

18 Johnny Cake Hill
Mon.-Sat. 9 to 5
Sun. 1 to 5
508- 997-0046

Amos Haskins

The whaling industry in New Bedford allowed many African Americans to achieve a high level of economic success because the skills required to excel in that industry—strength, endurance, fearlessness, intelligence, and quick reflexes—were rewarded irrespective of the color of one's skin. This museum documented the contributions of African American involved in the whaling industry.

Some of those individuals involved in that industry included: Lewis Temple, who invented the toggle harpoon; Paul Cuffe, a successful sea merchant who owned ten ships at one time; Amos Haskins, a Native American ship Captain of the Wampanoag Tribe; and John Maslow, an African American ship builder.

Amos Haskins (1816–1861) was the first, and one of the few, Native American Captains of a whaling ship. He became Captain of the ship, the *Massasoit*, in 1851. Haskins's 22 person crew included twelve people of color, three of them in the highest ranks under the Captain, including the 1st, 2nd, and 3rd mates.

Haskins continued the tradition of intermarriage

New Bedford Whaling Museum

with African Americans when he married Elizabeth Farmer with whom he had five daughters. Haskins suffered the fate of many mariners when he died at sea in 1861.

5 54TH INFANTRY RECRUITMENT PLAZA MEMORIAL
William Street and Acushnet Avenue

The 54th Regiment was the first Regiment of African American soldiers from New England to participate in the Civil War. African American citizens of New Bedford actively recruited soldiers to join the 54th to fight to end slavery. On February 10th, 1863, the city began that recruitment effort at this site.

In April of 1861, they issued the following declaration:

"Whereas, In view of the probable departure from our city within a short time of a large portion of our patriotic military companies, called out for defense of our common country, in which case the citizens of New Bedford would naturally have a feeling of insecurity for their persons and property in the excited state of the public mind incident upon the existence of actual war, therefore,

Resolved, That as true and loyal citizens (although exempt by law from military duty,) we hold ourselves in readiness to organize military companies to be officered

54th Regiment Recruiting Station Memorial

and equipped, and to drill regularly for the protection and maintenance of peace and good order, and for the security and defense of our city and State against any and all emergencies,

Resolved, That the proceedings of this meeting be laid before the Mayor of this city and the Governor of this State, and we pledge them four hundred men will fight for liberty, to be ready at any moment to rally to their support wherever our services may be required."

–declaration by New Bedford African Americans, 1861

54th Regiment Recruiting Station Signage

New Bedford has initiated plans to develop a memorial at this location for all African Americans who participated in the Civil War.

 ## 6 LIBERTY BELL PLAQUE

Corner of Purchase and William St.

In 1850, the United States Congress passed a more stringent version of the Fugitive Slave Law of 1793 to pacify Southerners and assist in the capture of fugitives from slavery. Many northern abolitionists actively used tactics of civil disobedience in their efforts to negate the effects of that law. In New Bedford, the mayor rang a bell, the Liberty Bell, to warn fugitives when U.S. marshals were nearby.

On March 16th, 1851, a rumor circulated that U.S. marshals with a posse of armed men were on their way to New Bedford to make a mass capture of fugitives in the town. This was believed to be in retaliation of the escape of Shadrach Minkins in Boston on February 15th of that year. The Liberty

Liberty Bell Plaque

Bell was rung and fugitives and those sympathetic to their cause gathered to decide what action to take. Some of the wealthiest citizens of New Bedford decided to assist a large group of fugitives to escape to Canada. That action did not have to be carried out because the marshals never came.

That incident illustrated that New Bedford citizens were ready to work together to handle such adversities. This plaque, on the exterior wall of Merchants National Bank Building, marked the site where the Liberty Bell hung at its location inside Liberty Hall which stood at this site during the mid-1800s.

 7 ## FREDERICK DOUGLASS PLAQUE
New Bedford City Hall
133 William St.

Frederick Douglass (1818–1895), one of the most famous African Americans in history, fought relentlessly to end slavery and to gain equal rights for African Americans and women. Douglass disguised himself as a sailor to escape slavery in Maryland. He lived in New Bedford with his wife, Anna Douglass, after his initial excape from slavery. The city of New Bedford dedicated this plaque in 1995, on the centennial of the death of Frederick Douglass. See more on Douglass under other sites throughout this book.

"If there is no struggle, there is no progress. Those who profess to favor freedom, and yet depreciate agitation, are men who want crops without plowing up the ground. They want rain without thunder and lightning. They want the ocean without the awful roar of its many waters. This struggle may be a moral one; or it may be a physical one; or it may be both moral and physical; but it must be a struggle. Power concedes nothing without a demand. It never did and it never will. Find out just what any people will quietly submit to and you have found out the exact measure of injustice and wrong which will be imposed upon them, and these will continue till they are resisted with either words or blows, or with both. The limits of tyrants are prescribed by the endurance of those whom they oppress. In the light of these ideas, Negroes will be hunted at the North, and held and flogged at the South so long as they submit to those devilish outrages, and make no resistance, either moral or physical. Men may not get all they pay for in this world; but they must certainly pay for all they get. If we ever get free from the oppressions and wrongs heaped upon us, we must pay for their removal. We must do this by labor, by suffering, by sacrifice, and if need be, by our lives and the lives of others."

–Frederick Douglass

Frederick Douglass Plaque

Bedford. The congregation changed the name to the Douglass Memorial AME Zion Church in the 1930s. In 1995, the church closed, and the building became the location of an art gallery, *Gallery X*.

Douglass Memorial AME Zion

> "Where justice is denied, where poverty is enforced, where ignorance prevails, and where any one class is made to feel that society is an organized conspiracy to oppress, rob and degrade them, neither persons nor property will be safe."
> —FREDERICK DOUGLASS

8 FREDERICK DOUGLASS MEMORIAL AFRICAN METHODIST EPISCOPAL ZION CHURCH BUILDING
169 William St.

Originally known as the African Methodist Episcopal Church, this was the church home of Frederick Douglass when he and his family lived in New

9 LEWIS TEMPLE MONUMENT
613 Pleasant St.

Whaling was one of the most dangerous professions in the late 19th century. The extremely high demand for whale oil lamps and other products from the whale increased the pressure for many to pursue the whale at the risk of their lives and sometimes the lives of entire crews. Much of this danger was due to the fact that the process to catch a whale was incredibly difficult because of its enormous size and the primitive tools used to accomplish this task.

Lewis Temple Monument

In 1848, Lewis Temple (1800-1854), a local blacksmith, invented a *"toggle"* harpoon. This harpoon had a point that pivoted which made it more difficult for captured whales to escape once they were struck. It also allowed the whalers to pursue the whale at a greater distance, which made it possible for more men to survive the perilous voyage. This invention revolutionized the whaling industry. The sculptor of this monument, African American artist, James Toatley, based the likeness of Temple on a photograph of Temple's son, Lewis Temple, Jr.

10 NEW BEDFORD FREE PUBLIC LIBRARY
613 Pleasant St.

This library has collected the papers of Paul Cuffe, the influential African American sea merchant. During the period from 1800 until his death in 1817, Cuffe was the wealthiest and most influential African American in the United States. See more on Cuffe under Westport sites.

New Bedford Free Public Library

11 SITE: HENRY *"BOXCAR"* BROWN & JOSEPH RICKETSON HOUSE
UGRR Station
169 Union St.

Joseph Ricketson (NAA) harbored many fugitives from bondage in his home. Henry *"Boxcar"* Brown was one of those fugitves whose dramatic escape captured the attention of many Northerners. Henry Brown (1815-1875) lived in Richmond, VA, with his wife and three children. When his family was sold, Brown decided to escape bondage regardless of the personal danger. He developed a plan to ship himself to a free state with the aid of a cooperative white shopkeeper. Brown built a wooden crate with the help of a friend and then paid the shopkeeper $86 to ship his body to Philadelphia.

March 29, 1849
Brown's Journey: Richmond to Philadelphia
Distance   350 miles
Time   27 hours
Cost $86.00

Brown at 5'8" and 200 lbs., had to squeeze himself into the three foot long and two foot wide box which had only three air holes. His journey began on March 29th, 1849, and ended in Philadelphia, 27 hours and 350 miles later. Despite labels of *"This Side Up with Care,"* baggage handlers treated the package carelessly. At one point, workers turned the box upside down and Brown stayed in that upside down position for nearly two hours. That experience would have killed him but fortunately, two workers turned the box on its side in order to sit on it.

Illustration of Arrival of Boxcar Brown

Brown's dramatic escape made him a popular speaker on the anti-slavery circuit, but it also made him a prime target for fugitive bounty hunters. Brown's prominence forced him to stay on the move. He moved from Philadelphia to New York, and then from New York to New Bedford. In New Bedford, Henry Brown stayed with the Ricketson family in their house on this site. Brown eventually moved to England to escape the reach of the bounty hunters. There he continued to speak out against enslavement until after the Civil War.

Henry Brown

(12) ELISHA THORNTON, JR. HOUSE
UGRR Station
20 Seventh St.

One of the fugitives that Elisha Thornton (NAA) assisted was William Winters. Winters lived with the Thorntons during 1855 and 1856. Thornton's Quaker background encouraged his abolitionist views.

(13) NATHAN & MARY "POLLY" JOHNSON HOUSE FREDERICK & ANNA DOUGLASS

UGRR Station
21 Seventh St.
New Bedford
Historical Society
508-979-8828
www.nbhistoricalsociety.org

Nathan Johnson (1797–1880) and his wife, Mary *"Polly"* Johnson (1784–1871) achieved success as members of the African American business community in New Bedford. Married in 1819, in the next few decades, they became prosperous business owners and property owners; in fact, Polly Johnson's confectionary shop was renowned throughout New Bedford.

Nathan & Polly Johnson House

The Johnsons had the economic resources to be active participants on the Underground Railroad, and it was here, at their home, that Frederick Douglass (1818–1895) first stayed when he arrived in New Bedford on Sept. 17th, 1838, from his famous escape from bondage at the age of twenty-one. When Douglass arrived at the Johnson's home in New Bedford, he was Frederick Augustus Bailey. He allowed Nathan Johnson to select a new last name for him. Johnson selected the name Douglass after a character in the novel, *Lady of the Lake* by Sir Walter Scott, that he recently read.

Born in Maryland, the son of an enslaved mother and a white father, the first seven years of Douglass's life were hard, but at least he was able to live with his grandparents and an aunt. That familial security ended when at age eight, a ship carpenter in Baltimore hired Douglass as a helper. Douglass spent the next seven years of his life in Baltimore where he learned to read and write. Douglass also became familiar with the abolition movement while he worked on the docks.

After the stint in Baltimore, a farmer named Edward Covey (NAA) used Douglass as hired help. In both these arrangements, Thomas Auld (NAA), Douglass' enslaver, received all

Frederick Douglass, older

of his wages and Douglass received zero. For the next two years of his life, Douglass had to work around the clock and he was beaten daily by Covey. In his own words, Douglass was, *"broken in body, soul and spirit."*

Frederick Douglass vowed that he would escape, and in 1838, he succeeded. In New Bedford, Douglass became active in the abolitionist movement. On one occasion, William Lloyd Garrison (NAA), the publisher of the *"Liberator Newspaper,"* heard Douglass speak and encouraged him to become a public speaker on the abolitionist lecture circuit.

Letter to Thomas Auld, Douglass' Former Master On The Tenth Anniversary of Douglass' Escape from Bondage, September 3, 1848. Excerpt:

"Since I left you, I have had a rich experience. I have occupied stations which I never dreamed of when a slave. Three out of the ten years since I left you, I spent as a common laborer on the wharves of New Bedford, Massachusetts. It was there I earned my first free dollar. It was mine. I could spend it as I pleased. I could buy hams or herring with it, without asking any odds of any body. That was a precious dollar to me. You remember when I used to make seven or eight, or even nine dollars a week in Baltimore, you would take every cent of it from me every Saturday night, saying that I belonged to you, and my earnings also. I never liked this conduct on your part—to say the best, I thought it a little mean. I would not have served you so. But let that pass. I was a little awkward about counting money in the New England fashion when I first landed in New Bedford. ... at one time a man actually charged me with being a runaway, whereupon I was silly enough to become one by running away from him, for I was greatly afraid he might adopt measures to get me again into slavery, a condition I then dreaded more than death.

I soon, however, learned to count money, as well as to make it, and got on swimmingly. I married soon after leaving you: in fact, I was engaged to be married before I left you; and instead of finding my companion a burden, she was truly a helpmeet. She went to live at service, and I to work on the wharf, and though we toiled hard the first winter, we never lived more happily. After remaining in New Bedford for three years, I met with Wm. Lloyd Garrison, a person of whom you have possibly heard, as he is pretty generally known among slaveholders. He put it into my head that I might make myself serviceable to the cause of the slave by devoting a portion of my time to telling my own sorrows, and those of other slaves which had come under my observation. This was the commencement of a higher state of existence than any to which I had ever aspired. I was thrown into society the most pure, enlightened and benevolent that the country affords. Among these I have never forgotten you, but have invariably made you the topic of conversation—thus giving you all the notoriety I could do, I need not tell you that the opinion formed of you in these circles, is far from being favorable. They have little respect for your honesty, and less for your religion."

–Frederick Douglass

Anna Douglass

 14 **OLD FRIENDS MEETING HOUSE**
17-19 Seventh St.

Nathan and Mary Johnson, prosperous African American business and property owners in New Bedford, owned this Quaker Meeting House. It was the first public house of worship in New Bedford. Many African Americans became Quakers because the Quakers were very vocal in their views against slavery.

Old Friends Meetinghouse

15 HISTORIC BETHEL AME CHURCH
532 County St.
(County & Mill St.)

This is the current location of the Bethel AME Church of New Bedford. It was formerly the Christian Science Church.

Historic Bethel A.M.E. Church

16 SITE: LUCY FAGGINS "FREEDOM LAWSUIT" CAPT. JOSEPH CUNBAR HOUSE
26 South Sixth St.

The story of Lucy Faggins illustrated the united front of the African American community of New Bedford to protect one of their own. Lucy Faggins was originally enslaved in Richmond, Virginia. In 1841, a Southerner, Henry Ludlum (NAA), needed to come North for an extended period on business. Ludlum basically *"rented"* Lucy's services from the family in Virginia who enslaved her for the one year he was scheduled to remain North.

When Lucy arrived in New Bedford, she let it be known to the African American community that she was bound against her will. Ludlum attempted to isolate Lucy and limit her access to that community because they sought to free Lucy through legal channels on the basis that Massachusetts was a free state. Judge Wilde (NAA) of Boston issued a writ of habeas corpus for Lucy to appear in court where he promptly ruled that she was free from bondage.

17 DAVID & WILLIAM COFFIN HOUSE
34 South Sixth St.

David Coffin (NAA) was one of the wealthiest businessmen in 19th century New Bedford. His nephew, William Coffin (NAA) lived with his uncle's family at this residence. William was one of the most active abolitionists in the New Bedford community.

18 OUR LADY OF ASSUMPTION CHURCH
47 S. Sixth St.

The Cape Verdean Islands were a fertile source to supply sailors for American whale ships. Many Cape Verdeans relocated to New Bedford because of their participation in that industry. Eventually, the Cape Verdean immigrants established a vibrant community in the city.

432

This Roman Catholic Church served as the religious center for that Cape Verdean community in New Bedford.

Our Lady of Assumption Church Sign

Our Lady of Assumption Church

 **MARY ROTCH HOUSE**
46 South Sixth St.

Mary Rotch (NAA) was one of the many influential anti-slavery activists in New Bedford.

 WILLIAM ROTCH, JR. HOUSE
396 County St.

William Rotch, Jr. (NAA), was one of New Bedford's wealthiest businessmen in the early to mid-19th century. He was also an staunch abolitionist and anti-slavery activist. Rotch regularly employed people of color to work on his ships and at his house.

 WILLIAM ROTCH RODMAN HOUSE
UGRR Station
388 County St.

William Rotch Rodman (NAA) was another wealthy New Bedford businessman who also was deeply involved in abolitionist and anti-slavery activites. Rodman also employed known fugitives to work at his estate. One such person was John Jacobs, the brother of Harriet Jacobs of Cambridge. Harriet was well known for the seven years she spent in an attic to be near her two children in North Carolina.

 LOUM SNOW HOUSE
UGRR Station
465 County St.

Loum Snow (NAA), a wealthy citizen of New Bedford, was believed to have assisted many individuals including Nancy Carney, William Carney's wife, in their escape from slavery.

SECOND BAPTIST CHURCH
Middle St.

This building is the oldest structure built specifically for African American worship in New Bedford. Second Baptist Church originated from a break from the Third Christian Church in 1844 that was the result of philosophical differences.

Second Baptist fell victim to more internal disagreements, which resulted in another split in 1858 that formed Salem Baptist Church. In 1895, Second Baptist Church and Salem Baptist Church reunited again to form a single congregation under the banner of Salem Baptist Church at a different location.

 SITE: BETHEL AME CHURCH
Kempton Street

Bethel African Methodist Episcopal Church of New Bedford was formed in 1822 as the first AME Church in New England. Parishioners constructed the first church building in 1842. A fire destroyed it a decade later and the congregation rebuilt at this site. The New England AME held its first conference at this church in 1852. The church eventually relocated to County and Mill St. The city demolished the structure in 1972 to clear land for the Carney Memorial Academy.

 SGT. WILLIAM H. CARNEY HOUSE
128 Mill St.

Sergeant William H. Carney (1840–1908) was the first African American to receive a Congressional Medal of Honor for his bravery during the Union Army's attack on Fort Wagner in the Civil War. Carney served in the 54th Regiment of Massachusetts. At the Battle of Fort Wagner, Carney rescued the flag of the United States in the charge on the fort at the risk of his own safety. The Confederate troops enjoyed a strategic advantage in that assault and nearly 100 troops from the 54th were either killed or wounded that day. The movie, *"Glory"* which starred Denzel Washington, immortalized that battle.

Sgt. Carney

434

Carney's parents were enslaved in Norfolk, Virginia on the large plantation of Major Carney. At Major Carney's death, his will stipulated the emancipation of all those enslaved by him. Included in that group was Carney's father, William Carney, and his mother, Ann Dear Carney. The Carney's remained in Viginia after they were manumitted.

Education for African Americans, free or enslaved, was against the law in Virginia, so the Carneys sent their son to a secret school. Even though their family was free, life for all for African Americans in the South remained difficult and perilous. The perilous nature of this existence for free African Americans was due to the constant threat of kidnappers who sold those captured into slavery with unscrupulous slave dealers. These were the main reasons the Carneys relocated their family to the North to the busy port town of New Bedford, MA.

Sgt. Carney House

Full of youthful enthusiasm, William H. Carney enlisted in the 54th Regiment as soon as the unit was formed. For Carney and other free African Americans who joined the military, to fight in the Civil War was a moral imperative that they would die for, and many of them did. In the assault on Fort Wagner, despite the barrage of intense gunfire and despite the fact that he suffered from bullet wounds that nearly caused him to bleed to death, Carney held onto the American flag throughout the battle and did not allow it to touch the ground.

Sgt. Carney House Sign

"...On the 18th of July, 1863, about noon, we commenced to draw near this great fort, under a tremendous cannonading from the fleet, directed upon the fort. When we were within probably a thousand yards of the fort, we halted and lay flat upon the ground, waiting for the order to charge. The brave Colonel Shaw and his adjutant, in the company with General Strong, came forward and addressed the regiment with encouraging words. General Strong said to the regiment: "Men of Massachusetts, are you ready to take the fort tonight?" And the regiment spontaneously answered in the affirmative. Then followed three cheers for Colonel Shaw; three cheers for Governor Andrews of Massachusetts, and three cheers for General Strong.

"We were all ready for the charge, and the regiment started to its feet, the charge being fairly commenced. We had got but a short distance when we were opened upon with musketry, shell, grape and canister, which mowed down our men right and left. As the color-bearer became disabled, I threw away my gun and sized the colors, making my way to the head of the column; but before I reached there the line had descended the embankment into the ditch and was making its way upon Wagner itself. While going down the embankment one column was staunch and full. As we ascended the breastworks, the volleys of grapeshot which came from right and left, and of musketry in front, mowed them down as a scythe would do.

In less than twenty minutes I found myself alone, struggling upon the ramparts, while all around me were the dead and wounded, lying upon one another. Here I said, "I cannot go into the fort alone," and so I halted and knelt down, holding the flag in my hand. While there, the musket balls and grapeshot were flying all around me, and as they stuck, the sand would fly in my face. I knew my position was a critical one, and I began to watch to see if I would be left alone.

Discovering that the forces had renewed their attack farther to the right, and the enemy's attention being drawn thither, I turned (and) discovered a battalion of men coming towards me on the ramparts of Wagner. They proceeded until they were in front of me, and I raised my flag and started to join them, when, from the light of the cannon discharged on the fort, I saw they were (the) enemie (sic). I wound the colors round the staff and made my way down the parapet into the ditch, which was without water when I crossed it before, but was now filled with water that came up to my waist.

Out of the number that came up with me there was now no man moving erect, save myself, although they were not all dead, but wounded. In rising to see if I could determine my course to the rear, the bullet I now carry in my body came whizzing like a mosquito, and I was shot. Not being prostrated by the shot, I continued my course, yet had not gone far before I was struck by a second shot.

Soon after I saw a man coming towards me, and when within hailing distance I asked him who he was. He replied, "I belong to the 100th New York," and then inquired if I were wounded. Upon my replying in the affirmative, he came to my assistance and helped me to the rear. "Now then," he said, "let me take the colors and carry them for you." My reply was that I would not give them to any man unless he belonged to the 54th Regiment. So we pressed on, but did not go far before I was wounded in the head. We came at length within hailing distance of the rear guard, who caused us to halt, and upon asking us who we were, and finding I was wounded, took us to the rear through the guard. An officer came, and after taking my name and regiment, put us in the charge of the hospital corps, telling them to find my regiment. When we finally reached the latter the men cheered me and the flag. My reply was "Boys, I only did my duty. The old flag never touched the ground."

-- Sgt. William Carney

 ## MONUMENT TO BLACK VETERANS
Rockdale Ave. & Court St.

The City of New Bedford dedicated this monument in 1976 to honor all African Americans who served in the military.

Monument to Black Veterans

 ## UNITED HOUSE OF PRAYER
419 Kempton St.

The charismatic Bishop Charles M. Grace (1884-1960), popularly known as *"Daddy Grace,"* led more than 3 million followers during the 1930s and 1940s in his religious organization known as the United House of Prayer. This facility was the mother church for that organization. Born Marcelino

United House of Prayer

Manuel de Graco in the Cape Verdes Islands, Daddy Grace's family emigrated to New Bedford in 1902. Marcelino worked on various odd jobs before he started his ministry as a faith-healer in 1919.

Daddy Grace

Although Daddy Grace preached a philosophy of self-reliance, his church did an extensive amount of charitable work in the community such as the soup kitchens they operated for those in need. Those soup kitchens fed hundreds at a time when all Americans, and especially African Americans, suffered from the financial hardships imposed by the depression of the 1930s and its aftermath.

28 UNION BAPTIST CHURCH
109 Court St.

In 1895, Salem Baptist Church and Second Baptist Church merged to form Union Baptist Church, one of the oldest African American churches in New Bedford. The congregation included distinguished members of the community such as Sgt. William H. Carney. The National Register for Historic Places listed the building in 1975.

Union Baptist Church

29 REV. WILLIAM JACKSON HOUSE
UGRR Station
198 Smith St.

Rev. William Jackson (b.1818) dedicated his life to uplift his race in whatever capacity he could. Rev. Jackson pastored Second Baptist Church in 1851. He next founded Salem Baptist Church in 1855. Prior to the Civil War, Jackson used his house to harbor fugitives from slavery.

During the Civil War, he served as Chaplain of the Massachusetts 54th Regiment and later, as Chaplain of the Massachusetts 55th Regiment. Rev.

William Jackson was one of the first African American commissioned officers.

Rev. William Jackson Homestead

 MARTHA & HENRY ONLEY HOUSE

UGRR Station
147 Smith St., corner of Cedar St.

The Onley family actively organized the African American civic and cultural community in New Bedford in the mid-1800s. Prior to the Civil War, the family harbored fugitives from slavery in their house. They also help found Salem Baptist Church. After the war, they organized the Martha Briggs Literary

Onley Residence

Society, named after the first African American graduate of New Bedford High School, Martha Briggs.

Mary Hudson Onley, granddaughter of Martha and Henry Olney, was the first African American graduate of Bridgewater State University, in 1912. The College established the *Mary Hudson Olney Achievement Award* in 1997 to honor her.

Mary Hudson Onley

 JAMES & ANNA REED HOUSE
172 Arnold St.

James and Anna Reed worked together to visually document New Bedford's African American history from 1880 to 1914. James took the photographs and Anna colored and hand-tinted the images. The Reed family occupied this octagon house, one of only two in the city, for over 100 years until 1991.

32 SITE: MARTHA BAILEY BRIGGS HOUSE
29 Allen St.

Martha Bailey Briggs (1838-1889), an educational pioneer, was the first African American to graduate from New Bedford High School. Briggs set up a part-time school in her parent's home on Allen St. for African Americans who were recent arrivals to the city.

Martha Bailey Briggs

Briggs eventually relocated to Washington, D.C. where she was principal of the Miner Normal School, the precursor to the Miner Teacher's College of Howard University. The District of Colombia named two elementary schools after her to honor her leadership in education.

33 RURAL CEMETERY
149 Dartmouth St.

Some of the prominent African American citizens of New Bedford buried here included Lewis Temple, Nathaniel Johnson, Amos Haskins, William Bush, and Martha Bailey Briggs. Abolitionist, Daniel Drayton (NAA) was also buried here.

Rural Cemetery

Drayton (1802–1857) lived in Philadelphia and he sailed ships between Savannah, GA and St. John's, New Brunswick. This work sensitized him to the efforts of many individuals who constantly attempted to escape slavery. In 1847, he finally successfully assisted a family in their efforts.

Captain Drayton's most ambitious abolitionist effort was his participation in the attempted escape of 77 individuals on April 18th, 1848, onboard the ship, *"The Pearl"* in the Chesapeake Bay harbor in Washington D.C. The leaders of the escape intended to sail 225 nautical miles south along the Potomac River and north along the Chesapeake Bay and the Delaware River until they reached New Jersey, a free state. A windstorm forced the group to delay their journey in Chesapeake Bay. Betrayal and the realization by many wealthy whites in D.C. that many of their enslaved staff were absent led to a search and the ship was discovered in Chesapeake Bay by a police boat.

Three days of pro-slavery riots erupted in D.C. at the discovery. All of the fugitives were sent to New Orleans to be sold at the slave market as punishment. The incident influenced Harriet Beecher Stowe to write, *Uncle Tom's Cabin*. It also influenced Congress to pass the Compromise of 1850 which strengthened the ability of U.S. marshals to capture fugitives. Drayton and an accomplice, Edmund Sayres (NAA) were sentenced for 77 counts for each individual they tried to assist and transport in that escape.

Daniel Drayton

Drayton was released in 1852 because of a successful petition for his pardon. The four years Drayton served took a toil on his morale and health. He made several trips to New Bedford as a public speaker in an effort to raise money to support his destitute family. Those efforts were not successful and in 1857 he committed suicide in a New Bedford hotel.

 ## LEWIS TEMPLE HOUSE
54 Bedford St.

A local blacksmith, Lewis Temple (1800–1854) invented a *"toggle"* harpoon in 1848. That invention made it more difficult for captured whales to escape, and it increased the profit and safety of the entire industry. Temple arrived in New Bedford from Virginia in 1829. He married Mary Clark of Baltimore, shortly after he arrived in the whaling capital. The couple settled in this house where they raised their family.

Lewis Temple House

 ## WILLIAM PIPER HOUSE
58 Bedford St.

William Piper was a fugitive from slavery who settled in New Bedford around 1825. Piper was employed by the businessman, William Rotch Rodman (NAA) for most of the time he lived in New Bedford. The house remained in Piper's family until 1870.

CUFFE LAWTON HOUSE
62 Bedford St.

Cuffe Lawton (b. 1789) relocated to New Bedford from Newport, Rhode Island around 1826. In Rhode Island, Lawton was active in several mutual aid and anti-slavery groups. In New Bedford, he most likely continued those activities while employed as a laborer in the whaling industry. He purchased his home in 1834.

 THOMAS THOMPSON HOUSE
61 Bedford St.

Thomas Thompson was a tailor in New Bedford during the 1850s. He lived at this house with his family and two white families. This was at a time when segregation of living accommodations was the norm. The vibrant New Bedford maritime economy encouraged a liberal attitude that did not exist in other places towards conservative social conventions.

 GEORGE FLETCHER HOUSE
114 Seventh St.

George Fletcher was a fugitive from slavery in Washington, D.C. He and his brother, David, worked as laborers and saved enough money to open an oyster café on Union St. George purchased this house in 1844.

 WILLIAM HENRY JOHNSON HOUSE
46 Wing St.

William Henry Johnson was one of the many fugitives who made New Bedford home. Johnson escaped slavery in Virginia around 1830. He worked as a laborer in various New Bedford businesses and one job as a janitor in a law firm feed his interest in the law. He studied with a local attorney in his spare time to achieve his dream to become a licensed attorney. Johnson was a fervent anti-slavery acitivst.

 CAPE VERDEAN AMERICAN VETERANS MEMORIAL SQUARE
County and Washington St.

In 1976, New Bedford constructed this monument to honor all Cape Verdeans who served in the United States military.

Memorial Sq. for Cape Verdean Veterans

MONTE PLAYGROUND

Acushnet Ave. and Manuel Costa Way (formerly Cannon St.)

In 1935, Joseph P. Monte was the first Cape Verdean to receive a Purple Heart. He served in the first World War.

Manuel Costa (1918–1992), of Cape Verdean descent, was a popular New Bedford activist who mentored many youth in the community.

 ## ANDREW ROBESON (NAA) HOUSES

UGRR Station
34 William St. &
47R North Second St.

 ## WILLIAM ROTCH (NAA) HOUSE

UGRR Station
Mariner's Home, Johnny Cake Hill, 33 William St.

 ## LOCAL RESOURCES

Black Heritage Train of New Bedford
www.newbedfordhistory.org/history

Underground Railroad Walking Tour
www.nbhistoricalsociety.org

PLYMOUTH

 ## PARTING WAYS, NEW GUINEA SETTLEMENT

Plymouth Rd (Route 80) and Carver Rd

Parting Ways, New Guinea
1st known settlement in U.S. founded by freed African Americans
• Cato Howe
• Plato Turner
• Prince Goodwin
• Quamony Quash

In 1792, the town of Plymouth awarded to Cato Howe (d. 1824) 93 acres of land located on Plymouth Road, now Route 80, in West Plymouth, near the Kingston border. That land was a reward for his heroic service from 1775 until 1780 in the American Revolution. Howe also received a pension for his war service. That service included a stint at Valley Forge.

Howe invited three other African American war veterans, Plato Turner, Prince Goodwin and Quamony Quash, to join him. The group brought their families and they cleared and lived on the land. They named the settlement, Parting Ways, New Guinea Settlement. The name, Parting Ways, implied a clear desire for separation. That name and the fact that the land was located so far out of town suggested that the relationship between the African Americans and the local community was not totally amicable.

Parting Ways Cemetery

James Thurston Burr

Howe was a free man prior to his war service. Plato Turner (d. 1819) obtained his freedom before he enlisted. Turner served from 1776 to 1781. He also received a lifetime pension for his service. Quamony Quash (d. 1833) served in the regiment of his enslaver from 1775 until 1782. He received his freedom and a pension for his service. Prince Goodwin (d. 1819) served in the summer of 1777. He did not receive a pension nor his freedom for his service.

The poor soil and harsh conditions caused the settlers to have a brutal life. In 1824, when Cato Howe died, Plymouth allowed the families to continue to live at Parting Ways rather than sell the land. James Thurston Burr, Plato Turner's grandson, moved there in 1861 and he remained at the settlement until his house burned down in 1908. Burr was the last person to live on the settlement. He lived in a house

that dated from the time of the initial settlement of 1792. The foundation of his house was the site of archeological research started by Prof. Deetz (NAA) of Brown University in 1976. Based on the outlines of the foundation, the original structure was very similiar to Yoruba architecture from West Africa in its plan and layout.

The four patriots, Howe, Turner, Goodwin, and Quash, were buried in the Parting Ways Cemetery on the site. The National Register of Historic Places listed the site of the Turner Burr House and the Cemetery on its register. In 2009, the town of Plymouth set aside 27 acres at the site for a museum to be dedicated to study the lives of colonial African Americans.

1749 COURTHOUSE MUSEUM
11 Lincoln St. in Town Sq.
www.pilgrimhallmuseum.org

This museum is the oldest wooden court structure in the United States that still exists. It contains artifacts from the Parting Ways Settlement.

 BRITON HAMMOND GEN. JOHN WINSLOW HOUSE
7 North St.

In 1760, Hammond published the first African American narrative, *A Narrative of the UnCommon Sufferings and Surprising Deliverance of Briton Hammond....* It described his adventures when he was captured at sea and the many times he escaped. Hammond was in service to the Winslow (NAA) family who had residences in Plymouth and Marshfield. See more on Hammond under Marshfield sites.

 BETHEL AME CHURCH
6 Sever St.

In 1855, when the population of Plymouth was 6,846, there were just 138 African American citizens in the town. They formed an African Methodist Episcopal Church in 1866 and purchased this property for $1,000. The original trustees of the church were property owners and prominent members of the community: Edward Giles, Charles B. Allen, Amos Goodwin, William H. Gray, Allen Mellencourt, Aaron C. Joseph, and George Lyle.

Bethel AME Church

 CAESAR V. WATSON "FREEDOM LAWSUIT"
Site Unknown

In 1771, Caesar filed a *"Freedom Lawsuit"* in Plymouth against Elkanah Watson. At some point, Caesar entered the service of a French Navy Captain, the Chevalier de Drucour, although Caesar was originally enslaved by Watson. Drucour manumitted Caesar on July 1st, 1758, and gave him documentation to prove his status. Caesar returned to Plymouth and re-entered the service of Watson. There was confusion about Caesar's status and after 12 years, he brought this suit against Watson. Caesar won his lawsuit. Watson engaged John Adams in his appeal but the appeal was also not successful.

6 KWASHI KWANDI
LeBaron Alley

Kwashi Kwandi, a kidnapped child in 18th century Plymouth, displayed a high level of self-determination while he was still an adolescent. He refused to accept a new given name, Julius Ceasar, in lieu of his birth name, Kwashi Kwandi. Kwashi meant a male child born on Sunday in the language of the Akan tribe of Ghana, West Africa. The Plymouth family punished Kwashi severely in attempts to destroy his will but he consistently refused to answer to the new name. The family eventually acknowledged that he would never accept the new name and Kwashi Kwandi he remained until his death.

7 GEORGE & SHERRY LYLE
UGRR Station
Court St.

George was a fugitive from slavery himself in the mid-1800s. Once he settled in Plymouth, he used his house as an Underground Railroad Station. Lyle was one of the original Trustees of the Bethel AME Church.

8 NATHANIEL MORTON (NAA) HOUSE
UGRR Station
Site Unknown

9 LOCAL RESOURCES:
Plymouth Antiquarian Society
126 Water St.
508-746-0012
www.plymouthantiquarian society.org

The Plymouth Antiquarian Society holds Black History Walking Tours several times each year. Contact the society for exact times.

446

CAPE COD AND THE ISLANDS

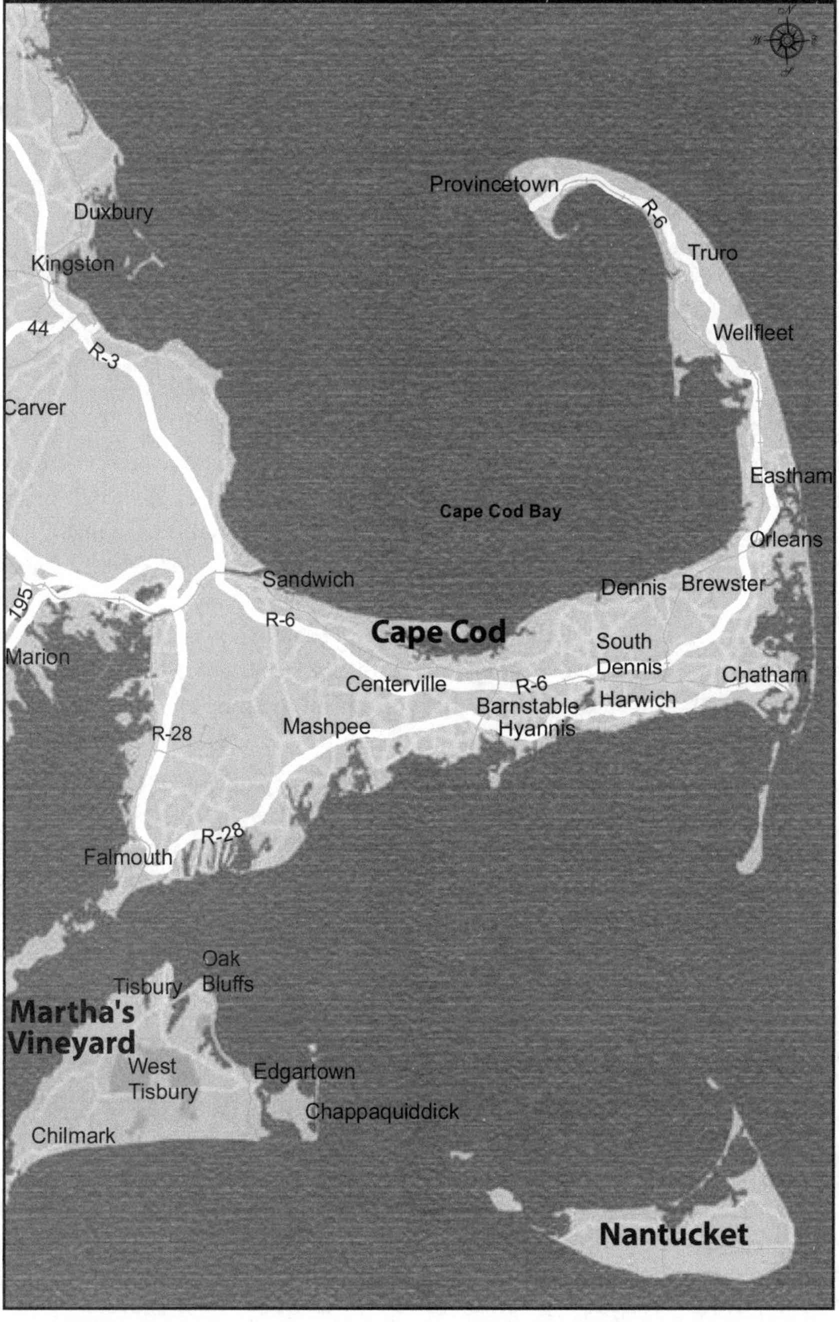

HARWICH

 CAPTAIN JONATHAN WALKER "THE MAN WITH THE BRANDED HAND"
Harwich Historical Society
80 Parallel St.
508-432-8089
www.harwichhistorical
society.org

Captain Jonathan Walker

Jonathan Walker (1799 - 1878) (NAA), a native of Harwich, was influenced to participate in the abolitionist movement because of his family's involvement. Early anti-slavery activity took him to Mexico in 1835 to assist in the settlement of fugitives there. Walker subsequently relocated his family to Pensacola, FL, where he continued his abolitionist activities.

In 1844, Walker was captured in an attempt to assist seven fugitives in their escape to the Bahamas. That capture led to a conviction and a four part sentence: one hour in a public pillory where he was subjected to all manner of public harassment, both verbal and physical; an eleven month prison sentence; payment of court costs and a $600.00 fine; and lastly, his right palm was branded with the initials, "SS" (for "Slave Stealer"), by a U.S. marshal.

It was the last part of that sentence which led to Walker's notoriety. His subsequent engagements to speak pub-licly in New England always ended dramatically. He held up his hand for the audience to view and stated that it was, *"the seal, the coat of arms of the United States."* Walker's memoir, *Trial and Imprisonment of Jonathan Walker,* shared the experience for a larger audience. A poem written by John Greenleaf Whittier, *"The Branded Hand,"* added to Walker's popularity. A photograph of the branded hand is in the collection of the Massachusetts Historical Society. A plaque to honor Walker was installed in the Harwich Historical Society building.

The Branded Hand

"The Branded Hand"

By John Greenleaf Whittier, excerpt:

"Welcome home again, brave seaman!
with thy thoughtful brow and gray,
And the old heroic spirit of our earlier,
better day;
With that front of calm endurance,
on whose steady nerve in vain
Pressed the iron of the prison,
smote the fiery shafts of pain.
Is the tyrant's brand upon thee?
Did the brutal cravens aim
To make God's truth thy falsehood,
His holiest work thy shame?
When, all blood-quenched, from the
torture the iron was withdrawn,
How laughed their evil angel!
the baffled fools to scorn!

…

Then lift that manly right-hand,
bold ploughman of the wave!
It branded palm shall prophesy,
"Salvation to the Slave!"
Hold up its fire-wrought language,
that whoso reads may feel
His heart swell strong within him,
his sinews change to steel."

CENTERVILLE

 ## CAPTAIN AUSTIN BEARSE (NAA)

Site unknown

Capt. Bearse (1808–1881) (NAA) was a dedicated member of the Boston Vigilance Society. He operated two boats that he utilized to pick up fugitives in Boston harbor after they managed to escape as ship stowaways. It was his task to deliver funds to various individuals to defray the expenses to assist fugitives to the next station, or to feed, and clothe them. He also posted notices, distributed flyers, and collected and distributed donations of clothes.

Bearse came to his abolitionist work because of his early work on ships that traded with Southern plantations in rice, cotton, and enslaved individuals. The experiences that influenced him the most were the many suicides he witnessed when families were broken up. Bearse documented his experiences in a memoir, *Reminiscences of Fugitive-Slave Law Days in Boston*.

 ## SOLDIER'S MONUMENT

Main St. and Park Ave.

Centerville erected this monument in honor of it citizens who served during the Civil War. The town suffered 31 casualties during that engagement.

MASHPEE

① MASHPEE WAMPANOAG TRIBAL MUSEUM
414 Main St.
508-477-9339

James Mye, Wampanoag

The Wampanoags lived in Southeastern Massachusetts and on the Cape when the Europeans first arrived in the early 17th century. The history of members of the Wampanoags and other indigenous tribes was intertwined with the history of African Americans in Massachusetts due to the high level of inter-marriage that occurred between the two groups. This museum structure was originally the home of Timothy Pocknet, a Wampanoag tribal member. Pocknet's second wife was Leah Lewis Queppish. Queppish's father was a fugitive from slavery. The level of inter-marriage resulted in descendents who possessed pronounced African physical features. This photograph of James Mye, a Wampanoag tribal member, indicated the type of physical traits shared between the two groups.

Wampanoag Museum

The initial contact with Europeans in the early 17th century, introduced a bacterial infection into the Wampanoag Tribe that killed many of the elderly and the very young of the population. The devastation from that infection set the stage for distrust of the Europeans and tension developed between the two groups. Chief Massasoit (1580-1662), the leader of the Wampanoag Confederacy and a skilled diplomat, negotiated peace treaties with the Massachusetts Bay Colony that lasted nearly half a century. This stability allowed the settlers to gain a critical foothold in their new settlements.

Shortly after Massasoit's death, peace began to unravel and the unrest evolved into what was known as, *"King Phillip's War."* Massasoit's second son, Metacomet, became leader of the Confederacy after the death of his brother, Wamsutta, whom Metacomet believed the English murdered. The English gave Metacomet the name, King Phillip, hence the name of the rebellion,

King Phillip's War. Metacomet's goal was to retake land that the settlers controlled. The indigenous tribes conducted guerilla raids on the settlements that shocked the settlers because of their brutality.

King Phillip's War had begun to deal a blow to the colonists who thought that they could freely develop the land when the English came to the aid of the settlers. That intervention altered the outcome of the rebellion and history. Metacomet's capture in 1676 ended the war. The English quartered and beheaded Chief Metacomet at his execution. To behead a political leader was a symbolic gesture with spiritual connotations. A head separated from the body in the physical world meant that the soul would never find peace in the after-world. It was the ultimate insult to inflict upon a leader and its purpose was to intimidate his followers into submission. The English killed forty percent of the Wampanoag Tribe during the prolonged war. The survivors were sold into slavery and the rest were corralled onto a reservation in Mashpee.

Wampanoag Hut

2 AFRICAN AMERICAN PARTICIPATION IN THE AMERICAN REVOLUTION AND THE CIVIL WAR

Freed Africans intermarried regularly into the Wampanoag Tribe. By the time of the American Revolution, the town contained three hundred and twenty-seven people of African descent. Fourteen of those were married to Native American women. Twenty-four men from the Wampanoag community enlisted in the American Revolution:

American Revolution Enlistees:

Francis Webquish	Samuel Moses
Demps Squibs	Mark Negro
Tom Caesar	Joseph Asher
James Keeter	Joseph Keeter
Daniel Pocknit	Job Rimmon
George Shaun	Castel Barnet
Joshua Pognit	James Rimmon
David Hatch	James No Cake
Abel Hoswitt	Elisha Keeter
John Pearce	John Mapix
Amos Babcock	Hosea Pognit
Church Ashur	Gideon Tumpum

(Colored Patriots of the American Revolution by William Nell

At the start of the Civil War, twenty-seven men from this community enlisted in Barnstable County's required regiment of four hundred troops. At the end of the war, over seventy-three people of African and Native American descent had left widows among the African and Native American community of Mashpee.

Town of Nantucket Map

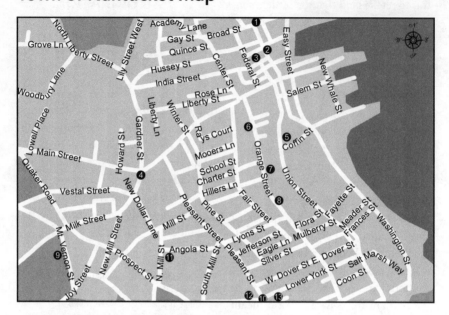

NANTUCKET

① ABSALOM BOSTON AND WHALING MUSEUM
15 Broad St.

Exhibits about African Americans who contributed to the whaling industry in Nantucket have been included in this museum. One of the lives explored was that of Absalom Boston. Absalom Boston (1785–1855) was a *"Black Jack,"* a name used to identify an African American ship captain.

Absalom Boston

NANTUCKET ISLAND

When the English established Nantucket and other coastal towns in Massachusetts during the late 1600s, members of the Quaker sect were the predominant settlers of those areas. Their religious opposition to slavery was well established by the time that African Americans were drawn to Nantucket to participate in the strong economy established by the whaling industry during 1760 to 1875.

The African American community in this early period was small and tightly knit, 275 people out of a total population of 7,300. They developed businesses and institutions to help the community achieve progress. The neighborhood known as *"New Guinea,"* was the center of that community. The colonists gave that name to predominantly African American neighborhoods throughout New England during the colonial period, to reflect the African heritage of the residents.

Boston achieved fame in 1822 when he engaged an all-African American crew on his whaling ship, *"Industry,"* for an expedition that lasted six months. The voyage was a success and Captain Boston returned with seventy barrels of oil and, even more importantly, he experienced no loss of life. Captain Boston's continued success allowed him to expand his entrepreneurial endeavors. Boston's leadership established many civic initiatives in his community.

Whaling Museum

2 DREAMLAND THEATER
17 South Water Street

Built in 1831, this structure originally was a Quaker Meeting House. It hosted abolitionist speakers when they visited the island. Subsequent uses, and several moves later, it evolved into a hat factory, a skating rink, and part of the Nantucket Hotel. Today, it enjoys renewed popularity as the Dreamland Movie Theater.

3 NANTUCKET ATHENAEUM
Federal and India Street

The Nantucket Athenaeum was the public library for the community. In 1834, the town relocated it to a building that was formerly the Universalist Church. The Athenaeum was a popular venue for public speakers especially abolitionists. Based on the powerful testimony and delivery of the first public speech of Frederick Douglass, which was delivered here, William Lloyd Garrison (NAA) convinced him to join the Massachusetts Anti-Slavery Society as a speaker.

August 12, 1841 Frederick Douglass gave his 1st public speech

Athenaeum

In August of 1842, another historic event took place at the Athenaeum, a six-day anti-slavery convention. That convention evolved into a series of events that polarized the town, the *"Brotherhood of Thieves Riots."* Scheduled to speak at the convention were many anti-slavery luminaries such as Frederick Douglass, William Lloyd Garrison, and Charles Lenox Remond. Remond proposed that the way to fight slavery was with rifles, and he advocated for the dissolution of the Union.

The speaker who literally, *"brought the house down,"* was Stephen S. Foster (NAA). Foster trained in the ministry but left that profession to become an anti-slavery orator. He strongly felt that the Christian clergy encouraged and condoned slavery, a belief shared by many anti-slavery activists, both white and black.

Early during the convention's proceedings, Foster delivered a fiery speech that equated Southern and Northern Christian clergy with a, *"brotherhood of thieves,"* who encouraged slavery because they directly benefited from that system. News of his speech spread across the island like wildfire, stoked by newspaper quotes of his specific reference to the clergy as, *"Pimps of Satan."*

After the speech was published, unruly mobs gathered around the Athenaeum, and the management asked the convention to move elsewhere. The convention moved around for the next three days, but each day, and at each subsequent venue, rioters disrupted the convention and injured several individuals. Finally, the town forced the organizers to end the convention early. Local abolitionist, Nathaniel Barney (NAA) encouraged Foster to publish his speech a year later.

The Brotherhood of Thieves: A True Picture of the American Church and Clergy: A Letter to Nathaniel Barney of Nantucket by Stephen S. Foster, excerpt:

"...In exposing the deep and fathomless abominations of these pious thieves, who gain their livelihood by preaching sermons and stealing babies, I am not at liberty to yield to any intimidations, however imposing the source....

...The fact that my charges against the religious sects of our country were met with violence and outrage, instead of sound arguments and invalidating testimony, is strong presumptive evidence of their truth....

...I said at your meeting...,that the American church and clergy, as a body, were thieves, adulterers, man-stealers, pirates, and murderers; that the Methodist Episcopal Church was more corrupt and profligate than any house of ill-fame in the city of New York; that the Southern Ministers of that body were desirous of perpetuating slavery for the purpose of supplying themselves with concubines from among its hapless victims; and that many of our clergymen were guilty of enormities that would disgrace an Algerine pirate!!!

These sentiments called forth a burst of holy indignation from the pious and dutiful advocates of the church and clergy, which overwhelmed the meeting with repeated shows of stones and rotten eggs,...

...This violence and outrage on the part of the church were, no doubt, committed to the glory of God and the honor of religion, although the connection between rotten eggs and holiness of heart is not very obvious. It is, I suppose, one

of the mysteries of religion which laymen cannot understand without the aid of clergy; and I therefore suggest that the pulpit make it a subject of Sunday discourse. But are not the charges here alleged against the clergy strictly and literally true? I maintain that they are true to the very letter; that the clergy and their adherents are literally, and beyond all controversy, a "brotherhood of thieves;..."

-- Stephen S. Foster

4 PRINCE BOSTON V. SWAIN FAMILY "WAGE LAWSUIT" "FREEDOM LAWSUIT"

Site: Old Courthouse Monument Sq., Milk and Main Street

The Old Courthouse was the place where Absalom Boston's uncle, Prince Boston, successfully made legal challenges to the status quo about the rights of enslaved individuals, and he challedged that system not once but twice. The Swain family of Nantucket, wealthy merchants, enslaved Prince Boston's parents, Boston and Maria. The parents and their youngest son, Peter, were freed in 1760, but each of their other six children, including Seneca Boston, Absalom's father, and Prince Boston, his uncle, had to remain enslaved until the age of 28.

The law allowed enslavers to appropriate the earnings of the individuals whom they enslaved. After Prince Boston worked for three and one-half months on a ship, the "Friendship," in 1770, John Swain, one of the Swain sons, tried to appropriate his wages

when the ship returned to Nantucket. Prince Boston took his case to the Court of Common Pleas in Nantucket and won the first lawsuit for lost wages brought by an African American.

Monument Sq.

This victory inspired him to pursue another lawsuit in 1772, this time for freedom from slavery. Prince Boston filed this *"Freedom Lawsuit"* even though he would have obtained his freedom in 1778, when he reached the age of 28, per the stipulations of William Swain's will. The success of this second lawsuit effectively ended slavery on Nantucket. That spirit of defiance continued throughout the Boston family.

5 MARY ELLEN PLEASANT & SITE: GRANDMA HUSSEY'S STORE
Somewhere on Union Street

Born in Virginia, Mary Ellen Pleasant (1814–1904) arrived on Nantucket in 1827 as a bonded servant, to the Hussey (NAA) family, active abolitionists and prominent shopkeepers on Nantucket. Grandma Hussey, the family matriarch, ran a retail store somewhere on Union St. While Pleasant worked there, she developed her own entrepreneurial skills. During that time, Pleasant became great friends with Phoebe Hussey Garner (NAA), a granddaughter of the Hussey family. Phoebe introduced Pleasant to many of those active in the abolition movement on Nantucket.

In 1852, Mary Pleasant moved to Boston where she entered into a relationship that allowed her to acquire the capital to move west. Pleasant relocated to San Francisco where she acquired a fortune with businesses that catered

to the gold rush community. Pleasant used that fortune to finance anti-slavery activities. In San Francisco, Pleasant became known as the, *"mother of human rights,"* because of her numerous lawsuits against discrimination.

 6 UNITARIAN CHURCH
11 Orange Street

Absalom Boston (1785-1855) married his first wife here in 1814. This church also hosted lectures by Frederick Douglass in 1885, and Booker T. Washington in 1904.

Unitarian Church

Mary Ellen Pleasant

 7 SHERBURNE HOUSE
30 Orange Street

Frederick Douglass and his wife, Anna, stayed with the Sherburnes (NAA) when they visited the island in 1885.

8 ANNA GARDNER HOUSE
40 Orange Street

Oliver and Hannah Gardner (NAA), members of the Quaker Community of Nantucket and active abolitionists, sheltered Arthur Cooper in 1822 when he fled slavery in Virginia. Their daughter, Anna Gardner (1816-1901), taught at the African Meeting House School, a part of the Nantucket Public Schools, from 1836 to 1840.

Gardner House

Anna Gardner, organizer of Nantucket's first Anti-Slavery Convention in 1841, tutored Eunice Ross, a local African American teenager, to take the entrance exams for the local high school. Ross passed the exams in 1840, but the school board denied her admission to the high school. Anna Gardner resigned her post at the African School in protest. After the Civil War, Gardner went to North Carolina to teach the newly emancipated citizens.

9 COLORED CEMETERY
Off Prospect Street

Many African Americans significant to the history of Nantucket were buried in the Colored Cemetery. Some of those individuals include Arthur Cooper (1789-1853), the fugitive from bondage whose escape galvanized the town; James Crawford (d. 1888), the minister of African Baptist Church; and Eunice Ross (1824-1895), whose fight to enter Nantucket High School eventually led the way to school desegregation across the state.

10 FIVE CORNERS
Intersection of York St., Pleasant St., Atlantic Ave., & West York St.

The African American community of New Guinea in Nantucket centered around this intersection of York St., Pleasant St., West York St., and Atlantic Ave. Absalom Boston, entrepreneur and civic leader, owned at least three houses in this area, and several businesses.

This area was also the base of operations of Edward J. Pompey, a prominent civil rights activist of Nantucket and the local distributor of the abolitionist press. Pompey and Boston led the charge to integrate public schools on Nantucket Island in the early 1840s.

ARTHUR COOPER HOUSE

Somewhere on Angola Street

Arthur Cooper (1789-1859) pastored the Zion Church in Nantucket, an AME congregation. In 1820, after he escaped slavery in Virginia with his free wife, Mary, and their children, Cooper settled his family in Nantucket. In 1822, when a bounty hunter located Cooper and attempted to take him and his family by force back into bondage, the local African American community united with local Quakers and surrounded the house. The bounty hunter was forced to flee.

Oliver and Hannah Gardner provided shelter in their home for the Coopers after the bounty hunter fled to get help. The bounty hunter appealed to the local magistrate, but that official refused to intervene and the Coopers were able to remain in Nantucket.

Arthur Cooper

 ## AFRICAN MEETING HOUSE
AKA: AFRICAN BAPTIST CHURCH
AKA: PLEASANT BAPTIST CHURCH

29 York Street
Black Heritage Trail of Nantucket
www.afroammseum.org/bhtn

The African Meeting House served as the hub of the African American community on Nantucket in the 1800s. The Trustees of the African Baptist Society built this structure in 1824 with funds donated by prominent members of the African American community, notably Absalom Boston. It functioned as a church, school, and general meeting place. The church held its services in the building and the children of New Guinea were educated here when Nantucket opened public schools in 1825.

African Meeting House

Abolitionist and fugitive from slavery, Rev. James Crawford, pastored the African Baptist Church after he relocated to Nantucket in 1848 with his wife Ann. Rev Crawford was instrumental in the successful efforts to secure the freedom of two enslaved women. In 1857, Diana Williams Read (1815–1860) of Charleston, SC, and her daughter, Cornelia Williams Read of Wilmington, NC, were about to be sold when Ann Crawford, Rev. Crawford's wife, and Diana Williams Read's sister learned about the sale.

Diana arrived in Nantucket shortly after Crawford raised the $700 to secure her freedom. Another $1,000 was raised to secure Cornelia's freedom. Crawford, who possessed a light complexion and blue eyes, travelled to North Carolina to retrieve her. Cornelia eventually married William B. Gould, another fugitive who dramatically escaped slavery on the Cape Fear River in Wilmington, North Carolina on September 21st, 1862. See more on Gould under Dedham sites.

Rev. James Crawford

The school was also part of Nantucket history. In 1840, when Eunice Ross aged out of the African Meeting House School, her teacher, Anna Gardner (NAA), the daughter of island abolitionists, Oliver and Hannah Gardner (NAA), tutored her to take the entrance exam for Nantucket High, the one public high school on the island. Ross passed the exam and requested admission to the high school, but the school board denied her admission. Anna Gardner quit her position as teacher at the African Meeting House School in protest.

The issue of school integration polarized the island community. Elections for the School Board in 1842 reflected this heated issue. Six New Guinea residents were among the fifty-nine people who ran for the thirteen positions. One of those six, Edward J. Pompey, the distributor of the abolitionist press on the island, received over fifty votes, but that was not enough to win election. William Starbuck (NAA), the foremost segregationist on the ballot, received over 600 votes. During this time, Absalom Boston filed a lawsuit on behalf of Eunice Ross and his daughter, Phoebe Ann Boston, who also passed the entrance exam, to integrate the schools.

Several individuals and groups sent various petitions to the State Legislature to address the issue. The petitions advocated both sides of the issue, to integrate the system, and to maintain the status quo. Eunice Ross sent in a petition that stated that, despite the fact that she qualified for admission based on the rigorous entrance exam, the school board still denied her admission to the high school. In 1845, the Massachusetts State Legislature passed House Bill No. 45, which provided for a public education for all students through high school.

Despite this victory, Nantucket schools remained segregated until the voters ousted the School Board and voted in a board more amenable to integration. In 1846, the new School Board finally admitted Eunice Ross and Phoebe Ann Boston to Nantucket High School. The School Board closed the African Meeting House School that year and those students entered the other public schools on the island.

The Museum of African American History in Boston acquired this structure in 1989. The musem subsequently renovated it as the Nantucket branch of the museum.

Seneca Boston House

African American entrepreneur, Florence Higginbotham purchased the house in 1920. In 1933, she purchased the African Meeting House next door in order to preserve its legacy. The Museum of African American History purchased both properties in 1989, and they have restored both.

Florence Higginbotham

 ### 13 SENECA BOSTON & THANKFUL MICAH HOUSE
27 York Street

Seneca Boston and Thankful Micah purchased this house in 1774. They were the parents of Absalom Boston, the first African American ship captain to operate a ship with an all-Black crew during this time. Absalom Boston (1785–1855) spent his childhood in this home.

14 LOCAL RESOURCES
Nantucket Historical Association
15 Broad St.
508-224-1894
www.nha.org

Martha's Vineyard map

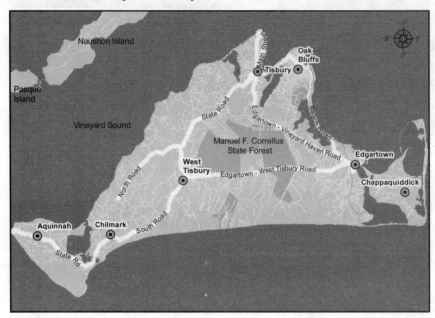

Town of Oak Bluffs Map

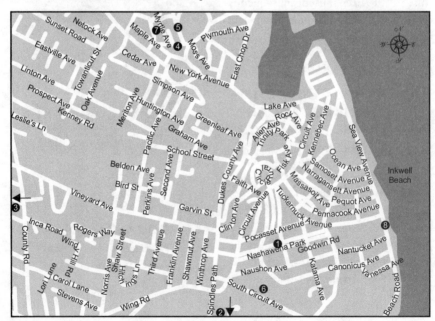

MARTHA'S VINEYARD

Colonists settled Martha's Vineyard around 1640. The vineyard part of the name was due to the wild grapes which dominated the original flora of the island. The early population of approximately 3,000 Wampanoags who lived throughout the island was decimated to about 350 by 1750 because of the diseases brought to the island by the European settlers and the wars waged to protect the native land against the intruders.

By the 1820s, Martha's Vineyard was the epicenter of the whaling industry. That economic boom resulted in elegant mansions that were built all over the island. When the whaling industry began to fade around 1870, the tourist industry was poised to take its place. Today, tourism is the dominant industry on Martha's Vineyard.

Most of the African American heritage sites in this section were based on sites documented by a group, co-founded by Elaine Cawley Weintraub and Carrie Camillo Tankard, that established the official African American Heritage Trail of Martha's Vineyard. Exploration of the trail is accessible through self-guided tours or through tours escorted by members of the Heritage Trail group. See local resources section.

Born in Washington, D.C., Edward Brooke graduated from Howard University. After he served five years in the army in World War II, Brooke attended and received his law degree from Boston University. Prior to his election to the senate, the people of Massachusetts elected him as Attorney General for the state. That election win made him the first African American elected as an Attorney General in the United States.

Edward Brooke, III

OAK BLUFFS

 SENATOR EDWARD W. BROOKE SUMMER COTTAGE
Nashawena Park

Edward William Brooke III (1919-2015) was the first African American member of the United States Senate with his 1966 landslide victory over Endicott Peabody (NAA) in Massachusetts. Brooke served as Republican Senator until his defeat by Paul Tsongas (NAA) in 1978. Edward Brooke spent many summers at this cottage with his family.

 REV. JOHN SAUNDERS
Pulpit Rock Way
Farm Neck

Fugitive from slavery, John Saunders escaped from Virginia around 1787 with his wife, Priscilla. They settled in this area of Vineyard Haven where Saunders zealously preached Methodist theology. The locals named this area,

Pulpit Rock Way after a large rock near here upon which Saunders allegedly preached his sermons.

3 EASTVILLE CEMETERY
Near Lagoon Pond

Rebecca Michael was one of the African American residents buried in Eastville Cemetery. Michael was the mother of Captain William A. Martin, the only African American whaling captain, or *"Black Jack,"* to come from Martha's Vineyard.

4 ADAM CLAYTON POWELL COTTAGE
Dorothy West Avenue

Politician, Adam Clayton Powell, Jr. (1908-1972), served in the United States House of Representatives from 1945 to 1971 for the District of Harlem

Powell Cottage

in New York City. Powell spent family summer vacations here from 1933 until his divorce from his first wife, Isabel Powell, in 1945.

Powell's leadership of the Education and Labor Committee in the administrations of President John F. Kennedy (NAA) and President Lyndon B. Johnson (NAA) allowed him to spearhead influential social and civil rights legislation through the U.S. Congress during his tenure in the House of Representatives. He was often ostracized by his fellow Congressmen because of what they perceived as his radical positions on certain issues.

Adam Clayton Powell, Jr.

> *"Unless man is committed to the belief that all mankind are his brothers, then he labors in vain and hypocritically in the vineyard of equality."*
> —ADAM CLAYTON POWELL, JR.
>
> ---
>
> *"Freedom is an internal achievement rather than an external adjustment."*
> —POWELL

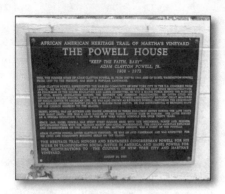

Powell Plaque

 ## 6 LADY PIONEERS OF HOSPITALITY TIVOLI INN
121 Lower Circuit Avenue

Circuit Avenue was one of the few areas in Oak Bluffs where African Americans could purchase property. In the 1890s, two African American entrepreneurs, Louisa Izett and Georgia O'Brien, opened a boarding house at this location, *"Aunt Georgia's Inn."* It served as a staple in the community until the 1930s. Today, it is the Tivoli Inn.

 ## 5 SHEARER COTTAGE
Rose Ave.

Charles and Henrietta Shearer of Everett, MA, purchased this home in 1903 as a summer home for their family. The family expanded the summer home in 1912 when they began to cater to African Americans who visited the island but were not welcomed at other hospitality establishments. The Shearer Cottage is the oldest inn on the island in continuous operation that caters to a primarily African American clientele.

Tivoli Inn

 ## 7 DOROTHY WEST COTTAGE
Myrtle Avenue

Boston born writer, Dorothy West (1907-1998), worked from the period of the Harlem Renaissance in the 1920s up through the 1990s. West relocated to Harlem after she won several literary contests. In Harlem, she eventually founded the magazine, *"Challenge,"* which published the work of other Harlem Renaissance writers.

Shearer Cottage

INK WELL BEACH
Seaview Ave.

African American politicians, enter-tainers, entrepreneurs, intellectuals and artists, all flocked to this popular sum-mer destination since the early 1900s. The name, *"Ink Well Beach"* originated because the beach was so popular with African American visitors.

Dorothy West

In 1943, West relocated to Martha's Vineyard where she worked as a jour-nalist. West's novel, *The Living is Easy* was first published in 1945. She pub-lished her last novel, *The Wedding*, in the mid-1990s. The producer, Oprah Winfrey made it into a movie.

Dorothy West Cottage

EDGARTOWN

 NANCY MICHAEL
Memorial Wharf
Dock St.

Nancy Michael (1772-1857) was the daughter of Rebecca Amos of Chil-mark and the grandmother of William Martin, the only African American whaling captain, *"Black Jack,"* from Martha's Vineyard. In 1779, Nancy, and her brother, Pero, age 19, were trans-ferred to Joseph Allen of Tisbury, just four years before slavery was effectively ended in Massachusetts in 1783. Nancy took on the surname of Michael and kept that name throughout her life.

Nancy moved to Edgartown during her adult years and remained there until her death. In Edgartown, Nancy Michael told the fortunes of sailors to earn income. The Edgartown commu-nity renamed her, *"Black Nance."* They sought her out to bless, or curse, those about to undertake ocean voyages. Her daughter, Rebecca Michael, was born in 1809. Rebecca's son was William Martin. The town installed a plaque at Memorial Wharf to honor the memory of Nancy Michael.

② Lois Mailou Jones Cottage
Pacific Ave.

Artist and educator, Lois Mailou Jones (1905–1998) enjoyed a career that spanned from the period of the Harlem Renaissance in the early 1930s until her death. Born in Boston in 1905, Jones spent summers on Martha's Vineyard while still a child and she continued that tradition throughout her adult life.

Jones taught at Howard University from 1927 to 1977. During that time and after retirement, she travelled widely. Lois Mailou Jones was a world famous artist whose work varied in style from the figurative to the abstract.

Lois Mailou Jones

The Metropolitan Museum of Art in New York City and the Museum of Fine Arts in Boston both have collected her paintings.

CHAPPAQUIDDICK

① Capt. William A. Martin House

The son of Rebecca Michael of Edgartown, Captain William A. Martin (1829-1907) worked in the maritime industry. In 1857, Martin married Sarah Brown, a Native American from Chappaquiddick Island. Chappaquiddick had a predominantly Native American community and Martin and Brown made that community their home.

Although Martin's early life was mired in poverty, he obtained an education and rose up through the ranks of the whaling industry. In 1853, he became First Mate and Keeper of the Log on the whaling vessel, the *Europa*. That journey lasted until 1857. By 1867, Martin had risen in rank to become the Joint Master and Keeper of the Log Book on the *Eunice H. Adams* ship during a voyage that lasted three years.

By 1878, Martin obtained the rank of Ship Captain and he led several successful whaling voyages after that time. Martin's life illustrated how individuals achieved success through diligence and persistence.

JEFFERS LANE CEMETERY CHAPPAQUIDDICK INDIAN BURIAL GROUND

32 Jeffers Lane

Jeffers Lane Cemetery was originally part of the Chappaquiddick Indian Plantation. The Plantation was the name given the Native American Reservations which held their communal land. Those plantations were systematically eliminated through a land-grab effort that was legally titled, "*The Act to Enfranchise the Indians of Massachusetts, 1869.*" That Act of Enfranchisement was allegedly a vehicle to give Native Americans full citizenship rights including the vote, but the price they had to pay was to give up their communal lands that was divided among the tribal members who could prove a relationship to the plantation.

That effort sounded innocent enough but once the Native population became absorbed into the general population, they lost control of any sovereign rights they were entitled to as a separate united entity. Many of the population lost their land because they were subjected to frivolous criminal charges. They often had to borrow against their property in order to defend themselves. Since the system was not in their favor, court costs often were as much as the criminal charges. The goal was to divest the Native population of their valuable land holdings,

by any means possible. Unfortunately, that effort was largely successful.

Jeffers Lane Cemetery was part of the original Chappaquiddick Indian Burial Ground before the land was divided. Sixteen Wampanoag Tribal members have headstones in the cemetery: Charles, John, Lydia, and Susan Webquish; William, Sarah, Gladys, and Harriet Belain; Lydia B. Gardner; Matilda and Moses Jeffers; Frances Goodridge; Robert and Sarah (Brown) Martin and her husband, William A. Martin; and Lawrence Prince, husband of Love (Madison) Prince. Ten other headstones that are no longer legible also are on the grounds and presumed to represent the gravesite of other Tribal members.

CHILMARK

 REBECCA AMOS SITE

North Road, Flanders Farm

Rebecca Amos was the great grandmother of William Martin, the only African American whaling captain from Martha's Vineyard. Rebecca survived the Middle Passage from Guinea, West Africa to Cape Cod where Cornelius Bassett of Chilmark continued her enslavement. In 1779, two of her three children, including Nancy Michael, were included in a property sale to Joseph Allen of Tisbury. Rebecca married Native American, Elisha Amos.

Elisha owned over 80 acres of land in Chilmark that Rebecca inherited at his death. The North Road property is the site of the land that Elisha left to Rebecca in his will and on which she lived until her death in 1801. Flanders Farm is the site of Cornelius Bassett's property where the Bassett family enslaved Rebecca Amos.

 LOCAL RESOURCES

African American Heritage Trail of Martha's Vineyard
www.myheritagetrail.org

Cousen Rose Gallery
71 Circuit Ave.
508-693-6656
www.cousenrose.com

MENEMSHA

 RANDAL BURTON & EDGAR JONES ESCAPE

In the mid-1850s, the Wampanoag Tribal community near Menemsha assisted two fugitives from slavery, Randall Burton and Edgar Jones, in their escapes. Tribal history and the placement of a memorial marker in Menemsha both document that assistance. Both escapes occurred after the Fugitive Slave Act of 1850 made it a Federal crime to assist a fugitive from slavery.

In the instances of both men, tribal members hid them on tribal land while the local sheriffs searched. At an opportune time, they were smuggled out of the community.

CENTRAL MASSACHUSETTS SITES

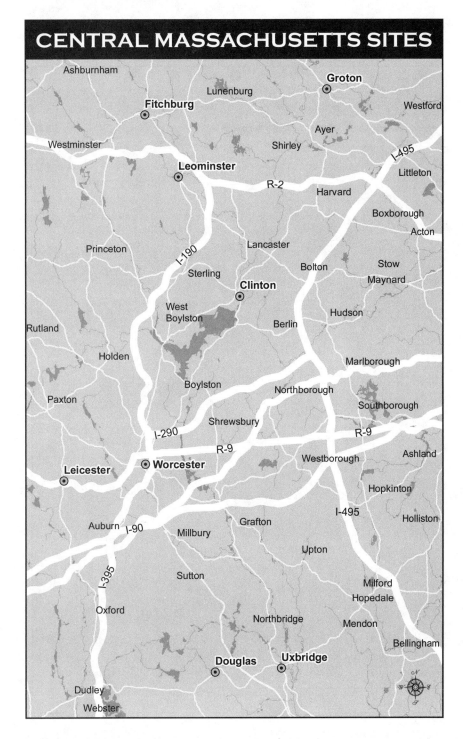

Worcester Map

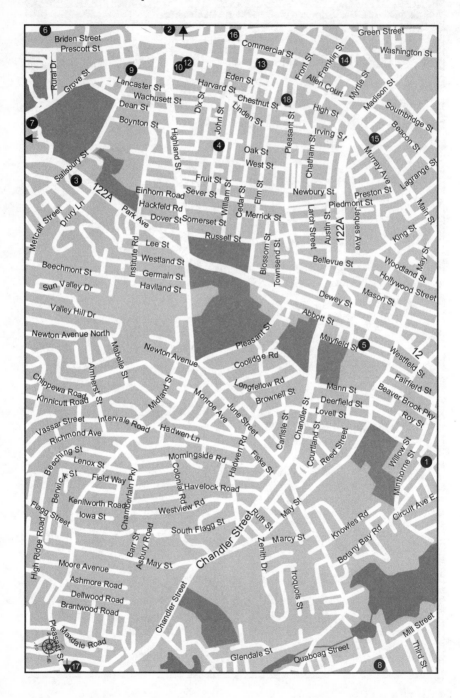

WORCESTER

1 MARSHALL *"MAJOR"* TAYLOR

4 Hobson Avenue

Marshall *"Major"* Taylor (1878–1948), also known as the *"Worcester Whirlwind"* or the *"Colored Cyclone,"* captivated fans as a world champion cyclist at a time when cycling was the biggest sports attraction in this country. Crowds of 20,000 to 30,000 spectators turned out and paid to attend cycling events to cheer on their favorite cyclist. Taylor was born outside of Indianapolis, Indiana. When he was eight years old, Louis *"Birdie"* Munger (NAA) an Indianapolis bicycle manufacturer, hired him to help in Munger's cycling shop.

"Major" Taylor on Bicycle

Taylor soon developed an intense interest in cycling. His nickname came from the military uniform he wore while he performed bicycle tricks in front of Munger's shop. Taylor won his first bike race in Indianapolis at the age of 13. When Munger moved to Worcester, MA, to expand his bicycle factory, he took Taylor with him. In Worcester, Taylor was able to freely train and compete, something he was not able to do in Indianapolis.

Early in his career, Taylor finished an arduous six-day, 1,732 mile race at Madison Square Garden in New York City. That event made Taylor decide to specialize in short sprints instead of long distance races.

Taylor's 1-mile world record in 1898 lasted for 28 years. That victory led him to win the world championship the next year.

August 27th, 1898
Taylor Set a
World Record for
1 mile @ 1 minute:
41.4 seconds

Taylor settled in Worcester while he continued his career as a cyclist. He lived at this home with his family until 1930. In his autobiography, *The Fastest Bicycle Rider in the World*, Taylor encouraged African American athletes to be persistent but fair while they pursued their dreams:

Marshall "Major" Taylor with Family

"...My personal observation and experiences indicate to me that while the majority of white people are considerate of my people, the minority are so bitter in their race prejudice that they actually overshadow the goodwill entertained for us by the majority.

Now a few words of advice to boys, and especially to those of my own race, my heart goes out to them as they face life's struggles. I can hardly express in words my deep feeling and sympathy for them, knowing as I do, the many serious handicaps and obstacles that will confront them in almost every walk of life. However, I pray they will carry on in spite of that dreadful monster prejudice, and with patience, courage, fortitude, and perseverance achieve success for themselves. I trust they will use that terrible prejudice as an inspiration to struggle on to the heights in their chosen vocations. ...

It is my thought to present the facts to the rising generation of my people without coloring or shading them in the least. In a word I do not want to make their futures appear more rosy than they will be, nor do I wish to discourage them in the slightest degree as they face life and its vicissitudes. My idea in giving this word to the boys and girls of my race is that they may be better prepared than I was to overcome these sinister conditions.

...I would advise all youths aspiring to athletic fame or a professional career to practice clean living, fair play and good sportsmanship. These rules may seem simple enough, but it will require great morale and physical courage to adhere to them. But if carried out in the strict sense of the word it will surely lead to a greater success than could otherwise be attained. Any boy can do so who has will power and force of character, even as I did, despite the fact that no one of my color was able to offer me advice gained through experience as I started up the ladder to success.

Last, but not least, I would urge all boys aspiring to an athletic career to strictly observe the rules of the game, to practice good sportsmanship and fairplay, and also to be able to abide by an unfavorable decision with the same grace that they accept a victory. To these ideals which were instilled in me when I was a youth, I attribute in a large degree the success that was mine on the bicycle tracks of the world."

–Marshall "Major" Taylor

Taylor Family Home

② WILLIAM & CHARLES BROWN HOUSE
4 Palmer Street

William Brown was one of the first successful African American entrepreneurs in Worcester. He founded the family's upholstery business in 1841, as a free man. His son, Charles, continued that business into the 20th century.

William & Charles Brown House

③ AMERICAN ANTIQUARIAN SOCIETY
185 Salisbury Street at Park Avenue
508-755-5221

This historical society holds the family papers of William Brown and many other prominent African Americans of Worcester.

④ JOHN STREET BAPTIST CHURCH
43 John Street

This 1891 church is Worcester's oldest African American church still in operation.

John Street Baptist Church

⑤ HOME FOR AGED COLORED PEOPLE
63 Parker Street

A charity group established this home in 1898, to care for elderly African Americans.

⑥ DAVID ROLSTON HOUSE
32 Burncoat Street

David Rolston, a successful manufacturer of tin cylinders, built this house in 1883. Rolston's economic success made it possible for his children to receive a good education. In 1906, the Worcester School Board appointed his daughter, Edith Marietta, as the city's first African American school principal.

David Rolston House

7 ESTELLA & BENJAMIN CLOUGH HOUSE
4 Stowell Avenue

The Clough family represented many firsts for the African American community in Worcester. The patriarch, Francis Clough, a successful entrepreneur, owned a barbershop in Worcester in the latter half of the 19th century. Francis was appointed as one of the first African American jurors in the state in 1860. His son, Benjamin Clough, was Worcester's first African American postal carrier, a position of great prestige because of the high degree of trust implied by the appointment. His daughter, Jennie Clough, was the first African American teacher in the Worcester School system.

8 "MAJOR" TAYLOR BICYCLE PATH
Along Mill Street

Worcester named this bicycle path after Marshall *"Major"* Taylor, the world champion cyclist.

9 NATIONAL GUARD MUSEUM & ARCHIVES
44 Salisbury Street
Open Mon. to Friday,
9 AM to 4 PM

The National Guard Museum and Archives is the official repository of documents and records for all Massachusetts volunteer regiments, including those who served in the Civil War.

10 WALKER V. JENNISON "FREEDOM LAWSUIT" SITE: WORCESTER DISTRICT COURT
2 Main St.

In 1781, a famous lawsuit was tried at a State Court near this location. Quock Walker vs. Nathaniel Jennison (NAA). That lawsuit, and another, Brom and Bett vs. Ashley (NAA) in Sheffield, paved the way to end the enforcement of slavery in Massachusetts. Although their legal challenges were based on charges of physical abuse and broken promises of freedom, as were previous successful *"Freedom Lawsuits,"* an additional reason was brought into the equation, the Massachusetts State Constitution. That document, passed in 1781, declared: *"...all men are born free and equal."*

The Walker v. Jennison lawsuits involved a total of three cases. The first lawsuit was filed by Quock Walker of Barre, against Nathaniel Jennison. Walker won on a charge of *"injury without right"* because a previous owner, James Caldwell (NAA), had already granted Walker his freedom.

The second lawsuit was filed by Nathaniel Jennison v. the Caldwell brothers. Jennison charged that the two Caldwell brothers (NAA), interfered with his property when they assisted Walker in his escape. Jennison won the second lawsuit.

The third lawsuit was the Commonwealth v. Jennison. The Massachusetts Attorney General charged Jennison in 1781 with criminal assault and battery on Walker. That trial did not come before the Massachusetts Supreme Court until April, 1783. In his decision, the Supreme Judicial Court Chief Justice William Cushing (NAA) ruled against Jennison and stated that involuntary servitude was incompatible with the new state constitution.

The institution of slavery ceased to be enforced in Massachusetts from that moment. Levi Lincoln (NAA), Walker's attorney, was later appointed Attorney General of the United States under President Thomas Jefferson. Massachu-

setts Superior Court Chief Justice William Cushing went on to be appointed as one of the first Justices of the United States Supreme Court.

> *"...your Constitution of Government, by which the people of this Commonwealth have solemnly bound themselves sets out with declaring that all men are born free and equal.... This being the case, I think the idea of slavery is inconsistent with our own conduct and constitution; and there can be no such thing as perpetual servitude of a rational creature.... and liberty can only be forfeited by some criminal conduct or relinquished by personal consent or contract."*
> —*Chief Justice William Cushing,*
> *1783*

11 FIRST AFRICAN AMERICAN JURORS SITE: WORCESTER SUPERIOR COURT
Site unknown

The first African American jurors in the state were appointed in Worcester in 1860. That year, Francis Clough, a businessman and barber, and William Jenkins, a fugitive from slavery and barber, were appointed to a jury trial in Worcester.

(12) FREE CHURCH
UGRR Station
90 Main St.

Thomas Wentworth Higginson (NAA) (1823–1911) pastored this Unitarian congregation from 1852 to 1862. A fervent abolitionist, Higginson belonged to the *"Secret Committee of Six"*, the group that financed John Brown's raid on Harper's Ferry in 1859.

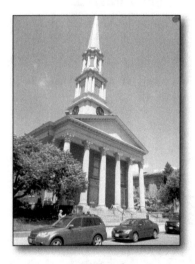

Free Church

(13) MECHANICS HALL
321 Main St.

When Mechanics Hall was completed in 1857, it immediately became one of the most popular venues for performances and public speakers in the city. Frederick Douglass was one of the famous abolitionists to speak there.

Mechanics Hall

(14) "MAJOR" TAYLOR STATUE
Worcester Public Library, 3 Salem St., Rear

The city of Worcester dedicated this memorial in 2008 to honor one of the city's most famous residents, Marshall *"Major"* Taylor. The memorial was completed by sculptor, Tody Mendez (NAA).

Major Taylor Statue

15 "A WALL FOR QUOCK WALKER" HAROLD DONOHUE FEDERAL BLDG.
595 Main St.

This mural was commissioned as part of the Federal Government's Art in Architecture program. It was completed by artist, Michael Hachey (NAA). Hachey depicted scenes from Worcester's legal history that led to the end of the practice of slavery in Massachusetts and the critical role Quock Walker played in that history. Two of the panels from the five panel mural are depicted here.

16 MARSHALL "MAJOR" TAYLOR STREET

This street in downtown Worcester was renamed to honor one of Worcester's beloved sons, Marshall "Major" Taylor.

17 LIBERTY FARM FOSTER (NAA) HOUSE
UGRR Station
116 Mower Street

Ardent abolitionists and feminists, Abbey Kelley Foster (NAA) (1811-1887) and Stephen S. Foster (NAA) (1809-

A Wall for Quock Walker

1881), lived at this house from 1847 to 1881. The couple actively lectured on both the rights of women and the abolition of slavery. Also, in the period prior to the Civil War, fugitives from slavery frequently used the Foster home as a safe haven in their escape from bondage. The name, *"Liberty Farm,"* derived from the couples' use of their home to harbor fugitives.

> *"...any law, constitution, court, or government, any church, priesthood, creed, or Bible, any Christ, or any God, that, by silence or otherwise, authorizes man to enslave man, merits the scorn and contempt of mankind."*
> --STEPHEN S. FOSTER

Stephen Foster gave a highly charged speech which was popularly titled, *"The Brotherhood of Thieves,"* at the 1843 Anti-Slavery Convention on Nantucket Island. This speech declared the Christian clergy complicit in the perpetuation of slavery because they benefited from the system. A riot broke out in the town of Nantucket after the speech and several people were injured. See Nantucket sites.

After the Civil War, the Fosters fought for the enfranchisement of women. They often refused to pay property taxes to protest women's lack of vote. When this occurred, the state seized and auctioned off their house to pay the taxes. Their friends diligently repurchased it and returned it to the couple.

Liberty Farm

Stephen & Abbey Foster

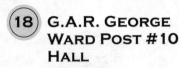 **G.A.R. George Ward Post #10 Hall**
55 Pearl St.

This was one of the few G.A.R. Posts which permitted African American veterans to join. The Massachusetts Colored Veterans Association of Worcester held its first meeting at this post on May 28th, 1886.

 Edward Earle (NAA) House

UGRR Station
Site Unknown

20 Charles Hadwen (NAA) House

UGRR Station
Site Unknown

21 Eli Thayer
Site Unknown

Eli Thayer (1819–1899) (NAA) from Worcester was one of the primary organizers of the New England Emigrant Aid Society in 1854. The goal of the company was to give financial assistance to anti-slave settlers in the new Kansas territory. The company was based in downtown Boston. Thayer later served as a United States Representative.

LEICESTER

---

1 Peter Salem Cabin Site
Peter Salem St.

Peter Salem (1750–1816) achieved fame as one of the heroes of the Battle of Bunker Hill of June 17th, 1775, when he shot and killed Major Pitcairn, the highest ranked British officer in that battle. After the war, Salem lived for a brief time in Salem, MA. He later built and lived in a cabin in Leicester. Salem died in Framingham and was buried there. See Charlestown and Framingham sites.

 Samuel May Jr. House

UGRR Station
Becker College
May Residence Hall
Main St.

Rev. Samuel May, Jr. (1810–1899) (NAA) was the Pastor of Leicester Unitarian Church and the co-founder of the Leicester Anti-Slavery Society. May was also a member of the Boston Vigilance Committee from 1850 until 1861.

CLINTON

GALLERY OF AFRICAN ART
62 High St.
978-368-1840
www.galleryofafricanart.
org
Daily: 10 a.m. to 5:30 p.m.

This gallery was created to celebrate the music and art of the African Diaspora. It evolved from the private collection of Gordon Lankton (NAA). In addition to the art collection, it has developed a wide array of education programs, interactive workshops, concerts of African music, and a variety of artist-in-residence programs.

GROTON

PRIMUS & MARGARET LEW FAMILY
Pepperell Section

Primus Lew and Margaret Lew were the parents of Barzillai Lew, a veteran of the American Revolution. They were free and owned a farm in this section of Groton. The couple had three children, two sons and a daughter. Primus was a musician and a veteran of the French and Indian War, as was his son, Barzillai. Barzillai Lew (1743–1822), their first son, was born on November 5th, 1743. Barzillai followed in his father's footsteps when he also served in the French and Indian War in 1760, where he was also a fifer. The family's reputation as talented musicians extended into the twentieth century.

DR. AMOS FARNSWORTH (NAA) HOUSE
UGRR Station
Site Unknown

REV. SOLOMON S. YOUNG (NAA) HOUSE
UGRR Station
Site Unknown

FITCHBURG

MR. & MRS. SAMUEL CROCKER (NAA) HOUSE
UGRR Station
Site Unknown

BENJAMIN S. SNOW (NAA) HOUSE

UGRR Station
Site Unknown

LEOMINISTER

 ## JONATHAN & FRANCIS DRAKE (NAA) HOUSE

UGRR Station
21 Franklin St.

This was one of the safe houses where Shadrach Minkins stayed after his famous jail break in February of 1851. During his stay, Mrs. Drake disguised him as a female in order to attend Sunday worship services.

 ## REV. JOEL BINGHAM (NAA) HOUSE

UGRR Station
Site Unknown

 ## JOEL SMITH (NAA) HOUSE

UGRR Station
Site Unknown

ASHBY

 ## PRINCE ESTERBROOKS GRAVE

First Parish Burial Ground
New Ipswich Rd.

Prince Esterbrooks (1740–1830) served with the Lexington Minutemen. He was one of the first Patriots shot at the Battle of Lexington and Concord. After his military service, Esterbrooks settled in the town of Ashby. The town of Lexington dedicated a memorial in his honor on the Town Common in April of 2008. See Lexington sites.

Esterbrooks Gravesite

NORTH ASHBURNHAM

 ## ALVIN WARD (NAA) HOUSE
UGRR Station
323 Lake Road

This was one of the stops of Shadrach Minkins in his escape from the Federal jail enroute to Canada. Minkins became sick at this station and he had to stay here for a short time before he proceeded to the next stop. Two other fugitives who stayed here were Levin Evans and Edward Ross.

 ## ENOCH WHITMORE (NAA) HOUSE
UGRR Station
Tuckerman Road

BARRE

 ## QUOCK WALKER "FREEDOM LAWSUIT"
Caldwell Farm, Site Unknown

Quock Walker took refuge on the Caldwell Farm in Barre after he fled the Jennison Farm in his escape from bondage in 1781. The successful lawsuits of Quock Walker and Elizabeth "Mum Bett" Freeman and Brom led to the end of slavery in Massachusetts. Quock Walker, enslaved by Nathaniel Jennison, (NAA) escaped his cruel bondage in Worcester County. Jennison, who possessed a cruel and bossy personality, considered those he enslaved as chattel property that he could treat in any manner he saw fit. Quock Walker eventually tired of the cruel and shameful treatment that he received on the Jennison farm and he ran away to the Caldwell Farm in Barre.

When Jennison located Walker, he beat him severely. Walker sued in 1781 for damages for assault and battery. Attorneys, Levi Lincoln (NAA) and Caleb Strong (NAA), defended him in the case. Jennison told the court that it was his right as Walker's owner to use whatever means were within his power to bring him back, even physical violence. The court disagreed. Walker won his case and the court awarded him 50 pounds in damages. See more on these cases in Worcester sites and Sheffield sites.

Quock Walker's extended family relocated to Cambridge and Lowell. They became leaders in the African American community in those towns. See Walker Lewis in Lowell sites. Levi Lincoln was appointed Attorney General of the United States under President Thomas Jefferson. Massachusetts Superior Court Chief Justice William Cushing wrote the decision, *"slavery is in-*

consistent with this state's constitution." Cushing was eventually appointed as one of the first Justices of the United States Supreme Court.

EAST DOUGLAS

 REV. SOLOMON P. SNOW (NAA) HOUSE
UGRR Station
Weslayan Methodist Church
Site Unknown

UXBRIDGE

 EFFINGHAM L. CAPRON (NAA) HOUSE
UGRR Station
Site Unknown

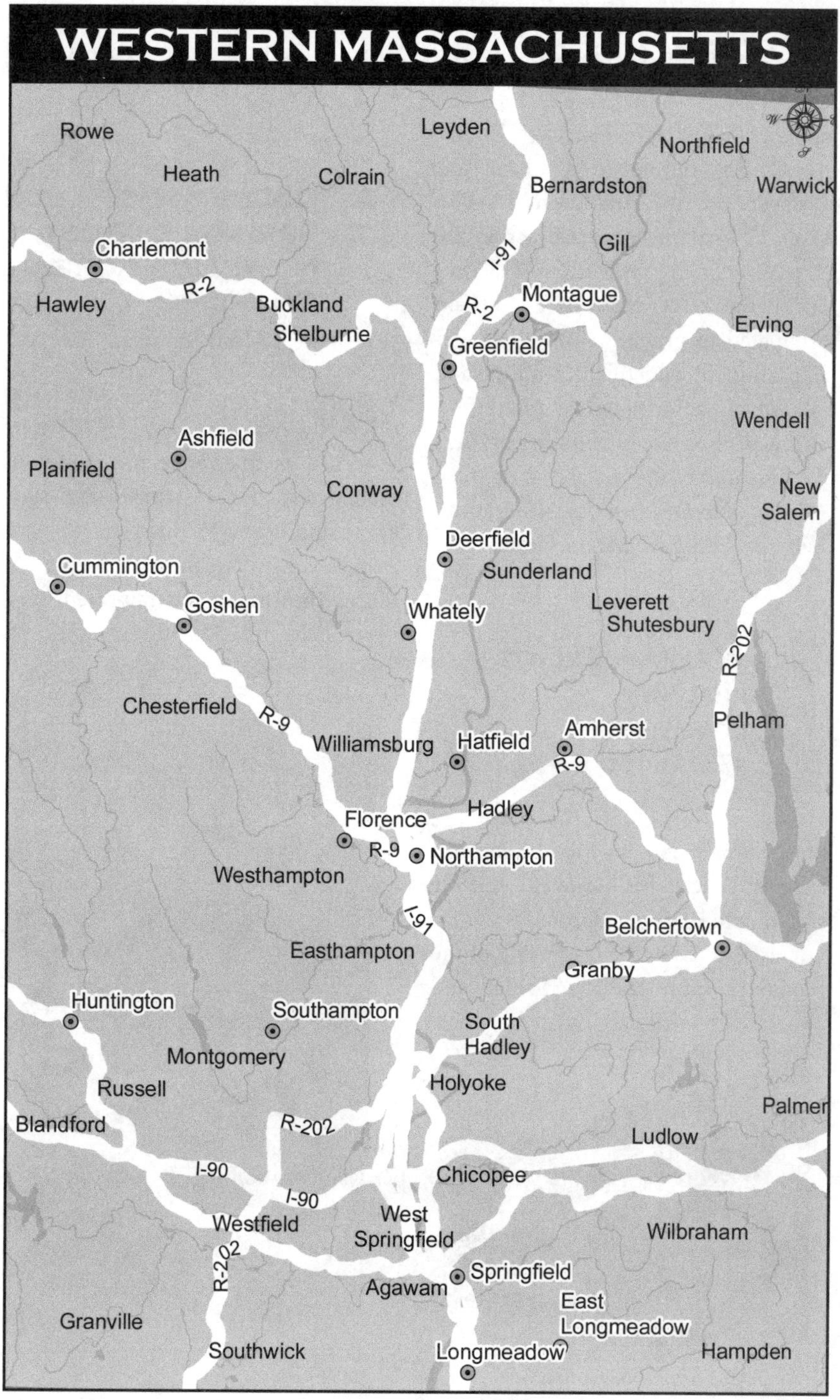

WESTERN MASSACHUSETTS

Rowe

Leyden

Northfield

Heath

Colrain

Bernardston

Warwick

Gill

Charlemont

R-2

Buckland

Shelburne

Montague

R-2

Erving

Hawley

Greenfield

Wendell

Ashfield

Plainfield

Conway

New
Salem

Deerfield

Cummington

Sunderland

Leverett

Goshen

Whately

Shutesbury

R-202

Chesterfield

R-9

Williamsburg

Hatfield

Amherst

Pelham

R-9

Hadley

Florence

R-9

Northampton

Westhampton

I-91

Belchertown

Easthampton

Granby

Huntington

Southampton

Montgomery

South
Hadley

Russell

Holyoke

Palmer

Blandford

R-202

Ludlow

I-90

I-90

Chicopee

Westfield

West
Springfield

Wilbraham

R-202

Agawam

Springfield

Granville

East
Longmeadow

Southwick

Longmeadow

Hampden

GREENFIELD

Greenfield and other parts of Franklin County developed a strong anti-slavery focus during the mid-1800s. Over 200 groups organized across the state to fight the institution of slavery during the 1830s, and thirteen of them originated in Franklin County. Several prominent Greenfield families and individuals contributed to that effort. This aspect of Greenfield's history was documented in the research pamphlet, *"The Road to Freedom: Anti-slavery Activity in Greenfield, Massachusetts."*

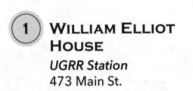

1 WILLIAM ELLIOT HOUSE
UGRR Station
473 Main St.

William *"Billy"* Elliot (NAA) had a lifelong commitment to the abolition of slavery. He used his home as a reliable stop on the Underground Railroad. Elliot also served in the leadership of the Franklin County Abolition Society and

Billy Elliot House.

he was a member of the Free Soil Party which tried to limit the expansion of slavery into the new territories.

2 COLDBROOK SPRINGS BAPTIST NOW: ZION KOREAN CHURCH
463 Main St

Coldbrook Springs Baptist Church was originally located in Barre, MA, where it served as the venue for numerous meetings and lectures for the anti-slavery community. William Lloyd Garrison frequently lectured from its podium. The church was relocated to its current site in 1936.

Coldbrook Springs Baptist Church

3 LEAVITT HOUSE
NOW: GREENFIELD PUBLIC LIBRARY
402 Main St.

The Leavitt (NAA) family consisted of three brothers, Roger, Jonathan, and Hart, and their off-spring, most of whom were active in the abolitionist movement. Roger, the President of the Franklin County Anti-Slavery Society, led abolitionist activities in Charlemont where he operated a large farm. Jonathan gained prominence as a judge, and Hart was a local merchant and one of the founders of the Franklin County Anti-Slavery Society.

Leavitt Family House

4 SITE: MARSH (NAA) HOUSE
UGRR Station
39 Bank Row

Dexter and Eunice Marsh were typical of the many people who made the anti-slavery movement such a force in the North, average, working-class citizens who opposed slavery on moral grounds. Dexter's father, Joshua Marsh, had a reputation as a staunch abolitionist, and it was no surprise when Dexter continued in his father's footsteps. The family's house at this site was well-known as a safe haven for fugitives from bondage.

5 SITE: WASHINGTON HALL
253 Main St.

Washington Hall was a popular venue for speakers on the anti-slavery lecture circuit.

6 SITE: DR. CHARLES AND MRS. EMELINE FISK (NAA) HOUSE
UGRR Station
Main St. and Fiske Ave.

7 SITE: JOHN PUTNAM BARBERSHOP
308 Main St.

Barbershops occupied a place of importance in the African American community throughout our history. This was a place where community members shared valuable information. African American barber, John Putnam, seized the opportunity presented by his business to gather and disperse information critical to those who worked on the Underground RailRoad. See more on Putnam under site #9.

John Putnam

300-man militia to escort Sims to the wharves. When abolitionists solicited funds to buy Sims freedom, Devens offered to donate the entire cost himself. The offer was refused by the man who enslaved Sims.

In another case, a fugitive, Robert Wright, hid in Greenfield for fear of a return to bondage. Devens suggested that the individual who enslaved Wright should be contacted to negotiate a purchase. Local anti-slavery activists initiated contact and when the enslaver agreed to a sale, Devens made a substantial contribution to that effort.

8 CHARLES DEVENS HOUSE
70 Devens St.

Charles Devens, Jr. (NAA) was appointed as a United States marshal in 1849, a year before the Fugitive Slave Act of 1850 was passed and a year before the resolve of the Federal government was tested by the fugitive court cases that rocked the nation. When the Fugitive Slave Act of 1850 was passed, Devens found himself in the position of enforcer of laws that he did not agree with.

After the bold rescue of fugitive, Shadrach Minkins, in February, 1851, the federal government decided not to take any chances with future cases. When fugitive, Thomas Sims was captured in April of 1851, Devens task was to ensure that Sims was successfully returned to bondage. Devens used a

Charles Devens, Jr.

Devens volunteered for military duty after Fort Sumter and he rose to the rank of Union general in the war. After the war, Devens continued his service to his country. He served on the Massachusetts Supreme Court and as U.S. Attorney General. While he lived in Washington, D.C., Devens obtained federal employment for Thomas Sims. Fort Devens in Massachusetts was named in honor of General Devens, Jr. The City of Worcester installed a statue in the downtown area to honor his service to his state and his country.

Devens House

9 SITE: JOHN AND JULIA PUTNAM HOUSE
UGRR Station
175 Wells St.

Although John and Julia Putnam were both born in Massachusetts, they decided to dedicate their limited resources to assist those who risked their life to escape slavery. They used John Putnam's barbershop on Main St. as an information resource for those who worked for the Underground Railroad. The couple also hid individuals in their house who sought shelter during their escape.

10 SAMUEL WELLS (NAA) HOUSE
UGRR Station
Site Unknown

MONTAGUE

1 REV. ERASTUS ANDREWS (NAA) HOUSE
UGRR Station
Site Unknown

2 KENDALL ABBOTT (NAA) HOUSE
UGRR Station
Site Unknown

3 JOSHUA MARSH (NAA) HOUSE
UGRR Station
Site Unknown

DEERFIELD

THE TOWN OF Deerfield created a brochure and self-guided tour of African American Historic Sites in the town to document and preserve that aspect of its history. That brochure formed the basis of the sites listed in this guide. That brochure documented the location of the houses of various enslaved individuals prior to the date that Massachusetts abolished slavery in the state in 1783. That documentation of the African American heritage of Deerfield confirmed the extent to which enslaved individuals intermingled in the daily life of the communities in which they lived.

1. JENNY, CATO AND TITUS, VETERANS OF THE FRENCH & INDIAN WAR SITE: REV. ASHLEY HOUSE
129 Old Main St.

Mother and infant, Jenny (d. 1808) and Cato (d.1825), were enslaved by Rev. Jonathan Ashley (NAA) as early as 1738. Despite the fact that Jenny served the family for seventy years, her primary wish on her death in 1808, was for her spirit to return to Africa. Cato, who learned to read, also served the family and he served in the French and Indian War.

Titus was enslaved in 1750. He also served in the French and Indian War. Titus was sold in 1760.

2. CAESAR, VETERAN OF THE FRENCH AND INDIAN WAR, AND MESECK SITE: HINSDALE HOUSE
128 Old Main St.

Two enslaved individuals, Caesar and Meseck, both lived here between 1740 and 1760. Caesar was a veteran of the French and Indian War.

3. CAESAR, VETERAN OF THE FRENCH & INDIAN WAR SITE: JONATHAN HOYT HOUSE
113 Old Main St.

Many enslaved individuals were given names with Roman origins by their enslavers. Caesar was one of the more popular Roman names for enslaved males. The Caesar of the Hoyt (NAA) residence was baptized in 1741, and he served in the French and Indian War.

4. POMPEY, ADAM, & PETER SITE: THOMAS WELLS HOUSE
103 Old Main St.

Thomas Wells enslaved at least three males at his house on this site between 1730 and 1750: Pompey, Adam, and Peter.

5 PETER, ISHMAIL, & HARTFORD SITE: THOMAS DICKINSON HOUSE
99 Old Main St.

Thomas Dickinson (NAA) was the nephew of Thomas Wells. Legal ownership of Peter who was considered Wells personal property, passed to Dickinson upon Wells death in 1750. Dickinson also enslaved two other males, Ishmail and Hartford.

93 Main St.

Thomas Dickinson House

6 NEGRO FEMALE DR. THOMAS WILLIAMS HOUSE
93 Old Main St.

The names of many enslaved individuals were never documented and they were simply listed on property inventories as Negro girl or Negro boy, etc. This was the case with one individual who lived at the Williams (NAA) house. Dr. Williams was the village doctor and he provided medical care for all the residents of the village, white and black.

7 PRINCE, POMPEY, ADAM, & TITUS SITE: JOSEPH BARNARD HOUSE
72 Old Main St.

Prince, Pompey, Adam, and Titus all worked for Joseph Barnard around his house and at his store. One of them, Prince, was enslaved by Joseph Barnard in 1743. The others were enslaved by Barnard's uncle, Samuel Barnard (NAA). Despite the close relationship between enslaved individuals and their enslavers, a desire for freedom remained a high priority for those enslaved. When Prince ran away in 1749, Barnard posted a reward for his return.

8 SITE: FOURTH MEETINGHOUSE
Old Main Street and Town Commons

Many baptisms of the enslaved population of Deerfield, including Lucy Terry's six children, occurred here. At least

494

one marriage of an enslaved couple occurred here, that of Caesar and Hagar.

Terry & Prince House

9 CIVIL WAR MONUMENT
Old Main Street and Town Commons

10 TOWN BURYING GROUND
Old Albany Road

This was the primary burial place for the village of Deerfield. Many of the local enslaved population were buried here.

Ebenezer Wells House

11 CAESAR, LUCY TERRY & ABIJAH PRINCE
Ebenezer Wells House
52 Old Main Street and Memorial Street

Caesar and Lucy Terry (1724-1821), were both enslaved by Ebenezer Wells (NAA). They were baptized at the Fourth Meetinghouse in 1735. In 1744, Lucy joined the Church as a member. Lucy authored the oldest recorded poem written by an African American, *"Bars Flight,"* in 1746. Lucy Terry entertained the locals with stories in the tradition of an African griot, a person who verbally documented local history and passed it on to new generations through storytelling.

During Terry's life, the competition for food and the desire of the indigenous people to protect their land from the encroachment of the white settlers strained the relationship between the two groups. This tension often resulted in raids by the indigenous population on the settlements. One such raid on Deerfield, Massachusetts, occurred on August 25th, 1746. Lucy Terry's poem, *"Bars Flight,"* described this bloody raid. *"Bars Flight,"* the best contemporary account of that important historical event, was passed verbally from generation to generation until it was documented in a book in 1855, on the history of the region.

"BARS FLIGHT"

August 'twas the twenty fifth
Seventeen hundred forty-six
The Indians did in ambush lay
Some very valiant men to slay
The names of whom I'll not leave out
Samuel Allen like a hero fout
And though he was so brave and bold
His face no more shall we behold.
Eleazer Hawks was killed outright
Before he had time to fight
Before he did the Indians see
Was shot and killed immediately.
Oliver Amsden he was slain
Which caused his friends
much grief and pain.
Samuel Amsden they found dead
Not many rods off from his head.
Adonijah Gillet we do hear
Did lose his life which was so dear.
John Saddler fled across the water
And so excaped the dreadful slaughter.
Eunice Allen see the Indians comeing
And hoped to save herself by running
And had not her petticoats stopt her
The awful creatures had not
cotched her
And tommyhawked her on the head
And left her on the ground for dead.
Young Samuel Allen, Oh! lack a-day
Was taken and carried to Canada"

– Lucy Terry

In 1756, Lucy Terry married Abijiah Prince, a freed African American, who owned a farm in southern Vermont. Before the couple relocated to Vermont, they lived with their family in this addition to the Ebenezer Wells house.

The couple had six children, two of whom, Caesar Prince and Fetus Prince, served in the American Revolution. Prince's courage and determination foretold the rhetoric of the founding fathers for, *"life, liberty, and the pursuit of happiness."* In 1785, the family successfully challenged a wealthy white neighbor in Vermont in a land dispute.

Lucy Terry Prince wanted for her children what every mother wanted, for them to have an opportunity to achieve all they were capable of. To this end, in 1785, Prince made a three hour presentation before the Board of Trustees of Williams College to have one of her sons admitted as a student. She was unsuccessful in that effort but her courage to confront the Board of white, male, landed gentry should be forever honored. Lucy Terry Prince and her family were highly regarded in the community and her obituary was published in two newspapers.

12 MEMORIAL HALL MUSEUM
8 Memorial Street

Memorial Hall Museum features a memorial dedicated to those enslaved Africans throughout Deerfield's history. The Museum also has a memorial dedicated to Frank and Parthena, an enslaved married couple killed in 1704 during a French and Indian attack on their village. The African drum surrounded by cowrie shells represented the African heritage of the couple.

Memorial Hall Museum

Memorial to Frank and Parthena

13 PHILLIS, HUMPHRY, AND CESAR TIMOTHY CHILDS HOUSE
43 Old Main St.

The first individual enslaved by Childs (NAA) was Phillis in 1741. Records documented the participation of two other individuals who were also enslaved by Childs in the community of Deerfield, Humphry and Cesar. Humphry was treated by Dr. Williams, and Cesar made purchases at the local store.

14 CAESAR, FRENCH & INDIAN WAR SITE: SAMUEL CHILDS HOUSE
40 Old Main Street

Caesar, enslaved by Samuel Childs (NAA), was a veteran of the French and Indian War (1754-1763).

15 PETER, NEGRO FEMALE & TWO CHILDREN (CAESAR) SITE: SAMUEL DICKINSON HOUSE
36 Old Main St.

Four enslaved individuals resided with Samuel Dickinson (NAA), Peter, a Negro female, and her two children, one of whom was named Caesar.

16 POMPEY, CAESAR, & NEGRO FEMALE SITE: CAPT. JONATHAN WELLS HOUSE
37 Old Main St.

The individuals enslaved by Capt. Jonathan Wells (NAA) were fully integrated into the Deerfield community. Both Pompey and Caesar were baptized, Pompey in 1735. Caesar also was accepted as a member of the Fourth Meeting House.

17 NEGRO FEMALE & NEGRO MALE SITE: JONATHAN WELLS (NAA) HOUSE
29 Old Main St.

18 TITUS, REBEL AGAINST BONDAGE SITE: DANIEL ARMS HOUSE
8 Old Main Street

Titus, a resident of Deerfield during the mid-1700s, rebelled regularly against his enslaver, Daniel Arms (NAA), with daily acts of defiance. Arms constantly punished and eventually sold Titus because he consistently refused to obey Arms.

19 PVMA LIBRARY
6 Memorial Street

The PVMA (Pocumtuck Valley Memorial Assoc.) Library contains documents from the life of Lucy Terry. Those documents include her marriage license, documents on the birth of her six children, and her obituary.

20 REV. SAMUEL WILLARD HOUSE
UGRR Station
Old Main Street

The Willard (NAA) house is now part of Deerfield Academy.

21 LOCAL RESOURCES
African American Historic Sites of Deerfield
www.americancenturies.
mass.edu/activities/afram/
afram.

WHATELY

---

1 MR. CRAFT (NAA) HOUSE
UGRR Station
Site Unknown

(2) **DEACON JOHN M. BARDWELL (NAA) HOUSE**
UGRR Station
Site Unknown

(3) **DEACON DEXTER MORTON (NAA) HOUSE**
UGRR Station
Site Unknown

(4) **DANIEL F. MORTON (NAA) HOUSE**
UGRR Station
Site Unknown

(5) **OSEE MONSON (NAA) HOUSE**
UGRR Station
Site Unknown

(6) **THOMAS NASH (NAA) HOUSE**
UGRR Station
Site Unknown

CHARLEMONT

(1) **HART AND MARY LEAVITT (NAA) HOUSE**
UGRR Station
Avery Brook Road

(2) **ROGER HOOKER AND KEZIAH LEAVITT (NAA) HOUSE**
UGRR Station
Harris Mountain Road

ASHFIELD

(1) **HOSEA BLAKE (NAA) HOUSE**
UGRR Station
Site Unknown

GOSHEN

(1) **GEORGE & TRYPHENA CATHCART ABELL (NAA) HOUSE**
UGRR Station
Site Unknown

499

CUMMINGTON

Cummington was the epicenter of a quartet of villages that hosted a very active anti-slavery community in the years prior to the Civil War. That history was documented in the publication, *"Finding Aid: The Antislavery Movement in Cummington, MA,"* created by Stephanie Pasternak for the Cummington Historical Commission. That resource served as the basis of the sites listed here.

 ### KINGMAN FARM KINGMAN TAVERN MUSEUM
UGRR Station
Main St.

Levi Kingman (1789–1880) (NAA) was part of the strong abolitionist community that operated in the Cummington area. He lived here from 1817, until 1871. Prior to the Civil War, Kingman operated an Underground Railroad Station in his home.

 ### HIRAM BROWN HOUSE
Main St.

Hiram Brown (1803–1897) (NAA) was one of the local lights of the anti-slavery movement in Cummington. Brown was the organizer of many anti-slavery conventions that attracted attendees from miles around. Brown's views and activism caused his entire family to be excommunicated in 1854, from their local congregation, the Village Congregational Society.

CUMMINGTON HILL

 ### WILLIAM PACKARD HOUSE
Bryant Road

William Packard (1791–1870) (NAA) was an active abolitionist in the community. In 1835, he spearheaded a petition that requested the U.S. Congress to end the slave trade.

 ### SITE: F.H. (NAA) & MELISSA EVERETT DAWES (NAA) HOUSE
UGRR Station
Route 112 / Powell Road

 ### SITE: ALDEN TOWER (NAA) HOUSE
UGRR Station
Trouble St

4 SITE: ARUNAH BARTLETT (NAA) HOUSE
UGRR Station
Trouble St.

LIGHTENING BUG

1 PHILLIP ALLEN HOUSE
Site Unknkown

Phillip Allen, an African American resident, purchased property here in 1817.

2 JAMES W. BRIGGS (NAA) HOUSE
UGRR Station
Site Unknown

WEST CUMMINGTON

1 UNIVERSALIST CHURCH NOW, WEST CUMMINGTON CHURCH PARISH HOUSE
West Main St.

The membership of this congregation included the foremost abolitionists

from the area, Alden Tower (NAA), Arunah Bartlett (NAA), and John Everett (NAA).

HATFIELD

1 AMOS NEWPORT "FREEDOM LAWSUIT" JOSEPH BILLINGS HOUSE
Main St., west side near Billings Way

Amos Newport was one of several African Americans who demanded their rights to the same freedoms enjoyed by white citizens. Those demands were made before slavery ceased to be enforced in the state. Joseph Billing (NAA) enslaved Newport in 1729, while Newport was in his late teens. By 1766, Newport was fed up with Billing's mistreatment and he sued for his freedom.

Nearly two dozen *"Freedom Lawsuits"* had been successfully tried in the state by that time. Newport initiated his lawsuit because of mistreatment but that argument was not used as the basis of his lawsuit. Instead, Newport argued that he was a free individual and no one had a right of ownership of him. That initial lawsuit failed because Billings's bill of sale documented the transaction that allegedly transferred ownership of Newport to Billings. John Adams represented Billings, the defendant. Newport appealed the case and lost again. Newport ended his efforts in debt because of fees incurred to undertake his lawsuits.

When he advocated for his freedom in 1766, Newport anticipated the promise of the Declaration of Independence of 1776, and the promise of the Massachusetts state constitution.

Several of Newport's descendants relocated to Amherst. A great-great grandson, F. Dwight Newport, and Dwight's son, Edward Foster Newport, both attended Amherst College where they were employed as athletic trainers. The college named Newport House in their honor.

Florence Map

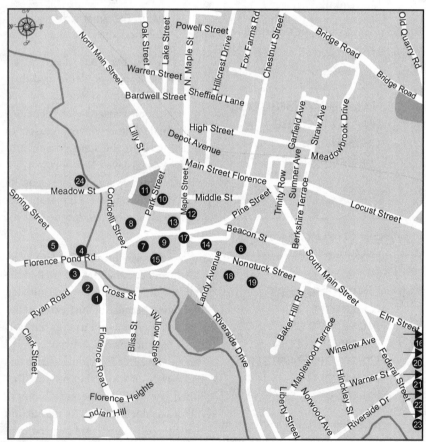

FLORENCE/NORTHAMPTON

AFRICAN AMERICANS in Florence and Northampton actively participated in the colonial struggle for freedom from British tyranny. A recent congressional proposal to develop a memorial dedicated to African American participation in Massachusetts in the Revolutionary War prompted Northampton to submit ten names for inclusion.

Later, Florence and Northampton provided solace and safe haven for fugitives from slavery in the South. That progressive attitude led to the development of a utopian community in the 1840s, the *Northampton Association of Education & Industry* (NAEI). The NAEI promoted equality of the races and sexes. Three well known members of the NAEI were Sojourner Truth, David Ruggles, and Lydia Child (NAA). The town established a self-guided tour of its African American heritage sites to document that history.

 DAVID RUGGLES HOUSE
47 Florence Road

David Ruggles (1810-1849), a noted African American abolitionist, helped between 400 to 600 individuals escape slavery through his activity on the Underground Railroad. Ruggles moved to Northampton from New York City in 1842, for health reasons. After he regained his health, Ruggles established a facility for hydrotherapy in Florence, the Northampton Water Cure, at this location. Originally located on Spring St., this house was relocated to this site in 1851.

Ruggles was one of seven children born in Connecticut to free parents. He inherited his entrepreneurial spirit from his parents, his mother was a caterer, and his father was a blacksmith. Ruggles received his education at a school sponsored by members of the Methodist community. In 1828, Ruggles moved to New York City where he opened a combination grocery and bookstore, the first African American owned bookstore in the country. At that this time, Ruggles was very involved with the anti-slavery movement.

David Ruggles

In the early 1830s, a fire set by a mob destroyed his store and as a result, Ruggles became even more active in the anti-slavery movement. He worked for the abolitionist weekly, the "*Emancipator,*" for a while, first, to solicit subscribers and later, as a writer.

In 1835, Ruggles co-founded and became secretary of the New York Committee of Vigilance. That organization encouraged civil disobedience and self-defense for those who managed to emancipate themselves from slavery. Two well-known fugitives who Ruggles personally assisted on their journey to freedom, were Basil Dorsey who eventually settled in Florence, and Frederick Douglass.

Ruggles and Douglass became close friends and the marriage of Frederick Douglass and Anna Murray took place at the shop of David Ruggles. The Committee of Vigilance was so successful in its efforts to assist fugitives from slavery that other Underground Railroad associations based their structure and techniques on its model. Ruggles also wrote for, and published the periodical, the *"Mirror of Liberty,"* from 1838 to 1841.

On July 23rd, 1836, the New York Sun published this letter by Ruggles that complained of the frequency that freed African Americans were kidnapped in the North:

Ruggles House

"It is too bad to be told, much less to be endured!—On Saturday, 23rd instant, about 12 o'clock, Mr. George Jones, a respectable free colored man, was arrested at 21 Broadway, by certain police officers, upon the pretext of his having "committed assault and battery." Mr. Jones, being conscious that no such charge could be sustained against him, refused to go with the officers. His employers, placing high confidence in his integrity, advised him to go and answer to the charge, promising that any assistance should be afforded to satisfy the end of justice. He proceeded with the officers, accompanied with a gentleman who would have stood his bail—he was locked up in Bridewell—his friend was told that "when he was wanted he could be sent for." Between the hours of 1 and 2 o'clock, Mr. Jones was carried before the Hon. Richard Riker, Recorder of the City of New York. In the absence of his friends, and in the presence of several notorious kidnappers, who preferred and by oath sustained that he was a runaway slave, poor Jones,... was by the Recorder pronounced to be a SLAVE!

In less than three hours after his arrest, he was bound in chains, dragged through the streets, like a beast to the shambles! My depressed countrymen, we are all liable; your wives and children are at the mercy of merciless kidnappers.

We have no protection in law, because the legislators withhold justice. We must no longer depend on the interposition of Manumission or Anti-Slavery Societies, in the hope of peaceable and just protection; where such outrages are committed, peace and justice cannot dwell. While we are subject to be thus inhumanly practiced upon, no man is safe; we must look to our own safety and protection from kidnappers, remembering that "self-defense is the first law of nature."

Let a meeting be called—let every man who has sympathy in his heart to feel when bleeding humanity is thus stabbed afresh, attend the meeting let a remedy be prescribed to protect us from slavery. Whenever necessity requires, let that remedy be applied. Come what, any thing is better than slavery."

—David Ruggles

Riker's Island, the site of one of New York's state prisons, was named to honor Judge Riker and his family. Today, it is notorious for the harsh conditions that the majority African American and Latino inmates have to endure. New York City residents have mounted a petition to have the complex renamed because of the family's affiliations with slavery.

Ruggles's tireless work for the anti-slavery movement led him to financial ruin and physical collapse. The stress that he constantly experienced led to near blindness. The New York Committee of Vigilance forced Ruggles out of the organization because of a legal dispute with another newspaperman, Samuel Cornish, to whose newspaper, the *"Colored American,"* Ruggles regularly contributed. Despite those set-backs, Ruggles continued to promote the position of a united front as the best defense to fight slavery.

"While every man's hand is against us, our every hand is against each other. I speak plainly, because truth will set us free. Are we not guilty of cherishing, to an alarming extent, the sin of sectarian, geographical, and complexional proscription? The spirit abroad is this: Is that brother a Methodist? He is not one of us. A Baptist? He is not one of us. A Presbyterian? He is not one of us. An Episcopalian? He is not one of us. A Roman Catholic? He is not one of us. Does he live above human creeds, and enjoy the religion of the heart? He is of Beelzebub.

Again, Is that brother from the east? He is not of us. From the west? He is not of us. From the north? He is not of us. From the south? He is not of us. From the middle States? He is not of us. Is he a foreigner? He can never be of us. But, forsooth, is that brother of a dark complexion? He is of no worth. Is he of a light

complexion? He is of no nation. Such, sir, are the visible lines of distinction, marked by slavery for us to follow. If we hope for redemption from our present condition, we must repent, turn, and UNITE in the hallowed cause of reform.
–David Ruggles, The Liberator newspaper, Sept. 24, 1841.

> *"Slaves, though we be enrolled, Minds are never to be sold."*
> –DAVID RUGGLES

> *"A man is sometimes lost in the dust of his own raising."*
> –DAVID RUGGLES

> *"Prejudice is not so much dependent upon natural antipathy as upon education."*
> –DAVID RUGGLES

David Ruggles moved to Northampton in 1842, on the encouragement of Lydia Child (NAA), one of the founders of the NAEI. In Florence, Ruggles's experiments with hydrotherapy resulted in an improvement to his health to the extent that he became a passionate advocate of the cure. In 1846, Ruggles operated a hydrotherapy facility that treated between 30 and 40 patients during its peak until his own death in 1849 from a bowel inflammation.

Ruggles and Douglass remained close friends and when Douglass began his *"North Star"* newspaper in January of 1848, Ruggles wrote this testimonial:

Northampton, Jan. 1, 1848
"DEAR FRIENDS DOUGLASS AND DELANEY,

The specimen number of the North Star, is just what it should be—a beacon of liberty, to illuminate the pathway of the bleeding, hunted fugitive of the South; and to arouse our disfranchised fellow countrymen and women of the North, who are lulled to sleep by the siren song of Liberty, while we are slaves, to all intents, purposes, and constructions, in any State within this SLAVEHOLDING UNION. Let it be seen and felt, that while our brethren and sisters of the South are slaves to individuals, we, of the North, are slaves to the mass. Let the whole truth in regard to our real condition be so clearly shown, that our colored brethren, who believe themselves free, may understand, that in the United States of American, there are no "free colored men;" and that there never can be, so long as there is no concert of action..."; to sustain such an engine in our cause—my word to all is, Let him who would be a slave, refuse to sustain it!
Ever yours in Human Freedom, DAVID RUGGLES"

2 LAURA WASHINGTON & GEORGE HODESTIA HOUSE
9 Florence Road

Florence was an attractive destination for many African Americans in the early 1840s who were attracted by its progressive views toward racial harmony. Two of Florence's early African American residents, Laura Washington and George Hodestia, shared this home on Florence Road. George Hodestia escaped bondage from Maryland.

3 CYNTHIA DORSEY HOUSE
15 Ryan Road

Cynthia Dorsey was the second wife of Basil Dorsey, a prominent African American resident of Florence. This property was part of six acres of land that Basil Dorsey purchased in 1852. At some point after that land purchase, Cynthia Dorsey built her house on this site.

Cynthia Dorsey House

4 BASIL DORSEY HOUSE
4 Florence Road

Basil Dorsey (1810–1872) escaped slavery in Maryland with three of his brothers. The group traveled to Pennsylvania where Dorsey's freed wife, Louisa, and their children, joined him. When bounty hunters found Dorsey, the local officials imprisoned him as a run-away. Fortunately for Dorsey, the judge dismissed the case.

Dorsey and his family continued north. Louisa died in childbirth and Dorsey settled in Florence, Massachusetts in 1844, with his other children. Dorsey later married Cynthia Jones of Pittsfield. He ultimately attained a level of prosperity through his job at a local textile mill.

5 HENRY ANTHONY HOUSE
40 Spring St.

One of the first African Americans to settle in Florence, Henry Anthony (d. 1880) escaped bondage in the mid-1830s from Maryland. Anthony built this house around 1840. Anthony was

Henry Anthony House

one of six fugitives who signed a petition to protest the Fugitive Slave Act of 1850. That act of protest exposed their location to potential bounty hunters and put them in jeopardy for capture.

Nonotuck Silk Mill

6 NONOTUCK SILK MILL / NAEI / CRITCHLOW DAGUERROTYPE FACTORY
Nonotuck Street

In 1842, a group of progressive citizens founded the Northampton Association of Education and Industry (NAEI) in the village of Florence. The NAEI was one of the few utopian communities created at this time to develop a new paradigm for community. It refused to depend on the exploitation of enslaved labor as the foundation of its economy, and it sought to recognize the equality of the races and sexes.

The industries the association sought to develop were silk manufacturing and the cultivation of sugar beets, two commodities that did not depend on forced labor as did their counterparts, cotton and sugar. The silk factory for the Northampton Association of Education and Industry was located in this mill complex. The radical philosophy of the NAEI, which at its peak included over 200 members, made it a hub for abolitionist activity. Numerous abolitionist lecturers, such as William Lloyd Garrison (NAA) and Frederick Douglass, spoke at its assemblies.

The association closed in 1846 because it was not economically sustainable. Its radical philosophy reflected the extent that people grappled with the inequality that existed in the United States. Among the several prominent African Americans who joined the collective were Sojourner Truth, David Ruggles, Stephen Rush, and George Washington Sullivan.

7 FLORENCE CONGREGATIONAL
130 Pine St.

The Florence Congregational Church was a popular venue for many abolitionist speakers who visited Florence. Those speakers included Frederick Douglass and William Lloyd Garrison (NAA).

Florence Congregational Church

8 SOJOURNER TRUTH MEMORIAL
Pine and Park Streets

Sojourner Truth (1797-1883), a famous civil rights advocate for African Americans and women, lived in Florence from 1843 to 1857. The town installed this memorial in 2002, to recognize her important legacy.

Born Isabella Baumfree on a Dutch plantation in upstate New York, Truth spoke Dutch until the age of nine when the family that enslaved her sold her away from her biological family. Truth escaped bondage in 1826, with one of her children. Two other children remained enslaved. Although New York State abolished enslavement the next year in 1827, illegal sales continued to occur and one of Sojourner Truth's sons was a victim of this insidious practice. A plantation in Alabama purchased him but Truth successfully sued the sellers and was able to obtain his return.

In 1843, Isabella Baumfree changed her named to Sojourner Truth, and she began her life's mission to speak out against slavery, and for the rights of women. That same year, Truth joined the Northampton Association of Education and Industry (NAEI). Its mission to advocate for the total equality of people regardless of their sex or race aligned with her own beliefs. Her autobiography, *The Narrative of Sojourner Truth: A Northern Slave*, which was published in 1850, made her a popular speaker on the abolitionist and women's right lecture circuit.

Sojourner Truth Statue

Truth delivered her famous, *"Aren't I a Woman"* speech at the 1851 Women's Rights Convention in Akron, Ohio. Well-intentioned abolitionist writers retitled the speech, *"Ain't I a Woman,"* when it was published. They gave it what they perceived to be a more Southern African American dialect, to appeal to Northern whites who believed that the majority of African Americans spoke in such a dialect. That alteration of her original speech only reinforced negative stereotypes of African Americans. Fortunately, twentieth century historians have corrected that alteration.

"...That man over there says that women need to be helped into carriages, and lifted over ditches, and to have the best place everywhere. Nobody ever helps me into carriages, or over mud-puddles, or gives me any best place! And aren't I a woman? Look at me! Look at my arm! I have ploughed and planted, and gathered into barns, and no man could beat me! And aren't I a woman? I could work as much and eat as much as a man - when I could get it - and bear the lash as well! And aren't I a woman? I have borne five children, and seen most all sold off to slavery, and when I cried out with my mother's grief, none but Jesus heard me! And aren't I a woman?..."

—Sojourner Truth

 ## 9 CHARLES ROBERTS DORSEY HOUSE
114 Pine St.

Charles Roberts Dorsey, the son of Basil Dorsey, built this house on Pine St. Basil Dorsey was one of the prominent African American citizens of Florence. Charles was a teamster in a local quarry.

Charles Roberts Dorsey House

 ## 10 SOJOURNER TRUTH HOUSE
35 Park St.

Abolitionist and feminist, Sojourner Truth lived in this house from 1850 to 1857, after the NAEI (Northampton Association for Education and Industry) disbanded. Truth's speeches against enslavement and for the rights of women were reinforced by her own history which gave a personal moral imperative to the causes for which she spoke.

Sojourner Truth House

"When I left the house of bondage I left everything behind. I wasn't goin' to keep nothin' of Egypt on me, an' so I went to the Lord an' asked him to give me a new name. and the Lord gave me Sojourner because I was to travel up an' down the land showin' the people their sins an' being a sign unto them. Afterward I told the Lord I wanted another name 'cause everybody else had two names; and the Lord gave me Truth, because I was to declare the truth to the people."

–Sojourner Truth

"We'll have our rights; see if we don't; and you can't stop us from them; see if you can. You may hiss as much as you like, but it is comin'. Women don't get half as much rights as they ought to; we want more, and we will have it."

–Sojourner Truth

"...if I have to answer for the deeds done in my body just as much as a man, I have a right to have just as much as a man. There is a great stir about colored men getting' their rights, but not a word about the colored women; and if colored men get their rights, and not colored women theirs, you see the colored men will be masters over the women, and it will be just as bad as it was before. So I am for keeping the thing going while things are stirring; because if we wait till it is still, it will take a great while to get it going again."

–Sojourner Truth

Sojourner Truth

PARK STREET CEMETERY
Park St. near
West Center St.

African Americans important in the history of Florence who were buried in the Park Street Cemetery included: Basil Dorsey, Charles Roberts Dorsey, and Henry Anthony.

 SAMUEL L. HILL HOUSE
UGRR Station
29-33 Maple St.

Samuel L. Hill (NAA), the founder of the Nonotuck Silk Mill Company, also co-founded the Northampton Association for Education and Industry (NAEI).

Samuel Hill House

 HAMMOND HOUSE
UGRR Station
26 Maple St.

Abolitionist and artist, Elisha Hammond (NAA) painted a well-known portrait of Frederick Douglass in 1844.

He was also a fervent abolitionist who used his home as a station on the Underground Railroad.

Elisha Hammond House

 BASIL DORSEY & THOMAS JONES HOUSE
191 Nonotuck St.

Basil Dorsey, a fugitive from slavery in Maryland, settled in Florence where he gained prominence as an active member of the community. See other sites in Florence. Dorsey built this house around 1850. He sold it after he purchased his freedom in the early 1850s.

Thomas H. Jones (1806-1890) briefly lived in this house with his family in

Basil Dorsey / Thomas H. Jones House

the mid to late 1850s. Jones experienced the harsh realities of slavery first-hand after his first wife's mistress moved from Wilmington, NC, and forced the family to break up. Jones married again, this time to Mary Moore who had three children by a previous marriage.

Jones was able to purchase Mary's freedom but not that of her children. Soon after they discovered plans to sell the children, Jones sent Mary and two of the children ahead to Brooklyn and later escaped himself. Jones preached and gave abolitionist lectures to raise money in the North to free the last child left behind. The family purchased this home in 1854.

 15 DAVID RUGGLES CENTER
225 Nonotuck St.
Open by appointment only

Organizers of the David Ruggles Center dedicated the facility on May 4th, 2009. It serves as an education center for all things related to the rich Underground Railroad history of Florence.

David Ruggles Center

 16 SETH HUNT (NAA) HOUSES
UGRR Stations
22 Conz St. /
115 Bridge St.

 17 J.PAYSON WILLSTON (NAA) HOUSE
UGRR Station
Maple and Pine St.

18 GEORGE BENSON HOUSE
UGRR Station
Somewhere on Nonotuck St.

George Benson (NAA) was an active participant in the Northampton Association of Education and Industry. He was also William Lloyd Garrison's brother-in-law.

 19 WILLIAM ADAM (NAA) HOUSE
UGRR Station
Somewhere on Nonotuck St.

 20 MISS COCHRAN (NAA) COTTAGE
UGRR Station
48 Pomeroy Terrace

21 SESSIONS (NAA) HOUSE
UGRR Station
109 Elm St.

22 JONATHAN HUNT MILLS (NAA) HOUSE
UGRR Station
45 Elm St.

23 SAMUEL BOTTOM (NAA) HOUSE
UGRR Station
Main St.

24 ROSS FARM
UGRR Station
123 Meadow St.

The 300-acre Ross Farm was the center of the residential community of the Northampton Association for Education and Industry (NAEI). The original owner, Theodore Burt (NAA), built this farmhouse in 1825. From 1841 to 1845, Samuel Hill (NAA) lived here. Hill was a member of the NAEI and participant on the Underground Railroad. When the NAEI disbanded in 1845, Austin Ross (NAA) purchased the property. Ross also operated the property as a stop on the Underground Railroad before the Civil War and as a dairy farm from 1845 to 1902.

Ross Farm

25 AFRICAN AMERICAN VETERANS OF THE AMERICAN REVOLUTION

Daniel Alvord, Samuel Blackman, Thomas Clark, John Cowell, Barnabas Cole, John Elliot, Asa Lewis, Cato Lewis, Prince Peter, and John Pond were all Florence veterans of the American Revolution.

26 LOCAL RESOURCES
African American Heritage Trail of Florence
www.davidrugglescenter.org

Amherst Map

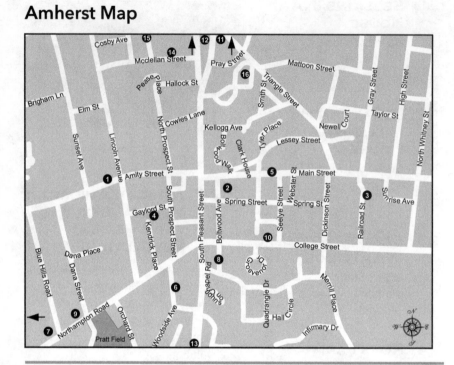

AMHERST

① SITE: AMHERST ACADEMY
Amity St.

Originally built in 1814, Amherst Academy was the predecessor to Amherst College. By 1861, the Academy building was no longer operated by the College as an educational facility. Rather than demolish the building, the President of Amherst College offered it to the African American community for their use as a place of worship. Two of the congregations that used the facility were Zion Mission Chapel and Grace Church. The facility was finally demolished in 1869.

② TOWN HALL TABLETS, AMHERST TOWN HALL
4 Boltwood Ave.

In 1893, the town inscribed the names of over 300 Amherst residents who served in the Civil War on six memorial tablets. Twenty-one of those honored were African American veterans of the Massachusetts 54th Volunteer Regiment and the Massachusetts 5th Calvary.

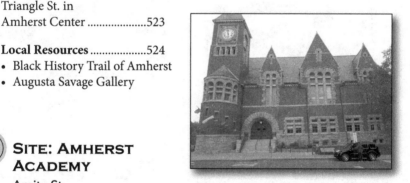

Amherst Town Hall

③ SITE: HENRY JACKSON HOUSE
Somewhere on Railroad St.

Henry Jackson (1817-1902) became one of the heroes of Amherst when he and two friends, Lewis Frazier and William Jennings, orchestrated the rescue of eleven-year-old Angeline Palmer. Angeline, an African American orphan, worked as an indentured servant for the family of Mason and Susan Shaw (NAA) of Belchertown which was ten miles south of Amherst. The trio discovered that the Shaws planned to sell Angeline into slavery when they visited Mrs. Shaw's family in Georgia. See Belchertown site.

Henry Jackson

After Angeline was rescued, the sheriff arrested the three African American men and indicted them with conspiracy to kidnap Angeline. They spent three months in jail for the offense but many in the community considered their actions heroic.

During the Civil War, Frazier and Jennings served in the 54th Regiment and 5th Calvary. Henry Jackson became a successful Amherst entrepreneur. He was buried in West Cemetery.

 HOPE COMMUNITY CHURCH
16 Gaylord St.

When Amherst College students worshipped here in the 1820s, Hope Community Church was born. The original name of the church was Zion Methodist Chapel. A series of prior locations culminated in a permanent home with a new structure at the 16 Gaylord St. location. The church closed in the 1960s and reopened in 1970. The church is now a National Historic Landmark.

Hope Community Church

 FIRST CONGREGATIONAL
165 Main St.

English and African American residents of Amherst worshipped together when this church which was established in 1739. After the African American members increased in numbers over the years, they petitioned for a separate church, and in 1868, the A.M.E. Zion Church was formed. Famous members of First Congregational were Noah Webster (NAA) of Webster's Dictionary and Emily Dickinson (NAA) and her family.

First Congregational Church members were very active during the Civil Rights Movement in the 1960s. Martin Luther King, Jr. spoke here on April 17th, 1961.

First Congregational Church

6 GOODWIN MEMORIAL A.M.E. ZION
41 Woodside Ave.

Goodwin Memorial A.M.E. Zion was organized when African American members split from First Congregational Church. The congregation originally met in Amherst Academy. When the school demolished the building in 1869, the congregation built Zion Methodist Chapel. In 1904, a splinter group developed into Hope Church and the rest of the members joined the A.M.E. denomination. This structure was built in 1910. In 1967, the church changed its name to Goodwin Memo-

rial A.M.E. to honor one of the founders, Moses Goodwin.

Goodwin Memorial A.M.E. Zion

7 HAZEL AVE. / BAKER ST. / NORTHAMPTON RD.

Hazel Ave., Baker St., and Northampton Rd. were the nucleus of an African American community that dated from the 1860s.

8 CHARLES HAMILTON HOUSTON & JOHNSON CHAPEL AT AMHERST COLLEGE
Quadrangle of Amherst College

Johnson Chapel served as a popular venue for notable speakers who visited the Amherst campus. Some of the figures who spoke here included Martin Luther King, Jr. who visited on April 17th, 1961, and Associate Justice Thurgood Marshall of the U.S. Supreme Court who visited in 1978. Marshall's mentor, Charles Hamilton Houston, graduated from Amherst College in 1915. Houston carved his initials in the tower the year of his graduation as was the custom at the time.

Johnson Chapel

After graduation from Amherst College and Harvard Law School, Houston began his career at the NAACP in Washington, D.C., where he established the legal defense arm of the NAACP. That group set about the task to systematically dismantled segregation laws throughout the country. See more on Houston under Cambridge sites.

9 NEWPORT DORM
193-194 Northampton Rd.

Amherst College named this house to honor two of its African American alumni, F. Dwight Newport and Edward Foster Newport. Both Newports attended Amherst College and they returned to work there as athletic train-

ers. Their ancestor, Amos Newport of Hatfield, was also a trailblazer. He filed a *"Freedom Lawsuit"* in 1766. See Hatfield site. Newport House was built on the site of the original Zion Chapel.

Newport House

10 CHARLES DREW HOUSE, AMHERST COLLEGE
Amherst College
56 College Street

After Charles Drew (1904–1950) graduated from Amherst College in 1926, he trained as a surgeon at Columbia University. Drew was one of the foremost medical pioneers of the twentieth century. His discovery of how to store blood plasma for long periods of time allowed the plasma to be used safely in future surgeries. This medical breakthrough revolutionized surgeries in War II and the survival rates of patients increased exponentially.

His discovery led to the American Red Cross to appoint Drew as first Director of its Blood Bank. Drew resigned that position when the armed forces instituted the policy of separation of blood plasma based on the racial identity of the donor. Drew's life ended after a tragic automobile accident.

Charles Drew

"...Excellence of performance will transcend artificial barriers created by man."
– CHARLES DREW

Charles Drew House

A special theme house, the Charles Drew Memorial Culture House on the Amherst College campus, was dedicated to honor Dr. Drew in 1986. The fraternity, Phi Kappa Psi, converted this mid-1800s house into a fraternity house in 1922. In 1948, after the fraternity admitted an African American member, Tom Gibbs, the national committee suspended them. To protest, Amherst College ended the tradition of fraternity houses on campus and created the concept of theme houses instead.

 W.E.B.DuBois LIBRARY AT UMASS AMHERST
154 Hicks Way

A prominent intellectual of the twentieth century, W.E.B. DuBois (1868-1963) was born in Great Barrington, Massachusetts. DuBois fought his entire life for the right and necessity of individual African Americans to develop their intellectual capacity to the greatest level possible in order for all African Americans to thrive.

This position put him in direct conflict with Booker T. Washington, the other primary African American spokesperson at the turn of the century. Washngton felt that African Americans should develop economically at the expense of intellectual growth. Dubois co-founded the NAACP in 1905. Under his leadership, it became synonymous with the spirit of militant protest and self-assertion for African Americans.

UMASS Amherst completed this library in 1974, and they renamed it in 1996, to honor W.E.B. DuBois. The Special Collections and Archives of the library contain a large collection of his writings.

12 W.E.B. DuBois Dept. of Afro-American Studies at UMASS Amherst

329 New Africa House
180 Infirmary Way

One of the remnants of the civil rights movement of the 1960s was a heightened appreciation for, *"Black Pride,"* and awareness of racial identity. One of the manifestations of this new awareness was a demand by African American college students for more African American faculty on campuses across the country. The response by the University of Massachusetts at Amherst resulted in three key decisions: they developed a stellar Black Studies Department during the 1970s and 1980s; they were one of the first universities in the country to divest themselves of investments in companies in South Africa; and they developed culturally relevant courses.

> **Prominent Artists who joined UMass Amherst Black Studies Dept. during the 1970s and 1980s**
> - Pearl Primus, dancer and anthropologist;
> - Molefi Asante, writer;
> - Max Roach, jazz musician;
> - Billy Taylor, jazz musician;
> - Yusef Lateef, jazz musician;
> - John Edgar Wideman, writer;
> - James Baldwin, writer;
> - Chinua Achebe, writer;
> - Richard Yarde, artist;
> - Nelson Steven, artist and one of the founders of the Afri-Cobra movement.

13 Caesar Prutt House

459 South Pleasant S.

Caesar Prutt (1727–1807) was a veteran of three separate wars; the French and Indian War, the Seven Years War, and the American Revolution. Although Prutt never challenged his enslaved status throughout the period that the practice was legal in Massachusetts, he lived his life on his terms. Prutt carried firearms freely, and he earned independent wages which he spent at his discretion.

Caesar Prutt House

MOSES GOODWIN HOUSE
43 McClellan St.

Moses Goodwin (1860–1923), one of the founders of the local A.M.E. Zion Church, lived here. The church was renamed the Goodwin Memorial AME Zion Church in 1963, to honor Goodwin's memory. This house remained in the Goodwin family until 1993.

Moses Goodwin House

 ERWIN & HELEN PETTIJOHN
44 Beston St.

The Pettijohn family's roots in Amherst date back to the early 1700s. The most recent Pettijohns, Erwin and Helen Pettijohn, resided at this residence until Helen died in 1986. Erwin was a successful contractor who employed many community residents in his business.

Pettijohn House

 WEST CEMETERY
Triangle St. in Amherst Center

Many prominent African American citizens and African American veterans of the Civil War were buried in West Cemetery. In 2000, the National Register of Historic Places listed West Cemetery, which was founded in 1737, as an historic resource. Some of the Civil War veterans interred here:

Massachusetts 5th Calvary:
- Charles H. Thompson
- John D. Thompson
- Arthur Jackson
- Samuel Freeman
- Jarvis Jackson
- Windsor Jackson
- Howard E. Paxen
- Joseph J. Solomon
- Lorenzo Sugland
- Christopher Thompson
- Henry Thompson
- Charles Turner
- Charles Waters
- William Williamson

Massachusetts 54th Regiment:
- Charles A. Finnemore
- Sanford Jackson (the husband of Angeline Palmer)
- Jason Champlin
- Francis W. Jennings
- William Jennings (also served in the Massachusetts 5th Calvary)
- William H.H. Jennings
- John N. Langley
- Alexander Taylor
- James Thompson

LOCAL RESOURCES
Black History Trail of Amherst
www.amherstblackhistory.jimdo.com

Augusta Savage Gallery
103 New African House,
UMass Amherst
180 Infirmary Way
413-545-5177
www.fac.umass.edu/online/AugustaSavage

Shaw House

BELCHERTOWN

 ANGELINE PALMER, SHAW HOUSE
32 Park St.

By 1840, Massachusetts had long abolished slavery, but some northern whites continued to kidnap freed African Americans to sell in the South. That year, eleven-year-old Angeline Palmer, an orphan who worked as an indentured servant for the family of Mason and Susan Shaw (NAA) of Belchertown, found herself in the middle of such a plot.

Angeline's half-brother, Lewis Frazier, worked as a laborer in Amherst, which was ten miles north of Belchertown. When a servant in the Shaw household overheard the couple discuss a plan to sell Angeline into slavery in Georgia when they planned to visit Mrs. Shaw's relatives, the servant passed the information on to Frazier. Frazier shared the information with two of his friends, Henry Jackson and William Jennings. All three men were in their mid-twenties. Outraged, the young men quickly took the information to the Amherst Board of Selectmen. The Selectmen refused to believe the plot because the Shaws were respected members of the Belchertown community.

Jackson, Frazier, and Jennings decided to take matters into their own hands and arranged to rescue Angeline as she returned from a visit to her grandmother in Amherst two days before the scheduled trip to Georgia. A nervous Angeline, remember, she was only eleven, shared the plot with her grandmother who did not feel comfortable with the plans so the grandmother shared them with the sheriff.

The sheriff returned Angeline to Belchertown by a different route than the route expected by the rescuers. When the rescuers approached the stagecoach that Angeline was supposed to be in and did not find her, they panicked. Meanwhile, Jackson, who had previously overheard the sheriff's plans, found Angeline at the Shaw's house. He rescued her from the Shaw family and took her to live with a couple in North Amherst.

The sheriff arrested the three African American men on the charged that they kidnapped Angeline. The trio spent three months in jail for the offense but many in the community considered their actions heroic.

Springfield Map

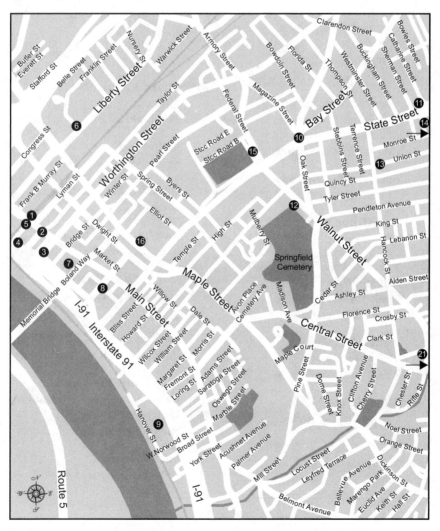

SPRINGFIELD

SPRINGFIELD played an important role in the history of African Americans. John Brown, the fervent white abolitionist, settled in Springfield at the time that he formulated his tactics for the overthrow of slavery. There, Brown found a receptive audience for his beliefs. Springfield residents such as Thomas Thomas, Primus Mason, Eli Baptist, and Rev. John Mars were already key participants in the Underground Railroad and other anti-slavery activity even before Brown arrived. Springfield provided the fertile soil of an anti-slavery community where African Americans were fully integrated in activities to assert their rights as true citizens.

1 MASSASOIT HOTEL
UGRR Station
Main St. and Gridiron St.

The Massasoit Hotel, owned and operated by the Chapin (NAA) family, was an important station on the Underground Railroad. Secret space underneath the main stair was used to hide fugitives until it was safe for

Massasoit Hotel

them to move on. The prominence of the Massasoit Hotel in the community illustrated the extent that prominent citizens of Springfield were involved in the anti-slavery movement.

2 SITE: REV. OSGOOD HOUSE
UGRR Station
Main St. near Hampden St.

Rev. Dr. Samuel Osgood (NAA) was one of many Springfield residents who joined the fight to end slavery. His house was a stop on the Underground Railroad. That stop was referred to as the, *"prophet's chamber."* Osgood was also an active member of the Hampden County Anti-Slavery Society.

3 SITE: THOMAS THOMAS CAFÉ
59 Worthington St.

Thomas Thomas (1817–1893) owned and operated a restaurant at this location from 1872, until his death. Prior to that, he operated another restaurant on Main St. for eleven years. Although Springfield was a place of refuge for fugitives from enslavement, African Americans there still experienced economic hardships and limited opportunities. Despite those limitations, Thomas's quick mind and flexible attitude allowed him to seek and take advantage of a wide variety of opportunities.

Thomas Thomas

Born enslaved in Oxford, MD, Thomas's ambition and industriousness made it possible for him to purchase his freedom with income earned from extra work. Thomas immediately left Oxford after he manumitted himself. For several years he was a drifter who traveled from place to place but he always managed to find work. While employed in Springfield, IL, Thomas made the acquaintance of Abraham Lincoln.

Work on a steamboat on the Mississippi and Arkansas rivers provided Thomas with an opportunity to trade in consumer commodities such as eggs and potatoes. Unfortunately, his success was short-lived. The authorities jailed him in New Orleans for violation of the restrictions on free movement for African Americans. In fact, some southern states had laws that required freed men to leave within six months or risk re-enslavement. After that experience, Thomas relocated to Spring-field, MA, in 1844, where he became a fixture in the abolitionist community.

When John Brown arrived in Springfield in 1847, he and Thomas quickly developed a relationship built on trust and respect. Officially, John Brown hired Thomas to work in his warehouse. Unofficially, Thomas assisted Brown in the development of his network of associates in the African American community. Thomas introduced John Brown to the congregation of the Sanford St. Church, also known as the Free Church. Brown decided to join the congregation while he lived in Springfield. That congregation was the primary source of members for the League of Gileadites, the citizen militia that Brown organized to defend fugitives from capture.

Thomas Thomas was also one of the founders of the Springfield Order of Masons. He resided on Auburn St. at the time of his death.

 SITE: PERKINS & BROWN WAREHOUSE #1
UGRR Station
Gridiron St. and Columbus Ave.-Demolished

John Brown and his partner, Simon Perkins (NAA) of Akron, OH, located their wool trading business in these two warehouses. Their close proximity to the railroad station facilitated the transport of the wool.

⑤ SITE: PERKINS & BROWN WAREHOUSE #2

UGRR Station
Main St. and Gridiron St.
near the Massasoit Hotel.

⑥ SITE: JOHN BROWN HOUSE

51 Franklin Street

John Brown (1800-1859) (NAA), a pivotal personality in the years prior to the Civil War, lived in Springfield from 1846 until 1851. His dedication to end slavery and his willingness to put his life and the lives of his family at risk in that fight made him a hero of mythical proportions to those enslaved and to those repulsed by the institution of slavery. More than any other event, Brown's raid on Harper's Ferry, a Federal arsenal, on Oct. 16th, 1859, was the single, most decisive event that precipitated the Civil War.

John Brown

Brown grew up on a farm in Ohio. He often accompanied his father as he made beef deliveries to the army during the war of 1812. Brown's observations on those trips had a powerful effect on him. They gave Brown an appreciation of the necessity for strict discipline in order to achieve military objectives and a greater appreciation of the sacredness of every life. Those impressions influenced the development of Brown's strategy to create an insurrection of the enslaved population in the United States.

By 1839, John Brown had developed such abhorrence to slavery that he decided to dedicate his life to abolish it. His adult occupations as a wool farmer, a leather tanner, and a surveyor, were simply means to finance his goal to end slavery. He relocated to Massachusetts in the mid-1840s to work as an intermediary for wool farmers in Ohio. He was a partner with Simon Perkins (NAA) in this business venture. The first warehouse Brown rented for their business was located at Gridiron St. and Columbus Ave. The second warehouse was located at Main St. and Gridiron St. near the Massasoit Hotel.

During his stay in Massachusetts, Brown joined an African American church, the First Congregational Church. It was also known as the, *"Free Church."* It was in Springfield that Brown began to develop his plans for a major insurrection against enslavement. He first organized the *"League of Gileadites,"* an African American militia to confront fugitive bounty hunters. The responsibilities of the fifty members of the League were to aid and assist fugitives from bondage in response to the Fugitive Slave Act of 1850. After the formation of this group, bounty hunters were not able to capture any fugitives in Springfield. The charter that John Brown wrote for the League of Gileadites included advice on how members should conduct themselves when confronted by bounty hunters:

"...Nothing so charms the American people as personal bravery. The trial for life of one bold and to some extent successful man, for defending his rights in good earnest, would arouse more sympathy throughout the nation than the accumulated wrongs and sufferings of more than three millions of our submissive colored population. ...Colored people have more fast friends amongst the whites than they suppose, and would have ten times the number they now have were they but half as much in earnest to secure their dearest rights as they are to ape the follies and extravagances of their white neighbors, and to indulge in idle show, in ease, and in luxury...Should one of your number be arrested, you must collect together as quickly as possible, so as to outnumber your adversaries who are taking an active part against you. Let no able-bodied man appear on the ground unequipped, or with his weapons exposed to view; let that be understood beforehand. Your plans must be known only to yourself, and with the understanding that all traitors must die, wherever caught and proven to be guilty. Give all cowards an opportunity to show it on condition of holding their peace. Do not delay one moment after you are ready; you will lose all your resolution if you do. Let the first blow be the signal for all to engage, and when engaged do not do your work by halves; but make clean work with your enemies, and be sure you meddle not with any others. By going about your business quietly, you will get the job disposed of before the number that an uproar would bring together can collect; and you will have the advantage of those who come out against you, for they will be wholly unprepared with either equipment or matured plans–all with them will be confusion and terror. Your enemies will be slow to attack you after you have once done up the work nicely; and if they should they will have to encounter your white friends as well as you, for you may safely calculate on a division of the whites, and by that means get to an honorable parley.

Be firm, determined, and cool; but let it be understood that you are not to be driven to desperation without making it an awful dear job to others as well as to you. Give them to know distinctly that those who live in wooden houses should not throw fire, and that you are just as able to suffer as your white neighbors. After effecting a rescue, if you are assailed, go into the houses of your most *prominent and influential white friends with your wives, and that will effectually fasten upon them the suspicion of being connected with you, and will compel them to make a common cause with you, ...You may make a tumult in the court-room where a trial is going on by burning gunpowder freely in paper packages, if you cannot think of any better way to create a momentary alarm,...*

A lasso might possibly be applied to a slave-catcher for once with good effect. Hold on to your weapons, and never be persuaded to leave them, part with them, or have them far away from you. Stand by one another, and by your friends, while a drop of blood remains; and be hanged, if you must, but tell no tales out of school. Make no confession.

AGREEMENT
As citizens of the United States of America, trusting in a Just and Merciful God, whose spirit and all-powerful aid we humbly implore, we will ever be true to the Flag of our beloved Country, always acting under it. We whose names are hereunto affixed do constitute ourselves a branch of the United States League of Gileadites. That we will provide ourselves at once with suitable implements, and will aid those who do not possess the means, if any such are disposed to join us. We invite every colored person whose heart is engaged for the performance of our business, whether male or female, old or young...."

–League of Gileadites

John Brown's business venture in Springfield was not a success. The wool merchants to whom he supplied wool sued the firm for breach of contract in several lawsuits.

Brown's company won some of those lawsuits and they lost some, but the cumulative financial strain eventually put Brown and Perkins out of business. That business failure triggered John Brown's relocation from Springfield.

In the early 1850s, John Brown and his seven sons and a son-in-law moved to *"Bleeding Kansas,"* so named because of the fierceness of the fight to determine whether the state would become a free state or slave state. Since that decision would be decided by ballot, both sides tried to reinforce the population with settlers of their respective beliefs. The violence was very intense. One particular campaign left one of Brown's sons dead, one became a prisoner, and another son and his son-in-law were wounded. Although Brown's family suffered personally, his campaigns were considered successful because they freed several enslaved individuals. Those Kansas victories led to Brown's nickname, *"Osawatomie Brown."*

The victories in Kansas convinced John Brown that only a large-scale insurrection would effectively end slavery in the United States. He returned to Massachusetts in January of 1857, to raise funds to continue his efforts of surprise raids. Here he met with key individuals, the *"Secret Committee of Six."* The group raised funds for Brown to continue his successful raids in Kansas and for the defense of *"Free State"* settlers, many of whom had relocated from Massachusetts with the assistance of the New England Emigrant Aid Society. The *"Secret Committee of Six"* later funded Brown's raid on Harper's Ferry in 1859.

Secret Committee of Six
- Thomas Wentworth Higginson
- Gerrit Smith
- Rev. Theodore Parker
- Dr. Samuel Gridley Howe
- George Luther Stearns
- Franklin Sanborn

Over twenty documented insurrections against enslavement had been attempted in North America previously. They inspired John Brown to not only believe in the righteousness of his cause, but to believe that their goals could be successful with the right strategy. Also, the only successful insurrection in the Western Hemisphere, the Haitian Revolution of the 1790s led by a formerly enslaved leader, Toussaint L'Ouverture, inspired many to believe that such a revolt could be successfully carried out in the United States.

Well-known Revolts in U.S.

1712	Unknown Individuals	New York, NY
1741	Unknown Individuals	New York, NY
1800	Gabriel Prosser	Henrico Cty, VA
1822	Denmark Vesey	Charleston, SC
1831	Nat Turner	Southampton, VA

Those insurrection attempts so terrorized the local white populations, especially that of Nat Turner which took the life of 51 whites, that the punishment of the leaders was especially brutal in order to put fear into the very souls of anyone who even contemplated participation in a revolt. In one instance, the Denmark Vesey revolt, the severed heads of the insurrectionists were put on pikes at the entrance to town. Despite that threat, enslaved individuals continued attempts to organize revolts.

John Brown's insurrection at Harper's Ferry and Gabriel Prosser's revolt in Virginia were both based on the capture of an arsenal for the eventual distribution of weapons. A high level of secrecy was critical as the revolt was planned because of the high potential for betrayal. Brown carried out his plans with only twenty-one men, sixteen whites and five blacks. The excerpt below is from John Brown's last speech at his trial:

"... I wish to say, furthermore, that you had better, all you people at the South, prepare yourselves for a settlement of that question that must come up for settlement sooner than you are prepared for it. The sooner you are prepared the better. You may dispose of me very easily. I am nearly disposed of now; but this question is still to be settled, this negro question, I mean; the end of that is not yet."

"...I deny everything but what I have all along admitted–the design on my part to free the slaves....had I so interfered in behalf of the rich, the powerful... or in behalf of any of their friends,...and suffered and sacrificed what I have in this interference, it would have been all right, and every man in this court would have deemed it an act worthy of reward rather than punishment.

...This court acknowledges, as I suppose, the validity of the law of God. I see a book kissed here which I suppose to be the Bible, or at least the New Testament. That teaches me that all things whatsoever I would that men should do to me, I should do even so to them. It teaches me, further, to "remember them that are in bonds, as bound with them." I endeavored to act up to that instruction. I say, I am yet too young to understand that God is any respecter of persons. I believe that to have interfered as I have done as I have always freely admitted I have done in behalf of His despised poor, was not wrong, but right. Now, if it is deemed necessary that I should forfeit my life for the furtherance of the ends of justice, and mingle my blood further with the blood of my children and with the blood of millions in this slave country whose rights are disregarded by wicked, cruel, and unjust enactments, I submit; so let it be done!..."

–John Brown

Intellectuals, both here and abroad, displayed an outburst of support for John Brown and what he attempted. Henry David Thoreau gave a speech on October 30th, 1859, in which he pled for John Brown's life. He praised Brown's actions but acknowledged the fact that Brown would probably still be executed. Thoreau stated:

"...These men, in teaching us how to die, have at the same time taught us how to live. If this man's acts and words do not create a revival, it will be the severest possible satire on the acts and words that do. It is the best news that America has ever heard. It has already quickened the feeble pulse of the North, and infused more and more generous blood into her veins and hearts than any number of *years of what is called commercial and political prosperity could. How many a man who was lately contemplating suicide has now something to live for!*

One writer says that Brown's peculiar monomania made him to be "dreaded by the Missourians as a supernatural being." Sure enough, a hero in the midst of us cowards is always so dreaded. He is just that thing. He shows himself superior to nature. He has a spark of divinity in him...."

–Henry David Thoreau

On Feb. 8th, 1861, just a little over one year after John Brown's execution for his failed attempt to capture Harper's Ferry, seven Southern states seceded from the Union and formed the Confederate States.

> **Original Seven Confederate States**
> - Alabama
> - Florida
> - Georgia
> - Louisiana
> - Mississippi
> - South Carolina
> - Texas

The primary reason was a disagreement about the expansion of slavery in the new territories. On April 12th, 1861, the Southern Confederation's attack on Fort Sumter in South Carolina was the official commencement of the Civil War.

 7 PAN AFRICAN MUSEUM

1500 Main St.
413-733-1823
www.pahmusa.mysite.com

Permanently displayed in this museum is the exhibit, *"Forgotten Images of the Pioneer Valley."* It also regularly featured exhibits on the African American history of greater Springfield. Every third Sunday, the museum presents free tours of the sites on the Underground Railroad of downtown Springfield.

 8 FIRST CHURCH OF SPRINGFIELD WILLIAM GREEN JENNY CUMFREY WILLIAMS

Site: Court Square

William Green, a fugitive from Maryland, escaped to Springfield where he married Parthenia Peters in 1841. The couple attended First Church of Springfield at this location. Green worked on the Underground Railroad and he was active in the League of Gileadites, the organization that provided armed resistance to fugitive bounty hunters. In 1853, Green followed in the footsteps of many fugitives and documented his story in a written narrative, *A Narrative of Events in the Life of William Green, Formerly a Slave, Written by Himself.*

Around 1800, Jenny Cumfrey was one of many fugitives who made

Springfield home. The difference in her situation was that Cumfrey did not escape from the deep South but from New York state, Massachusetts's neighbor to the west. She married Jack Williams at the First Church of Springfield in 1802. The couple settled into a reasonably comfortable domestic routine until Peter Van Geyseling (NAA) arrived from New York in 1808 to claim Jenny as his property. The Springfield community, white and black, raised the funds to purchase Jenny's freedom and prevented her return to slavery.

New York State Gradual Emancipation Act of 1799
All enslaved individuals born after July 4th, 1799, would be free but indentured until adulthood.

New York State Emancipation Act of 1817
All enslaved individuals born before July 4th, 1799 would be freed in 1827.

Order of Emancipation in Northern States
1774	Rhode Island
1777	Vermont
1780	Pennsylvania
1783	Massachusetts
1784	Connecticut
1799	New York

Maine never allowed slavery in its borders.

9 NAISMITH BASKETBALL HALL OF FAME
1150 West Columbus Ave.
10 a.m. to 4 p.m. daily

This museum was named after the creator of the game of basketball, James

Naismith (NAA). The museum first opened in 1968, and it was relocated in 1985, to accommodate its large number of visitors. Many African American giants of the sport were inducted into the Basketball Hall of Fame.

10 LITTLE HAYTI
Area of State St. to Bay Rd.

Little Hayti received its name because of the large number of African Americans who chose to settle there. African American developer, Primus Mason, developed the area in the mid-1800s with two partners, William Clark and Emptson Brown. African Americans throughout the north recognized a need to settle in close proximity to one another and the reasonably priced properties in this neighborhood of Springfield accommodated that need.

11 MASON SQUARE
Old Hill, Upper Hill, Bay, and McKnight Neighborhoods

In 1989, Springfield renamed this area Mason Sq. to honor Primus Mason (1817–1892). Although Primus Mason was born into a life of poverty, he always nurtured a desire to contribute to the well-being of his fellow citizens. Mason raised himself out of poverty and provided for his neighbors through numerous endeavors. That altruistic trait made him a true hero of his community.

Primus Mason was born in Monson, MA. At an early age, he was hired out as a laborer to help support his family. His employer was so cruel that Mason eventually ran away to Springfield when he was twenty. Mason could not read or write until he was over forty, yet he took any job that was available. One of his jobs, that of a horse undertaker, was a job that many other individuals shunned.

Mason's frugal lifestyle allowed him to accumulate capital to fund his many ventures. One venture, depleted his savings by $1,000 when he withdrew funds to finance a trip to California to try his luck in the Gold Rush. After that unsuccessful venture, Mason returned to Springfield where he resumed his investments in real estate.

Mason's real estate acumen enabled him to become one of Springfield's wealthiest citizens. He used his wealth

Primus Mason

to benefit his fellow citizens at every opportunity. His generosity continued even after his death. In his will, Mason left an estate valued at over $40,000 to establish the Springfield Home for Aged Men.

 ## SPRINGFIELD HOME FOR AGED MEN
Walnut St.

Primus Mason established this Home for Aged Men through his will. Mason wanted this home to be a place:

> *"...where old men who are worthy may feel at home."*
> —PRIMUS MASON

 ## ST. JOHN'S CONGREGATIONAL
UGRR Station
643 Union St.

African American abolitionists established the Sanford St. Church in 1844 as the first African American church in Springfield. The church was renamed St. John's Congregational Church in 1892 to honor its most famous member, John Brown. Brown joined the congregation in 1846. The church was known as the *"Free Church"* in the years prior to the Civil War because of the activist position its members took on the issue of slavery. John Brown became a trusted member of the congregation and he recruited from its members to form his radical group, the League of Gileadites, formed in January, 1851. A bible which John Brown donated to the congregation has been permanently displayed in the church.

Sanford Street Church was led at that time by Rev. John Mars. Rev. Mars was a self-emancipated person from Connecticut who was outspoken in his opposition to slavery. He advised his congregation to, *"turn plowshares into swords,"* to defend themselves against bounty hunters. On Oct. 4th, 1850, Mars along with two other members of the community, John B. Smith, and B.B. Young, sent this letter to *"The Liberator"* newspaper to protest the Fugitive Slave Act of 1850:

St. John's Congregational Church

"Whereas, a Bill entitled the Fugitive Slave Bill has recently passed both Houses of Congress...

1. *Resolved, That in the event of this Bill becoming a law, we, the citizens of Springfield, feel called upon to express, in the most decided manner, and in language not to be misunderstood, our disapprobation of the same, or of any further legislation having a tendency to oppress mankind.*
2. *Resolved, That we will repudiate all and every law that has for its object the oppression of any human being, or seeks to assign us degrading positions.*
3. *And whereas, we hold to the declaration of the poet, "that he who would be free, himself must strike the blow," and that resistance to tyrants is obedience to God,*
4. *Resolved, That we do welcome to our doors everyone who feels and claims for himself the position of a man, and has broken from the Southern house of bondage, and that we feel ourselves justified in using every means which the God of love has placed in our power to sustain our liberty.*
5. *And, whereas, active vigilance is the price of liberty, we resolve ourselves into a Vigilance Association, to look out for the ...fugitive, and also for the oppressor, ...*

> 6. *Resolved, That should the task-master presume to enter our dwellings, and attempt to reclaim any of our brethren whom he may call his slaves, we feel prepared to resist his pretensions.*
>
> 7. *Resolved, That as the passage of the Fugitive Slave Bill is an encroachment upon the sovereign rights of the Free States, and as the soil of the State of Massachusetts is thereby made slave-hunting-ground, and her citizens slave-hunters, that it behooves her, as a free Sovereign State, to exercise her legal authority in sustaining herself against being made a participant in so disgraceful an act."*

Throughout the Civil War, Rev. Mars spearheaded efforts to organize African American troops. He was one of the earliest African American commissioned officers with his appointment as Chaplain.

Eli Baptist and Thomas Thomas were two other crucial members of the Free Church. Both men were very active in the efforts to defend fugitives in Springfield. They later organized self-help and mutual aid groups such as the Union Mutual Beneficial Society and the Springfield branch of the Masonic Lodge.

 ANNIE MCTIER HOUSE

20-24 Wilbraham Ave.

Annie McTier was the first African American female in Springfield to register to vote after female citizens in the United States won the right to vote on Aug. 18th, 1920.

 SPRINGFIELD ARMORY

One Armory Sq., Suite 2.
413-734-8551

This facility was opened in 1777, as the Springfield Arsenal. It was renamed in 1794, when it began to manufacture small arms. The Springfield Rifle, a weapon used by troops throughout the Civil War, was manufactured here. It weighed nine pounds, was fifty-six inches in length, and it fired two to four rounds per minute. This single-shot rifle was popular because it could be easily and successfully used by inexperienced troops because of its range (100 to 400 yards), its accuracy, and its reliability. Today, the Springfield Armory is maintained by the National Park Service as a National Historic Site.

LYMAN & MERRIE WOOD MUSEUM

21 Edwards St
800-625-7738

One of the permanent exhibits of the Lyman and Merrie Wood Museum is the exhibit, *"John Brown, Abraham Lincoln and the Civil War."* That exhibit contains many artifacts and documents from the period that John Brown lived in Springfield.

 ## JUPITER RICHARDS

Revolutionary War Veteran

Jupiter Richards was a veteran of the American Revolution where he served as a member of the 2nd Massachusetts Volunteer Infantry Regiment. His war service lasted for seven years.

 ## DR. JEFFERSON CHURCH (NAA) HOUSE

UGRR Station
Site Unknown

 ## JOSEPH C. BUELL (NAA) HOUSE

UGRR Station
Site Unknown

 ## JOHN HOLLAND (NAA) HOUSE

UGRR Station
Site Unknown

 ## CHIEF JUSTICE RODERICK IRELAND

Terrence St., now
Chief Justice Roderick L. Ireland Way

Roderick Ireland (b. 1944), the first African American Justice of the Massachusetts Supreme Court, was born in Springfield and raised on this street. Ireland received degrees from Lincoln University, Columbia Law School, Harvard Law School, and a PhD. from Northeastern University.

In 1971, Ireland began his legal career as a staff attorney for the Roxbury Defender's Committee, a non-profit that offered legal services to those who could not afford an attorney. In his first term (1975–1979), Gov. Michael Dukakis (NAA) appointed Ireland to the Boston Juvenile Court in 1977. In his third term (1987–1990), Gov. Dukakis appointed him to the Massachusetts Court of Appeals. Gov. William Weld (NAA) appointed him as Associated Justice of the Massachusetts Supreme Judicial Court in 1997. Gov. Deval Patrick nominated Ireland to become the Chief Justice of the Massachusetts Supreme Judicial Court in 2010.

The City of Springfield honored Ireland in June of 2015, and renamed Terrence St. where he grew up as, Chief Justice Roderick L. Ireland Way.

22 DRED SCOTT CASE CALVIN CHAFFEE & ELIZA SANFORD EMERSON CHAFFEE
Site Unknown

Massachusetts had an interesting tangential link to the legal case that riveted U.S. citizens in the mid 19th century, the Dred Scott case. It puzzled legal minds, then and now, by the lack of logic of its majority decision, that African Americans enslaved or free, could never be U.S. citizens, and therefore, had no legal right to sue in U.S. courts. That decision was made despite the fact that Scott had previously won his case in a Missouri state court. This case revealed the legal complexity the United States created for itself when it did not end slavery in the Constitution.

That initial ambiguity eventually led to confusion about which government entity, Congress or the states, had the power to regulate slavery. The confused outcome of the Dred Scott case was one of several factors that pushed the United States into the Civil War. In that landmark U.S. Supreme Court decision, only two justices voted in the minority. One of them, Justice Benjamin Robbins Curtis of Massachusetts, resigned his lifetime judgeship to protest that pernicious decision.

Dred Scott (1799–1858) was born enslaved by Peter Blow (NAA) in Virginia. He was taken to Alabama to work on the Blow family farm in 1818. After the farm failed, the family relocated to Missouri with Scott in 1830. There the family sold Scott to a surgeon

Dred Scott

in the U.S. Army, Dr. Emerson (NAA). When Dr. Emerson was sent to a post in Illinois, he took Scott with him. In Illinois in 1837, Scott married Harriet Robinson, another enslaved person. Robinson's enslaver transferred Harriet to Dr. Emerson after the marriage.

Meanwhile, Dr. Emerson married Eliza Sanford (NAA) in 1838. After a brief stay in Louisiana, the Emersons returned to Missouri in 1840. When Dr. Emerson died in 1843, his widow inherited his estate which included the Scott family. Mrs. Emerson leased them out for hire.

Dred Scott attempted to purchase his family's freedom in 1846, but Eliza refused and Scott decided to sue in St. Louis Circuit Court. A Missouri legal precedent, *"Once free, always free,"* made Scott optimistic of victory because he and his family had lived briefly in the free state of Illinois. Scott won that first court case. Eliza, who had relocated to Springfield, MA in 1850, to marry Calvin Chaffee (NAA), won an appeal in 1852.

In 1853, Scott sued again, but this time in federal court. After Eliza's marriage, she passed ownership of the Scott family to her brother, John Sanford (NAA), a resident of New York state. When Scott lost the federal court appeal, he decided to take his case to the U.S. Supreme Court. That case was not heard by the Supreme Court until 1857. In an ironic twist, Dred Scott was assisted financially with his legal expenses by descendents of the Blow family who had become abolitionists.

Calvin Chaffee was a professed abolitionist with political aspirations. The local public soon became aware of the hypocrisy of Chaffee's situation, that of an abolitionist married to a slave owner. The public pressure on the Chaffees led to the Scott family's manumission on May 26th, 1857. Dred Scott enjoyed his freedom for only a short time, he died the next year.

 LOCAL RESOURCES
African American Heritage Trail
www.ourpluralhistory.stcc.edu/maps/aaht.

Springfield History Library
21 Edwards St.
www.springfieldmuseums.org

EAST LONGMEADOW

 ELIJAH BURT (NAA) HOUSE
UGRR Station
201 Chestnut St.

Elijah Burt House

SOUTHAMPTON

 HON. SAMUEL C. POMEROY (NAA) HOUSE
UGRR Station
Site Unknown

HUNTINGTON

 ASA MERRITT (NAA) HOUSE
UGRR Station
Site Unknown

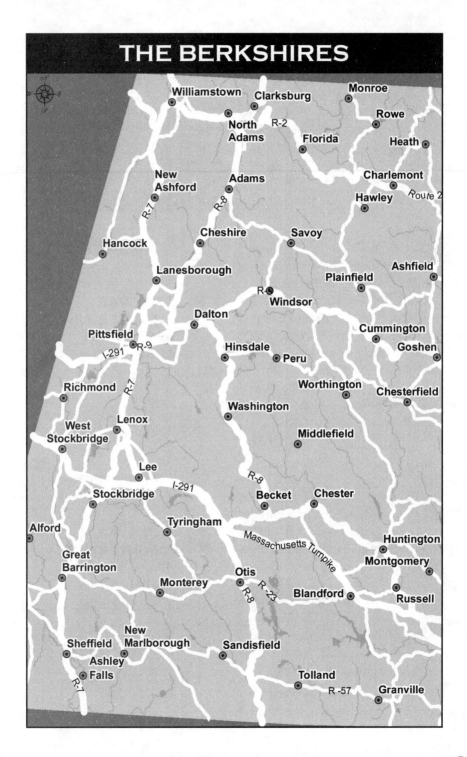

THE BERKSHIRES

Williamstown

Clarksburg

Monroe

Rowe

North Adams

R-2

Florida

Heath

New Ashford

Adams

Charlemont

Hawley

Route 2

R-7

R-8

Hancock

Cheshire

Savoy

Lanesborough

Ashfield

Plainfield

R-9

Windsor

Dalton

Cummington

Goshen

Pittsfield

I-291

R-9

Hinsdale

Peru

R-7

Worthington

Chesterfield

Richmond

Washington

West Stockbridge

Lenox

Middlefield

Lee

R-8

I-291

Stockbridge

Becket

Chester

Tyringham

Alford

Massachusetts Turnpike

Huntington

Montgomery

Great Barrington

Otis

R-23

Monterey

R-8

Blandford

Russell

New Marlborough

Sheffield

Sandisfield

Ashley Falls

R-7

Tolland

R-57

Granville

543 🐾

THE AFRICAN AMERICAN population of the Berkshires was always small but active. That community made significant contributions to the legacy of this state. The successful "Freedom Lawsuit" of Mum Bett Freeman influenced the cessation of slavery in this state. This region also supplied a high proportion of African American volunteers to all of this country's wars. Also, the foremost African American intellectual of the twentieth century, W.E.B. DuBois, was born and raised in the Berkshires. Those contributions were documented in the publication, *African American Heritage in the Upper Housatonic Valley,* edited by David Levinson. The region also established a series of brochures on African American history in the region, *African American Heritage in the Upper Housatonic Valley.* Both of those resources were invaluable in my research.

The dominant occupation of African American men in the region before the Civil War was that of farm laborer. The rise of the tourist industry in the late nineteenth century changed that employment trend. By the end of WWI, the majority of African American males worked in the hospitality industry or in service related jobs that were dependent on the tourist industry. The majority of African American women worked as domestics in private residences. Later they did the same work in the hospitality industry.

The high percentage of employed African Americans was a source of customers for businesses that supported that community. Most of those businesses were located in Pittsfield. They were primarily service related businesses such as barbershops, tailors, and taxis, but they also included some restaurants and other limited retail establishments.

CHESTER

 ## CIVIL WAR VOLUNTEER IN MASS. 54TH REGIMENT

Justin M. Duncan enlisted in March of 1863.

BECKET

 ## CIVIL WAR VOLUNTEER IN MASS. 55TH REGIMENT

Anthony L. King enlisted in August of 1864.

2 JACOB'S PILLOW DANCE RETREAT

UGRR Station
358 George Carter Road
413-243-0745
www.jacobspillow.org

George Carter (NAA) founded Jacob's Pillow farm in1790. The name derived from the Biblical references to Jacob's Ladder and the appearance of the road that zigged-zagged from the bottom of the hill to the farm at the top. The Pillow in the name was a reference to the shape of several boulders on the site. The farm was a stop on the Underground Railroad in the mid-1800s.

Ted Shawn (NAA), a pioneer of modern dance, purchased the farm as a retreat in 1930. He and his wife, Ruth St. Denis (NAA), another modern dance pioneer, developed summer dance programs at the site in the mid-1930s, and Jacob's Pillow Dance was born. Warren Davis, a lumberman from Great Barrington, located, felled, and hand-hewed the beams that span the central space in the main theater.

Some of the most famous African Americans in modern dance have appeared at Jacob's Pillow. They included Asadata Dafora, Pearl Primus, Carmen de Lavallade, Geoffrey Holder, Katherine Dunham, Alvin Ailey, the Dance Theatre of Harlem, Bill T. Jones, Savion Glover, and many others. The dance troupe, the Zaccho Dance Theatre, developed a site specific performance, *"Invisible Wings,"* in 1998. That performance was based on Jacob's Pillow's history as a site on the Underground Railroad. The summer festival season runs from the third week of June through the third week of August.

Jacob's Pillow

HINSDALE

 VETERAN'S MEMORIAL
Lawn of Town Library
58 Maple St.

This memorial was dedicated by the town in 1923. On it are engraved the names of Hinsdale residents who served in this country's wars. The Civil War veterans listed included several members of the Mass. 54th Regiment. Charles W. Potter enlisted in July of 1863. Lorenzo S. Duncan, Thompson Freeman, and Frank Hamilton II all enlisted in December of 1864.

 CIVIL WAR VOLUNTEERS IN THE MASSACHUSETTS 5TH CALVARY:
William Michaels enlisted in March of 1864, and William F. Thompson enlisted in October of 1865.

PERU

 AUGUSTUS C. FRISSELL (NAA) HOUSE
UGRR Station
Site Unknown

 CIVIL WAR VOLUNTEER IN MASS. 54TH REGIMENT

Joseph Kelson enlisted in Dec. of 1863.

DALTON

 ZENAS MARSHALL CRANE (NAA) HOUSE
UGRR Station
Site Unknown

2 HOOSE FAMILY HOUSE
Corner of Gulf St. and High St.

The Hoose family was prominent in the African American community throughout the Berkshires. The family originally settled in Dalton in the late 1700s, and members spread throughout the Berkshires from there. The mother of Ulysses Franklin Grant of Williamstown, the National Baseball Hall of Famer, was Frances Hoose. Another family member, Hannah Hoose of Pittsfield, was the first African American female in the country to enlist in WWII. A young male of the family, Edward Hoose of Dalton, joined the Mass. 54th Regiment at the age of 21. This ancestral home of the family is the oldest home built by African Americans in the Berkshires.

③ WIZARD'S GLEN
UGRR Station
Gulf Road

A small group of African Americans coalesced around Wizard's Glen during the 1820s, to form a tight-knit but short-lived community. Local legend described a cave that once existed underneath the road. It was believed the cave was used as a stop on the Underground Railroad. Those who settled in Wizard's Glen lived a modest but comfortable existence.

④ CENTER CEMETERY
Main St.

Civil War veterans buried here were N. Barnes, a veteran of the Mass. 55th Regiment, and Henry Jones. Other notable members of the African American community of Dalton buried here included George W. Hoose of the Hoose family.

⑤ CIVIL WAR VOLUNTEERS: MASS. 54TH

Edward Hoose enlisted in Dec. of 1863.

MASS. 55TH:

Milton M. Gardner enlisted in August of 1864.

SAVOY

① ANDREW J. BABBIT (NAA) HOUSE
UGRR Station
Site Unknown

ADAMS

① ROBERT KIRKPATRICK (NAA) HOUSE
UGRR Station
Site Unknown

② MASS. 54TH VOLUNTEER

Jeremiah L. W. Bradley of South Adams enlisted in December of 1863.

NORTH ADAMS

① HENRY L. DAWES (NAA) HOUSE
UGRR Station
Site Unknown

HENRY P. PHILLIPS (NAA) HOUSE

UGRR Station
Site Unknown

MARGARET ALEXANDER HART

North Adams
Normal School, now,
Massachusetts College of
Liberal Arts
375 Church St.

In 1935, Williamstown native, Margaret Alexander Hart (1911–2004), was the first African American to graduate from the Massachusetts College of Liberal Arts. After she completed a post-graduate degree at Columbia University in New York City, she taught in Virginia. Hart returned to Pittsfield in 1940, when her father became ill.

Pittsfield hired her as the first African American teacher in the school system and she remained there throughout her career. Hart was twice honored by Massachusetts College of Liberal Arts: in 1996, they awarded her an honorary doctorate; and in 2004, they named a scholarship after her.

WILLIAMSTOWN

DR. SABIN (NAA) HOUSE

UGRR Station
Site Unknown

SITE: ULYSSES FRANKLIN GRANT HOUSE

Spring St.

Ulysses Franklin Grant (1865–1937) achieved considerable success as a professional athlete. He was born in Pittsfield on August 1st, 1865, but he spent his childhood in Williamstown. Grant played for the Buffalo Bisons from 1886 to 1888. African Americans were banned from the league in 1890. Grant played second baseman most of his professional career. Small in stature at 5'-7" tall and 155 lbs., Grant displayed considerable power at the bat, he was frequently the foremost hitter in the league at the bat. His speed also allowed him to steal bases on a regular basis.

Despite Grant's talents and the talent of other African American athletes on the field, racism prevailed. African American players had to construct special wooden shin guards to protect themselves from the attempts of other players to injure them. African American players formed the Negro Leagues to continue to participate in the sport after they were banned from the league.

Ulysses Franklin Grant

Grant played professionally until 1903. He worked the remainder of his life as a waiter in New York City until his death on May 27th, 1937. Considered one of the best players of the 19th century, Grant was elected to the National Baseball Hall of Fame in 2006. His grave at East Ridgelawn Cemetery in Clifton, NJ remained unmarked until 2011.

NEW ASHFORD

(1) CIVIL WAR VOLUNTEERS IN THE 5TH CALVARY

Isaac Johnson enlisted in March, 1864.

LANESBOROUGH

(1) LYMAN W. HALL (NAA) HOUSE
UGRR Station
Site Unknown

(2) AMERICAN REVOLUTIONARY WAR VETERANS:

Four African Americans from Lanesborough were documented as veterans of the Revolutionary War: Negro Cato, William Johnson, Monday Manley, and Primus Putnam.

(3) CIVIL WAR VOLUNTEERS FROM LANESBOROUGH MASS. 54TH

Henry E. Jones enlisted in November of 1863 and William Parret enlisted in July of 1863. Charles Hamilton also enlisted into the 54th Regiment. Hamilton was the grandfather of Charles Persip, the first African American recruit from the Berkshires in World War I.

MASS. 5TH:

Sylvester Moores enlisted in March, 1864.

CHESHIRE

 ALONZO CUMMINGS (NAA) HOUSE
UGRR Station
Site Unknown

 **AMERICAN REVOLUTION VETERANS:**

Two African Americans participated in the war from Cheshire: Brister and Cyrus.

Pittsfield Map

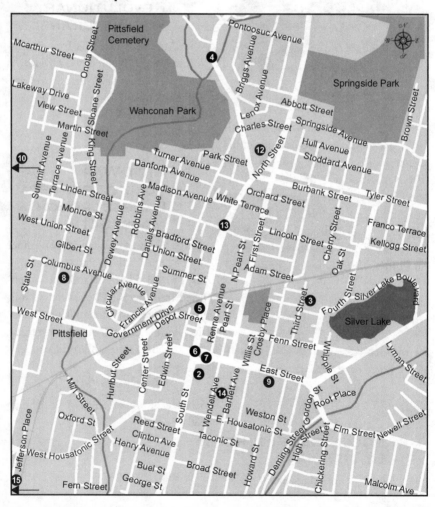

PITTSFIELD

PITTSFIELD, the largest town in Berkshire County, was settled around 1750, and African Americans have been part of its history from the start. In 1790, Pittsfield contained 45 African American residents and by 1840, that number had grown to 202. That small figure was relatively sizeable in comparison to the African American population in other towns in the Berkshires. Due to its critical mass of African American residents, Pittsfield always served as a center for African American civic and community life in the Bekshires.

African Americans contributed to the Pittsfield community in several ways. One family in particular, the Persips, distinguished themselves through service in the military through several generations. Another resident, Hannah Hoose, was the first African American female in the entire country to enlist in the military at the start of World War II. Pittsfield also hosted a very active NAACP chapter throughout the civil rights movement of the late 1950s, and early 1960s. An African American Heritage Trail of the town, www.AfricanAmericanTrail.org, was established to document and share the town's heritage.

1 JAMES MARS
Site Unknown

One of the important African American historical figures of the Berkshires, James Mars (c.1790–1880), was not originally from Massachusetts. Mars was enslaved in Connecticut for the first twenty-five years of his life. He worked as an indentured servant for the next twenty years. In 1784, Connecticut law granted freedom to African Americans born after March 1st, 1784, once they reached the age of twenty-five. The state did not abolish slavery completely until 1848. Based on Connecticut law, Mars' indentured servant status was illegal. Mars relocated to Hartford where he became a community activist.

In Hartford, Mars co-founded the Talcott St. Congregational Church and the North African School. He also sponsored several petitions in the General Assembly of Connecticut on behalf of the African American community in that state. His desire to vote led him to relocate his family to Pittsfield, MA, in the late 1840s. African Americans had won the right to vote in Massachusetts in 1783 after a challenge by Paul Cuffe of Westport.

James Mars

Mars wrote an autobiography, *Life of James Mars, a Slave Born and Sold in Connecticut.* He did not want history to forget that slavery existed in Connecti- cut. The book was published in 1868. Mars died in Ashley Falls, MA, and he was buried in Connecticut.

> "...One thing in my history I have not mentioned, which I think of importance. Although born and raised in Connecticut, yes, and lived in Connecticut more than three-fourths of my life, it has been my privilege to vote at five Presidential elections. Twice it was my privilege and pleasure to help the lamented and murdered Lincoln, and if my life is spared I intend to be where I can show that I have the principles of a man, and act like a man, and vote like a man but not in my native state; I cannot do it there, I must remove to the old Bay State for the right to be a man. Connecticut, I love thy name, but not their restrictions. I think the time is not far distant when the colored man will have his rights in Connecticut...."
>
> – *James Mars, excerpt from his autobiography.*

 BERKSHIRE MUSEUM

39 South St.
www.berkshiremuseum.org

On display at the Berkshire Museum are two artifacts used at the discovery of the North Pole, the sledge used by Admiral Robert E. Peary (NAA), and the polar fur suit worn by Matthew Henson. Peary and Henson were accompanied on their journey by four Inuit guides, Egingwah, Seeglo, Ootah, and Ooqueah.

Born in Nanjemoy, Maryland to a family of freed sharecroppers, Henson (1866–1955) moved to Baltimore at the age of twelve where he became a cabin boy on a merchant ship. He travelled the world for the next five years. Henson met Peary in 1887, and the two developed a mutual respect that led to their long-term professional relationship.

Matthew Henson

The two men explored the Artic for the next twenty years. In 1909, during their eighth attempt to reach the North Pole, Peary, Henson, and their four Inuit guides journeyed toward their destination. Exhaustion and frostbite forced Peary to ride in the dog sledge while Henson continued on foot with the guides. Because of that unplanned occurrence, Henson became the first documented person to set foot on the North Pole on April 6th, 1909. He also planted the American flag on the Pole that day.

Berkshire Museum

Admiral Peary immediately received many accolades for the successful expedition to the North Pole but Henson's contributions to that effort were not recognized until years later. In 1944, the U.S. Congress awarded Matthew Henson a Congressional Medal of Honor. In 1988, his grave and that of his wife were removed from Woodlawn Cemetery in Brooklyn, NY, and they were reinterred in Virginia at Arlington National Cemetery near the location of the grave and monument to Admiral Peary. A monument was also erected at Henson's gravesite.

③ REV. SAMUEL HARRISON HOUSE
82 Third St.

Rev. Samuel Harrison (1818 - 1900) was the chaplain for the Massachusetts 54th Regiment during the first part of the Civil War. Harrison was one of the chaplains who provided spiritual leadership to the regiment in their protest against the United States government for the disparity in pay between white and black troops.

Rev. Samuel Harrison

Harrison was born in Philadelphia to a widowed mother who was enslaved by the Bolton family. After Samuel Harrison was born, mother and son were emancipated and they moved to New York City. Harrison relocated to Philadelphia at the age of nine to apprentice to an uncle who was a shoemaker.

In 1850, after he trained in the ministry in Newark, NJ, Harrison relocated his family to Pittsfield where he was ordained as pastor of the Second Congregational Church. Harrison retired from the pulpit in 1862, in order to work on the war effort. He served as chaplain from November 12th, 1863, until March 14th, 1864, when he had to resign due to illness. After he resigned, Harrison continued to advocate the cause of the soldiers for equal pay. His house was listed on the National Register of Historic Places in 2006.

Harrison House

4 PITTSFIELD CEMETERY
203 Wahconah St.

Five members of the Mass. 54th Regiment, George Green, Moses Foster, Samuel Servius Jones, Charles Potter, and Rev. Samuel Harrison, were buried at Pittsfield Cemetery. Both Green and Foster were buried in unmarked graves. Jones was buried in the Orchard Hill section of the cemetery. Potter was buried in the Pontoosuc Hill section.

Harrison was buried in the High Grove section with his wife, Ellen, and other family members.

Pittsfield Cemetery

5 PERSIP PARK
167 North St. (North & Columbus Ave.)

This park was dedicated on March 26th, 1983, to honor Alfred Persip and his family whose military service extended through several generations, from the Civil War through the second World War. A maternal grandfather, Charles Hamilton, served in the Civil War as part of the Massachusetts's 54th Regiment. Alfred K. Persip (1895–1983) was the first African American from the Berkshires to enlist in the military at the onset of World War I. Two of his brothers, Charles (1892–1982) and John (1887–1983), also volunteered and saw service in World War I. Three Persips enlisted in the military in World War II; Earl G. Persip Jr., Edward L. Persip, and Kenneth E. Persip.

In World War I, Alfred Persip served in the all-Black, 372nd Regiment under the French. After the war, the French government awarded the entire unit the Croix de Guerre, the highest French military honor, for their distinguished service. African Americans chose to volunteer for military service in World War I for the same reason that they volunteered in earlier wars, to prove their patriotism.

The military service of African Americans in World War I was particularly ironic because of the treatment many African American soldiers received upon their return to the states. Vicious attacks on African American veterans and riots across the country occurred just after the war ended. Many white Americans refused to accept the fact that those veterans were entitled to the same rights as all citizens.

Persip Park

In response to that violence, DuBois wrote an 1919 editorial for "Crisis" magazine that was entitled, *"Returning Soldier:"*

…We are returning from war. … tens of thousands of black men were drafted into a great struggle. … against the threat of German race arrogance, we fought gladly and to the last drop of blood: for America and her highest ideals, we fought in far-off hope: for the dominant southern oligarchy entrenched in Washington, we fought in bitter resignation. For the America that represents and gloats in lynching, disfranchisement, caste, brutality and devilish insult –, we were also forced by vindictive fate to fight, also.

But today we return! We return from the slavery of uniform which the world's madness demanded us to don to the freedom of civil garb. We stand again to look America squarely in the face and call a spade a spade. … This country of ours, despite all its better souls have done and dreamed, is yet a shameful land.

It lynches.

And lynching is a barbarism of a degree of contemptible nastiness unparalleled in human history.…

It disfranchises its own citizens.

Disfranchisement is the deliberate theft and robbery of the only protection of poor against rich and black against white. The land that disfranchises its citizens and calls itself a democracy lies and knows it lies.

It encourages ignorance.

It has never really tried to educate the Negro. A dominant minority does not want Negroes educated............

It steals from us.

It organizes industry to cheat us. It cheats us out of our labor. It confiscates our savings. It reduces our wages. It raises our rent. It steals our profit. It taxes us without representation. It keeps us consistently and universally poor, and then feeds us on charity and derides our poverty.

It insults us.

It has organized a ... world-wide propaganda of deliberate and continuous insult and defamation of black blood wherever found... And it looks upon any attempt to question or even discuss this dogma as arrogance, unwarranted assumption and treason.

This is the country to which we Soldiers of Democracy return. This is the fatherland for which we fought! But it is our fatherland. It was right for us to fight. The faults of our country are our faults. Under similar circumstances, we would fights again. But by the God of Heaven, we are cowards and jackasses if now that the war is over, we do not marshal every ounce of brain and brawn to fight a sterner, longer, more unbending battle against the forces of hell in our own land.

We return.

We return from fighting.

We return fighting.

Make way for Democracy! We saved it in France, and by the Great Jehovah, we will save it in the United States of America or know the reason why."

–W.E.B. DuBois

6 SYLVANUS GRANT AND THE PITTSFIELD ELM

Site: Park Square, North and South Sts.

One of the landmarks of downtown Pittfield in the mid-nineteenth century was a distinguished 350-year-old elm tree which the locals named the Pittsfield Elm. In 1863, this tree, which stood 128-feet tall and spanned 28-feet in diameter, was irreparably damaged by lightning and it had to be removed. The size of the tree and its central location required the skills of an extremely experienced lumberman and Sylvanus Grant (1844–1927) of Lenox was selected to carry out the task. Sylvanus was the cousin of famed baseball player, Frank Grant.

7 CIVIL WAR MEMORIAL

Park Sq.

Four members of the Massachusetts 54th Regiment were listed on this me-

Civil War Statue at Park Sq.

morial to honor those who died during the Civil War; Eli Franklin, Levi Bird, Henry Wilson, and John Van Blake. The monument was dedicated in 1872.

OTHER VOLUNTEERS IN MASSACHUSETTS 54TH REGIMENT:

Orrin Duncan, Edward B. Emerson, Merrick Fletcher, Moses Foster, Alexander Gaines, George W. Green, Henry Hamilton, Paul Hamilton, Rev. Samuel Harrison, Samuel D. Jackson, Samuel Jones, William Peters, Charles A. Potter, George A. Ringgold, and George A. Wilson all volunteered in the Massachusetts 54th Regiment.

MASSACHUSETTS 5TH CALVARY:

Richmond Birdsound, Augustus Fields, John E. Gillard, Benjamin F. Porter, and John A. William were volunteers in the Massachusetts 5th Calvary.

MASSACHUSETTS 55TH REGIMENT:

Daniel F. Philips enlisted in June of 1863.

MASS. 52ND REGIMENT:

Abraham Reynolds enlisted in March of 1865.

U.S. COLORED ARTILLERY:

Richmond Birdsound enlisted in March of 1865.

UNION NAVY:

Joshua Foster and Mason Jones served as landsmen in the war. Theodore Gunn was a seaman.

8 SECOND CONGREGATIONAL
50 Onota St.

Seven African Americans, John L. Brown, Catherine Fields, Delilah Potter, Morris Potter, William Potter, Mary Richards, and David S. Thomas, became frustrated with the racism they experienced as members of First Congregational Church so they founded Second Congregational Church in 1846. Second Congregational was the first African American church founded in Berkshire County. Rev. Samuel Harrison served as its first minister in 1850.

Second Congregational Church

9 JUDGE JOHN GARRETT PENN PITTSFIELD HIGH SCHOOL
300 East Street

John Garrett Penn (b.1932), a graduate of Pittsfield High School, served as a Federal Judge in Washington, D.C. After he received his law degree from Boston University in 1957, he went on to enjoy a stellar legal career. President Nixon (NAA) appointed Penn to the Superior Court of Washington, D.C. in 1970. In 1979, President Carter (NAA) promoted him to the Federal Bench. From 1992 until 1997, Penn served as the Chief Justice of the United States District Court for the District of Columbia.

Judge Garrett Penn

Pittsfield High School

10 STEPHANIE WILSON TACONIC HIGH SCHOOL
96 Valentine Road

Stephanie Wilson, one of only five African American female astronauts, was born in Boston but raised in Pittsfield. Astronaut Stephanie Wilson was one of the Space Shuttle Discovery crew when the spaceship launched in 2006. Wilson, a graduate of the Pittsfield school system, attended Stearns Elementary, Crosby Middle School, and Taconic High School.

Stephanie Wilson

Taconic High School

Wilson, a Harvard graduate, was especially proud of her African American heritage. She requested that NASA play, *"Lift Every Voice and Sing,"* as one of the wake-up songs when she was in space.

 11 ULYSSES FRANKLIN GRANT
Site Unknown

Baseball Hall of Fame member, Ulysses Franklin Grant was born in Pittsfield on August 1st, 1865. See Williamstown sites.

12 HENRY JENKINS ROBERTS SITE: BERKSHIRE MEDICAL INSTITUTE
725 North St.

In 1847, the first African Americans graduated from medical school in the United States, David Peck and Henry Jenkins Roberts. David Peck graduated from Rush Medical School in Chicago, and Henry Jenkins Roberts (1821–1863) graduated from the Berkshire Medical Institute in Pittsfield, MA. The Berkshire Medical Institute lasted from 1822 to 1867.

Roberts was born free in Virginia but his mother relocated the family to Liberia after the death of her husband in 1829. The distinguished family included his brother, Joseph Jenkins Roberts, the first President of Liberia. The Berkshire Medical Institute only allowed African Americans to study there on the condition that they not practice in the U. S.

BERKSHIRE COUNTY NAACP

467 North St.

The Berkshire County Chapter of the NAACP was founded in 1918, at the earliest stages of the NAACP's development. This chapter was particularly active in the Civil Rights Movement of the 1960s. They invited several national Civil Rights leaders to speak in Pittsfield and they staged a sit-in at the local Woolworth's to support the parallel protests at various Woolworths in the South.

 ### CHARLES A. PERSIP AMERICAN LEGION POST 68

41 Wendell Ave.

In 1983, this American Legion post was named to honor Charles A. Persip (1892–1982), a World War I veteran. His advocacy on behalf of veterans earned him the nickname, *"Mr. American Legion"* during his lifetime. Two of Persip's brothers were also World War I veterans.

*Charles A. Persip
American Legion Post 68*

 ### SITE: HENRY S. JACKSON BLACKSMITH SHOP

Stearnsville Section, North side of Lebanon Ave. near Melbourne Rd.

Henry S. Jackson originally escaped slavery in Washington, D.C., prior to his relocation to Pittsfield in 1858. He operated a blacksmith shop near this site. During the Civil War, Jackson led the local recruitment office for the Mass. 54th Regiment.

 ### DR. JOHN MILTON BREWSTER (NAA) HOUSE

UGRR Station
Site Unknown

 ### JOHN BROWN (NAA) HOUSE

UGRR Station
Site Unknown

John Brown was the cousin of the abolitionist, John Brown, of Harper's Ferry.

WILLIAM M. WALKER (NAA) HOUSE

UGRR Station
Site Unknown

19 OLIVER LOUIS WOOD (NAA) HOUSE

UGRR Station
Site Unknown

20 ISAAC GRIFFIN (NAA) HOUSE

UGRR Station
Site Unknown

21 VETERANS OF THE AMERICAN REVOLUTION

Six African Americans from Pittsfield participanted in the American Revolutionary War: Jabez Abro, Anthony Clever, Prince Hall, Jeffrey Hazard, Negro Titus, and Ezegial Comer.

22 LOCAL RESOURCES

African American Heritage Trail of Pittsfield
www.africanamericantrail.org

Berkshire Athenaeum
1 Wendell Ave.

Berkshire Historical Society
7780 Holmes Road

LENOX

1 SITE: JAMES VAN DER ZEE HOUSE

Taconic St.
Beneath Route 7 Bypass at Hubbard St.

James Van der Zee (1886–1983) was born and spent his youth in Lenox, MA. Van der Zee was the renown photographer of the Harlem Renaissance, the movement of African American culture based in New York City in the 1920s.

Van der Zee enjoyed a happy, secure childhood in Lenox that encouraged his development in art and music. When he moved from Lenox to Harlem in 1906, Van der Zee enrolled in the Carlton Conservatory where he studied piano and violin. Throughout his adult life, Van Der Zee maintained a close connection to his hometown and he often spent part of each summer in Lenox.

*James Van der Zee
with his father and brothers*

A job as a darkroom assistant in 1915, reinvigorated his interest in photography and he set up a studio shortly thereafter. James Van der Zee was the official photographer of the Universal Negro Improvement Association, UNIA, the self-empowerment organization started by Marcus Garvey in Harlem, and the unofficial photographer of the Harlem Renaissance. Van der Zee's photographs have been placed in museum collections across the country.

② Dr. John Milton (NAA) House
UGRR Station
Site Unknown

③ Church on the Hill Cemetery
169 Main St.

The Grand Army of the Republic (GAR) was a fraternal organization for Union veterans, both white and black, of the Civil War. Grand Army of the Republic headstones were placed at the gravesites of four Civil War veterans who were members of the Mass. 54th Regiment; Jeremiah Bradley, Samuel Weaver, Jacob Adams, and George M. Brown.

The GAR was a strong advocate for African American veterans to receive their full rights which included the right to a government pension. The group was formed in 1866, and it disbanded in 1956, when the last Union Civil War veteran died.

Church on the Hill & Cemetery

The GAR originated the Memorial Day holiday in 1868, to commemorate the death of Civil War soldiers killed in the war. The holiday was originally known as *"Decoration Day,"* a day when the graves of those veterans were decorated. The holiday was later expanded to include those who lost their life during any United States war. The GAR placed headstones on the graves of many Civil War veterans, both white and black.

Anna Kneeland Haggety Shaw (NAA), the widow of Col. Robert Gould Shaw (NAA), was also buried here. Col. Shaw of the Mass. 54th Regiment of the Civil War was killed along with many of his troops at the assault on Fort Wagner on July 18th, 1863.

④ CHARLES T. WAY HOUSE NOW, PLEASANT VALLEY HOUSE

472 West Mountain Rd., (off Route 7 and West Dugway Road)

Charles T. Way was a veteran of the Mass. 54th Regiment, the grandson of Revolutionary War veteran, Agrippa Hull, and a prominent member of African American society of the Berkshires. Although he lived in Stockbridge after the war, he retired to Lenox to live with his niece and her husband, Wellington and Henrietta Crockett from 1906 until 1922. Mrs. Crockett sold the property to the Pleasant Valley Wildlife Sanctuary in 1929. They converted the house into the Superintendent's office of the Wildlife Sanctuary shortly after the property was transferred.

Charles T. Way House

⑤ HENRY WARD BEECHER (NAA) HOUSE

Blossom Hill, now Cranwell Resort

Henry Ward Beecher (1813–1887) (NAA), an abolitionist and a minister, lived here with his family. Beecher was the brother of Harriet Beecher Stowe (NAA), the famous author. Harriet Beecher Stowe's novel, *Uncle Tom's Cabin*, galvanized abolitionists in their fight against slavery.

⑥ AFRICAN AMERICAN VOLUNTEERS IN THE CIVIL WAR

MASSACHUSETTS 54TH REGIMENT:

Fourteen African Americans from Lenox volunteered for service in the Massachusetts 54th Regiment. In March of 1863 they were; Jacob Adams, John Hall, Thomas Jackson, George G. Peters, Peter H. Pruyn, Charles Van Allen, Henry Van Alstine, John E. Vosburght, George E. Waterman, and Samuel Weaver. Henry J. Carter volunteered in April of 1863. In September of 1864, two individuals volunteered, David Addison and Edward Porter. Charles F. Patterson was another volunteer but his date of enlistment was not known.

MASSACHUSETTS 5TH CALVARY:

Two individuals volunteered for the 5th Regiment in September of 1864, Alexander Adams and Alfred Michael.

LEE

1 COL. JARED BRADLEY (NAA) HOUSE
UGRR Station
Bradley St. in East Lee

2 DR. FRANK FREEMAN (NAA) HOUSE
UGRR Station
Prospect St.

3 JUDGE BRANNING (NAA) HOUSE
UGRR Station
Franklin St.

4 AMERICAN REVOLUTIONARY WAR VETERANS:

Negro Peter from Lee was a veteran of the American Revolution.

5 AFRICAN AMERICAN VOLUNTEERS IN THE CIVIL WAR FROM LEE AND THE WAR MEMORIAL PLAQUE MEMORIAL HALL
32 Main St.

Memorial Hall

MASS. 54TH REGIMENT:

This Civil War Plaque commemorated those soldiers from Lee who lost their lives during the Civil War. The three Mass. 54th Regiment soldiers included on the plaque were all casualties of the assault on Fort Wagner. Henry F. Burghardt enlisted on March 30th, 1863, and he died in the original battle of Fort Wagner. Aaron Spencer also enlisted on March 30th, 1863, and he died during the subsequent siege of Fort Wagner. George M. Pell enlisted July 15th, 1863 and he died of illness on Morris Island.

Two other African Americans from Lee, James E. Sharts and William H. Sharts, most likely brothers, enlisted in the 54th Regiment on March 30th, 1863. They both survived the war.

MASS. 5TH CALVARY VOLUNTEERS:

Four individuals from Lee volunteered in the Massachusetts 5th Regiment. George R.W. Chadwell and Frederick B. Randolph both volunteered on January 29th, 1864. In June of that same year, Thomas Watson and Henry Weaver volunteered.

MASS. 55TH REGIMENT:

Dexter M. Jackson enlisted in the 55th in January of 1864.

6 | PLESSY V. FERGUSON CASE ALBION WINEGAR TOURGEE & HENRY BILLINGS BROWN

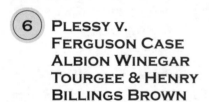

Two individuals with direct connections to Lee, MA, Albion Winegar Tourgee (1838–1905) and Henry Billings Brown (1836–1913) landed on opposite sides of one of the most important legal cases about the civil rights of African Americans in United States history, Plessy v. Ferguson of 1896. The decision from that case institutionalized the doctrine of, *"separate but equal,"* the legal precedent used to uphold a plethora of *"Jim Crow"* laws enacted throughout the South. Albion Winegar Tourgee was attorney for the plaintiff, Homer Adolph Plessy, and Henry Billings Brown wrote the majority opinion for the Supreme Court.

Tourgee lived with relatives in Lee in his youth. After he became an attorney, he set up his practice in New York state. His reputation as a fighter for the civil rights of African Americans made him a logical choice as attorney for the plaintiff in the Louisiana case. Brown was born in Lee into a wealthy, merchant-class family. He studied at Harvard and Yale.

The genesis of this important civil rights case was the intention of a group of African American leaders in Louisiana to challenge the Louisiana state law that instituted separate accommodations on railroad coaches. Their eventual goal was a repeal of that law. In 1892, the group engaged Homer Plessy to sit in a railroad coach designated for whites only by state law. Plessy possessed a very light complexion and many often mistook him to be white. The group made prior arrangements for Plessy to be *'discovered'* by someone who knew his true racial identity, and to be arrested. A lawsuit to challenge state law quickly followed the arrest.

Homer Plessy

The Louisiana judge who presided over that case, Judge John Howard Ferguson (NAA), ruled that the state had the right to regulate railroad companies within their state boundaries and thus, were allowed to require companies to institute separate accommodations in public places based on race. The Plessy camp appealed that decision to the U.S. Supreme Court. The case was heard in 1896. In a 7 to 1 vote, the Supreme Court upheld the state's right to enforce separate accommodations based on race. That decision had significant impact on the institutionalization of racist policies in public accommodations in this country.

In a bit of historical irony, the only judge to dissent from that opinion, Justice John Marshall Harlan (1833–1911) (NAA), was a born and bred Southerner. A native of Kentucky, Harlan's family's wealth was created before the Civil War by the institution of slavery. The judge who wrote the opinion for the majority was Harvard educated Justice Henry Billings Brown. Brown was a born and bred Northerner whose state of birth, Massachusetts, was probably the most active in the country in the fight against slavery.

U.S. Supreme Court Justice Stephen J. Field (NAA) of Stockbridge also sat on the bench for this trial and he also sided with the majority opinion. That occurrence gave Massachusetts the dubious distinction that two of her native-born sons participated in the enactment of one of the most deleterious judgments to come from the United States Supreme Court.

Plessy v. Ferguson
Albion W. Tourgee, Council for Plaintiff:

"...the act prohibited must be of a character to affect the general health or public morals of a whole community, not merely to minister to the wishes of one class or another. What is the act prohibited in the statue in question in this case? The sitting of a white man or woman in the car in which a colored man or woman sits or the sitting of a colored man or woman in the car in which white men or women are sitting,---is this dangerous to the public health? Does this contaminate public morals? If it does from whence comes the contamination? Why does it contaminate any more than in the house or on the street? Is it the white who spreads the contagion or the black? And if color breeds contagion in a railway coach, why exempt nurses from the operation of the Act?

The title of an Act does not make it a "police provision" and a discrimination intended to humiliate or degrade one race in order to promote the pride or ascendency in another, is not made a "police regulation" by insisting that the one will not be entirely happy unless the other is shut out of their presence. Haman was troubled with the same sort of unhappiness because he saw Mordecai the Jew sitting at the King's gate. He wanted a "police regulation" to prevent his being contaminated by the sight. He did not set out the real cause of his zeal for the public welfare: neither does this statue. He wanted to "down" the Jew: this act is intended to "keep the negro in his place." The exemption of nurses shows that the real evil lies not in the color of the skin but in the relation the colored person sustains to the white. If he is a dependent it may be endured: if he is not, his presence is insufferable. Instead of being intended to promote the general comfort and moral well-being, this act is plainly and evidently intended to promote the happiness of one class by asserting its supremacy and the inferiority of another class. Justice is pictured blind and her daughter, the Law, ought at least to be color-blind...

...We insist that the State has no right to compel us to ride in a car "set apart" for a particular race, whether it is as good as another or not."

Justice Henry Billings Brown delivered the majority opinion of the Court:

... the case reduces itself to the question whether the statute of Louisiana is a reasonable regulation, and with respect to this there must necessarily be a large discretion on the part of the legislature. In determining the question of reasonableness it is at liberty to act with reference to the established usages, customs, and traditions of the people, and with a view to the promotion of their comfort and the preservation of the public peace and good order. Gauged by this standard, we cannot say that a law which authorizes or even requires the separation of the two races in public conveyances is unreasonable, or more obnoxious to the Fourteenth Amendment than the acts of Congress requiring separate schools for colored children in the District of Columbia, the constitutionality of which does not seem to have been questioned,... Legislation is powerless to eradicate racial instincts or to abolish distinctions based upon physical differences, and the attempt to do so can only result in accentuating the difficulties of the present situation. If the civil and political rights of both races be equal one cannot be inferior to the other civilly or politically. If one race be inferior to the other socially, the Constitution of the United States cannot put them upon the same plane...

Justice John Marshall Harlan, dissenting opinion:

...The white race deems itself to be the dominant race in this country. ...But in view of the Constitution, in the eye of the law, there is in this country no superior, dominant, ruling class of citizens. There is not caste here. Our Constitution is color-blind, and neither knows nor tolerates classes among citizens. In respect of civil rights, all citizens are equal before the law. The humblest is the peer of the most powerful. The law regards man as man, and takes no account of his surroundings or of his color when his civil rights as guaranteed by the supreme law of the land are involved. It is, therefore, to be regretted that this high tribunal, the final expositor of the fundamental law of the land, has reached the conclusion that it is competent for a State to regulate the enjoyment by citizens of their civil rights solely upon the basis of race.

In my opinion, the judgment this day rendered will, in time, prove to be quite as pernicious as the decision made by this tribunal in the Dred Scott case. ... The destinies of the two races, in this country, are indissolubly linked together, and the interests of both require that the common government of all shall not permit the seeds of race hate to be planted under the sanction of law.... If evils will result from the commingling of the two races upon public highways established for the benefit of all, they will be infinitely less than those that will surely come from state legislation regulating the enjoyment of civil rights upon the basis of race. We boast of the freedom enjoyed by our people above all other peoples. But it is difficult to reconcile that boast with a state of the law which, practically puts the brand of servitude and degradation upon a large class of our fellow citizens, our equals before the law. The thin disguise of 'equal' accommodations for passengers in railroad coaches will not mislead any one, nor atone for the wrong this day done...

For the reasons stated, I am constrained to withhold my assent from the opinion and judgment of the majority."

WEST STOCKBRIDGE

 **WEST STOCKBRIDGE CEMETERY**
Route 41

Mass. 54th Regiment veteran, Charles T. Way was buried here. Veteran of the American Revolution, Agrippa Hull was his grandfather. Another relative was David Gunn, Sr.

 **AMERICAN REVOLUTION VETERANS:**

Frank Duncan was a veteran of the American Revolution.

3 CIVIL WAR VOLUNTEERS

MASSACHUSETTS 5TH CALVARY:
Robert H. Roberson and Albert M. Rogers both enlisted in January of 1864.

RICHMOND

 AMERICAN REVOLUTIONARY WAR VETERANS:

Three African Americans served in the American Revolution from Richmond; Ishmael Richards, Thomas Smith, and John Van Huff.

 AFRICAN AMERICAN VOLUNTEERS IN THE CIVIL WAR

MASSACHUSETTS 55TH REGIMENT:
Franklin J. Dickerson enlisted in the 55th Regiment in December of 1863.

STOCKBRIDGE

STOCKBRIDGE was incorporated in 1739, and the first documented free Africans in the Berkshires, Cuffee and Nana Negro, lived there as early as 1746. Later in the century, another resident of the town, Elizabeth Freeman, created history when she sued for her freedom from bondage in Ashley Falls. Her lawsuit and that of another African, Quock Walker, led to the abolition of slavery in Massachusetts in 1783. The importance of the legacy of Stockbridge in African American history was established despite its small African American population. In 1790, there were 64 African American residents and by 2000, that figure had shrunk to 28.

One famous visitor to Stockbridge in the mid-1800s, was Harriet Beecher Stowe (NAA), the author of *Uncle Tom's Cabin*. Stowe frequently visited her daughter who married a Stockbridge minister. Another visitor was Booker T. Washington. Washington spoke at the Congregational Church on several occasions to raise funds to assist Tuskegee Institute in Alabama.

The other well-known African American school in the South, Hampton Institute, also in Alabama, also had strong Stockbridge connections. The founder, Samuel Chapman Armstrong (NAA), was related by birth and marriage to two Stockbridge residents, Reuben Chapman (NAA) and Emmeline Dean Walker (NAA).

Another resident of Stockbridge, Stephen J. Field (NAA), was one of the seven United States Supreme Court Justices to rule in favor of the doctrine of *"separate but equal"* in the Plessy v. Ferguson court case of 1896. Today, Stockbridge is a key tourist destination in the resort region of the Berkshires.

 ## CUFFEE AND NANA NEGRO
Site unknown but near Mohawk Lake

In 1746, Cuffee (d. 1763) and Nana Negro were the first free African Americans to live in the Berkshires when they were manumitted by Elias Van Schaack (NAA). The purchase of property was a privilege that only freed individuals could exercise so many African Americans exercised that privilege as soon as they were legally able. In 1758, Cuffee Negro purchased 100 acres of land near what is now Monument Mountain. That was followed by another purchase of 100 acres in western Stockbridge in 1761. These purchases are proof of Cuffee Negro's shrewd capacity to negotiate and transact business in his lifetime.

 ## SITE: ELIZABETH FREEMAN HOUSE
End of Cherry Hill Road

Elizabeth Freeman purchased a 19-acre farm at this location after she ended her employment with the Sedgwick family. The purchase of this farm made Freeman the second largest African

American landowner in the area after Agrippa Hull. Freeman was a skilled nurse and mid-wife and she used those skills to support herself and her family. Freeman lived here with her daughter, Betsy, and her extended family. W.E.B. DuBois believed that Betsy was his great-grandmother.

3 SITE: AGRIPPA HULL FARM
Across the Housatonic River, exact site unknown

Agrippa Hull (1759–1848) was born free in Northampton, Massachusetts. His father died when Hull was still very young and his mother sent him to live in Stockbridge with another free African American family. Hull enlisted in the Continental Army at the start of the American Revolution. He was assigned as aide to Tadeuz Kosciuszko (NAA), a Polish military engineer.

Agrippa Hull

Hull was Kosciuszko's aide for over fifty months and he served a total of six and a half years in the army. Kosciuszko was chief military engineer for General Washington and Washington personally signed Hull's discharge papers. After the war, Kosciuszko invited Hull to join him in Poland but Hull declined the invitation and chose to move back to Stockbridge instead.

The veteran's pension that Hull received made it possible for him to purchase the first of numerous plots of land that he eventually owned. Agrippa Hull and his wife, Margaret "Peggy" Timbroke, were early entrepreneurs in Stockbridge. In addition to the land speculation that he engaged in, Hull developed a local reputation as an organizer of social events with Peggy as the caterer. Agrippa Hull also work for two decades for Theodore Sedgwick, the attorney who filed the lawsuit on behalf of Elizabeth "Mumbett" Freeman. At his death, Hull was the largest African American landowner in Stockbridge.

It is believed that Kosciuszko's relationship with Agrippa Hull influenced his attitude toward slavery. In his will, Kosciuszko requested that his estate be used to purchase freedom for as many enslaved individuals as his money could buy and to bequeath to them sufficient funds for their education and maintenance and 100 acres of land each. Unfortunately, upon Kosciuszko's death in 1817, the executer of his estate, Thomas Jefferson, decided not to use his friend's sizable American estate (around $15,000) to honor Kosciusz-ko's request. Kosciuszko's contribution to the American Revolution was honored with a statue of him erected in the Boston Gardens. See more on Kosciuszko under Beacon Hill sites.

 4 **STOCKBRIDGE PUBLIC LIBRARY**
36 Main St.

Several artifacts important to African American history reside here. Those items include the papers of Theodore Sedgwick, the attorney who defended Elizabeth "Mum Bett" Freeman in her lawsuit for freedom, and a painting of Agrippa Hull who was a veteran of the American Revolution.

A memorial plaque in the library was installed to commemorate local participants in the Civil War. Included were six members of the 54th Regiment; John Clough, Charles Piper, Charles T. Way, John Q. Williams, Valorous Williams, and Luther Willard.

 5 **CIVIL WAR MEMORIAL: GREAT WAR OF THE REBELLION**
Pine and Main Streets

This Civil War Memorial was dedicated in 1866. It listed the name of Mass. 54th Regiment veteran, Luther Willard. Stockbridge suffered a total of 28 casualties in that war.

Civil War Memorial

OTHER CIVIL WAR VOLUNTEERS

MASS. 54TH REGIMENT:
John I. Clow, John Q. Williams, and Velorous W. Williams all enlisted in December of 1863. Charles T. Way enlisted in May of 1863, and Charles H. Piper enlisted in July of 1863.

MASS. 5TH CALVARY:
Theodore Martin enlisted in January of 1864.

UNION NAVY:
Daniel Collier and Ira E. Jackson both were from Stockbridge.

 6 **THEODORE SEDGWICK HOUSE**
22 Main St.

Theodore Sedgwick successfully represented Elizabeth *"Mum Bett"* Freeman when she filed a, *"Freedom Lawsuit,"* against the Ashleys of Ashley Falls. After the lawsuit, Freeman entered into employment with the Sedgwick family. She worked for the family for many years as a nanny and a housekeeper. When the Sedgwicks moved from Sheffield to Stockbridge, Elizabeth Freeman moved with them. Sedgwick family members were staunch anti-slavery advocates. One son, Theodore Sedgwick II (1780–1839) (NAA), frequently lectured on the abolition of slavery. His sister, Catherine Sedgwick (NAA), wrote a short biography of Elizabeth Freeman and the obituary for her headstone.

Theodore Sedgwick House

7 CONGREGATIONAL CHURCH
4 Main St.

The Congregational Church documented several African American members as part of its early history. In 1782, Clarisa Benny was baptized into the church. Her parents, Joab and Rose Benny, were married in 1756, but they were not listed as members. Joab and Rose Benny were also two of the earliest African American property owners in Stockbridge. In 1755, they purchased 50 acres near Evergreen Hill.

In 1785, Edward (no last name) and Priscilla (no last name) were baptized into the church. In 1809, Tamar (no last name) became a church member. In 1819, these African Americans were listed as members; Richard Cady, Thomas Dunkins, Betty Freeman (Elizabeth Freeman's daughter), Agrippa Hull, Enoch Humphrey, Thomas Kellis, Rose Salter, and Horace Weston. Between 1827 and 1844, church records listed six African American members: Mary E. Howell, Agrippa Hull, Betsey Jackson, My Slocomb Jackson, Sherman Mars, and Mary Hull Way.

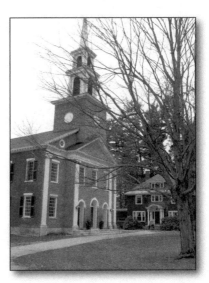

Congregational Church of Stockbridge

8 STOCKBRIDGE CEMETERY
50 Main St.

Elizabeth Freeman (1742–1829) and Agrippa Hull (1759–1848) were both buried in Stockbridge Cemetery. Elizabeth Freeman was buried here in the Sedgwick family plot, the *"Sedgwick Pie."* The following quote was inscribed on her headstone:

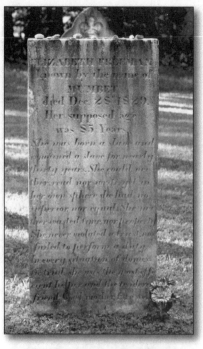

Elizabeth "Mumbett" Freeman Headstone

> ### Elizabeth Freeman.
> *Known by the name of Mumbet…*
> *She was born a slave and remained a slave for nearly 30 years. She could neither read nor write yet in her own sphere she had no superior or equal. She neither wasted time nor property. She never violated a trust nor failed to perform a duty. In every situation of domestic trial she was the most efficient helper, and the tenderest friend.*
> *Good mother, farewell.*
>
> *– Catherine Sedgwick (NAA)*

In the old section of the cemetery, Civil War veterans, Valorous Williams of Stockbridge, and David H. Van of Great Barrington, were buried. The GAR placed stone markers on their graves.

9 NORMAN ROCKWELL MUSEUM
9 Glendale Rd., Route 183.
10 am to 4 pm weekdays
www.nrm.org
413-298-4100

Norman Rockwell (1894–1978) (NAA) was an important painter whose art celebrated and documented the daily routines of the average person. Rockwell became a popular artist because many of his paintings graced the cover of the widely distributed magazine, *"Saturday Evening Post."* Rockwell also completed paintings during the late 1950s through the mid-1960's that documented the turmoil of the civil rights crisis in America.

Several of those paintings displayed at the museum include: *"The Problem We All Live With,"* which represented the school desegregation crisis from a child's point of view; *"Murder in Mississippi,"* a depiction of the murder of three civil rights workers in Mississippi; *"The Golden Rule,"* a painting of a representation of Jesus Christ in the center surrounded by many different races and nationalities of the world in obvious harmony; and *"New Kids in the Neighborhood,"* a portrayal of neighborhood youngsters as they checked out the new kids on the block, except in this case, the new kids were African Americans who moved into a white neighborhood. In several of the paintings, Rockwell used local African American children, members of the Gunn family, as models for the paintings.

Norman Rockwell Museum

 10 DAVID LESTER AND SINCLARA HICKS GUNN HOUSE
2 East St., (east of Route 7)

David Lester Gunn's (1899–1986) family was one of the pillars of the African American community in the Berkshires. One of Gunn's ancestors was Mary Gunn, an adopted daughter of Agrippa Hull, the American Revolutionary War veteran.

After David Gunn attended an historically black college in the South, he returned to the Berkshires in 1942. His appointment in 1943 as a basketball and baseball coach for a local public school made him the first African American appointed to such a position in the county. Gunn was active in many community and social organizations such as the Prince Hall Masonic Temple and the Berkshire County NAACP.

 11 REVOLUTIONARY WAR VETERANS

In addition to Agrippa Hull, quite a few African Americans from Stockbridge were veterans of the American Revolution; Samuel Adderthorn, Frank Duncan, Caesar Freeman, William Erving, Negro Guy, Humphrey Hubbard, James Storm, Festus Prince, Negro Humphrey, Cato Mumford, Titus Pomp, and Prince Wanton.

GREAT BARRINGTON

1 DuBois Site: W.E.B. DuBois Boyhood Home National Historic Landmark

DuBois Park
612 W. Route 23,
¼ mile past Route 71

William Edward Burghardt DuBois (1868–1963), born in Great Barrington, was one of the most influential African American intellectuals in world history. In 1895, Du Bois was the first African American to receive a Ph.D. from Harvard University. DuBois co-founded the NAACP in 1910, and he was at the forefront of all civil rights activity in the first half of the twentieth century. The United States Postal Service issued two stamps to honor DuBois's contribution to American history, one was issued in 1992, and the other was issued in 1998. See more on DuBois under Cambridge, Amherst, and Pittsfield sites.

DuBois Boyhood Home Sign

This five-acre site was the homestead of DuBois's maternal grandparents, the Burghardts, or, *"the black Burghardts,"* as DuBois referred to them with pride. DuBois's family presence in Great Barrington dated back to the late 1700s and his family's ownership of this homestead dated back to the 1820s. Two other Burghardt families owned homesteads within a ¼ mile distance on either side of this one, Ira Burghardt and Harlow Burghardt, Uncle Ira and Uncle Harlow as DuBois called them. That proximity facilitated a strong family kinship in which W.E.B. DuBois was thoroughly integrated. Alfred DuBois, his father, was never fully accepted by the Burghardt clan and Alfred abandoned DuBois and his mother, Mary Sylvina Burghardt DuBois, when W.E.B. DuBois was a toddler. Poverty forced the single mother to move back to her family's home early in DuBois's childhood.

WEB DuBois as a Child

DuBois maintained an affinity to the family homestead throughout his life. An anonymous benefactor purchased the property and gave it to DuBois in 1928. He kept the property with a goal to renovate it. Lack of funds and steady deterioration forced the house to be demolished in 1954.

In 1968, the W.E.B. DuBois Memorial Foundation was formed to establish a suitable memorial to DuBois in his hometown. In 1979, the site was recognized as a National Historic Landmark. UMass Amherst was designated as the custodian of the site. The University undertook archeological research on the site and in 2008, it built an interpretive display at the site so that visitors could learn more about DuBois's legacy.

An effort to document additional sites critical to understand the importance of W.E.B. DuBois to the heritage of the Berkshires and the rest of the state was commissioned by the group, *"Friends of W.E.B. DuBois."* The DuBois Downtown Great Barrington Heritage Trail was the outcome of that effort.

"The most important thing to remember is this: To be ready at any moment to give up what you are for what you might become."
-W.E.B. DuBois

"...The equality in political, industrial, and social life which modern men must have in order to live, is not to be confounded with sameness. On the contrary, in our case, it is rather insistence upon the right of diversity; - upon the right of a human being to be a man even if he does not wear the same cut of vest, the same curl of hair or the same color of skin. Human equality does not even entail, as it is sometimes said, absolute equality of opportunity; for certainly the natural inequalities of inherent genius and varying gifts make this a dubious phrase. But there is more and more clearly recognized minimum of opportunity and maximum of freedom to be, to move and to think, which the modern world denies to no being which it recognizes as a real man."

–W.E.B. DuBois

"Now is the accepted time, not tomorrow, not some more convenient season. It is today that our best work can be done and not some future day or future year. It is today that we fit ourselves for the greater usefulness of tomorrow. Today is the seed time, now are the hours of work, and tomorrow comes the harvest and the playtime."

–W.E.B. DuBois

2 ELM COURT NEIGHBORHOOD
Elm Street and Rosseter

After the Clinton A.M.E. Zion Church was built on Elm St. in 1887, this area became a nucleus for African American residents and businesses in Great Barrington.

3 WARREN H. DAVIS HOUSE
11 Rosseter St.

Warren H. Davis (1884–1960) was a prolific entrepreneur who milled and sold lumber. Davis moved to Great Barrington in 1902. Over the course of his career, he was involved in over 228 land transactions. He purchased 5,000 acres of forest in 1920 and quickly sold it to the Commonwealth of Massachusetts. That transaction became the core of Beartown State Forest. Davis retained the lumber rights to that forest for nine years after the sale.

Warren Davis House

Davis was an experienced and gifted lumberman. He selected and hewed by hand the logs used as beams in the great theater space of Jacob's Pillow in Becket. Warren Davis also operated the Harlem Inn Restaurant with his life partner, Maybelle Gunn. The restaurant was located in Copake, NY, a small town just across the state line in New York.

4 CLINTON A.M.E. ZION CHURCH
9 Elm Court

The Clinton African Methodist Episcopal Zion Church originated in the 1860s as the A.M.E. Zion Society. From its start, the Society was the main social and civic organization for the small community of African Americans in Great Barrington. The population of that community numbered 131 in 1860. Even today, the African American population continues to represent just a small fraction of the total population. The 2000 census listed 157 African American residents out of a total population of 7,527.

Clinton A.M.E. Zion Church

The Society built this structure on Elm Court in 1887 and renamed itself, Clinton A.M.E. Zion Church. The church was the oldest African American church built in Berkshire County. It was added to the National Register of Historic Places in 2008.

5 DuBois Site: DuBois Mural

Taconic St. Parking Lot on the side of Carr Hardware

The Railroad Street Youth Project painted this mural in 2003, to document DuBois's legacy.

6 Sumner Hall
306 Main St.

Sumner Hall was a large meeting space on the second floor of this block of commercial spaces. The A.M.E. Zion Society occasionally held services in Sumner Hall before the Clinton A.M.E. Zion Church was built in 1887. Sumner Hall was converted into apartments in the 1970s.

Sumner Hall Block

7 Brom & Bett "Freedom Lawsuit" Site: Great Barrington Courthouse, now Town Hall
334 Main St.

The court where Theodore Sedgwick argued the lawsuit of Brom & Bett vs. Ashley and Ashley in 1781, was located here before the town demolished it. Sedgwick won the case on August 21st, 1783. That lawsuit and the Quock Walker lawsuit in Worcester led to the cessation of the enforcement of slavery in Massachusetts after 1783. After her successful lawsuit, Bett changed her name to Elizabeth Freeman. Freeman (1742–1829) had this to say about her life as a slave:

> *"Anytime, anytime, while I was a slave if one minute's freedom had been offered to me, and I had been told I must die at the end of that minute, I would have taken it, just to stand one minute on God's earth a free woman, I would."*
> -- ELIZABETH FREEMAN

(8) DuBois Site: St. James Episcopal Church
Main St. & Taconic Ave.

DuBois attended services at this church with his mother until 1878. The church was located next door to the Sumner's (NAA) residence. Mary Burhardt DuBois worked for that family in 1870, and they lived in an apartment over the stables of the house.

St. James Episcopal Church

(9) DuBois Site: Kellogg Terrace/ Searles Castle
389 Main St.

Searles Castle was constructed in the 1880s, as an opulent forty-room mansion for Mary Hopkins (NAA). DuBois worked on the construction site as a time-keeper while he was in high school. Originally known as Kellogg Terrace, the estate was renamed as Searles Castle after Hopkins married Edward Francis Searles (NAA).

Kellogg Terrace / Searles Castle

(10) Site: May Edward Chinn
Bottom of Church St.

May Edward Chinn (1896–1980) achieved recognition as both an accomplished pianist and as a physician. Chinn's first degree in music allowed

May Edward Chinn

her to travel as Paul Robeson's piano accompanist. In 1926, Chinn was the first African American to graduate from New York University's Bellevue Medical School, today known as New York University.

Chinn focused her medical career on the development of methods to detect cancer with Dr. George Papanicolaou. Papanicolaou was known for the development of the *"Pap"* test to detect cervical cancer. Dr. Chinn was awarded an honorary degree by Columbia University in 1980, to acknowledge her scientific contributions.

  DuBois Site: DuBois Birth Place
Bottom of Church St.

At the time of the birth of DuBois, Mary and Alfred DuBois rented a small cottage at the bottom of Church Street from Thomas Jefferson McKinley (c. 1784 - 1896). McKinley relocated to Great Barrington after he manumitted himself from slavery in South Carolina. McKinley owned two cottages on this site, one he lived in, and the other he rented out. The cottages were demolished shortly after McKinley's death to make space for a manufacturing plant.

  DuBois Site: DuBois River Garden Park & Housatonic River Walk

W.E.B. Dubois was very fond of the Housatonic River. It flowed a short distance from his early home at the bottom of Church Street. Although the river was polluted throughout his youth from paper mills, DuBois envisioned a day when the river would be rescued to its rightful place as a focus of the town. In a visit to Great Barrington in 1930, DuBois delivered a speech at an annual alumni meeting for the high school. In that speech, he admonished the town because it had turned its back on the river. The visionary speech predated the ecology movement of the later part of the 20th century. It was also clairvoyant as it foretold a time when cities would recognize their rivers as great amenities to be embraced.

> *"...we should rescue the Housatonic and clean it as we have never in all the years thought before of cleaning it, and seek to restore its ancient beauty; making it the center of a town, of a valley, and perhaps–who knows?–of a new measure of civilized life."*
> -- DuBois

> "For this valley, the river must be the center. Certainly it is the physical center, perhaps, in a sense, the spiritual center. Perhaps from that very freeing of spirit will come other freedoms and inspirations and aspirations which may be steps toward the diffusion and diversification and enriching of culture throughout this land."
> -- DuBois

The town took DuBois's words to heart and by 2002, the labor of over 1,600 volunteers transformed one-half mile of the river near DuBois's childhood home into a riverwalk with a park dedicated to DuBois at the entrance to the riverwalk.

 13 MASON LIBRARY
231 Main St.

The Mason Library was frequently used by James Weldon Johnson (see site #17) as a peaceful place to write when he summered at Mary White Ovington's estate, *"Riverbank"*. Ovington (NAA) was a strong NAACP supporter. Johnson continued to visit the library after he purchased his summer home, *"Five Acres,"* in Great Barrington.

DuBois River Garden Park

Mason Library

Housatonic River Walk

 14 DuBois SITE: FIRST CONGREGATIONAL
251 Main St..

The First Congregational Church of Great Barrington was first organized in 1742. As early as 1746, an individ-

585

ual by the name of Simon, was the first African American resident to become a member. W.E.B. DuBois and his mother, Mary DuBois, were also members of the congregation. They attended services from 1867 through 1886. The family lived for a while in a cottage behind the church. After DuBois gained admission to Fisk University, the church provided financial assistance to enable him to continue his studies.

First Congregational Church

15 DuBois Site: Mahaiwe Cemetery
S. Main St. and Silver St.

The Mahaiwe Cemetery was the primary place for burial of African Americans in Great Barrington prior to 1895. After that year, the Ellwood Cemetery surpassed it in popularity. Three veterans of the Mass. 54th Regiment were buried here. Corp. Levi Jackson and

Francis Jackson share a single headstone. Those two and James H. Jackson were all buried in the Negro section of the cemetery, in the east side along South Main St.

Members of the DuBois family were also buried here. His son, Burghardt, died in 1899, as a toddler during the period that DuBois taught in Atlanta, GA. Rather than bury him in Georgia, DuBois and his wife Nina, chose to bury him in Great Barrington, the place of his birth. His wife of fifty-five years, Nina Gomer DuBois, was also buried in Mahaiwe Cemetery at her death in 1950, as was their daughter, Yolanda who died in 1960. The Burghardts, DuBois's family on his mother's side, maintained a family plot here as well.

Mahaiwe Cemetery

16 Russell (NAA) House Now, Community Health Program
UGRR Station
Castle St.

(17) JAMES WELDON JOHNSON SUMMER HOME, "FIVE ACRES"

101 Alford Road at
Seekonk Rd.

James Weldon Johnson (1871-1938), author, poet, civil rights activist, and the first African American Executive Secretary of the NAACP, used this cottage as a summer retreat from the early 1920s until his death from an automobile accident. Many of his literary efforts were produced here. Early in his career, Johnson served as Executive Secretary of the NAACP at the insistence of W.E.B. DuBois. Prior to his appointment, all the Executive Secretaries of the NAACP had been white men.

Johnson began his career as a high school principal and an attorney in his hometown of Jacksonville, FL. He also served as a diplomat in the administration of President Theodore Roosevelt (NAA). Despite these accomplishments, Johnson is most well-known for his literary achievements. His popular novel, *The Autobiography of An Ex-Colored Man*, dealt with the controversy of those who chose to pass as white.

James W. Johnson

African American students across the country regularly recite Johnson's poem, *"The Creation,"* at Black history events. He was also a lyricist whose popular song, *"Lift Every Voice and Sing,"* became the *"Negro National Anthem."* Johnson wrote the lyrics to this song in 1913, to commemorate the fiftieth anniversary of the Emancipation Proclamation. His brother, J. Rosamund Johnson wrote the music.

> **"Lift Every Voice and Sing"**
> *Lyrics by James Weldon Johnson*
>
> *Lift every voice and sing,*
> *till earth and Heaven ring,*
> *Ring with the harmonies of liberty;*
> *Let our rejoicing rise,*
> *high as the listening skies,*
> *Let it resound loud as the rolling sea.*
>
> *Sing a song full of the faith*
> *that the dark past has taught us,*

Johnson Cottage

*Sing a song full of the hope
that the present has brought us;
Facing the rising sun of
our new day begun,
Let us march on till victory is won.*

*Stony the road we trod,
bitter the chastening rod,
Felt in the days when hope
unborn had died;
Yet with a steady beat,
have not our weary feet,
Come to the place for which
our fathers died.*

*We have come over a way
that with tears has been watered,
We have come, treading our path
through the blood of the slaughtered;
Out from the gloomy past,
till now we stand at last
Where the white gleam of
our bright star is cast.*

*God of our weary years,
God of our silent tears,
Thou Who hast brought us thus far
on the way;
Thou Who hast by Thy might,
led us into the light,
Keep us forever in the path, we pray.*

*Lest our feet stray from the places,
our God, where we met Thee.
Lest our hearts, drunk with the wine
of the world, we forget Thee.
Shadowed beneath Thy hand,
may we forever stand,
True to our God,
true to our native land."*

⑱ GEORGE W. STANLEY (NAA) HOUSE

UGRR Station
Site Unknown

⑲ E. WHITING (NAA) HOUSE

UGRR Station
Site Unknown

⑳ VETERANS OF THE AMERICAN REVOLUTION

Three African Americans from Great Barrington were veterans of the war; York Kilborn, Negro Morton, and John Adams.

㉑ VOLUNTEERS IN THE CIVIL WAR

MASS. 54TH REGIMENT:

All of the recruits to the 54th from Great Barrington enlisted in 1863. Eight recruits enlisted in March; Ralph B. Garnder, Franklin Gover, Francis J. Jackson, James H. Jackson, Levi H. Jackson, William A. Stevens, Jacob H. Thomas, and Charles P. Thompson. Abraham A. Jackson enlisted in July. John R. Ferris and Edward H. Williams enlisted in November, and the last recruit that year was David H. Van Allen who enlisted in December.

MASS. 5TH CALVARY:

Six individuals volunteered for the 5th Calvary from Great Barrington. Othello Jackson, John McArthur, George W. Suma, and Jacob H. Thomas all enlisted in March of 1864. John Carr enlisted in June of 1864. Timothy Pelton enlisted in August of 1865.

SHEFFIELD

1 SITE: NEW GUINEA NEIGHBORHOOD

NE corner of Bear's Den Rd. and Berkshire School Road

Around 1800, this area of Sheffield was known as New Guinea because many African Americans settled here after their escape from slavery in New York State before that state abolished slavery in 1799. The African American population in the town was always small. In 1790, thirty-seven African Americans were listed on the census and in 2000, that number was thirty- five.

2 EDWARD AUGUSTUS CROSLEAR SITE: HOME AND FARM

NE corner of Bear's Den Rd. and Berkshire School Rd.

After the Civil War, Edward Augustus Croslear, a veteran of the Mass. 54th

Regiment, and another veteran, Edward Moore, purchased property in this area. Croslear co-founded the first African American church in Sheffield.

3 SHEFFIELD CENTER CEMETERY

Berkshire School Rd.

Two veterans of the Civil War were buried here, Edward Augustus Croslear and William Jones. Both were buried in the northwest section of the cemetery.

4 SITE: CONWAY (NAA) HOUSE

UGRR Station
Bow Wow Road

5 VETERANS OF THE CIVIL WAR

MASS. 54TH REGIMENT:

Five individuals enlisted in March of 1863; David Addison, Milo J. Freeland, Nathaniel H. Johnson, Edward Moore, and Henry J. Tucker. December of 1863 also saw five enlistees, Edward A. Croslear, John C. Harris, George Jarvis, William Jones, and Ira Waterman. The last person to enlist in the 54th Regiment from Sheffield, Norman Johnson, did so in July of 1863.

MASS. 5TH CALVARY:

Daniel Brown, George Hicks, and George Mars enlisted in January of

1864. Frances Boyd, Albert Frasier, and Robert Millier all enlisted in April of 1864. Benjamin Simons enlisted in May of 1864, and Edward Johnson enlisted in November of that year.

 6 LOCAL RESOURCES
Sheffield Historical Society
159-161 Main St.

The Sheffield Historical Society is an excellent resource on African American history in the area.

ASHLEY FALLS

 1 ELIZABETH "MUM BETT" FREEMAN COLONEL JOHN ASHLEY HOUSE
117 Cooper Hill Road
1 -5 p.m. Memorial Day to Columbus Day. / Fee.
413- 229-8600

Elizabeth *"Mum Bett"* Freeman (1742–1829) fled from this house in 1781, after Mrs. Ashley (NAA) severely burned her arm with an iron poke. Elizabeth's successful lawsuit against the Ashleys led to her freedom and helped to end slavery in Massachusetts. Originally located on Rannapo Road, the house was moved to this location in 1930.

Col. John Ashley House

The poke that Mrs. Ashley used was meant for Mum Bett's sister, Lizzie. Elizabeth received the injury instead when she rushed between the poke and Lizzie. Enraged that Mrs. Ashley would attempt to burn either of them, Elizabeth fled five miles in the middle of winter to the house of Theodore Sedgwick (NAA).

Elizabeth whose name was Bett from birth, was originally from Claverack, NY, where she had been enslaved by the family of Pieter Hogeboom. When the daughter of the family, Hannah Hogeboom, married John Ashley, Bett was brought to Massachusetts to serve Hannah. John Ashley owned a 3,000 acre farm in Sheffield. In addition to Mum Bett, the Ashleys enslaved four other individuals, John, Zack, Harry, and Lizzie. The family had a history of mistreatment of those they held in bondage and in 1781, Zack sued Col. Ashley for mistreatment. The case was delayed and later settled out of court after Freeman's victory.

Elizabeth "Mum Bett" Freeman

Theodore Sedgwick, an attorney, successfully filed a lawsuit on Elizabeth's behalf for her freedom. Another enslaved individual, Brom, a male who had been enslaved by one of the Ashley's sons, Gen. John Ashley, was added as a plaintiff. The addition of Brom to the lawsuit made it more likely to be heard in court since women did not have the right to file lawsuits as individuals at that time. Elizabeth was also awarded damages for the burns that she received. This lawsuit and that of Quock Walker in Worcester effectively ended slavery in Massachusetts after 1783. Sedgwick later became a Justice of the Massachusetts Supreme Court.

Elizabeth Freeman settled in Stockbridge and married a veteran of the American Revolution. They had one child and her husband died soon after. Freeman purchased a small house and lived with her daughter and her extended family. At her death, she was buried in the Sedgwick family plot, the *"Sedgwick Pie,"* in Stockbridge, MA. This memory of Elizabeth Freeman by Judge Sedgwick's son, who was also named Theodore, indicated the level of respect that she commanded.

"…On the contrary, without ever claiming superiority, she uniformly, in every case, obtained an ascendency over all those with whom she was associated in service. Her spirit of fidelity to her employers was such as has never been surpassed. This was exemplified in her whole life. I can convey an idea of it only by the relation of a single incident.

The house of Mr. Sedgwick, in this town, was attacked by a body of insurgents, during the Shay's war, so well remembered in this vicinity. Mr. Sedgwick was then absent in Boston, and Mum Bett was the only guardian of the house. She assured the party that Mr. Sedgwick was absent, but suffered them to search the house to find him, which they did, by feeling under the beds and other places of concealment, with the points of their bayonets. She did not attempt to resist, by direct force, the rifling of property, which was one of the objects of the insurgents. She, however, assumed a degree of authority; told the plunderers that they 'dare not strike a woman,' and attended them in their exploring the house, to prevent wanton destruction. She escorted them into the cellar with a large kitchen shovel in her hand, which she intimated that she would use in case of necessity. One of the party broke off the neck of a bottle of porter. She told him that if he or his companions desired to drink porter, she would fetch a corkscrew, and draw a cork, and they might drink like gentlemen; but that, if the neck of another bottle should be broken she would lay the man that broke it flat with her shovel....

Understanding, ... that they intended to take with them, in their retreat, a very fine gray mare that was in the stable,..., she left the house and went directly to the stable. Before the rioters were apprised of her intention, she led the animal to a gate that opened upon the street, stripped off the halter, and, by a blow with it incited the mare to a degree of speed that soon put her out of danger from the pursuit of the marauders.

Even in her humble station, she had, when occasion required it, an air of command which conferred a degree of dignity, and gave her an ascendency over those of her rank, which is very unusual in persons of any rank or color. Her determined and resolute character, which enabled her to limit the ravages of a Shay's mob, was manifested in her conduct and deportment, during her whole life. She claimed no distinction; but it was yielded to her from her superior experience, energy, skill, and sagacity.

–Theodore Sedgwick II

2 BROM GEN. JOHN ASHLEY HOUSE

Cooper Hill Road and Rannapo Road

Brom, an enslaved male servant in the household of Gen. John Ashley (NAA), was the lead plaintiff in the successful Brom & Bett vs. Ashley and Ashley lawsuit of 1781. Gen. Ashley was the son of Col. Ashley. The lawsuit was initiated by Mum Bett, who changed her name to Elizabeth Freeman after the lawsuit, but women did not have the legal right to bring a lawsuit so Brom was encouraged to participate. Both plaintiffs sued for damages because of physical abuse they received and for their freedom. Their success laid the groundwork for the end of slavery in Massachusetts in 1783. Slavery was never abolished in this state, it just ceased to be enforced after this lawsuit and the 1781 lawsuit of Quock Walker of Worcester.

3 SITE: COL. ASHLEY HOUSE

Rannapo Road

This was the original location of Col. Ashley's house. It was relocated in 1930.

THEODORE SEDGWICK HSE
Opposite the Village Green

Theodore Sedgwick (1746–1813) was the attorney who defended Brom and Elizabeth *"Mum Bett"* Freeman in their lawsuit. It was to this house that Elizabeth Freeman walked approximately five miles in the winter to escape from the Ashleys. Freeman lived with the Sedgwicks here before they all relocated to Stockbridge. Sedgwick was an ambitious politician who later became a Justice of the Massachusetts Supreme Court.

Theodore Sedgwick

 ## HISTORIC DISTRICT MARKER
Town Green in front of Post Office

This marker was placed to document Elizabeth *"Mumbett"* Freeman's role to end slavery in Massachusetts.

LOCAL RESOURCES:
African America Heritage Self-guided Trails of the Upper Housatonic Valley: www.AfricanAmericanTrail.org

---

NEW MARLBOROUGH

 ## MARGARET ETZEL (NAA) HOUSE
UGRR Station
Beech Plain Road

 ## CIVIL WAR VOLUNTEERS:

MASSACHUSETTS 5TH CALVARY:
Edward B. Benton was the sole volunteer from New Marlborough.

SANDISFIELD

 REV. HIGBY (NAA) PARSONAGE
UGRR Station
Site unknown

TYRINGHAM

 VOLUNTEERS IN THE MASS. 54TH
Amos Williams enlisted in July of 1863. William T. Taylor enlisted in December of 1863.

OTIS

 VOLUNTEERS IN THE MASS. 5TH
Three African Americans from Otis volunteered in the 5th Regiment; Joshua Rodman and Charles Van Hoesen both enlisted in January of 1864, and Homer C. Dolphin enlisted in March of that year.

MONTEREY

 VOLUNTEERS IN THE MASS. 54TH
Five African American recruits from Monterey enlisted in the 54th Regiment. William Wells enlisted in November of 1863. The remainder, Charles Jackson, Jeremiah Nokes, Charles Swan, and Henry Swan, all enlisted in December of that year.

METRO BOSTON EVENTS

January
- Martin Luther King Jr. Birthday Celebrations
- Regattaabar Jazz Festival

February
- Black History Month Celebrations

March
- Evacuation Day Re-enactment (17th)

April
- Boston Marathon
- Boston Red Sox Baseball Season

May
- Malcolm X Memorial Program / Roxbury Community College
- Wake Up the Earth Festival JP
- Franklin Park Kite Festival

June
- Boston Gay Pride Parade
- Cambridge River Festival
- Jacob's Pillow Dance Festival

July
- Puerto Rican Festival
- Boston Pops 4th of July Celebration
- Cape Verdean Festival
- Festival Betances at Villa Victoria, Boston
- Lowell Folk Festival
- African American Church Picnic at Salem Willows Park

August
- Roxbury Film Festival
- Caribbean Parade and Carnival, Roxbury
- Newport Jazz Festival, RI

September
- Berklee Beantown Jazz Festival, Boston
- Tanglewood Jazz Festival
- Boston Children's Chorus Season
- New England Patriots Football Season
- New Bedford Waterfront Festival

October
- Roxbury Open Studios
- John Coltrane Memorial Concert, Berklee College of Music
- Boston Bruins Hockey Season
- Haunted Happenings, Salem
- Boston Book Festival, Copley Sq., Boston
- Jamaica Plain Lantern Festival

November
- Dimock St., Steppin' Out Event, Boston
- Boston Celtics Basketball Season

December
- Black Nativity Concerts
- Urban Nutcracker Performances
- First Night Boston Celebration

GENERAL RESOURCES

Color Magazine
www.color-magazine.com

Ethnic Online
www.ethniconline.net

Museum of African American History, Boston & Nantucket
www.maah.org

The Bay State Banner Newspaper
www.baystatebanner.com

Unity First Magazine
www.unityfirst.com

Black Heritage Trails in Massachusetts:

1. African American Heritage in the Upper Housatonic Valley (the Berkshires):

2. African American Heritage Sites: Salem

3. African American Heritage Trail: Cambridge

4. African American Heritage Trail: Concord

5. African American Heritage Trail : Florence

6. African American Heritage Trail of Martha's Vineyard

7. African American Heritage Trail: Springfield

8. African American Historic Sites: Deerfield

9. Behind the Mansions: New Bedford

10. Black Heritage Trail: Boston

11. Black Heritage Sites in Nantucket's New Guinea

12. Black Heritage Trail of New Bedford, Mass

13. Black Heritage Trail, Nantucket

14. Black History Trail: Amherst

15. Black Springfield: A Historical Study

16. Fifty Sites in Great Barrington, associated with W.E.B. DuBois

17. Mount Auburn Cemetery: African American Heritage Trail

18. The Road to Freedom: Greenfield and the Underground Railroad

19. Walking Tour of Downtown Lowell: A Dozen Sites Associated with Anti-slavery in the Spindle City, 1830–1860

BIBLIOGRAPHY

A Black Colonizationist, Memoir of Captain Paul Cuffee, A Man of Colour
By Paul Cuffee

A Brave Black Regiment. The History of the Fifty-Fourth Regiment, or Mass. Voluntary Infantry, 1863-65.
By Luis Fenollosa Emilio

A Cultural Guide to African American Heritage in New England
by Linda Cline and Robert Hayden. 1992

"A Guide to the Parks of Boston's Emerald Necklace"
by Boston Parks and Recreation

A History of Negro Troops in the War of Rebellion
By George Washington Williams

A Legacy Remembered: the African American Community of West Medford
By Robert Furey, Wallace Kountze, Dorothy E. Tucker, John Reid, and Maureen Sonnie

A Narrative in the Life of William Green, formerly a Slave, Written by Himself
By William Green

A Narrative of the Life and Travels of Mrs. Nancy Prince
By Nancy Prince

A Narrative of the Uncommon Sufferings and Surprising Deliverance of Briton Hammon, A Negro Man, -- Servant to General Winslow, of Marshfield, in New-England.
By Briton Hammon

A Respectable Man of Color - Beyond the Legend of Cuffee Dole
By Christine Comiskey

A Treatise on the Intellectual Character & Civil & Political Condition of the Colored People of the U. S.; & the Prejudice Exercised Toward Them; ...
By Hosea Easton

"Aboard the Underground Railroad"
by the National Park Service, U.S. Dept of the Interior, www.nps.gov

"African American Churches of Beacon Hill"
www.nps.gov

"African American Heritage in the Upper Housatonic Valley:
Pittsfield, Massachusetts;
Mum Bett's Trail;
Jacob's Pillow Dance;
W.E.B. Du Bois in Gt. Barrington;
54th Massachusetts Regiment"
www.AfricanAmericanTrail.org

African American Heritage in the Upper Housatonic Valley
Edited by David Levinson with Rachel Fletcher, Frances Jones-Sneed, Elaine S. Gunn, and Bernard A. Drew
www.berkshirepublishing.com

"African American Heritage Sites in Salem"
by the National Park Service, U.S. Dept. of the Interior

African American Heritage Trail: Cambridge
by the Cambridge Historical Commission. 2000

"African American Heritage Trail: Concord"
www.RobbinsHouse.org

"African American Heritage Trail : Florence"
www.davidrugglescenter.org

"African American Heritage Trail: Martha's Vineyard"
by Elaine Cawley Weintraub
www.myheritagetrail.org

"African American Heritage Trail: Springfield"
www.ourpluralhistoy.stcc.edu

"African American Historic Sites in the Village of Deerifield, Massachusetts, 1695 - 1783"
www.americancenturies.mass.edu

"African American History in Medford"
by Medford Historical Society
www.medfordhistorical.org

African American Lives
Edited by Henry Louis Gates Jr. and Evelyn Brooks Higginbotham

"African Americans and the End of Slavery in Massachusetts"
www.masshist.org/endofslavery

African Americans in Boston: More Than 350 Years
by Robert Hayden

"African Americans in the Revolutionary Period"
www.nps.gov/revwar

African Americans on Martha's Vineyard and Nantucket: A History …
By Robert Hayden

African Americans on Martha's Vineyard: From Enslavement to Presidential Visit
By Tom Dresser

A.I.A. (American Institute of Architects) Guide to Boston
By Susan and Michael Southworth

"Albert Parsons"
www.wikipedia.org/wiki/Albert_Parsons

"American Memorials Directory"
www.americanMemorialsDirectory.com

An Appeal in Favor of that Class of Americans Called Africans
By Lydia Maria Child

"Andover Stories: When Andover's Finest Went Underground"
By Gail Ralston
www.andovertownsman.com

Army Life of a Black Regiment
By Thomas Wentworth Higgison

"B Company 54th Mass Vol. Infantry Regiment"
www.54thmass.org

"Behind the Mansions: A New Bedford Neighborhood"
National Park Service

"Belinda Slave Petition"
www.celebrateboston.com

"Biographies of Patriots of Color at The Battle of Bunker Hill"
www.nps.gov/bost/learn/education

Black Bostonians
By James Oliver Horton and Lois E. Horton

"Black Heritage Sites in Nantucket's New Guinea"
www.afroammuseum.org

Black Heritage Sites: The North
By Nancy C. Curtis, Ph. D.

"Black Heritage Trail: Boston"
www.nps.gov

"Black Heritage Trail of New Bedford, Mass"
www.newbedfordhistory.org/histor.

"Black Heritage Trail, Nantucket"
www.afroammuseum.org/bhtn

"Black History Articles"
Bay State Banner
www.baystate-banner.com/archives

"Black History of Amherst, MA"
www.amherstblackhistory.jimdo.com

"Black History Trail Proposal for Worcester Area"
By Linda Bock
www.telegram.com/article/20140224/NEWS/302249971

Black Jacks: African American Seamen in the Age of Sail
By W. Jeffrey Bolster

Black Pioneers of Science and Invention
By Louis Haber

"Black Springfield: A Historical Study"
by Imani Kazani
www.scholarworks.umass.edu

Black Walden: Slavery and Its Aftermath in Concord
By Elise Lemire

Boston: A Topographical History
By Walter Muir Whitehill

Boston Confronts Jim Crow: 1890–1920
By Mark R. Schneider

Boston Women's Heritage Trail: Seven Self-guided Walks Through Four Centuries
by Polly Kaufman, Jean Gibran, Sylvia McDowell, and Mary Smoyer.

"Bostonian Society Historical Markers"
www.bostonhistory.org

Boston's Abolitionists
By Kerri Greenidge

Boston's Histories
Ed. By Thomas O'Connor

"Power and Social Responsibility: Entrepreneurs and the Black Community in Antebellum Boston"
by Lois E. Horton & James Oliver Horton

"Brookline in the Civil War"
By Katherine Robinson Briggs

"Caning of Charles Sumners"
www.wikipedia.org/wiki/CaningofCharlesSumners

"Cato Freeman: From Slave to Land Owner"
By Bryan McGonigle
www.patch.com/massachusetts/nortandover/

Charles Benson: Mariner of Color in the Age of Sail
By Michael Sokolow

"Charles Street Meeting House"
www.nps.gov

Civil Disobedience
By Henry David Thoreau

Civil Rights and the American Negro: A Documentary History
Edited by Albert P. Blaustein and Robert L. Zangrando

Clotel
By William Wells Brown

Colored Patriots of the American Revolution
By William Nell

Common Ground
By George Lukas

Courage and Conscience: Black & White Abolitionists in Boston
Ed. Donald M. Jacobs

"Cuff Dole: Wanted Man"
By J.L. Bell
www.boston1775.blogspot.com

"Daniel Drayton: New Bedford Whaling"
www.nps.gov

"Daniel Saunders, Sr. (1796–1872) Lawrence, MA"
www.queencityma.wordpress.com

David Ruggles: A Radical Black Abolitionist & the Underground Railroad in New York City
by Graham Russell Gao Hodges

"David Ruggles in Florence, Massachusetts"
www.davidrugglesinflorence.blogspot.com

David Walker's Appeal To the Coloured Citizens of the World
Edited by Peter P. Hinks

"Dedication of the Memorial Hall, in Dedham, September 29, 1868"
By Dedham, MA

Defenders of Liberty: African Americans in the Revolutionary War
By Lt. Col. Michael Lee Lanning

Diary of a Contraband: The Civil War Passage of a Black Sailor
Edited by William B. Gould IV
www.goulddiary.stanford.edu

"Discovery Details Wenham's Civil War Monument's History"
By Lucy R. Sprague Frederikson

"Dred Scott"
www.wikipedia.org/wiki/DredScott

"Dorchester's Homage to its Civil War Heroes"
By Anthony Sammarco
Dorchester Community News, Feb. 7, 1992

"Dr. Cornelius N. Garland"
Crisis Magazine, January, 1920

Empire of Cotton
By Sven Becket

"Exploring Boston's Neighborhoods"
Boston Landmarks Commission.
1994–2001

Faith and Boundaries: Colonists, Christianity and Community Among the Wampanoag Indians of Martha's Vineyard 1600–1871
By David J. Silverman

"Famous Trials"
By Douglas O. Linder
University of Missouri–Kansas City

"Fifty-Fifth Regiment Massachusetts Volunteer Infantry–Three Years"
www.massachusettscivilwar.com

"Fifth-Fourth Regiment Massachusetts Volunteer Infantry–Three Years"
www.massachusettscivilwar.com

"Fifty Sites in Great Barrington, Massachusetts, Associated with the Civil Rights Activist, W.E.B. DuBois"
By the Great Barrington Land Conservancy and Great Barrington Historical Society

Forbidden Fruit: Love Stories from the Underground Railroad
By Betty DeRamus

Forged in Battle: The Civil War Alliances of Black Soldiers and White Officers
By Joseph T. Glathaar

"Freedom on Nantucket: The Reverend James Crawford & William Benjamin Gould"
By Helen Hannon, Historic Nantucket, Winter, 2008
www.nha.org

"Freedom Stories of the Pioneer Valley"
"Amos Newport"
by Robert H. Romer

"The Rescue of Angeline Palmer"
by Cliff McCarthy

"Jenny Cumfrey Williams"
"William Green"
by Cliff McCarthy

"Jupiter Richards"
by Cliff McCarthy & Richard Colton
www.freedomstoriespv.wordpress.com

Friends of Liberty
by Graham Russell Hodges and Gary Nash

From Your Loving Son: Civil War Correspondence and Diaries of Private George F. Moore and His Family
Published by Sudbury Historical Society

"From Slavery to Freedom: Black History Walking Tour (Plymouth)"
By Casey Meserve
www.patch.com

"Fugitive Slave Traffic and the Maritime World of New Bedford"
By Kathryn Grover
www.umassd.edu

"Gloucester Eagle Scout Renovates Riverdale Civil War Memorial"
By Jane Fosberry
www.

"Hardtack History / Hardtack Recipes"
www.kenanderson.net/hardtack

"Harriet E. Wilson"
www.wikipedia.org

Harvard and Slavery: Seeking a Forgotten History
By Sven Beckert, Katherine Stevens and the students of the Harvard and Slavery Research Seminar

"Henry Ladsworth Longfellow Poems"
www.hwlongfellow.org/poems

"Historical Sites of Danvers"
By the Danvers Preservation Commission

"Historic Northampton"
www.historic-northampton.org

"Historic Resource Study: Boston African American National Historic Site"
By Kathryn Grover and Janine V. da Silva, 2002

"History of 55th Massachusetts Volunteer Infantry"
www.coax.net

"History of African Americans in South Danvers"
By Nancy Barthelemy
The South Danvers Observer
www.peabodylibrary.org

History of New Bedford and Vicinity, 1602–1892,
by Leonard B. Ellis

"History of Dedham, Massachusetts, 1793–1999"
www.wikipedia.org

Hobomok, A Tale of Early Times
By Lydia Maria Child

Hotel Keepers, Head Waiters, and Housekeepers' Guide
By Tunis G. Campbell

How Hair is Wove
By James Babcock

I Love Boston Guide
By Marilyn J. Appleberg

Incidents in the Life of a Slave Girl
By Linda Brent (Harriet Jacobs)

In Small Things Forgotten: An Archaeology of Early American Life
By James F. Deetz

In their Footsteps: The American Visions Guide to African-American Heritage Sites
By Henry Chase

"Issac Royall House"
www.royallhouse.org

"James George Barbadoes"
www.wikipedia.org/James_George_Barbadoes

John Stewart Rock: Teacher Healer Counselor
By J. Harlan Buzby

"Jonathan Walker"
www.nps.gov

Journal
By Henry David Thoreau

"Legal Papers of John Adams, Volume 2"
www.masshist.org/publications

Legendary Locals of Boston's South End
By Hope J. Shannon

"Leonard Grimes"
www.nps.gov

"Letter from Paul Revere to Jeremy Belknap, circa 1798"
www.masshist.org/database

Life of James Mars, a Slave Born and Sold in Connecticut
By James Mars

Lighting the Trail: The African American Heritage of Martha's Vineyard
By Elaine Cawley Weintraub

"Local Historian Unearths Beverly's African American History"
By Tala Strauss
www.boston.com

"Longfellow House–Washington's Headquarters National Historic Site"
www.wikipedia.org/wiki/Longfellow House

"Lucy Parsons"
www.wikipedia.org/wiki/Lucy Parsons

Lucy Terry Prince–Singer of History
By David R. Proper
www.memorialhall.mass.edu

Maria W. Stewart, American's First Black Woman Political Writer: Essays & Speeches
By Marilyn Richardson

"Major Taylor Association"
www.majortaylorassociation.org

Mapping Boston
Ed. Alex Krieger and David Cobb

"Massachusetts General Colored Association"
www.wikipedia.org/wiki/Massachusetts General Colored

"Massachusetts Historical Society Online Collections"
www.masshist.org

"Massachusetts Towns in the Civil War, ca 1861–1865: Wayland, MA as a Case Study"

Memoir of James Jackson, the Attentive and Obedient Scholar
By Susan Paul

Memoir of Rev. Charles T. Torrey, Who Died in the Penitentiary of Maryland, Where He Was Confined for Showing Mercy to the Poor
By J.C Lovejoy

"Missouri Compromise"
www.wikipedia.org/wiki/MissouriCompromise

"Mount Auburn Cemetery: Aboard the Underground Railroad"
www.nps.gov

"Mount Auburn Cemetery: African American Heritage Trail"
www.mountauburn.org/tag/african-american-heritage-trail

Mr. and Mrs. Prince
By Gretchen Holbrook Gerzina

"My View: Black History Month: Remembering Heroes of Civil War, Anti-Slavery Movement" (newspaper article)
By David Goss, The Salem News, Feb. 13, 2012

"Names of the Ipswich Slaves"
By Gordon Harris
www.ipswich.wordpress.com

Nantucket Historical Association
www.nha.org

"The Brotherhood of Thieves Riot of 1842"
by Susan F. Beegel

"Black-White Relations on Nantucket"
by Robert Johnson

"Seizing Agency: Black Nantucket and the Abolitionist Press, 1832-48"
by Justin A. Pariseau

"The Portrait of Absalom Boston"
by Frances Ruley Karttunen

"The African Meeting House"
by Helen Seager

"The Courts of Nantucket"
by Allen Coffin

"African-American Women in Nineteenth-Century Nantucket: Wives, Mothers, Modistes, and Visionaries"
by Gloria Davis Goode

"'I Will Take to the Water': Frederick Douglass, the Sea, and the Nantucket Whale Fishery"
by Nathaniel Philbrick

"The Integration of Nantucket Public Schools"
by Barbara White

Narrative of the Life of Frederick Douglass, An American Slave
By Frederick Douglass

Narrative of the Sufferings of Lewis and Milton Clarke
By Lewis and Milton Clarke

"Nathaniel Ward"
www.historicipswich.org

"Natick Civil War Monument Needs Repairs"
By Charlie Breitrose / MetroWest Daily News

National Archives
www.archives.gov

National Register of Historic Places Listings
www.nps.gov/nr

Native American Whalemen and the World: Indigenous Encounters and the Contingency of Race
By Nancy Shoemaker

New Bedford Historical Society:
   "Mary J. 'Polly' Johnson"
   "Thomas H. Jones"
   "Jeremiah Burke Sanderson"
   "Martha Bailey Briggs"
   "Lewis Temple"
   "William Bush"
   "Sergeant William H. Carney"
   "Paul Cuffe Sailed the Seas,..."
   "Amos Haskins"
www.nbhistoricalsociety.org

"Northampton Association of Education & Industry"
www.historic-northampton.org

"NRHP Nomination for Bethel African American AME Church and Parsonage"

One Minute a Free Woman: Elizabeth Freeman and the Struggle for Freedom
By Emilie Piper and David Levinson

Other Brahmins, Boston's Black Upper Class
By Adelaide Cromwell

Our Nig, or Sketches from the Life of a Free Black
By Harriet Wilson

"Our Plural History–Springfield, MA"
www.ourpluralhistory.stcc.edu/resistingslavery

"Paul Revere's Ride: Awakening Abolitionists"
by Jill Lepore, American Educator, Summer, 2011

"Parting Ways, New Guinea, Settlement"
www.partingways.org

"Pearl Incident"
www.wikipedia.org

People of the Underground Railroad: A Biographical Dictionary
By Tom Calarco

Personal Memoir of Daniel Drayton, For Four Years and Four Months a Prisoner
By Daniel Drayton

Phillis Wheatley
By William Henry Robinson, PhD.

"Pingrey's Plain, the "Gallow's Lot"
By Godon Harris
www.ipswich.wordpress.com

Poems of Various Subjects, Religious and Moral
By Phillis Wheatley

Poems on Slavery, 1842
By Henry Wadsworth Longfellow

"Poets, Shoemakers, and Freedom Seekers: Abolitionists and the Underground Railroad in Essex County"
By National Park Service, U.S. Dept. of the Interior

"Preserving Three Hundred-fifty Years of Change in the Blackstone Block"
By Miguel Gomez-Ibanez
www.historicnewengland.org

Prince Esterbrooks, Slave & Soldier
By Alice Hinkle

"Prince Hall Freemasonry"
www.wikipedia.org/wiki/Prince_Hall_Freemasonry

"Prince, Nancy Gardner (1799–c. 1856)
www.blackpast.org

"Profiles in Courage: African-Americans in Lowell"
By Martha Mayo
www.library.uml.edu

"Quock Walker and Emancipation in Massachusetts"
By Patrick Browne

"Quock Walker, 28, Kicks the Legs Out From Under Slavery in Massachusetts"
www.newenglandhistoricalsociety.com/quock-walker-28-kicks-the-legs-out-from-under-slaver-in-massachusetts/

"Remembering Brookline's Civil War Dead"
By Ken Liss / Wicked Local

Reminiscences of Fugitive-Slave Law Days in Boston
By Capt. Austin Bearse

"Remond Family"
By Jim Mcallister, The Salem News, Jan. 15, 2007

Report of the Arguments of Counsel and of the Opinion of the Court in the Case of Commonwealth vs. Aves Tried and Determined in the Supreme Judicial Court of Massachusetts
By Anonymous

"Rev. Charles Torrey"
www.wikipedia.org

Ripples of Hope: Great American Civil Rights Speeches
Edited by Josh Gottheimer

"Saint John's Baptist Church: A History"
www.sjbc.org

"Salem's Forgotten Soldiers of Freedom"
By David Goss
www.gordon.edu

Sarah's Long Walk
By Stephen Kendrick and Paul Kendrick

"Sarah Parker Remond: A Daughter of Salem, Massachusetts"
By Marilyn Richardson
www.sarahparkerremond.wordpress.com

Schooling Citizens: The Struggle for African American Education in Ante-Bellum America
By Hillary J. Moss

Second Wind
By Bill Russell

Services of Colored Americans in the Wars of 1776 and 1812
By William Nell

Shadrach Minkins, From Fugitive Slave to Citizen
By Gary Collison

"Slave Gravestones of Essex County"
Primary Research: Local History, Closer to Home
www.primaryresearch.org

Slavery in the Connecticut Valley of Massachusetts
By Robert H. Romer

Slave Testimony: Two Centuries of
Letters, Speeches, Interviews, and
Autobiographies
Edited by John W. Blassingame

"Slavery & Freedom: African-Americans
in Beverly, 1750–1850"
By Terri McFadden
www.beverlyhistoricalsociety.org

"Stoneham, MA: 400 Years of History"
By Marina Memmo
www.stonehamhistory.com

"Streets of Salem: Civil War
Remembrance"
By Donna Seger

"St. Paul's Churchyard"
www.stpauls-nbpt.org

Summary of the Life of James Mars, A
Slave Born and Sold in Connecticut
By James Mars

"The 54th Mass. Volunteer Infantry
Regiment"
www.northaginstsouth.com

The African American Experience: Black
History and Culture
Edited by Kai Wright

"The African Meeting House: A Gathering
Place for Freedom"
www.afroammuseum.org

The Black Past: Remembered and
Reclaimed
www.BlackPast.org

The Blackman, His Antecedents, His
Genius, and His Achievements
By William Wells Brown

The Black Presence in the Era of the
American Revolution 1770-1800
By Sidney Kaplan

"The Boston Vigilance Committee: A
Reconsideration"
By Gary Collison
History Journal of Massachusetts, 1984

"The Branded Hand"
By John Greenleaf Whittier
www.readbookonline.net

The Brotherhood of Thieves: A True
Picture of the American Church and
Clergy: A Letter to Nathaniel Barney of
Nantucket
by Stephen S. Foster

"The Case of Lucy Faggins"
By William C. Nell
The Liberator Newspaper, 16 July 1841

The Complete Guide to Boston's
Freedom Trail
by Charles Bahne. 1985

"The Dark 'Fugitive Slave' History of
Riker's Island"
By Brenton Mock
www.citylab.com

"The David Walker Memorial Project"
www.davidwalkermemorial.org

"The Drinking Gourd Project: African
American and Abolitionist Heritage Tours
of Concord, MA"
www.drinkinggourd.cchumanrights.org

The Fastest Bicycle Rider in the World
By Marshall "Major" Taylor

The History of the Negro Race in
America 1619–1880
By George Washington Williams

The House Servant's Directory, 1827
By Robert Roberts

The Hidden History of Mass.: A Guide
for Black Folks
by Dr. Tingba Apidta. 1995

"The John Brown Bell"
By Joan Abshire
www.marlboroughhistory.org

The Journals of Charlotte Forten Grimke,
ed. by Brenda Stevenson

"The Liberator Files: Boston-based Abolitionist newspaper, published by William Lloyd Garrison 1831–1865"
www.theliberatorfiles.com

The Life and Letters of John Brown
By Franklin Sanborn

"The Mark of Belinda Royall"
www.medfordhistorical.org

The Narrative Life of Lunsford Lane
By Lunsford Lane

The Narrative of Sojourner Truth: A Northern Slave
By Sojourner Truth

The Negro in the American Revolution
By Benjamin Quarles

The North End: A Brief History of Boston's Oldest Neighborhood
By Alex Goldfeld

The Plymouth Colony Archive Project: Parting Ways: In Small Things Forgotten: An Archeology of Early American Life
By James F. Deetz

The House Servant's Directory, or a Monitor for Private Families, 1827
By Robert Roberts

"The Puritan Origins of Black Abolitionism in Massachusetts"
By Christopher Cameron
www.academia.edu

"The Quock Walker Case"
www.mass.gov/courts/court-info/sjc/edu-res-center/jn-adams/the-quock-walker-case.

"The Remonds of Salem, Massachusetts: A Nineteenth-Century Family Revisited"
By Dorothy Burnett Porter
www.americanantiquarian.org

The Road to Freedom: Greenfield and the Underground Railroad
Greenfield Human Rights Commission and the Greenfield Historical Commission
Project Director, Joan Featherman and Project Author, Jill Ogline

The Souls of Black Folk
By WEB DuBois

The Struggle for Freedom and the History of African Americans in Western Massachusetts
By Wayne E. Phaneuf

The Underground Railroad in Massachusetts
By Wilbur H. Siebert

"The Underground Railroad in Massachusetts: Statement of Historic Context"
www.nps.gov

"The Underground Railroad: New Bedford"
By National Park Service, U.S. Dept. of the Interior
www.cr.nps.gov/history/ugrr.htm

"The Untold Story of the Royall House Slaves"
By Helene Ragovia
www.tuftsjournal.tufts.edu

The Wampanoag Tribe of Martha's Vineyard: Colonization to Recognition
By Tom Dresser

"The War of the Rebellion–The Great Civil War"
www.miltonhistoricalsociety.org

"The Worldly Remonds of Salem"
By Donna Seger
www.streetsofsalem.com

"Then and Now: Primus Avenue on Beacon Hill, Early Urban Renewal"
www.bostonzest.com

To Free a Family: The Journey of Mary Walker
By Sydney Nathans

Toussaint L'Ouverture
By John R. Beard

Trial and Imprisonment of Jonathan Walker
By Capt. Jonathan Walker

Two Years Before the Mast
By Richard Henry Dana, Jr.

Tyrannicide: Forging an American Law of Slavery in Revolutionary South Carolina and Massachusetts
By Emily Blanck

Uncle Tom's Cabin
By Harriet Beecher Stowe

"Uncovering the Stories of Black Families in Springfield and Hampden County, Massachusetts: 1650–1865"
By Joseph Carvarho III
www.AmericanAncestors.org

"Underground Railroad Monument Unveiled in Lawrence"
By Laura Crimaldi
www.bostonglobe.com

Walden Pond
By Henry David Thoreau

Walking Tours of Civil War Boston
By Barbara Berenson and R. Marc Kantrowitz

"Walking Tour of Downtown Lowell: A Dozen Sites Associated with Anti-slavery in the Spindle City, 1830–1860"
By Gray Fitzsimons
www.

"W.E.B. Du Bois Boyhood Homesite and Great Barrington: A Plan for Heritage Conservation…"
Final Planning Report, July 2009
By Michael Singer Studio & el.
www.library.umass.edu/spcoll/duboishome

"We Meete the Enemie in dire combat…"
www.marlborough-ma.gov

"William B. Gould I"
www.wikipedia.org

"William Matthew Prior: Artist, Businessman, & Visionary"
By Jacquelyn Oak
www.afanews.com

INDEX